SOUTH CAROLINA EDITION

McDougal Littell
Science

McDougal Littell Science
SOUTH CAROLINA

GRADE
7

Chemical
Interactions

Human Biology

Matter

Cells and
Heredity

Ecology

GRADE 7 CONTENTS

South Carolina Standards — xxiv
Introducing Science — xxviii
Unifying Principles of Science — xxx
The Nature of Science — xxxvi
The Nature of Technology — xl
Using *McDougal Littell Science* — xlii

Unit 1 Cells and Heredity
The Cell
How Cells Function
Cell Division
Patterns of Heredity
DNA and Modern Genetics

Unit 2 Human Biology
Systems, Support, and Movement
Absorption, Digestion, and Exchange
Transport and Protection
Control and Reproduction
Growth, Development, and Health

Unit 3 Ecology
Ecosystems and Biomes
Interactions Within Ecosystems
Human Impact on Ecosystems

Unit 4 Matter
Introduction to Matter
Properties of Matter

Unit 5 Chemical Interactions
Atomic Structure and the Periodic Table
Chemical Bonds and Compounds
Chemical Reactions
Solutions

South Carolina Essentials
Bacteria and Protists
Infectious and Noninfectious Diseases
Characteristics of Soil
Location and Movement of Water on Earth

Student Resource Handbooks
Scientific Thinking Handbook — R2
Lab Handbook — R10
Math Handbook — R36
Note-Taking Handbook — R45
Appendix — R52
Glossary — R54
Index — R73
Acknowledgments — R93

ISBN-10: 0-618-91745-4
ISBN-13: 978-0-618-91745-7

2 3 4 5 6 7 8 VJM 11 10 09 08 07

Internet Web Site: http://www.mcdougallittell.com

Science Consultants

Chief Science Consultant

James Trefil, Ph.D. is the Clarence J. Robinson Professor of Physics at George Mason University. He is the author or co-author of more than 25 books, including *Science Matters* and *The Nature of Science.* Dr. Trefil is a member of the American Association for the Advancement of Science's Committee on the Public Understanding of Science and Technology. He is also a fellow of the World Economic Forum and a frequent contributor to *Smithsonian* magazine.

Rita Ann Calvo, Ph.D. is Senior Lecturer in Molecular Biology and Genetics at Cornell University, where for 12 years she also directed the Cornell Institute for Biology Teachers. Dr. Calvo is the 1999 recipient of the College and University Teaching Award from the National Association of Biology Teachers.

Kenneth Cutler, M.S. is the Education Coordinator for the Julius L. Chambers Biomedical Biotechnology Research Institute at North Carolina Central University. A former middle school and high school science teacher, he received a 1999 Presidential Award for Excellence in Science Teaching.

Instructional Design Consultants

Douglas Carnine, Ph.D. is Professor of Education and Director of the National Center for Improving the Tools of Educators at the University of Oregon. He is the author of seven books and over 100 other scholarly publications, primarily in the areas of instructional design and effective instructional strategies and tools for diverse learners. Dr. Carnine also serves as a member of the National Institute for Literacy Advisory Board.

Linda Carnine, Ph.D. consults with school districts on curriculum development and effective instruction for students struggling academically. A former teacher and school administrator, Dr. Carnine also co-authored a popular remedial reading program.

Donald Steely, Ph.D. serves as principal investigator at the Oregon Center for Applied Science (ORCAS) on federal grants for science and language arts programs. His background also includes teaching and authoring of print and multimedia programs in science, mathematics, history, and spelling.

Sam Miller, Ph.D. is a middle school science teacher and the Teacher Development Liaison for the Eugene, Oregon, Public Schools. He is the author of curricula for teaching science, mathematics, computer skills, and language arts.

Vicky Vachon, Ph.D. consults with school districts throughout the United States and Canada on improving overall academic achievement with a focus on literacy. She is also co-author of a widely used program for remedial readers.

Content Reviewers

John Beaver, Ph.D.
Ecology
Professor, Director of Science Education Center
College of Education and Human Services
Western Illinois University
Macomb, IL

Donald J. DeCoste, Ph.D.
Matter and Energy, Chemical Interactions
Chemistry Instructor
University of Illinois
Urbana-Champaign, IL

Dorothy Ann Fallows, Ph.D., MSc
Diversity of Living Things, Microbiology
Partners in Health
Boston, MA

Michael Foote, Ph.D.
The Changing Earth, Life Over Time
Associate Professor
Department of the Geophysical Sciences
The University of Chicago
Chicago, IL

Lucy Fortson, Ph.D.
Space Science
Director of Astronomy
Adler Planetarium and Astronomy Museum
Chicago, IL

Elizabeth Godrick, Ph.D.
Human Biology
Professor, CAS Biology
Boston University
Boston, MA

Isabelle Sacramento Grilo, M.S.
The Changing Earth
Lecturer, Department of the Geological Sciences
San Diego State University
San Diego, CA

David Harbster, MSc
Diversity of Living Things
Professor of Biology
Paradise Valley Community College
Phoenix, AZ

Richard D. Norris, Ph.D.
Earth's Waters
Professor of Paleobiology
Scripps Institution of Oceanography
University of California, San Diego
La Jolla, CA

Donald B. Peck, M.S.
Motion and Forces; Waves, Sound, and Light;
 Electricity and Magnetism
Director of the Center for Science Education (retired)
Fairleigh Dickinson University
Madison, NJ

Javier Penalosa, Ph.D.
Diversity of Living Things, Plants
Associate Professor, Biology Department
Buffalo State College
Buffalo, NY

Raymond T. Pierrehumbert, Ph.D.
Earth's Atmosphere
Professor in Geophysical Sciences (Atmospheric Science)
The University of Chicago
Chicago, IL

Brian J. Skinner, Ph.D.
Earth's Surface
Eugene Higgins Professor of Geology and Geophysics
Yale University
New Haven, CT

Nancy E. Spaulding, M.S.
Earth's Surface, The Changing Earth, Earth's Waters
Earth Science Teacher (retired)
Elmira Free Academy
Elmira, NY

Steven S. Zumdahl, Ph.D.
Matter and Energy, Chemical Interactions
Professor Emeritus of Chemistry
University of Illinois
Urbana-Champaign, IL

Susan L. Zumdahl, M.S.
Matter and Energy, Chemical Interactions
Chemistry Education Specialist
University of Illinois
Urbana-Champaign, IL

Safety Consultant

Juliana Texley, Ph.D.
Former K–12 Science Teacher and School Superintendent
Boca Raton, FL

English Language Advisor

Judy Lewis, M.A.
Director, State and Federal Programs for reading proficiency
and high risk populations
Rancho Cordova, CA

Teacher Panel Members

Carol Arbour
Tallmadge Middle School,
Tallmadge, OH

Patty Belcher
Goodrich Middle School,
Akron, OH

Gwen Broestl
Luis Munoz Marin Middle School,
Cleveland, OH

Al Brofman
Tehipite Middle School,
Fresno, CA

John Cockrell
Clinton Middle School,
Columbus, OH

Jenifer Cox
Sylvan Middle School,
Citrus Heights, CA

Linda Culpepper
Martin Middle School,
Charlotte, NC

Melvin Figueroa
New River Middle School,
Ft. Lauderdale, FL

Doretha Grier
Kannapolis Middle School,
Kannapolis, NC

Robert Hood
Alexander Hamilton Middle School,
Cleveland, OH

Scott Hudson
Covedale Elementary School,
Cincinnati, OH

Loretta Langdon
Princeton Middle School,
Princeton, NC

Carlyn Little
Glades Middle School,
Miami, FL

Ann Marie Lynn
Amelia Earhart Middle School,
Riverside, CA

James Minogue
Lowe's Grove Middle School,
Durham, NC

Kathleen Montagnino-DeMatteo
Jefferson Davis Middle School,
West Palm Beach, FL

Joann Myers
Buchanan Middle School,
Tampa, FL

Barbara Newell
Charles Evans Hughes Middle School,
Long Beach, CA

Anita Parker
Kannapolis Middle School,
Kannapolis, NC

Greg Pirolo
Golden Valley Middle School,
San Bernardino, CA

Laura Pottmyer
Apex Middle School,
Apex, NC

Lynn Prichard
Williams Middle Magnet School,
Tampa, FL

Jacque Quick
Walter Williams High School,
Burlington, NC

Robert Glenn Reynolds
Hillman Middle School,
Youngstown, OH

Stacy Rinehart
Lufkin Road Middle School,
Apex, NC

Theresa Short
Abbott Middle School,
Fayetteville, NC

Rita Slivka
Alexander Hamilton Middle School,
Cleveland, OH

Marie Sofsak
B F Stanton Middle School,
Alliance, OH

Nancy Stubbs
Sweetwater Union Unified School District,
Chula Vista, CA

Sharon Stull
Quail Hollow Middle School,
Charlotte, NC

Donna Taylor
Bak Middle School of the Arts,
West Palm Beach, FL

Sandi Thompson
Harding Middle School,
Lakewood, OH

Lori Walker
Audubon Middle School & Magnet Center,
Los Angeles, CA

Teacher Lab Evaluators

Andrew Boy
W.E.B. DuBois Academy,
Cincinnati, OH

Jill Brimm-Byrne
Albany Park Academy,
Chicago, IL

Gwen Broestl
Luis Munoz Marin Middle School,
Cleveland, OH

Al Brofman
Tehipite Middle School,
Fresno, CA

Michael A. Burstein
The Rashi School,
Newton, MA

Trudi Coutts
Madison Middle School,
Naperville, IL

Jenifer Cox
Sylvan Middle School,
Citrus Heights, CA

Larry Cwik
Madison Middle School,
Naperville, IL

Jennifer Donatelli
Kennedy Junior High School,
Lisle, IL

Melissa Dupree
Lakeside Middle School,
Evans, GA

Carl Fechko
Luis Munoz Marin Middle School,
Cleveland, OH

Paige Fullhart
Highland Middle School,
Libertyville, IL

Sue Hood
Glen Crest Middle School,
Glen Ellyn, IL

William Luzader
Plymouth Community Intermediate School,
Plymouth, MA

Ann Min
Beardsley Middle School,
Crystal Lake, IL

Aileen Mueller
Kennedy Junior High School,
Lisle, IL

Nancy Nega
Churchville Middle School,
Elmhurst, IL

Oscar Newman
Sumner Math and Science Academy,
Chicago, IL

Lynn Prichard
Williams Middle Magnet School,
Tampa, FL

Jacque Quick
Walter Williams High School,
Burlington, NC

Stacy Rinehart
Lufkin Road Middle School,
Apex, NC

Seth Robey
Gwendolyn Brooks Middle School,
Oak Park, IL

Kevin Steele
Grissom Middle School,
Tinley Park, IL

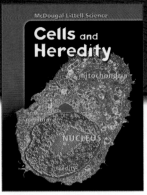

McDougal Littell Science
Cells and Heredity

mitochondria

membrane

NUCLEUS

eEdition

UNIT 1
Cells and Heredity

Unit Features

SCIENTIFIC AMERICAN **FRONTIERS IN SCIENCE** *Genes That Map the Body*   2

TIMELINES IN SCIENCE *The Story of Genetics*   128

1 The Cell   6

the BIG idea

All living things are made up of cells.

1 **The cell is the basic unit of living things.**   9
CHAPTER INVESTIGATION *Using a Microscope*   16
2 **Microscopes allow us to see inside the cell.**   18
MATH IN SCIENCE *Using Scientific Notation*   25
3 **Different cells perform various functions.**   26
THINK SCIENCE *Cells and Spacesuits*   33

2 How Cells Function   38

the BIG idea

All cells need energy and materials for life processes.

1 **Chemical reactions take place inside cells.**   41
SCIENCE ON THE JOB *Natural Dyes and Cells*   46
2 **Cells capture and release energy.**   47
MATH IN SCIENCE *Interpreting Graphs*   55
3 **Materials move across the cell's membranes.**   56
CHAPTER INVESTIGATION *Diffusion*   64

How do plants like these sunflowers change energy from the Sun?
page 38

3 Cell Division   70

the **BIG** idea

Organisms grow, reproduce, and maintain themselves through cell division.

1. **Cell division occurs in all organisms.**   73
   CONNECTING SCIENCES *Chemical Dyes Show Nerve Growth*   79

2. **Cell division is part of the cell cycle.**   80
   CHAPTER INVESTIGATION *Stages of the Cell Cycle*   86

3. **Both sexual and asexual reproduction involve cell division.**   88
   MATH IN SCIENCE *Using Exponents*   93

4 Patterns of Heredity   98

the **BIG** idea

In sexual reproduction, genes are passed from parents to offspring in predictable patterns.

1. **Living things inherit traits in patterns.**   101
   CHAPTER INVESTIGATION *Offspring Models*   108

2. **Patterns of heredity can be predicted.**   110
   MATH IN SCIENCE *Using Punnett Squares*   116

3. **Meiosis is a special form of cell division.**   117
   THINK SCIENCE *Are Traits Linked?*   123

5 DNA and Modern Genetics   132

the **BIG** idea

DNA is a set of instructions for making cell parts.

1. **DNA and RNA are required to make proteins.**   135
   CHAPTER INVESTIGATION *Extract and Observe DNA*   142

2. **Changes in DNA can produce variation.**   144
   MATH IN SCIENCE *Finding Percent of a Whole*   149

3. **Modern genetics uses DNA technology.**   150
   EXTREME SCIENCE *Modern Genetics Meets the Dodo and the Solitaire* 155

Visual Highlights

Parts of a Eukaryotic Cell	22
Levels of Organization	30
Photosynthesis	49
Cellular Respiration	51
Cell Division	83
Punnett Square and Probability	113
Meiosis	121
Translation	140

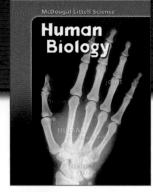

eEdition

UNIT 2
Human Biology

Unit Features

SCIENTIFIC AMERICAN **FRONTIERS IN SCIENCE** *Surprising Senses*   162

TIMELINES IN SCIENCE *Seeing Inside the Body*   254

6 Systems, Support, and Movement   166

the BIG idea

The human body is made up of systems that work together to perform necessary functions.

1. **The human body is complex.**   169
   THINK SCIENCE *What Does the Body Need to Survive?*   173
2. **The skeletal system provides support and protection.**   174
   MATH IN SCIENCE *Comparing Rates*   181
3. **The muscular system makes movement possible.**   182
   CHAPTER INVESTIGATION *A Closer Look at Muscles*   188

7 Absorption, Digestion, and Exchange   194

the BIG idea

Systems in the body obtain and process materials and remove waste.

1. **The respiratory system gets oxygen and removes carbon dioxide.**   197
   SCIENCE ON THE JOB *Breathing and Yoga*   204
2. **The digestive system breaks down food.**   205
   MATH IN SCIENCE *Choosing Units of Length*   211
3. **The urinary system removes waste materials.**   212
   CHAPTER INVESTIGATION *Modeling a Kidney*   216

What materials does your body need to function properly? page 194

Red blood cells travel through a blood vessel. How do you think blood carries materials around your body? page 222

8 Transport and Protection 222

the **BIG** idea

Systems function to transport materials and to defend and protect the body.

1. **The circulatory system transports materials.** 225
   CHAPTER INVESTIGATION *Heart Rate and Exercise* 232

2. **The immune system defends the body.** 234
   MATH IN SCIENCE *Making a Line Graph* 242

3. **The integumentary system shields the body.** 243
   EXTREME SCIENCE *Artificial Skin* 249

9 Control and Reproduction 258

the **BIG** idea

The nervous and endocrine systems allow the body to respond to internal and external conditions.

1. **The nervous system responds and controls.** 261
   CHAPTER INVESTIGATION *Are You a Supertaster?* 268

2. **The endocrine system helps regulate body conditions.** 270
   CONNECTING SCIENCES *Heating and Cooling* 277

3. **The reproductive system allows the production of offspring.** 278
   MATH IN SCIENCE *Solving Proportions* 285

10 Growth, Development, and Health 290

the **BIG** idea

The body develops and maintains itself over time.

1. **The human body changes over time.** 293
   SCIENCE ON THE JOB *Aging the Face* 299

2. **Systems in the body function to maintain health.** 300
   MATH IN SCIENCE *Choosing a Data Display* 307

3. **Science helps people prevent and treat disease.** 308
   CHAPTER INVESTIGATION *Cleaning Your Hands* 314

Visual Highlights

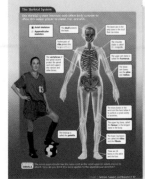

The Skeletal System 177
Muscle Tissue 185
Respiratory System 201
Digestive System 209
Circulatory System 228
Growth of the Fetus 283
Pathogens and Disease 311

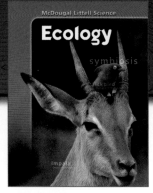

Ecology

eEdition

Unit Features

SCIENTIFIC AMERICAN **FRONTIERS IN SCIENCE** *Ecosystems on Fire* 322

TIMELINES IN SCIENCE *Wilderness Conservation* 394

11 Ecosystems and Biomes 326

((the **BIG** idea))

Matter and energy together support life within an environment.

1 Ecosystems support life. 329
  CHAPTER INVESTIGATION *Soil Samples* 334

2 Matter cycles through ecosystems. 336
  MATH IN SCIENCE *Adding Integers* 341

3 Energy flows through ecosystems. 342
  CONNECTING SCIENCES *Biomagnification* 349

4 Biomes contain many ecosystems. 350

How many living and nonliving things can you identify in this photograph? page 326

How do living things interact? page 362

12 Interactions Within Ecosystems   362

the BIG idea

Living things within an ecosystem interact with each other and the environment.

1 **Groups of living things interact within ecosystems.**   365
CHAPTER INVESTIGATION *Estimating Populations*   372

2 **Organisms can interact in different ways.**   374
THINK SCIENCE *Where Are the Salamanders?*   382

3 **Ecosystems are always changing.**   383
MATH IN SCIENCE *Multiplying a Fraction by a Whole Number*   389

13 Human Impact on Ecosystems   398

the BIG idea

Humans and human population growth affect the environment.

1 **Human population growth presents challenges.**   401
SCIENCE ON THE JOB *Ecology in Urban Planning*   408

2 **Human activities affect the environment.**   409
MATH IN SCIENCE *Finding Volumes*   417

3 **People are working to protect ecosystems.**   418
CHAPTER INVESTIGATION *Cleaning Oil Spills*   426

Visual Highlights

Energy Flows Through Ecosystems   347
Aquatic Biomes   356
Levels in the Environment   369
Symbiotic Relationships   380
Ecosystem Recovery   421

UNIT 4

Matter

eEdition

UNIT 4
Matter

Unit Feature

 FRONTIERS IN SCIENCE *Exploring the Water Planet*   434

14 Introduction to Matter   438

the **BIG** idea

Everything that has mass and takes up space is matter.

1. **Matter has mass and volume.**   441
   CHAPTER INVESTIGATION *Mass and Volume*   446

2. **Matter is made of atoms.**   448
   EXTREME SCIENCE *Particles Too Small to See*   452

3. **Matter combines to form different substances.**   453
   MATH IN SCIENCE *Making a Circle Graph*   458

4. **Matter exists in different physical states.**   459

What matter can you identify in this photograph? page 438

What properties could help you identify this sculpture as sugar? page 470

15 **Properties of Matter** 470

the BIG idea

Matter has properties that can be changed by physical and chemical processes.

1 **Matter has observable properties.** 473
MATH IN SCIENCE *Solving Proportions* 481

2 **Changes of state are physical changes.** 482
CHAPTER INVESTIGATION *Freezing Point* 488

3 **Properties are used to identify substances.** 490
CONNECTING SCIENCES *Separating Minerals* 495

Visual Highlights

States of Matter 461
Physical Changes 477

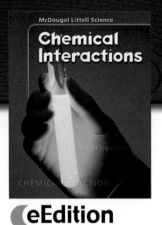

McDougal Littell Science
Chemical Interactions

eEdition

UNIT 5
Chemical Interactions

Unit Features

SCIENTIFIC AMERICAN **FRONTIERS IN SCIENCE** *Medicines from Nature*   502

TIMELINES IN SCIENCE *The Story of Atomic Structure*   604

16 Atomic Structure and the Periodic Table   506

the **BIG** idea

A substance's atomic structure determines its physical and chemical properties.

1 Atoms are the smallest form of elements.   509
CONNECTING SCIENCES *Elements of Life*   516

2 Elements make up the periodic table.   517
CHAPTER INVESTIGATION *Modeling Atomic Masses*   524

3 The periodic table is a map of the elements.   526
MATH IN SCIENCE *Using Scientific Notation*   533

17 Chemical Bonds and Compounds   538

the **BIG** idea

The properties of compounds depend on their atoms and chemical bonds.

1 Elements combine to form compounds.   541
MATH IN SCIENCE *Calculating Ratios*   546

2 Chemical bonds hold compounds together.   547
THINK SCIENCE *Stick to It*   555

3 Substances' properties depend on their bonds.   556
CHAPTER INVESTIGATION *Chemical Bonds*   560

How do these skydivers stay together? How is this similar to the way atoms stay together? page 538

Why might some substances dissolve in the seawater in this photograph, but others do not? page 608

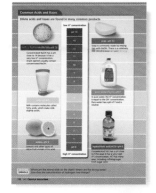

18 Chemical Reactions — 566

the BIG idea

Chemical reactions form new substances by breaking and making chemical bonds.

1. **Chemical reactions alter arrangements of atoms.** — 569
   MATH IN SCIENCE *Analyzing Line Graphs* — 577
2. **The masses of reactants and products are equal.** — 578
   SCIENCE ON THE JOB *Chemistry in Firefighting* — 585
3. **Chemical reactions involve energy changes.** — 586
   CHAPTER INVESTIGATION *Exothermic or Endothermic?* — 592
4. **Life and industry depend on chemical reactions.** — 594

19 Solutions — 608

the BIG idea

When substances dissolve to form a solution, the properties of the mixture change.

1. **A solution is a type of mixture.** — 611
2. **The amount of solute that dissolves can vary.** — 617
   CONNECTING SCIENCES *Cool, Clear Water* — 624
3. **Solutions can be acidic, basic, or neutral.** — 625
   CHAPTER INVESTIGATION *Acids and Bases* — 632
4. **Metal alloys are solid mixtures.** — 634
   MATH IN SCIENCE *Calculating Percentages* — 639

Visual Highlights

The Periodic Table of the Elements — 520
Comparing Bonds — 552
Balancing Equations with Coefficients — 583
Chemical Reactions in Catalytic Converters — 597
Common Acids and Bases — 630

Features

Math in Science

CELLS AND HEREDITY
Using Scientific Notation 25
Interpreting Graphs 55
Using Exponents 93
Using Punnett Squares 116
Finding Percent of a Whole 149

HUMAN BIOLOGY
Comparing Rates 181
Choosing Units of Length 211
Making a Line Graph 242
Solving Proportions 285
Choosing a Data Display 307

ECOLOGY
Adding Integers 341
Multiplying a Fraction by a Whole Number 389
Finding Volumes 417

MATTER
Making a Circle Graph 458
Solving Proportions 481

CHEMICAL INTERACTIONS
Using Scientific Notation 533
Calculating Ratios 546
Analyzing Line Graphs 577
Calculating Percentages 639

Think Science

CELLS AND HEREDITY
Making Comparisons 33
Determining Relevance 123

HUMAN BIOLOGY
Inferring 173

ECOLOGY
Inferring 382

CHEMICAL INTERACTIONS
Isolating Variables 555

Connecting Sciences

CELLS AND HEREDITY
Life Science and Physical Science ... 79

HUMAN BIOLOGY
Life Science and Physical Science ... 277

ECOLOGY
Life Science and Physical Science ... 349

MATTER
Physical Science and Earth Science .. 495

CHEMICAL INTERACTIONS
Physical Science and Life Science ... 516
Physical Science and Earth Science .. 624

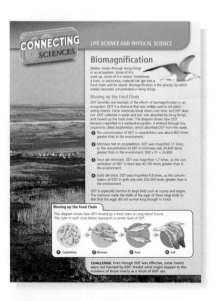

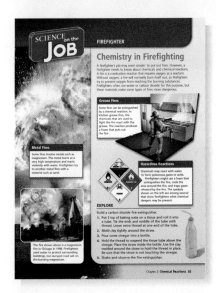

Science on the Job

CELLS AND HEREDITY
Natural Dyes and Cells   46

HUMAN BIOLOGY
Breathing and Yoga   204
Aging the Face   299

ECOLOGY
Ecology in Urban Planning   408

CHEMICAL INTERACTIONS
Chemistry in Firefighting   585

Extreme Science

CELLS AND HEREDITY
Modern Genetics Meets the Dodo
and the Solitaire   155

HUMAN BIOLOGY
Artificial Skin   249

MATTER
Particles Too Small to See   452

Frontiers in Science

CELLS AND HEREDITY
Genes That Map the Body   2

HUMAN BIOLOGY
Surprising Senses   162

ECOLOGY
Ecosystems on Fire   322

MATTER
Exploring the Water Planet   434

CHEMICAL INTERACTIONS
Medicines from Nature   502

Timelines in Science

CELLS AND HEREDITY
The Story of Genetics   128

HUMAN BIOLOGY
Seeing Inside the Body   254

ECOLOGY
Wilderness Conservation   394

CHEMICAL INTERACTIONS
The Story of Atomic Structure   604

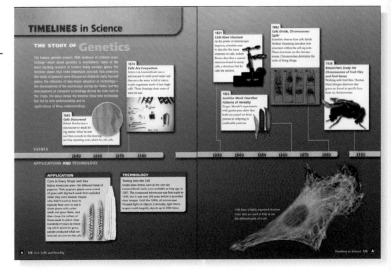

Internet Resources @ ClassZone.com

Simulations

CELLS AND HEREDITY
Virtual Cell Tour	7
Cells through Different Microscopes	19
Stages of Cell Division	71
Mendel's Experiment	99
Punnett Squares	111

HUMAN BIOLOGY
Human Body Systems	167
Assemble a Skeleton	176

ECOLOGY
Carrying Capacity	363

MATTER
Weight on Different Planets	443
Gas Behavior	465
Physical and Chemical Changes	471

CHEMICAL INTERACTIONS
Build an Atom	512
Mixing Alloys	609

Visualizations

CELLS AND HEREDITY
Photosynthesis	39
Active Transport	60
Mitosis	82
Protein Synthesis	141

HUMAN BIOLOGY
Lung and Diaphragm Movement	195
Peristalsis	206
Heart Pumping Blood	223
Skin Healing	247
Fertilization and Implantation of an Egg Cell	280
Human Aging	291

ECOLOGY
Nitrogen Cycle	340
Human Population Growth	402

CHEMICAL INTERACTIONS
Radioactive Decay	532
Ionic and Covalent Bonds	539
Polar Electron Cloud	551
Concentration and Reaction Rate	574
Endothermic and Exothermic Reactions	590
Supersaturated Solutions and Precipitation	618

Career Centers

Molecular Biology	5
Neurobiology	165
Ecology	325
Volcanology	437
Chemistry	505

Resource Centers

CELLS AND HEREDITY
Resources for the following topics may be found at ClassZone.com: *Cell Structures; Unicellular Organisms; Macromolecules; Diffusion; Nerve Regeneration; Cell Cycle; Asexual Reproduction; Sexual Reproduction; Meiosis; Genetics Research; Human Genome Project; DNA; Mutations; DNA Technology.*

HUMAN BIOLOGY
Resources for the following topics may be found at ClassZone.com: *Shackleton Expedition; Skeletal System; Muscles; Respiratory System; Urinary System; Circulatory System; Blood Types; Lymphatic System; Skin; Current Medical Imaging Techniques; Senses; Nervous System; Endocrine System; Human Health; Nutrition; Fighting Disease.*

ECOLOGY
Resources for the following topics may be found at ClassZone.com: *Prairie Ecosystems; Ecosystems; Cycles in Nature; Land and Aquatic Biomes; Symbiotic Relationships; Succession; Conservation Efforts; The Environment; Urban Expansion; Natural Resources; Ecosystem Recovery.*

MATTER
Resources for the following topics may be found at ClassZone.com: *Scale Views of Matter; Volume; Scanning Tunneling Microscope Images; Mixtures; Chemical Properties of Matter; Melting Points and Boiling Points; Separating Materials from Mixtures.*

CHEMICAL INTERACTIONS
Resources for the following topics may be found at ClassZone.com: *Periodic Table; Atom; Elements Important to Life; Chemical Formulas; Properties of Ionic and Covalent Compounds; Balancing Chemical Equations; Catalysts in Living Things; Atomic Research; Aquifers and Purification; Acids and Bases; Alloys.*

Math Tutorials

CELLS AND HEREDITY
Using Scientific Notation	25
Interpreting Graphs	55
Using Exponents	93
Using Punnett Squares	116
Finding Percent of a Whole	149

HUMAN BIOLOGY
Comparing Rates	181
Choosing Units of Length	211
Making a Line Graph	242
Solving Proportions	285
Choosing a Data Display	307

ECOLOGY
Adding Integers	341
Multiplying a Fraction by a Whole Number	389
Finding Volumes	417

MATTER
Making a Circle Graph	458
Solving Proportions	481

CHEMICAL INTERACTIONS
Using Scientific Notation	533
Calculating Ratios	546
Analyzing Graphs	577
Calculating Percentages	639

NSTA SciLinks

Codes for use with the NSTA SciLinks site may be found on every chapter opener.

Content Review

There is a content review for every chapter at ClassZone.com

Test Practice

There is a standardized test practice for every chapter at ClassZone.com

Explore the Big Idea

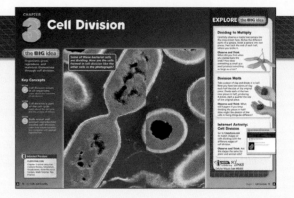

Chapter Opening Inquiry

Each chapter opens with hands-on explorations that introduce the chapter's Big Idea.

Cells and Heredity

Seeing and Understanding; Bits and Pieces	7
Leaves Underwater; Just a Spoonful of Sugar	39
Dividing to Multiply; Division Math	71
How Are Traits Distributed? Combinations	99
What Is the Pattern? What Vegetable Is That?	133

Human Biology

How Many Bones Are in Your Hand? How Does It Move?	167
Mirror, Mirror; Water Everywhere	195
Blood Pressure; Wet Fingers	223
Color Confusion; Eggs	259
How Much Do You Exercise? How Safe Is Your Food?	291

Ecology

How Do Plants React to Sunlight? What Is Soil?	327
How Do Living Things Interact Where You Live? How Many Roles Can a Living Thing Have in an Ecosystem?	363
How Many is Six Billion? How Easily Does Polluted Water Move Through Plants?	399

Matter

What Has Changed? Where Does the Sugar Go?	439
Float or Sink; Hot Chocolate	471

Chemical Interactions

That's Far! Element Safari	507
Mixing It Up; The Shape of Things	539
Changing Steel Wool; A Different Rate	567
Does It Dissolve? Acid Test	609

Chapter Investigations

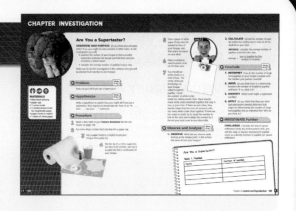

Full-Period Labs

The Chapter Investigations are in-depth labs that let you form and test a hypothesis, build a model, or sometimes design your own investigation.

Cells and Heredity

Using a Microscope	16
Diffusion	64
Stages of the Cell Cycle	86
Offspring Models	108
Extract and Observe DNA	142

Human Biology

A Closer Look at Muscles	188
Modeling a Kidney	216
Heart Rate and Exercise	232
Are You a Supertaster?	268
Cleaning Your Hands	314

Ecology

Soil Samples	334
Estimating Populations	372
Cleaning Oil Spills *Design Your Own*	426

Matter

Mass and Volume	446
Freezing Point	488

Chemical Interactions

Modeling Atomic Masses	524
Chemical Bonds	560
Exothermic or Endothermic?	592
Acids and Bases	632

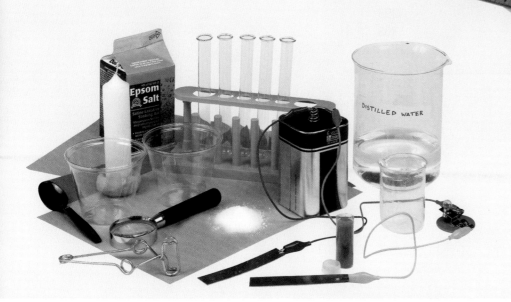

Explore

Introductory Inquiry Activities

Most sections begin with a simple activity that lets you explore the Key Concept before you read the section.

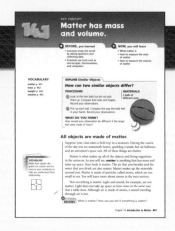

Cells and Heredity

Activity and Life	9
Specialization	26
Food Molecules	41
Diffusion	56
Cell Division	73
Probability	110
Meiosis	117
Templates	135
Codes	144

Human Biology

Levers	174
Muscles	182
Breathing	197
Digestion	205
Waste Removal	212
The Circulatory System	225
Membranes	234
The Skin	243
Smell	261
Reproduction	278
Growth	293
The Immune System	308

Ecology

Your Environment	329
The Water Cycle	336
Energy	342
Counting Animals	365
Population Growth	383
Sharing Resources	401
Environmental Impacts	418

Matter

Similar Objects	441
Mixed Substances	453
Solids and Liquids	459
Physical Properties	473
Identifying Substances	490

Chemical Interactions

The Size of Atoms	509
Similarities and Differences of Objects	517
Compounds	541
Bonds in Metals	556
Chemical Changes	569
Energy Changes	586
Mixtures	611
Solutions and Temperature	617
Acids and Bases	625

Investigate

Skill Labs

Each Investigate activity gives you a chance to practice a specific science skill related to the content that you're studying.

Cells and Heredity

Plant and Animal Cells	*Observing*	21
Cell Models	*Making models*	31
Oil and Water	*Observing*	44
Fermentation	*Observing*	53
Cells	*Making models*	62
Chromosomes	*Making models*	76
Cell Division	*Making models*	84
Asexual Reproduction	*Drawing conclusions*	91
Multiple Probabilities	*Analyzing data*	114
Fertilization	***Design Your Own***	119
Neutral Mutations	*Making models*	146

Human Biology

Systems	*Predicting*	170
Movable Joints	*Observing*	179
Lungs	*Making models*	199
Chemical Digestion	*Making models*	207
Antibodies	*Making models*	239
Skin Protection	*Observing*	245
Response to Exercise	*Observing*	274
Life Expectancy	*Graphing*	297
Food Labels	*Analyzing*	303

Ecology

Carbon	*Observing*	339
Decomposers	*Observing*	345
Climate	*Graphing Data*	355
Species Interactions	*Analyzing Data*	377
Limiting Factors	***Design Your Own***	385
Resources	*Interpreting*	404
Particles in the Air	*Observing*	411

Matter

Mass	*Modeling*	449
Mixtures	*Inferring*	456
Liquids	*Measuring*	463
Chemical Changes	*Measuring*	479
Separating Mixtures	***Design Your Own***	493

Chemical Interactions

Masses of Atomic Particles	*Modeling*	513
Radioactivity	*Modeling*	531
Element Ratios	*Modeling*	543
Crystals	*Observing*	553
Chemical Reactions	*Inferring*	574
Conservation of Mass	*Measuring*	579
Sugar Combustion	*Inferring*	595
Solutions	*Observing*	613
Solubility	***Design Your Own***	620
Alloys	*Observing*	637

These pages list all of the standards for Grade 7 Science. The charts show you where each standard is covered in your book.

Scientific Inquiry

Standard 7-1: The student will demonstrate an understanding of technological design and scientific inquiry, including process skills, mathematical thinking, controlled investigative design and analysis, and problem solving.

7-1.1 Use appropriate tools and instruments (including a microscope) safely and accurately when conducting a controlled scientific investigation.

7-1.2 Generate questions that can be answered through scientific investigation.

7-1.3 Explain the reasons for testing one independent variable at a time in a controlled scientific investigation.

7-1.4 Explain the importance that repeated trials and a well-chosen sample size have with regard to the validity of a controlled scientific investigation.

7-1.5 Explain the relationships between independent and dependent variables in a controlled scientific investigation through the use of appropriate graphs, tables, and charts.

7-1.6 Critique a conclusion drawn from a scientific investigation.

7-1.7 Use appropriate safety procedures when conducting investigations.

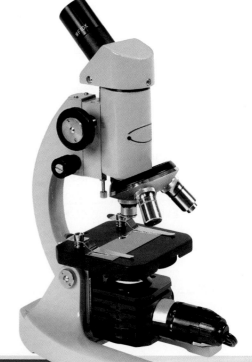

Standard	Labs & Handbooks	Pages
7-1.1– 7-1.7	All Chapter Investigations	Example: 426–427
	Lab Handbook	R10–R35

Cells and Heredity

Standard 7-2: The student will demonstrate an understanding of the structure and function of cells, cellular reproduction, and heredity. (Life Science)

7-2.1 Summarize the structures and functions of the major components of plant and animal cells (including the cell wall, the cell membrane, the nucleus, chloroplasts, mitochondria, and vacuoles).

7-2.2 Compare the major components of plant and animal cells.

7-2.3 Compare the body shapes of bacteria (spiral, coccus, and bacillus) and the body structures that protists (euglena, paramecium, amoeba) use for food gathering and locomotion.

7-2.4 Explain how cellular processes (including respiration, photosynthesis in plants, mitosis, and waste elimination) are essential to the survival of the organism.

7-2.5 Summarize how genetic information is passed from parent to offspring by using the terms genes, chromosomes, inherited traits, genotype, phenotype, dominant traits, and recessive traits.

7-2.6 Use Punnett squares to predict inherited monohybrid traits.

7-2.7 Distinguish between inherited traits and those acquired from environmental factors.

Standard	Chapters	Pages
7-2.1	1, 2	18–24, 47–54, 56–63
7-2.2	1, 2	18–24, 47–54
7-2.3	1, South Carolina Essentials	16–17, 645–646
7-2.4	2, 3	47–54, 56–63, 73–78, 80–85
7-2.5	3, 4	73–78, 101–107
7-2.6	4	110–115
7-2.7	4	101–107

Human Body Systems and Disease

Standard 7-3: The student will demonstrate an understanding of the functions and interconnections of the major human body systems, including the breakdown in structure or function that disease causes. (Life Science)

7-3.1 Summarize the levels of structural organization within the human body (including cells, tissues, organs, and systems).

7-3.2 Recall the major organs of the human body and their function within their particular body system.

7-3.3 Summarize the relationships of the major body systems (including the circulatory, respiratory, digestive, excretory, nervous, muscular, and skeletal systems).

7-3.4 Explain the effects of disease on the major organs and body systems (including infectious diseases such as colds and flu, AIDS, and athlete's foot and noninfectious diseases such as diabetes, Parkinson's, and skin cancer).

Standard	Chapters	Pages
7-3.1	6	169–172
7-3.2	7, 8, 9	197–215, 225–231, 261–276
7-3.3	6, 7, 8, 9	174–187, 197–215, 225–248, 261–284
7-3.4	8, South Carolina Essentials	234–241, 647

Ecology: The Biotic and Abiotic Environment

Standard 7-4: The student will demonstrate an understanding of how organisms interact with and respond to the biotic and abiotic components of their environment. (Earth Science, Life Science)

7-4.1 Summarize the characteristics of the levels of organization within ecosystems (including populations, communities, habitats, niches, and biomes).

7-4.2 Illustrate energy flow in food chains, food webs, and energy pyramids

7-4.3 Explain the interaction among changes in the environment due to natural hazards (including landslides, wildfires, and floods), changes in populations, and limiting factors (including climate and the availability of food and water, space, and shelter).

7-4.4 Explain the effects of soil quality on the characteristics of an ecosystem.

7-4.5 Summarize how the location and movement of water on Earth's surface through groundwater zones and surface-water drainage basins, called watersheds, are important to ecosystems and to human activities.

7-4.6 Classify resources as renewable or nonrenewable and explain the implications of their depletion and the importance of conservation.

Standard	Chapters	Pages
7-4.1	12	365–371
7-4.2	11	336–340
7-4.3	12	383–388
7-4.4	11, South Carolina Essentials	329–333, 648–650
7-4.5	11, 13, South Carolina Essentials	329–333, 336–340, 409–416, 651–654
7-4.6	13	401–407, 409–416, 418–425

The Chemical Nature of Matter

Standard 7-5: The student will demonstrate an understanding of the classifications and properties of matter and the changes that matter undergoes. (Physical Science)

7-5.1 Recognize that matter is composed of extremely small particles called atoms.

7-5.2 Classify matter as element, compound, or mixture on the basis of its composition.

7-5.3 Compare the physical properties of metals and nonmetals.

7-5.4 Use the periodic table to identify the basic organization of elements and groups of elements (including metals, nonmetals, and families).

7-5.5 Translate chemical symbols and the chemical formulas of common substances to show the component parts of the substances (including NaCl [table salt], H_2O [water], $C_6H_{12}O_6$ [simple sugar], O_2 [oxygen gas], CO_2 [carbon dioxide], and N_2 [nitrogen gas]).

7-5.6 Distinguish between acids and bases and use indicators (including litmus paper, pH paper, and phenolphthalein) to determine their relative pH.

7-5.7 Identify the reactants and products in chemical equations.

7-5.8 Explain how a balanced chemical equation supports the law of conservation of matter.

7-5.9 Compare physical properties of matter (including melting or boiling point, density, and color) to the chemical property of reactivity with a certain substance (including the ability to burn or to rust).

7-5.10 Compare physical changes (including changes in size, shape, and state) to chemical changes that are the result of chemical reactions (including changes in color or temperature and formation of a precipitate or gas).

Standard	Chapters	Pages
7-5.1	14, 16	448–451, 509–515
7-5.2	16, 17, 19	509–515, 541–545, 611–616
7-5.3	16, South Carolina Essentials	526–532, 655
7-5.4	16	517–523
7-5.5	17	541–545
7-5.6	19	625–631
7-5.7	18	569–576, 578–584
7-5.8	18	578–584
7-5.9	15	473–480
7-5.10	15	473–480, 482–487

Introducing Science

Scientists are curious. Since ancient times, they have been asking and answering questions about the world around them. Scientists are also very suspicious of the answers they get. They carefully collect evidence and test their answers many times before accepting an idea as correct.

In this book you will see how scientific knowledge keeps growing and changing as scientists ask new questions and rethink what was known before. The following sections will help get you started.

Unifying Principles of Science   xxx

What do scientists know? These pages introduce unifying principles that will give you a big picture of science.

The Nature of Science   xxxvi

How do scientists learn? This section provides an overview of scientific thinking and the processes that scientists use to ask questions and to find answers.

The Nature of Technology   xl

How do we use what scientists learn? These pages introduce you to how people develop and use technologies to design solutions to real-world problems.

Using McDougal Littell Science   xlii

How can you learn more about science? This section provides helpful tips on how to learn and use science from the key parts of this program—the text, the visuals, the activities, and the Internet resources.

What Is Science?

Science is the systematic study of all of nature, from particles too small to see to the human body to the entire universe. However, no individual scientist can study all of nature. Therefore science is divided into many different fields. For example, some scientists are biologists, others are geologists, and still others are chemists or astronomers.

All the different scientific fields can be grouped into three broad categories: life science, earth science, and physical science.

- Life science focuses on the study of living things; it includes the fields of cell biology, botany, ecology, zoology, and human biology.
- Earth science focuses on the study of our planet and its place in the universe; it includes the fields of geology, oceanography, meteorology, and astronomy.
- Physical science focuses on the study of what things are made of and how they change; it includes the fields of chemistry and physics.

McDougal Littell Science, Grade 7

McDougal Littell Science pulls together units from the different categories of science to give you a broad picture of how scientists study nature. For example, life scientists, earth scientists, and physical scientists all study energy from different points of view. In Unit 1 you will learn that biologists study how energy is used by individual cells. In Unit 4 you will see how oceanographers study deep-sea organisms that depend on chemicals as their ultimate source of energy. Finally in Unit 5 you will see that chemists study the energy released during chemical reactions.

Even though science has many different fields, all scientists have similar ways of thinking and approaching their work. For example, scientists use instruments as well as their minds to look for patterns in nature. Scientists also try to find explanations for the patterns they discover. As you study each unit, you will in part focus on the patterns that scientists have found within that particular specialized branch. At the same time, as you move from one unit to another, you will be blending knowledge from the different branches of science together to form a more general understanding of our universe.

Unifying Principles

As you learn, it helps to have a big picture of science as a framework for new information. McDougal Littell Science has identified unifying principles from each of the three broad categories of science: life science, earth science, and physical science. These unifying principles are described on the following pages. However, keep in mind that the broad categories of science do not have fixed borders. Earth science shades into life science, which shades into physical science, which shades back into earth science.

the BIG idea

Each chapter begins with a big idea. Keep in mind that each big idea relates to one or more of the unifying principles.

What Is Life Science?

Life science is the study of the great variety of living things that have lived or now live on Earth. Life science includes the study of the characteristics and needs that all living things have in common. It is also a study of changes—both daily changes and those that take place over millions of years. Probably most important, in studying life science you will explore the many ways that all living things—including you—depend on Earth and its resources.

Living things, such as these birds, have certain characteristics that distinguish them from nonliving things. One important characteristic is the ability to grow. If all goes well, these warbler chicks will grow to become adult birds that can feed and take care of themselves.

UNIFYING PRINCIPLES of Life Science

All living things share common characteristics.

Despite the variety of living things on Earth, there are certain characteristics common to all. The basic unit of life is the **cell.** Any living thing, whether it has one cell or many, is described as an **organism.** All organisms are characterized by

- organization—the way that an organism's body is arranged
- growth—the way that an organism grows and develops over its lifetime
- reproduction—the way that an organism produces offspring like itself
- response—the ways an organism interacts with its surroundings

All living things share common needs.

All living things have three basic needs: energy, materials, and living space. Energy enables an organism to carry out all the activities of life. The body of an organism needs water and other materials. Water is important because most of the chemical reactions in a cell take place in water. Organisms also require other materials. Plants, for example, need carbon dioxide to make energy-rich sugars, and most living things need oxygen. Living space is the environment in which an organism gets the energy and materials it needs.

Living things meet their needs through interactions with the environment.

The **environment** is everything that surrounds a living thing. This includes other organisms as well as nonliving factors, such as rainfall, sunlight, and soil. Any exchange of energy or materials between the living and nonliving parts of the environment is an **interaction.** Plants interact with the environment by capturing energy from the Sun and changing that energy into chemical energy that is stored in sugar. Animals can interact with plants by eating the plants and getting energy from the sugars that the plants have made.

The types and numbers of living things change over time.

A **species** is a group of living things so closely related that they can produce offspring together that can also reproduce. Scientists have named about 1.4 million different species. The great variety of species on Earth today is called **biodiversity.** Different species have different characteristics, or **adaptations,** that allow the members of that species to get their needs met in a particular environment. Over the millions of years that life has existed on Earth, new species have come into being and others have disappeared. The disappearance of a species is called **extinction.** Fossils of now extinct organisms is one way that scientists have of seeing how living things have changed over time.

What Is Earth Science?

Earth science is the study of Earth's interior, its rocks and soil, its oceans, its atmosphere, and outer space. For many years, scientists studied each of these topics separately. They learned many important things. More recently, however, scientists have looked more and more at the connections among the different parts of Earth—its oceans, atmosphere, living things, and rocks and soil. Scientists have also been learning more about other planets in our solar system, as well as stars and galaxies far away. Through these studies they have learned much about Earth and its place in the universe.

When a wolf eats a rabbit, matter and energy move from one living thing into another. When a wolf drinks water warmed by the Sun, matter and energy move from Earth's waters into one of its living things.

UNIFYING PRINCIPLES of Earth Science

Heat energy inside Earth and radiation from the Sun provide energy for Earth's processes.

Energy is the ability to cause change. All of Earth's processes need energy to occur. Earth's interior is very hot. This heat energy moves up to Earth's surface, where it provides the energy to build mountains, cause earthquakes, and make volcanoes erupt. Earth also receives energy from the Sun as **radiation**—energy that travels across distances in the form of certain types of waves. Energy from the Sun causes winds to blow, ocean currents to flow, and water to move from the ground to the atmosphere and back again.

Physical forces, such as gravity, affect the movement of all matter on Earth and throughout the universe.

What do the stars in a galaxy, the planet Earth, and your body have in common? For one thing, they are all made of matter. **Matter** is anything that has mass and takes up space. Rocks are matter. You are matter. Even the air around you is matter. Everything in the universe is also affected by the same physical forces. A **force** is a push or a pull. Forces affect how matter moves everywhere in the universe.

Matter and energy move among Earth's rocks and soil, atmosphere, waters, and living things.

Think of Earth as a huge system, or an organized group of parts that work together. Within this system, matter and energy move among the different parts. The four major parts of Earth's system are the

- **atmosphere,** which includes all the air surrounding the solid planet
- **geosphere,** which includes all of Earth's rocks and minerals, as well as Earth's interior
- **hydrosphere,** which includes oceans, rivers, lakes, and every drop of water on or under Earth's surface
- **biosphere,** which includes all the living things on Earth

Earth has changed over time and continues to change.

Events are always changing Earth's surface. Some events, such as the building or wearing away of mountains, occur over millions of years. Others, such as earthquakes, occur within seconds. A change can affect a small area or even the entire planet

What Is Physical Science?

Physical science is the study of what things are made of and how they change. It combines the study of both physics and chemistry. Physics is the study of matter, energy, and forces, and it includes such topics as motion, light, and electricity and magnetism. Chemistry is the study of the structure and properties of matter. It focuses especially on how substances change into different substances.

The force of the rushing water pushes the rafts forward, while the force from the people paddling helps to steer the rafts.

UNIFYING PRINCIPLES of Physical Science

Matter is made of particles too small to see.

The tiny particles that make up all matter are called **atoms.** Just how tiny are atoms? They are far too small to see even through a powerful microscope. In fact, an atom is about a million times smaller than the period at the end of this sentence. There are more than 100 basic kinds of matter called **elements.** The atoms of any element are all alike but different from the atoms of any other element. Everything around you is made of atoms and combinations of atoms.

Matter changes form and moves from place to place.

You see objects moving and changing all around you. All changes in matter are the result of atoms moving and combining in different ways. Regardless of how much matter may change, however, under ordinary conditions it is never created or destroyed. Matter that seems to disappear merely changes into another form of matter.

Energy changes from one form to another, but it cannot be created or destroyed.

All the changes you see around you depend on energy. Energy, in fact, means the ability to cause change. Using energy means changing energy. But energy is never created or destroyed, no matter how often it changes form. This fact is known as the **law of conservation of energy.** The energy you may think you've lost when a match has burned out has only been changed into other forms of energy that are less useful to you.

Physical forces affect the movement of all matter on Earth and throughout the universe.

A **force** is a push or a pull. Every time you push or pull an object, you are applying a force to that object, whether or not the object moves. There are several forces—several pushes or pulls—acting on you right now. All these forces are necessary for you to do the things you do, even sitting and reading. **Gravity** keeps you on the ground. Gravity also keeps the Moon moving around Earth, and Earth moving around the Sun. **Friction** is the force that opposes motion. The friction between the bottoms of your shoes and the floor makes it possible for you to walk without slipping. Too much friction between a heavy box and the floor makes it hard to push the box across the floor.

The Nature of Science

You may think of science as a body of knowledge or a collection of facts. More important, however, science is an active process that involves certain ways of looking at the world.

Scientific Habits of Mind

Scientists are curious. They are always asking questions. A scientist who observes that the number of plants in a forest preserve has decreased might ask questions such as, "Are more animals eating the plants?" or "Has the way the land is used affected the numbers of plants?" Scientists around the world investigate these and other important questions.

Scientists are observant. They are always looking closely at the world around them. A scientist who studies plants often sees details such as the height of a plant, its flowers, and how many plants live in a particular area.

Scientists are creative. They draw on what they know to form a possible explanation for a pattern, an event, or a behavior that they have observed. Then scientists create a plan for testing their ideas.

Scientists are skeptical. Scientists don't accept an explanation or answer unless it is based on evidence and logical reasoning. They continually question their own conclusions as well as conclusions suggested by other scientists. Scientists trust only evidence that is confirmed by other people or methods.

A white-tailed deer feeds on many plants, including the trillium shown here.

By measuring the growth of this tree, a scientist can study interactions in the ecosystem.

Science Processes at Work

You can think of science as a continuous cycle of asking and seeking answers to questions about the world. Although there are many processes that scientists use, scientists typically do each of the following:

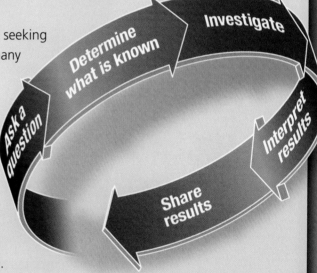

- Observe and ask a question
- Determine what is known
- Investigate
- Interpret results
- Share results

Observe and Ask a Question

It may surprise you that asking questions is an important skill. A scientific investigation may start when a scientist asks a question. Perhaps scientists observe an event or a process that they don't understand, or perhaps answering one question leads to another.

Determine What Is Known

When beginning an inquiry, scientists find out what is already known about a question. They study results from other scientific investigations, read journals, and talk with other scientists. A biologist who is trying to understand how the change in the number of deer in an area affects plants will study reports of censuses taken for both plants and animals.

Investigate

Investigating is the process of collecting evidence. Two important ways of collecting evidence are observing and experimenting.

Observing is the act of noting and recording an event, a characteristic, a behavior, or anything else detected with an instrument or with the senses. For example, a scientist notices that plants in one part of the forest are not thriving. She sees broken plants and compares the height of the plants in one area with the height of those in another.

An **experiment** is an organized procedure during which all factors but the one being studied are controlled. For example, the scientist thinks the reason some plants in the forest are not thriving may be that deer are eating the flowers off the plants. An experiment she might try is to mark two similar parts of an area where the plants grow and then build a fence around one part so the deer can't get to the plants there. The fence must be constructed so the same amounts of light, air, and water reach the plants. The only factor that changes is contact between plants and the deer.

Close observation of the Colorado potato beetle led scientists to a biological pesticide that can help farmers control this insect pest.

Forming hypotheses and making predictions are two other skills involved in scientific investigations. A **hypothesis** is a tentative explanation for an observation or a scientific problem that can be tested by further investigation. For example, since at least 1900, Colorado potato beetles were known to be resistant to chemical insecticides. Yet the numbers of beetles were not as large as expected. It was hypothesized that bacteria living in the beetles' environment were killing many beetles. A **prediction** is an expectation of what will be observed or what will happen and can be used to test a hypothesis. It was predicted that certain bacteria would kill Colorado potato beetles. This prediction was confirmed when a bacterium called *Bt* was discovered to kill Colorado potato beetles and other insect pests.

Interpret Results

As scientists investigate, they analyze their evidence, or data, and begin to draw conclusions. **Analyzing data** involves looking at the evidence gathered through observations or experiments and trying to identify any patterns that might exist in the data. Often scientists need to make additional observations or perform more experiments before they are sure of their conclusions. Many times scientists make new predictions or revise their hypotheses.

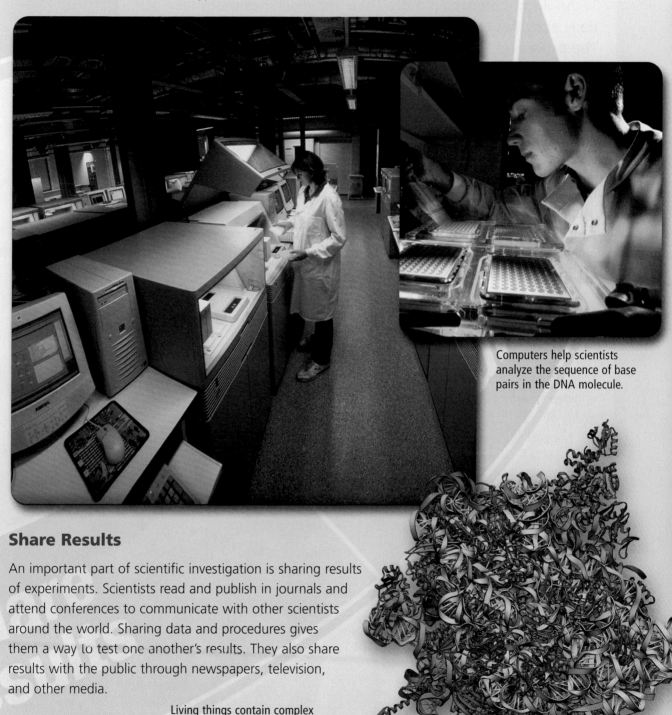

Computers help scientists analyze the sequence of base pairs in the DNA molecule.

Share Results

An important part of scientific investigation is sharing results of experiments. Scientists read and publish in journals and attend conferences to communicate with other scientists around the world. Sharing data and procedures gives them a way to test one another's results. They also share results with the public through newspapers, television, and other media.

Living things contain complex molecules such as RNA and DNA. To study them, scientists often use models like the one shown here.

The Nature of Technology

Imagine what life would be like without cars, computers, and cell phones. Imagine having no refrigerator or radio. It's difficult to think of a world without these items we call technology. Technology, however, is more than just machines that make our daily activities easier. Like science, technology is also a process. The process of technology uses scientific knowledge to design solutions to real-world problems.

Science and Technology

Science and technology go hand in hand. Each depends upon the other. Even designing a device as simple as a toaster requires knowledge of how heat flows and which materials are the best conductors of heat. Scientists also use a number of devices to help them collect data. Microscopes, telescopes, spectrographs, and computers are just a few of the tools that help scientists learn more about the world. The more information these tools provide, the more devices can be developed to aid scientific research and to improve modern lives.

The Process of Technological Design

Heart disease is among the leading causes of death today. Doctors have successfully replaced damaged hearts with hearts from donors. Medical engineers have developed pacemakers that improve the ability of a damaged heart to pump blood. But none of these solutions is perfect. Although it is very complex, the heart is really a pump for blood; thus, using technology to build a better replacement pump should be possible. The process of technological design involves many choices. In the case of an artificial heart, choices about how and what to develop involve cost, safety, and patient preference. What kind of technology will result in the best quality of life for the patient?

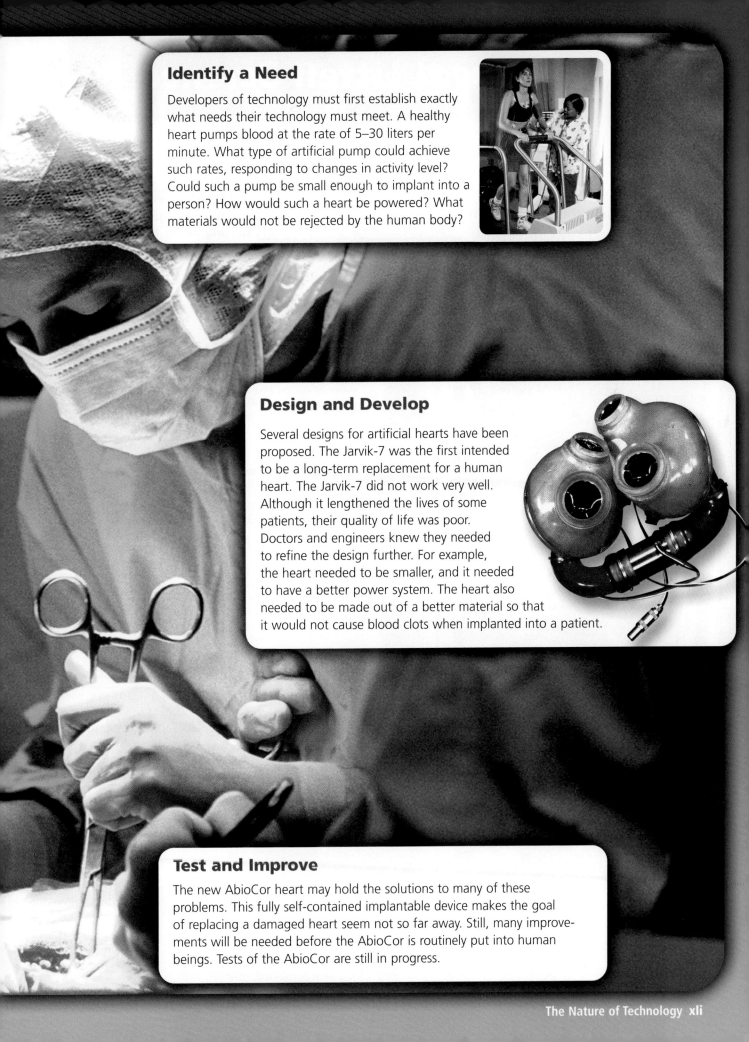

Identify a Need

Developers of technology must first establish exactly what needs their technology must meet. A healthy heart pumps blood at the rate of 5–30 liters per minute. What type of artificial pump could achieve such rates, responding to changes in activity level? Could such a pump be small enough to implant into a person? How would such a heart be powered? What materials would not be rejected by the human body?

Design and Develop

Several designs for artificial hearts have been proposed. The Jarvik-7 was the first intended to be a long-term replacement for a human heart. The Jarvik-7 did not work very well. Although it lengthened the lives of some patients, their quality of life was poor. Doctors and engineers knew they needed to refine the design further. For example, the heart needed to be smaller, and it needed to have a better power system. The heart also needed to be made out of a better material so that it would not cause blood clots when implanted into a patient.

Test and Improve

The new AbioCor heart may hold the solutions to many of these problems. This fully self-contained implantable device makes the goal of replacing a damaged heart seem not so far away. Still, many improvements will be needed before the AbioCor is routinely put into human beings. Tests of the AbioCor are still in progress.

Using McDougal Littell Science

Reading Text and Visuals

This book is organized to help you learn. Use these boxed pointers as a path to help you learn and remember the **Big Ideas** and **Key Concepts**.

Read the Big Idea.

As you read **Key Concepts** for the chapter, relate them to **the Big Idea.**

Take notes.

Use the strategies on the **Getting Ready to Learn** page.

CHAPTER 1
The C

the **BIG** idea

All living things are made up of cells.

Key Concepts

SECTION 1
The cell is the basic unit of living things.
Learn why cells are important to the study of life.

SECTION 2
Microscopes allow us to see inside the cell.
Learn what microscopes have shown about the inner structure of cells.

SECTION 3
Different cells perform various functions.
Learn about different types of cells in both unicellular and multicellular organisms.

Internet Preview

CLASSZONE.COM
Chapter 1 online resources: Content Review, two Simulations, two Resource Centers, Math Tutorial, Test Practice

6   Unit: Cells and Heredity

CHAPTER 1
Getting Ready to Learn

CONCEPT REVIEW

- Living things share certain characteristics that distinguish them from nonliving things.
- Living things have common needs, including energy, matter, and living space.

VOCABULARY REVIEW

See Glossary for definitions.

cell
DNA
genetic material
theory

CONTENT REVIEW
CLASSZONE.COM
Review concepts and vocabulary.

TAKING NOTES

MAIN IDEA WEB

Write each new blue heading, or main idea, in the top box. In the boxes around it, take notes about important terms and details that relate to the main idea.

VOCABULARY STRATEGY

Write each new vocabulary term in the center of a **four square** diagram. Write notes in the squares around each term. Include a definition, some characteristics, and some possible examples of the term. If possible, write some things that are not examples of the term.

See the Note-Taking Handbook on pages R45–R51.

8   Unit: Cells and Heredity

SCIENCE NOTEBOOK

All living things are made of cells.

| The cell is the smallest unit that performs the activities of life. | Multicellular organisms have many different types of cells working together. | In a unice organism single cell carries ou the activiti of life. |

Definition	Characteristics
Any living thing	Needs energy, materials from the environment, and living space. Grows, develops, responds to environment, reproduces. Is made up of one or more cells.
Examples	Nonexamples
Dogs, cats, birds, insects, moss, trees, bacteria	Rocks, water, dirt

ORGANISM

KEY CONCEPT

1.1 The cell is the basic unit of living things.

BEFORE, you learned

- Living things have common characteristics
- Living things have common needs
- A theory is something that explains what is observed in nature

NOW, you will learn

- How living things are different from nonliving things
- How the microscope led to the discovery of cells
- About the cell theory

Remember what you know.

Think about concepts you learned earlier and preview what you'll learn now.

VOCABULARY

organism p. 9
unicellular p. 11
multicellular p. 11
microscope p. 12
bacteria p. 14

EXPLORE Activity and Life

Does a candle show signs of life?

PROCEDURE

① Carefully light one candle.

② Sit quietly and observe the candle. Note its behavior. What does the flame do? What happens to the wax?

MATERIALS
- small candle
- candleholder
- matches

WHAT DO YOU THINK?
- How does a lit candle seem alive?
- How do you know for sure that it is not?

Living things are different from nonliving things.

MAIN IDEA WEB
Make a main idea web about living things, including how they differ from nonliving things.

You know life when you see it. Perhaps your class takes a field trip to a local state park to collect water samples. You are surrounded by trees. There is a stream, with rocks covered with moss and green algae. There are fish and frogs; there are birds and insects. You are surrounded by life. But how would you define it?

One way to answer the question is to think about what makes a living thing different from a nonliving thing. You might ask if a thing uses energy. Or maybe you would observe it to see if it moves. You could investigate whether it consumes food and water. These are characteristics of living things, or organisms. Any individual form of life that uses energy to carry out its activities is an **organism.** Most organisms move. All organisms get water and other materials from the environment.

Chapter 1: The Cell **9**

Reading Text and Visuals

Cells come from other cells.

The studies of Hooke and Leeuwenhoek made people ask if all living things have cells. People continued to observe samples taken from all sorts of living matter. They continued to find cells, although often these cells looked very different from one another. Still, it was clear that all living matter was made of cells.

There was another important question scientists were trying to answer: Where do cells come from? The answer to this question was settled by the 1850s. People studying all types of living cells observed the same thing—that cells divide. One living cell divides into two living cells. Here, under the microscope, was evidence of where cells come from. Life comes from life—that is, one cell comes from another cell.

CHECK YOUR READING What do scientists mean when they say that life comes from life? Your answer should include the word *cells*.

The observations and evidence gathered over a long time by many scientists are summarized in the three concepts of the cell theory:

1. Every living thing is made of one or more cells.

2. Cells carry out the functions needed to support life.

3. Cells come only from other living cells.

The Cell Theory

The importance of the cell to life is summarized in the cell theory.

1 Every living thing is made up of one or more cells. A polar bear is a multicellular organism.

2 Cells carry out the functions needed to support life. Fat cells are animal cells that provide energy as well as insulation.

3 Cells come only from other living cells. Each polar bear cub began as a single cell.

400×

Read one paragraph at a time.

Look for a topic sentence that explains the main idea of the paragraph. Figure out how the details relate to that idea. One paragraph might have several important ideas; you may have to reread to understand.

Answer the questions.

Check Your Reading questions will help you remember what you read.

Study the visuals.

- Read the title.
- Read all labels and captions.
- Figure out what the picture is showing. Notice the information in the captions.

Doing Labs

To understand science, you have to see it in action. Doing labs helps you understand how things really work.

① Read the entire lab first.

② Form a hypothesis.

③ Follow the procedure.

④ Record the data.

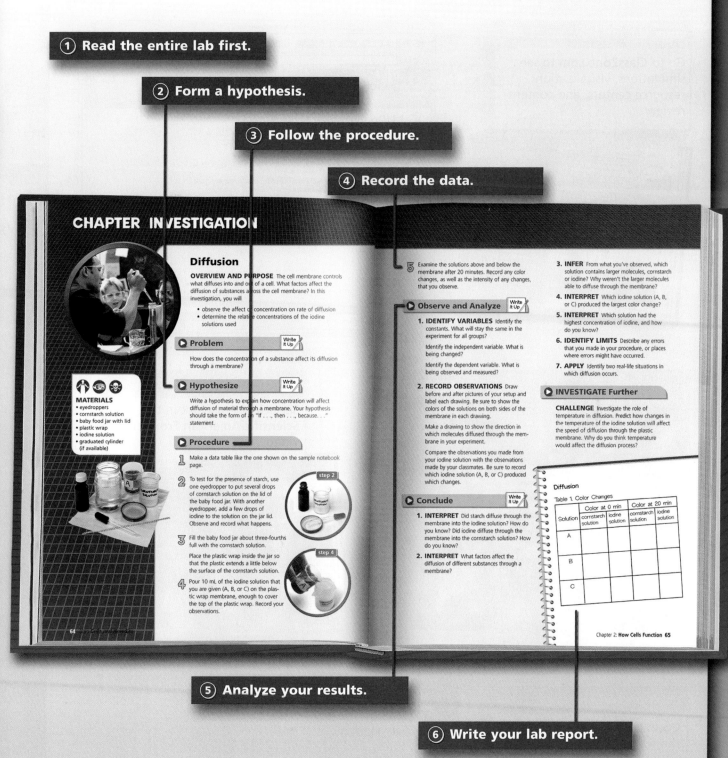

CHAPTER INVESTIGATION

Diffusion

OVERVIEW AND PURPOSE The cell membrane controls what diffuses into and out of a cell. What factors affect the diffusion of substances across the cell membrane? In this investigation, you will

- observe the affect of concentration on rate of diffusion
- determine the relative concentrations of the iodine solutions used

▶ **Problem**   Write It Up

How does the concentration of a substance affect its diffusion through a membrane?

▶ **Hypothesize**   Write It Up

Write a hypothesis to explain how concentration will affect diffusion of material through a membrane. Your hypothesis should take the form of an "If . . . , then . . . , because. . ." statement.

▶ **Procedure**

MATERIALS
- eyedroppers
- cornstarch solution
- baby food jar with lid
- plastic wrap
- iodine solution
- graduated cylinder (if available)

1. Make a data table like the one shown on the sample notebook page.

2. To test for the presence of starch, use one eyedropper to put several drops of cornstarch solution on the lid of the baby food jar. With another eyedropper, add a few drops of iodine to the solution on the jar lid. Observe and record what happens. *step 2*

3. Fill the baby food jar about three-fourths full with the cornstarch solution.

   Place the plastic wrap inside the jar so that the plastic extends a little below the surface of the cornstarch solution.

4. Pour 10 mL of the iodine solution that you are given (A, B, or C) on the plastic wrap membrane, enough to cover the top of the plastic wrap. Record your observations. *step 4*

64

5. Examine the solutions above and below the membrane after 20 minutes. Record any color changes, as well as the intensity of any changes, that you observe.

▶ **Observe and Analyze**   Write It Up

1. **IDENTIFY VARIABLES** Identify the constants. What will stay the same in the experiment for all groups?

   Identify the independent variable. What is being changed?

   Identify the dependent variable. What is being observed and measured?

2. **RECORD OBSERVATIONS** Draw before and after pictures of your setup and label each drawing. Be sure to show the colors of the solutions on both sides of the membrane in each drawing.

   Make a drawing to show the direction in which molecules diffused through the membrane in your experiment.

   Compare the observations you made from your iodine solution with the observations made by your classmates. Be sure to record which iodine solution (A, B, or C) produced which changes.

▶ **Conclude**   Write It Up

1. **INTERPRET** Did starch diffuse through the membrane into the iodine solution? How do you know? Did iodine diffuse through the membrane into the cornstarch solution? How do you know?

2. **INTERPRET** What factors affect the diffusion of different substances through a membrane?

3. **INFER** From what you've observed, which solution contains larger molecules, cornstarch or iodine? Why weren't the larger molecules able to diffuse through the membrane?

4. **INTERPRET** Which iodine solution (A, B, or C) produced the largest color change?

5. **INTERPRET** Which solution had the highest concentration of iodine, and how do you know?

6. **IDENTIFY LIMITS** Describe any errors that you made in your procedure, or places where errors might have occurred.

7. **APPLY** Identify two real-life situations in which diffusion occurs.

▶ **INVESTIGATE Further**

CHALLENGE Investigate the role of temperature in diffusion. Predict how changes in the temperature of the iodine solution will affect the speed of diffusion through the plastic membrane. Why do you think temperature would affect the diffusion process?

Diffusion
Table 1. Color Changes

Solution	Color at 0 min		Color at 20 min	
	cornstarch solution	iodine solution	cornstarch solution	iodine solution
A				
B				
C				

Chapter 2: **How Cells Function** 65

⑤ Analyze your results.

⑥ Write your lab report.

Using Technology

The Internet is a great source of information about up-to-date science. The ClassZone Web site and NSTA SciLinks have exciting sites for you to explore. Video clips and simulations can make science come alive.

Look for red banners.

Go to **ClassZone.com** to see simulations, visualizations, resource centers, and content review.

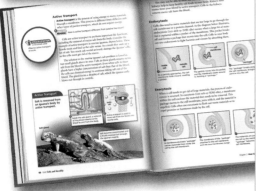

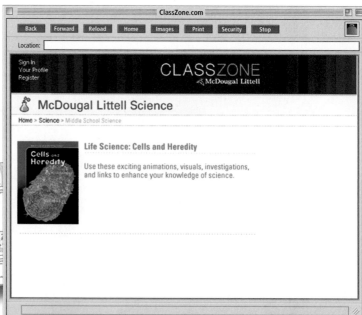

Watch the video.

See science at work in the **Scientific American Frontiers** video.

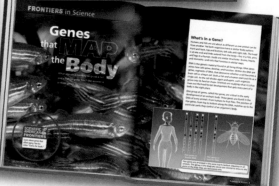

Look up SciLinks.

Go to **scilinks.org** to explore the topic.

Heredity **Code: MDL034**

UNIT 1

Cells and Heredity

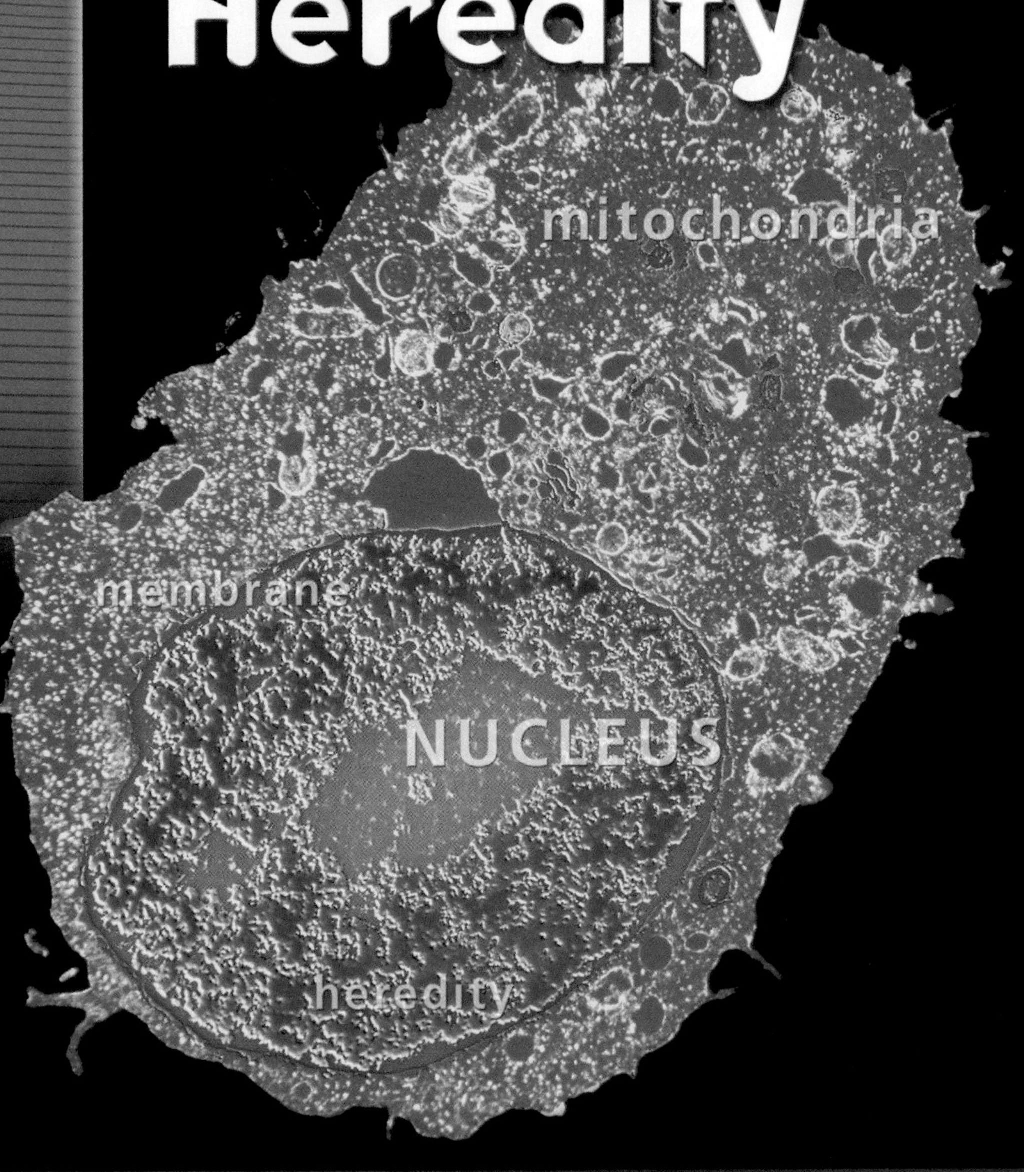

mitochondria

membrane

NUCLEUS

heredity

Contents Overview

Frontiers in Science
Genes That Map the Body   2

Timelines in Science
The Story of Genetics   128

Chapter 1	The Cell	6
Chapter 2	How Cells Function	38
Chapter 3	Cell Division	70
Chapter 4	Patterns of Heredity	98
Chapter 5	DNA and Modern Genetics	132

Genes that MAP the Body

What signals a monkey to grow a tail and a fish to grow fins? The answer is in their genes.

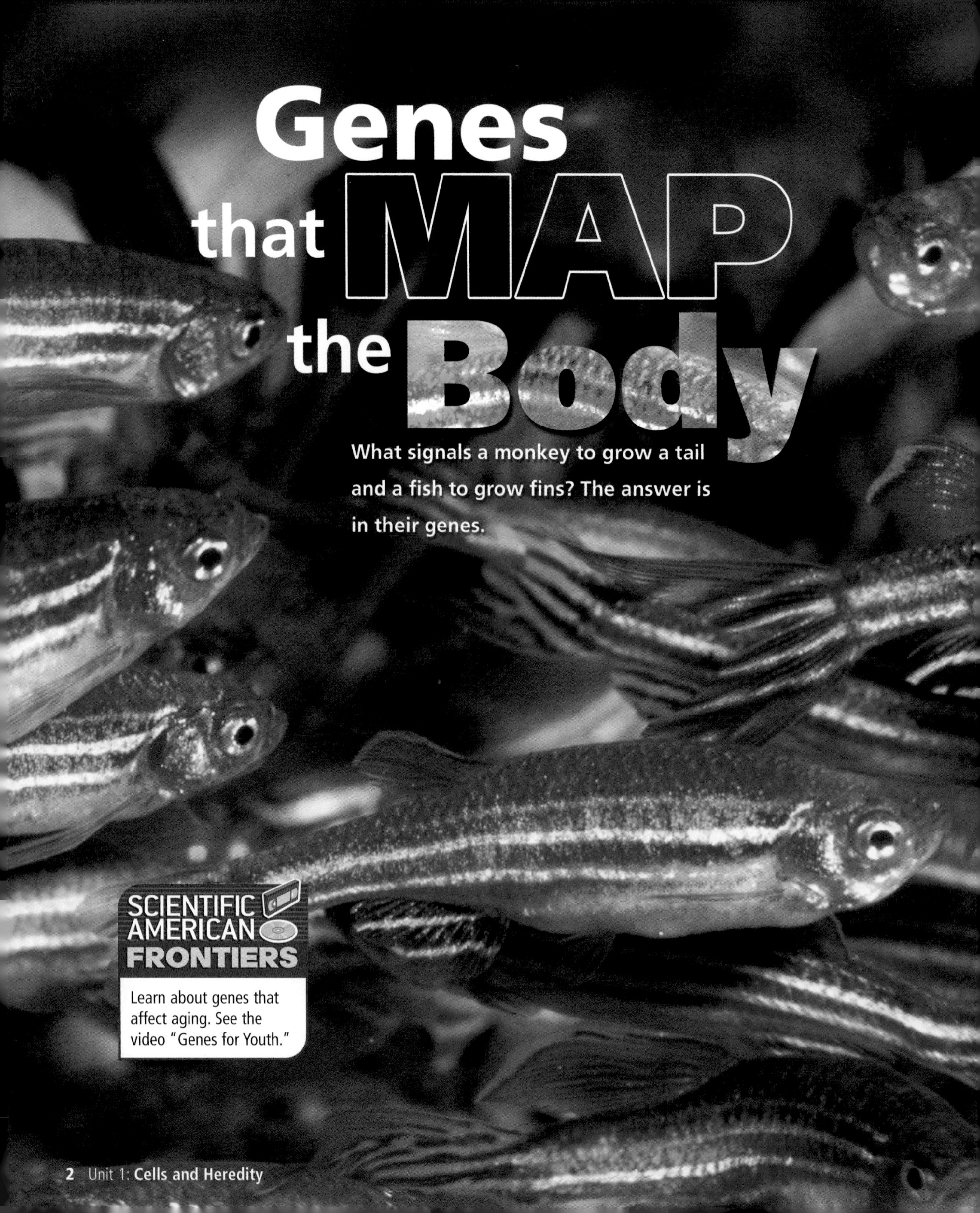

SCIENTIFIC AMERICAN FRONTIERS

Learn about genes that affect aging. See the video "Genes for Youth."

What's in a Gene?

Humans and fish are about as different as one animal can be from another. Yet both organisms have a similar body pattern: front and back, top and bottom, left side and right side. The head is at one end and limbs extend from the body—fins in a fish, arms and legs in a human. Inside are similar structures—brains, hearts, and stomachs—and cells that function in similar ways.

DNA is the genetic material found in all living things. DNA determines how cells grow, develop, and function. Within the DNA are genes, segments of DNA, that determine whether a cell becomes a brain cell or a heart cell. Both a fish and a human start out life as a single cell. As the cell divides again and again, each organism grows into its familiar shape. Scientists are studying what it is that maps out the head-to-tail development that gets every part of a body in the right place.

One group of genes, called *Hox* genes, are critical in the early development of an animal's body. These genes are found in the DNA of every animal—from humans to fruit flies. The position of *Hox* genes, from top to bottom along the DNA, matches up to the particular parts they control of an organism's body.

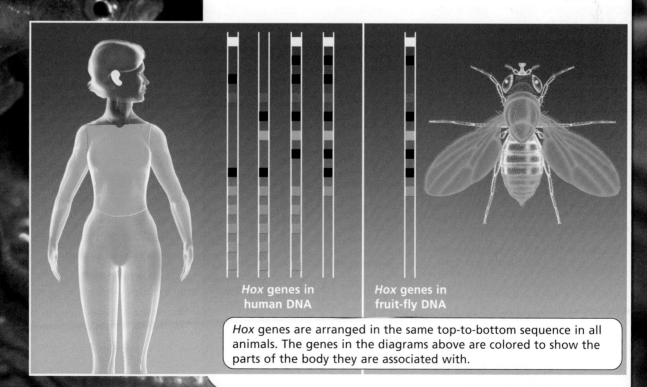

Hox genes in human DNA

Hox genes in fruit-fly DNA

Hox genes are arranged in the same top-to-bottom sequence in all animals. The genes in the diagrams above are colored to show the parts of the body they are associated with.

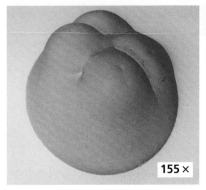

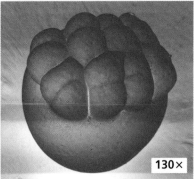

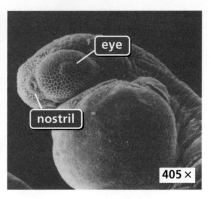

The egg of a zebrafish starts to divide after fertilization.

SOURCE for three images, Dr. Richard Kessel and Dr. Gene Shih/Visuals Unlimited

The egg now has 16 cells, all of which are similar in size and shape.

Many hours later, the cells have started to develop into different parts of the body.

How *Hox* Genes Work

Hox genes act like switches. A particular *Hox* gene turns on the development of a particular structure in an animal's body. One type of *Hox* gene switches on the development of structures in the head—for example, eyes and ears. Another switches on the development of limbs—the arms, legs, fins, or wings of an animal. The position of the genes within an animal's DNA matches to the part of the body it controls. *Hox* genes at the top control development of parts of the head. Those toward the middle control development of the main part of the body and the limbs.

How a Limb Develops

What happens if a *Hox* gene gets out of position? If the *Hox* gene that controls the development of legs in a fruit fly is placed in with the *Hox* genes that control development of the head, the fruit fly will grow legs from its head. The gene functions as it should, it's just that it's not doing its job in the right place.

Another interesting thing about *Hox* genes is that they are active only for a certain period of time. They "switch off" when the part of the body they control has developed. Studies of the zebrafish have provided clues as to how this happens.

SCIENTIFIC AMERICAN FRONTIERS

View the "Genes for Youth" segment of your Scientific American Frontiers video to learn about the role of genes in aging.

IN THIS SCENE FROM THE VIDEO ▶ biologist Cynthia Kenyon observes the activity level of some unusual worms that remain active much longer than other worms.

Kenyon is interested in what controls aging in worms. She studies how the genes in long-living worms affect the activity of their cells. She looks for differences between the cells of unusual worms and those of normal worms. Because cells of animals function in similar ways, she is interested in how

UNDERSTANDING AGING A multicellular organism starts life as a single cell. As an organism grows, it goes through different stages of development. Think of the differences between a baby, a teenager, a young adult, and an older person.

what she learns about aging in worms might apply to other animals. Even though a worm is far less complex an animal than a human, studying these worms may provide clues into how humans age.

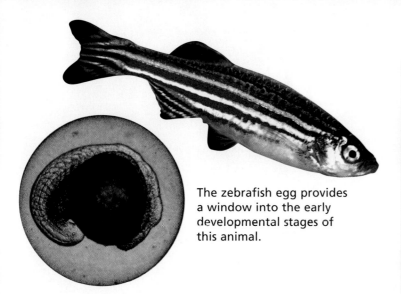

The zebrafish egg provides a window into the early developmental stages of this animal.

A Window on Development

Zebrafish are tiny fish that hatch in about three days. Scientists can actually see through the fish egg to watch its body develop. Working with the *Hox* genes of zebrafish, one researcher studied the amount of time that the *Hox* gene that controls fin development was active. The gene "turned on" for a short period of time, the fin developed, then the gene "turned off."

This research led scientists to think about the length of time the same *Hox* gene is active in other animals. It's possible that limbs are longer in larger animals because their *Hox* genes are active for a longer period of time. Researchers are excited because what they learn about the *Hox* genes of a simple animal can provide clues into the development of larger, more complex animals.

UNANSWERED Questions

There are many unanswered questions about the role *Hox* genes play in the development of body plans:

- Which *Hox* genes control which stages of development and how long are the genes active?
- What is it that signals the genes to "turn on and off"?
- How can research on *Hox* genes be used by medical researchers to help them treat genetic diseases or disorders that affect how a body develops?

UNIT PROJECTS

As you study this unit, work alone or with a group on one of the projects below.

Design an Experiment

Use fast plants to observe differences among plants.

- Follow directions for growing fast plants.
- Observe the plants as they grow and identify different characteristics.
- Use your observations to form a question about genes and plant characteristics.
- Design an experiment to answer your question.

Living Cell

Work cooperatively to present a "living cell" demonstration. Model cell processes, such as photosynthesis and cellular respiration.

- Design a model that shows parts of the cell at work.
- Include structures such as membranes, the nucleus, chloroplasts, and mitochondria. Represent energy and materials that move into and out of a cell.
- Have one student narrate each process.

DNA Detective Work

Prepare an oral presentation about how DNA technology is used to solve crimes.

Explain the science behind police and detective work.

 CAREER CENTER
CLASSZONE.COM

Learn more about careers in molecular biology.

1 The Cell

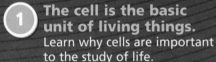

the BIG idea

All living things are made up of cells.

Key Concepts

SECTION

1 The cell is the basic unit of living things.
Learn why cells are important to the study of life.

SECTION

2 Microscopes allow us to see inside the cell.
Learn what microscopes have shown about the inner structure of cells.

SECTION

3 Different cells perform various functions.
Learn about different types of cells in both unicellular and multicellular organisms.

Internet Preview

CLASSZONE.COM

Chapter 1 online resources: Content Review, two Simulations, two Resource Centers, Math Tutorial, Test Practice

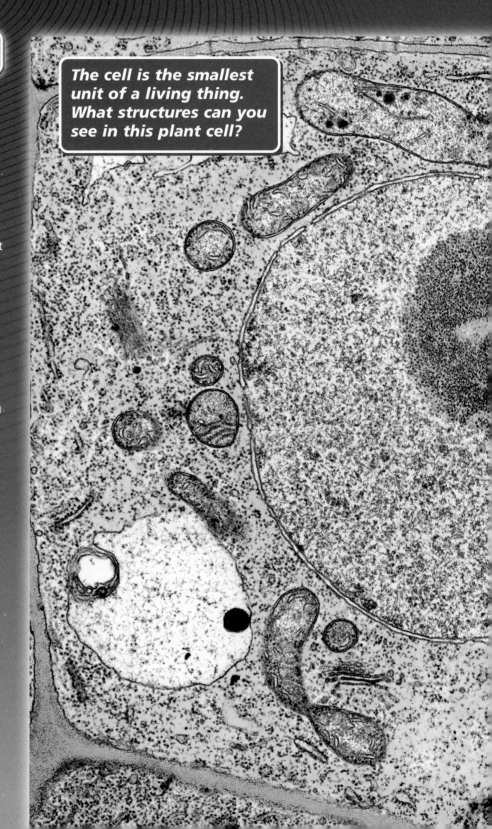

The cell is the smallest unit of a living thing. What structures can you see in this plant cell?

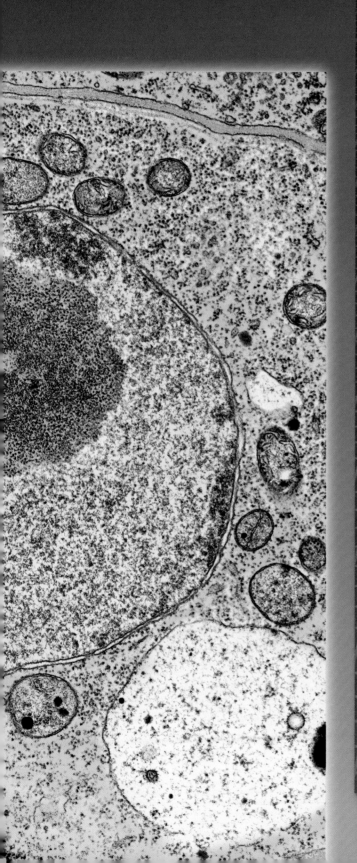

Seeing and Understanding

Cut out a color photograph or drawing from a magazine or newspaper and place it on a flat surface. Use a magnifying glass to look at the image. Start with the magnifying glass right on top of the image and then slowly move the magnifying glass away, studying the photograph as you do.

Observe and Think What happens as you move the magnifying glass away from the image? How can a simple magnifying tool help you understand better how the image was printed?

Bits and Pieces

Find a sentence approximately ten words long in a newspaper or magazine and cut it out. Then cut the sentence into words. Ask a friend to put the words back together into a sentence.

Observe and Think What clues can your friend use to put the sentence back together? How can the parts of something help you understand how the whole works?

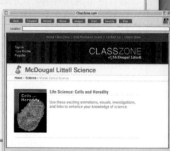

Internet Activity: Cells

Go to **ClassZone.com** to take a virtual tour of a cell.

Observe and Think What functions do the different parts of the cell perform?

Getting Ready to Learn

◀ CONCEPT REVIEW

- Living things share certain characteristics that distinguish them from nonliving things.
- Living things have common needs, including energy, matter, and living space.

◀ VOCABULARY REVIEW

See Glossary for definitions.

cell

genetic material

organism

theory

 CONTENT REVIEW
CLASSZONE.COM
Review concepts and vocabulary.

▶ TAKING NOTES

MAIN IDEA WEB

Write each new blue heading, or main idea, in the top box. In the boxes around it, take notes about important terms and details that relate to the main idea.

VOCABULARY STRATEGY

Write each new vocabulary term in the center of a **four square** diagram. Write notes in the squares around each term. Include a definition, some characteristics, and some possible examples of the term. If possible, write some things that are not examples of the term.

See the Note-Taking Handbook on pages R45–R51.

SCIENCE NOTEBOOK

All living things are made of cells.

The cell is the smallest unit that performs the activities of life.	Multicellular organisms have different types of cells working together.	In a unicellular organism a single cell carries out all the activities of life.

Definition	Characteristics
Any living thing	Needs energy, materials from the environment, and living space. Grows, develops, responds to environment, reproduces. Is made up of one or more cells.

ORGANISM

Examples	Nonexamples
Dogs, cats, birds, insects, moss, trees, bacteria	Rocks, water, dirt

1.1 The cell is the basic unit of living things.

◀ BEFORE, you learned

- Living things have common characteristics
- Living things have common needs
- A theory is something that explains what is observed in nature

▶ NOW, you will learn

- How living things are different from nonliving things
- How the microscope led to the discovery of cells
- About the cell theory

VOCABULARY

unicellular p. 11
multicellular p. 11
microscope p. 12
bacteria p. 14

EXPLORE Activity and Life

Does a candle show signs of life?

PROCEDURE

1. Carefully light one candle.

2. Sit quietly and observe the candle. Note its behavior. What does the flame do? What happens to the wax?

WHAT DO YOU THINK?

- How does a lit candle seem alive?
- How do you know for sure that it is not?

MATERIALS
- small candle
- candleholder
- matches

Living things are different from nonliving things.

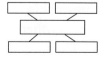

MAIN IDEA WEB
Make a main idea web about living things, including how they differ from nonliving things.

You know life when you see it. Perhaps your class takes a field trip to a local state park to collect water samples. You are surrounded by trees. There is a stream, with rocks covered with moss and green algae. There are fish and frogs; there are birds and insects. You are surrounded by life. But how would you define it?

One way to answer the question is to think about what makes a living thing different from a nonliving thing. You might ask if a thing uses energy. Or maybe you would observe it to see if it moves. You could investigate whether it consumes food and water. These are characteristics of living things, or organisms. Any individual form of life that is capable of growing and reproducing is an organism. All organisms get water and other materials from the environment.

Characteristics of Life

Living things have these characteristics:

- organization
- the ability to develop and grow
- the ability to respond to the environment
- the ability to reproduce

An organism's body must be organized in a way that enables it to meet its needs. Some organisms, like bacteria, are very simple. A more complex organism, such as the kingfisher shown in the photograph below, is organized so that different parts of its body perform different jobs, called functions. For example, a kingfisher has wings for flying, a heart for pumping blood, and eyes for seeing.

Another characteristic of organisms is that they grow and, in most cases, develop into adult forms. Some organisms change a great deal in size and appearance throughout their lifetimes, whereas others grow and change very little. Organisms also respond to the world outside them. Think of how the pupils of your eyes get smaller in bright light. Finally, organisms can reproduce, producing new organisms that are similar to themselves.

 CHECK YOUR READING What four characteristics are common to all living things?

Needs of Life

Organisms cannot carry out the activities that characterize life without a few necessities: energy, materials, and living space. What does it mean to need energy? You know that if you want to run a race, you need energy. But did you know that your body also needs energy to sleep or to breathe or even to think? All organisms require a steady supply of energy to stay alive. Where does this energy come from, and how does an organism get it?

APPLY Identify three living things in this photograph. How do they meet their needs?

Food is a source of **energy** and **materials**.

Water provides **materials** and **living space**.

The energy used by almost all forms of life on Earth comes from the Sun. Some organisms, like plants and some bacteria, are able to capture this energy directly. Your body, like the bodies of other animals, uses food as a source of energy. The food animals eat comes from plants or from organisms that eat plants. Food also provides the materials necessary for growth and reproduction. These materials include substances such as carbon dioxide, nitrogen, oxygen, and water. Finally, all organisms need space to live and grow. If any one of these requirements is missing, an organism will die.

All living things are made of cells.

The cell is the smallest unit of a living thing. Some organisms are made of a single cell. These organisms are **unicellular** and usually too small for you to see directly. Pond water is full of tiny unicellular organisms. Most of the organisms you can see, such as a frog or a water lily, are made up of many cells. Organisms made up of many cells are called **multicellular** organisms.

The needs and characteristics of a single cell in a unicellular organism are the same as those for any organism. Each of the tiny single-celled organisms found in a drop of pond water performs all the activities that characterize life. Multicellular organisms, like a frog or a water lily, have bodies that are more complex. Different parts of the body of a multicellular organism perform different functions. A water lily's roots hold it in the soil and its leaves capture energy from the Sun. A frog moves with its arms and legs and eats with its mouth.

Multicellular organisms have different types of cells that make up their body parts and help the organisms meet their needs. Roots are made of root cells, which are different from leaf cells. Muscle cells have special parts that allow them to move. In a multicellular organism, many cells work together to carry out the basic activities of life.

VOCABULARY
Add four squares for *unicellular* and *multicellular* to your notebook. You may want to add to your lists of characteristics and examples as you read through the chapter.

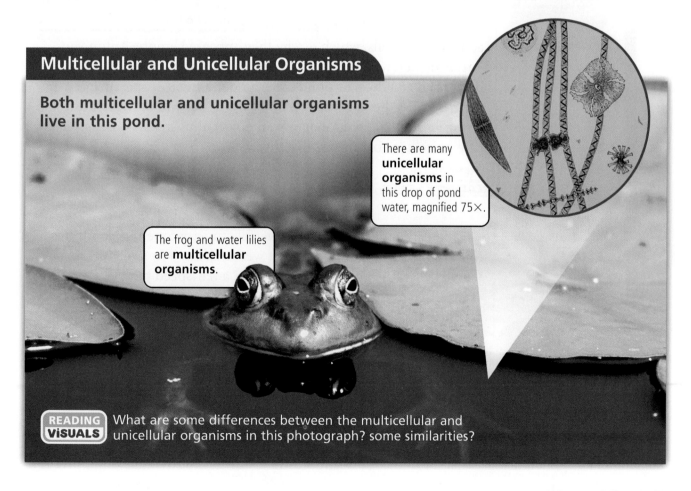

Multicellular and Unicellular Organisms

Both multicellular and unicellular organisms live in this pond.

There are many **unicellular organisms** in this drop of pond water, magnified 75×.

The frog and water lilies are **multicellular organisms**.

READING VISUALS What are some differences between the multicellular and unicellular organisms in this photograph? some similarities?

The microscope led to the discovery of cells.

READING **TiP**

The word *microscopic* is an adjective made from the noun *microscope*. Things that are microscopic are too small to see without the use of a microscope.

Most cells are microscopic, too small to see without the aid of a microscope. A **microscope** is an instrument which makes an object appear bigger than it is. It took the invention of this relatively simple tool to lead to the discovery of cells. In the 1660s, Robert Hooke began using microscopes to look at all sorts of materials. Anton van Leeuwenhoek took up similar work in the 1670s. They were among the first people to describe cells.

Robert Hooke gave the cell its name. While looking at a sample of cork, a layer of bark taken from an oak tree, he saw a group of similarly shaped compartments that looked to him like tiny empty rooms, or cells. You can see from his drawing, shown at right, how well these cells fit Hooke's description. Hooke used a microscope that magnified objects 30 times (30×). In other words, objects appeared thirty times larger than their actual size.

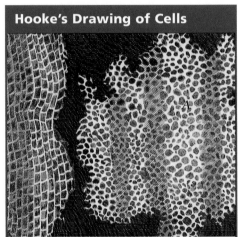

Hooke's Drawing of Cells

Robert Hooke published this drawing of dead cork cells in 1665. The microscope he used, shown at left, has two lenses.

The bark cells Hooke saw were actually dead cells, which is why they appeared empty. Anton van Leeuwenhoek was one of the first people to describe living cells. He looked at a drop of pond water under a microscope. Imagine his surprise when he saw that a drop of water was full of living things! Using lenses that could magnify an object almost 300×, he observed tiny unicellular organisms like those shown on page 11.

CHECK YOUR **READiNG** How did the invention of the microscope change the study of biology?

You can understand how powerful a microscope is if you think of how big a penny would be if it were increased in size 30 ×. It would be a little bigger than the tire of a ten-speed bicycle. Enlarged 300 ×, that penny would be so big that you would need a tractor-trailer to move it. Magnify your best friend 30× (supposing a height of 1.5 meters, or almost 5 ft), and your friend would appear to be 45 meters (147 ft) tall. That's almost the height of Niagara Falls. Change the magnification to 300 ×, and your friend would appear to be 450 meters (1470 ft) tall—taller than the Empire State Building.

Cells come from other cells.

The studies of Hooke and Leeuwenhoek made people ask if all living things have cells. People continued to observe samples taken from all sorts of living matter. They continued to find cells, although often these cells looked very different from one another. Still, it was clear that all living matter was made of cells.

There was another important question scientists were trying to answer: Where do cells come from? The answer to this question was settled by the 1850s. People studying all types of living cells observed the same thing—that cells divide. One living cell divides into two living cells. Here, under the microscope, was evidence of where cells come from. Life comes from life—that is, one cell comes from another cell.

 CHECK YOUR READING What do scientists mean when they say that life comes from life? Your answer should include the word *cells*.

The observations and evidence gathered over a long time by many scientists are summarized in the three concepts of the cell theory:

1 Every living thing is made of one or more cells.

2 Cells carry out the functions needed to support life.

3 Cells come only from other living cells.

The Cell Theory

The importance of the cell to life is summarized in the cell theory.

1 **Every living thing is made up of one or more cells.** A polar bear is a multicellular organism.

2 **Cells carry out the functions needed to support life.** Fat cells are animal cells that provide energy as well as insulation.

400×

3 **Cells come only from other living cells.** Each polar bear cub began as a single cell.

The cell theory is important to the study of biology.

The three ideas on page 13 are so important that they are grouped together using the word *theory*. A scientific theory is a widely accepted explanation of things observed in nature. A theory must be supported by evidence, including experimental evidence and observations. A theory proves its value when it explains new discoveries and observations.

CHECK YOUR READING What are two characteristics of a scientific theory?

Theories are important for a number of reasons. Certainly they satisfy scientists' desire to understand the natural world, and they serve as foundations for further research and study. Theories can also lead to research that has some practical benefit for society.

Louis Pasteur

The work of the French scientist Louis Pasteur shows how an understanding of cell theory can have practical uses. Pasteur lived in the 1800s, when there was no mechanical refrigeration in homes. People were used to having foods spoil, like milk going sour. During this time, many people died from diseases such as typhoid fever, tuberculosis, and diphtheria. Pasteur's work showed that microscopic organisms were involved both in the spoilage of food and in disease.

Pasteur observed that milk that turned sour contained large numbers of tiny single-celled organisms called **bacteria** (bak-TEER-ee-uh). He developed a process, now known as pasteurization, in which heat is used to kill the bacteria. Killing the bacteria keeps milk fresh longer. The fact that bacteria cause milk to sour or "sicken" made Pasteur wonder whether microscopic organisms could also be the cause of sickness in humans and animals.

The milk that you get from the school cafeteria has been pasteurized so that it will stay fresh longer.

Bacteria and Spontaneous Generation

Using a microscope to study air, water, and soil, Pasteur found microorganisms everywhere. He found bacteria in the blood of animals, including people who were sick. Pasteur referred to the microorganisms he observed as "germs." He realized that an understanding of germs might help prevent disease. Pasteur's work led to the first animal vaccinations for cholera and anthrax and to a treatment for rabies in humans.

At the time that Pasteur was doing his research, there were scientists who thought that bacteria grew from nonliving materials, an idea called spontaneous generation. Pasteur conducted a now-

Pasteur's Experiments

Pasteur's experiments showed that bacteria are present in the air. They do not appear spontaneously.

— End of flask is sealed.

1 Broth is boiled to destroy any living bacteria, and the flask is sealed.

2 A few days pass, and the broth is still clear. No bacteria have grown.

3 More days pass, and the broth is still clear. No bacteria have grown.

— End of flask is sealed.

1 Broth is boiled to destroy any living bacteria, and the flask is sealed.

— End of flask is broken. Exposure to air is the variable.

2 A few days pass, and the broth is clear. The end of the flask is then broken to expose the broth to the air.

3 Two to three days pass, and the broth is cloudy because of the growth of bacteria.

famous series of experiments that did not support the idea of spontaneous generation and confirmed the cell theory. He showed that cells come only from other cells. Two of Pasteur's experiments are shown above. Both began with a sealed flask containing boiled broth. In the first experiment, the flask remained sealed, while in the second experiment, the top of the flask was broken to expose the contents to air. Bacteria grew only in the second flask.

1.1 Review

KEY CONCEPTS

1. Name four characteristics of living things.
2. How did the microscope change human understanding of life?
3. Explain the three concepts that make up the cell theory.

CRITICAL THINKING

4. **Analyze** Relate the characteristics of a scientific theory to the cell theory.
5. **Compare and Contrast** Draw a Venn diagram to compare and contrast multicellular and unicellular organisms.

◔ CHALLENGE

6. **Synthesize** Explain how Pasteur's experiment supported the cell theory and failed to support the theory of spontaneous generation.

CHAPTER INVESTIGATION

Using a Microscope

OVERVIEW AND PURPOSE The smallest forms of life are not visible to the human eye. You will use a light microscope as a tool to observe very small unicellular and multicellular organisms. Then you will compare the organisms you see under the microscope to the Identification Key. Refer to pages R14 and R15 of the Lab Handbook for more information about using a microscope and preparing a slide.

▶ Procedure

1. Make a data table like the one shown on page 17. To observe the microscopic organisms, you need to make a wet-mount slide. Obtain a slide and use the eyedropper to place 2–3 drops of pond water in the center of the slide.

2. Obtain a cover slip for your slide. Place one edge of the cover slip on the slide, at the left edge of the pond water. Slowly lower the cover slip as if you were closing the cover of a book. The cover slip should lie flat on the slide. If you see air bubbles, pick up the cover slip and lower it again.

   step 2

3. Clean the lenses of the microscope with lens paper. Choose the lowest magnification, then place the slide on the stage. Start with the objective at its lowest point and raise the objective to focus. First focus with the coarse adjustment, which is usually the larger knob. Begin your search for living organisms. Use the fine adjustment to make the image clearer. Be patient when looking for life on your slide. It may take some time.

4. When you find something interesting, carefully switch to a higher magnification. Turn the nose of the microscope until another objective snaps into place. Use only the fine adjustment when viewing at high power, to avoid scratching the microscope or the slide. Move the slide gently from side to side as you look through the microscope. Search different parts of the sample for different organisms.

   step 4

MATERIALS
- slides
- eyedropper
- pond water
- cover slip
- light microscope
- lens paper
- Identification Key

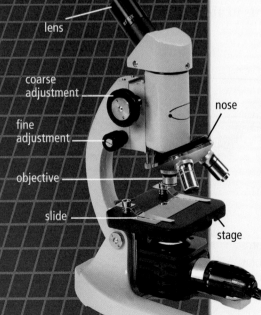

lens

coarse adjustment

fine adjustment

objective

slide

nose

stage

Euglena
(unicellular)

Paramecium
(unicellular)

Stentor
(unicellular)

Desmid
(unicellular)

Water flea
(multicellular)

Hydra
(multicellular)

Copepod
(multicellular)

Volvox
(multicellular)

5 Make a sketch of each of the different organisms that you see. Record any movement or behavior you observe. Include the magnification of the objective lens that you used.

▶ Observe and Analyze

1. **CLASSIFY** Use the Identification Key above to identify the organism. If you cannot make an identification, write *unknown*.

▶ Conclude

1. **COLLECT DATA** Compare your sketches with those of your classmates. How many different organisms in total did your class find? How many were identified as unicellular? How many were identified as multicellular?

2. **COMMUNICATE** Why is the microscope an important tool for studying cells and entire organisms?

3. **INTERPRET** Using what you learned in this chapter and in this investigation, explain the ways in which you would use the different objectives on a microscope.

4. **APPLY** Many diseases, such as strep throat, are caused by microscopic organisms. Why might a microscope be an important tool for a doctor?

5. **APPLY** How might the way a biologist uses a microscope be different from the way a doctor uses a microscope?

▶ INVESTIGATE Further

Collect a small sample of soil from outside the school or your home. Mix the soil with enough tap water to make it liquid. Then take a sample of the soil mixture and examine it under the microscope. Sketch some of the organisms you see. Are they similar to those in the pond-water sample? Why do you think different types of organisms live in different environments?

Using a Microscope

Table 1. Identifying Microorganisms

Organism 1
  Magnification used:
  Movement/behavior:
  Sketch:

  Name:

Organism 2
  Magnification used:
  Movement/behavior:
  Sketch:

  Name:

1.2 Microscopes allow us to see inside the cell.

STANDARDS

7–2.1 Summarize the structures and functions of the major components of plant and animal cells (including the cell wall, the cell membrane, the nucleus, chloroplasts, mitochondria, and vacuoles).

7–2.2 Compare the major components of plant and animal cells.

VOCABULARY

cell membrane p. 20
cytoplasm p. 20
nucleus p. 20
eukaryotic cell p. 20
prokaryotic cell p. 20
organelle p. 20
cell wall p. 21
chloroplast p. 23
mitochondria p. 23

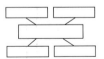

MAIN IDEA WEB
Make a main idea web that explains the importance of the microscope.

BEFORE, you learned

- Some organisms are unicellular and some are multicellular
- A microscope is necessary to study most cells
- The cell theory describes the cell as the fundamental unit of life

NOW, you will learn

- About different types of microscopes
- About prokaryotic and eukaryotic cells
- How plant and animal cells are similar and different

THINK ABOUT

How small are cells?

Because cells are so small, describing them requires a very small unit of measure: the micrometer (μm). A micrometer is one millionth of a meter. Most cells range in size from about 1 micrometer (some bacteria) to 1000 micrometers (some plant and animal cells). To get a sense of the sizes of cells, consider that it would take about 17,000 tiny bacterial cells lined up to reach across a dime. How many of these cells might fit on your fingertip?

The microscope is an important tool.

The invention of the light microscope led to the discovery of cells and to the development of cell theory. In light microscopes, lenses are used to bend light and make objects appear bigger than they are. Modern light microscopes can magnify objects up to 1000 times.

The light microscope is still used today to study cells. Over many years scientists have found ways to make light microscopes more useful. Cell samples are treated with dyes to make structures in the cells easier to see. Scientists use video cameras and computer processing to observe the movement of cell parts and materials within cells. One important advantage of light microscopes is that scientists can observe living cells with them.

Two other types of microscopes are important in the study of cells. The scanning electron microscope (SEM) and the transmission electron microscope (TEM) can produce images of objects as small as 0.002 micrometers. The light microscope can be used only for objects that are larger than 0.2 micrometers. Therefore, although a light microscope can be used to see many of the parts of a cell, only the SEM and TEM can be used for looking at the details of those parts.

In both the SEM and the TEM, tiny particles called electrons, not light, are used to produce images. The advantage of these microscopes is that they can magnify objects up to a million times. The disadvantage is that they cannot be used to study live specimens.

SIMULATION
CLASSZONE.COM
View cells through different types of microscopes.

 CHECK YOUR READING Compare light microscopes with electron microscopes. What are the advantages and disadvantages of each?

To be viewed with an SEM, a cell sample is coated in a heavy metal, such as gold. Then a beam of electrons is run back and forth over the surface of the cell. The electrons bounce off the coating and are read by a detector that produces a three-dimensional image of the surface.

A cell viewed with a TEM is sliced extremely thin. Electrons pass through a section. Images produced by a TEM appear two-dimensional.

Electron Microscopes

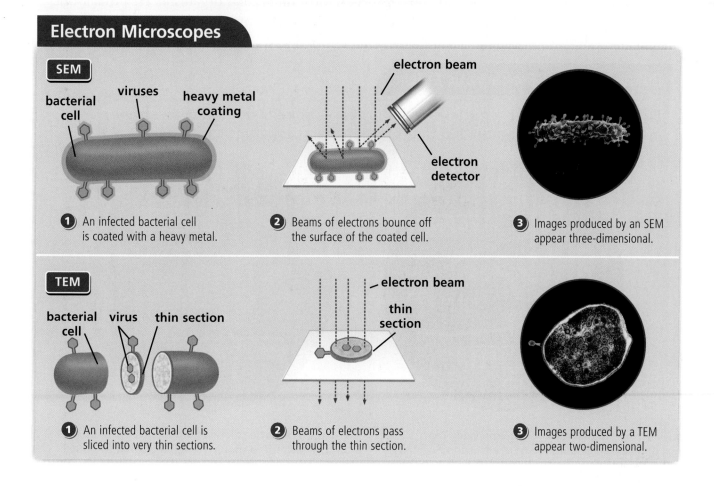

SEM

electron beam

bacterial cell   viruses   heavy metal coating

electron detector

1. An infected bacterial cell is coated with a heavy metal.

2. Beams of electrons bounce off the surface of the coated cell.

3. Images produced by an SEM appear three-dimensional.

TEM

bacterial cell   virus   thin section

electron beam

thin section

1. An infected bacterial cell is sliced into very thin sections.

2. Beams of electrons pass through the thin section.

3. Images produced by a TEM appear two-dimensional.

Cells are diverse.

Very early on, the people studying cells knew that cells have a great diversity of sizes and shapes. As microscopes were improved, scientists could see more and more details of cells. What they saw was that the inside of one cell can be very different from that of another cell.

Every cell has a boundary that separates the inside from the outside. That boundary is the **cell membrane,** a protective covering that encloses the entire cell. Any material coming into or out of the cell must pass through the cell membrane. Contained inside the cell membrane is a gelatin-like material called **cytoplasm** (SY-tuh-PLAZ-uhm). Most of the work of the cell is carried out in the cytoplasm.

Scientists separate cells into two broad categories based on one key difference: the location of the genetic material cells need to reproduce and function. In a **eukaryotic cell** (yoo-KAR-ee-AHT-ihk) the genetic material is in a structure called the **nucleus** (NOO-klee-uhs), a structure enclosed by its own membrane. Scientists use the word **organelle** (AWR-guh-NEHL) to describe any part of a cell that is enclosed by membrane.

In a **prokaryotic cell** (proh-KAR-ee-AWT-ihk) there is no separate compartment for the genetic material. Instead, it is in the cytoplasm. There are no organelles. Most unicellular organisms are prokaryotic cells. Almost all multicellular organisms are eukaryotic.

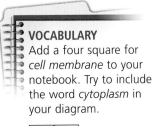

VOCABULARY
Add a four square for *cell membrane* to your notebook. Try to include the word *cytoplasm* in your diagram.

Eukaryotic and Prokaryotic Cells

Eukaryotic cells have a nucleus while prokaryotic cells do not. On average, eukaryotic cells are about 100 times larger than prokaryotic cells.

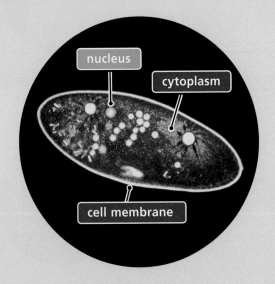

nucleus
cytoplasm
cell membrane

A **eukaryotic cell** has a nucleus. The paramecium shown here is magnified 133×.

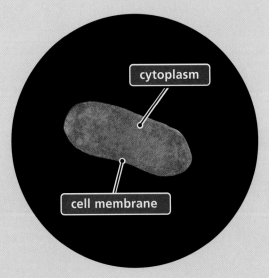

cytoplasm
cell membrane

A **prokaryotic cell** does not have a nucleus. The bacterium shown here is magnified 12,000×.

INVESTIGATE Plant and Animal Cells

How do plant and animal cells compare?

PROCEDURE

1. Choose the objective lens with the lowest magnification. Place the plant-cell slide on the stage and turn on the light source. Handle the slide carefully.

2. Observe the cells at low magnification. Make a drawing of one of the cells.

3. Observe the cells at high magnification. Fill in details. Return to the low-magnification lens before removing the slide.

4. Repeat steps 1–3 with the animal-cell slide.

WHAT DO YOU THINK?

- Compare the drawings you made. How are the plant and animal cells alike, and how are they different?
- Compare the thickness of plant cell's cell membrane and cell wall with the thickness of the animal cell's cell membrane.

CHALLENGE Placing a ruler on top of the slides, view each slide at low power. Estimate and compare the sizes of the two cells.

SKILL FOCUS
Observing

MATERIALS
- prepared slides
- microscope
- *for Challenge:* millimeter ruler

TIME
30 minutes

Plants and animals have eukaryotic cells.

Plant and animal cells, like all eukaryotic cells, are divided into two main compartments. The nucleus, usually the largest organelle, is the compartment that stores the instructions a cell needs to function. You will learn more about how cells use this information in Chapter 5.

Surrounding the nucleus is the cytoplasm. The cell membrane is the boundary between the cytoplasm and the outside of the cell. Plant cells also have cell walls. A **cell wall** is a tough outer covering that lies just outside the cell membrane. The cell wall supports and protects the cell. Having a cell wall is one important way in which plant cells differ from animal cells.

Find out more about cell structures.

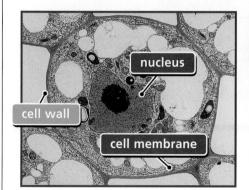
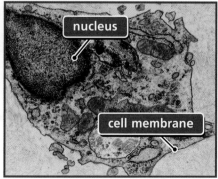

Both a plant cell (shown at left magnified 1750×) and an animal cell (shown at right magnified 12,000×) have a nucleus and a cell membrane. Plant cells also have a cell wall.

Parts of a Eukaryotic Cell

Plant Cell

Found in plant cells, not animal cells:

- chloroplast
- central vacuole
- cell wall

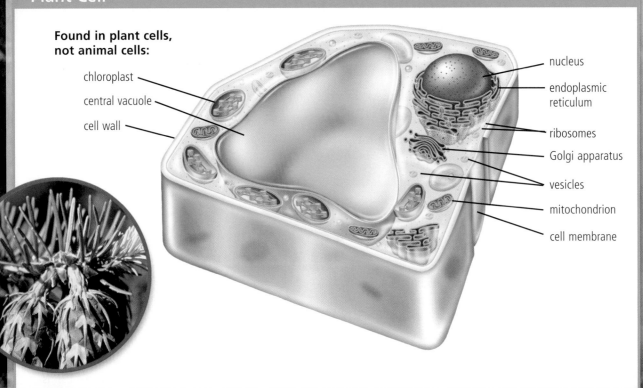

- nucleus
- endoplasmic reticulum
- ribosomes
- Golgi apparatus
- vesicles
- mitochondrion
- cell membrane

Animal Cell

Found in animal cells, not plant cells:

- lysosome

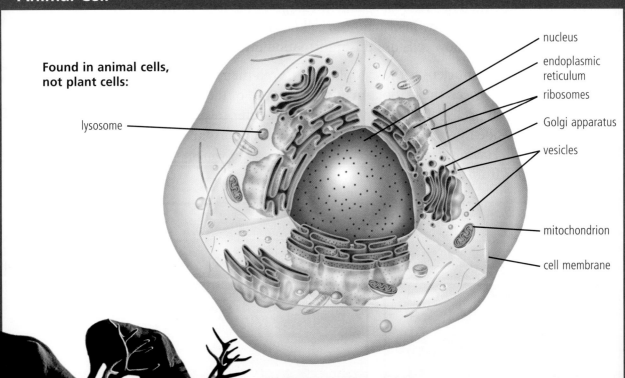

- nucleus
- endoplasmic reticulum
- ribosomes
- Golgi apparatus
- vesicles
- mitochondrion
- cell membrane

Structures That Process Information

The nucleus is often the largest organelle in a cell. It contains information a cell needs to function. Some of the information is translated by ribosomes, tiny structures located in the cytoplasm and the endoplasmic reticulum. Ribosomes use the information to build important molecules called proteins.

Organelles That Provide Energy

No cell can stay alive without energy. Cells need energy to perform all the activities of life. Plants get their energy directly from the Sun. Within plant cells are **chloroplasts** (KLAWR-uh-PLASTS), organelles in which the energy from sunlight is used to make sugar. Plants use some of the sugar immediately, to keep their cells functioning. The rest of the sugar is stored in the cells.

Animal cells do not contain chloroplasts. As a result, animals are not able to use the energy of the Sun directly. Instead, animals get their energy from food. Much of the food an animal uses for energy comes from the sugar that plant cells have stored. Animals can get this energy by eating plants or by eating animals that have eaten plants.

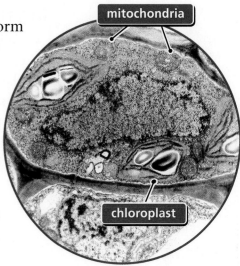

This plant cell is magnified 6000×.

CHECK YOUR READING How can a chloroplast, a structure found in plant cells but not in animal cells, provide energy for both plants and animals?

Both plant cells and animal cells must be able to use energy to do work. The energy is made available by organelles found in all eukaryotic cells. **Mitochondria** (MY-tuh-KAHN-dree-uh) are the organelles that use oxygen to get energy from processing food.

Organelles That Process and Transport

You know that plant and animal cells get their energy from the sugars that the organisms make or consume. Sugars are also an important part of the starting materials that cells use to maintain themselves and grow. The job of making cell parts from the starting materials that enter a cell is divided among a number of structures in the cytoplasm.

In the illustrations on page 22, you can see that the endoplasmic reticulum is a system of twisting and winding membranes. Some of the endoplasmic reticulum contains ribosomes, which manufacture proteins. The endoplasmic reticulum manufactures parts of the cell membrane.

The endoplasmic reticulum is also part of the cellular transport system. Portions of endoplasmic reticulum break off to form small packages called vesicles. The vesicles transport processed materials to an organelle called the Golgi apparatus. The folded membranes of the Golgi apparatus make it look something like a stack of pancakes. The Golgi apparatus takes the materials manufactured by the endoplasmic reticulum and finishes processing them.

Organelles for Storage, Recycling, and Waste

Cells store water, sugar, and other materials, which they use to function. Cells must also store waste materials until they can be removed. Inside plant and fungus cells are sacs called vacuoles. Vacuoles are enclosed by a membrane and can hold water, waste, and other materials. Vacuoles function with the cell membrane to move materials either into or out of the cell. A plant cell has a large central vacuole in which water and other materials can be stored. Water in the vacuole provides support for smaller plants.

Animal cells do not have central vacuoles. What animal cells do have are similar structures called lysosomes. Lysosomes are vesicles that contain chemicals that break down materials taken into the cell, as well as old cell parts. Remember that animals, unlike plants, take in food. Nutrients brought into the cell need to be broken down, as well as wastes contained.

central vacuole

 CHECK YOUR READING Compare and contrast lysosomes and central vacuoles.

1.2 Review

KEY CONCEPTS

1. What advantages and disadvantages does a light microscope have in comparison with an electron microscope?

2. What is the difference between a eukaryotic cell and a prokaryotic cell?

3. List three structures found in plant cells that are not in animal cells.

CRITICAL THINKING

4. **Synthesize** What organelles can be said to act like an assembly line within a cell? Explain.

5. **Compare and Contrast** Make a Venn diagram comparing and contrasting plant and animal cells.

◆ CHALLENGE

6. **Synthesize** Identify the type of microscope used to capture the image at the right, and indicate whether the cell is a plant cell or an animal cell. How do you know?

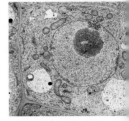

(magnified 27,900×)

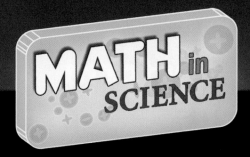

MATH in SCIENCE

MATH TUTORIAL
CLASSZONE.COM

Click on Math Tutorial for more help with scientific notation.

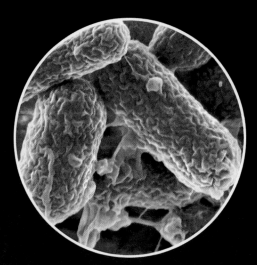

How many bacteria can fit on the head of a pin? The bacteria are magnified 50,000× in this photograph. The head of the pin below is magnified 7×.

Comparing Sizes

Measuring the sizes of very small things like atoms or very large things like planets requires numbers with many places. For example, the diameter of the nucleus of a cell is around 1/100,000 of a meter, while the diameter of Earth is 12,756,000 meters. How can you compare these sizes?

Example

(1) Express a large number as a number between 1 and 10 multiplied by a power of 10.

$12{,}756{,}000 = 1.2756 \times 10^7$

The exponent is the number of places following the first place.

(2) Express any number smaller than 1 as a negative power of 10.

$\dfrac{1}{100{,}000} = 0.00001 = 1 \times 10^{-5}$

The exponent is the number of places following the decimal point.

(3) Compare −5 and 7 to see that 7 is 12 more than −5.

ANSWER Earth's diameter is roughly 10^{12} times bigger than the diameter of a cell's nucleus.

Answer the following questions.

1. An oxygen atom measures 14/100,000,000,000 of a meter across. Write the width of the oxygen atom as a decimal number.

2. Write the width of the oxygen atom in scientific notation.

3. A chloroplast measures 5 millionths of a meter across. Write its width in standard form and in scientific notation.

4. A redwood tree stands 100 meters tall. There are 1000 millimeters in a meter. Express the height of the redwood tree in millimeters. Write the number in scientific notation.

5. A typical plant cell measures 1 millionth of a meter in width. Express the width in standard form and in scientific notation.

CHALLENGE The yolk of an ostrich egg is about 8 centimeters in diameter. The ostrich itself is about 2.4 meters tall. Write each of these lengths in the same unit, and express them in scientific notation. Then tell how many times taller the ostrich is than the yolk.

KEY CONCEPT

Different cells perform various functions.

 BEFORE, you learned

- Modern microscopes reveal details of cell structures
- Some cells are prokaryotic and some are eukaryotic
- Plant and animal cells have similarities and differences

NOW, you will learn

- How organisms are classified into three domains
- About specialization in multi-cellular organisms
- How cells, tissues, and organs are organized

VOCABULARY

specialization p. 28
tissue p. 29
organ p. 30

EXPLORE Specialization

How do roots differ from leaves?

PROCEDURE

1. Soak the grass plant in a cup of water to clean away any dirt.

2. Compare the color of the roots with the color of the blades or leaves. Record your observations.

3. Wash your hands when you have finished.

WHAT DO YOU THINK?

- How does the color of the grass roots compare with that of the grass blades?
- Chloroplasts contain a chemical that gives leaves their green color. What does this suggest to you about the functions of the grass blades and roots?

MATERIALS

- grass plants
- cup
- water

Organisms can be classified by their cell type.

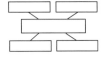

MAIN IDEA WEB
Make a web of the important terms and details about the main idea: *Organisms can be classified by their cell type.*

Look around you at this moment. The living organisms you see may number 10, 20, 100, or 1000, depending on where you are. What you are not seeing, but what is also there, is a huge number of unicellular organisms. For example, there are at least 2–3 million bacteria living on each square centimeter of your skin.

Most of the organisms alive on Earth today are made of a single cell. One of the most interesting scientific discoveries made recently had to do with a group of unicellular organisms. These organisms were found living where no one expected to find any life at all.

Archaea and Bacteria

In the early 1980s, scientists discovered unicellular organisms living in rather extreme environments. Some were living deep in the ocean, at thermal vents where there is extreme heat and little oxygen. Others were found in the salty waters of the Great Salt Lake and in the hot sulfur springs of Yellowstone Park.

At first, these organisms were referred to as archaebacteria. The organisms were similar in appearance to bacteria. The prefix *archae* comes from a Greek word that means "ancient." Many of these organisms live in environments that scientists think are like the environments of ancient Earth.

REMINDER

The genetic material in a prokaryotic cell is not enclosed in a nucleus. In eukaryotic cells genetic material is stored in a nucleus.

thermal vent

archaea

Archaea are prokaryotic organisms that can live in extreme environments like these thermal vents. In a thermal vent, temperatures can reach 600 degrees Celsius.

It took a while for scientists to realize that these organisms that looked like bacteria were genetically very different from bacteria. Scientists decided to establish a separate category for them, a domain called Archaea (AHR-kee-uh). A domain is a broad category of living things that is based on characteristics of their cells. Scientists have identified three domains. Bacteria are classified in the domain Bacteria. A third domain includes organisms with eukaryotic cells.

Organisms that belong to the domains Bacteria and Archaea are similar in some important ways. They are prokaryotes, which are unicellular organisms with prokaryotic cells. Their cytoplasm contains ribosomes but no organelles, so the structure of a prokaryote is simple. Another feature of a prokaryote is a tough cell wall that protects the organism.

RESOURCE CENTER
CLASSZONE.COM

Learn more about unicellular organisms.

 CHECK YOUR READING Why did scientists decide to establish separate domains for archaea and bacteria?

SOUTH CAROLINA
Essentials

See the South Carolina Essentials, pages 645–646, to read about the body shapes of bacteria and body structures that protists use for food gathering and locomotion.

Eukarya

The third domain is the domain Eukarya. Organisms in this domain have cells with a nucleus. This domain includes almost all the multicellular organisms on Earth: plants, animals, and fungi. It also includes many unicellular organisms called protists. The cells of unicellular eukaryotes are more complex in structure and larger than the cells of prokaryotes.

CHECK YOUR READING How are eukaryotes different from prokaryotes?

The paramecium is one of the most complex of all unicellular eukaryotes. Its body is lined with hairlike strands, called cilia (SIHL-ee-uh), that allow it to move. It has dartlike structures that carry a substance used in healing and, perhaps, defense. Along the outside of the cell is a long oral groove lined with cilia that leads to a mouth pore. In addition to a nucleus, the cell of a paramecium has organelles that enable it to digest food and remove water and wastes. The paramecium has all it needs to live as a single cell. By comparison, in most multicellular eukaryotes, no individual cell can survive on its own.

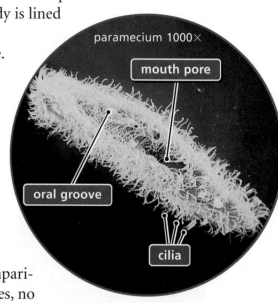
paramecium 1000×
mouth pore
oral groove
cilia

Cells in multicellular organisms specialize.

VOCABULARY
Remember to add a four square for *specialization* to your notebook.

Most multicellular organisms consist of many different types of cells that do different jobs. For example, most animals have blood cells, nerve cells, and muscle cells. The cells are specialized. **Specialization** of cells means that specific cells perform specific functions. This specialization is why a single cell from a multicellular organism cannot survive on its own. A blood cell can help you fight infection or deliver oxygen to your muscles, but it cannot cause your body to move as a muscle cell can. Plants have cells that function in photosynthesis, and other cells that draw water from the soil, and still others that function mainly to support the plant's weight.

CHECK YOUR READING What does it mean for a cell to be specialized?

Specialization

A fully grown salamander has many specialized cells.

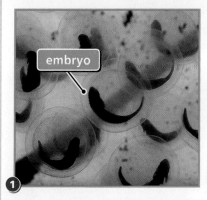

embryo

larva

adult

1 A salamander, like all multicellular organisms, begins life as an egg. After fertilization, the egg develops into an embryo.

2 As the cells divide, they begin to specialize. The amount of specialization depends on the complexity of the organism.

3 A salamander's body has many specialized cells. These include skin cells, blood cells, bone cells, muscle cells, and nerve cells.

A multicellular organism is a community of cells.

Cells in a multicellular organism are specialized. The ways in which the cells work together and interact depend on the organism. You can think of the cells of an organism as members of a community. The size and complexity of the community differ from organism to organism.

A sponge is an animal that is fairly simple in its organization. It spends its life attached to the ocean floor, filtering food and other nutrients from the water. Like all animals, the sponge is organized at a cellular level. Different types of cells in its body perform different functions. For example, certain cells take in food, and other cells digest it. However, cells in a sponge are not very highly specialized. A piece broken from a living sponge will actually regenerate itself as new cells replace the lost ones.

In more complex organisms, such as plants and animals, cells are not only specialized but grouped together in tissues. A **tissue** is a group of similar cells that are organized to do a specific job. If you look at your hand, you will see the top layer of tissue in your skin. Humans have two layers of skin tissue, layered one on top of the other. Together these skin tissues provide protection and support.

CHECK YOUR READING In what way is a tissue an organization of cells?

Levels of Organization

Levels of organization in multicellular organisms include cells, tissues, organs, organ systems, and the organism itself.

Plant cell

Tissue

Organ: leaf

Organ system:
leaves, stems, roots

Organism: lilac tree

Animal cell

Tissue

Organ: eye

Organ system:
eyes, brain, nerves

Organism: tarsier

Different tissues working together to perform a particular function represent another level of organization, the **organ.** The eye is an organ that functions with the tarsier's brain to allow sight. A leaf is an organ that provides a plant with energy and materials. It has tissue that brings in water and nutrients, tissue that uses the Sun's energy to make sugar, and tissue that moves sugar to other parts of the plant.

CHECK YOUR READING   What is the relationship between tissues and organs?

Different organs and tissues working together form an organ system. An organism may have only a few organ systems. The organ systems of plants include roots, stems, and leaves. Other organisms have many organ systems. Humans have 11 major organ systems, made up of about 40 organs and over 200 types of tissue. The human nervous system, for example, includes the brain, the spinal cord, nerves, and sensory organs, such as the ears and eyes.

An organism itself represents the highest level of organization. It is at this level that we see all the characteristics we associate with life. If an organism is a complex organism—a human, for example— it will consist of trillions of cells grouped into tissues, organs, and organ systems. However, a simple organism, like a sponge, meets its needs with a body made up of only a few types of specialized cells.

CHECK YOUR READING What level of organization is an organism? What do we see at this level of organization?

INVESTIGATE Cell Models

What are some of the limitations of using a model to represent a cell?

PROCEDURE

1. Work with a partner to choose a type of cell to model and to determine the types of organelles to include.

2. Using the poster board as a base, construct the model from available supplies. Make the model as accurate as you can.

3. Use a marker to label each organelle, and include a description of its function.

4. Compare your cell model with those made by your classmates.

WHAT DO YOU THINK?

- What are some of the limitations of using a model to represent a cell?

- What are some of the benefits of making a three-dimensional model of a cell?

CHALLENGE Think of something to which you might compare the activities of a cell—perhaps the activities of a factory or a school. Add labels to your model to show how the comparison applies to each of the cell's structures.

SKILL FOCUS
Making models

MATERIALS
- craft supplies
- scissors
- glue
- poster board
- markers

TIME
30 minutes

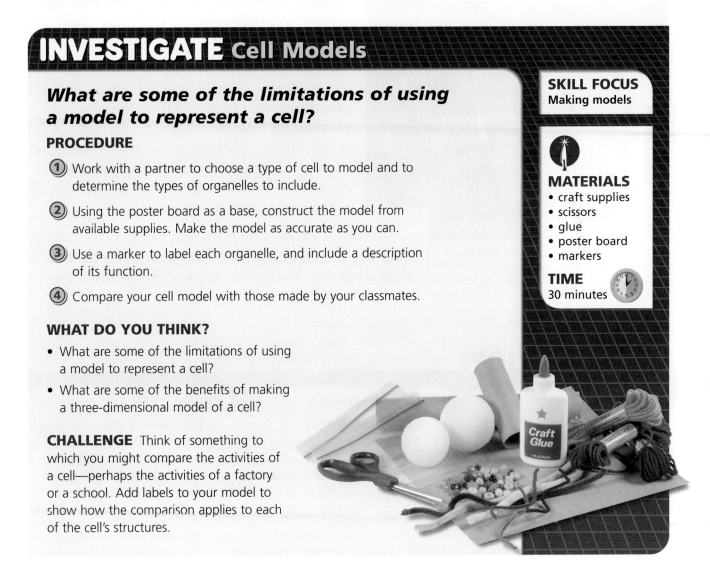

Scientists use models to study cells.

Scientific Models

Scientists use several different types of models.

Any drawing or photograph on a flat page is two-dimensional. In addition, diagrams of cells are often simplified to make them easier to understand. If you look at plant or animal cells under a microscope, you will notice some differences between real cells and the diagrams on page 22. In order to study cell structures and their functions, scientists use many types of models, including three-dimensional models. One of the most important discoveries in science involved the use of models.

DNA is the genetic material common to all cells. You will read more about the structure and function of DNA later in this unit. In the early 1950s, scientists had a good idea what DNA was made up of. The problem was that they could not figure out how all the pieces of the molecule fit together.

A scientist named Rosalind Franklin used x-rays to produce images of DNA. The x-ray provided an important clue as to the shape of the molecule. Two other scientists, James Watson and Francis Crick, were then able to put together a three-dimensional model of DNA and present it to the world in 1953.

Watson and Crick used a model made from wire and tin.

Today's scientists have many different tools for making models. The images at the left show a computer model of DNA along with Watson and Crick's famous model.

1.3 Review

KEY CONCEPTS

1. What are the three domains, and what type of cells do the organisms in each domain have?

2. Define specialization in your own words.

3. Describe the levels of organization in a tree.

CRITICAL THINKING

4. **Synthesize** In what way does a specialized cell in a multicellular organism differ from the cell of a unicellular organism?

5. **Compare and Contrast** How is a model similar to the real object it represents? How is it different?

⬥ CHALLENGE

6. **Evaluate** The organism below is called *Chlamydomonas*. What domain does it belong to, and what do the internal structures tell you about it?

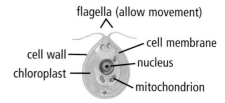

flagella (allow movement)
cell membrane
cell wall
nucleus
chloroplast
mitochondrion

Think SCIENCE

Cells and Spacesuits

What do a space suit and a unicellular organism have in common? Both have to support life. And both can support life in difficult environments. What are some of the similarities—and differences—between the cell body of a unicellular organism and a space suit that supports an astronaut in outer space?

▶ Some Features of Spacesuits

FEATURE	FUNCTION
Strong outer material...	...protects the astronaut from space particles.
A special jet-propelled backpack...	...helps the astronaut move in the weightlessness of space.
Tanks of compressed air...	...provide oxygen for the astronaut to breathe.

▶ Some Features of Cells

FEATURE	FUNCTION
Tail-like flagella on the outside of some cells...	...help cells move.
An outer membrane...	...keeps harmful particles out.
Tiny openings in a cell's membrane...	...let oxygen move into the cell.

▶ Make Comparisons

On Your Own Match each cell feature with a similar spacesuit feature. What characteristics do the cell and spacesuit have in common? What is one key difference?

As a Group Use your comparisons to make a Venn diagram.

CHALLENGE An analogy uses a familiar thing to help explain or describe something new. Come up with your own analogies to describe the cell or some of its organelles.

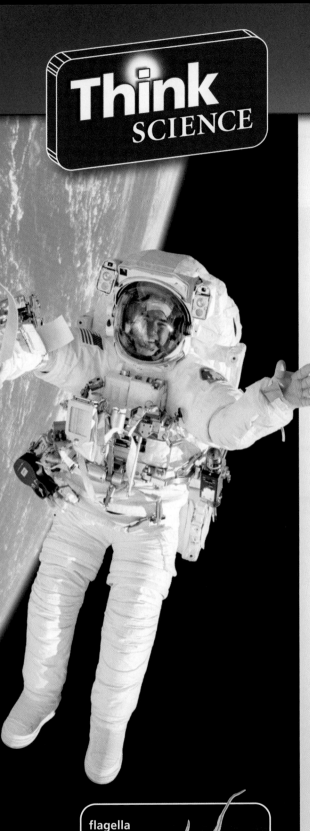

flagella

This cell has flagella, which help it move.

the BIG idea

All living things are made up of cells.

CONTENT REVIEW
CLASSZONE.COM

KEY CONCEPTS SUMMARY

1 **The cell is the basic unit of living things.**

All living things are made up of one or more cells. **Organisms** share the following characteristics:

- organization
- ability to grow and develop
- ability to respond
- ability to reproduce

Multicellular organisms include this frog and these water-lily plants.

Many unicellular organisms live in pond water.

VOCABULARY
unicellular p. 11
multicellular p. 11
microscope p. 12
bacteria p. 14

2 **Microscopes allow us to see inside the cell.**

A **prokaryotic cell** is relatively simple in structure, with no nucleus or other organelles. A **eukaryotic cell** is more complex, with many different organelles inside it.

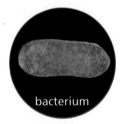
bacterium

plant cell

animal cell

A bacterium consists of a single prokaryotic cell.

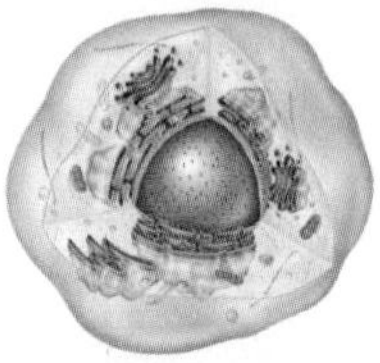

Plants and animals are made up of many eukaryotic cells.

VOCABULARY
cell membrane p. 20
cytoplasm p. 20
nucleus p. 20
eukaryotic cell p. 20
prokaryotic cell p. 20
organelle p. 20
cell wall p. 21
chloroplast p. 23
mitochondria p. 23

3 **Different cells perform various functions.**

- The single cell of a unicellular organism does all that is necessary for the organism to survive.
- A multicellular organism is a community of **specialized** cells.
- Scientific models make it easier to understand cells.

tarsier

The tarsier has many levels of organization in its body.

VOCABULARY
specialization p. 28
tissue p. 29
organ p. 30

Reviewing Vocabulary

1–5. *Use a vocabulary term to identify each numbered part of this plant cell.*

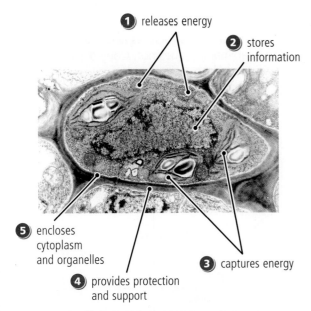

① releases energy

② stores information

③ captures energy

④ provides protection and support

⑤ encloses cytoplasm and organelles

In one or two sentences, describe how the terms in each of the following pairs are related. Underline each term in your answer.

6. unicellular, multicellular

7. cell, organelle

8. prokaryotic cell, eukaryotic cell

9. tissue, organ

Reviewing Key Concepts

Multiple Choice *Choose the letter of the best answer.*

10. Which statement about cells is part of the cell theory?
  a. Cells are found in most living things.
  b. Cells with cell walls do not have cell membranes.
  c. All cells capture energy from sunlight.
  d. Cells come only from other living cells.

11. What structure does a plant cell have that is not found in an animal cell and that allows a plant cell to capture energy from the Sun?
  a. cell wall
  b. chloroplast
  c. mitochondrion
  d. central vacuole

12. Which technology was important to the development of the cell theory?
  a. computer
  b. scientific model
  c. microscope
  d. refrigeration

13. Organisms can be divided into domains on the basis of the characteristics of their cells. What are these domains?
  a. Archaea, Bacteria, and Eukarya
  b. prokaryotes and eukaryotes
  c. plants, animals, and bacteria
  d. unicellular and multicellular

14. A complex multicellular organism has different levels of organization. What is the order of these levels?
  a. cell membrane, cytoplasm, nucleus
  b. tissues, organs, organ systems
  c. tissues, organs, specialized cells
  d. cell membrane, organelles, nucleus

15. What is the function of the genetic material in a cell?
  a. provides transport of materials from the nucleus to the cell membrane
  b. breaks down materials brought into the cell
  c. provides information a cell needs to function and grow
  d. controls what comes into a cell and what goes out

Short Answer *Write a short answer to each question.*

16. What are four characteristics common to all living things?

17. What are three needs common to all living things?

Chapter 1: **The Cell** 35

Thinking Critically

Questions 18–20 refer to polar bears and their cells as examples of animals and animal cells.

18. **PREDICT** Some polar bears go through long periods of sleep during the cold winter months. In what two ways might their fat cells help the bears survive during these periods?

19. **PROVIDE EXAMPLES** Animals do not get energy directly from the Sun as plants do. Give one or two examples of body systems in a polar bear that help it obtain and process food.

20. **COMPARE AND CONTRAST** Consider the fat cells in a polar bear and compare them with the single body cell of a bacterium. How are the cells alike, and how are they different?

21. **CONNECT** The cell theory applies to all organisms, including you. State the three parts of the cell theory and describe briefly how they relate to you.

22. **ANALYZE** Louis Pasteur designed the swan-necked flask to use in his experiments. In one experiment, he used two sealed flasks of nutrient broth. One flask he heated; the other he left untouched. Bacteria grew in the untouched flask. Nothing grew in the flask that had been heated, or sterilized. How did this experiment provide evidence against the theory of spontaneous generation?

Both ends of flasks are sealed.

23. **PREDICT** What would happen if the neck of the sterilized swan-necked flask were broken?

24. **IDENTIFY CAUSE** Why does pasteurized milk eventually spoil?

25. **COMPARE AND CONTRAST** A plant cell has a number of structures and organelles that an animal cell does not. Copy the table below and place a check in the appropriate box of each row. The first two are done for you.

	Animal Cell	Plant Cell
Cell wall		✓
Cell membrane	✓	✓
Cytoplasm		
Nucleus		
Central vacuole		
Chloroplast		
Mitochondrion		

the BIG idea

26. **CLASSIFY** Look again at the photograph on pages 6–7. Can you identify any of the structures shown? Can you identify the type of microscope used to make the photograph? How do you know?

27. **CONNECT** What are three ways that an understanding of cells has changed the way people live? **Hint:** Think about Pasteur and his work.

UNIT PROJECTS

If you are doing a unit project, make a folder for your project. Include in your folder a list of the resources you will need, the date on which the project is due, and a schedule to track your progress. Begin gathering data.

The Euglena Puzzle

*Read the following description of euglenas and how scientists classify them.
Then answer the questions below.*

Plants and animals are typically multicellular organisms. For a long time, scientists tried to classify any unicellular organism that had a nucleus as either a single-celled plant or a single-celled animal. One group of unicellular organisms, *Euglenas,* was particularly difficult to classify. These tiny organisms can be found living in most ponds. What is puzzling about *Euglenas* is that they have characteristics of both plants and animals.

Some scientists argued that *Euglenas* are more like plants because many of them have chloroplasts. Chloroplasts are cellular structures that enable both plants and *Euglenas* to capture energy from the Sun. Other scientists argued that *Euglenas* are more like animals because they can take in food particles from the water. *Euglenas* also have flagella, tail-like structures that enable them to swim. The *Euglena* even has an eyespot for sensing light.

1. What cellular structures enable plants and *Euglenas* to capture energy from the Sun?

   a. flagella   **c.** nuclei

   b. chloroplasts   **d.** eyespots

2. What cellular structures are common to plants, animals, and *Euglenas*?

   a. flagella   **c.** nuclei

   b. chloroplasts   **d.** eyespots

3. In what way are *Euglenas* different from both plants and animals?

   a. They have no nuclei.   **c.** They live in ponds.

   b. They are unicellular.   **d.** They get energy
                                        from food.

4. What does an eyespot do?

   a. senses light   **c.** provides energy

   b. captures food   **d.** senses movement

5. Having flagella makes *Euglenas* similar to animals because it allows *Euglenas* to do what?

   a. eat food   **c.** sense light

   b. get energy   **d.** move about

Extended Response

Answer the following questions in detail. Include some of the terms in the word box. In your answers, underline each term you use.

sunlight	energy	food
eyespot	flagellum	move

6. A jar of water containing *Euglenas* is placed in a sunny window. After a while, a noticeable cloud forms in the water, near where the light shines into the water. Over the course of the day, the position of the Sun changes. As it does, the cloud keeps moving toward the light. On the basis of your reading, what do you think is happening and why?

7. Suppose there is a small pond near your school. The pond is surrounded by many tall trees that tend to block sunlight around the edges of the pond. In this situation, explain why it is an advantage for *Euglenas* to have the characteristics they do. Which of these characteristics do you associate with plants? with animals?

CHAPTER

2 How Cells Function

the **BIG** idea

All cells need energy and materials for life processes.

How do plants like these sunflowers change energy from the Sun?

Key Concepts

SECTION

1 **Chemical reactions take place inside cells.**
Learn why water and four types of large molecules are important for cell functions.

SECTION

2 **Cells capture and release energy.**
Learn about the process of photosynthesis and the two ways cells release energy.

SECTION

3 **Materials move across the cell's membranes.**
Learn about the different ways materials move through cells.

Internet Preview

CLASSZONE.COM

Chapter 2 online resources: Content Review, two Visualizations, two Resource Centers, Math Tutorial, and Test Practice.

EXPLORE (the BIG idea)

Leaves Underwater

Put a dish, two plant leaves, and two baby food jars in a sink full of water. Fill one jar with water and both leaves, then turn the jar upside down on the dish. Fill the other jar with just water and do the same. Remove your set-up from the sink and place it in sunlight for two hours.

Observe and Think
What happened in the jars? Why do you think these things happened?

Just a Spoonful of Sugar

Pour a little warm water into each of two cups. Stir eight spoonfuls of sugar into one of the cups. Drop several raisins into each cup and wait for six hours. After six hours, compare the raisins in each cup.

Observe and Think How are the raisins different? How would you explain your observation?

Internet Activity: Photosynthesis

Go to **ClassZone.com** to examine how plants use sunlight to make sugar molecules.

Observe and Think
What are the starting materials of photosynthesis? What are the products?

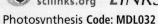

NSTA
scilinks.org
SCiLINKS

Photosynthesis **Code: MDL032**

Getting Ready to Learn

◀ CONCEPT REVIEW

- Cells are the basic units of living things.
- Some cells have organelles that perform special functions for the cell.
- Animal cells and plant cells have similar structures, but plant cells have cell walls and chloroplasts.

◀ VOCABULARY REVIEW

cell membrane, p. 20

organelle, p. 20

chloroplast, p. 23

mitochondria, p. 23

ⓘ CONTENT REVIEW
CLASSZONE.COM
Review concepts and vocabulary.

▶ TAKING NOTES

OUTLINE

As you read, copy the headings on your paper in the form of an outline. Then add notes in your own words that summarize what you read.

VOCABULARY STRATEGY

Draw a **word triangle** diagram for each new vocabulary term. On the bottom line, write and define the term. Above that, write a sentence that uses the term correctly. At the top, draw a small picture to show what the term looks like.

See the Note-Taking Handbook on pages R45–R51.

SCIENCE NOTEBOOK

OUTLINE

I. ALL CELLS ARE MADE OF THE SAME ELEMENTS.

  A. ALL MATTER IS MADE OF ELEMENTS.

     1. 6 make up most of human body

     2. elements interact to produce new materials
       a. smallest unit of element is atom

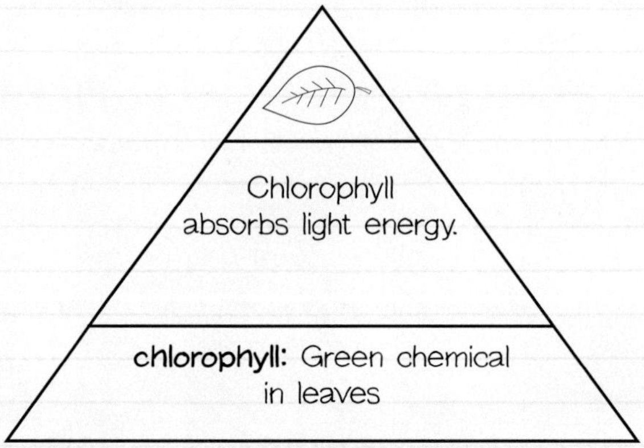

Chlorophyll
absorbs light energy.

chlorophyll: Green chemical
in leaves

2.1 Chemical reactions take place inside cells.

◀ **BEFORE,** you learned

- All living things are made of cells
- Cells need energy to sustain life
- Plant and animal cells have similarities and differences

▶ **NOW,** you will learn

- About the types of elements found in all cells
- About the functions of large molecules in the cell
- Why water is important to the activities of the cell

VOCABULARY

chemical reaction p. 42
carbohydrate p. 42
lipid p. 43
protein p. 43
nucleic acid p. 43

EXPLORE Food Molecules

How are different types of molecules important in your everyday life?

PROCEDURE

① Examine the foods shown in the photograph. Protein, carbohydrates, and lipids (fats) are important substances in the food you eat. Locate at least one source of protein, carbohydrates, and lipids in the food.

② Use your textbook and additional resource materials to find out a little more about these molecules in our food supply.

WHAT DO YOU THINK?
What foods do you eat that supply protein, carbohydrates, and lipids?

MATERIALS
- notebook
- reference materials

OUTLINE
Continue the outline begun on page 40.

I. Main idea
  A. Supporting idea
    1. Detail
    2. Detail
  B. Supporting idea

All cells are made of the same elements.

The microscope allowed people to observe the tiny cells that make up all living things. Even smaller, too small for a light microscope to show, is the matter that makes up the cell itself.

All matter in the universe—living and nonliving—can be broken down into basic substances called elements. About a hundred different elements are found on Earth. Each element has its own set of properties and characteristics. For example, the characteristics of oxygen include that it is colorless, odorless, and on Earth, it exists in the form of a gas.

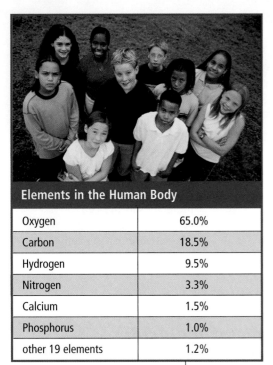

Elements in the Human Body	
Oxygen	65.0%
Carbon	18.5%
Hydrogen	9.5%
Nitrogen	3.3%
Calcium	1.5%
Phosphorus	1.0%
other 19 elements	1.2%

Source: CRC Handbook of Chemistry and Physics

Of all the elements found on Earth, about 25 are essential for life. As you can see from the table, just 6 elements account for about 99 percent of the mass of the human body. But very little of this matter exists as pure elements. Instead, most is in the form of compounds, which are substances made up of two or more different elements. For example, water is a compound made of hydrogen and oxygen.

The smallest unit of any element is called an atom. In a compound, atoms of two or more elements are joined together by chemical bonds. Most compounds in cells are made up of atoms bonded together in molecules. For example, a molecule of water is made of one atom of oxygen bonded to two atoms of hydrogen.

Most activities that take place within cells involve atoms and molecules interacting. In this process, called a **chemical reaction,** bonds between atoms are broken and new bonds form to make different molecules. Energy is needed to break bonds between atoms, and energy is released when new bonds form. Cells use chemical energy for life activities.

Large molecules support cell function.

In living things, there are four main types of large molecules: (1) carbohydrates, (2) lipids, (3) proteins, and (4) nucleic acids. Thousands of these molecules work together in a cell. The four types of molecules in all living things share one important characteristic. They all contain carbon atoms. These large molecules are made up of smaller parts called subunits.

Carbohydrates

sugars
\

Carbohydrates are used for structure and energy storage. Carbohydrates, such as cellulose, are made of **sugars.**

Carbohydrates (KAHR-boh-HY-DRAYTS) provide the cell with energy. Simple carbohydrates are sugars made from atoms of carbon, oxygen, and hydrogen. Inside cells, sugar molecules are broken down. This process provides usable energy for the cell.

Simple sugar molecules can also be linked into long chains to form more complex carbohydrates, such as starch, cellulose, and glycogen. Starch and cellulose are complex carbohydrates made by plant cells. When a plant cell makes more sugar than it can use, extra sugar molecules are stored in long chains called starch. Plants also make cellulose, which is the material that makes up the cell wall. Animals get their energy by eating plants or other animals that eat plants.

Lipids

Lipids are the fats, oils, and waxes found in living things. Like carbohydrates, simple lipids are made of atoms of carbon, oxygen, and hydrogen and can be used by cells for energy and for making structures. However, the atoms in all lipids are arranged differently from the atoms in carbohydrates. Many common lipids consist of a molecule called glycerol bonded to long chains of carbon and hydrogen atoms called fatty acids. This structure gives lipids unique properties. One extremely important property of lipids is that they cannot mix with water.

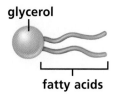

glycerol

fatty acids

Lipids make up the membranes surrounding the cell and organelles. Lipids are made of **fatty acids** and **glycerol.**

How do cells use carbohydrates and lipids?

Proteins

Proteins are made of smaller molecules called amino acids. Amino acids contain the elements carbon, oxygen, hydrogen, nitrogen, and sometimes sulfur. In proteins, amino acids are linked together into long chains that fold into three-dimensional shapes. The structure and function of a protein is determined by the type, number, and order of the amino acids in it.

Your body gets amino acids from protein in food, such as meat, eggs, cheese, and some beans. After taking in amino acids, your cells use them to build proteins needed for proper cell functioning. Some amino acids can be made by the body, but others must be taken in from an outside food source.

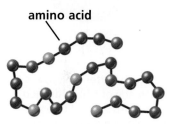

amino acid

Proteins are made up of **amino acids.** Proteins carry out most of the chemical activity in cells.

There are many types of proteins. Enzymes are proteins that control chemical reactions in the cells. Other proteins support the growth and repair of living matter. The action of proteins in your muscles allows you to move. Some of the proteins in your blood fight infections. Another protein in your blood delivers oxygen to all the cells in your body. Proteins are also important parts of cell membranes. Some proteins in the cell membrane transport materials into and out of the cell.

Nucleic Acids

Nucleic acids (noo-KLEE-ihk) are the molecules that hold the instructions for the maintenance, growth, and reproduction of a cell. There are two types of nucleic acids: DNA and RNA. Both DNA and RNA are made from carbon, oxygen, hydrogen, nitrogen, and phosphorus. The subunits of nucleic acids are called nucleotides.

DNA provides the information used by the cell for making proteins a cell needs. This information takes the form of a code contained in the specific order of different nucleotides in the DNA.

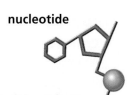

nucleotide

Nucleic acids store and translate the genetic information a cell needs to function. Nucleic acids, such as DNA, are made up of **nucleotides.**

The pattern of nucleotides in DNA is then coded into RNA, which delivers the information into the cytoplasm. Other RNA molecules in the cytoplasm produce the proteins.

 CHECK YOUR READING What is the function of DNA and RNA?

About two thirds of every cell is water.

hydrogen

oxygen

Each **water** molecule is made of two **hydrogen** atoms bonded to one **oxygen** atom.

All of the chemical reactions inside the cell take place in water. Water is also in the environment outside the cell. For example, water inside cells makes up about 46 percent of your body's mass, and water outside the cells in body fluids accounts for another 23 percent.

A water molecule consists of two atoms of hydrogen bonded to one atom of oxygen. Because of its structure, a water molecule has a slight positive charge near the hydrogen atoms and a slight negative charge near the oxygen atom. Molecules that have slightly charged ends are said to be polar. Like a magnet, the ends of a polar molecule attract opposite charges and repel charges that are the same. Because water is a polar molecule, many substances dissolve in water. However, not all materials dissolve in water. If you have ever shaken a bottle of salad dressing, you've probably observed that oil and water don't mix.

INVESTIGATE Oil and Water

What happens when you combine oil and water?

PROCEDURE

① Put a small amount of oil into one beaker and an equal amount of milk into another.

② Put water into a third beaker and add enough food coloring to make the water darkly colored.

③ Add equal amounts of the colored water to the beaker of oil and the beaker of milk. Stir the liquids to mix them. Record your observations.

WHAT DO YOU THINK?

• Compare and contrast the behavior of the mixture of oil and water with that of the mixture of milk and water.

• Why does a mixture of oil and water behave differently from a mixture of milk and water?

CHALLENGE The outside of a cell is surrounded by water. Explain how the water-hating nature of lipids can keep a cell's inside separated from its outside.

SKILL FOCUS
Observing

MATERIALS
• vegetable oil
• milk
• water
• 3 beakers
• food coloring
• stirring stick

TIME
10 minutes

Cell Membrane

The cell membrane is made of a double layer of lipids.

Lipids have a water-loving head and a water-hating tail.

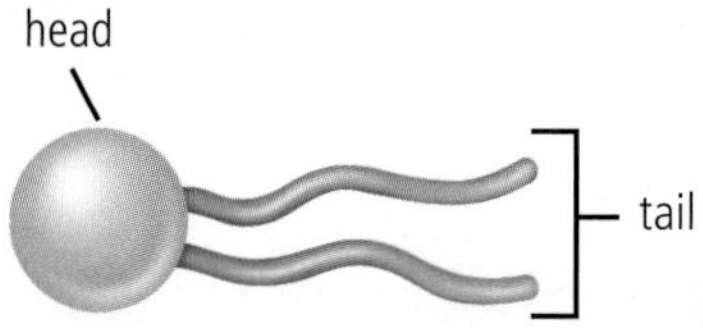

head

tail

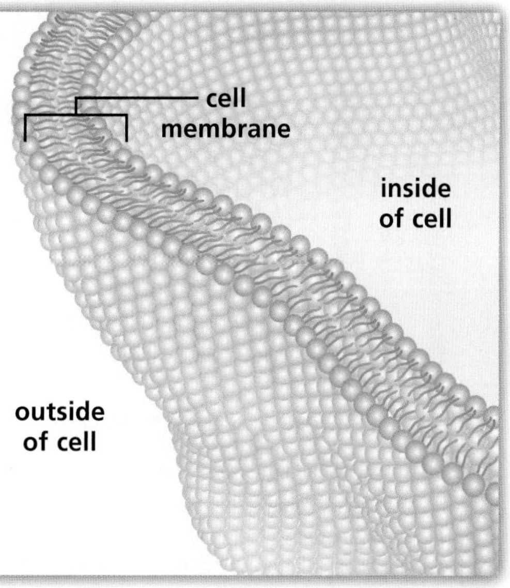

cell membrane

inside of cell

outside of cell

Most lipids do not dissolve in water. A special type of lipid is the major molecule that makes up cell membranes. These special lipid molecules have two parts: a water-loving head and two water-hating tails. In other words, the head of the lipid molecule is polar, while the tails are nonpolar.

Why is it important that cell membranes contain lipids? Remember that cell membranes function as boundaries. That is, they separate the inside of a cell from the outside. Most of the material inside and outside the cell is water. As you can see in the diagram above, the water-hating tails in the lipids repel the water while the head clings to water.

READING TiP

As you read about the properties of cell, notice the arrangements of lipids in the diagram of the cell.

2.1 Review

KEY CONCEPTS

1. Explain how just a few elements can make up all living things.

2. What functions do proteins, carbohydrates, lipids, and nucleic acids perform?

3. What does it mean to describe water molecules as being polar?

CRITICAL THINKING

4. **Compare and Contrast** How are carbohydrates and lipids similar? How are they different?

5. **Draw Conclusions** What do the major types of molecules that make up living things have in common?

● CHALLENGE

6. **Model** Some people have compared the nucleic acids DNA and RNA to a blueprint for life. How are DNA and RNA like blueprints? How are they different?

SCIENCE on the JOB

TEXTILE DESIGNER

Natural Dyes and Cells

Where does the blue in your blue jeans come from? How about the red, yellow, green, or pink in your favorite wool or cotton sweater? Most fabrics are colored with dyes made up in labs, but some designers prefer to use natural dyes and natural cloth. All textile designers must understand the science of dyes and fibers to produce the colors they want.

Fibers

Natural fibers come either from plants or animals. Wool is an animal fiber. Silk, too, is made up of animal cells. Cotton, linen, and rayon are fibers made from plants. Plant fibers have thick cell walls, made mostly of cellulose. Animal fibers, on the other hand, contain mainly proteins.

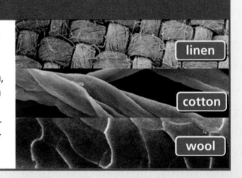

linen

cotton

wool

silk

Dyes

Most natural dyes come from plants, but sometimes insects are used too. The indigo plant is used for most blue, including the original blue jeans. Insects are most often used to make reds. All dyes are made of molecules—carbon, oxygen, hydrogen, and other atoms. The molecules of the dye bind to the molecules of the fibers, adding the dye's color to the fiber.

Color Fixers

A mordant is a chemical compound that combines with dye as a color fixer, or color keeper. The mordant must strengthen the bonds between natural dye molecules and fibers. A stronger bond means the color is less likely to fade or wash out of the fibers. Most mordants are liquid solutions containing metals, such as chromium.

EXPLORE

1. **EXPERIMENT** Design an experiment using onion skins, beets, or blackberries to color white wool and white cotton. The procedure should include chopping the plant and heating it with water to make the dye. Be sure that your experiment procedure includes only one variable. Your experiment should start with a question, such as How do the dyes differ? Or Which dye works best?

2. **CHALLENGE** Using different mordants with the same dye can give different colors. For example, dandelion leaf dye gives yellow-green, gray-green, tan, or gold with different mordants. Explain why this happens.

KEY CONCEPT

2.2 Cells capture and release energy.

SOUTH CAROLINA

McDougal Littell Science

STANDARDS

7–2.4 Explain how cellular processes (including respiration, photosynthesis in plants, mitosis, and waste elimination) are essential to the survival of the organism.

VOCABULARY

chemical energy p. 47
glucose p. 47
photosynthesis p. 48
chlorophyll p. 48
cellular respiration p. 50
fermentation p. 52

OUTLINE

Remember to include this heading in your outline of this section.

I. Main idea
  A. Supporting idea
    1. Detail
    2. Detail
  B. Supporting idea

◀ **BEFORE, you learned**

- The cell is the basic unit of all living things
- Plant cells and animal cells have similarities and differences
- Plants and animals need energy and materials

▶ **NOW, you will learn**

- Why cells need energy
- How energy is captured and stored
- How plants and animals get energy

THINK ABOUT

What do these cells have in common?

Both muscle cells and plant cells need energy to live. Your muscle cells need energy to help you move and perform other functions. Even though plant cells don't move in the same way that muscles move, they still need energy. How do human muscle cells and plant cells get energy?

leaf cells

muscle cells

All cells need energy.

To stay alive, cells need a constant supply of energy. Animal cells get energy from food, while plant cells get energy from sunlight. All cells use chemical energy. **Chemical energy** is the energy stored in the bonds between atoms of every molecule. To stay alive, cells must be able to release the chemical energy in the bonds.

A major energy source for most cells is stored in a sugar molecule called **glucose.** When you need energy, cells release chemical energy from glucose. You need food energy to run, walk, and even during sleep. Your cells use energy from food to carry out all of their activities.

Think about muscle cells. When you run, muscle cells release chemical energy from glucose to move your legs. The more you run, the more glucose your muscle cells need. You eat food to restore the glucose supply in muscles. But how do plant cells get more glucose? Plants transform the energy in sunlight into the chemical energy in glucose.

Some cells capture light energy.

The source of energy for almost all organisms ultimately comes from sunlight. Plants change the energy in sunlight into a form of energy their cells can use—the chemical energy in glucose. All animals benefit from the ability of plants to convert sunlight to food energy. Animals either eat plants, or they eat other animals that have eaten plants.

Photosynthesis (FOH-toh-SIHN-thih-sihs) is the process that plant cells use to change the energy from sunlight into chemical energy. Photosynthesis takes place in plant cells that have chloroplasts. Chloroplasts contain **chlorophyll** (KLAWR-uh-fihl), a light-absorbing pigment, or colored substance, that traps the energy in sunlight.

The process of photosynthesis involves a series of chemical steps, or reactions. The illustration on the next page shows an overview of how photosynthesis changes starting materials into new products.

READING TiP

As you read each numbered item here, find the number on the diagram on page 49.

1 **The starting materials** of photosynthesis are carbon dioxide and water. The plant takes in carbon dioxide from the air and water from the soil.

2 **The process** takes place when carbon dioxide and water enter the plant's chloroplasts. Chlorophyll captures energy from sunlight, which is used to change carbon dioxide and water into new products.

3 **The products** of photosynthesis are oxygen and sugars such as glucose. The plant releases most of the oxygen to the air as a waste product and keeps the glucose for its energy needs.

CHECK YOUR READING Summarize photosynthesis. Remember that a summary includes only the most important information.

Plants do not immediately use all of the glucose they make. Some of the glucose molecules are linked together to build large carbohydrates called starch. Plants can store starch and later break it back down into glucose or other sugars when they need energy. Sugars and starches supply food for animals that eat plants.

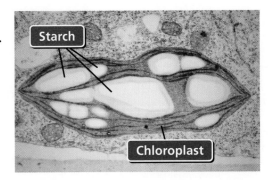

The starch in this plant cell stores energy.

Chloroplast

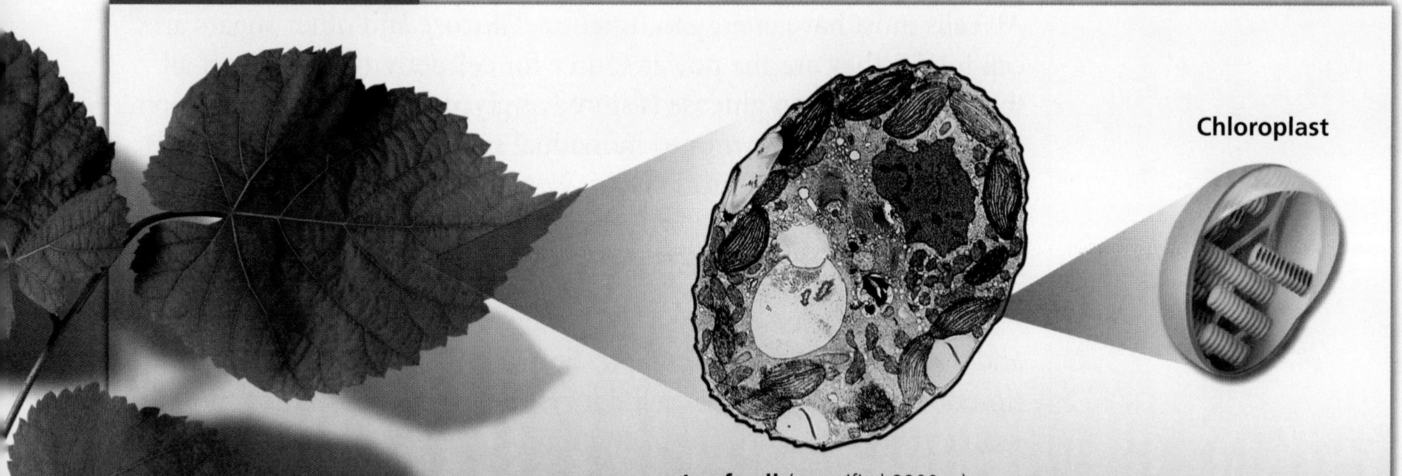

Leaf cell (magnified 2200×)

1 **The starting materials** Carbon dioxide from the air and water from the soil enter the chloroplasts.

2 **The process** Inside the chloroplasts, chlorophyll captures energy from sunlight. This energy is used to change starting materials into new products.

3 **The products** Glucose supplies energy and is a source of materials for the plant; most oxygen is released into the air.

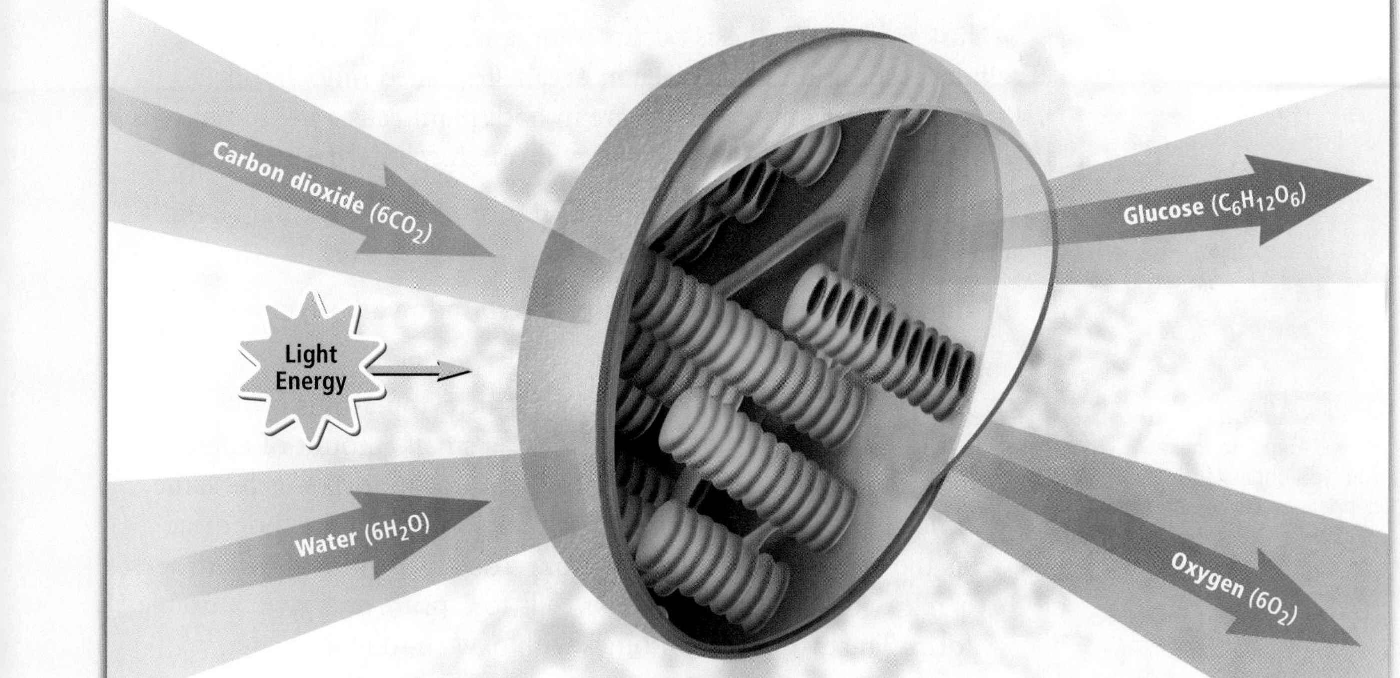

Carbon dioxide ($6CO_2$)

Glucose ($C_6H_{12}O_6$)

Light Energy

Water ($6H_2O$)

Oxygen ($6O_2$)

Chloroplast

Water $6H_2O$	+	Carbon dioxide $6CO_2$	+	Light Energy		Glucose $C_6H_{12}O_6$	+	Oxygen $6O_2$

READING VISUALS What part of the diagram shows starting materials being changed?

All cells release energy.

All cells must have energy to function. Glucose and other sugars are cell food—they are the power source for cell activities in almost all living things. When glucose is stored as glycogen or taken in as starch, it must be broken down into individual sugar molecules before cells are able to use it. Chemical energy is stored in the bonds of sugars. When a sugar molecule is broken down, a usable form of energy is released for the cell's life functions.

Cells can release energy in two basic processes: cellular respiration and fermentation. Cellular respiration requires oxygen, but fermentation does not. In addition, cellular respiration releases much more usable energy than does fermentation.

 What is released when a sugar molecule is broken down?

Cellular Respiration

In **cellular respiration,** cells use oxygen to release energy stored in sugars such as glucose. In fact, most of the energy used by the cells in your body is provided by cellular respiration.

Just as photosynthesis occurs in organelles called chloroplasts, cellular respiration takes place in organelles called mitochondria. Remember that mitochondria are in both plant cells and animal cells, so both kinds of cells release energy through cellular respiration.

Like photosynthesis, cellular respiration is a process that changes starting materials into new products.

❶ **The starting materials** of cellular respiration are sugars—such as glucose—and oxygen.

❷ **The process** begins when glucose in the cytoplasm is broken down into smaller molecules. This releases a small amount of energy. These molecules then move into the mitochondria. At the same time, oxygen enters the cell and travels into the mitochondria. As the smaller molecules are broken down even further, hydrogen is released in a way that allows cells to capture energy in a usable form. The hydrogen combines with oxygen to make water.

❸ **The products** are energy, carbon dioxide, and water.

Some of the energy released during cellular respiration is transferred to other molecules, which then carry the energy where it is needed for the activities of the cell. The rest of the energy is released as heat. Carbon dioxide formed during cellular respiration is released by the cell.

 What are the three products of cellular respiration?

Cellular Respiration

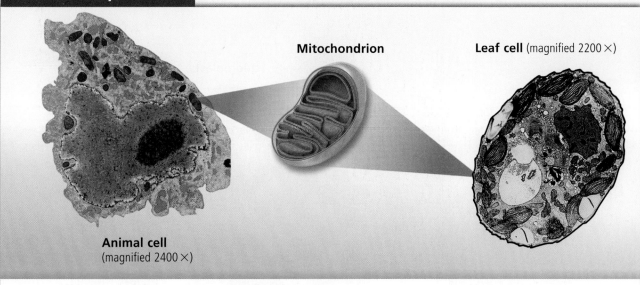

Mitochondrion

Leaf cell (magnified 2200 ×)

Animal cell
(magnified 2400 ×)

① **The starting materials** Glucose and oxygen enter the cell. Glucose is split into smaller molecules.

② **The process** Inside the mitochondria more chemical bonds are broken in the smaller molecules. Oxygen is needed for this process.

③ **The products** Energy is released, and water and carbon dioxide are produced.

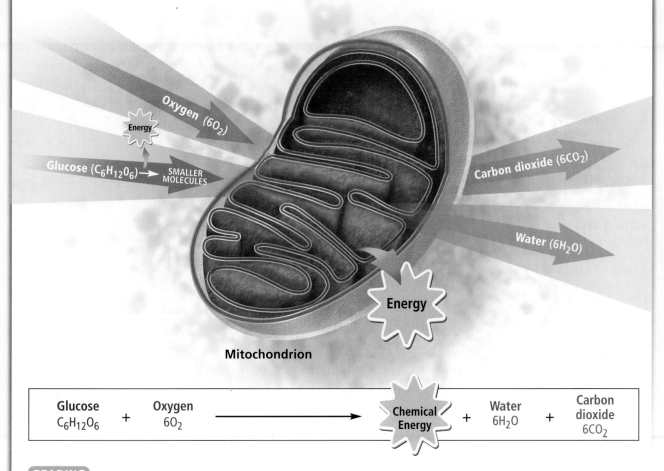

Energy

Oxygen ($6O_2$)

Glucose ($C_6H_{12}O_6$) → SMALLER MOLECULES

Carbon dioxide ($6CO_2$)

Water ($6H_2O$)

Energy

Mitochondrion

Glucose $C_6H_{12}O_6$	+	Oxygen $6O_2$	⟶	Chemical Energy	+	Water $6H_2O$	+	Carbon dioxide $6CO_2$

READING ViSUALS Where in the process is energy released?

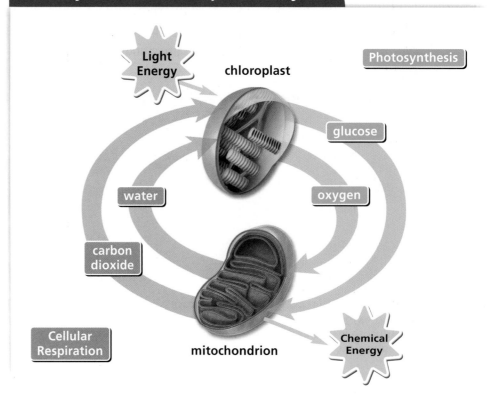

Photosynthesis and Respiration Cycle

Light Energy
chloroplast
Photosynthesis
glucose
water
oxygen
carbon dioxide
Cellular Respiration
mitochondrion
Chemical Energy

You may find it interesting to compare cellular respiration with photosynthesis. The diagram above highlights the cycle that occurs between photosynthesis and cellular respiration. Notice that the starting materials of one process are also the products of the other process. This cycle does not necessarily occur in the same cell, or even in the same organism.

Fermentation

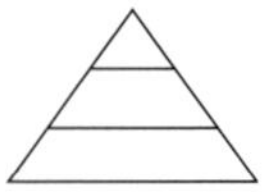

Fermentation is the process by which cells release energy without oxygen. Recall that in cellular respiration the cell first breaks glucose into smaller molecules. This releases a small amount of energy. Without oxygen, cellular respiration cannot continue. In eukaryotic cells, instead of entering the mitochondria, these smaller molecules stay in the cytoplasm, where fermentation occurs.

There are two main types of fermentation: alcoholic fermentation and lactic acid fermentation. Both types of fermentation break sugars down to small molecules. In the absence of oxygen, different reactions occur that produce either alcohol and carbon dioxide or lactic acid. In both cases, a small amount of energy is released.

 CHECK YOUR READING Use a Venn diagram to compare and contrast fermentation and cellular respiration.

VOCABULARY
Add a word triangle for *fermentation* to your notebook. Your triangle could include a sketch of a loaf of bread.

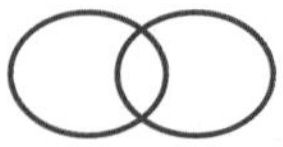

The production of many foods that people eat every day involve either alcoholic fermentation or lactic acid fermentation. Three important foods are bread, yogurt, and cheese.

Bread is often made by mixing flour, milk, and sugar with a microorganism you know as yeast. Yeast runs out of oxygen and uses fermentation to convert the sugar into alcohol and carbon dioxide. Bubbles of carbon dioxide gas forming inside the dough cause it to rise. When the dough is baked, the small amount of alcohol evaporates, the yeast is killed, and the carbon dioxide bubbles give the bread a light, spongy structure.

Some bacteria release energy through lactic acid fermentation. These bacteria convert the sugar found in milk into lactic acid and are used to make yogurt, cheese, and sourdough bread. Lactic acid changes the acidity of a bread mixture to give it a slightly sour flavor. In yogurt and cheese, the buildup of lactic acid causes the milk to partially solidify, producing the creamy texture of yogurt. If fermentation continues for a long time, the milk eventually turns into cheese.

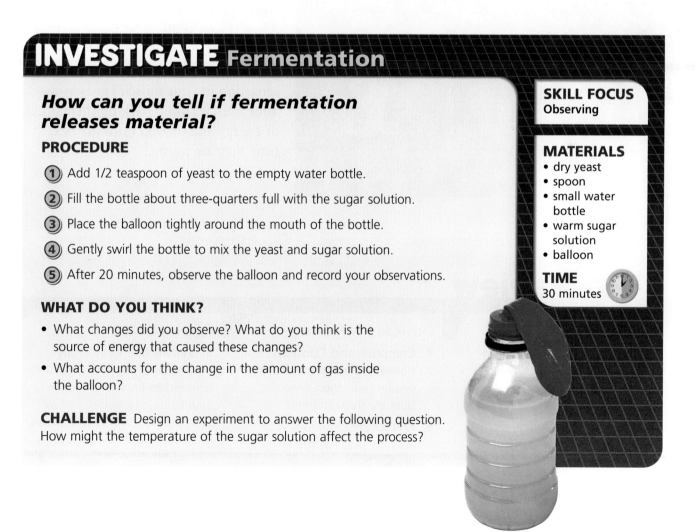

INVESTIGATE Fermentation

How can you tell if fermentation releases material?

PROCEDURE

1. Add 1/2 teaspoon of yeast to the empty water bottle.
2. Fill the bottle about three-quarters full with the sugar solution.
3. Place the balloon tightly around the mouth of the bottle.
4. Gently swirl the bottle to mix the yeast and sugar solution.
5. After 20 minutes, observe the balloon and record your observations.

WHAT DO YOU THINK?

- What changes did you observe? What do you think is the source of energy that caused these changes?
- What accounts for the change in the amount of gas inside the balloon?

CHALLENGE Design an experiment to answer the following question. How might the temperature of the sugar solution affect the process?

SKILL FOCUS
Observing

MATERIALS
- dry yeast
- spoon
- small water bottle
- warm sugar solution
- balloon

TIME
30 minutes

Energy and Exercise

Your muscle cells, like some organisms, are able to release energy by both cellular respiration and fermentation. While you are at rest, your muscle cells use specialized molecules to store both energy and oxygen.

During hard or prolonged exercise, your muscle cells may use up all their stores of energy and oxygen. Then your muscle cells rely on fermentation to break down sugars. There is much less energy available to cells that use fermentation, which is why you cannot continue to run rapidly for long distances. When your cells use fermentation to release energy, one of the waste products is lactic acid, which can cause a burning sensation in your muscles.

APPLY Why might these students feel a burning sensation in their arm muscles while doing pull-ups?

When you stop after this type of exercise, your muscles continue to hurt and you continue to breathe hard for many minutes. During this time, your muscles are playing catch-up. They use the oxygen brought into your blood by your heavy breathing to finish breaking down the byproducts of fermentation. As the lactic acid is converted into carbon dioxide and water, the burning sensation in your muscles goes away. Your muscles build back up their stores of energy and oxygen until the next time they are needed.

2.2 Review

KEY CONCEPTS

1. Which form of energy is especially important for living things? Why?

2. How is photosynthesis important to life on Earth?

3. What starting materials do cells need for cellular respiration?

CRITICAL THINKING

4. **Compare and Contrast** How are photosynthesis and cellular respiration similar? How are they different?

5. **Predict** Suppose that in a lab you could remove all the oxygen from a terrarium. What would happen to the plants? Why?

⚫CHALLENGE

6. **Synthesize** In everyday language, the word *respiration* refers to breathing. How is breathing related to *cellular respiration*? **Hint:** The air we breathe out contains more carbon dioxide than the air we breathe in.

MATH in SCIENCE

MATH TUTORIAL
CLASSZONE.COM
Click on Math Tutorial for more help with interpreting line graphs.

Carbon Dioxide Levels in Biosphere 2

Biosphere 2 is a research and education center in Arizona that can house people, plants, and animals. It was built to find out whether people could get the food and breathable air needed to survive in a small sealed environment over a two-year period.

Example

Data on carbon dioxide levels in the air of Biosphere 2 were collected at 15-minute intervals for several weeks. The graph below shows the amounts of carbon dioxide (CO_2) in the air on January 20, 1996.

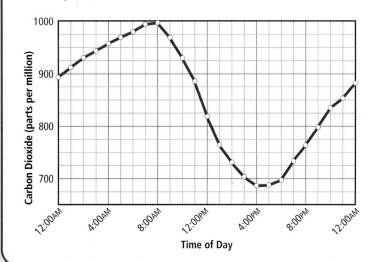

Answer the following questions.

1. What intervals are shown on the *x*-axis? What is shown on the *y*-axis?

2. At what time of day does the carbon dioxide concentration reach its highest point? About how many parts per million of CO_2 are in the air at that time?

3. Between what hours is the CO_2 level decreasing?

CHALLENGE The data in the graph were collected on a sunny day. How might the graph look different if the day had been overcast?

2.3 Materials move across the cell's membranes.

STANDARDS

7–2.1 Summarize the structures and functions of the major components of plant and animal cells (including the cell wall, the cell membrane, the nucleus, chloroplasts, mitochondria, and vacuoles).

7–2.4 Explain how cellular processes (including respiration, photosynthesis in plants, mitosis, and waste elimination) are essential to the survival of the organism.

VOCABULARY

diffusion p. 56
passive transport p. 58
osmosis p. 59
active transport p. 60

VOCABULARY
Add a word triangle for *diffusion* to your notebook. Your triangle could include a sketch of the sun.

◀ BEFORE, you learned

- All cells have an outer covering called the cell membrane
- Cells need starting materials for life-sustaining processes
- Cells need to get rid of waste products

▶ NOW, you will learn

- How materials move into and out of the cell through the cell membrane
- How energy is involved in transporting some materials into and out of cells
- How surface area affects transport in cells

EXPLORE Diffusion

How do particles move?

PROCEDURE

1. Fill the beaker with tap water.
2. Add 3 drops of food coloring to the water.
3. For 10 minutes, observe what happens. Write down your observations.

WHAT DO YOU THINK?
- What changes did you observe?
- What might have caused the changes?

MATERIALS
- beaker
- water
- food coloring

Some materials move by diffusion.

When you walk toward the shampoo section in a store, you can probably smell a fragrance even before you get close. The process by which the scent spreads through the air is an example of diffusion. **Diffusion** (dih-FYOO-zhuhn) is the process by which molecules spread out, or move from areas where there are many of them to areas where there are fewer of them.

Diffusion occurs because the molecules in gases, liquids, and even solids are in constant motion in all directions. This random movement of molecules tends to spread molecules out until they are evenly distributed. But diffusion does more than just spread a scent around a room. Cells use diffusion to carry out important life functions. Diffusion helps cells maintain conditions necessary for life. For example, the oxygen needed for respiration enters cells by diffusion. Similarly, the carbon dioxide produced by respiration leaves cells by diffusion.

Concentration

Diffusion occurs naturally as particles move from an area of higher concentration to an area of lower concentration. The concentration of a substance is the number of particles of that substance in a specific volume. For example, if you dissolved 9 grams of sugar in 1 liter of water, the concentration of the sugar solution would be 9 g/L. When there is a difference in the concentration of a substance between two areas, diffusion occurs.

Generally, the greater the difference in concentration between two areas, the more rapidly diffusion occurs. As the difference in concentration decreases, diffusion slows down. The number of particles moving to one area is balanced by the number moving in the other direction. Particles are still moving in all directions, but these movements do not change the concentrations.

 CHECK YOUR READING Summarize what happens during diffusion. (Remember, a summary includes only the most important information.)

Concentration and Diffusion

A sugar cube dissolving in water provides an example of diffusion.

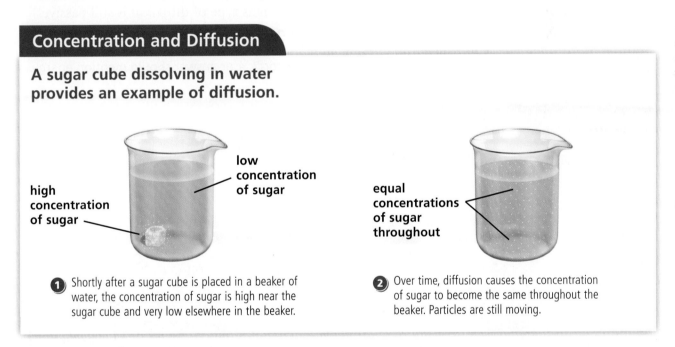

high concentration of sugar

low concentration of sugar

equal concentrations of sugar throughout

1 Shortly after a sugar cube is placed in a beaker of water, the concentration of sugar is high near the sugar cube and very low elsewhere in the beaker.

2 Over time, diffusion causes the concentration of sugar to become the same throughout the beaker. Particles are still moving.

Diffusion in Cells

Diffusion is one way by which materials move in and out of cells. Small molecules such as oxygen can pass through tiny gaps in the cell membrane by diffusion. For example, consider the conditions that result from photosynthesis in a leaf cell.

RESOURCE CENTER
CLASSZONE.COM

Learn more about diffusion.

- Photosynthesis produces oxygen inside the cell.
- The concentration of oxygen molecules becomes higher inside the cell than outside.
- Oxygen molecules move out of the cell by diffusion.

In a plant cell, some of the oxygen produced by photosynthesis is used in cellular respiration. The remaining oxygen diffuses out of the cell. Much of it escapes to the air. Some of it diffuses to other cells where there is a lower concentration of oxygen. This process of diffusion continues from one cell to the next.

Diffusion is a form of passive transport. In **passive transport,** materials move without using the cell's energy. Cells benefit from passive transport because some materials can move through various cell membranes without any input of energy. Whether or not a substance can diffuse across a cell membrane depends on how well the substance dissolves in the lipids that make up the cell membrane. A special form of passive transport allows polar substances, such as glucose, salts, and amino acids, to pass through cell membranes.

All cells need the food energy supplied by glucose. Yet glucose is produced in just some plant cells. Polar substances move into the cell through protein channels—or openings—in their membranes that are specific for each substance. This type of diffusion is still passive transport because it uses no energy.

 CHECK YOUR READING What is passive transport? Your answer should mention energy.

VOCABULARY
Add a word diagram for *passive transport* to your notebook. You may want to use words instead of a sketch in part of your triangle.

Passive Transport

Materials move across a cell membrane continuously.

= oxygen
= glucose

Different concentrations

More **oxygen** moves out of the cell than into the cell.

outside of cell

inside of cell

Special **proteins** allow passive transport of some molecules, such as glucose.

The concentration of oxygen is greater inside the cell than outside.

Equal concentrations

Equal amounts of **oxygen** move into and out of the cell.

The concentration of oxygen is the same inside and outside the cell.

Osmosis

You have read about the importance of water. Water molecules move through cell membranes by diffusion. The diffusion of water through a membrane is given a special name, **osmosis** (ahz-MOH-sihs). If the concentration of water is higher outside a cell than inside, water moves into the cell. If the concentration of water is lower outside a cell, water moves out of the cell.

You can easily observe the effect of osmosis on plants. If you forget to water a plant, it wilts. Why? The soil dries out, and the plant's roots have no water to absorb. As a result, water leaves the plant cells by osmosis and they shrink. If you water the plant, water becomes available to enter the shrunken cells by osmosis. The leaves will return to normal as water moves into the cells.

Without water, a plant droops. The cells have little water in their vacuoles, shown in blue. (magnified 1200 ×)

Water moves into leaf cells by osmosis and fills the vacuoles, shown in blue. (magnified 1200 ×)

Some transport requires energy.

Not all materials that move in and out of a cell can do so by diffusion. For cells to carry out life functions, materials must often move from areas of low concentration into areas of high concentration. This process of moving materials against a concentration requires energy.

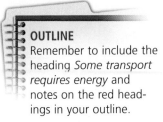

OUTLINE
Remember to include the heading *Some transport requires energy* and notes on the red headings in your outline.

Active Transport

Active transport is the process of using energy to move materials through a membrane. This process is different from diffusion and other types of passive transport, which do not require energy.

 CHECK YOUR READING How is active transport different from passive transport?

VISUALIZATION
CLASSZONE.COM

Observe active transport at work.

Cells use active transport to perform important life functions, including the removal of excess salt from the body. Consider the example of active transport in marine iguanas, shown below. These lizards swim and feed in the salty ocean. As a result they soak up a lot of salt. Too much salt would seriously damage the iguanas' cells, so the cells must get rid of the excess.

The solution to the marine iguana's salt problem is found in two small glands above its eyes. Cells in these glands remove excess salt from the blood by active transport. Even when cells in these glands have a higher concentration of salt than that of the blood, the cells use chemical energy to continue taking salt out of the blood. The gland forms a droplet of salt, which the iguana easily blows out through its nostrils.

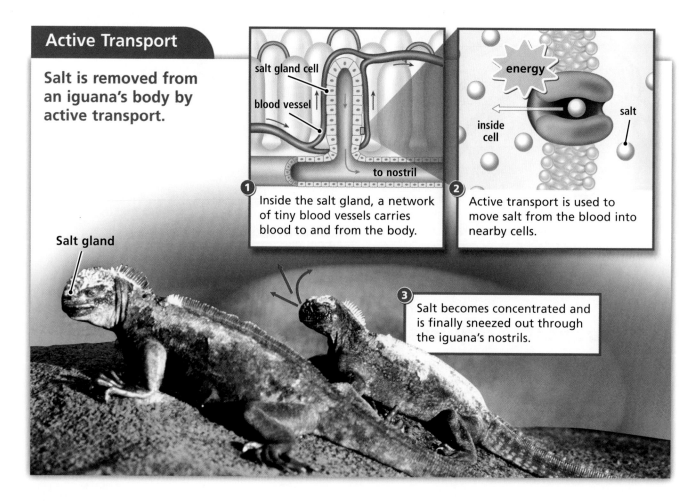

Active Transport

Salt is removed from an iguana's body by active transport.

salt gland cell

blood vessel

to nostril

energy

inside cell

salt

Salt gland

1 Inside the salt gland, a network of tiny blood vessels carries blood to and from the body.

2 Active transport is used to move salt from the blood into nearby cells.

3 Salt becomes concentrated and is finally sneezed out through the iguana's nostrils.

You may not be able to blow salt out of your nostrils, but your kidneys help to keep healthy salt levels in your body. Kidneys filter wastes from your blood by active transport. Cells in the kidneys remove excess salt from the blood.

Endocytosis

Cells also need to move materials that are too large to go through the cell membrane or a protein channel. As the diagram below illustrates, endocytosis (EHN-doh-sy-TOH-sihs) occurs when a large bit of material is captured within a pocket of the membrane. This pocket breaks off and forms a package that moves into the cell. Cells in your body can use endocytosis to fight bacteria and viruses by absorbing them.

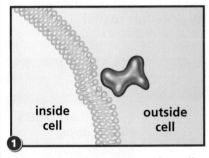
As a particle approaches, the cell membrane folds inward, creating a pocket.

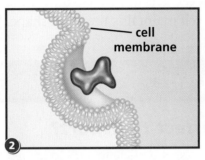
The particle moves into the pocket, and the membrane closes around it, forming a "package."

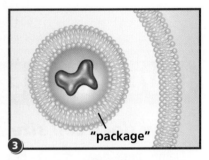
The "package" breaks away from the cell membrane, bringing the particle into the cell.

Exocytosis

When a cell needs to get rid of large materials, the process of endocytosis is reversed. In exocytosis (EHK-soh-sy-TOH-sihs), a membrane within the cell encloses the material that needs to be removed. This package moves to the cell membrane, joins with it, and the material is expelled. Cells often use exocytosis to flush out waste materials or to expel proteins or hormones made by the cell.

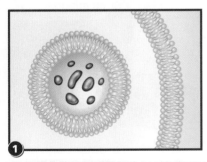
A membrane-enclosed "package" carries materials from inside the cell to the cell membrane.

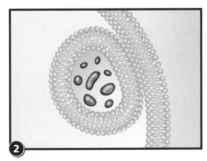
The membrane of the "package" attaches to the cell membrane, and the two membranes merge.

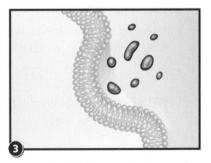
The materials are pushed out of the cell as the membrane of the "package" becomes part of the cell membrane.

Cell size affects transport.

Most cells are very small. In fact, most cells are too small to be seen without a microscope. The average cell in your body is about 50 micrometers (0.05 mm) in diameter. Most of the cells on this planet are bacteria, which are only 3 to 5 micrometers in diameter. How can something as important as a cell be so tiny? Actually, if cells were not so small, they could never do their jobs.

Everything the cell needs or has to get rid of has to go through the cell membrane. The amount of cell membrane limits the ability of cells to either get substances from the outside or transport waste and other materials to the outside. This ability is related to surface area. The relationship between surface area and volume controls cell size. As a cell gets larger, its volume increases faster than its surface area if the cell maintains the same shape. Why does this matter?

INVESTIGATE Cells

How does cell size affect transport?

Demonstrate how small size helps make it possible for cells to get resources.

PROCEDURE

1. Cut a large piece of egg white from the egg.

2. Use a knife to trim the egg white into one small cube, about 1 cm square, and one large cube, about 2 cm square.

3. Pour 100 mL of water into the beaker. Add 10 drops of blue food coloring and stir. Place both cubes into the solution. Let both stand in the colored water overnight.

4. Remove each gently from the water with a spoon. Place both on a paper towel. With the knife, cut each in half. Use the ruler to measure how far the blue water penetrated into the surface of each one.

WHAT DO YOU THINK?

- Record your observations. Which piece of egg was penetrated more, compared to its total diameter, by the blue water?

- Why was there a difference in water penetration?

CHALLENGE What do you predict would happen to an egg left in its shell?

SKILL FOCUS
Modeling

MATERIALS
- 2 hard-boiled, peeled eggs
- knife
- ruler
- 100 mL water
- glass beaker
- dark blue food coloring
- spoon
- paper towel

TIME
30 minutes

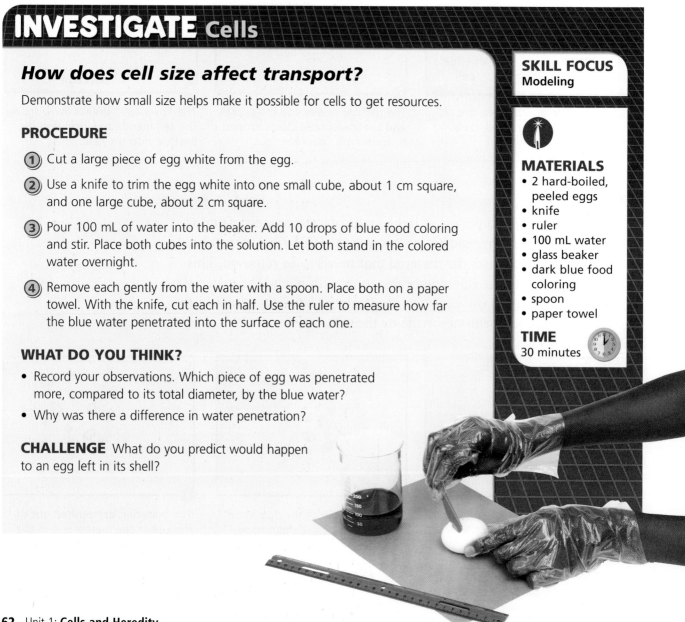

Surface Area and Volumes of Cubes				
	Number of Cubes	Side Length	Surface Area	Volume
4 cm	1	4 cm	96 cm^2	64 cm^3
2 cm	8	2 cm	192 cm^2	64 cm^3
1 cm	64	1 cm	384 cm^2	64 cm^3

As the cell gets bigger, there comes a time when its surface area is not large enough to allow resources to travel to all parts of the cell. So the cell stops growing. Bird eggs and frog eggs are much larger than typical cells, but they have a storehouse of food and also rapidly divide to give rise to multicellular embryos. In fact, this multicellular embryo is a good illustration of another way cells get around the surface-area-to-volume problem: they divide. The ratio of surface area to volume in newly divided cells is much higher, giving more surface area for exchanging materials with the outside of cells.

A cell's shape also affects its surface area. For example, some single-celled organisms are thin and flat, providing increased surface area. Other cells, such as nerve cells and muscle cells, are long and skinny, which also gives them a higher ratio of surface area to volume.

READING TIP

Look at the chart above. Notice that the volumes are all the same, but the surface area changes.

2.3 Review

KEY CONCEPTS

1. How are the processes of diffusion and osmosis alike?

2. What is the difference between active and passive transport? Use the term *energy* in your answer.

3. How does the surface area of a cell limit the growth of the cell?

CRITICAL THINKING

4. **Apply** If you put a bouquet of carnations in water, through what process does the water enter the stems?

5. **Predict** If a marine iguana were to spend a few days in a freshwater tank, would it continue to blow salt droplets from its nostrils? Why or why not?

⚠ CHALLENGE

6. **Predict** Freshwater protozoa, which are unicellular organisms, have a greater concentration of salt inside them than does the surrounding water. Does water diffuse into or out of the protozoa?

CHAPTER INVESTIGATION

Diffusion

OVERVIEW AND PURPOSE The cell membrane controls what diffuses into and out of a cell. What factors affect the diffusion of substances across the cell membrane? In this investigation, you will

- observe the effect of concentration on rate of diffusion
- determine the relative concentrations of the iodine solutions used

▶ Problem

How does the concentration of a substance affect its diffusion through a membrane?

▶ Hypothesize

Write a hypothesis to explain how concentration will affect diffusion of material through a membrane. Your hypothesis should take the form of an "If . . ., then . . ., because. . ." statement.

MATERIALS
- eyedroppers
- cornstarch solution
- baby food jar with lid
- plastic wrap
- iodine solution
- graduated cylinder (if available)

▶ Procedure

1. Make a data table like the one shown on the sample notebook page.

2. To test for the presence of starch, use one eyedropper to put several drops of cornstarch solution on the lid of the baby food jar. With another eyedropper, add a few drops of iodine to the solution on the jar lid. Observe and record what happens.

step 2

3. Fill the baby food jar about three-fourths full with the cornstarch solution.

   Place the plastic wrap inside the jar so that the plastic extends a little below the surface of the cornstarch solution.

step 4

4. Pour 10 mL of the iodine solution that you are given (A, B, or C) on the plastic wrap membrane, enough to cover the top of the plastic wrap. Record your observations.

5 Examine the solutions above and below the membrane after 20 minutes. Record any color changes, as well as the intensity of any changes, that you observe.

▶ Observe and Analyze   Write It Up

1. **IDENTIFY VARIABLES** Identify the constants. What will stay the same in the experiment for all groups?

   Identify the independent variable. What is being changed?

   Identify the dependent variable. What is being observed and measured?

2. **RECORD OBSERVATIONS** Draw before and after pictures of your setup and label each drawing. Be sure to show the colors of the solutions on both sides of the membrane in each drawing.

   Make a drawing to show the direction in which molecules diffused through the membrane in your experiment.

   Compare the observations you made from your iodine solution with the observations made by your classmates. Be sure to record which iodine solution (A, B, or C) produced which changes.

▶ Conclude   Write It Up

1. **INTERPRET** Did starch diffuse through the membrane into the iodine solution? How do you know? Did iodine diffuse through the membrane into the cornstarch solution? How do you know?

2. **INTERPRET** What factors affect the diffusion of different substances through a membrane?

3. **INFER** From what you've observed, which solution contains larger molecules, cornstarch or iodine? Why weren't the larger molecules able to diffuse through the membrane?

4. **INTERPRET** Which iodine solution (A, B, or C) produced the largest color change?

5. **INTERPRET** Which solution had the highest concentration of iodine, and how do you know?

6. **IDENTIFY LIMITS** Describe any errors that you made in your procedure, or places where errors might have occurred.

7. **APPLY** Identify two real-life situations in which diffusion occurs.

▶ INVESTIGATE Further

CHALLENGE Investigate the role of temperature in diffusion. Predict how changes in the temperature of the iodine solution will affect the speed of diffusion through the plastic membrane. Why do you think temperature would affect the diffusion process?

Diffusion

Table 1. Color Changes

Solution	Color at 0 min		Color at 20 min	
	cornstarch solution	iodine solution	cornstarch solution	iodine solution
A				
B				
C				

Chapter Review

the BIG idea

All cells need energy and materials for life processes.

CONTENT REVIEW
CLASSZONE.COM

KEY CONCEPTS SUMMARY

1 **Chemical reactions take place inside cells.**

All cells are made of the same elements. Cells contain four types of large molecules—**carbohydrates, lipids, proteins,** and **nucleic acids**—that support cell function.

About two thirds of every cell is water. The properties of water are important to cell function.

carbohydrates

lipids

proteins

nucleic acids

VOCABULARY
chemical reaction p. 42
carbohydrate p. 42
lipid p. 43
protein p. 43
nucleic acid p. 43

---

2 **Cells capture and release energy.**

All cells need energy. Some cells capture light energy through **photosynthesis.** All cells release chemical energy from glucose.

Cellular respiration and **fermentation** are two ways that cells release energy from glucose.

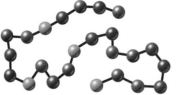

Light Energy

Cellular Respiration

glucose

water

oxygen

Photosynthesis

carbon dioxide

Chemical Energy

VOCABULARY
chemical energy p. 47
glucose p. 47
photosynthesis p. 48
chlorophyll p. 48
cellular respiration p. 50
fermentation p. 52

---

3 **Materials move across the cell's membranes.**

Passive transport is the movement of materials from an area of higher concentration to an area of lower concentration. **Diffusion** and **osmosis** are examples of passive transport.

Active transport is the movement of materials from an area of lower concentration to an area of higher concentration. Cells need energy to perform active transport.

passive transport

active transport

VOCABULARY
diffusion p. 56
passive transport p. 58
osmosis p. 59
active transport p. 60

Reviewing Vocabulary

Use words from the vocabulary lists on page 66 to answer these questions.

1. Which molecule stores information?

2. Which word describes the process when two or more atoms bond together?

3. What kind of energy do cells use?

4. Which term describes the process in which cells release energy without using oxygen?

5. Which process occurs in chloroplasts?

6. From what sugar molecule do many living things release energy?

7. Which chemical that aids in photosynthesis do you find in a chloroplast?

8. Which word means "diffusion of water across cell membranes"?

9. Choose two pairs of opposite processes.

10. Use a Venn diagram to compare and contrast passive transport and active transport.

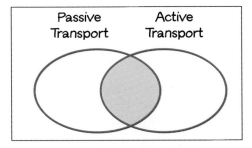

Reviewing Key Concepts

Multiple Choice *Choose the letter of the best answer.*

11. The fats, oils, and waxes found in living things are known as
    a. lipids   **c.** carbohydrates
    b. proteins   **d.** glucose

12. What do cells use as a source of energy and for energy storage?
    a. proteins   **c.** cytoplasm
    b. water   **d.** carbohydrates

13. Leaf cells use chlorophyll to absorb
    a. oxygen   **c.** carbon dioxide
    b. light energy   **d.** glucose

14. The cells of a redwood tree require oxygen for the process of
    a. photosynthesis   **c.** fermentation
    b. cellular respiration **d.** endocytosis

15. In fermentation, cells release energy without
    a. alcohol   **c.** glucose
    b. water   **d.** oxygen

16. Both a whale and a seaweed use which of the following to change glucose into energy?
    a. water   **c.** cellular respiration
    b. photosynthesis   **d.** bonding

17. The movement of materials across a cell membrane, requiring energy, is called
    a. diffusion   **c.** passive transport
    b. osmosis   **d.** active transport

Short Answer *Write a short answer to each question.*

18. Why is water needed by cells?

19. Describe the main function of nucleic acids.

20. What is the role of chlorophyll in a plant's leaves?

21. Explain why a carrot feels spongy after being soaked in salt water.

22. Explain how the ways in which plants and animals get their energy differ.

Thinking Critically

23. **RECOGNIZE CAUSE AND EFFECT** Explain why chemical reactions are essential to living creatures.

24. **MODEL** How does a glass filled with oil and water illustrate the properties of a cell membrane? What properties does it not illustrate?

The illustration below summarizes the relationship between photosynthesis and cellular respiration. Use it to answer the next three questions.

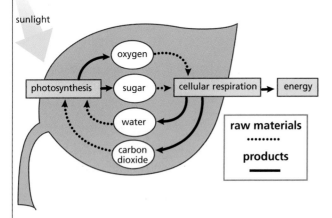

25. **OBSERVE** What are the starting materials of photosynthesis? What are the starting materials of cellular respiration?

26. **OBSERVE** What are the products of photosynthesis? What are the products of cellular respiration?

27. **DRAW CONCLUSIONS** What does the diagram above reveal about the connections between photosynthesis and cellular respiration?

Process	Requires Energy?	Moves from Higher to Lower Concentration?
Diffusion	no	yes
Osmosis		
Active transport		
Passive transport		

28. **CHART INFORMATION** Copy and complete this chart. The first line is done for you.

29. **INFER** The French scientist Louis Pasteur mixed yeast and grape juice in a sealed container. When he opened the container, the grape juice contained alcohol. Explain what happened.

30. **DRAW CONCLUSIONS** Why would it be harmful to your health to drink seawater?

31. **PREDICT** Look at the diagram at the right. The bag has pores that are bigger than the sugar molecules. What will be true of the concentration of the sugar water after a few hours?

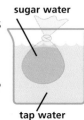
sugar water

tap water

the BIG idea

32. **COMPARE AND CONTRAST** Look again at the picture on pages 38–39. Why do you think the sunflowers are facing the Sun?

33. **INFER** Does your body get all its energy from the Sun? Explain.

34. **WRITE** Imagine that your community has a high level of carbon dioxide emission from cars and factories. A developer wants to build a shopping center on the remaining forest land. Would this action increase or decrease carbon dioxide levels? Why? Write a paragraph explaining your answer.

UNIT PROJECTS

Check your schedule for your unit project. How are you doing? Be sure that you have placed data or notes from your research in your project folder.

Analyzing Data

Elodea plants in beakers of water were placed at different distances from a light source. The number of bubbles that formed on the plants was counted and recorded. The data table shows the results.

Beaker	Distance from light	Bubbles per minute
1	200 cm	2
2	100 cm	10
3	50 cm	45
4	20 cm	83

Study the data and answer the questions below.

1. What gas do the bubbles consist of?

   a. carbon dioxide   **c.** water vapor

   b. hydrogen   **d.** oxygen

2. What is the relationship between the distance from the light source and the rate of bubble formation?

   a. The rate increases as the distance increases.

   b. The rate decreases as the distance increases.

   c. The rate stays the same as the distance increases.

   d. The rate changes in a way unrelated to distance.

3. If another beaker with *elodea* were placed 150 cm from the light, about how many bubbles would form each minute?

   a. 1   **c.** 11

   b. 7   **d.** 24

4. What is the independent variable in this experiment?

   a. type of plant   **c.** distance from light

   b. number of bubbles   **d.** amount of time

5. Which graph best represents the data shown in the table?

a.
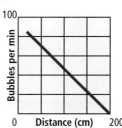

c.
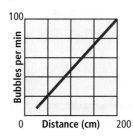

b.
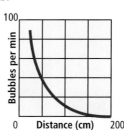

d.
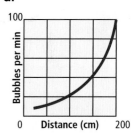

Extended Response

Answer each question. Include some of the terms shown in the word box. In your answers underline each term you use.

chemical energy	cellular respiration
osmosis	chloroplasts
fermentation	glucose
photosynthesis	diffusion

6. A person rides his bicycle several miles. What process is used by the cells in his legs to release energy at the beginning of the ride? At the end of the ride? Explain.

7. A student places a plant in a sealed container and puts the container on a window sill. She leaves the plant there for a week. Will the plant have the starting materials it needs to carry out photosynthesis during the entire week? Explain.

3 Cell Division

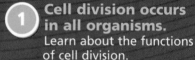

the BIG idea

Organisms grow, reproduce, and maintain themselves through cell division.

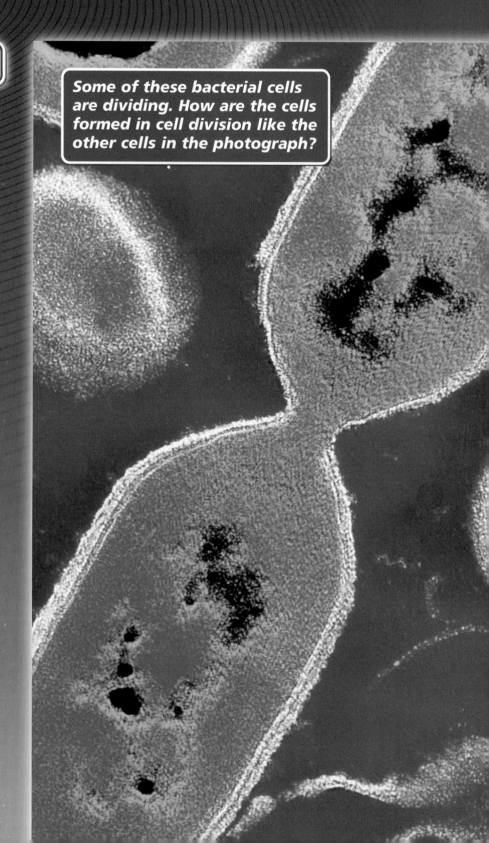

Some of these bacterial cells are dividing. How are the cells formed in cell division like the other cells in the photograph?

Key Concepts

SECTION

1 Cell division occurs in all organisms.
Learn about the functions of cell division.

SECTION

2 Cell division is part of the cell cycle.
Learn about the cell cycle and the process of mitosis.

SECTION

3 Both sexual and asexual reproduction involve cell division.
Learn how sexual reproduction compares with asexual reproduction.

 Internet Preview

CLASSZONE.COM

Chapter 3 online resources: Content Review, Simulation, Visualization, three Resource Centers, Math Tutorial, Test Practice

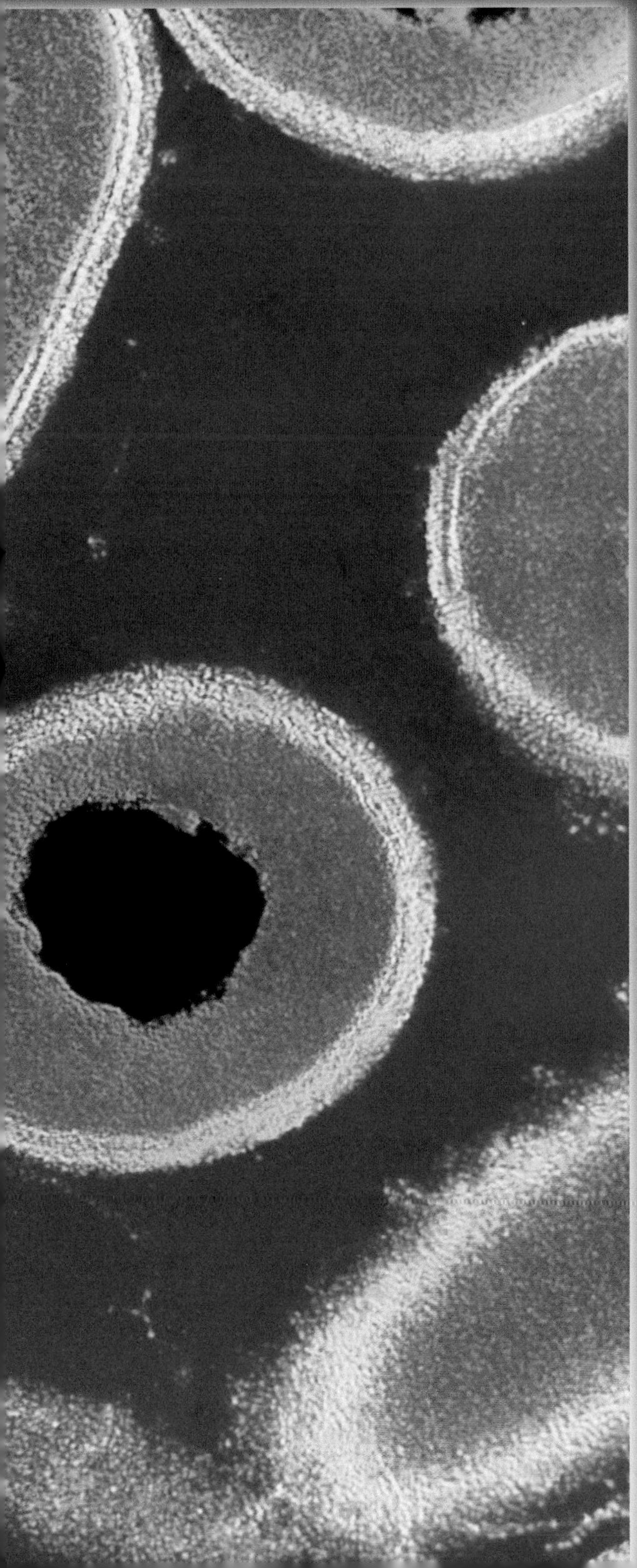

EXPLORE (the BIG idea)

Dividing to Multiply

Carefully observe a maple tree samara like the ones shown here. Notice the different parts of a samara. Break a samara into two pieces. Peel back the end of each half, where you broke it.

Observe and Think
What did you find when you peeled back the ends? How does something as small as a seed produce something as large as a tree?

Division Math

Take a piece of clay and divide it in half. Now you have two pieces of clay, each half the size of the original piece. Divide each of the two new pieces in half, producing 4 pieces, each a quarter the size of the original piece.

Observe and Think What will happen if you keep dividing the pieces in half? How might the division of the cells in living things be different?

Internet Activity: Cell Division

Go to **ClassZone.com** to match images of cells dividing with the different stages of cell division.

Observe and Think Are the stages the same for plant and animal cells?

NSTA
scilinks.org
SCiLINKS

Cellular Mitosis **Code: MDL033**

Getting Ready to Learn

◀ CONCEPT REVIEW

- The cell is the basic unit of structure and function in living things.
- All cells come from other cells.
- DNA provides the instructions a cell needs to function and reproduce.

◀ VOCABULARY REVIEW

cell membrane p. 20

nucleus p. 20

cycle *See Glossary.*

CONTENT REVIEW
CLASSZONE.COM
Review concepts and vocabulary.

▶ **TAKING NOTES**

COMBINATION NOTES

To take notes about a new concept, first make an informal outline of the information. Then make a sketch of the concept and label it so you can study it later.

VOCABULARY STRATEGY

Write each new vocabulary term in the center of a **frame game** diagram. Decide what information to frame it with. Use examples, description, parts, sentences that use the term in context, or pictures. You can change the frame to fit each term.

See the Note-Taking Handbook on pages R45–R51.

SCIENCE NOTEBOOK

NOTES

Mitosis has four phases

- prophase: chromosomes become visible

- metaphase: chromosomes line up in middle

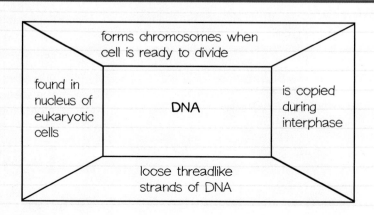

forms chromosomes when cell is ready to divide

found in nucleus of eukaryotic cells

DNA

is copied during interphase

loose threadlike strands of DNA

3.1

Cell division occurs in all organisms.

STANDARDS

7–2.4 Explain how cellular processes (including respiration, photosynthesis in plants, mitosis, and waste elimination) are essential to the survival of the organism.

7–2.5 Summarize how genetic information is passed from parent to offspring by using the terms *genes, chromosomes, inherited traits, genotype, phenotype, dominant traits,* and *recessive traits.*

VOCABULARY

DNA p. 74
chromosome p. 75

◀ BEFORE, you learned

- Cells come from other cells
- Cells take in and release energy and materials
- In a multicellular organism, some cells specialize

▶ NOW, you will learn

- How genetic material is organized in cells
- About the functions of cell division in multicellular organisms

---

EXPLORE Cell Division

How is organization helpful?

PROCEDURE

① Work with two other students. Obtain paired and unpaired groups of socks.

② Two of the students put on blindfolds. One takes the paired group of socks and the other takes the unpaired group.

③ Each blindfolded student tries to separate his or her group of socks into two piles of single socks, one from each pair. The third student keeps track of time and stops the activity after 2 min.

MATERIALS
- 2 blindfolds
- socks
- stopwatch

WHAT DO YOU THINK?
Which group of socks was more accurately separated into two identical sets? Why?

Cell division is involved in many functions.

▼ **REMINDER**

Most multicellular organisms are made up of eukaryotic cells. Most genetic material in eukaryotic cells is contained in the nucleus.

Cell division occurs in all organisms, but performs different functions. Unicellular organisms reproduce through cell division. In multicellular organisms, cell division is involved in growth, development, and repair, as well as in reproduction.

You are probably bigger this year than you were last year. One characteristic of all living things is that they grow. Your body is made up of cells. Although cells themselves grow, most growth in multicellular organisms occurs when cells dividing produce new cells. In this chapter you will read about cell division in eukaryotic cells.

The genetic material of eukaryotic cells is organized in chromosomes.

The genetic material of a cell contains information needed for the cell's growth and other activities. When a cell divides into two new cells, each new cell receives a full set of genetic material. The genetic material in cells is contained in DNA molecules.

DNA

VOCABULARY
Make a frame game diagram for the term *DNA*. You can change the frame if you need to.

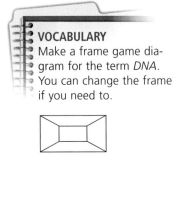

The genetic material in cells is DNA—deoxyribonucleic acid (dee-AHK-see-RY-boh-noo-KLEE-ihk). **DNA** is a chemical that contains information for an organism's growth and functions. You read in Chapter 1 that James Watson and Francis Crick worked with other scientists to build a model of DNA in 1953. They showed that DNA is made of two strands of molecules joined in a structure that resembles a twisted ladder or a double helix. You will learn more about DNA later in the unit.

 What is DNA?

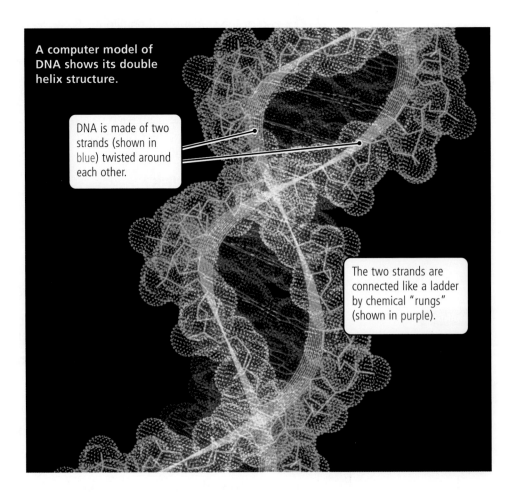

A computer model of DNA shows its double helix structure.

DNA is made of two strands (shown in blue) twisted around each other.

The two strands are connected like a ladder by chemical "rungs" (shown in purple).

Chromosomes

In a eukaryotic cell, most of the cell's DNA is in the nucleus. During most of a cell's life cycle, DNA exists as a mass of loose strands. While the DNA is spread throughout the nucleus, the cell performs the functions needed for survival. During this time, the DNA is duplicated, or copied.

DNA is wrapped around proteins like thread around a spool and compacted into structures called **chromosomes** (KROH-muh-SOHMZ). Before division, the chromosomes compact more and become visible under a light microscope. During division, a duplicated chromosome can be seen as two identical structures called chromatids that are held together by a centromere.

Within each species of organism, the number of chromosomes is constant. For example, humans have 46 chromosomes. Fruit flies, however, have 8 chromosomes, and corn plants have 20.

READING **TiP**

Compare the diagram of DNA with the computer model on page 74.

⬤ CHECK YOUR READING   Describe the relationship between DNA and chromosomes.

Organization of Genetic Material

The DNA in chromosomes is wrapped around a protein core until it is very condensed.

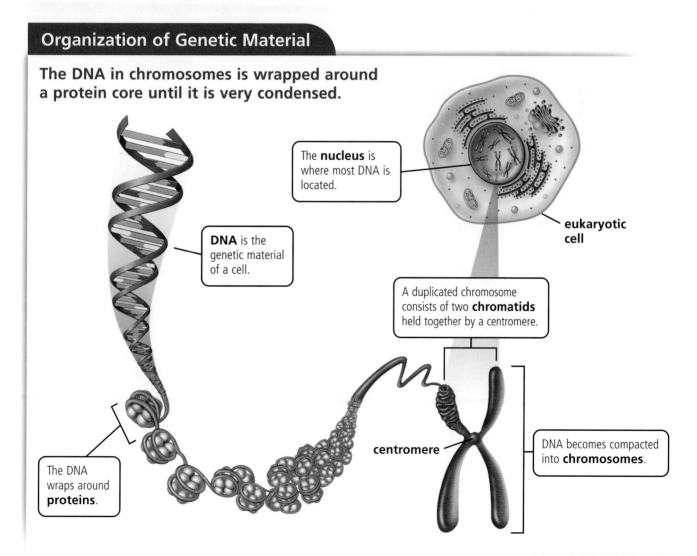

The **nucleus** is where most DNA is located.

DNA is the genetic material of a cell.

eukaryotic cell

A duplicated chromosome consists of two **chromatids** held together by a centromere.

The DNA wraps around **proteins**.

centromere

DNA becomes compacted into **chromosomes**.

How does DNA fit inside the nucleus?

PROCEDURE

1. Select four pieces of yarn of different colors and four craft sticks. Push the yarn together into a loose ball. Observe how much space it takes up and how the individual pieces are organized.

2. Wrap each piece of yarn around a craft stick. Wrap the yarn so that the coils are tightly packed but do not overlap.

WHAT DO YOU THINK?

- What did you observe about the loosely balled yarn?
- What does the loosely balled yarn represent?
- What does the yarn on the craft sticks represent?
- Why does the yarn on the craft sticks take up less space than the ball of yarn?

CHALLENGE How does the yarn's being wrapped on the craft sticks make it easier to separate the different colors?

SKILL FOCUS
Modeling

MATERIALS
- yarn
- craft sticks

TIME
20 minutes

Cell division is involved in growth, development, and repair.

COMBINATION NOTES
Remember to take notes and draw sketches to help you understand the main idea: *Cell division is involved in growth, development, and repair.* Be sure to include the red heads in your notes.

Multicellular organisms vary greatly in size and complexity. You may not think that you have much in common with an ant or an oak tree. Actually, you share many characteristics with these organisms. One of the most important characteristics is that both you and they are made of trillions of cells. But, like most organisms, you and they started out as single cells. In multicellular organisms, cell division is essential for three major functions: growth, development, and repair.

Through cell division, a single cell becomes two cells. Those two cells divide into four, and the four cells divide into eight, and so on. A multicellular organism grows because cell division increases the number of cells in it. As the organism develops and its cells divide, many of the cells become specialized, and most of them continue to divide.

Even when growth and development appear to stop, cell division is still occurring. When an organism ages or is injured, the worn-out or damaged cells need to be replaced by new cells formed when healthy cells divide. For example, the cells that make up the lining of your throat have a short life span—two to three days. Living throat cells are constantly dividing and replacing the cells that have died.

Growth

In general, a large organism does not have larger cells than a small organism; it simply has many more cells than the small organism. When you were small, your body contained fewer cells than it has now. By the time you reach adulthood, your body will be made up of about 100 trillion cells.

Individual cells grow in size, but there are limits to the size that cells can reach. As you learned in Chapter 2, cells need a high ratio of surface area to volume in order to function. As a cell grows, that ratio decreases. When the cell divides into two smaller cells, the ratio of surface area to volume for each cell increases.

Scientists are still searching for answers about how cell size is related to the control of cell division. Some scientists think that there is no single factor that controls cell division. Instead, they think that many cell processes added together control when a cell divides.

CHECK YOUR READING Describe how the number of cells in a multicellular organism changes as the organism grows.

Growth and Development

Organisms, like this sea turtle, grow and develop through cell division.

① The embryo growing inside this egg started as a single cell.

② When it hatches, the baby turtle has trillions of cells.

③ The adult turtle has more than a hundred times the cells of the baby turtle.

READING TiP
Connect what you have read about growth and development with the series of sea turtle photographs above.

Development

Although multicellular organisms begin as single cells, they grow into larger organisms through cell division. However, cell division alone does not allow organisms to develop. If cell division were the only process occurring in cells, all multicellular organisms would end up as spheres of identical cells. But during development, cells become specialized to perform particular functions.

These cells may take on shapes or structures that help them to perform their functions. Some cells might become layered skin cells, while others might become long, thin nerve cells. These cells still have the same set of genetic material as all the other cells in an organism's body, but as the organism develops they specialize.

CHECK YOUR READING Give two examples of specialized cells from the paragraph above.

Repair

You may have cut yourself at one time or another. Perhaps you have even broken a bone in your arm or leg. The body repairs injuries like these by means of cell division. For example, when your skin is cut, skin cells on either side of the cut make new cells to heal the wound. You can see the process of healing in the diagram below.

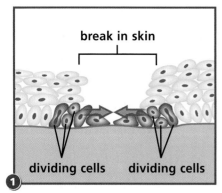

break in skin

dividing cells   dividing cells

① Cells in the lower layer begin to divide quickly and move into the break.

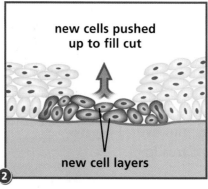

new cells pushed up to fill cut

new cell layers

② New cells begin to fill the area as cells continue to divide.

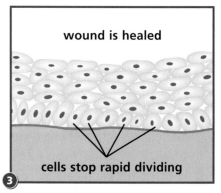

wound is healed

cells stop rapid dividing

③ Cells stop their rapid dividing once the break is filled.

As cells age and die, they need to be replaced. In the human body—which is made up of about 200 different types of cells—cells are replaced at different rates. Your skin cells wear out quickly, so they need to be replaced often. Every minute or so, your skin loses about 40,000 cells, which are replaced with new ones. In contrast, most of the cells in your brain live a long time and do not divide very often.

CHECK YOUR READING   What role does cell division play in healing the body?

3.1 Review

KEY CONCEPTS

1. Why is cell division important?
2. How is genetic material organized in eukaryotic cells?
3. Explain how cell division is involved in the growth, development, and repair of an organism.

CRITICAL THINKING

4. **Summarize** Explain how DNA compacts before a eukaryotic cell divides.
5. **Infer** Why do you think that injuries to the skin generally heal faster than injuries to the brain?

⬥ CHALLENGE

6. **Apply** Describe the stages of development in a multicellular organism that is familiar to you.

Chemical Dyes Show Nerve Growth

For years, the medical community has agreed that nerve tissue, once damaged, does not repair itself. In fact, the opinion was that new nerve cells didn't grow in adults at all. However, a surprising discovery has shown that new nerve cells do grow in the mature brains of both monkeys and people!

Elizabeth Gould noticed that new nerve cells can grow in adult brains

The Discovery

The discovery involves a chemical known as bromodeoxyuridine (BrdU), which can be used to detect new cancer cells.

1 BrdU highlights the DNA of cells that are reproducing, such as cancer cells.

2 BrdU also makes it possible to count the new cells that are being created, because they stand out as well.

3 The cells that have been highlighted with BrdU can be seen under a microscope when they are illuminated with a special light.

When scientists used this technique to examine certain areas in the brains of monkeys and of adult humans who had died of cancer, they found that new nerve cells had grown in the brains of each. Thus, the chemical properties of BrdU allowed scientists to discover new nerve cells growing in places where scientists had previously never expected to see them.

Hope for the Future

If new nerve cells grow in these tissues, it may be possible to stimulate growth in damaged nerve tissue such as that in the spinal cord. If researchers discover how new growth in nerve cells is stimulated, there may be new hope for people who have nervous systems damaged by accidents or by diseases such as Parkinson's disease.

EXPLORE

1. **SYNTHESIZE** How could you use chemicals, such as small dots with a pen, in an experiment to show how your fingernails grow?

2. **CHALLENGE** What are some possible effects of being able to grow new nerve cells?

RESOURCE CENTER
CLASSZONE.COM
Find out more about new nerve cell growth.

3.2

Cell division is part of the cell cycle.

STANDARDS

7–2.4 Explain how cellular processes (including respiration, photosynthesis in plants, mitosis, and waste elimination) are essential to the survival of the organism.

VOCABULARY

cell cycle p. 80
interphase p. 81
mitosis p. 81
cytokinesis p. 81

◀ **BEFORE,** you learned

- Cells come from other cells through cell division
- A cell must have a full set of genetic material to function
- Cell division enables multi-cellular organisms to develop, grow, and repair themselves

▶ **NOW,** you will learn

- About two main stages in the cell cycle
- About the changes that occur in cells before mitosis
- About the events that take place during mitosis

THINK ABOUT

What is a cycle?

Many things in your everyday life are cycles. A cycle is any activity or set of events that regularly repeats. Cycles can be short, like the sequence of events that make your heart beat, or they can be very long, like the turning of our galaxy. One example of a cycle is shown at the right. The photographs show a tree during four seasons in a northern climate. How are these seasons a cycle?

The cell cycle includes interphase and cell division.

All living things live, grow, reproduce, and die in a process called a life cycle. The life cycle of a tree, for example, begins with a seed. Under the right conditions, the seed begins to grow. It produces a very small plant, which may grow over many years into a towering tree. When it is mature, the tree makes its own seeds, and the cycle begins again.

Cells have a life cycle too, called the cell cycle. The **cell cycle** is the normal sequence of development and division of a cell. The cell cycle consists of two main phases: one in which the cell carries out its functions, called interphase, and one in which the cell divides, which can include mitosis and cytokinesis. All cells divide, but only eukaryotes undergo mitosis. Each phase in the cell cycle requires a certain period of time—from hours to days or years, depending on the type of cell.

RESOURCE CENTER
CLASSZONE.COM

Learn about the cell cycle.

Interphase

Interphase is the part of the cell cycle during which a cell is not dividing. Much activity takes place in this phase of the cell's life. During interphase, the cell grows to about twice the size it was when it was first produced. The cell also engages in normal life activities, such as transporting materials in and transporting wastes out. Also, cellular respiration occurs, which provides the energy the cell needs.

Changes that occur during interphase prepare a cell for division. Before a cell can divide, it duplicates its DNA exactly. Correct copying of the DNA is very important. It ensures that, after cell division, each new cell gets a complete set of DNA.

CHECK YOUR READING What cell processes occur during interphase?

VOCABULARY
Make a frame game diagram for *interphase*.

Cell Division Phase

Mitosis is the part of the cell cycle during which the nucleus divides. Prokaryotes do not undergo mitosis because they have no nucleus. In most cells, mitosis is the shortest period in the life cycle. The function of mitosis is to move the DNA and other material in the parent cell into position for cell division. When the cell divides, each new cell gets a full set of DNA and other cell structures. **Cytokinesis** (SY-toh-kuh-NEE-sihs) is the division of the parent cell's cytoplasm. Cytokinesis occurs immediately after mitosis.

Cell Cycle

The events that happen during the life of a cell are called the cell cycle.

1 **Interphase**
The **cell cycle** begins with interphase, which is the longest part of the cell cycle.

2 **Cell Division Phase**
After **mitosis** and **cytokinesis** there are two cells. The cell cycle then begins again for each cell.

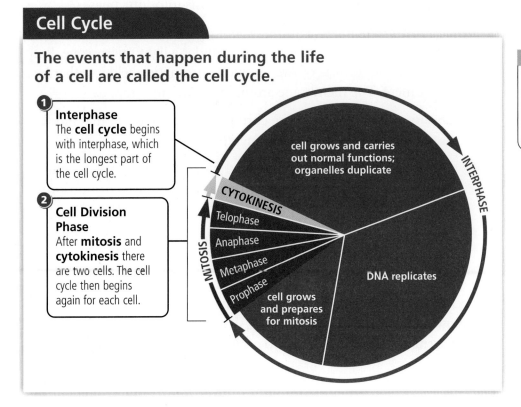

INTERPHASE

cell grows and carries out normal functions; organelles duplicate

CYTOKINESIS

Telophase
Anaphase
Metaphase
Prophase

MITOSIS

DNA replicates

cell grows and prepares for mitosis

READING TiP

The arrows in the Cell Cycle diagram represent the passage of time. Interphase is in red, mitosis is in purple, and cytokinesis is in yellow.

As a result of mitosis and cytokinesis, the original—or parent—cell splits into two genetically identical daughter cells. In this case, the term *daughter cell* does not imply gender. It is a term scientists use to refer to these new cells. Each daughter cell receives a complete set of DNA from the parent cell.

Cell division produces two genetically identical cells.

Recall that many cells in your body are continually dividing into new cells. The new cells help your body grow, develop, repair itself, and replace worn-out parts. Though your body cells divide at different rates, the same process—mitosis—divides their genetic material.

Cell division produces daughter cells that are genetically identical to each other, as well as to their parent cell, which no longer exists. Being genetically identical to their parent cell helps the new cells function properly. A skin cell, for example, divides and produces skin cells genetically identical to it.

CHECK YOUR READING How are daughter cells like the parent cell?

Steps of Mitosis

The process of mitosis is essential in evenly dividing the genetic material between the daughter cells. Although mitosis is a continuous process, scientists divide the events of mitosis into four phases.

1. **Chromosomes form.** During prophase, the DNA in the nucleus of a cell condenses and becomes visible under a light microscope. Each chromosome consists of two identical chromatids held together by a centromere. The membrane around the nucleus disappears.

2. **Chromosomes line up.** The chromosomes line up in the middle of the cell. This stage is called metaphase.

3. **Chromosomes separate.** During the stage called anaphase, the chromatids split, resulting in two separate identical chromosomes. These chromosomes are pulled to opposite sides of the cell.

4. **Nuclei form.** A new nuclear membrane forms around each group of chromosomes during telophase. The chromosomes return to their threadlike form.

Mitosis is finished, and the cell's genetic material has been divided. Following telophase the parent cell's cytoplasm is divided to complete the parent cell's division into two entirely separate daughter cells.

Cell Division

Before mitosis, the cell's DNA is copied during interphase.

Interphase

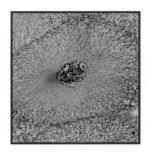

The cell has grown and is ready to divide.

The nucleus contains two complete copies of DNA.

Mitosis produces two new cells with identical copies of DNA.

Chromosome

chromatids

centromere

❶ Chromosomes condense.
Prophase

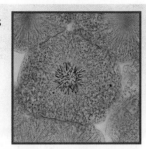

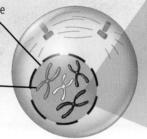

The nuclear membrane disappears.

Long strands of DNA condense to distinct chromosomes, each with two chromatids that are exact copies of each other.

❷ Chromosomes line up.
Metaphase

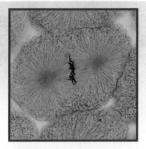

Chromosomes line up in the middle of the cell.

❸ Chromosomes separate.
Anaphase

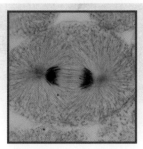

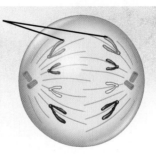

Chromatids of each chromosome split into two separate chromosomes.

Separated chromosomes pull to the opposite ends of the cell.

❹ Nuclei form.
Telophase,
Cytokinesis

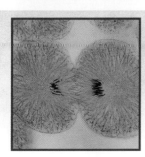

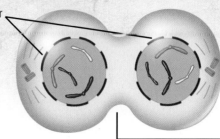

New nuclear membranes form.

Cell pinches and divides

Division of the Cytoplasm

READING TiP

As you read about cytokinesis refer to the images of plant and animal cells on page 85.

Cytokinesis, or the division of the parent cell's cytoplasm, immediately follows mitosis in eukaryotic cells. Cytokinesis differs slightly in animal cells and plant cells.

During cytokinesis in an animal cell, a fiber ring forms in the center of the dividing cell. The fiber ring contracts, pulling the cell membrane inward. Eventually, the cell is pinched into two daughter cells.

In a plant cell, the cell wall prevents the cell membrane from being pulled inward. A structure called a cell plate grows between the two new nuclei. The cell plate develops into a membrane and eventually becomes part of the cell wall of each of the new cells.

 CHECK YOUR READING How does cytokinesis differ in plant cells and animal cells?

INVESTIGATE Cell Division

How can you model mitosis?

PROCEDURE

1. Divide the poster board into six spaces, and draw arrows from one space to the next to indicate a cycle. Label the spaces, in order, "Interphase," "Prophase," "Metaphase," "Anaphase," "Telophase," and "Cytokinesis."

2. In each space, make a model of a cell and its DNA in the indicated phase. Make sure you represent the cell membrane, the nuclear membrane—when it is present—and the DNA.

WHAT DO YOU THINK?

- In which phases is the nuclear membrane present?
- In which phases are the chromosomes condensed?
- What do the arrows in your model show?

CHALLENGE How do you think cell division would differ in prokaryotic cells? Do you think cell division in prokaryotic cells would be more or less complex than in eukaryotic cells? Make drawings to show how you think a prokaryotic cell might divide.

SKILL FOCUS
Making models

MATERIALS
- poster board
- markers
- pipe cleaners
- packing peanuts
- glue
- scissors
- yarn

TIME
30 minutes

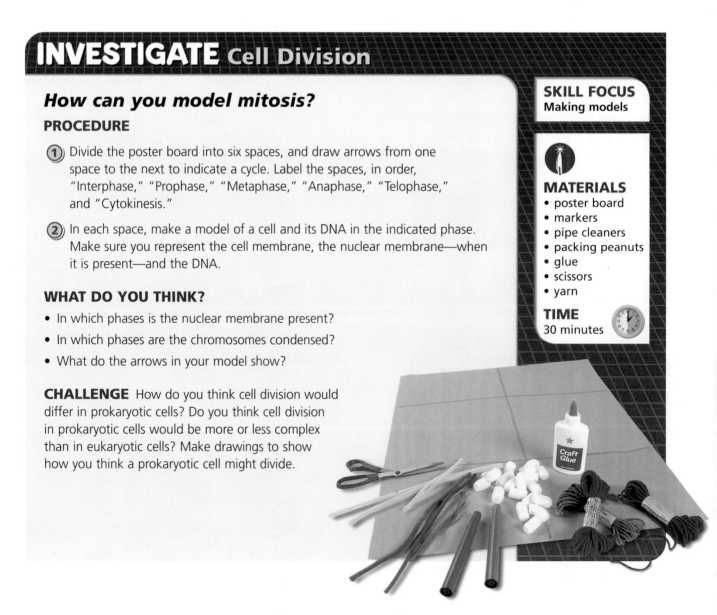

Cytokinesis

Cytokinesis happens in both plant and animal cells.

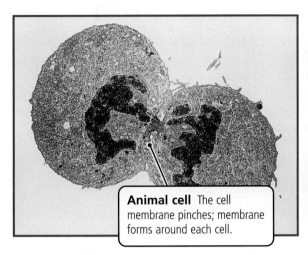

Animal cell The cell membrane pinches; membrane forms around each cell.

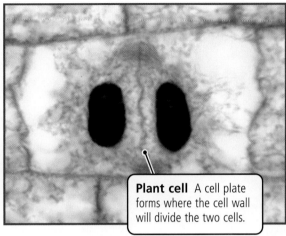

Plant cell A cell plate forms where the cell wall will divide the two cells.

READING VISUALS **COMPARE AND CONTRAST** How does the process of cytokinesis in the animal cell on the left differ from that of the plant cell on the right?

The two daughter cells are now completely separated. Each is surrounded by a cell membrane. Each daughter cell has some of its parent cell's cytoplasm. Though daughter cells are genetically identical to their parent cell, they are smaller. After division, cells may enter a period of growth, during which they take in the resources they need to increase the amount of their cytoplasm and to grow to full size. When cells are fully grown, they are about the same size as the parent cell was before division.

CHECK YOUR READING What happens to cells after cytokinesis?

3.2 Review

KEY CONCEPTS

1. What are the two main parts of the cell cycle?

2. Describe the state of a cell about to start mitosis.

3. How is the genetic material in two daughter cells similar to the genetic material in a parent cell?

CRITICAL THINKING

4. **Sequence** Describe in order the steps that occur during mitosis.

5. **Compare and Contrast** How is cytokinesis in plant cells similar to cytokinesis in animal cells? How is it different?

CHALLENGE

6. **Infer** You know that mitosis does not happen in prokaryotes. Do you think cytokinesis happens in prokaryotes? Explain your answer.

CHAPTER INVESTIGATION

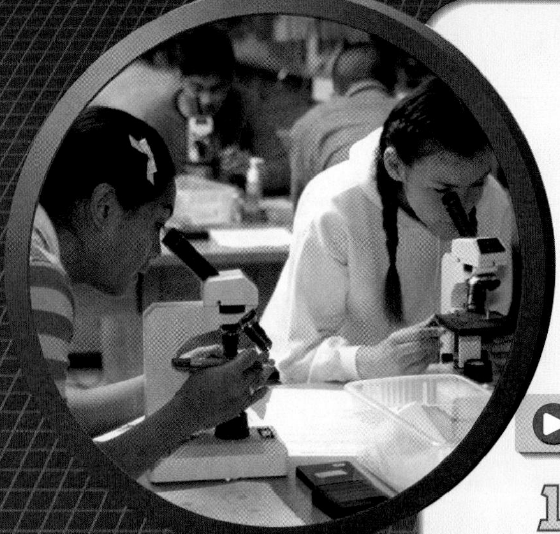

Stages of the Cell Cycle

OVERVIEW AND PURPOSE In this activity you will observe cells from an onion root tip that are undergoing mitosis. You will identify and draw cells in different stages of mitosis and the cell cycle. Then you will count the number of cells in each stage. Remember to record this information in your **Science Notebook.**

▶ Procedure

1. Make a data table like the one shown on the sample notebook page.

2. Obtain a prepared slide of an onion root tip. Place the slide on the microscope stage. Using the low-power objective, adjust the focus until the root tip is clear.

    step 2

3. Move the slide until you are looking at the region just above the root tip. The cells in this area were in the process of mitosis when the slide was made.

4. Look at the boxlike cells arranged in rows. The DNA in these cells has been stained to make it more visible. Select a cell in interphase. Switch to high power and sketch this cell in your notebook.

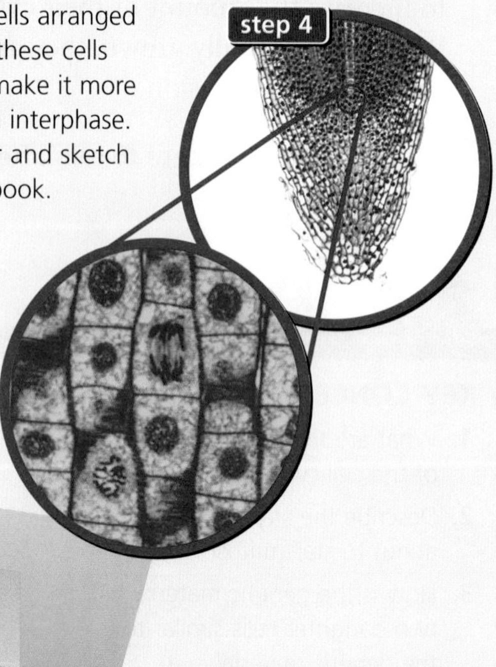

    step 4

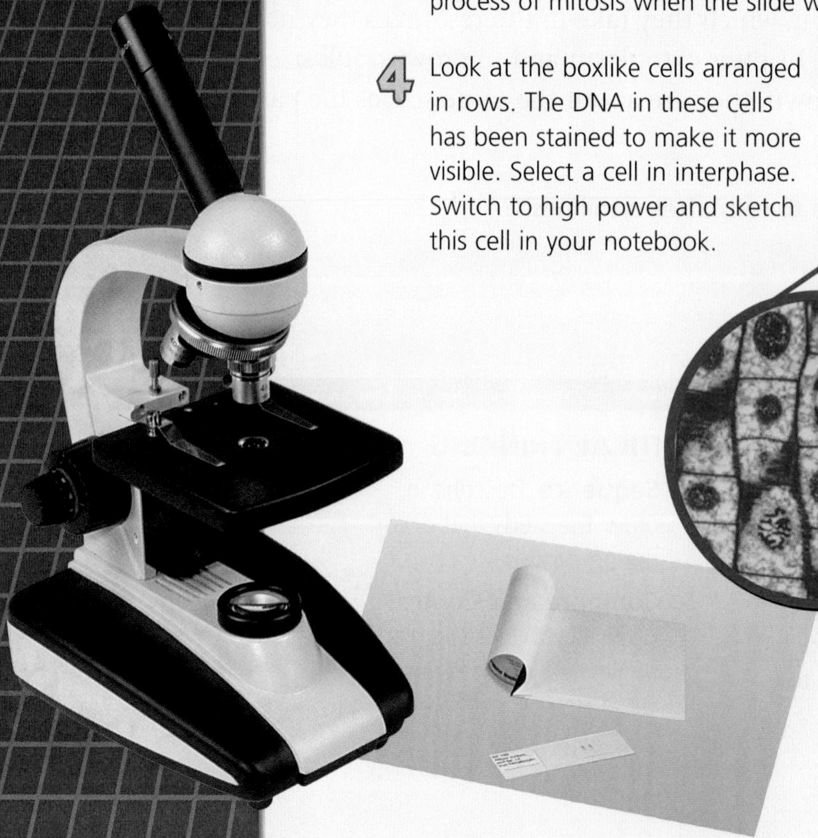

MATERIALS
- prepared slides of onion root tip cells
- light microscope

5. Repeat step 3 for cells in the various stages of mitosis: prophase, metaphase, anaphase, and telophase. Refer to the diagram on page 83 to identify cells in each stage.

6. Arrange your sketches to represent the order of the process of mitosis.

7. Under low-power magnification, choose 25 cells at random. Decide which stage of the cell cycle each cell is in. Record the number of cells in each stage in your data table.

▶ Observe and Analyze

Write It Up

1. **OBSERVE** Look at your sketches of the stages of mitosis. Describe the events in each stage.

2. **ANALYZING DATA** Was there any one stage of the cell cycle that was occurring in the majority of cells you observed? If so, which was it?

▶ Conclude

Write It Up

1. **INFER** What might the differences in the number of cells in each stage of the cell cycle mean?

2. **IDENTIFY LIMITS** Were there any cells that were difficult to classify as being in one particular phase of the cell cycle? What do these cells suggest to you about the process of mitosis?

3. **APPLY** Where does new root growth take place? Explain your answer.

▶ INVESTIGATE Further

CHALLENGE From your data table, calculate the percent of cells in each stage of the cell cycle. Use those numbers to predict how much time a cell spends in each stage. You can base your calculation on a total cell cycle of 24 hours.

Stages of the Cell Cycle

Table 1. Number of Cells in Each Stage of the Cell Cycle

Stage	Number of Cells Observed
Interphase	
Prophase	
Metaphase	
Anaphase	
Telophase	

KEY CONCEPT
3.3 Both sexual and asexual reproduction involve cell division.

◀ **BEFORE,** you learned	▶ **NOW,** you will learn
• Cells go through a cycle of growth and division • Mitosis produces two genetically identical cells	• About cell division and asexual reproduction • How sexual reproduction and asexual reproduction compare

VOCABULARY

asexual reproduction
p. 88
binary fission p. 89
regeneration p. 90

THINK ABOUT

How does cell division affect single-celled organisms?

In multicellular organisms, cell division functions in growth, repair, and development. But in unicellular organisms, each cell is itself an organism. Unicellular organisms, like this paramecium, also undergo cell division. What are some possible results of cell division in unicellular organisms? How might they compare with the results of cell division in multicellular organisms?

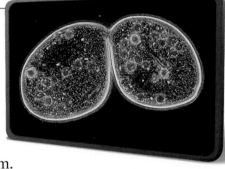

COMBINATION NOTES
Begin taking notes on the main idea: *Asexual reproduction involves one parent.* Be sure to include sketches of each method of reproducing.

Asexual reproduction involves one parent.

Mitosis and cytokinesis are the processes by which eukaryotic cells divide. In multicellular organisms, the daughter cells that result are separate cells but do not live independent lives. For example, new skin cells are part of skin tissue and cannot live independently. In multicellular organisms, mitosis and cytokinesis are not considered methods by which an organism reproduces.

Most unicellular organisms, and a few multicellular organisms, use cell division to reproduce, in a process called asexual reproduction. In **asexual reproduction,** one organism produces one or more new organisms that are identical to itself and that live independently of it. The organism that produces the new organism or organisms is the parent. Each new organism is an offspring. The offspring produced by asexual reproduction are genetically identical to the parent.

Cell Division in Unicellular Organisms

Cell division and reproduction are the same thing in all single-celled organisms. However, the process of cell division in prokaryotes and in single-celled eukaryotes differs.

Binary fission is the form of asexual reproduction occurring in prokaryotes. Binary fission occurs when the parent organism splits in two, producing two completely independent daughter cells. Genetically, the daughter cells are exactly like the parent cell. Since all prokaryotic organisms are single-celled, cell division and reproduction by binary fission are the same process for them.

In single-celled eukaryotic organisms, however, reproduction by cell division involves mitosis and cytokinesis. The unicellular organism undergoes mitosis, duplicating and separating its chromosomes. Then its cytoplasm is divided through cytokinesis. The result is two separate, independent, and genetically identical offspring. Examples of single-celled eukaryotic organisms that reproduce by cell division include algae, some yeasts, and protozoans, such as paramecium.

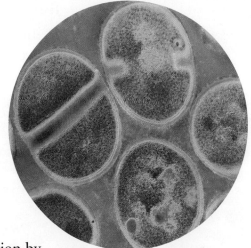

Binary fission results in two nearly equal, independent cells, as shown in these bacteria.

Budding

Both unicellular and multicellular organisms can reproduce by budding. Budding is a process in which an organism develops tiny buds on its body. Each bud forms from the parent's cells, so the bud's genetic material is the same as the parent's. The bud grows until it forms a complete or nearly complete new organism that is genetically identical to the parent.

In some budding organisms, buds can form from any part of the body. In other organisms, buds can be produced only by specialized cells in particular parts of the body. A new organism produced by budding may remain attached to its parent. Most often, when a bud reaches a certain size, it breaks free of the parent and becomes a separate, independent organism.

Some yeast and single-celled organisms reproduce asexually by budding. But budding is most notable in multicellular organisms. Hydras are freshwater animals that are famous for reproducing by budding. Among plants, the kalanchoe (KAL-uhn-KOH-ee) produces tiny buds from the tips of its leaves. Each kalanchoe bud that lands on a suitable growing surface will develop into a mature kalanchoe plant that is genetically identical to the parent plant.

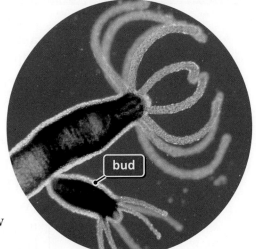

bud

Budding Hydras reproduce by pinching off small buds.

How is budding different in unicellular and multicellular organisms?

Regeneration

In certain multicellular organisms, specialized cells at the site of a wound or lost limb are able to become different types of tissues. The process of new tissue growth at these sites is called **regeneration.**

Regeneration
This starfish is regenerating its legs that were lost.

Although one function of regeneration is the regrowth of damaged or missing body parts, in some organisms asexual reproduction is another function of regeneration.

Regeneration can be observed in many animals called starfish. If a starfish is cut in half, each half can regenerate its missing body parts from its own cells. The result is two complete, independent, and genetically identical starfish. Sometimes a starfish will drop off one of its limbs. The animal will eventually form a new limb. In these cases, regeneration is considered a form of asexual reproduction.

The growth of plants from cuttings is also a kind of asexual reproduction through regeneration. Cells near a cut made in a plant's stem begin to produce the missing part of the plant. Once the missing part is grown, the cutting can be planted in soil. The cutting will grow into a new, independent plant that is genetically identical to the plant from which the cutting was taken.

CHECK YOUR READING Describe the process of regeneration in starfish.

Asexual Reproduction and Health

RESOURCE CENTER
CLASSZONE.COM

Learn more about asexual reproduction.

You have probably had the following experience. In the morning you feel fine. By afternoon, you have a strange feeling that something is not quite right, but you are well enough to function normally. You may even continue to feel well at dinner, and you eat heartily. Then, later that evening, it hits you. You're sick. That tickle in your throat has become a sore throat requiring a visit to the doctor and antibiotics. How did you get so sick so fast?

You could have picked up bacteria in school that morning. Perhaps another student coughed, spreading the bacteria that cause strep throat. A population of bacteria, like populations of other organisms that reproduce asexually through binary fission, increases in number geometrically. Two cells become 4, which become 8, which become 16, and so on.

The reason you get sick so fast is that for many bacteria the generation time is very short. Generation time is the time it takes for one generation to produce offspring—the next generation. In fact, some types of bacteria can produce a new generation of cells in less than 30 minutes. In about an hour the number of bacteria can increase to four times the starting number.

Although all offspring are genetically identical, the rare genetic random change does occasionally occur during cell division. The rapid reproduction rate makes it more likely that some offspring will have a random genetic change, which may be beneficial.

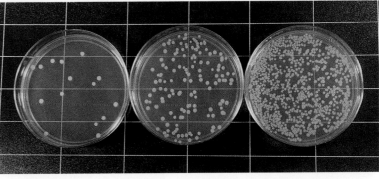

Asexual reproduction
These bacteria are quickly multiplying through asexual reproduction.

INVESTIGATE Asexual Reproduction

Which parts of plants can reproduce?

Some organisms can regenerate offspring from any part of their body. Others can regenerate offspring from only one specialized body part. In this activity, you will discover if a houseplant regenerates from various parts.

PROCEDURE

1. Obtain a plant part (leaf, stem, stem with leaf, or root) from your teacher. Also get one flowerpot filled with potting soil.

2. Dip the plant part in water and set it into the soil, about 1 in. deep, but make sure that most of the plant part is above the level of the soil. Water the soil lightly.

3. Place all the class's pots on the same window sill. Observe your plant part every day for two to three weeks. Record your observations.

WHAT DO YOU THINK?

- Which plant parts, if any, were able to regenerate a new plant?

- What can you conclude about the ability of different plant parts to grow into new plants?

CHALLENGE How does the plant in the experiment compare with the kalanchoe plant you read about in the text? What accounts for plants' different abilities to produce viable offspring?

SKILL FOCUS
Drawing conclusions

MATERIALS
- houseplant
- flowerpot
- soil
- water

TIME
15 minutes

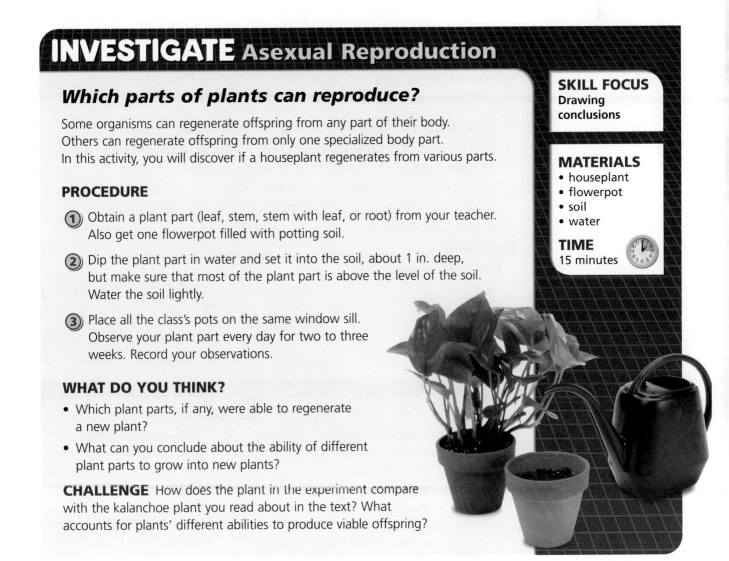

Sexual reproduction involves two parent organisms.

Reproduction of multicellular organisms often involves sexual reproduction as well as asexual cell division. The table shows some differences between asexual and sexual reproduction.

Comparing Asexual and Sexual Reproduction	
Asexual Reproduction	**Sexual Reproduction**
Cell Division	Cell division and other processes
One parent organism	Two parent organisms
Rate of reproduction is rapid	Rate of reproduction is slower than rate for asexual reproduction
Offspring identical to parent	Offspring have genetic information from two parents

If you grow a plant from a cutting, the new plant will be identical to the parent. However, plants that grow from seeds contain genetic material from two parents. Plants growing from seeds and animals growing from eggs are examples of organisms that reproduce through sexual reproduction.

Cell division is part of both sexual and asexual reproduction. The process of mitosis produces cells identical to the parent cells. The diversity of life on Earth is in part possible because of the combining of genetic materials from two parents in sexual reproduction. In the next chapter, you will read about cell processes involved in sexual reproduction.

 List two major differences between asexual and sexual reproduction.

 Review

KEY CONCEPTS

1. How does binary fission relate to cell division?

2. What is a bud, and where does it form on an organism that reproduces asexually?

3. Compare sexual and asexual reproduction.

CRITICAL THINKING

4. **Predict** Do you think prokaryotes undergo regeneration? Why or why not?

5. **Compare and Contrast** How is binary fission in prokaryotic organisms similar to and different from mitosis and cytokinesis in single-celled eukaryotic organisms?

CHALLENGE

6. **Synthesize** Some bacteria can exchange pieces of genetic material with one another through a process called conjugation. What effect might this exchange have on the offspring of the bacteria that underwent conjugation?

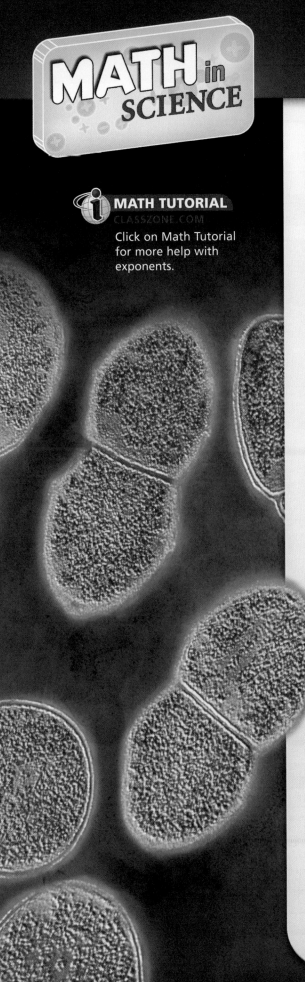

MATH in SCIENCE

MATH TUTORIAL
CLASSZONE.COM

Click on Math Tutorial for more help with exponents.

Divide and Multiply

Each time a parent cell divides, the result is two new cells. The new cells are a new generation that in turn divides again. The increase in the number of cells can be shown using exponents. Each cell of each new generation produces two cells. This type of increase in the number of objects is often called exponential growth.

Example

What is the numerical sequence when cells divide to form new cells? You can model this type of progression by using a plain piece of paper.

(1) To represent the first division, fold the piece of paper in half.

(2) Fold it in half again, and it will show the second division. Fold it again and again to represent succeeding divisions.

(3) Write the sequence that shows the number of boxes on the paper after each fold.

2, 4, 8, 16, . . .

(4) Notice that after one division (fold), there are 2 cells (boxes), or 2^1. Two divisions yield $2 \cdot 2$ cells, or 2^2. And after three divisions, there are $2 \cdot 2 \cdot 2$ cells, or 2^3.

ANSWER The sequence can be written with exponents:
$2^1, 2^2, 2^3, 2^4, . . .$

Answer the following questions.

1. Suppose the cells divide for one more generation after the 4 described above. How can this be written as an exponent of 2? How many cells will there be?

2. How many cells would exist in the tenth generation? Write the number using an exponent.

3. Suppose you took the paper in the example and folded it in thirds each time, rather than in half. Make a table showing the number of boxes after each folding. Use numbers with exponents to write the sequence.

4. Write the following number sequence as a sequence of numbers with exponents: 5, 25, 125, 625, . . .

5. Write the following number sequence as a sequence of numbers with NO exponents: $10^1, 10^2, 10^3, 10^4, . . .$

CHALLENGE Before you begin folding, you have a single sheet of paper, or 1 box. The parent cell is also a single unit. Use this information to explain why $2^0 = 3^0$.

Chapter Review

the **BIG** idea

Organisms grow, reproduce, and maintain themselves through cell division.

CONTENT REVIEW
CLASSZONE.COM

KEY CONCEPTS SUMMARY

1 Cell division occurs in all organisms.

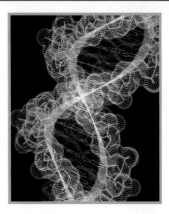

- In unicellular organisms functions of cell division include reproduction

- In multicellular organisms functions of cell division include growth, development, and repair.

VOCABULARY
DNA p. 74
chromosome p. 75

---

2 Cell division is part of a cell cycle.

The **cell cycle** has two main phases, **interphase** and **mitosis.** Most of the life cycle of a cell is spent in interphase. During mitosis, cells divide.

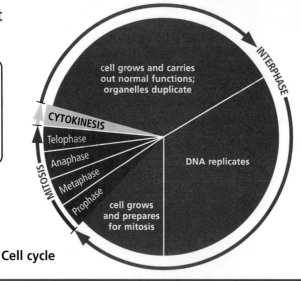

INTERPHASE

cell grows and carries out normal functions; organelles duplicate

CYTOKINESIS
Telophase
Anaphase
Metaphase
Prophase
MITOSIS

DNA replicates

cell grows and prepares for mitosis

Cell cycle

VOCABULARY
cell cycle p. 80
interphase p. 81
mitosis p. 81
cytokinesis p. 81

---

3 Both sexual and asexual reproduction involve cell division.

Some organisms reproduce asexually. Both asexual and sexual reproduction involve cell division.

Comparing Asexual and Sexual Reproduction	
Asexual Reproduction	**Sexual Reproduction**
Cell Division	Cell division and other processes
One parent organism	Two parent organisms
Rate of reproduction is rapid	Rate of reproduction is slower than rate for asexual reproduction
Offspring identical to parents	Offspring have genetic information from two parents

VOCABULARY
asexual reproduction p. 88
binary fission p. 89
regeneration p. 90

Reviewing Vocabulary

On a separate sheet of paper, write a sentence describing the relationship between the two vocabulary words in each pair.

1. cell cycle, interphase

2. mitosis, cytokinesis

3. chromosome, DNA

4. parent, offspring

Reviewing Key Concepts

Multiple Choice *Choose the letter of the best answer.*

5. Most of the growth in your body occurs because your cells
   a. grow larger   c. make proteins
   b. take in oxygen   d. divide

6. The stage in a cell's life when it is not in the process of dividing is called
   a. interphase   c. mitosis
   b. the cell cycle   d. cell division

7. What material in the cell makes up chromosomes?
   a. carbohydrates   c. the nucleus
   b. chromatids   d. nucleic acids

8. What ratio increases when a cell divides into two smaller cells?
   a. volume to length
   b. length to width
   c. surface area to volume
   d. width to surface area

9. The process of cytokinesis results in
   a. two daughter cells that are different from one another
   b. two genetically identical daughter cells
   c. identical pairs of chromosomes
   d. identical pairs of chromatids

10. What is the step that follows mitosis, in which the cytoplasm divides?
    a. prophase   c. anaphase
    b. synthesis   d. cytokinesis

11. A cell's chromosomes must be duplicated before mitosis occurs so that
    a. they can form chromatids
    b. they can attach to the spindle
    c. each daughter cell gets a full number of chromosomes
    d. each daughter cell does not have to duplicate its own chromosomes

12. Binary fission differs from mitosis because the new cells
    a. cannot function without the parent
    b. grow from missing limbs
    c. have half the normal number of chromosomes
    d. live independently of the parent cell

13. If a starfish is cut in half, it can regrow its missing body through
    a. binary fission   c. healing
    b. budding   d. regeneration

14. Which is an example of reproduction?
    a. binary fission in unicellular organisms
    b. cell division in a multicellular organism
    c. cell division around a broken bone
    d. division of cytoplasm

15. Which sequence is correct for mitosis?
    a. chromosomes form, chromosomes separate, chromosomes line up, nuclei form
    b. chromosomes form, chromosomes line up, chromosomes separate, nuclei form
    c. chromosomes line up, nuclei form, chromosomes separate, chromosomes form
    d. chromosomes separate, chromosomes form, nuclei form, chromosomes line up

Short Answer *Write a short answer to each question.*

16. What is the difference between cytokinesis in plant and animal cells?

17. Describe what happens in a cell during interphase. Your answer should mention DNA.

18. Describe the functions of cell division in both unicellular and multicellular organisms.

19. IDENTIFY CAUSE Describe some of the reasons that cells divide.

This illustration shows a plant and the cutting that was taken from it, which is growing in a container of water. Use the illustration to answer the next six questions.

20. OBSERVE From which part of the plant was the cutting taken?

21. INFER Where did the cutting get the genetic information that controls its development?

22. INFER What is the genetic relationship between the original plant and the cutting?

23. SYNTHESIZE What process causes both the cutting and the original plant to grow?

24. SUMMARIZE Write a brief summary of the process that causes growth in both plants.

25. PREDICT These plants can also reproduce from fertilized seeds. How is the cutting the same as the plant that would grow from a seed? How is the cutting different?

26. CALCULATE A single bacterium enters your body at 10:00 A.M. These bacteria reproduce at a rate of one generation every 30 minutes. How many bacteria of this type will be in your body by 8:00 P.M. that evening?

The diagrams below show 4 parts of a process. Use them to answer the following three questions.

a.   c.

b.   d.

27. SEQUENCE What is the correct order of the four diagrams above?

28. SYNTHESIZE Draw two diagrams, one showing what you would see before the process shown above begins, and one showing what you would see after the conclusion of the process.

29. MODEL On a separate sheet of paper, draw your own simple model of the process of mitosis.

the BIG idea

30. SUMMARIZE Look again at the question on the photograph on pages 70–71. Now that you have studied this chapter, how would you change your answer to the question?

31. SYNTHESIZE How do the concepts in this chapter relate to the concepts in the cell theory?

UNIT PROJECTS

If you need to do an experiment for your unit project, gather the materials. Be sure to allow enough time to observe results before the project is due.

Analyzing Data

This diagram shows the length of the cell cycle for a typical skin cell in the human body.

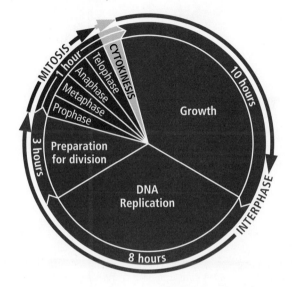

Use the diagram to answer the questions below.

1. How long does the growth phase of the cell cycle take?

   a. 1 hour   **c.** 8 hours

   b. 3 hours   **d.** 10 hours

2. How much time does the cell cycle spend in interphase?

   a. 1 hour   **c.** 21 hours

   b. 10 hours   **d.** 22 hours

3. What is the total length of time it takes for the skin cell to complete one full cell cycle?

   a. 10 hours   **c.** 21 hours

   b. 18 hours   **d.** 22 hours

4. What phase of the cell cycle takes about 8 hours?

   a. DNA replication

   b. mitosis

   c. growth

   d. preparation for cell division

5. Suppose another type of skin cell takes 44 hours to complete one cell cycle. If all of the phases are proportional to the length of time shown in the diagram, how long will the preparation for cell division phase last?

   a. 3 hours   **c.** 10 hours

   b. 6 hours   **d.** 20 hours

6. According to the diagram, what is the second stage in mitosis?

   a. prophase   **c.** telophase

   b. metaphase   **d.** cytokinesis

Extended Response

Answer the two questions. Include some of the terms shown in the word box. Underline each term you use in your answers.

cell cycle	metaphase	mitosis
anaphase	prophase	telophase

7. A scientist is studying the stages of cell division in the cells of an onion root. The scientist counts 100 cells and identifies which stage of cell division each cell is in at a given moment. He counts a total of 85 cells in interphase, 8 cells in prophase, 3 cells in metaphase, and 2 cells each in anaphase and telophase. A typical onion cell takes about 12 hours to complete the cell cycle. Using the information in the diagram and the data given here, how can you account for these numbers?

8. Your science class is investigating the effect of temperature on the rate of mitosis in onion plants. You hypothesize that the higher the temperature, the faster cells undergo mitosis. How could you set up an experiment to support your hypothesis? Describe the materials you would use and the steps you would take in your procedure.

CHAPTER

Patterns of Heredity

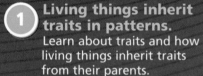

In sexual reproduction, genes are passed from parents to offspring in predictable patterns.

Key Concepts

SECTION

1 **Living things inherit traits in patterns.**
Learn about traits and how living things inherit traits from their parents.

SECTION

2 **Patterns of heredity can be predicted.**
Learn how math can be used to predict patterns of heredity.

SECTION

3 **Meiosis is a special form of cell division.**
Learn about the process of meiosis.

 Internet Preview

CLASSZONE.COM

Chapter 4 online resources: Content Review, two Simulations, two Resource Centers, Math Tutorial, Test Practice

What similarities can you see between this mother wolf and her two offspring?

EXPLORE (the BIG idea)

How Are Traits Distributed?

Ask 10 people you know if they are left-handed or right-handed, if they have dimples, and if they can roll their tongue. For each trait, write down how many people have that trait.

Observe and Think Were any of the traits evenly distributed? Why do you think that is?

Combinations

Take one bag with 4 blue slips of paper and one bag with 4 red slips of paper. Consider different ways to mix or combine the materials in the bags.

Observe and Think How many ways could you think of mixing the materials? How were the combinations similar and different?

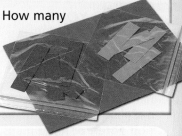

Internet Activity: Mendel's Experiment

Go to **ClassZone.com** to try a virtual version of Mendel's experiments with peas. Learn about heredity as you breed plants with different traits.

Observe and Think What does Mendel's experiment teach us about heredity?

NSTA
scilinks.org
SCiLINKS

Heredity Code: MDL034

CHAPTER 4
Getting Ready to Learn

◀ CONCEPT REVIEW

- Life comes from life.
- Mitosis produces identical cells.
- Some organisms reproduce with asexual reproduction.

◀ VOCABULARY REVIEW

chromosome p. 75

mitosis p. 81

asexual reproduction p. 88

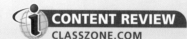

CONTENT REVIEW
CLASSZONE.COM
Review concepts and vocabulary.

▶ TAKING NOTES

CHOOSE YOUR OWN STRATEGY

Take notes using one or more of the strategies from earlier chapters—**main idea webs, combination notes,** or **mind maps.** Feel free to mix and match the strategies, or use an entirely different note-taking strategy.

VOCABULARY STRATEGY

Think about a vocabulary term as a **magnet word** diagram. Write the other terms or ideas related to that term around it.

See the Note-Taking Handbook on pages R45–R51.

SCIENCE NOTEBOOK

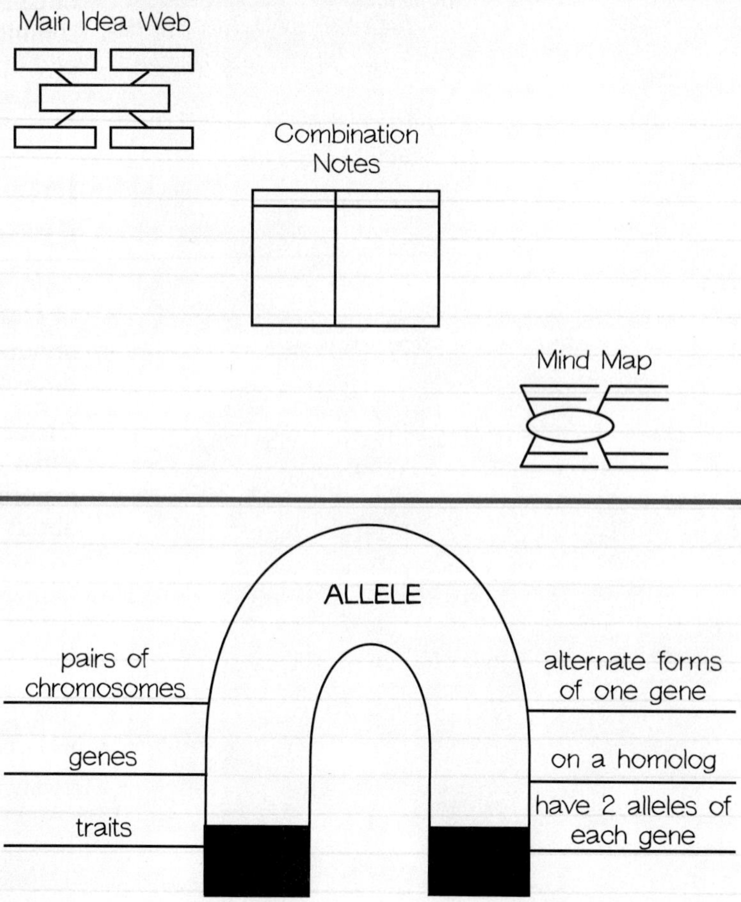

Main Idea Web

Combination Notes

Mind Map

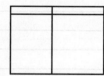

ALLELE

pairs of chromosomes

genes

traits

alternate forms of one gene

on a homolog

have 2 alleles of each gene

4.1

Living things inherit traits in patterns.

McDougal Littell Science
SOUTH CAROLINA

STANDARDS

7–2.5 Summarize how genetic information is passed from parent to offspring by using the terms *genes, chromosomes, inherited traits, genotype, phenotype, dominant traits,* and *recessive traits.*

7–2.7 Distinguish between inherited traits and those acquired from environmental factors.

VOCABULARY

sexual reproduction p. 102
gene p. 102
heredity p. 102
allele p. 103
phenotype p. 106
genotype p. 106
dominant p. 107
recessive p. 107

▶ **BEFORE, you learned**

- Life comes from life
- Cells contain chromosomes
- Some organisms reproduce with asexual reproduction

▶ **NOW, you will learn**

- How genes for traits are passed from parent to offspring
- About discoveries made by Gregor Mendel
- About dominant and recessive alleles

THINK ABOUT

What characteristics might be inherited?

Make a list of characteristics you can observe about the girl in the photograph to the right. Perhaps your list includes the fact that she has pale skin, or that she can read. Some of these characteristics are qualities or abilities learned or acquired from the environment around her. However, some of the characteristics were probably inherited from her parents. Of the characteristics on your list, which do you think were inherited and which do you think were acquired?

NOTETAKING STRATEGY
Take notes on the idea that parents and offspring are similar by using a strategy from an earlier chapter or one of your own.

Parents and offspring are similar.

You are an individual who has a unique combination of characteristics. These characteristics are also known as traits. Many of your traits may resemble those your parents have, including your hair color, eye color, and blood type. These characteristics are called inherited traits.

Some traits are acquired, not inherited. An acquired trait is developed during your life. Learned behaviors are one type of acquired trait. For example, your ability to read and write is an acquired trait—a skill you learned. You were not born knowing how to ride a bike, and if you have children, they will not be born knowing how to do it either. They will have to learn the skill just as you did.

Some acquired traits are not learned but result from interaction with the environment. Skin color, for example, has both an inherited component and an environmental one. The skin color of many light-skinned people darkens when they are exposed to the Sun.

 CHECK YOUR READING How are inherited traits and acquired traits different? Give one example of each.

 **RESOURCE CENTER**
CLASSZONE.COM

Find out more about sexual reproduction.

In this chapter, you will learn about inheritance that happens through sexual reproduction. During **sexual reproduction** a cell containing genetic information from the mother and a cell containing genetic information from the father combine into a completely new cell, which becomes the offspring. You will learn more about the mechanics of sexual reproduction in Section 4.3.

Genes are on chromosome pairs.

Inherited traits are controlled by the structures, materials, and processes you learned about in Chapters 1 and 2. In turn, these structures, materials, and processes are coded for by genes. A **gene** is a unit of heredity that occupies a specific location on a chromosome and codes for a particular product. **Heredity** is the passing of genes from parents to offspring.

Individuals inherit their genes from their parents. The genes code for the expression of traits. It is important to understand that an organism does not inherit the traits themselves from its parents. It inherits the genes that code for the traits it has. Most traits are not coded for by just one gene. Some characteristics are affected by many genes in complicated ways. We have much to learn about which genes might affect which characteristics.

In most eukaryotes, cells contain pairs of chromosomes, with one chromosome of each pair coming from each of two parents. The chromosomes in a pair are called homologs. They resemble each other, having the same size and shape, and carrying genetic information for particular traits.

On each homolog are sites where specific genes are located. Let us say, for example, that the gene that determines

Chromosomes and Genes

The letters on the pair of chromosomes below represent alleles.

Chromosomes come in pairs. Each member in a pair is called a homolog.

A **gene** occupies a specific location on both chromosomes in a pair.

Alleles are alternate forms of the same gene.

whether or not a plant is tall is located at place A on a pair of homologs. Though both homologs have the gene for height at site A, the genes may not be identical. They may be variations instead. The various forms of the same gene are called **alleles** (uh-LEELZ).

Thus, the homolog from one parent might have an allele for regular height at site A, while the gene from the other parent might have an allele for short height at site A. The alleles on a pair of homologs may or may not be different. Though any one plant can have only two alleles of a gene, there can be many alleles for a particular gene within a population.

 CHECK YOUR READING What are alleles?

Each species has a characteristic number of chromosomes. Chimpanzees have 24 pairs of chromosomes, for a total of 48 chromosomes. Fruit flies have 4 pairs of chromosomes, or 8 in all. Humans have 23 pairs, for a total of 46 chromosomes. Scientists refer to chromosomes by their number. Human chromosomes are numbered 1 through 22; the 23rd pair are the sex chromosomes.

In humans, the sex chromosomes are called the X-chromosome and the Y-chromosome. A human female has two X-chromosomes, while a human male has one X-chromosome and one Y-chromosome. In addition to determining the sex of an offspring, the X- and Y-chromosomes contain important genes, just as the other, numbered chromosomes do.

READING TiP
The word *homolog* comes from the Greek words *homos,* which means "same," and *logos,* which means "proportion."

Human Chromosomes

Humans have 23 pairs of chromosomes, for a total of 46. One of these pairs, shown below, determines the sex of the offspring.

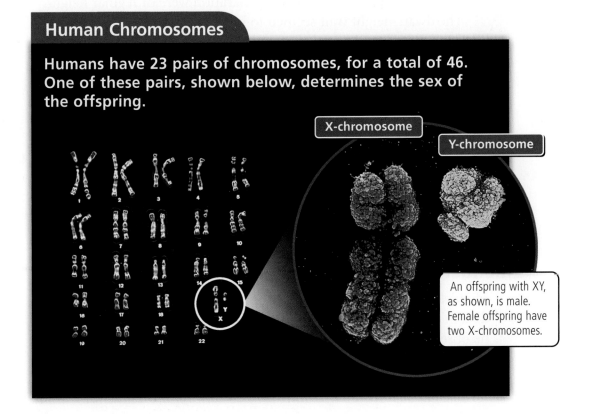

X-chromosome

Y-chromosome

An offspring with XY, as shown, is male. Female offspring have two X-chromosomes.

Gregor Mendel made some important discoveries about heredity.

The first major experiments investigating heredity were performed by a monk named Gregor Mendel, who lived in Austria during the mid-1800s. Before Mendel became a monk, he attended university and received training in science and mathematics. This training served him well when he began investigating the inheritance of traits among the pea plants in the monastery's garden.

Mendel took very detailed notes, carefully recording all the data from his many experiments. He worked with seven different traits: plant height, flower and pod position, seed shape, seed color, pod shape, pod color, and flower color. He studied each trait separately, always starting with plants that were true-breeding for that one particular trait. A true-breeding plant is one that will always produce offspring with a particular trait when allowed to self-pollinate.

READING TiP

The root of the word *trait* means to "draw out." It was originally used in the sense of drawing out a line. This same idea works in heredity if you think of drawing a connection between parents and offspring.

One Example

In his experiments with plant height, Mendel took two sets of plants, one true-breeding for plants of regular height and the other true-breeding for plants of short or dwarf height.

1. Instead of letting the plants self-pollinate as they do naturally, he deliberately paired as parents one plant from each set. Mendel called the plants that resulted from this cross the first generation. All of the plants from this first generation were of regular height. The dwarf-height trait seemed to have disappeared entirely.

2. Mendel then let the first-generation plants self-pollinate. He called the offspring that resulted from this self-pollination the second generation. About three fourths of the second-generation plants were of regular height, but about one fourth were of dwarf height. So the trait that seemed to disappear in the first generation reappeared in the second generation.

Mendel's experiments with other traits showed similar patterns.

 Summarize the pattern shown in Mendel's experiments with plant height.

Mendel's Conclusions

Mendel drew upon his knowledge of mathematics while analyzing his data in order to suggest a hypothesis that would explain the patterns he observed. Mendel realized that each plant must have two "factors" for each possible trait, one factor from each parent. Some traits, such as dwarf height, could be masked—dwarf height could be seen in the

Mendel's Pea Plants

Mendel observed variation in the height of pea plants (regular or dwarf height). By crossing plants with specific traits, he deduced that offspring get factors for each trait from both parents.

Parent Plants

X

regular   dwarf

1 **First generation** Crossing a true-breeding regular pea plant with a true-breeding dwarf pea plant produces all regular pea plants in the first generation.

regular   regular   regular   regular

X

2 **Second generation** Allowing the first generation pea plants to self-pollinate resulted in about three-fourths regular pea plants and one- fourth dwarf pea plants.

regular   regular   regular   dwarf

plant only if both of the plant's factors were for dwarf height. All of the plants in the first generation had one dwarf factor and one regular factor. A plant with one dwarf-height factor and one regular-height factor would be of regular height, because the regular-height factor masks the dwarf-height factor.

Later experiments allowed Mendel to draw a number of other conclusions about how these factors are distributed. Since the mid-1800s, Mendel's experiments and conclusions have been the basis for most of the scientific thought about heredity. Those things he called "factors" are what we now call genes and alleles.

CHECK YOUR READING How many factors or genes does each plant have for each possible trait?

Alleles interact to produce traits.

The pea-plant traits Gregor Mendel chose to study were all controlled by single genes, and each of the genes was on a different chromosome. As you learned earlier, most traits are not controlled by only one gene. However, simple examples such as Mendel's peas do help us better understand heredity.

Phenotype and Genotype

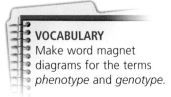

VOCABULARY
Make word magnet diagrams for the terms *phenotype* and *genotype*.

What color eyes do you have? The eye color you see when you look in the mirror is your phenotype. An organism's **phenotype** describes the actual characteristics that can be observed. Your height, the size of your feet, the presence or absence of a fold in your eyelids—all are observable traits and are part of your phenotype.

By contrast, the genes that control the development of eyefolds are part of your genotype. **Genotype** is the name for the genes an organism has. Your genotype is not always obvious from your phenotype. If you have eyefolds, your genotype definitely contains at least one eyefold-producing allele. But it may also have one allele for no eyefolds. Sometimes your genes contain information that is not expressed in your phenotype.

CHECK YOUR READING Which term describes characteristics that can be observed?

eye with folds at the corner of the eyelids

eye without folds at the corner of the eyelids

COMPARE The photograph above shows **phenotypes** of the eyefold gene. A person with eyefolds is shown to the left, a person without eyefolds to the right.

Dominant and Recessive Alleles

The eyefold gene, which controls the development of folds in the eye-lids, has two alleles: eyefolds and no-eyefolds. If you have even one copy of the allele for eyefolds, you will have eyefolds. This happens because the allele that codes for eyefolds is dominant. A **dominant** allele is one that is expressed in the phenotype even if only one copy is present in the genotype—that is, even if the other allele is an alternative form.

Suppose your genotype contains a no-eyefolds allele. The no-eyefolds allele is recessive. A **recessive** allele is one that is expressed in the phenotype only when two copies of it are present on the homologs. If one chromosome in the pair contains a dominant allele and the other contains a recessive allele, the dominant allele will be expressed in your phenotype. If you do not have eyefolds, it is because you got two no-eyefolds genes—one from each parent.

 CHECK YOUR READING — Under what conditions is a recessive allele expressed in an offspring's phenotype?

The interaction of dominant and recessive alleles means that it is possible for two brown-haired parents to have a blond child.

Hair color is determined by multiple genes, can be affected by the environment, and sometimes changes over time. However, in some cases it has a dominant-recessive pattern similar to that of the eyefold gene. As in the family shown at right, parents who both have brown hair can have a blond child. The allele for brown hair is dominant, so if both parents have alleles for both brown hair and blond hair, the brown-hair allele is more likely to be expressed. Their child, how-ever, could have two blond-hair alleles (one from each parent) and therefore have blond hair instead of brown.

4.1 Review

KEY CONCEPTS

1. Explain the difference between acquired and inherited traits.
2. Describe the conclusions that Mendel drew from his experiments with pea plants.
3. What type of alleles are expressed only if two identical copies exist on the homologs of the offspring?

CRITICAL THINKING

4. **Compare and Contrast** What is the difference between a genotype and a phenotype?
5. **Analyze** Explain why a person with an allele for a particular trait may not have a phenotype that shows the trait.

CHALLENGE

6. **Apply** In guinea pigs, the allele for black fur is dominant over the allele for brown fur. If you had two parent guinea pigs, each with brown fur, what color fur might the off-spring have, and why?

CHAPTER INVESTIGATION

Offspring Models

OVERVIEW AND PURPOSE Sexual reproduction combines genes from two parent organisms and results in diversity among offspring. In this activity, you will
- design a model of an offspring
- determine how the offspring exhibits portions of both genotype and phenotype from its parents

▶ Problem

How are traits passed from parent to offspring?

▶ Procedure

MATERIALS
- foam balls (body segments)
- colored toothpicks (antennae)
- small paperclips (wings)
- colored pipe cleaners (legs)
- colored pushpins (eyes)

1. Make data tables like those shown on the sample notebook page.

2. Your teacher will supply bags containing alleles written on slips. Capital letters represent dominant alleles, and lower-case letters represent recessive alleles. Each bag will have two alleles for one trait. Six of the bags, one for each of 6 traits, will represent the female parent's alleles. Another set of 6 bags will represent the male parent's alleles. From each bag, choose one allele.

3. In Table 1, record the alleles for both parents, and the allele pairs for the offspring. Then place the slips back into the bags. You will use the alleles to build a model offspring.

4. Use the information in the table below to determine the phenotype of the offspring. Write the phenotype in the fourth column in Table 1.

Genotypes and Phenotypes	
BB or Bb = 3 body segments	bb = 2 body segments
WW or Ww = 2 pairs of wings	ww = 1 pair of wings
AA or Aa = green antennae	aa = red antennae
PP or Pp = 3 pairs of legs	pp = 2 pairs of legs
CC or Cc = yellow legs	cc = orange legs
EE or Ee = blue eyes	ee = green eyes

5 Choose the materials you need to assemble the offspring. You can use toothpicks to attach the body segments. Push the pipe cleaners, toothpicks, and wings into the foam balls. **CAUTION:** Take care when handling the pushpins.

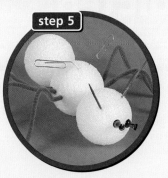

step 5

Observe and Analyze
Write It Up

1. **OBSERVE** Does your offspring look the way you would expect either parent to look? Explain.

2. **ANALYZE** How many different genotypes are possible for each trait? Explain.

Conclude
Write It Up

1. **INFER** What are the possible genotypes of the parents? Fill in Table 2.

2. **INTERPRET** Can you tell how the genotypes of the parents differ from that of the offspring? Explain.

3. **INTERPRET** How does your offspring model illustrate what you have learned about heredity?

4. **IDENTIFY LIMITS** What sources of error might you have experienced?

5. **APPLY** In humans, blue eyes are the phenotype for two recessive alleles. Can parents with blue eyes have a brown-eyed offspring? Explain.

INVESTIGATE Further

CHALLENGE Repeat the procedure, but this time use alleles taken from your model offspring and those of a model offspring made by one of your classmates. Record the genotype and determine the phenotype of this second-generation offspring.

Offspring Models

Table 1. Parent and Offspring Family Traits

	Female Allele	Male Allele	Offspring Genotype	Offspring Phenotype
Body segments				
Pairs of wings				
Antennae color				
Pairs of legs				
Color of legs				
Color of eyes				

Table 2. Possible Parent Genotypes

Trait	Female Parent	Male Parent
Body segments		
Pairs of wings		
Antennae color		
Pairs of legs		
Color of legs		
Color of eyes		

KEY CONCEPT

4.2 Patterns of heredity can be predicted.

McDougal Littell Science
SOUTH CAROLINA

STANDARDS

7–2.6 Use Punnett squares to predict inherited monohybrid traits.

VOCABULARY

Punnett square p. 110
ratio p. 112
probability p. 112
percentage p. 112

◀ **BEFORE, you learned**

- Genes are passed from parents to offspring
- Offspring inherit genes in predictable patterns

▶ **NOW, you will learn**

- How Punnett squares can be used to predict patterns of heredity
- How ratios and probability can be used to predict patterns of heredity

---

EXPLORE Probability

How can probability help predict results?

PROCEDURE

① Toss both coins 10 times. For each toss, record the combination of heads and/or tails.

② For each combination (two heads, two tails, or a head and a tail), add up the number of tosses.

WHAT DO YOU THINK?

- Which combination happened most often?
- If you tossed both coins one more time, which combination would be the most likely result? Can you know for sure? Why or why not?

MATERIALS
- two coins
- pencil and paper

Punnett squares show possible outcomes for inheritance.

NOTETAKING STRATEGY
Use a strategy from an earlier chapter or design one of your own to take notes on how Punnett squares show possible patterns of heredity.

Mendel noticed that traits are inherited in patterns. One tool for understanding the patterns of heredity is a graphic called a Punnett square. A **Punnett square** illustrates how the parents' alleles might combine in offspring.

Each parent has two alleles for a particular gene. An offspring receives one allele from each parent. A Punnett square shows how the parents' alleles may be passed on to potential offspring.

The Punnett square on page 111 shows how alleles for pea-plant height would be distributed among offspring in Mendel's first-generation cross. The dominant allele (D) is regular height, and the recessive allele (d) is dwarf height.

The top of the Punnett square shows one parent's alleles for this trait—two dominant regular alleles (DD). The side of the Punnett square shows the other parent's alleles for this trait—two recessive dwarf alleles (dd).

Each box in the Punnett square shows a way the alleles from each parent would combine in potential offspring. You can see that each potential offspring would have the same genotype: one dominant and one recessive allele (Dd). The phenotype of each offspring would show the dominant allele, in this case regular height.

What is a Punnett square?

READING TiP
As you read about Punnett squares, connect each sentence with the diagram below.

Using Punnett Squares

The Punnett square below shows the possible allele combinations for an offspring of one parent with two dominant (D) regular-height alleles and one parent with two recessive (d) dwarf-height alleles.

SIMULATION
CLASSZONE.COM
Predict offspring traits with virtual Punnett squares.

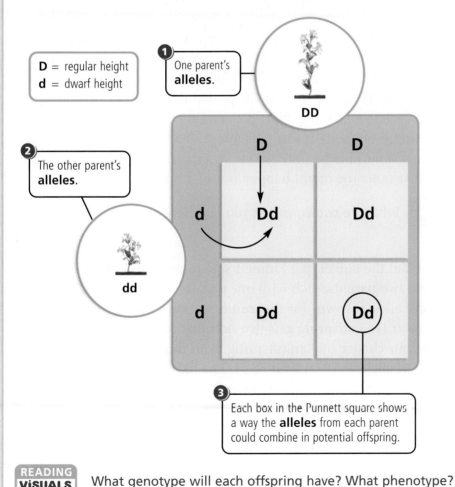

D = regular height
d = dwarf height

1 One parent's **alleles**.

DD

2 The other parent's **alleles**.

dd

	D	D
d	Dd	Dd
d	Dd	Dd

3 Each box in the Punnett square shows a way the **alleles** from each parent could combine in potential offspring.

READING VISUALS   What genotype will each offspring have? What phenotype?

Ratios and percentages can express the probability of outcomes.

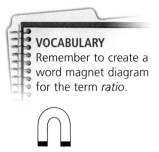

VOCABULARY
Remember to create a word magnet diagram for the term *ratio*.

The Punnett square on page 111 for the first generation of pea plants shows that all potential offspring will be of regular height, because they all have one dominant allele. You can say that 100 percent of the offspring will be of regular height. Or you could say that the ratio of regular-height offspring to total offspring is four to four. A **ratio** compares, or shows the relationship between, two quantities. A ratio is usually written 4:4 and read as "four to four." This can be interpreted as "four out of four." The Punnett square shows that four out of four offspring will express the dominant gene for regular height.

4:4
ratio of blue squares to total squares

1:4 red
3:4 blue

Punnett squares and the ratios they show express probability. **Probability** is the likelihood, or chance, of a specific outcome in relation to the total number of possible outcomes. The ratios derived from a Punnett square tell you the probability that any one offspring will get certain genes and express a certain trait. Another way of expressing probability is as a percentage. A **percentage** is a ratio that compares a number to 100. That is, it states the number of times a particular outcome might happen out of a hundred chances.

 What are two ways that you can express a probability?

Look at the guinea-pig Punnett square on page 113. This cross is between two parents, each with one dominant allele (black) and one recessive allele (brown) for the trait fur color. In this cross, only one in four (ratio 1:4) offspring gets two dominant alleles. That is, there is a one in four chance that an offspring from this cross will have two dominant alleles for black fur (BB). The likelihood that the offspring will get one dominant and one recessive allele (Bb) is 2:4—two out of every four offspring would have this genotype. Like the one offspring with two dominant alleles (BB), the two offspring with the genotype Bb will have black fur. This makes a total of three offspring (3:4) with the phenotype black fur. Only 1:4 offspring of this cross will have the genotype and phenotype brown fur (bb).

Punnett Square and Probability

The Punnett square below shows the possible ways alleles could combine in the offspring of two parent guinea pigs. Each parent has one dominant allele for black fur (B) and one recessive allele for brown fur (b).

B = black fur
b = brown fur

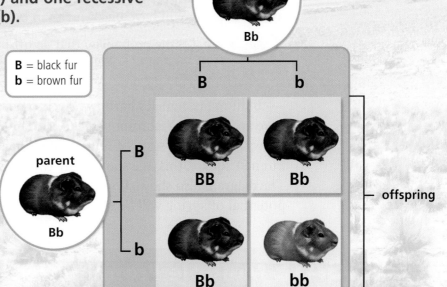

parent
Bb

parent
Bb

B   b

B

BB   Bb

b

Bb   bb

offspring

The table below shows the probability of the various genotypes and phenotypes from the Punnett square above. Each probability is shown as both a ratio and a percentage.

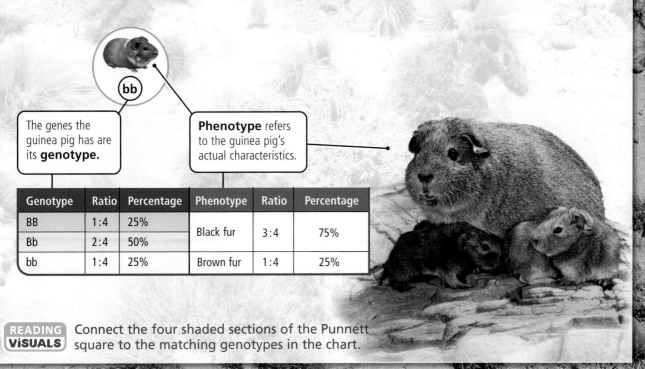

The genes the guinea pig has are its **genotype.**

Phenotype refers to the guinea pig's actual characteristics.

Genotype	Ratio	Percentage	Phenotype	Ratio	Percentage
BB	1:4	25%	Black fur	3:4	75%
Bb	2:4	50%			
bb	1:4	25%	Brown fur	1:4	25%

READING VISUALS Connect the four shaded sections of the Punnett square to the matching genotypes in the chart.

When one parent has two dominant alleles and the other has two recessive alleles, there is a 100 percent chance that an offspring will have the dominant phenotype. The pea-plant example on page 111 shows this pattern. All the offspring are of regular height. When both parents have one dominant and one recessive allele, there is a 75 percent chance that an offspring will have the dominant phenotype. The guinea-pig example on page 113 shows this pattern. Chances are that more offspring will have black fur than brown fur.

○ **CHECK YOUR READING** What is the probability that an offspring from the pea plant cross on page 111 will be of dwarf height?

In humans, females have two X-chromosomes (XX), and males have an X- and a Y-chromosome (XY). The Punnett square on page 115 shows the possible sexes of human offspring. Unlike the guinea-pig Punnett square, this one shows only two possible outcomes, XX and XY. The diagram also shows how to find the percentage chance that a potential offspring will be female.

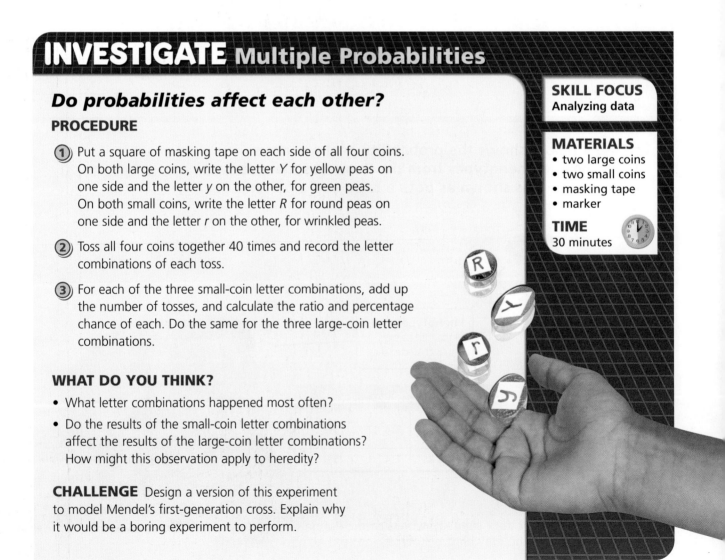

INVESTIGATE Multiple Probabilities

Do probabilities affect each other?
PROCEDURE

① Put a square of masking tape on each side of all four coins. On both large coins, write the letter *Y* for yellow peas on one side and the letter *y* on the other, for green peas. On both small coins, write the letter *R* for round peas on one side and the letter *r* on the other, for wrinkled peas.

② Toss all four coins together 40 times and record the letter combinations of each toss.

③ For each of the three small-coin letter combinations, add up the number of tosses, and calculate the ratio and percentage chance of each. Do the same for the three large-coin letter combinations.

WHAT DO YOU THINK?

• What letter combinations happened most often?

• Do the results of the small-coin letter combinations affect the results of the large-coin letter combinations? How might this observation apply to heredity?

CHALLENGE Design a version of this experiment to model Mendel's first-generation cross. Explain why it would be a boring experiment to perform.

SKILL FOCUS
Analyzing data

MATERIALS
• two large coins
• two small coins
• masking tape
• marker

TIME
30 minutes

Calculating Probability

Two humans, a female (XX) and a male (XY), have an offspring. The Punnett square below can be used to calculate the probability that an offspring will be female or male.

1 To find the percentage chance of a female offspring, first find the ratio by counting the number of XX offspring out of the four possible outcomes.

2 Two out of 4 (ratio 2 : 4, or 2/4) offspring will be female.

3 Multiply this ratio by 100 to find the probability as a percentage.

4 Two fourths equal 1/2, and 1/2 of 100 is 50. So there is a 50 percent chance that an offspring will be female.

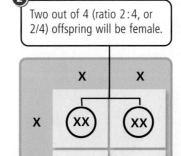

 Compare this Punnett square with the pea-plant Punnett square on page 111 and the guinea-pig Punnett square on page 113. How is it similar? How is it different?

It is important to realize that Punnett squares and probability do not guarantee the outcome of a genetic cross. They indicate the probability of different outcomes. While there is a 75 percent chance that an offspring will have black fur according to the Punnett square on page 113, you cannot know with any certainty what color fur a particular offspring will actually have. Actual experimental results may not match predicted outcomes.

 Can a Punnett square tell you the specific outcome of a genetic cross? Why or why not?

4.2 Review

KEY CONCEPTS

1. Explain how Punnett squares predict the outcomes of a genetic cross.
2. How are ratios and percentages related?
3. How can you find a percentage chance from a Punnett square?

CRITICAL THINKING

4. **Predict** Mendel studied the colors of flowers in his experiments with pea plants. Let P stand for purple and p stand for white. Purple is dominant. Make a Punnett square for a cross between two Pp plants. Find the percentage chance for each outcome.

⬥ CHALLENGE

5. **Apply** In pea plants, the allele for smooth peas is dominant over the allele for wrinkled peas. Create a Punnett square and calculate the probability that two smooth-pea plants will have an offspring with wrinkled peas if each parent has one smooth and one wrinkled allele.

MATH TUTORIAL
CLASSZONE.COM

Click on Math Tutorial for more help with probability.

Coat Coloring

The Shetland sheepdog, or Sheltie, has patches of color on its silky coat. A gene controls marbling of the colors, or merling. The merle gene comes in two forms: M for merle, or m for no merle.

A Sheltie with Mm has a merle coat.

A Sheltie with MM is mostly white.

A Sheltie with mm has solid patches, no merling

Example

One Sheltie parent has a merle coat (Mm), and one has no merling (mm). With these two parents, what is the probability of a puppy with a merle coat?

(1) Make a Punnett square. Put the alleles from one parent on top. Put those of the other on the side.

(2) Fill in the blocks by combining the alleles.

(3) The total number of blocks is the second part of a ratio. ___ : 4

(4) To find the probability of an outcome, count the blocks of that outcome.

ANSWER: There is a 2 : 4, or 2 out of 4 probability.

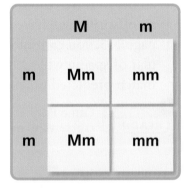

	M	m
m	Mm	mm
m	Mm	mm

Now, make your own Punnett square for Shelties.

1. Make a Punnett square to show two Sheltie parents, both with merle coats (Mm).

2. What is the probability of a merle puppy?

3. What are the chances of a puppy with no merling?

CHALLENGE Write each of the probabilities in questions 2 and 3 and the example as a percentage.

4.3 Meiosis is a special form of cell division.

 BEFORE, you learned

- Mitosis produces two genetically identical cells
- In sexual reproduction, offspring inherit traits from both parents
- Genetic traits are inherited in predictable patterns

 NOW, you will learn

- Why meiosis is necessary for sexual reproduction
- How cells and chromosomes divide during meiosis
- How meiosis differs from mitosis

VOCABULARY

gamete p. 118
egg p. 118
sperm p. 118
fertilization p. 118
meiosis p. 119

EXPLORE Meiosis

Why does sexual reproduction need a special form of cell division?

PROCEDURE

① Suppose the cells that combine during sexual reproduction are produced by mitosis, with the same pairs of chromosomes as most cells. Model this combination with the pipe cleaners; both red pipe cleaners and both blue pipe cleaners end up in the new cell.

② Now model a way for the new cell to end up with the same number of chromosomes as most other cells.

MATERIALS
- 2 blue pipe cleaners
- 2 red pipe cleaners

WHAT DO YOU THINK?
- What was wrong with the new cell produced at the end of step 1?
- Describe your model of the way a new cell could end up with the correct number of chromosomes.

Meiosis is necessary for sexual reproduction.

In Section 4.1 you learned that two cells combine during the process of sexual reproduction. One of the cells contains genetic information from the mother. The other contains genetic information from the father. The two cells combine into a completely new cell, which becomes the offspring.

 How does the genetic material of offspring produced by sexual reproduction compare with the genetic material of the parents?

Most human cells, which can be referred to as body cells, contain 46 chromosomes—the full number of chromosomes that is normal for a human being. Any cell that contains the full number of chromosomes (two sets) for a species is a 2n cell, also called a diploid cell. The 2n cells for a fruit fly, for example, contain 8 chromosomes.

Think about what would happen if two body cells were to combine. The resulting cell would have twice the normal number of chromosomes. Reproductive cells, called gametes, differ from body cells.

Gametes are cells that contain half the usual number of chromosomes—one chromosome from each pair. Gametes are 1n cells, also called haploid cells. Human gametes contain 23 unpaired chromosomes. The gametes of a fruit fly contain 4 unpaired chromosomes. Gametes are found only in the reproductive organs of plants and animals. An **egg** is a gamete that forms in the reproductive organs of a female. A gamete that forms in the reproductive organs of a male is a **sperm**.

During sexual reproduction two gametes combine to become a 2n cell that can grow into a new offspring. **Fertilization** is the process that takes place when a sperm and an egg combine to form one new cell. The diagram below shows what happens to the chromosomes in gametes during fertilization. In humans, an egg cell with 23 chromosomes joins a sperm cell with 23 chromosomes to form a new 2n cell with 46 chromosomes.

Fertilization

During fertilization, a 1n egg cell from a female combines with a 1n sperm cell from a male, producing a 2n fertilized egg cell, which develops into an offspring.

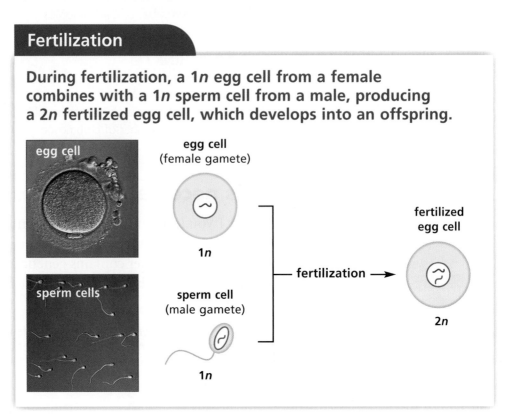

egg cell

egg cell (female gamete)

1n

sperm cells

sperm cell (male gamete)

1n

fertilization →

fertilized egg cell

2n

You know that body cells divide by the process called mitosis. Mitosis produces two daughter cells, each containing exact copies of the chromosomes in the parent cell. Each daughter cell formed by mitosis is a standard diploid ($2n$) cell.

But to produce gametes, which are haploid, a different kind of cell division is necessary. **Meiosis** is a special kind of cell division that produces haploid ($1n$) cells. During meiosis, a single cell goes through two cell divisions—meiosis I and meiosis II. Meiosis takes place only in the reproductive tissues of an organism.

Cells divide twice during meiosis.

Before meiosis begins, the chromosomes of the parent cell are copied. A cell that is ready to divide contains two copies of each chromosome pair—twice as many chromosomes as usual. So to end up with cells that have half the usual number of chromosomes, there must be two divisions.

Remember that the two chromosomes in a pair are called homologs. At the beginning of meiosis I, the cell has two copies of each homolog, attached together. During meiosis I the homologs separate. The starting cell divides into two cells. One cell contains the two copies of one homolog of each pair, while the other cell contains the two copies of the other homolog of each pair. Then, during meiosis II, each of the two cells is divided, producing four haploid cells. Each haploid cell has one unpaired set of chromosomes.

NOTETAKING STRATEGY
Use an earlier strategy or one that you think works well to take notes on the division of cells during meiosis.

Meiosis I

As you can see in the diagram on page 121, there are four steps in meiosis I: prophase I, metaphase I, anaphase I, and telophase I. Included in telophase I is a cytokinesis, the division of the cytoplasm. The diagram shows what would happen during meiosis I in a species that has four chromosomes in its 2*n* body cells.

READING TiP

As you read about meiosis I and meiosis II, match the numbers in the text to the numbers in the diagram on page 121.

1 Prophase I The duplicated chromosomes pair up with their partners. There are two sets of each of the chromosome pairs in the parent cell. The chromatids are attached together. There are pairs of doubled homologs.

2 Metaphase I The chromosome pairs line up along the center of the cell.

3 Anaphase I The two copies of one homolog are pulled apart from the two copies of the other homolog. This separating of the homologs is the most significant step of meiosis I.

4 Telophase I and Cytokinesis A new cell membrane forms at the center of the cell, dividing the parent cell into two daughter cells.

CHECK YOUR READING What happens to the parent cell during telophase I?

Meiosis II

RESOURCE CENTER
CLASSZONE.COM

Learn more about meiosis.

During meiosis I, two daughter cells are formed. The chromosomes of these two cells are not copied before meiosis II begins. Both of these cells divide during meiosis II, to produce a total of four daughter cells. The four steps in meiosis II, shown on page 121, are prophase II, metaphase II, anaphase II, and telophase II (with cytokinesis).

5 Prophase II In each daughter cell, there are two copies of each of *n* chromosomes. The copies are attached together.

6 Metaphase II Each duplicated chromosome lines up separately along each cell's center.

7 Anaphase II The two attached copies of each chromosome separate and are pulled to opposite poles in each cell.

8 Telophase II and Cytokinesis A new cell membrane forms in the center of each cell, as each cell divides into two 1*n* daughter cells, producing a total of four 1*n* cells.

During meiosis, one cell in an organism's reproductive system divides twice to form four 1*n* cells. In male organisms, these gametes become sperm. In female organisms, at least one of these cells becomes an egg. In some species, including humans, only one of the four daughter cells produced by a female during meiosis becomes an egg. The rest dissolve back into the organism or, in some cases, are never produced.

Meiosis

Meiosis reduces the number of chromosomes by half, producing four 1*n* cells.

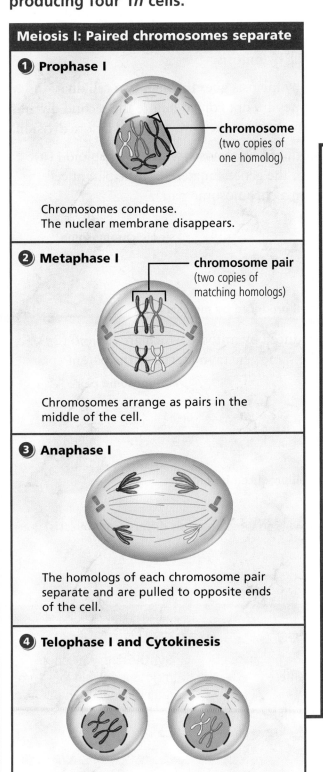

Meiosis I: Paired chromosomes separate

1 Prophase I

chromosome
(two copies of one homolog)

Chromosomes condense.
The nuclear membrane disappears.

2 Metaphase I

chromosome pair
(two copies of matching homologs)

Chromosomes arrange as pairs in the middle of the cell.

3 Anaphase I

The homologs of each chromosome pair separate and are pulled to opposite ends of the cell.

4 Telophase I and Cytokinesis

The cell divides into two daughter cells.

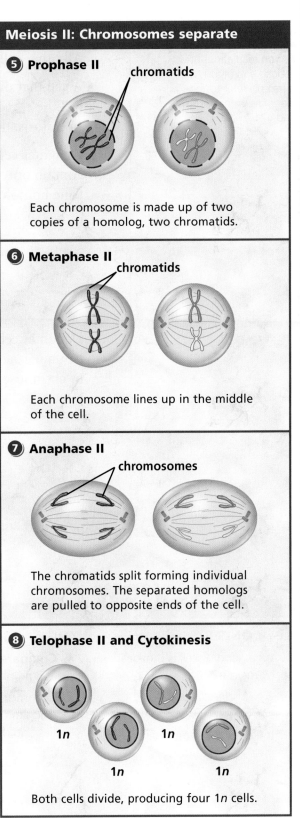

Meiosis II: Chromosomes separate

5 Prophase II

chromatids

Each chromosome is made up of two copies of a homolog, two chromatids.

6 Metaphase II

chromatids

Each chromosome lines up in the middle of the cell.

7 Anaphase II

chromosomes

The chromatids split forming individual chromosomes. The separated homologs are pulled to opposite ends of the cell.

8 Telophase II and Cytokinesis

1*n*   1*n*
1*n*   1*n*

Both cells divide, producing four 1*n* cells.

Meiosis and mitosis differ in some important ways.

You can see that the processes of meiosis and mitosis are similar in many ways. However, they also have several very important differences.

READING TiP

As you read about how meiosis and mitosis are different, refer to the diagrams on pages 83 and 121.

- Only cells that are to become gametes go through meiosis. All other cells divide by mitosis.

- A cell that divides by meiosis goes through two cell divisions, but the chromosomes are not copied before the second division. In mitosis, the chromosomes are always copied before division.

- Daughter cells produced by meiosis, which are haploid ($1n$), contain only half of the genetic material of the parent cell (one homolog from a chromosome pair).

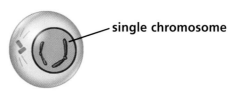

single chromosome

Cell produced by meiosis

- Daughter cells produced by mitosis, which are diploid ($2n$), contain exactly the same genetic material as the parent (pairs of chromosomes).

chromosome pair

Cell produced by mitosis

 CHECK YOUR READING What are four ways in which meiosis differs from mitosis?

 Review

KEY CONCEPTS

1. What kind of cell is produced by meiosis?

2. What is fertilization?

3. In your own words, describe the differences between meiosis and mitosis.

CRITICAL THINKING

4. **Compare** How do prophase I and prophase II differ?

5. **Communicate** Make a Venn diagram to show the similarities and differences between mitosis and meiosis.

● CHALLENGE

6. **Synthesize** Why does meiosis II result in four $1n$ cells rather than four $2n$ cells?

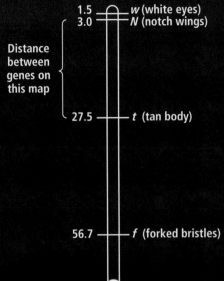

1.5 — w (white eyes)
3.0 — N (notch wings)

Distance between genes on this map

27.5 — t (tan body)

56.7 — f (forked bristles)

Genes have a particular location on a chromosome. A gene map shows the location.

Are Traits Linked?

Fruit flies are easy to breed in a laboratory and have an assortment of easily recognized genetic traits—different eye colors, body patterns, limb characteristics, and wing shapes. For these reasons, early geneticists studied fruit flies to learn how certain traits were inherited. Sometimes the experiments produced puzzling results. Here is an example from the laboratory of Thomas Hunt Morgan.

▷ Observations

- In a batch of fruit flies, most red-eyed individuals were born with short wings.
- In the same batch, at least one fruit fly was born with red eyes and normal-sized wings.

▷ Hypotheses

Morgan and his coworkers made these hypotheses about the inherited traits:

- The gene for red eyes and the gene for short wings are linked together on a fruit fly's chromosomes. These linked genes are usually inherited together.
- Sometimes during meiosis, one of the linked genes will "cross over" from one chromosome to a homologous one. When this happens, a fruit fly will be born with one but not both of the linked genes—red eyes without short wings.
- Genes that are farthest from each other on a chromosome are most likely to become separated and cross over during meiosis. Genes that are closest (linked) to each other are least likely to.

▷ Further Discoveries

By studying the results of many breeding experiments, Morgan and his student, Alfred Sturtevant, could determine which genes were closest and farthest from each other on the same chromosome. From this information, they drew a simple map showing the location of each of the fruit fly's linked genes.

▷ Determine Relevance

On Your Own Look at the map of a chromosome on this page. Which of the traits are most likely to be inherited together? Which might be most easily separated and cross over during meiosis?

As a Group Is it reasonable to think that information about a fruit fly's genes could apply to the genes of a human being? Discuss this topic in a small group and see if the group can agree.

4 Chapter Review

the BIG idea

In sexual reproduction, genes are passed from parents to offspring in predictable patterns.

CONTENT REVIEW
CLASSZONE.COM

KEY CONCEPTS SUMMARY

1 Living things inherit traits in patterns.

Offspring inherit **alleles**, which are forms of **genes**, from their parents. Alleles can be **dominant** or **recessive**. The alleles you have are your **genotype**; the observable characteristics that come from your genotype are your **phenotype**.

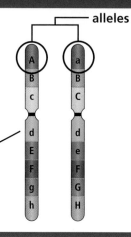

alleles

a gene

VOCABULARY
sexual reproduction p. 102
gene p. 102
heredity p. 102
allele p. 103
phenotype p. 106
genotype p. 106
dominant p. 107
recessive p. 107

2 Patterns of heredity can be predicted.

Punnett squares show possible outcomes of heredity. **Ratios** and **percentages** can be used with Punnett squares to express the **probability** of particular outcomes.

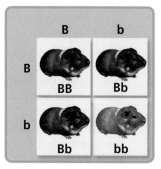

B = black fur
b = brown fur

VOCABULARY
Punnett square p. 110
ratio p. 112
probability p. 112
percentage p. 112

3 Meiosis is a special form of cell division.

- At the beginning of meiosis I, the parent cell has two copies of each chromosome pair.
- During meiosis I, the homologs of the chromosome pair separate; there are two cells, each with two copies of one homolog from each pair.
- During meiosis II, the two copies of each homolog separate; each daughter cell has one homolog.

 Meiosis I

Meiosis II

1n   1n

1n   1n

VOCABULARY
gamete p. 118
egg p. 118
sperm p. 118
fertilization p. 118
meiosis p. 119

Reviewing Vocabulary

Make a frame for each of the vocabulary terms listed below. Write the term in the center. Think about how each term is related to the Big Idea of the chapter. Decide what information to frame it with. Use definitions, examples, descriptions, parts, or pictures.

1. allele   **3.** ratio

2. heredity   **4.** probability

Describe how the vocabulary terms in the following pairs of words are related to each other. Explain the relationship in a one- or two-sentence answer. Underline each vocabulary word or term in your answers.

5. phenotype, genotype

6. dominant, recessive

Reviewing Key Concepts

Multiple Choice *Choose the letter of the best answer.*

7. Which is an example of an acquired trait?
  a. eye color   **c.** blood type
  b. hair color   **d.** ability to read

8. The unit of heredity that determines a particular trait is known as
  a. a chromosome   **c.** a gene
  b. a gamete   **d.** a phenotype

9. A human female would have which set of sex chromosomes?
  a. XX   **c.** XY
  b. YY   **d.** XxYy

10. If one copy of a dominant allele is present in a genotype, then the trait the allele codes for is
  a. expressed in the phenotype
  b. not expressed in the phenotype
  c. partially expressed in the phenotype
  d. not expressed in an offspring's phenotype

11. In guinea pigs, the allele for black fur (B) is dominant, and the allele for brown fur (b) is recessive. If a BB male mates with a Bb female, what percentage of offspring are likely to have black fur?
  a. 100 percent   **c.** 50 percent
  b. 75 percent   **d.** 25 percent

12. If one parent has two dominant alleles and another parent has two recessive alleles, the offspring will have
  a. the recessive phenotype
  b. the dominant phenotype
  c. two dominant alleles
  d. two recessive alleles

13. Cells that contain half the usual number of chromosomes are
  a. fertilized egg cells   **c.** alleles
  b. gametes   **d.** diploid cells

14. The process that produces haploid (1*n*) cells is known as
  a. mitosis   **c.** meiosis
  b. reproduction   **d.** fertilization

15. What happens when fertilization occurs?
  a. Two 2*n* cells combine in a new cell.
  b. Two 1*n* cells combine into a new cell.
  c. Two 2*n* daughter cells are produced.
  d. Two 1*n* daughter cells are produced.

16. Which does not occur during meiosis?
  a. Four haploid daughter cells are produced.
  b. Two diploid daughter cells are produced.
  c. Only cells that are gametes are produced.
  d. Daughter cells are produced that contain half the chromosomes of the parent cell.

Short Answer *Write a short answer to each question.*

17. In what case would a recessive allele be expressed in the phenotype of an offspring?

18. Describe the purpose of a Punnett square.

19. How does the number of chromosomes in a person's sex cells compare with the number of chromosomes in the body cells?

20. **INFER** How was Mendel able to infer that each offspring of two parent pea plants had a pair of "factors" for a particular trait?

21. **COMMUNICATE** Briefly describe how heredity works. Use the terms *gene* and *chromosome* in your explanation.

22. **APPLY** Can a dwarf pea plant ever have a dominant allele? Explain.

23. **ANALYZE** How is a Punnett Square used to show both the genotype and phenotype of both parents and offspring?

24. **APPLY** In rabbits, the allele for black fur is dominant over the allele for white fur. Two black rabbits have a litter of eight offspring. Six of the offspring have black hair and two have white hair. What are the genotypes of the parents? Explain.

Use the Punnett square below to answer the next two questions.

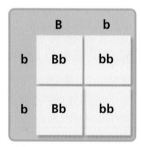

	B	b
b	Bb	bb
b	Bb	bb

25. **CALCULATE** A parent has one dominant allele for black fur (B) and one recessive allele for white fur (b). The other parent has two recessive alleles for white fur. In this cross what is the chance that an offspring will be born with black fur? With white fur?

26. **CALCULATE** What is the percentage chance that an offspring will have the recessive phenotype?

27. **ANALYZE** This diagram shows the process of fertilization. Which of the cells shown are haploid? Explain.

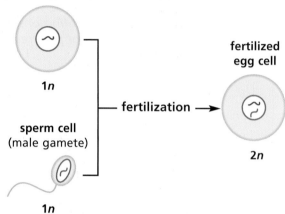

28. **SUMMARIZE** Briefly describe what happens during meiosis I and meiosis II. What is the function of meiosis?

the BIG idea

29. **INFER** Look again at the picture on pages 98–99. Now that you have finished the chapter, how would you change or add details to your answer to the question on the photograph?

30. **SYNTHESIZE** Write one or more paragraphs explaining how Mendel's observations of pea plants contributed to the study of modern genetics. Use these terms in your explanation.

gene	phenotype
allele	dominant
trait	recessive
genotype	

UNIT PROJECTS

If you need to create graphs or other visuals for your project, be sure you have grid paper, poster board, markers, or other supplies.

Analyzing data

The chart below shows the phenotypes of pea-plant offspring.

Phenotypes of Pea Plants	
Phenotype	Number of Offspring
Regular (D)	12
Dwarf (d)	4

Use the chart to answer the questions below.

1. What percentage of pea plants showed the dominant phenotype?
   a. 100 percent
   b. 75 percent
   c. 50 percent
   d. 25 percent

2. What percentage of pea plants showed the recessive phenotype?
   a. 100 percent
   b. 75 percent
   c. 50 percent
   d. 25 percent

3. What is the genotype of the dwarf pea plants?
   a. DD
   b. Dd
   c. dd
   d. cannot tell

4. What are the possible genotypes of the regular pea plants?
   a. DD and dd
   b. DD and Dd
   c. Dd and dd
   d. cannot tell

5. What are the genotypes of the parents?
   a. Dd and dd
   b. DD and Dd
   c. Dd and Dd
   d. dd and dd

6. Which statement is true, based on the data in the chart?
   a. If both parents were Dd, then none of the offspring would be dwarf.
   b. If both parents were DD, then none of the offspring would be dwarf.
   c. If one parent were Dd and the other were dd, then none of the offspring would be regular.
   d. If one parent were DD and the other parent were dd, then none of the offspring would be regular.

Extended Response

7. Traits for a widow's peak hairline (W) and curly hair (C) are controlled by dominant alleles. A family of eight has three children with widow's peaks. All six children have curly hair. Use your knowledge of heredity to write one or two paragraphs explaining the possible genotypes of the parents.

8. A student proposes a hypothesis that traits that are dominant are more common in the general population than traits with recessive alleles. Describe a procedure you might use to test this hypothesis.

TIMELINES in Science

THE STORY OF Genetics

The human genome project, DNA evidence in criminal cases, cloning—news about genetics is everywhere. Some of the most exciting research in science today involves genes. The timeline shows that some important concepts that underline the study of genetics were discovered relatively early. You will notice the influence of two major advances in technology— the development of the microscope during the 1600s, and the development of computer technology during the later half of the 1900s. The boxes below the timeline show how technology has led to new understanding and to applications of those understandings.

1674
Cells Are Everywhere
Anton van Leeuwenhoek uses a microscope to study pond water and discovers the water is full of micro-scopic organisms, some made of single cells. These drawings show some of what he saw.

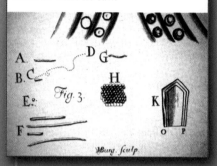

1665
Cells Discovered
Robert Hooke uses a microscope to study liv-ing matter. What he sees and then records in this drawing are tiny repeating units, which he calls cells.

EVENTS

| 1650 | 1660 | 1670 | 1680 |

APPLICATIONS AND TECHNOLOGY

APPLICATION

Corn in Every Shape and Size

Native Americans grew 700 different kinds of popcorn. Their popcorn plants were a kind of grass with big, hard seeds that exploded when they were heated. People who didn't want to have to explode their corn to eat it chose plants with softer seeds and grew them, and then chose the softest of those seeds to plant. Over hundreds of years, by choos-ing which plants to grow, people produced what we now eat as corn on the cob.

TECHNOLOGY

Seeing into the Cell

Single-glass lenses, such as the one van Leeuwenhoek used, were available as long ago as 1267. The compound microscope was first made in 1595, but it was over 200 years before it provided clear images. Until the 1930s, all microscopes focused light on objects. Eventually, light micro-scopes could magnify objects up to 2000 times.

1831
Cells Have Structure
As the power of microscopes improves, scientists start to describe the inner structure of cells. Robert Brown describes a central structure found in many cells, a structure that he calls the nucleus.

1882
Cells Divide, Chromosomes Split!
Scientists observe how cells divide. Walther Flemming describes how structures within the cell separate. These structures are the chromosomes. Chromosomes determine the traits of living things.

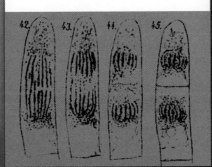

1928
Researchers Study the Chromosomes of Fruit Flies and Find Genes
Working with fruit flies, Thomas Hunt Morgan discovers that genes are found in specific locations on chromosomes.

1866
Austrian Monk Describes Patterns of Heredity
Gregor Mendel's experiments with garden peas show that traits are passed on from parents to offspring in predictable patterns.

| 1830 | 1840 | 1850 | 1860 | 1870 | 1880 | | 1930 |

Cells have a highly organized structure. Color dyes are used to help us see the different parts of a cell.

1944

DNA—Genetic Material

Researchers studying *Streptococcus* transformation find that bacterial cells get their characteristics from DNA.

1973

DNA Recombined

In an amazing breakthrough, scientists have cut DNA from two different sources and recombined the DNA. The new DNA molecule reproduces when placed inside a bacterium. Such bacteria can be used to make proteins useful to humans.

1951

Scientists Capture Image of DNA

Scientists searching for the secret of DNA structure get an enormous clue when Rosalind Franklin uses x-ray crystallography to create an image of DNA. Maurice Wilkins, James Watson, and Francis Crick are awarded the Nobel Prize in 1962 for building a model of the DNA double helix molecule.

1984

Chinese Scientists Alter Fish!

In an effort to produce fast-growing fish for food, a team working with Zuoyan Zhu has made the first genetically modified (GM) fish.

1950   1960   1970   1980

TECHNOLOGY

Seeing Molecules

In the 1930s, a microscope came into use that focuses a beam of electrons, instead of a beam of light, on an object. Now we can see things as small as the molecules inside cells.

The image of the chromosome at left was made using an electron microscope.

APPLICATION

DNA Frees Innocent Prisoner

Kevin Green was convicted of murder and spent 16 years in prison. While he was in jail, the California Department of Justice created a DNA database that contained the DNA fingerprints of many other convicted felons. When Green's defenders compared the DNA found at the murder scene with DNA fingerprints in the database, they found that it matched someone else's fingerprint. The real murderer confessed, and Green is now a free man, thanks to genetics.

1984
Living Things Have Genetic Fingerprints

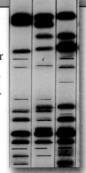

Human fingers have their own unique fingerprints. In a similar way, the DNA of different people has its own unique patterns. These DNA fingerprints are compared here.

2000
Scientists Sequence Human Genome

Two groups of researchers, Celera and the Human Genome Project, succeed in publishing the first draft of the sequence of DNA for all the chromosomes in the human body.

RESOURCE CENTER
CLASSZONE.COM
Find recent genetics updates.

1990   2000   Today

APPLICATION

Saved by a Gene Donor

In 1986 a baby girl named Ashanti DeSilva was born. One single mistake in her DNA meant that Ashanti's body could not make an important disease-fighting protein.

In 1981, researchers had figured out how to move a working gene from one mammal to another. Ashanti became the first person ever to receive a gene from someone else. Ashanti's doctors injected some of her white blood cells with healthy copies of the sick gene. Now her white blood cells worked. Researchers and doctors are trying to apply the same techniques to other genetic disorders. There is still much work to be done.

INTO THE FUTURE

Genetics is a young science. The timeline spans 350 years, but the real study of genetics began in 1900 with the rediscovery of the work of Gregor Mendel. Since then, scientists have determined the structure and function of DNA—and ways to use this knowledge.

In medicine, genetics is used to identify genes that play a role in inherited diseases. Questions remain about how this knowledge can be used to treat or even prevent disease.

In agriculture, genetics is used to modify the genes of plant and animal stocks to give them desirable traits, such as resistance to disease. Questions remain about what effect modified genes might have once they enter a population of plants or animals.

In biology, genetics is used to determine how different types of organisms have changed over time and how one species relates to another. Questions remain about whether similar genes found in different organisms behave in the same way.

In society, genetic profiles are used to help solve crimes or make identifications. Questions remain about how to protect individuals and their personal information.

ACTIVITIES

Reliving History

Use a hand lens or microscope to study water from a pond or puddle. See if your sample contains structures similar to those drawn by van Leeuwenhoek in 1674.

Writing About Science: Biography

Sharing information is important to scientific discovery. Learn more about individuals or groups involved in the discovery of DNA structure or sequencing the human genome. How important was cooperation in their work?

CHAPTER 5

DNA and Modern Genetics

the BIG idea

DNA is a set of instructions for making cell parts.

What can a model of DNA show you about its structure?

Key Concepts

SECTION

1 DNA and RNA are required to make proteins.
Learn about DNA, RNA, and protein synthesis.

SECTION

2 Changes in DNA can produce variation.
Learn about the effects of changes in DNA and how some changes can cause genetic disorders.

SECTION

3 Modern genetics uses DNA technology.
Learn about some applications of DNA technology and the Human Genome Project.

Internet Preview

CLASSZONE.COM

Chapter 5 online resources: Content Review, Visualization, four Resource Centers, Math Tutorial, Test Practice

EXPLORE (the **BIG** idea)

What Is the Pattern?

Sometimes by looking at the parts of a whole you can guess how the pieces fit together. Some evidence for the structure of DNA came when people noticed that certain types of chemical subunits came in pairs. Try this activity with a friend. Take 9 index cards and write 2 letters, A T or C G, on each card. Now cut the pairs in half and give your friend the individual pieces. See if he or she can find the pattern.

Observe and Think
How long did it take your friend to see the pattern? Were there any other clues that he or she used?

What Vegetable Is That?

Buy a broccoflower from your local supermarket. Describe what it looks like, what it tastes like, and how it smells.

Observe and Think What properties of each vegetable does the broccoflower have? What gives an organism its traits?

Internet Activity: Human Genome

Go to **ClassZone.com** to find out how scientists put together a sequence of the DNA in the human genome.

Observe and Think What are the benefits of having a map of the human genome?

NSTA
scilinks.org
SCiLINKS

Genetics Code: MDL035

Getting Ready to Learn

◀ CONCEPT REVIEW

- Traits are controlled by genes on chromosomes.
- Genes can be dominant or recessive.
- Cells have DNA, RNA, and proteins.

◀ VOCABULARY REVIEW

organelle p. 20

protein p. 43

gene p. 102

technology *See Glossary.*

ⓘ CONTENT REVIEW
CLASSZONE.COM
Review concepts and vocabulary.

▶ TAKING NOTES

SUPPORTING MAIN IDEAS

Make a chart to show main ideas and the information that supports them. Copy each blue heading; then add supporting information, such as reasons, explanations, and examples.

CHOOSE YOUR OWN STRATEGY

Take notes about new vocabulary terms using one or more of the strategies from earlier chapters —**four square, word triangle, frame game,** or **magnet word.** Feel free to mix and match the strategies, or use an entirely different vocabulary strategy.

See the Note-Taking Handbook on pages R45–R51.

SCIENCE NOTEBOOK

DNA sequences can change.

Variations in DNA make one organism different from another.

Human DNA has 6 billion base pairs; yeast DNA has 12 million base pairs.

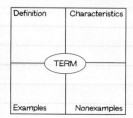
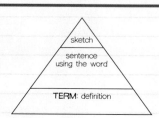
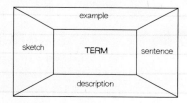
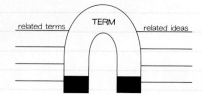

DNA and RNA are required to make proteins.

STANDARDS

7–2 The student will demonstrate an understanding of the structure and function of cells, cellular reproduction, and heredity.

VOCABULARY

replication p. 137
RNA p. 138

◀ **BEFORE,** you learned

- Traits pass from parents to off-spring in predictable patterns
- Traits are passed on through genes
- In sexual reproduction, off-spring get half their genes from each parent

▶ **NOW,** you will learn

- How the structure of DNA stores information the cell needs
- How DNA is copied
- How RNA uses the information from DNA to make proteins

EXPLORE Templates

How does a template work?

PROCEDURE

MATERIALS
- paper
- pencil

① Write a set of rules to describe how the characters in line A relate to the characters in line B.

A ☐ ⊙ ◯ △ △ ☐
B △ ◯ ⊙ ☐ ☐ △

② Place a piece of paper just under line C below. Use the rules from step 1 to produce a template—the corresponding pattern that goes with line C.

C ⊙ △ △ ☐ ◯ ◯

③ Give the rules and the template to a classmate to produce a copy of line C.

WHAT DO YOU THINK?
What is a template and how does it differ from a copy?

DNA is the information molecule.

SUPPORTING MAIN IDEAS
Make a chart of information supporting the main idea: *DNA is the information molecule.*

DNA is a molecule that stores information—that's all it does. You could compare the information in DNA to the books in your local library. You might find a book describing how to bake a cake, make a model sailboat, or beat your favorite computer game. The books, however, don't actually do any of those things—you do. The "books" in the DNA "library" carry all the information that a cell needs to function, to grow, and to divide. However, DNA doesn't do any of those things. Proteins do most of the work of a cell and also make up much of the structure of a cell.

Chapter 5: **DNA and Modern Genetics** 135

Proteins and Amino Acids

RESOURCE CENTER
CLASSZONE.COM

Learn more about DNA.

Proteins are large molecules that are made up of chains of amino acids. Twenty different amino acids come together in enough combinations to make up the thousands of different proteins found in the human body. Some proteins are small. For example, lysozyme is a digestive protein that is made up of a sequence of 129 amino acids. Some proteins are large. For example, dystrophin is a huge structural protein that is made up of 3685 amino acids.

CHECK YOUR READING What is the relationship between proteins and amino acids?

DNA stores the information that enables a cell to put together the right sequences of amino acids needed to produce specific proteins. Scientists describe DNA as containing a code. A code is a set of rules and symbols used to carry information. For example, your computer uses a code of ones and zeroes to store data and then translates the code into the numbers, letters, and graphics you see on a computer screen. To understand how DNA functions as a code, you first need to learn about the structure of the DNA molecule.

DNA and the Genetic Code

The DNA molecule takes the shape of a double-stranded spiral, which, as you can see from the diagram, looks something like a twisted ladder. In Chapter 2, you read about different subunits that make up the molecules found in cells. Nucleotide subunits make up each of the two strands of the DNA molecule. One part of the nucleotide forms the side rail of the DNA "ladder." The other part, the nucleotide base, forms the rung. Actually, two bases come together to form the rung, as one nucleotide base attaches to another from the opposite strand. You can see how the parts fit together in the diagram to the left.

There are four different nucleotides in DNA, identified by their bases: adenine (A), thymine (T), cytosine (C), and guanine (G). Because of differences in size and shape, adenine always pairs with thymine (A-T) and cytosine always pairs with guanine (C-G). The bases fit together like two pieces of a jigsaw puzzle. These bases are often referred to simply by their initials—A, T, C, and G. The phrase "all tigers can growl" may help you remember them.

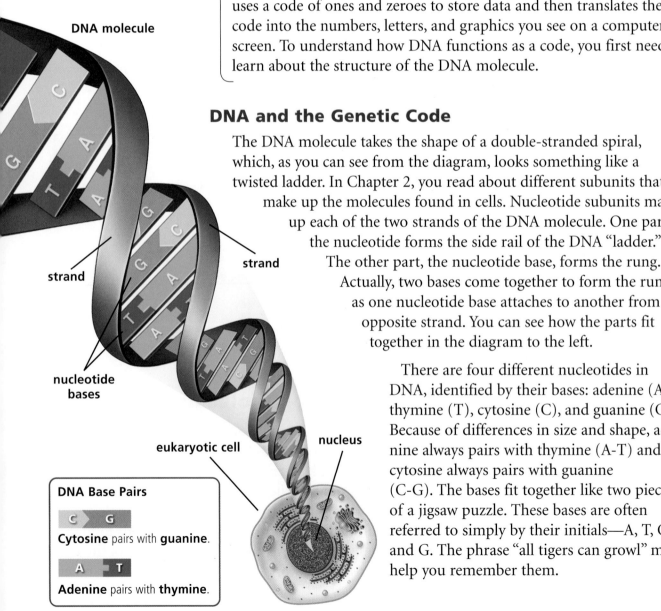

DNA molecule

strand

strand

nucleotide bases

eukaryotic cell

nucleus

DNA Base Pairs

C ▸ G

Cytosine pairs with **guanine**.

A ▸ T

Adenine pairs with **thymine**.

It is the sequence—the order—of bases in a strand of DNA that forms the code for making proteins. Like a list of ingredients in a recipe book, a set of bases specifies the amino acids needed to form a particular protein. The cookbook uses just 4 bases—A, T, G, and C—to code for 20 amino acids. A code of 2 bases to 1 amino acid gives only 16 possible combinations. However, a code of 3 bases to 1 amino acid gives 64 possible combinations.

The genetic code is, in fact, a triplet code. A specific sequence of 3 nucleotide bases codes for 1 amino acid. For example, the triplet T-C-T on a strand of DNA codes for the amino acid arginine. Some amino acids have two different codes. Others have three, and some have four. A gene is the entire sequence of the bases that codes for all the amino acids in a protein. Each gene is made up of a sequence of bases at a particular location on the DNA.

T–C–T
(DNA triplet)

codes for

arginine
(amino acid)

Replication

When a cell divides into two cells, each daughter cell receives an identical copy of the DNA. Before a cell divides, all of its DNA is copied, a process referred to as **replication.** Let's follow the process through for one DNA molecule. First, the two strands of DNA separate, almost like two threads in a string being unwound. Nucleotides in the area around the DNA match up, base by base, with the nucleotides on each DNA strand. C matches up with G, and A matches up with T. When replication is complete, there are two identical DNA molecules. Each molecule has one strand of old DNA and one strand of new DNA.

READING TiP

Replicate includes the root word meaning "to repeat."

Replication

Replication produces two identical molecules of DNA.

new strand

New DNA molecule

original strand

nucleotides

1 The DNA molecule opens up, separating into two strands.

2 Nucleotides match up and join to the open DNA strands.

3 Two identical DNA molecules are formed.

Original DNA molecule

original strand

new strand

New DNA molecule

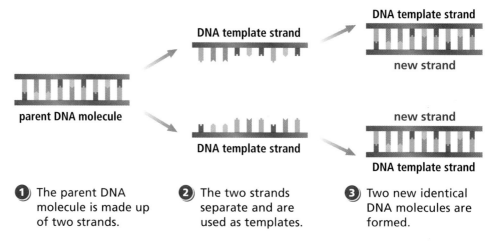

1 The parent DNA molecule is made up of two strands.

2 The two strands separate and are used as templates.

3 Two new identical DNA molecules are formed.

During replication, each strand of DNA is used as a template to produce a copy of the other strand. A template is a pattern or shape that produces a matching, or complementary, product. If you've ever made a plaster model of your hand, you've worked with a template. You press your hand into a soft material that leaves a mold of your hand. You then pour liquid plaster into the mold to produce a copy of your hand. The mold is a template. Its shape allows you to make a complementary shape that matches your hand.

RNA is needed to make proteins.

DNA is not used to make proteins directly. Translating the genetic code of DNA involves another type of molecule, RNA. **RNA,** or ribonucleic acid, carries the information from DNA to a ribosome, where the amino acids are brought together to form a protein. DNA actually codes for RNA. Three different types of RNA are involved in making proteins. They are named for their functions:

- messenger RNA (mRNA)
- ribosomal RNA (rRNA)
- transfer RNA (tRNA)

In prokaryotic cells, RNA and proteins are both made in the cytoplasm. In eukaryotic cells, DNA is copied in the nucleus, then RNA moves to the cytoplasm, where the proteins are made.

Transcription

The process of transferring information from DNA to RNA is called transcription. The chemical structure of RNA is quite similar to the structure of DNA. Both are made up of four types of nucleotide subunits. Three of the bases that make up RNA are the same as in DNA: guanine (G), cytosine (C), and adenine (A). However, the fourth base is uracil (U), not thymine.

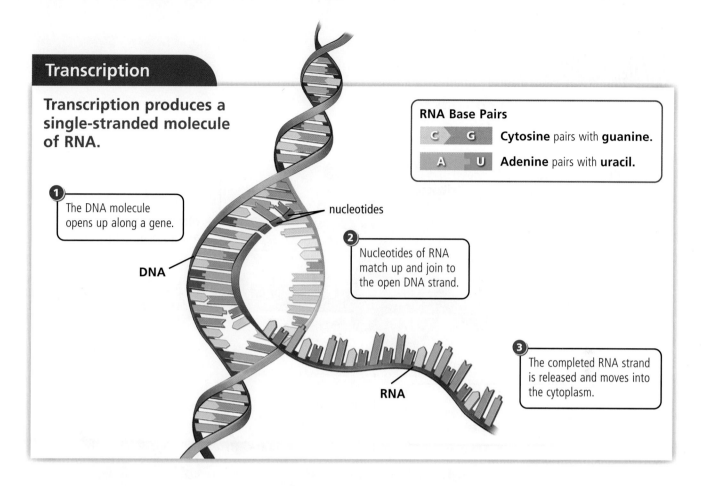

Transcription

Transcription produces a single-stranded molecule of RNA.

RNA Base Pairs

C — G **Cytosine** pairs with **guanine.**

A — U **Adenine** pairs with **uracil.**

1 The DNA molecule opens up along a gene.

nucleotides

DNA

2 Nucleotides of RNA match up and join to the open DNA strand.

3 The completed RNA strand is released and moves into the cytoplasm.

RNA

During transcription, DNA is again used as a template, this time to make a complementary strand of RNA. Only individual genes are transcribed, not a whole DNA molecule. The DNA again opens up, just where the gene is located. As shown in the diagram above, RNA bases match up to complementary bases on the DNA template. Adenine pairs with uracil (A-U) and cytosine pairs with guanine (C-G).

Transcription is different from replication in some important ways. Only one strand of DNA is transcribed, which means just a single strand of RNA is produced. When transcription is complete, the RNA is released, it does not stay attached to DNA. This means that many copies of RNA can be made from the same gene in a short period of time. At the end of transcription, the DNA molecule closes.

REMINDER

DNA base pairs:
  C-G, A-T
RNA base pairs:
  C-G, A-U

Translation

Replication and transcription involve passing along information that is coded in the language of nucleotide bases. To make proteins, cells have to translate this language of nucleotide bases into the language of amino acids. Three specific bases equal one amino acid. The actual assembly of the amino acids in their proper sequence is the translation. Translation takes place in the cytoplasm of a cell. It involves all three types of RNA.

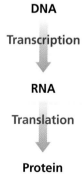

DNA

Transcription

RNA

Translation

Protein

Translation

The assembling of amino acids to form a protein occurs in the cytoplasm.

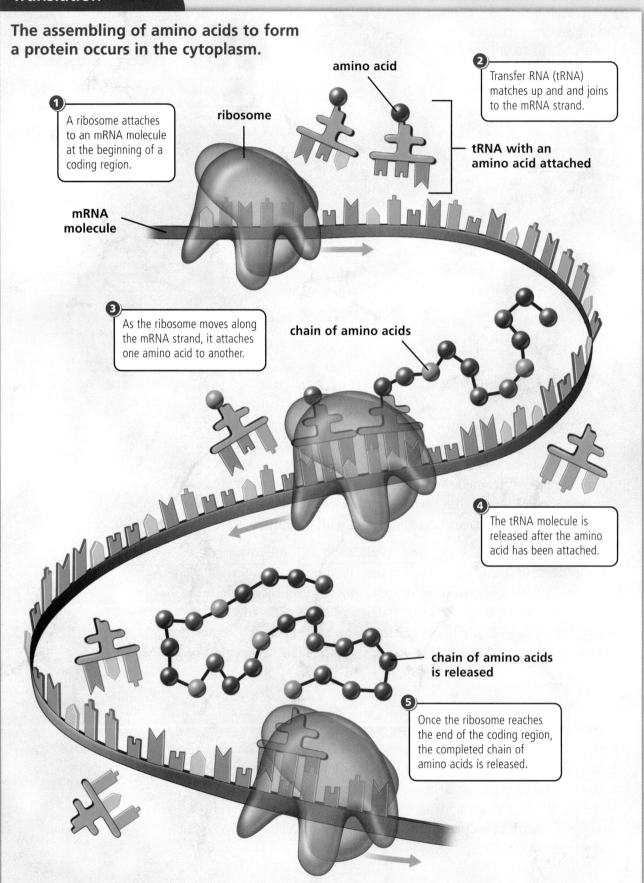

amino acid

2 Transfer RNA (tRNA) matches up and and joins to the mRNA strand.

1 A ribosome attaches to an mRNA molecule at the beginning of a coding region.

ribosome

tRNA with an amino acid attached

mRNA molecule

3 As the ribosome moves along the mRNA strand, it attaches one amino acid to another.

chain of amino acids

4 The tRNA molecule is released after the amino acid has been attached.

chain of amino acids is released

5 Once the ribosome reaches the end of the coding region, the completed chain of amino acids is released.

Proteins are made on ribosomes, structures that are made up of ribosomal RNA and proteins. If you think of DNA as a cookbook for making different proteins, and mRNA as a recipe for making a protein, then the ribosome is the place where the cooking gets done. In this analogy, tRNA gathers the ingredients, which are amino acids.

A tRNA molecule is shaped in such a way that one end of it can attach to a specific amino acid. The other end of tRNA has a triplet of bases that is complementary to a triplet of bases on mRNA. Transfer RNA does the actual translation of bases to amino acid when it matches up with mRNA. The diagram on page 140 shows the whole process.

Refer to the diagram on page 140 as you read the text. The numbers in the text match the numbers in the diagram.

1 Translation begins when a ribosome attaches to the beginning end of an mRNA molecule.

2 A tRNA molecule carrying an amino acid matches up to a complementary triplet on mRNA on the ribosome.

3 The ribosome attaches one amino acid to another as it moves along the mRNA molecule.

4 The tRNA molecules are released after the amino acids they carry are attached to the growing chain of amino acids.

5 The ribosome completes the translation when it reaches the end of the mRNA strand. The newly made protein molecule, in the form of a chain of amino acids, is released.

 Describe how the three different types of RNA work together in protein synthesis.

Watch an animation of how proteins are made.

The process of making proteins is basically the same in all cells. The flow of information in a cell goes from DNA to RNA to protein.

 Review

KEY CONCEPTS

1. Describe the shape of the DNA molecule and how nucleotide bases fit into that structure.

2. What is a protein and what is it made up of?

3. Identify three types of RNA involved in protein synthesis and briefly describe what they do.

CRITICAL THINKING

4. **Infer** What might happen if the wrong amino acid is put on a tRNA molecule?

5. **Apply** Copy the following sequence of DNA bases: A-T-C-A-G-G. Write the complementary mRNA and tRNA sequences for this.

CHALLENGE

6. **Synthesize** Study the sequences you wrote for question 5. How does the tRNA sequence compare to the original DNA sequence?

CHAPTER INVESTIGATION

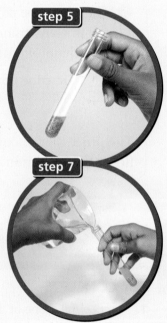

Extract and Observe DNA

OVERVIEW AND PURPOSE In this activity, you will work with several simple chemicals that can break down the membranes of a cell. You will extract DNA from raw wheat germ. Then you will examine the properties of the extracted DNA.

▶ Procedure

1. Make a table in your **Science Notebook** like the one shown on page 143.

2. Place a small scoop of wheat germ in a test tube. The wheat germ should be about 1 cm high in the test tube.

3. Add enough distilled water to wet and cover all of the wheat germ in the test tube.

4. Add 25–30 drops of detergent solution to the test tube.

5. For 3 minutes, gently swirl the test tube contents by rotating your wrist while holding the tube. Try not to make bubbles.

   step 5

6. Add 25–30 drops of the salt solution to the test tube, and swirl for 1 more minute.

7. Hold the test tube tilted at an angle. Slowly add alcohol so that it runs down the inside of the test tube and forms a separate layer on top of the the material already in the tube. Add enough alcohol to double the total volume you started with. Let the test tube stand for 2 minutes.

   step 7

MATERIALS
- raw wheat germ
- scoop
- test tube
- warm distilled water
- detergent solution
- salt solution
- cold ethyl or isopropyl alcohol
- bent paper clip

8 Watch for stringy, cloudy material to rise up from the bottom layer into the alcohol layer. This is the DNA.

9 Use the bent paper clip to remove some DNA. Be careful to probe only the alcohol layer and not disturb the material at the bottom of the test tube.

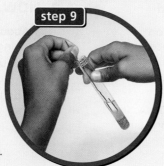

step 9

10 Wash your hands after working with the chemicals.

▶ Observe and Analyze

Write It Up

1. **OBSERVE** How do your observations of the DNA you just extracted compare with what you know about DNA. Record these comparisons in your notebook in a table similar to the one shown.

2. **INFER** What type of organism is wheat? Where is the DNA located in a wheat germ cell?

3. **INFER** What do you think was the purpose of using detergent in this experiment? Hint: How does soap work on greasy dishes?

4. **IDENTIFY LIMITS** What might happen if the wheat germ were not mixed properly with the detergent solution?

▶ Conclude

Write It Up

1. **INFER** If you had used cooked or toasted wheat germ in this experiment, you would not have gotten good results. Why do you think this is the case?

2. **INFER** Would this experiment work with cells from other organisms, such as bananas, onions, or cells from your own cheek? Why or why not?

3. **INFER** Would DNA from a single cell be visible to the naked eye?

4. **APPLY** The procedure that you performed today is used by many people to obtain DNA for further study. Give some examples of how DNA information is used in the world today.

▶ INVESTIGATE Further

CHALLENGE Repeat the experiment replacing the alcohol with water in step 7. Compare the results with the results you obtained using alcohol.

Extract and Observe DNA

Table 1. Properties and Observations

Properties of DNA	Observations

5.2 Changes in DNA can produce variation.

STANDARDS

7–2 The student will demonstrate an understanding of the structure and function of cells, cellular reproduction, and heredity.

VOCABULARY

mutation p. 145
pedigree p. 147

◀ **BEFORE, you learned**

- DNA contains information in the form of a sequence of bases
- Genes code for RNA and proteins
- DNA is transcribed into RNA, which is used to make proteins

▶ **NOW, you will learn**

- About mutations, any changes in DNA
- About the possible effects of mutations
- About pedigrees and how they are used

EXPLORE Codes

What happens to a code if small changes occur?

PROCEDURE

1. Language is a type of code. Look at the English sentence below.

   One day the cat ate the rat.

2. Insert an extra *a* into the word *cat* in the sentence above, but keep the spacing the same. That is, keep a space after every third letter.

WHAT DO YOU THINK?

- Does the sentence still make sense? How were the rest of the words affected?
- How would other small changes affect the meaning of the sentence? Try substituting, removing, and switching letters.

MATERIALS

- pencil
- paper

DNA sequences can change.

SUPPORTING MAIN IDEAS
In your notebook, organize information that supports this main idea: *DNA sequences can change.*

Differences, or variations, in DNA are what make one organism different from another. The number of differences in the DNA sequences between two species is large. Each human cell, with its 46 chromosomes, contains an astounding 3 billion base pairs in its DNA. A yeast cell, by comparison, has 12 million base pairs in its DNA.

The number of differences between any two individuals of the same species is small. For example, about 99.9 percent of the DNA in the cells of two different humans is the same. Just 0.1 percent variation in DNA makes you the unique person you are. That averages out to one base in a thousand.

How can there be such great variety among people if their DNA is so similar? The reason is that of the 6 billion base pairs in human DNA, only 5 percent are in the genes that code for RNA and proteins. As you learned in Chapter 4, genes and their interaction with the environment are what determine the traits of a person.

Differences in genes affect the height of people or the color of their eyes, hair, or skin. Genes produce variation because the type or amount of the proteins they code for can vary from person to person. For example, skin color comes from a protein called melanin. The amount of melanin an individual produces affects the color of their skin.

Many traits, including skin tones, are affected by genes.

Given the huge number of base pairs in the DNA of any organism, it is not surprising that errors occur when DNA is copied. DNA is also affected by the environment. For example, exposure to ultraviolet radiation or x-rays can damage DNA. Both natural and human-made toxins, which are harmful chemicals, can also damage DNA.

Any change in DNA is called a **mutation.** Cells have different ways to repair mistakes in a DNA sequence. Certain enzymes actually proofread DNA, for example correcting mismatched base pairs. Other enzymes enable damaged DNA to be fixed.

 What is a mutation?

When a mutation occurs in a gene, the coding region of DNA, the wrong amino acid might be placed in the amino-acid chain. If this happens, there are three possible outcomes.

❶ The mutation causes no effect. Since some amino acids have more than one code, a mutation may not change the resulting protein. Also, since each cell has two sets of DNA, even if one gene is not working, enough protein may be produced.

❷ The effect of a mutation is minor. A change in the genes that control the amount of melanin produced could affect not only how light or dark a person's skin is, it could also affect eye or hair color. The change, in this case, is a change in appearance.

❸ The effect of a mutation is great. The effect can be good, such as a plant having an increased resistance to disease. Or the effect can be bad, causing a genetic disorder or disease.

Remember, only 5 percent of human DNA is in genes. If a mutation occurs in a noncoding region of DNA, then chances are that the mutation will have no effect. Such a mutation is neutral.

VOCABULARY
Remember to choose a strategy from an earlier chapter or use one of your own to take notes on *mutation.*

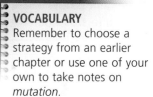 RESOURCE CENTER
CLASSZONE.COM

Find out more about mutations.

INVESTIGATE Neutral Mutations

How does a large number of noncoding sequences affect mutations?

PROCEDURE

1. Circle ten words on the page of a newspaper to represent genes. Place the newspaper on your desk.

2. Use a handful of paper-punch circles to represent mutations and scatter them onto the newspaper.

3. Count the number of paper-punch "mutations" that landed on "genes" and those that did not.

WHAT DO YOU THINK?

- What percentage of "mutations" affected gene sequences?
- What does this model suggest about the probability of mutations affecting genes that are only a small part of a DNA sequence?

CHALLENGE Most of the sequences in bacterial DNA are genes. How could you use the same model to evaluate the effect of mutations on bacterial DNA?

Mutations can cause genetic disorders.

A genetic disorder is a disease or condition that results from mutations that affect the normal functioning of a cell. Sometimes these disorders are inherited, passed on from parent to offspring. Examples of inherited disorders include Tay-Sachs disease, cystic fibrosis, sickle cell disease, and albinism. Other genetic disorders result from mutations that occur during a person's lifetime. Most cancers fall into this category.

CHECK YOUR READING What is a genetic disorder?

Sometimes a person carries a tendency for a disease, such as diabetes, glaucoma, Alzheimer's disease, or emphysema. In some cases, a person's behavior can help prevent the disease. Cigarette smoke is a leading cause of lung cancer. Smoke also greatly increases the risk of people with a genetic tendency for emphysema to develop that disease.

Sickle cell disease is an interesting example of how a mutation can have more than one effect. The mutation occurs in one of the genes that code for hemoglobin. Hemoglobin is a protein that carries oxygen in red blood cells. The mutation causes one amino acid to be replaced with another.

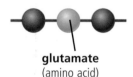

normal hemoglobin
(protein)

glutamate
(amino acid)

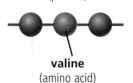

sickle cell hemoglobin
(protein)

valine
(amino acid)

Sickle cell disease is a recessive disorder. Only people who carry two recessive alleles are affected. Recall that an allele is one form of a gene. Because of the amino acid change, some red blood cells can take on a sickle shape. See the photograph at the right. The pedigree below shows the pattern of inheritance of the sickle cell allele through three generations of a family. A **pedigree** is a diagram of family relationships that includes two or more generations.

Sickle cell disease is a severe disease. Sickled red blood cells tend to break more easily than normal red blood cells. People with sickle cell disease do not get enough oxygen delivered to their body tissues, and the tissues become damaged. The disease is common in Africa and parts of India and the Middle East.

What is interesting about the sickle cell allele is that it provides protection against dying of malaria. Malaria is a severe disease, also common in Africa, India, and the Middle East. It is caused by microscopic organisms that reproduce in red blood cells. Scientists do not yet completely understand why people with the sickle cell allele are better able to survive malaria. However the effect of this protection is that the sickle allele remains common in populations that live in regions where malaria is common.

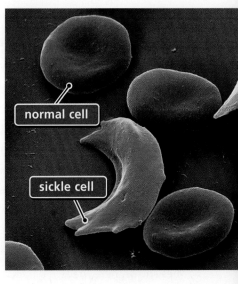
normal cell
sickle cell

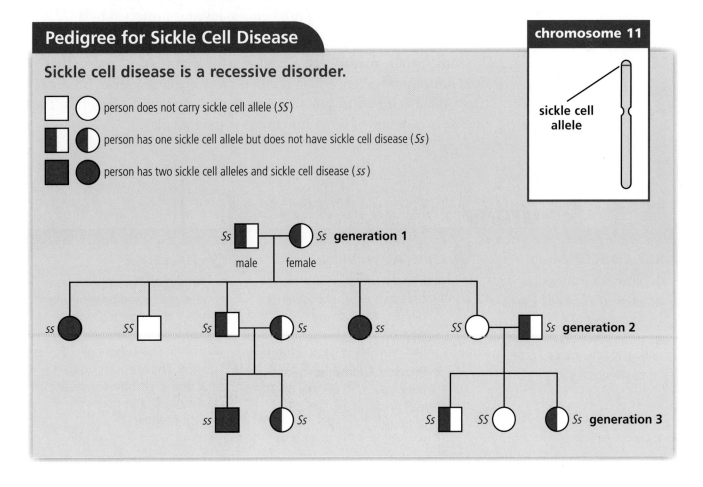

Pedigree for Sickle Cell Disease

chromosome 11

Sickle cell disease is a recessive disorder.

☐ ◯ person does not carry sickle cell allele (*SS*)

◧ ◐ person has one sickle cell allele but does not have sickle cell disease (*Ss*)

■ ● person has two sickle cell alleles and sickle cell disease (*ss*)

sickle cell allele

Ss ◧——◐ *Ss* **generation 1**
male   female

ss ● *SS* ☐ *Ss* ◧——◐ *Ss* ● *ss* *SS* ◯——◧ *Ss* **generation 2**

ss ■ ◐ *Ss*   *Ss* ◧ *SS* ◯ ◐ *Ss* **generation 3**

Cancer is a genetic disorder that affects the cell cycle.

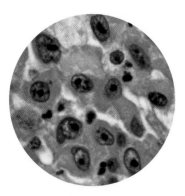

Cancer cells, such as the ones shown here, have abnormal shapes. Cancer cells reproduce uncontrollably and crowd out normal cells.

Cancer is not a single genetic disorder; but rather it is a group of disorders. All cancers are characterized by the uncontrolled division of cells. Normally, cells in a multicellular organism function to maintain the health of an organism. Cell division is controlled so that an organism has the number of cells it needs to function. Cancer cells are, in a way, "selfish" cells. Where normal cells stay within the same tissue, cancer cells spread quickly and can invade other tissues. A normal cell has a definite life span. Cancerous cells become "immortal"—they divide indefinitely.

 What is a characteristic of all cancers?

Most cancers are caused by mutations to DNA that happen during a person's lifetime. Some mutations come from mistakes made during replication. But many are caused by harmful chemicals often referred to as *carcinogens* (kahr-SIHN-uh-juhnz). Many plants naturally produce carcinogens in their tissues. Nicotine is a carcinogen naturally found in tobacco leaves. There are other carcinogens in tobacco.

Ultraviolet and nuclear radiation as well as x-rays can also cause cancer. That is why, if you get an x-ray at the doctor's or dentist's office, the part of your body not being x-rayed is protected by a lead apron.

Some people may inherit a tendency for a particular cancer. That does not mean the cancer will occur. Cancer involves a series of mutations. What is inherited is a mutation that is one step in the series. The disease occurs only if other mutations come into play.

5.2 Review

KEY CONCEPTS

1. What is a mutation?
2. How do mutations affect an organism?
3. What effect does cancer have on the cell cycle of a cancerous cell?

CRITICAL THINKING

4. **Infer** A mutation in a triplet code that ends up coding for the same amino acid is referred to as a silent mutation. In what sense is it silent?

5. **Provide Examples** Identify three causes of genetic disorders and give an example of each.

CHALLENGE

6. **Analyze** Why are genetic diseases carried by genes on the X chromosome more common in male offspring than female offspring? Hint: Think about how X and Y chromosomes are distributed in males and females.

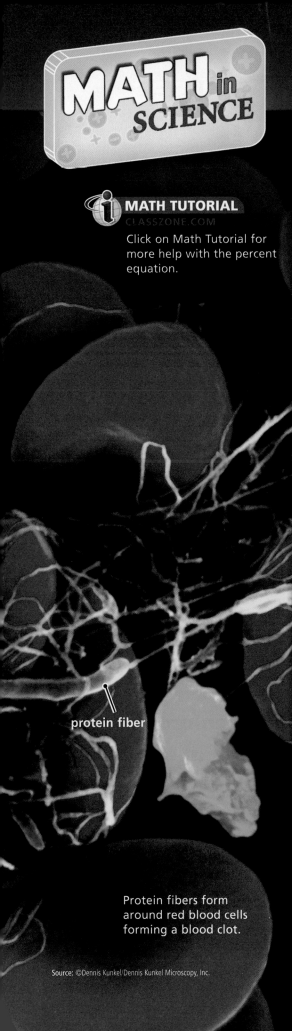

MATH in SCIENCE

MATH TUTORIAL
CLASSZONE.COM
Click on Math Tutorial for more help with the percent equation.

Percents and Populations

Hemophilia is a genetic disorder in which blood does not clot properly. In any group of people who have hemophilia, approximately 80 percent have type A, which is caused by a mutation in one gene. Usually about 12 percent have type B, a different gene mutation.

To express what part of a population carries a gene mutation, scientists can use percentages. Once you know the percentage of a population, you can find out how many individuals that percent represents.

Example

Suppose a doctor is treating a group of people who have the disease hemophilia. The group has 400 people. About how many individuals would you expect to have hemophilia A?

(1) Write the percent as a decimal.

$$80\% = 0.80$$

(2) Multiply the decimal number by the total population.

$$0.80 \cdot 400 = 320.00$$

(3) Be sure the answer has the same number of decimal places as the total number of decimal places in the original factors.

$$0.80 \cdot 400 = 320.00$$
2 decimal places

ANSWER There are probably about 320 people with hemophilia A.

Answer the following questions for a group of 400 hemophilia patients.

1. How many patients are likely to have hemophilia B?

2. Suppose a new doctor begins treatment of 20 percent of the hemophilia A patients. How many individuals is that?

3. In as many as 30 percent of cases of hemophilia, there is no family history of the disorder. In the group of 400, how many individuals probably did not have a family history of hemophilia?

CHALLENGE Write a fraction in simplest terms equal to each percentage: 80 percent, 30 percent, 12 percent, 3 percent. When you multiply these fractions by 400, do you get the same or different results as when you multiply 400 by the percentages? Explain why the results may be different.

protein fiber

Protein fibers form around red blood cells forming a blood clot.

Source: ©Dennis Kunkel/Dennis Kunkel Microscopy, Inc.

KEY CONCEPT

5.3 Modern genetics uses DNA technology.

 BEFORE, you learned

- Mutations are changes to DNA
- Not all mutations have an effect on an organism
- Mutations can lead to genetic disorders

 NOW, you will learn

- How scientists can change organisms by changing DNA
- About some applications of DNA technology
- About some issues surrounding the use of DNA technology

VOCABULARY

selective breeding p. 151
genetic engineering
 p. 151
genome p. 154
cloning p. 154

THINK ABOUT

What type of animal is this?

Look at the photograph of the animal to the right. The cells in this animal contain DNA from two different species. For a long time humans have been able to mix genes by breeding together animals of different but similar species. Now scientists have the technology to mix together genes from two very different species by inserting genes from one organism into the cells of another. What do the characteristics of this animal suggest about the source of its genes?

Changes in DNA can change an organism.

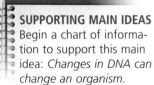

SUPPORTING MAIN IDEAS
Begin a chart of information to support this main idea: *Changes in DNA can change an organism.*

Organisms change over time. Changes come about because of mutations in DNA. Random changes in DNA may introduce new traits into an organism. Over time, certain traits may become more common in one group of organisms as they interact with the environment and each other.

Are all changes in a group of organisms random? There are dogs, such as bloodhounds, that are particularly well suited to tracking. There are cows that give large quantities of milk and crops that produce large quantities of grain. Changes such as these are not random, but result from careful breeding directed by humans.

Selective Breeding

For thousands of years, humans have been carefully selecting and breeding certain plants and animals that have desirable traits. As the years have passed, horses have gotten faster, pigs have gotten leaner, and corn has become sweeter. **Selective breeding** is the process of selecting and breeding parent organisms to pass on particular traits to the offspring.

Selective breeding can be successful as long as the desirable traits are controlled by genes. In fact, what these early farmers were actually selecting were alleles, particular versions of a gene. The alleles were already present in some members of the population. People were not changing DNA, but they were causing certain alleles to become more common in a particular breed. The different dog breeds are a good example of this. All dogs share a common ancestor, the wolf. However, thousands of years of selective breeding have produced dogs with a variety of characteristics.

Bloodhounds, with their strong sense of smell, are used in police work for tracking.

 How does selective breeding affect DNA?

Genetic Engineering

Within the last fifty years it has become possible to directly change the DNA of an organism. **Genetic engineering** is the process in which a sequence of DNA from an organism is first isolated, then inserted into the DNA of another organism, changing that organism's DNA. The DNA that is engineered often codes for some particular trait of interest. Using technology, scientists can take a gene from one species and transfer it into the DNA of an organism from another species. The resulting organisms are referred to as genetically modified (GM), or transgenic.

READING **TiP**
The root *trans-* means "across." *Transgenic* refers to the movement of genes across species.

 What are three steps involved in genetic engineering?

One application of genetic engineering across species involves making plants more insect-resistant. Genetic engineers have isolated genes in microorganisms that produce natural insect-killing chemicals, or pesticides. They have succeeded in transferring these genes into the DNA of crop plants, such as corn and soybeans. The cells of the genetically modified plants then produce their own pesticide, reducing the amount of chemical pesticide farmers need to use on their fields.

genetically modified tomatoes

These tomatoes have been genetically modified to grow in conditions that would not support naturally occurring tomatoes.

Genetic engineering can address very specific needs. For example, in many parts of the world, soils are poor in nutrients. Or the soil may contain salts. Such soil is not good for growing food crops. Genetic engineers have inserted a gene from a salt-tolerant cabbage into tomatoes. The salt-tolerant tomatoes can grow in soil that natural tomatoes cannot grow in. These tomatoes can also be grown using brackish water, which is water with a higher salt content than fresh water.

There are risks and benefits associated with genetic engineering.

Genetic engineering offers potential benefits to society, but also carries potential risks. Probably most people in the United States have eaten foods made from genetically modified corn or soybeans. The plants have bacterial genes that make them more resistant to plant-eating insects. This increases food production and reduces the amount of chemical pesticides needed. Less chemical pesticide on the ground reduces the risk of environmental pollution.

However, many people worry that the natural pesticides produced by a genetically modified plant might have some effect on humans. What if genetically modified plants cross-breed with other plants, and give protection to plants that are considered weeds? There is also the question of how to let people know if the food they eat is genetically modified. Many people think that such food should be labeled.

 CHECK YOUR READING What are some risks and benefits associated with using genetic engineering in food crops?

There is uncertainty about how the DNA of genetically modified organisms might affect natural populations. For example, scientists are working with salmon that are genetically modified to grow more quickly. Fish are an important food source, and natural fish populations are decreasing. However, the salmon are raised in pens set in rivers or the sea. If the fish escape, they may breed with fish from wild populations. Government officials have yet to decide whether the benefit of having these fast-growing fish is worth the risk to wild populations.

salmon pens

ANALYZE How would the genetic material of wild salmon change if they were to breed with genetically modified salmon?

DNA technology has many applications.

DNA technology is used in many different ways. It can be used to add nutrients to foods to make them more nutritious. It can be used to produce new and better drugs for treating disease. DNA technology can also be used to determine whether a particular drug might cause side effects in an individual. And it can be used to screen for and perhaps treat genetic disorders.

DNA Identification

You may have seen news stories about how DNA evidence is used to solve a crime. Law enforcement specialists gather as much DNA evidence as they can from a crime scene—for example, skin, hair, or blood. In a laboratory, they scan about ten regions of the DNA that are known to vary from individual to individual. They use this information to produce a DNA profile—a DNA fingerprint. This fingerprint is unique to a person, unless that person has an identical twin. If DNA analysis of tissue found at the crime scene matches the DNA fingerprint of a suspect, then police know the suspect was at the scene.

The more matches found between crime-scene DNA and the suspect's DNA, the higher the probability that the suspect is guilty. Experts currently recommend that at least four to six DNA regions be matched to establish a person's guilt. The chances are very small that another person would have exactly the same DNA profile for all the DNA regions tested. Of course, the courts also take other forms of evidence into account before an individual is convicted of a crime.

RESOURCE CENTER
CLASSZONE.COM

Learn more about DNA technology.

Studying Genomes

VOCABULARY
Don't forget to choose a strategy to take notes on the term *genome*.

One of the most challenging scientific projects ever undertaken was the Human Genome Project. A **genome** is all the genetic material in an organism. The primary goal of the project was to sequence the 3 billion nucleotide pairs in a single set of human chromosomes. The initial sequence was published in 2001. Scientists are now working to identify the approximately 30,000 genes within the human genome.

Scientists have completed sequencing the genomes of many organisms. These organisms, often referred to as model organisms, enable scientists to compare DNA across species. Many of the genes found in model organisms, such as the fruit fly and mouse, are also found in the human genome.

Scientists are aware that there are many ethical, legal, and social issues that arise from the ability to change DNA. We as a society have to decide when it is acceptable to change DNA and how to use the technology we have. **Cloning** is a technique that uses technology to make copies. It can be applied to a segment of DNA or to a whole organism. Cloning has been used in bacteria to produce proteins and drugs that help fight disease. Human insulin, which is used to treat people with a certain form of diabetes, is now produced in large quantities as the result of cloning techniques.

The same technology, which is so helpful in one application, can be a cause of concern when applied in a different way. In 1996, scientists produced the first clone of a mammal, a sheep named Dolly. All of Dolly's DNA came from a single body cell of another sheep. The ability to clone such a complex animal raised many concerns about future uses of cloning. This, as well as many other possible applications of technology, makes it important that people understand the science of genetics. Only then can they make informed decisions about how and when the technology should be used.

Dolly was the first successful clone of a mammal.

5.3 Review

KEY CONCEPTS

1. What is a genetically modified organism?

2. What is the Human Genome Project?

3. List three different applications of DNA technology.

CRITICAL THINKING

4. **Compare and Contrast** How is selective breeding different from genetic engineering? How is it the same?

5. **Analyze** Do you think a genetically modified trait in an organism can be undone? Why or why not?

⬤ CHALLENGE

6. **Analyze** Why might a genetically engineered drug, such as insulin, be better for treatment of disease than a drug that is manufactured chemically?

Modern Genetics Meets the Dodo and the Solitaire

Hunted to Extinction

The dodo bird was first sighted around 1600 by Portuguese sailors arriving on the shores of the island of Mauritius in the Indian Ocean. Portuguese sailors hunted the dodo, which was unable to fly, and used its meat for food. The bird, never having had contact with humans, did not run away. Only a mere 80 years later, the dodo was extinct.

DNA Evidence

Few bone specimens of the dodo bird remain today. Scientists collected and analyzed genetic material from preserved dodo specimens and specimens of another, similar extinct bird called the solitaire bird. The DNA evidence was compared with the genetic material of about 35 species of living pigeons and doves.

The model shows a solitaire bird, a close relative of the dodo.

The DNA had a story to tell. Evidence suggests that the dodo and solitaire bird were close relatives. Their nearest living relative is a species of pigeon found in nearby southeast Asia. From this evidence, scientists hypothesize that the dodo and solitaire birds species became separate almost 25 million years ago. In the geographic location of the island of Mauritius, the dodo developed its distinct characteristics, which eventually led to its extinction.

EXPLORE

1. **MAKE INFERENCES** How can scientists use what they know from analyzing dodo bones to help them form conclusions about the physical characteristics of the bird?

2. **CHALLENGE** Several factors contributed to the extinction of the dodo bird. Look online to find out more about these factors. How can learning about what happened to the dodo help save today's endangered species from extinction?

Chapter Review

the BIG idea

DNA is a set of instructions for making cell parts.

CONTENT REVIEW
CLASSZONE.COM

KEY CONCEPTS SUMMARY

1 **DNA and RNA are required to make proteins.**

DNA contains a code that enables a cell to make RNA and proteins. Replication copies the code before a cell divides.

- DNA's triplet code enables a cell to code for proteins
- mRNA, tRNA, and ribosomes translate the code into a sequence of amino acids.
- The amino acids form a protein needed for cell function.

DNA → RNA → Proteins

VOCABULARY
replication p. 137
RNA p. 138

2 **Changes in DNA can produce variation.**

Differences in DNA produce variations. Any change to DNA is a mutation. Many mutations have little or no effect. However, some mutations can change the way a cell works—sometimes helping an organism, sometimes hurting it.

Genetic disorders are caused by mutations in DNA. Some are inherited and can be followed through different generations of a family by using a pedigree. Other genetic disorders, such as cancer, are caused by mutations that occur during a person's lifetime.

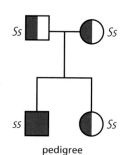
pedigree

VOCABULARY
mutation p. 145
pedigree p. 147

3 **Modern genetics uses DNA technology.**

Changes in DNA can change an organism. Selective breeding changes organisms by choosing desired traits already coded for by DNA.

Genetic engineering introduces changes to the DNA of an organism. It can be used to

- introduce new traits into an organism
- produce medicines and other products
- identify individuals
- clone genes as well as organisms
- sequence the genome of an organism

DNA technology raises important issues for society.

Dolly was the first clone of a mammal.

VOCABULARY
selective breeding p. 151
genetic engineering p. 151
genome p. 154
cloning p. 154

Reviewing Vocabulary

Copy the chart below and write the definition for each word. Use the meaning of the word's root to help you.

Term	Root Meaning	Definition
1. replication	to repeat	
2. mutation	to change	
3. genome	relating to offspring	
4. cloning	to branch off	

Reviewing Key Concepts

Multiple Choice *Choose the letter of the best answer.*

5. Genes are sequences of DNA, which are made up of
  a. nucleotides   **c.** phosphates
  b. chromosomes   **d.** ribosomes

6. What happens during replication?
  a. DNA is copied.
  b. RNA is copied.
  c. Ribosomes are made.
  d. Proteins are made.

7. Which base is found only in RNA?
  a. thymine
  b. guanine
  c. adenine
  d. uracil

8. The main function of mRNA in protein synthesis is to
  a. transfer amino acids to a ribosome
  b. carry proteins to the ribosome
  c. transcribe genes from DNA
  d. connect nucleotides together

9. Proteins are made up of a sequence of
  a. chromosomes   **c.** nucleotides
  b. amino acids   **d.** base pairs

10. Mutations are changes in
  a. DNA   **c.** tRNA
  b. the cell cycle   **d.** proteins

11. Which is a known cause of genetic mutations?
  a. poor nutrition
  b. malaria
  c. ultraviolet radiation
  d. cancer

12. A pedigree shows
  a. how proteins are synthesized
  b. how genes are inherited in a family
  c. where mutations are located in a sequence of DNA
  d. which triplet of bases matches up with a particular amino acid

13. The main goal of the Human Genome Project was to
  a. find cures for genetic diseases
  b. find all mutations in human DNA
  c. count the number of genes in human DNA
  d. sequence all DNA on human chromosomes

14. Genetic engineering involves
  a. inserting changed DNA into an organism
  b. cross-breeding plants
  c. testing new medicines for genetic diseases
  d. using x-rays to change DNA

Short Answer *Write a short answer to each question.*

15. DNA is described as the information molecule. What is the information that DNA carries?

16. What is the difference between selective breeding and genetic engineering?

17. List three applications of DNA technology and how these uses benefit humans.

Thinking Critically

Use the diagram to answer the next three questions.

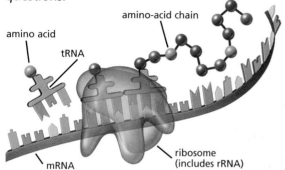

amino-acid chain

amino acid

tRNA

mRNA

ribosome
(includes rRNA)

18. ANALYZE How does the mRNA strand above compare with the DNA template that produced it? Use the words *guanine, cytosine, thymine, adenine, and uracil* in your answer.

19. SUMMARIZE Three types of RNA are needed for protein synthesis. What are the three types and what is the function of each?

20. APPLY A protein contains 131 amino acids. How many bases will there be on the mRNA strand corresponding to these amino acids and how do you know?

21. ANALYZE A cell contains two sets of DNA. If the gene on one molecule of DNA has a mutation, how will that affect the gene on the other molecule of DNA?

22. SYNTHESIZE A mutation occurs during DNA replication. The following sequence

A-T-T-A-C-A-G-G-G

is copied as,

A-T-A-C-A-G-G-G

with one base missing. How does that affect the triplet code?

23. SEQUENCE List the steps in making a protein. Start with a gene on a DNA molecule. Include the chemical subunits involved in each step.

24. EVALUATE A person who carries a gene for a genetic disorder may not get the disorder. How can that be?

25. INFER How might a scientist determine if a neutral mutation has occurred in an organism?

26. PREDICT A mutation in an Arctic hare causes brown spots to appear on normally white fur. Explain how the mutation might affect the ability of the hare to survive.

27. EVALUATE Doctors can sometimes cure cancer by removing cancerous cells from a person's body. Why is it important for the doctors to remove all the cells?

28. EVALUATE How might selective breeding of a type of animal limit genetic diversity within the breed?

29. EVALUATE If a scientist compares the genome of a mouse to that of a human and discovers that the two organisms have many of the same genes, what can the scientist infer about how the cells in the two organisms function?

the BIG idea

30. DRAWING CONCLUSIONS Look again at the photograph on pages 132–133. How have models helped scientists understand the function of DNA?

31. CONNECT A local newspaper has written an editorial against the use of genetic engineering. The writer argues that humans should never change the DNA in an organism, even though they have the technology to do so. Write a response to the editorial, stating whether you think the benefits humans get from genetic engineering are worth the risks.

UNIT PROJECTS

Evaluate all the data, results, and information from your project folder. Prepare to present your project. Be ready to answer questions posed by your classmates about your results.

Analyzing Data

Use the following information and the pedigree chart to answer the questions.

Red-green colorblindness is one of the most common genetic conditions in the human population. About 5 percent of males are red-green colorblind. A male receives just one allele for this trait, on the X chromosome he inherits from his mother. If he receives the allele for red-green colorblindness, he will be colorblind. His genotype will be cb/Y.

Females inherit two alleles for the trait. Colorblindness (cb) is recessive and the allele for regular color vision (Cb) is dominant. A female with both the recessive allele and the dominant allele will have normal color vision. Her genotype would be Cb/cb. However, if the female has a male child, her child may be colorblind. The pedigree chart shows colorblindness in three generations.

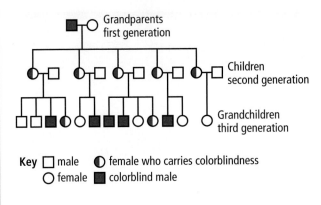

Grandparents
first generation

Children
second generation

Grandchildren
third generation

Key ☐ male   ◑ female who carries colorblindness
○ female   ■ colorblind male

1. How many individuals in the first generation are colorblind?
   a. two
   b. one
   c. none
   d. three

2. How many individuals in the second generation are female?
   a. none
   b. one
   c. two
   d. five

3. Which statement describes the pattern of inheritance for colorblindness?
   a. Grandmother and granddaughter are both colorblind.
   b. Grandmother and son are both colorblind.
   c. Grandfather and granddaughter are both colorblind.
   d. Grandfather and grandson are both colorblind.

4. What are the genotypes of the males in the third generation?
   a. Cb/Y, Cb/Y, Cb/Y, cb/Y, cb/Y, cb/Y, cb/Y
   b. cb/Y, cb/Y, cb/Y, cb/Y,cb/Y, cb/Y, cb/Y
   c. Cb/Y, Cb/Y, Cb/Y, Cb/Y, Cb/Y, Cb/Y, CbY
   d. Cb/Y, Cb/Y, cb/Y, cb/y, cb/y ,cb/Y, cb/Y

Extended Response

5. Write a paragraph explaining why a color-blind man who has three daughters and one son with normal color vision might have two grandsons who are color-blind. Use the terms in the vocabulary box in your answer. Underline each term.

6. The same color-blind man has four granddaughters. Would you predict the granddaughters to be colorblind? Explain why or why not. Use the terms in the vocabulary box.

genotype	phenotype	allele
recessive	dominant	generation

UNIT 2

Human Biology

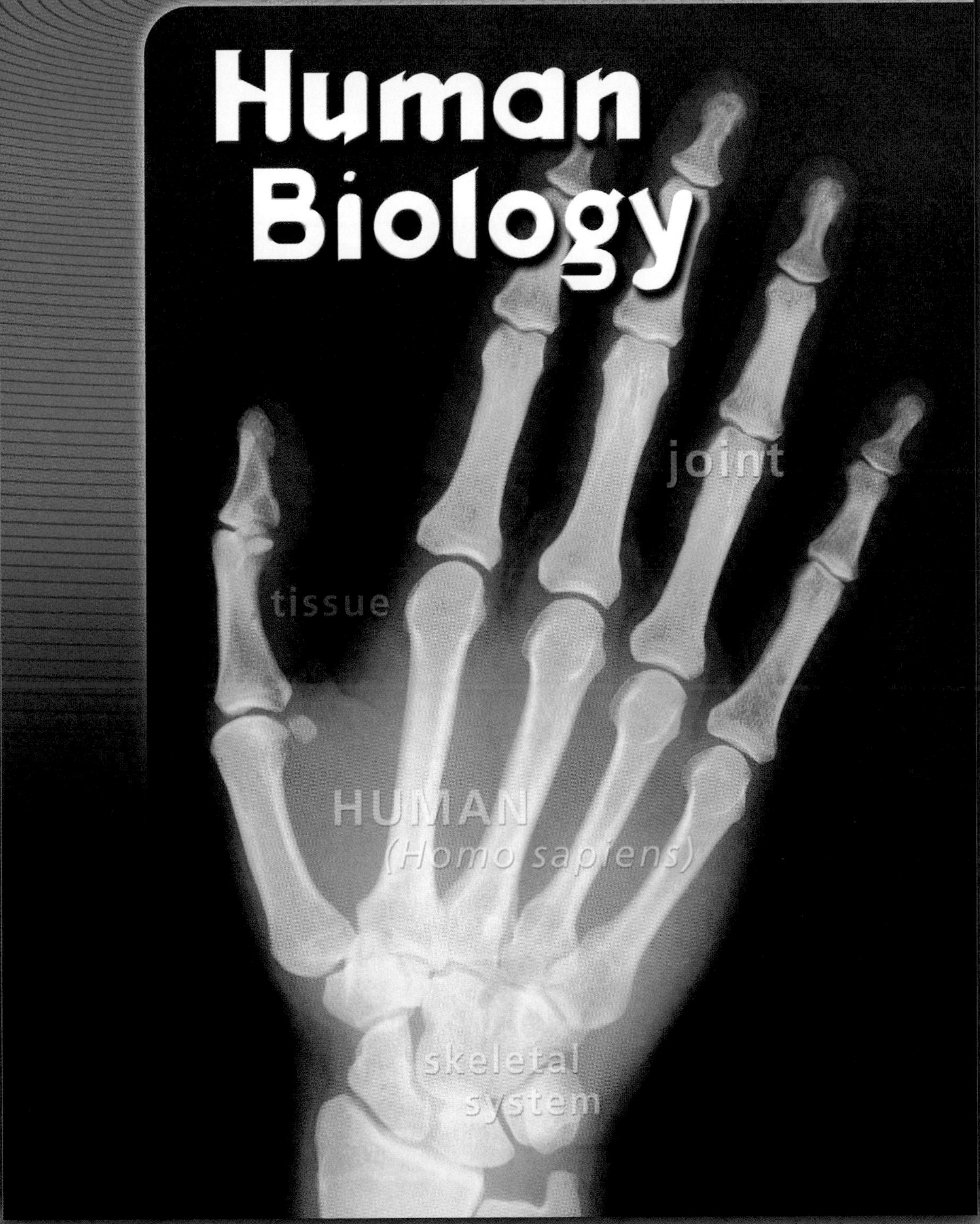

joint

tissue

HUMAN
(Homo sapiens)

skeletal
system

Contents Overview

Frontiers in Science
  Surprising Senses   162

Timelines in Science
  Seeing Inside the Body   254

Chapter 6   Systems, Support, and
                Movement   166

Chapter 7   Absorption, Digestion,
                and Exchange   194

Chapter 8   Transport and Protection 222

Chapter 9   Control and Reproduction 258

Chapter 10 Growth, Development,
                and Health   290

Surprising Senses

SCIENTIFIC AMERICAN FRONTIERS

Learn more about how the brain and senses work. See the video "Sight of Touch."

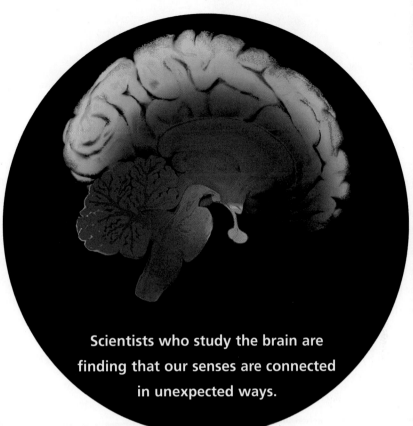

Scientists who study the brain are finding that our senses are connected in unexpected ways.

Senses and the Brain

One of the great mysteries still unsolved in science is what happens inside the brain. What is a thought? How is it formed? Where is it stored? How do our senses shape our thoughts? There are far more questions than answers. One way to approach questions about the brain is to study brain activity at times when the body is performing different functions.

Most advanced brain functions happen in the part of the brain called the cerebral cortex (suh-REE-bruhl KOR-tehks). That's where the brain interprets information from the senses. The cerebral cortex has many specialized areas. Each area controls one type of brain activity. Scientists are mapping these areas. At first, they studied people with brain injuries. A person with an injury to one area might not be able to speak. Someone with a different injury might have trouble seeing or hearing. Scientists mapped the areas in which damage seemed to cause each kind of problem.

Now scientists have even more tools to study the brain. One tool is called functional magnetic resonance imaging, or FMRI. Scientists put a person into a machine that uses radio waves to produce images of the person's brain. Scientists then ask the person to do specific activities, such as looking at pictures of faces or listening for specific sounds. The FMRI images show what parts of the person's brain are most active during each activity.

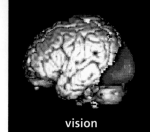  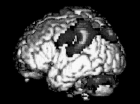 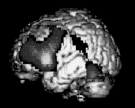

| vision | hearing | Braille reading | thought |

The PET scans show areas of the brain active during particular tasks. Braille is a textured alphabet read by the fingers. Braille reading activates areas associated with touch, vision, hearing, and thought.

Double Duty

Using FMRI and other tools, scientists have identified the parts of the cerebral cortex that are responsible for each of the senses. The vision area is located at the back of the brain. The smell, taste, touch, and hearing areas are all close together in the middle part of the brain.

People don't usually use just one sense at a time. Scientists have found some unexpected connections. In one study, Marisa Taylor-Clarke poked the arms of some volunteers with either one or two pins. Then she asked them how many pins they felt. Taylor-Clarke found that people who looked at their arms before the test did better than those who didn't. FMRI showed that the part of their brains responsible for touch was also more active when they used their sense of sight.

These connections in the brain show up even when one sense doesn't work. Many people who have hearing impairments read lips to understand what other people are saying. Scientists using FMRI discovered that these people use the part of the brain normally used for hearing to help them understand what they see. This is even true for people who have never been able to hear.

Scrambled Senses

Some people have more connections between their senses than most people have. They may look at numbers and see colors, or associate smells with shapes. Some even get a taste in their mouths when they touch something. All these are examples of synesthesia (sin-uhs-THEE-zhuh). About 1 in 200 people have some kind of synesthesia.

SCIENTIFIC AMERICAN FRONTIERS

View the "Sight of Touch" segment of your Scientific American Frontiers video to learn about another example of connections between the senses.

IN THIS SCENE FROM THE VIDEO ▶ Michelle, a research subject, reads Braille with her fingers after wearing a blindfold for three days.

SEEING BY TOUCHING Many blind people read using Braille, a system of raised dots used to represent letters. Some, such as Braille proofreader Gil Busch, can read Braille at astonishing speeds. Scientist Alvaro Pascual-Leone used MRI to study

Gil's brain. The visual area of Gil's brain was active while he read Braille.

Gil has been blind since birth, so his brain has had a long time to adjust. Pascual-Leone wanted to know whether the brain could rewire itself in a shorter time. He asked volunteer Michelle Geronimo to wear a blindfold for a week. During that time, she learned to read Braille and experienced the world as a blind person does. At the end of the week, Pascual-Leone was able to demonstrate that Michelle's brain had rewired itself, too. Her visual center was active when she read Braille.

FMRI has made it possible for scientists to learn more about synesthesia. One group of scientists studied people who saw colors when they heard words. FMRI showed that the visual areas of their brains were active along with the hearing areas. (For most people, only the hearing area would be active.)

But why does synesthesia happen? Some scientists think that people with synesthesia have more connections between areas of their brains. Every person has extra connections when they're born, but most people lose many of them in childhood. Perhaps people with synesthesia keep theirs. Another theory suggests that their brains are "cross-wired," so information goes in unusual directions.

Some people with synesthesia see this colorful pattern when they hear a dog bark.

As scientists explore synesthesia and other connections between the senses, they learn more about how the parts of the brain work together. The human body is complex. And the brain, along with the rest of the nervous system, has yet to be fully understood.

UNANSWERED Questions

Scientists have learned a lot about how senses are connected. Their research leads to new questions.

- How does information move between different areas of the brain?
- How and why does the brain rewire itself?
- How does cross-wired sensing (synesthesia) happen?

UNIT PROJECTS

As you study this unit, work alone or in a group on one of the projects below.

Your Body System

Create one or several models showing important body systems.

- Draw the outline of your own body on a large piece of craft paper.
- Use reference materials to help you place everything correctly. Label each part.

The Brain: "Then and Now"

Compare and contrast past and present understandings of the brain.

- One understanding is that each part of the brain is responsible for different body functions. This understanding has changed over time.
- Research the history of this idea.
- Prepare diagrams of then and now. Share your presentation.

Design an Experiment

Design an experiment that will test one of the senses. You should first identify a problem question you want to explore.

- The experiment may include a written introduction, materials procedure, and a plan for recording and presenting outcomes.
- Prepare a blank written experiment datasheet for your classmates to use.

CAREER CENTER
CLASSZONE.COM

Learn more about careers in neurobiology.

CHAPTER 6 Systems, Support, and Movement

the BIG idea

The human body is made up of systems that work together to perform necessary functions.

Key Concepts

SECTION

1 The human body is complex.
Learn about the parts and systems in the human body.

SECTION

2 The skeletal system provides support and protection.
Learn how the skeletal system is organized and what it does.

SECTION

3 The muscular system makes movement possible.
Learn about the different types of muscles and how they work.

What systems make it possible for this racer to move so fast?

 Internet Preview

CLASSZONE.COM

Chapter 6 online resources: Content Review, two Simulations, three Resource Centers, Math Tutorial, Test Practice

EXPLORE (the BIG idea)

How Many Bones Are in Your Hand?

Use a pencil to trace an outline of your hand on a piece of paper. Feel the bones in your fingers and the palm of your hand. At points where you can bend your fingers and hand, draw a circle. Each circle represents a joint where two bones meet. Draw lines to represent the bones in your hand.

Observe and Think How many bones did you find? How many joints?

How Does It Move?

The bones in your body are hard and stiff, yet they move smoothly. The point where two bones meet and move is called a joint. There are probably many objects in your home that have hard parts that move against each other: a joystick, a hinge, a pair of scissors.

Observe and Think What types of movement are possible when two hard objects are attached to each other? What parts of your body produce similar movements?

Internet Activity: The Human Body

Go to **ClassZone.com** to explore the different systems in the human body.

Observe and Think How are the systems in the middle of the body different from those that extend to the outer parts of the body?

Tissues and Organs **Code: MDL044**

Getting Ready to Learn

◀ CONCEPT REVIEW

- The cell is the basic unit of living things.
- Systems are made up of inter-acting parts that share matter and energy.
- In multicellular organisms cells work together to support life.

◀ VOCABULARY REVIEW

See Glossary for definitions.

cell
system

ⓘ CONTENT REVIEW
CLASSZONE.COM
Review concepts and vocabulary.

▶ TAKING NOTES

MAIN IDEA WEB

Write each new blue head-ing in a box. Then write notes in boxes around the center box that give important terms and details about that blue heading.

VOCABULARY STRATEGY

Write each new vocabulary term in the center of a **four square** diagram. Write notes in the squares around each term. Include a definition, some fea-tures, and some examples of the term. If possible, write some things that are not examples of the term.

See the Note-Taking Handbook on pages R45–R51.

SCIENCE NOTEBOOK

The cell is the basic unit of living things.

Tissues are groups of similar cells that function together.

The body has cells, tissues, and organs.

Organs are groups of tissues working together.

Definition	Features
Group of cells that work together	A level of organiza-tion in the body

TISSUE

Examples	Nonexamples
connective tissue, like bone	individual bone cells

6.1 The human body is complex.

McDougal Littell Science
SOUTH CAROLINA

STANDARDS

7–3.1 Summarize the levels of structural organization within the human body (including cells, tissues, organs, and systems).

VOCABULARY

tissue p. 170
organ p. 171
organ system p. 172
homeostasis p. 172

◀ BEFORE, you learned

- All living things are made of cells
- All living things need energy
- Living things meet their needs through interactions with the environment

▶ NOW, you will learn

- About the organization of the human body
- About different types of tissues
- About the functions of organ systems

THINK ABOUT

How is the human body like a city?

A city is made up of many parts that perform different functions. Buildings provide places to live and work. Transportation systems move people around. Electrical energy provides light and heat. Similarly, the human body is made of several systems. The skeletal system, like the framework of a building, provides support. The digestive system works with the respiratory system to provide energy and materials. What other systems in your body can you compare to a system in the city?

The body has cells, tissues, and organs.

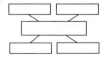

MAIN IDEA WEB
As you read this section, complete the main idea web begun on page 168.

Your body is made of many parts that work together as a system to help you grow and stay healthy. The basic level of organization in your body is the cell. Next come tissues, then individual organs, and then systems that are made up of organs. The highest level of organization is the organism itself. You can think of the body as having five levels of organization: cells, tissues, organs, organ systems, and the organism. Although these levels seem separate from one another, they all work together.

CHECK YOUR READING What are five levels of organization in your body?

INVESTIGATE Systems

How do the systems in your body interact?

PROCEDURE

1. Work with other classmates to make a list of everyday activities.

2. Discuss how your body responds to each task. Record your ideas.

3. Identify and count the systems in your body that you think are used to perform the task.

4. Have someone from your group make a chart of the different activities.

WHAT DO YOU THINK?

- Which systems did you name, and how did they work together to perform each activity?

- When you are asleep, what activities does your body perform?

CHALLENGE How could you make an experiment that would test your predictions?

SKILL FOCUS
Predicting

MATERIALS
large sheet of paper

TIME
20 minutes

Cells

The cell is the basic unit of life. Cells make up all living things. Some organisms, such as bacteria, are made of only a single cell. In these organisms the single cell performs all of the tasks necessary for survival. That individual cell captures and releases energy, uses materials, and grows. In more complex organisms, such as humans and many other animals and plants, cells are specialized. Specialized cells perform specific jobs. A red blood cell, for example, carries oxygen from the lungs throughout the body.

Tissues

A **tissue** is a group of similar cells that work together to perform a particular function. Think of a tissue as a brick wall and the cells within it as the individual bricks. Taken together, the bricks form something larger and more functional. But just as the bricks need to be placed in a certain way to form the wall, cells must be organized in a tissue.

 CHECK YOUR READING How are cells related to tissues?

The human body contains several types of tissues. These tissues are classified into four main groups according to their function: epithelial tissue, nerve tissue, muscle tissue, and connective tissue.

170 Unit 2: **Human Biology**

- Epithelial (ehp-uh-THEE-lee-uhl) tissue functions as a boundary. It covers all of the inner and outer surfaces of your body. Each of your internal organs is covered with a layer of epithelial tissue.

- Nerve tissue functions as a messaging system. Cells in nerve tissue carry electrical impulses between your brain and the various parts of your body in response to changing conditions.

- Muscle tissue functions in movement. Movement results when muscle cells contract, or shorten, and then relax. In some cases, such as throwing a ball, you control the movement. In other cases, such as the beating of your heart, the movement occurs without conscious control.

- Connective tissue functions to hold parts of the body together, providing support, protection, strength, padding, and insulation. Tendons and ligaments are connective tissues that hold bones and muscles together. Bone itself is another connective tissue. It supports and protects the soft parts of your body.

Organs

Groups of different tissues make up organs. An **organ** is a structure that is made up of two or more types of tissue that work together to carry out a function in the body. For example, the heart that pumps blood around your body contains all four types of tissues. As in cells and tissues, the structure of an organ relates to its function. The stomach's bag-shaped structure and strong muscular walls make it suited for breaking down food. The walls of the heart are also muscular, allowing it to function as a pump.

Levels of Organization

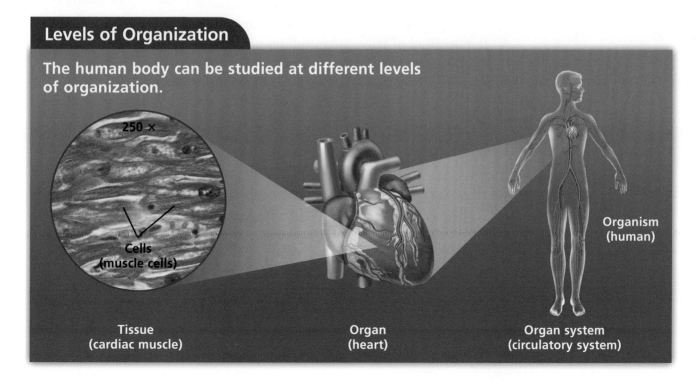

The human body can be studied at different levels of organization.

250 ×

Cells
(muscle cells)

Tissue
(cardiac muscle)

Organ
(heart)

Organ system
(circulatory system)

Organism
(human)

Organ Systems

An **organ system** is a group of organs that together perform a function that helps the body meet its needs for energy and materials. For example, your stomach, mouth, throat, large and small intestines, liver, and pancreas are all part of the organ system called the digestive system. The body is made up of many organ systems. In this unit, you will read about these systems. They include the skeletal, muscular, respiratory, digestive, urinary, circulatory, immune, nervous, and reproductive systems. Together, these systems allow the human organism to grow, reproduce, and maintain life.

The body's systems interact with one another.

READING **TiP**

VOCABULARY
The word *homeostasis* contains two word roots. *Homeo* comes from a root meaning "same." *Stasis* comes from a root meaning "stand still" or "stay."

The ability of your body to maintain internal conditions is called **homeostasis** (HOH-mee-oh-STAY-sihs). Your body is constantly regulating such things as your body temperature, the amount of sugar in your blood, even your posture. The processes that take place in your body occur within a particular set of conditions.

The body's many levels of organization, from cells to organ systems, work constantly to maintain the balance needed for the survival of the organism. For example, on a hot day, you may sweat. Sweating keeps the temperature inside your body constant, even though the temperature of your surroundings changes.

INFER This student is drinking water after exercising. Why is it important to drink fluids after you sweat?

 Review

KEY CONCEPTS

1. Draw a diagram that shows the relationship among cells, tissues, organs, and organ systems.

2. Make a chart of the four basic tissue groups that includes names, functions, and examples.

3. Identify three functions performed by organ systems.

CRITICAL THINKING

4. **Apply** How does drinking water after you sweat help maintain homeostasis?

5. **Compare and Contrast** Compare and contrast the four basic tissue groups. How would all four types of tissue be involved in a simple activity, like raising your hand?

CHALLENGE

6. **Apply** Describe an object, such as a car, that can be used as a model of the human body. Explain how the parts of the model relate to the body.

What Does the Body Need to Survive?

In 1914, Ernest Shackleton and 27 men set sail for Antarctica. Their goal was to cross the continent by foot and sled. The crew never set foot on Antarctica. Instead, the winter sea froze around their ship, crushing it until it sank. They were stranded on floating ice, over 100 miles from land. How long could they survive? How would their bodies respond? What would they need to stay alive?

You can make inferences in answer to any of these questions. First you need to recall what you know. Then you need new evidence. What was available to the explorers? Did they save supplies from their ship? What resources existed in the environment?

▶ Prior Knowledge

- The human body needs air, water, and food.
- The human body needs to maintain its temperature. The body can be harmed if it loses too much heat.

▶ Observations

Several of Shackleton's explorers kept diaries. From the diaries we know the following:

- The crew hunted seals and penguins for fresh meat.
- The temperature was usually below freezing.
- Tents and overturned lifeboats sheltered the crew from the wind.
- Their clothes were made of thick fabric and animal skins and furs.
- They melted snow and ice in order to have fresh water.

▶ Make Inferences

On Your Own Describe how the explorers met each of the needs of the human body.

As a Group How long do you think these 28 men could have survived these conditions? Use evidence and inferences in your answer.

CHALLENGE How might survival needs differ for sailors shipwrecked in the tropics compared to the Antarctic?

RESOURCE CENTER
CLASSZONE.COM

Learn more about Shackleton's expedition.

6.2 The skeletal system provides support and protection.

STANDARDS

7–3.3 Summarize the relationships of the major body systems (including the circulatory, respiratory, digestive, excretory, nervous, muscular, and skeletal systems).

VOCABULARY

skeletal system p. 174
compact bone p. 175
spongy bone p. 175
axial skeleton p. 176
appendicular skeleton p. 176

 BEFORE, you learned

- The body is made of cells, tissues, organs, and systems
- Cells, tissues, organs, and organ systems work together
- Systems in the body interact

▶ **NOW, you will learn**

- About different types of bone tissue
- How the human skeleton is organized
- How joints allow movement

EXPLORE Levers

How can a bone act as a lever?

PROCEDURE

① A lever is a stiff rod that pivots about a fixed point. Hold the bag in your hand and keep your arm straight, like a lever. Move the bag up and down.

② Move the handles of the bag over your elbow. Again hold your arm straight and move the bag up and down.

③ Now move the bag to the top of your arm and repeat the procedure.

MATERIALS
sports bag

WHAT DO YOU THINK?

- At which position is it easiest to move the bag?
- At which position does the bag move the farthest?
- How does the position of a load affect the action of a lever?

MAIN IDEA WEB
Make a web of the important terms and details about the main idea: *Bones are living tissue.*

Bones are living tissue.

Every movement of the human body is possible because of the interaction of muscles with the **skeletal system.** Made up of a strong connective tissue called bone, the skeletal system serves as the anchor for all of the body's movement, provides support, and protects soft organs inside the body. Bones can be classified as long bones, short bones, irregular bones, and flat bones. Long bones are found in the arms and legs. Short bones are found in the feet and hands. Irregular bones are found in the spine. Flat bones are found in the ribs and skull.

You might think that bones are completely solid and made up of dead tissue. They actually are made of both hard and soft materials.

Like your heart or skin, bones are living tissue. Bones are not completely solid, either; they have spaces inside. The spaces allow blood carrying nutrients to travel throughout the bones. Because bones have spaces, they weigh much less than they would if they were solid.

RESOURCE CENTER
CLASSZONE.COM

Explore the skeletal system.

Two Types of Bone Tissue

Every bone is made of two types of bone tissue: compact bone and spongy bone. The hard compact bone surrounds the soft spongy bone. Each individual bone cell lies within a bony web. This web is made up mostly of minerals containing calcium.

Compact Bone Surrounding the spongy, inner layer of the bone is a hard layer called **compact bone.** Compact bone functions as the basic supportive tissue of the body, the part of the body you call the skeleton. The outer layer of compact bone is very hard and tough. It covers the outside of most bones.

Spongy Bone Inside the bone, the calcium network is less dense. This tissue is called **spongy bone.** Spongy bone is strong but lightweight. It makes up most of the short, flat, and irregular bones found in your body. It also makes up the ends of long bones.

Marrow and Blood Cells

Within the spongy bone tissue is marrow, the part of the bone that produces blood cells. The new blood cells travel from the marrow into the blood vessels that run throughout the bone. The blood brings nutrients to the bone cells and carries waste materials away.

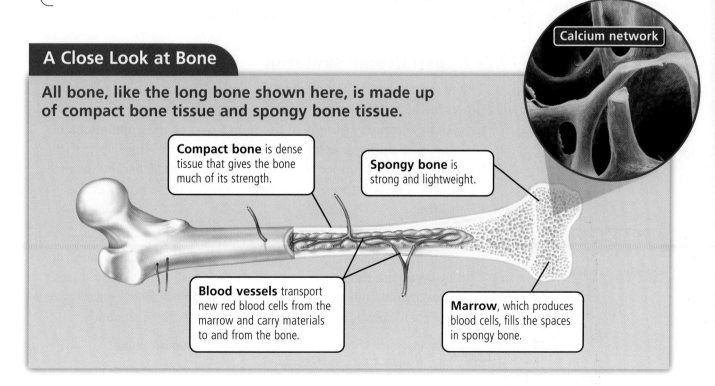

A Close Look at Bone

All bone, like the long bone shown here, is made up of compact bone tissue and spongy bone tissue.

Calcium network

Compact bone is dense tissue that gives the bone much of its strength.

Spongy bone is strong and lightweight.

Blood vessels transport new red blood cells from the marrow and carry materials to and from the bone.

Marrow, which produces blood cells, fills the spaces in spongy bone.

The skeleton is the body's framework.

Like the frame of a building, the skeleton provides the body's shape. The skeleton also works with other systems to allow movement. Scientists have identified two main divisions in the skeleton. These are the axial (AK-see-uhl) skeleton, which is the central part of the skeleton, and the appendicular (AP-uhn-DIHK-yuh-luhr) skeleton. Bones in the appendicular skeleton are attached to the axial skeleton. The diagram on page 177 labels some of the important bones in your skeleton.

The Axial Skeleton

VOCABULARY
Remember to add four squares for *axial skeleton* and *appendicular skeleton* to your notebook.

Imagine a line straight down your back. You can think of that line as an axis. Sitting, standing, and twisting are some of the motions that turn around the axis. The **axial skeleton** is the part of the skeleton that forms the axis. It provides support and protection. In the diagram, parts of the axial skeleton are colored in red.

The axial skeleton includes the skull, or the cranium (KRAY-nee-uhm). The major function of the cranium is protection of the brain. Most of the bones in the cranium do not move. The skull connects to the spinal column in a way that allows the head to move up and down as well as right and left.

Your spinal column makes up the main portion of the axial skeleton. The spinal column is made up of many bones called vertebrae. The many bones allow flexibility. If you run your finger along your back you will feel the vertebrae. Another set of bones belonging to the axial skeleton are the rib bones. The ribs function to protect the soft internal organs, such as the heart and lungs.

The Appendicular Skeleton

The diagram shows the bones in the appendicular skeleton in yellow. Bones in the **appendicular skeleton** function mainly to allow movement. The shoulder belongs to the upper part of the appendicular skeleton. The upper arm bone that connects to the shoulder is the longest bone in the upper body. It connects with the two bones of the lower arm. The wristbone is the end of one of these bones in the lower arm.

Assemble a skeleton.

The lower part of the body includes the legs and the hip bones. This part of the body bears all of the body's weight when you are standing. The leg bones are the strongest of all the bones in the skeleton. Just as the lower arm includes two bones, the lower leg has two bones. The larger of these two bones carries most of the weight of the body.

 How are the axial and appendicular skeletons alike? How are they different?

The Skeletal System

The skeletal system interacts with other body systems to allow this soccer player to stand, run, and kick.

- ■ axial skeleton
- □ appendicular skeleton

The **skull** protects the brain.

The lower jaw is the only bone in the skull that can move.

Twelve pairs of **ribs** protect the lungs and heart.

The shoulder blade is called the **scapula**.

The **vertebrae** of the spinal column protect the spinal cord and support the cranium and other bones.

The upper arm bone is called the **humerus**.

The lower arm bones are the **ulna** and **radius**.

The many bones in the wrist and the hand allow the hand to perform a great variety of activities.

The upper leg bone, called the **femur**, is the longest bone in the body.

The kneecap is called the **patella**.

The lower leg bones are called the **tibia** and the **fibula**.

There are 26 bones in the ankle and the foot.

READING VISUALS The word *appendicular* has the same root as the word *append,* which means to attach. How do you think this word applies to the appendicular skeleton?

The skeleton changes as the body develops and ages.

MAIN IDEA WEB Make a web of the important terms and details about the main idea: *The skeleton changes as the body develops and ages.*

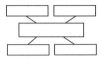

🔻 **REMINDER**

Density is the ratio of mass over volume. Bone density is a measure of the mass of a bone divided by the bone's volume.

You will remember that bones are living tissue. During infancy and childhood, bones grow as the rest of the body grows. Bones become harder as they stop growing. In adulthood, bones continue to change.

Infancy The skull of a newborn is made up of several bones that have spaces between them. As the brain grows, the skull also grows. During the growth of the skull, the spaces between the bones close.

Childhood Bone growth occurs at areas called growth plates. These growth plates are made of cartilage, a firm, flexible connective tissue. The length and shape of bones is determined by growth plates. Long bones grow at the ends of the bone surrounding growth plates.

Adolescence At the end of adolescence (AD-uhl-EHS-uhns) bones stop growing. The growth plate is the last portion of the bone to become hard. Once growth plates become hard, arms and legs stop growing and the skull plates fuse.

Adulthood Even after bones stop growing, they go through cycles in which old bone is broken down and new bone is formed. As people age, more bone is broken down than is formed. This can lead to a decrease in bone mass, which causes a decrease in bone density. The strength of bones depends upon their density. As people age, their bone density may decrease. Bones that are less dense may break more easily. Many doctors recommend that adults over a certain age get regular bone density tests.

Test of Bone Density

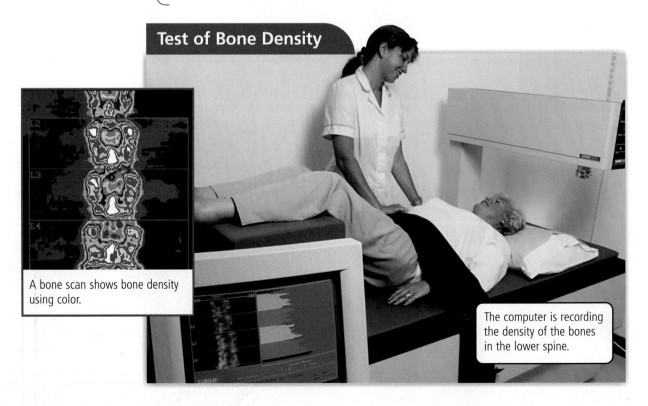

A bone scan shows bone density using color.

The computer is recording the density of the bones in the lower spine.

Joints connect parts of the skeletal system.

A joint is a place at which two parts of the skeletal system meet. There are three types of joints: immovable, slightly movable, and freely movable.

Immovable and Slightly Movable Joints An immovable joint locks bones together like puzzle pieces. The bones of your skull are connected by immovable joints. Slightly movable joints are able to flex slightly. Your ribs are connected to your sternum by slightly movable joints.

Freely Movable Joints Freely movable joints allow your body to bend and to move. Tissues called ligaments hold the bones together at movable joints. Other structures inside the joint cushion the bones and keep them from rubbing together. The entire joint also is surrounded by connective tissue.

Movable joints can be classified by the type of movement they produce. Think about the movement of your arm when you eat an apple. Your arm moves up, then down, changing the angle between your upper and lower arms. This is angular movement. The joint that produces this movement is called a hinge joint.

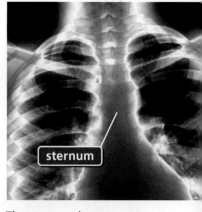
sternum

The sternum is an example of a slightly movable joint.

INVESTIGATE Movable Joints

How can you move at joints?

PROCEDURE

1. Perform several activities that involve your joints. Twist at the waist. Bend from your waist to one side. Reach into the air with one arm. Open and close your mouth. Push a book across your desk. Lift the book.

2. Record each activity and write a note describing the motion that you feel at each joint.

3. Try to see how many different ways you can move at joints.

WHAT DO YOU THINK?

- How was the motion you felt similar for each activity? How was it different?

- Based on your observations, identify two or more ways that joints move.

CHALLENGE Draw a diagram showing how you think each joint moves. How might you classify different types of joints based upon the way they move?

SKILL FOCUS
Observing

MATERIALS
book

TIME
20 minutes

179

Movable Joints

The joints in the elbow and hip allow different types of movement.

Angular movement (elbow)

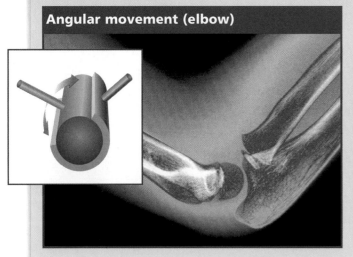

Rotational movement (hip)

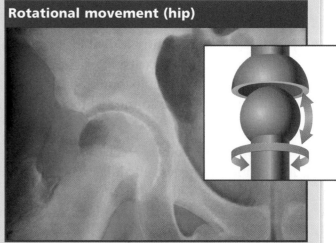

READING VISUALS **INFER** How do the structure and shape of each joint allow bones to move?

Your arm can also rotate from side to side, as it does when you turn a doorknob. Rotational movement like this is produced by a pivot joint in the elbow. You can also rotate your arm in a circle, like the motion of a softball pitcher winding up and releasing a ball. The joint in the shoulder that produces this type of rotational movement is called a ball-and-socket joint.

Joints also produce gliding movement. All joints glide, that is, one bone slides back and forth across another. In some cases, as with the joints in your backbone, a small gliding movement is the only movement the joint produces.

6.2 Review

KEY CONCEPTS

1. What are the functions of the two types of bone tissue?

2. What are the main divisions of the human skeleton?

3. Name three types of movement produced by movable joints and give an example of each.

CRITICAL THINKING

4. **Infer** What function do immovable joints in the skull perform? Think about the different stages of development in the human body.

5. **Analyze** Which type of movable joint allows the most movement? How does the joint's shape and structure contribute to this?

⬥ CHALLENGE

6. **Classify** The joints in your hand and wrist produce three different types of movement. Using your own wrist, classify the joint movement of the fingers, palm, and wrist. Support your answer.

Rates of Production

 MATH TUTORIAL

CLASSZONE.COM

Click on Math Tutorial for more help with unit rates.

Where do red blood cells come from? They are produced inside bone marrow at the center of long bones. An average of about 200 billion red blood cells per day are produced by a healthy adult. When a person produces too few red blood cells, a condition called anemia may occur. Doctors study rates of blood cell production to diagnose and treat anemia.

A rate is a ratio that compares two quantities of different units. The number of cells produced per 24 hours is an example of a rate.

Example

A healthy adult produces red blood cells at a rate greater than 166 billion cells per 24 hours. Suppose a man's body produces 8 billion red blood cells per 1 hour. Would he be considered anemic?

(1) Write the two rates as fractions.

$$\frac{8}{1} \qquad \frac{166}{24}$$

(2) Simplify the fractions, so that the denominators are both 1. To simplify, divide the numerator by the denominator.

$$\frac{8}{1} \qquad \frac{6.9}{1}$$

(3) Compare the two whole numbers. Is the first number $<$, $>$, or $=$ to the second number?

$$8 \qquad > \qquad 6.9$$

ANSWER The rate is greater than 6.9. The patient is not anemic.

Compare the following rates to see if they indicate that a person is anemic or normal.

1. For women, a normal rate is about 178 billion red blood cells per day. A certain woman produces 6 billion red blood cells per hour. Is her rate low or healthy?

2. Suppose a different woman produces 150 million (not billion) red blood cells per minute. How does that rate compare to 178 billion cells per day? Is it $<$, $>$, or $=$ to it?

3. Suppose a certain man is producing 135 million red blood cells per minute. Is that rate low or healthy?

CHALLENGE In the example above of a man producing 166 billion cells per day, calculate the percentage by which the rate would need to increase to bring it up to the average count of 200 billion per day.

6.3 The muscular system makes movement possible.

STANDARDS

7–3.3 Summarize the relationships of the major body systems (including the circulatory, respiratory, digestive, excretory, nervous, muscular, and skeletal systems).

VOCABULARY

muscular system p. 183
skeletal muscle p. 184
voluntary muscle p. 184
smooth muscle p. 184
involuntary muscle p. 184
cardiac muscle p. 184

BEFORE, you learned

- There are different types of bone tissue
- The human skeleton has two separate divisions
- Joints function in several different ways

NOW, you will learn

- About the functions of muscles
- About the different types of muscles and how they work
- How muscles grow and heal

EXPLORE Muscles

How do muscles change as you move?

PROCEDURE

① Sit on a chair with your feet on the floor.

② Place your hand around your leg. Straighten one leg as shown in the photograph.

③ Repeat step 2 several times.

WHAT DO YOU THINK?

- How did your muscles change during the activity?
- Record your observations.
- What questions do you have about the muscular system?

Muscles perform important functions.

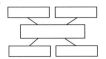

MAIN IDEA WEB
Make a web for the main idea: *Muscles perform important functions.*

Every movement of your body—from the beating of your heart, to the movement of food down your throat, to the blinking of your eyes—occurs because of muscles. Some movements are under your control, and other movements seem to happen automatically. However, muscles do more than produce movement. They perform other functions as well. Keeping body temperature stable and maintaining posture are two additional functions of muscles.

CHECK YOUR READING What are three functions that muscles perform?

Movement

The **muscular system** works with the skeletal system to allow movement. Like all muscles, the muscles that produce movement are made up of individual cells called muscle fibers. These fibers contract and relax.

Most of the muscles involved in moving the body work in pairs. As they contract, muscles shorten, pulling against bones. It may surprise you to know that muscles do not push. Rather, a muscle on one side of a bone pulls in one direction, while another muscle relaxes. Muscles are attached to bones by stretchy connective tissue.

RESOURCE CENTER
CLASSZONE.COM

Discover more about muscles.

Maintaining Body Temperature

Earlier you read that processes within the body require certain conditions, such as temperature and the right amount of water and other materials. The balance of conditions is called homeostasis. One of the functions of the muscular system is related to homeostasis. Muscles function to maintain body temperature.

When muscles contract, they release heat. Without this heat from muscle contraction, the body could not maintain its normal temperature. You may have observed the way your muscles affect your body temperature when you shiver. The quick muscle contractions that occur when you shiver release heat and raise your body temperature.

CHECK YOUR READING How do muscles help maintain homeostasis?

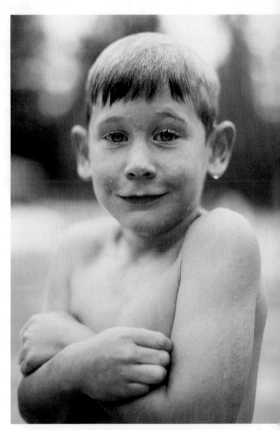

Muscles contract during shivering, raising body temperature.

Maintaining Posture

Have you ever noticed that you stand up straight without thinking about it, even though gravity is pulling your body down? Most muscles in your body are always a little bit contracted. This tension, or muscle tone, is present even when you are sleeping. The muscles that maintain posture relax completely only when you are unconscious.

Try standing on the balls of your feet for a few moments, or on one leg. When you are trying to balance or hold one position for any length of time, you can feel different muscles contracting and relaxing. Your muscles make constant adjustments to keep you sitting or standing upright. You don't have to think about these tiny adjustments; they happen automatically.

Your body has different types of muscle.

Your body has three types of muscle. All three types of muscle tissue share certain characteristics. For example, each type of muscle contracts and relaxes. Yet all three muscle types have different functions, and different types of muscle are found in different locations.

Skeletal Muscle

The muscles that are attached to your skeleton are called **skeletal muscles.** Skeletal muscle performs voluntary movement—that is, movement that you choose to make. Because they are involved in voluntary movement, skeletal muscles are also called **voluntary muscles.**

Skeletal muscle, like all muscle, is made of long fibers. The fibers are made up of many smaller bundles, as a piece of yarn is made up of strands of wool. One type of bundle allows your muscles to move slowly. Those muscles are called slow-twitch muscles. Another type of bundle allows your muscles to move quickly. These are called fast-twitch muscles. If you were a sprinter, you would want to develop your fast-twitch muscles. If you were a long distance runner, you would develop your slow-twitch muscles.

 CHECK YOUR READING What does it mean that skeletal muscles are voluntary muscles?

READING TIP

The root of the word *voluntary* comes from the Latin root *vol-*, meaning "wish." In the word *involuntary* the prefix *in-* suggests the meaning "unwished for." *Involuntary movement* means movement you can't control.

Smooth Muscle

Smooth muscle is found inside some organs, such as the intestines and the stomach. Smooth muscles perform automatic movement and are called **involuntary muscles.** In other words, smooth muscles work without your knowing it. You have no control over their movement. For example, smooth muscles line your stomach wall and push food through your digestive system. Smooth muscle fibers are not as long as skeletal muscle fibers. Also, unlike skeletal muscles, smooth muscles are not fast-twitch. Smooth muscles contract slowly.

VOCABULARY

Remember to add four squares for *involuntary muscles* and *voluntary muscles* to your notebook. Note differences in the two diagrams.

Cardiac Muscle

Your heart is made of **cardiac muscle.** Like smooth muscle, cardiac muscle moves without conscious control. Each cardiac muscle cell has a branched shape. The cells of the heart connect in a chain. These chains form webs of layered tissue that allow cardiac cells to contract together and make the heart beat. Just like the smooth muscle cells, the cardiac muscle cells contract slowly, except in emergencies.

 CHECK YOUR READING Compare and contrast the three types of muscle described: skeletal, smooth, and cardiac.

Muscle Tissue

The marchers in this band are using all three different types of muscle tissue.

250×

Cardiac muscle allows the hearts of the band members to pump blood as they march to the beat of the music.

150×

Smooth muscle in the air passages of the lungs allows the band members to breathe as they play their instruments.

360×

Skeletal muscle moves the legs of these marchers.

READING VISUALS Which movements of these band members are voluntary, and which are involuntary?

Skeletal muscles and tendons allow bones to move.

Skeletal muscles are attached to your bones by strong tissues called tendons. The tendons on the end of the muscle attach firmly to the bone. As the fibers in a muscle contract, they shorten and pull the tendon. The tendon, in turn, pulls the bone and makes it move.

You can feel your muscles moving your bones. Place your left arm, stretched out flat, in front of you on a table. Place the fingers of your right hand just above your left elbow. Bend your elbow and raise and lower your left arm. You are contracting your biceps. Can you feel the muscle pull on the tendon?

The dancers in the photograph are using many sets of muscles. The diagrams show how muscles and tendons work together to move bones. Muscles are shown in red. Notice how each muscle crosses a joint. Most skeletal muscles do. One end of the muscle attaches to one bone, crosses a joint, then attaches to a second bone. As the muscle contracts, it pulls on both bones. This pulling produces movement—in the case of these dancers, very exciting movement.

Skeletal muscles contract by shortening and pulling the tendon.

Muscle fibers can return to their original length after being shortened.

Muscles grow and heal.

Developing Muscles An infant's muscles cannot do very much. A baby cannot lift its head, because the neck muscles are not strong enough to support it. For the first few months of life, a baby needs extra support, until the neck muscles grow strong and can hold up the baby's head.

The rest of the skeletal muscles also have to develop and strengthen. During infancy and childhood and into adolescence, humans develop muscular coordination and become more graceful in their movements. Coordination reaches its natural peak in adolescence but can be further improved by additional training.

Exercise and Muscles When you exercise regularly, your muscles may get bigger. Muscles increase in size with some types of exercise, because their cells reproduce more rapidly in response to the increased activity. Exercise also stimulates growth of individual muscle cells, making them larger.

Stretching your muscles before exercise helps prevent injury.

You may have experienced sore muscles during or after exercising. During exercise, chemicals can build up in the muscles and make them cramp or ache. The muscle soreness you feel a day or so after exercise is caused by damage to the muscle fibers. The muscle fibers have been overstretched or torn. Such injuries take time to heal, because the body must remove injured cells, and new ones must form.

 Review

KEY CONCEPTS

1. What are the three main functions of the muscular system?
2. Make a rough outline of a human body and label places where you could find each of the three types of muscles.
3. Explain why you may be sore after exercise.

CRITICAL THINKING

4. **Apply** You are exercising and you begin to feel hot. Explain what is happening in your muscles.
5. **Analyze** Describe what happens in your neck muscles when you nod your head.

⬤ CHALLENGE

6. **Infer** The digestive system breaks down food and transports materials. How are the short length and slow movement of smooth muscle tissues in the stomach and intestines related to the functions of these organs?

CHAPTER INVESTIGATION

A Closer Look at Muscles

OVERVIEW AND PURPOSE You use the muscles in your body to do a variety of things. Walking, talking, reading the words on this page, and scratching your head are all actions that require muscles. How do your muscles interact with your bones? In this investigation you will

- examine chicken wings to see how the muscles and the bones interact
- compare the movement of the chicken wing with the movement of your own bones and muscles

▶ Problem

What are some characteristics of muscles?

▶ Hypothesize

Write a hypothesis to propose how muscles interact with bones. Your hypothesis should take the form of an "If . . . , then . . . , because . . ." statement.

▶ Procedure

MATERIALS
- uncooked chicken wing and leg (soaked in bleach)
- paper towels
- dissection tray
- scissors

1. Make a data table like the one shown on the sample notebook page. Put on your protective gloves. Be sure you are wearing gloves whenever you touch the chicken.

2. Obtain a chicken wing from your teacher. Rinse it in water and pat dry with a paper towel. Place it in the tray.

3. Extend the wing. In your notebook, draw a diagram of the extended wing. Be sure to include any visible external structures. Label the following on your diagram: lower limb, upper joint, and the wing tip.

4. Use scissors to remove the skin. Use caution so that you cut only through the skin. Peel back the skin and any fat so you can examine the muscles.

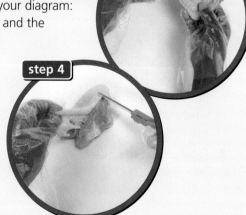

step 3

step 4

5 The muscles are the pink tissues that extend from one end of the bone to the other. Locate these in the upper wing and observe the way they move when you move the wing. Record your observations in your notebook.

6 Repeat this procedure for the muscles in the lower wing. In your notebook, draw a diagram of the muscles in the chicken wing.

7 There are also tendons in the chicken wing. These are the shiny white tissues at the end of the muscles. Add the tendons to your diagram.

8 Dispose of the chicken wing and parts according to your teacher's instructions. **Be sure to wash your hands well.**

▶ Observe and Analyze

Write It Up

1. **RECORD** Write a brief description of how the bones and muscles work together to allow movement.

2. **EVALUATE** What difficulties, if any, did you encounter in carrying out this experiment?

▶ Conclude

Write It Up

1. **INTERPRET** How does the chicken wing move when you bend it at the joint?

2. **OBSERVE** What happens when you pull on one of the wing muscles?

3. **COMPARE** Using your diagram of the chicken wing as an example, locate the same muscle groups in your own arm. How do they react when you bend your elbow?

4. **APPLY** What role do the tendons play in the movement of the muscles or bones?

▶ INVESTIGATE Further

CHALLENGE Using scissors, carefully remove the muscles and the tendons from the bones. Next find the ligaments, which are located between the bones. Add these to your diagram. Describe how you think ligaments function.

A Closer Look at Muscles
Problem What are some characteristics of muscles?

Table 1. Observations

Draw your diagrams	Write your observations
Extended wing	Muscles in the upper wing
Muscles in the wing	Muscles in the lower wing

Chapter Review

the **BIG** idea

The human body is made up of systems that work together to perform necessary functions.

CONTENT REVIEW
CLASSZONE.COM

◀ KEY CONCEPTS SUMMARY

1. The human body is complex.

You can think of the body as having five levels of organization: cells, tissues, organs, organ systems, and the whole organism itself. The different systems of the human body work together to maintain homeostasis.

Cells ① (cardiac muscle cells)

⑤ Organism (human)

② Tissue (cardiac muscle)   ③ Organ (heart)   ④ Organ system (circulatory system)

VOCABULARY
tissue p. 170
organ p. 171
organ system p. 172
homeostasis p. 172

2. The skeletal system provides support and protection.

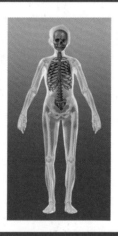

Bones are living tissue. The skeleton is the body's framework and has two main divisions, the **axial skeleton** and the **appendicular skeleton**. Bones come together at joints.

VOCABULARY
skeletal system p. 174
compact bone p. 175
spongy bone p. 175
axial skeleton p. 176
appendicular skeleton p. 176

3. The muscular system makes movement possible.

Types of muscle	Function
skeletal muscle, voluntary	moves bones, maintains posture, maintains body temperature
smooth muscle, involuntary	moves internal organs, such as the intestines
cardiac muscle, involuntary	pumps blood throughout the body

VOCABULARY
muscular system p. 183
skeletal muscle p. 184
voluntary muscle p. 184
smooth muscle p. 184
involuntary muscle p. 184
cardiac muscle p. 184

In one or two sentences describe how the vocabulary terms in each of the following pairs of words are related. Underline each vocabulary term in your answer.

1. cells, tissues

2. organs, organ systems

3. axial skeleton, appendicular skeleton

4. skeletal muscle, voluntary muscle

5. smooth muscle, involuntary muscle

6. compact bone, spongy bone

Reviewing Key Concepts

Multiple Choice *Choose the letter of the best answer.*

7. Which type of tissue carries electrical impulses from your brain?
   a. epithelial tissue
   b. muscle tissue
   c. nerve tissue
   d connective tissue

8. Connective tissue functions to provide
   a. support and strength
   b. messaging system
   c. movement
   d. heart muscle

9. Bone cells lie within a network made of
   a. tendons
   b. calcium
   c. marrow
   d. joints

10. The marrow produces
    a. spongy bone
    b. red blood cells
    c. compact bone
    d. calcium

11. Which bones are part of the axial skeleton?
    a. skull, shoulder blades, arm bones
    b. skull, spinal column, leg bones
    c. shoulder blades, spinal column, and hip bones
    d. skull, spinal column, ribs

12. Bones of the skeleton connect to each other at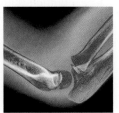
    a. tendons
    b. ligaments
    c. joints
    d. muscles

13. How do muscles contribute to homeostasis?
    a. They keep parts of the body together.
    b. They control the amount of water in the body.
    c. They help you move.
    d. They produce heat when they contract.

14. Cardiac muscle is found in the
    a. heart
    b. stomach
    c. intestines
    d. arms and legs

15. The stomach is made up of
    a. cardiac muscle
    b. skeletal muscle
    c. smooth muscle
    d. voluntary muscle

Short Answer *Write a short answer to each question.*

16. What is the difference between spongy bone and compact bone?

17. The root word *homeo* means "same," and the root word *stasis* means "to stay." How do these root words relate to the definition of *homeostasis*?

18. Hold the upper part of one arm between your elbow and shoulder with your opposite hand. Feel the muscles there. What happens to those muscles as you bend your arm?

19. **PROVIDE EXAMPLES** What are the levels of organization of the human body from simple to most complex? Give an example of each.

20. **CLASSIFY** There are four types of tissue in the human body: epithelial, nerve, muscle, and connective. How would you classify blood? Explain your reasoning.

21. **CONNECT** A clam shell is made of a calcium compound. The material is hard, providing protection to the soft body of a clam. It is also lightweight. Describe three ways in which the human skeleton is similar to a seashell. What is one important way in which it is different?

Use the diagram below to answer the next two questions

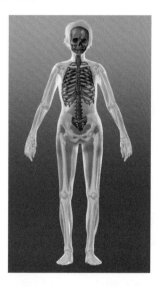

22. **SYNTHESIZE** Identify the types of joints that hold together the bones of the skull and sternum. How do these types of joints relate to the function of the skull and sternum?

23. **SYNTHESIZE** The human skeleton has two main divisions. Which skeleton do the arms and legs belong to? How do the joints that connect the arms to the shoulders and the legs to the hips relate to the function of this skeleton?

24. **COMPARE AND CONTRAST** How is the skeletal system of your body like the framework of a house or building? How is it different?

25. **SUMMARIZE** Describe three important functions of the skeleton.

26. **APPLY** The joints in the human body can be described as producing three types of movement. Relate these three types of movement to the action of brushing your teeth.

27. **COMPARE AND CONTRAST** When you stand, the muscles in your legs help to keep you balanced. Some of the muscles on both sides of your leg bones contract. How does this differ from how the muscles behave when you start to walk?

28. **INFER** Muscles are tissues that are made up of many muscle fibers. A muscle fiber can either be relaxed or contracted. Some movements you do require very little effort, like picking up a piece of paper. Others require a lot of effort, like picking up a book bag. How do you think a muscle produces the effort needed for a small task compared with a big task?

the **BIG** idea

29. **INFER** Look again at the picture on pages 166–167. Now that you have finished the chapter, how would you change or add details to your answer to the question on the photograph?

30. **SUMMARIZE** Write a paragraph explaining how skeletal muscles, bones, and joints work together to allow the body to move and be flexible. Underline the terms in your paragraph.

UNIT PROJECTS

If you are doing a unit project, make a folder for your project. Include in your folder a list of resources you will need, the date on which the project is due, and a schedule to track your progress. Begin gathering data.

Interpreting Diagrams

The action of a muscle pulling on a bone can be compared to a simple machine called a lever. A lever is a rod that moves about a fixed point called the fulcrum. Effort at one end of the rod can move a load at the other end. In the human body, a muscle supplies the effort needed to move a bone—the lever. The joint is the fulcrum, and the load is the weight of the body part being moved. There are three types of levers, which are classified according to the position of the fulcrum, the effort, and the load.

Read the text and study the diagrams, and then choose the best answer for the questions that follow.

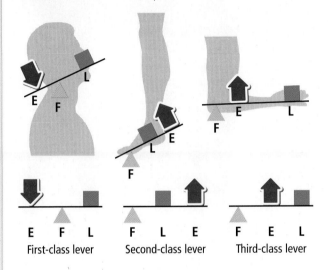

First-class lever   Second-class lever   Third-class lever

1. In a first-class lever
   a. the load is at end of the lever opposite the fulcrum
   b. the load is between the effort and the fulcrum
   c. the fulcrum is between the load and the effort
   d. the effort and load are on the same side

2. What is true of all levers?
   a. The fulcrum must be located at the center of a lever.
   b. The force of the load and effort point in the same direction.
   c. The load and effort are on the same side of the fulcrum.
   d. The lever exerts a force in a direction opposite the weight of the load.

3. The lever represents what structure in the human body?
   a. a joint   **c.** a muscle
   b. a bone   **d.** a ligament

4. The main point of the diagram is to show
   a. how bones work
   b. that there are three types of joints and how they are classified as levers
   c. where to apply a force
   d. the forces involved in moving parts of the body

Extended Response

Use the diagrams above and terms from the word box to answer the next question. Underline each term you use in your answer.

fulcrum	load	effort	rod
bone	muscle	joint	

5. Suppose you had a heavy box to lift. Your first thought might be to bend over, stretch out your arms, and grab the box. Your body would be acting as a simple machine. Identify the type of lever this is and the parts of this machine.

6. A doctor would advise you not to lift a heavy object, like a box, simply by bending over and picking it up. That action puts too much strain on your back. It is better to bend your knees, hold the box close to your body, and then lift. How does this way of lifting change how you are using your body?

CHAPTER

7 Absorption, Digestion, and Exchange

the BIG idea

Systems in the body obtain and process materials and remove waste.

Key Concepts

SECTION
1 **The respiratory system gets oxygen and removes carbon dioxide.**
Learn how the respiratory system functions.

SECTION
2 **The digestive system breaks down food.**
Learn how the digestive system provides cells with necessary materials.

SECTION
3 **The urinary system removes waste materials.**
Learn how the urinary system removes wastes.

Internet Preview

CLASSZONE.COM
Chapter 7 online resources:
Content Review, two
Visualizations, two Resource
Centers, Math Tutorial,
Test Practice.

What materials does your body need to function properly?

EXPLORE (the BIG idea)

Mirror, Mirror

Hold a small hand mirror in front of your mouth. Slowly exhale onto the surface of the mirror. What do you see? Exhale a few more times onto the mirror, observing the interaction of your breath with the cool surface of the mirror.

Observe and Think What did you see on the surface of the mirror? What does this tell you about the content of the air that you exhale?

Water Everywhere

Keep track of how much liquid you drink in a 24-hour period of time. Do not include carbonated or caffeinated beverages. Water, juice, and milk can count. Add up the number of ounces of liquid you drink in that period of time.

Observe and Think How many ounces did you drink in one day? Do you drink fluids only when you feel thirsty?

Internet Activity: Lung Movement

Go to **ClassZone.com** to watch a visualization of lung and diaphragm movement during respiration. Observe how movements of the diaphragm and other muscles affect the lungs.

Observe and Think How do the diaphragm and lungs move during inhalation? during exhalation? Why do movements of the diaphragm cause the lungs to move?

NSTA scilinks.org
SCi LINKS

Digestion **Code: MDL045**

Getting Ready to Learn

◀ CONCEPT REVIEW

- Cells make up tissues, and tissues make up organs.
- The body's systems interact.
- The body's systems work to maintain internal conditions.

◀ VOCABULARY REVIEW

homeostasis p. 172
smooth muscle p. 184
energy *See Glossary.*

ⓘ CONTENT REVIEW
CLASSZONE.COM
Review concepts and vocabulary.

▶ TAKING NOTES

OUTLINE

As you read, copy the blue headings on your paper in the form of an outline. Then add notes in your own words that summarize what you read.

VOCABULARY STRATEGY

Think about a vocabulary term as a **magnet word** diagram. Write the other terms or ideas related to that term around it.

See the Note-Taking Handbook on pages R45–R51.

SCIENCE NOTEBOOK

THE RESPIRATORY SYSTEM GETS OXYGEN AND REMOVES CARBON DIOXIDE.

A. Your body needs oxygen.
  1. Oxygen is used to release energy
  2. Oxygen is in air you breathe

B. Structures in the respiratory system function together
  1. nose, throat, trachea
  2. lungs

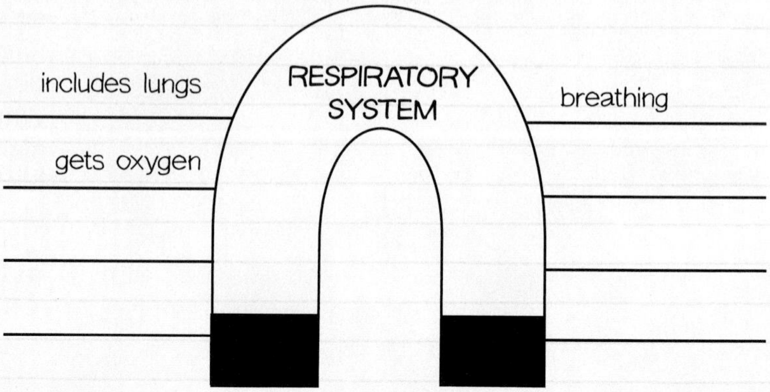

includes lungs   RESPIRATORY SYSTEM   breathing

gets oxygen

KEY CONCEPT

7.1 The respiratory system gets oxygen and removes carbon dioxide.

STANDARDS

7–3.2 Recall the major organs of the human body and their function within their particular body system.

7–3.3 Summarize the relationships of the major body systems (including the circulatory, respiratory, digestive, excretory, nervous, muscular, and skeletal systems).

VOCABULARY

respiratory system p. 197
cellular respiration p. 199

◀ **BEFORE, you learned**

- Cells, tissues, organs, and organ systems work together
- Organ systems provide for the body's needs
- Organ systems are important to the body's survival

▶ **NOW, you will learn**

- About the structures of the respiratory system that function to exchange gases
- About the process of cellular respiration
- About other functions of the respiratory system

EXPLORE Breathing

How do your ribs move when you breathe?

PROCEDURE

① Place your hands on your ribs.

② Breathe in and out several times, focusing on what happens when you inhale and exhale.

③ Record your observations in your notebook.

WHAT DO YOU THINK?

- What movement did you observe?
- Think about your observations. What questions do you have as a result of your observations?

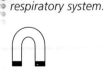

VOCABULARY
Make a word magnet diagram for the term *respiratory system.*

Your body needs oxygen.

During the day, you eat and drink only a few times, but you breathe thousands of times. In fact, breathing is a sign of life. The body is able to store food and liquid, but it is unable to store very much oxygen. The **respiratory system** is the body system that functions to get oxygen from the environment and remove carbon dioxide and other waste products from your body. The respiratory system interacts with the environment and with other body systems.

The continuous process of moving and using oxygen involves mechanical movement and chemical reactions. Air is transported into your lungs by mechanical movements, and oxygen is used during chemical reactions that release energy in your cells.

 CHECK YOUR READING What are the two main functions of your respiratory system?

Exchanging Oxygen and Carbon Dioxide

Like almost all living things, the human body needs oxygen to survive. Without oxygen, cells in the body die quickly. How does the oxygen you need get to your cells? Oxygen, along with other gases, enters the body when you inhale. Oxygen is then transported to cells throughout the body by red blood cells.

The air that you breathe contains only about 20 percent oxygen and less than 1 percent carbon dioxide. Almost 80 percent of air is nitrogen gas. The air that you exhale contains more carbon dioxide and less oxygen than the air that you inhale. It's important that you exhale carbon dioxide because high levels of it will damage, even destroy, cells.

In cells and tissues, proper levels of both oxygen and carbon dioxide are essential. Recall that systems in the body work together to maintain homeostasis. If levels of oxygen or carbon dioxide change, your nervous system signals the need to breathe faster or slower.

The photograph shows how someone underwater maintains proper levels of carbon dioxide and oxygen. The scuba diver needs to inhale oxygen from a tank. She removes carbon dioxide wastes with other gases when she exhales into the water. The bubbles you see in the water are formed when she exhales.

 CHECK YOUR READING What gases are in the air that you breathe?

Gas Exchange

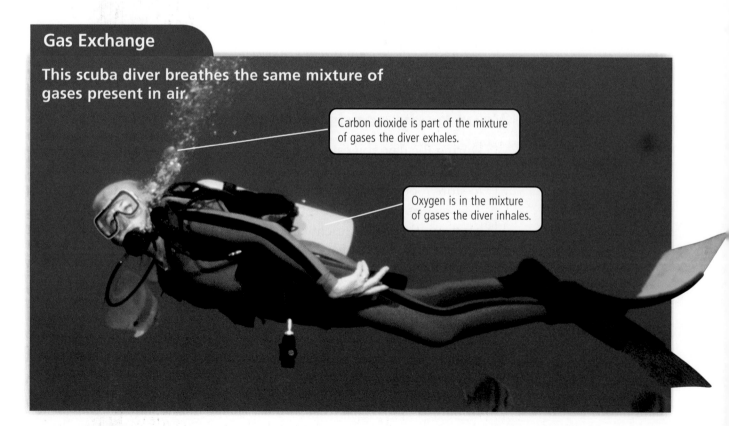

This scuba diver breathes the same mixture of gases present in air.

Carbon dioxide is part of the mixture of gases the diver exhales.

Oxygen is in the mixture of gases the diver inhales.

INVESTIGATE Lungs

How does air move in and out of lungs?

SKILL FOCUS
Making Models

PROCEDURE

1 Create a model of your lungs as shown. Insert an uninflated balloon into the top of the plastic bottle. While squeezing the bottle to force out some air, stretch the end of the balloon over the lip of the bottle. The balloon should still be open to the outside air. Tape the balloon in place with duct tape to make a tight seal

2 Release the bottle so that it expands back to its normal shape. Observe what happens to the balloon. Squeeze and release the bottle several times while observing the balloon. Record your observations.

WHAT DO YOU THINK?

- Describe, in words, what happens when you squeeze and release the bottle.

- How do you think your lungs move when you inhale? when you exhale?

CHALLENGE Design an addition to your model that could represent a muscle called the diaphragm. What materials do you need? How would this work? Your teacher may be able to provide additional materials so you can test your model. Be sure to come up with a comprehensive list of materials as well as a specific diagram.

MATERIALS
- one medium balloon
- 1-L clear plastic bottle with labels removed
- duct tape

TIME
15 minutes

Cellular Respiration

Inside your cells, a process called **cellular respiration** uses oxygen in chemical reactions that release energy. The respiratory system works with the digestive and circulatory systems to make cellular respiration possible. Cellular respiration requires glucose, or sugars, which you get from food, in addition to oxygen, which you get from breathing. These materials are transported to every cell in your body through blood vessels. You will learn more about the digestive and circulatory systems later in this unit.

During cellular respiration, your cells use oxygen and glucose to release energy. Carbon dioxide is a waste product of the process. Carbon dioxide must be removed from cells.

VOCABULARY
Add a magnet diagram for *cellular respiration* to your notebook. Include the word *energy* in your diagram.

 What three body systems are involved in cellular respiration?

Structures in the respiratory system function together.

OUTLINE

Add *Structures in the respiratory system function together* to your outline. Be sure to include the six respiratory structures in your outline.

I. Main idea
   A. Supporting idea
      1. Detail
      2. Detail
   B. Supporting idea

The respiratory system is made up of many structures that allow you to move air in and out of your body, communicate, and keep out harmful materials.

Nose, Throat, and Trachea When you inhale, air enters your body through your nose or mouth. Inside your nose, tiny hairs called cilia filter dirt and other particles out of the air. Mucus, a sticky liquid in your nasal cavity, also helps filter air by trapping particles such as dirt and pollen as air passes by. The nasal cavity warms the air slightly before it moves down your throat toward a tubelike structure called the windpipe, or trachea (TRAY-kee-uh). A structure called the epiglottis (EHP-ih-GLAHT-ihs) keeps air from entering your stomach.

Lungs The lungs are two large organs located on either side of your heart. When you inhale, air enters the throat, passes through the trachea, and moves into the lungs through structures called bronchial tubes. Bronchial tubes branch throughout the lungs into smaller and smaller tubes. At the ends of the smallest tubes, air enters tiny air sacs called alveoli. The walls of the alveoli are only one cell thick. In fact, one page in this book is much thicker than the walls of the alveoli. Oxygen passes from inside the alveoli through the thin walls and diffuses into the blood. At the same time, carbon dioxide waste passes from the blood into the alveoli.

CHECK YOUR READING Through which structures does oxygen move into the lungs?

Ribs and Diaphragm If you put your hands on your ribs and take a deep breath, you can feel your ribs expand. The rib cage encloses a space inside your body called the thoracic (thuh-RAS-ihk) cavity. Some ribs are connected by cartilage to the breastbone or to each other, which makes the rib cage flexible. This flexibility allows the rib cage to expand when you breathe and make room for the lungs to expand and fill with air.

A large muscle called the diaphragm (DY-uh-FRAM) stretches across the floor of the thoracic cavity. When you inhale, your diaphragm contracts and pulls downward, which makes the thoracic cavity expand. This movement causes the lungs to push downward, filling the extra space. At the same time, other muscles draw the ribs outward and expand the lungs. Air rushes into the lungs, and inhalation is complete. When the diaphragm and other muscles relax, the process reverses and you exhale.

RESOURCE CENTER
CLASSZONE.COM

Explore the respiratory system.

CHECK YOUR READING Describe how the diaphragm and the rib cage move.

Respiratory System

The structures in the respiratory system allow this flutist to play music.

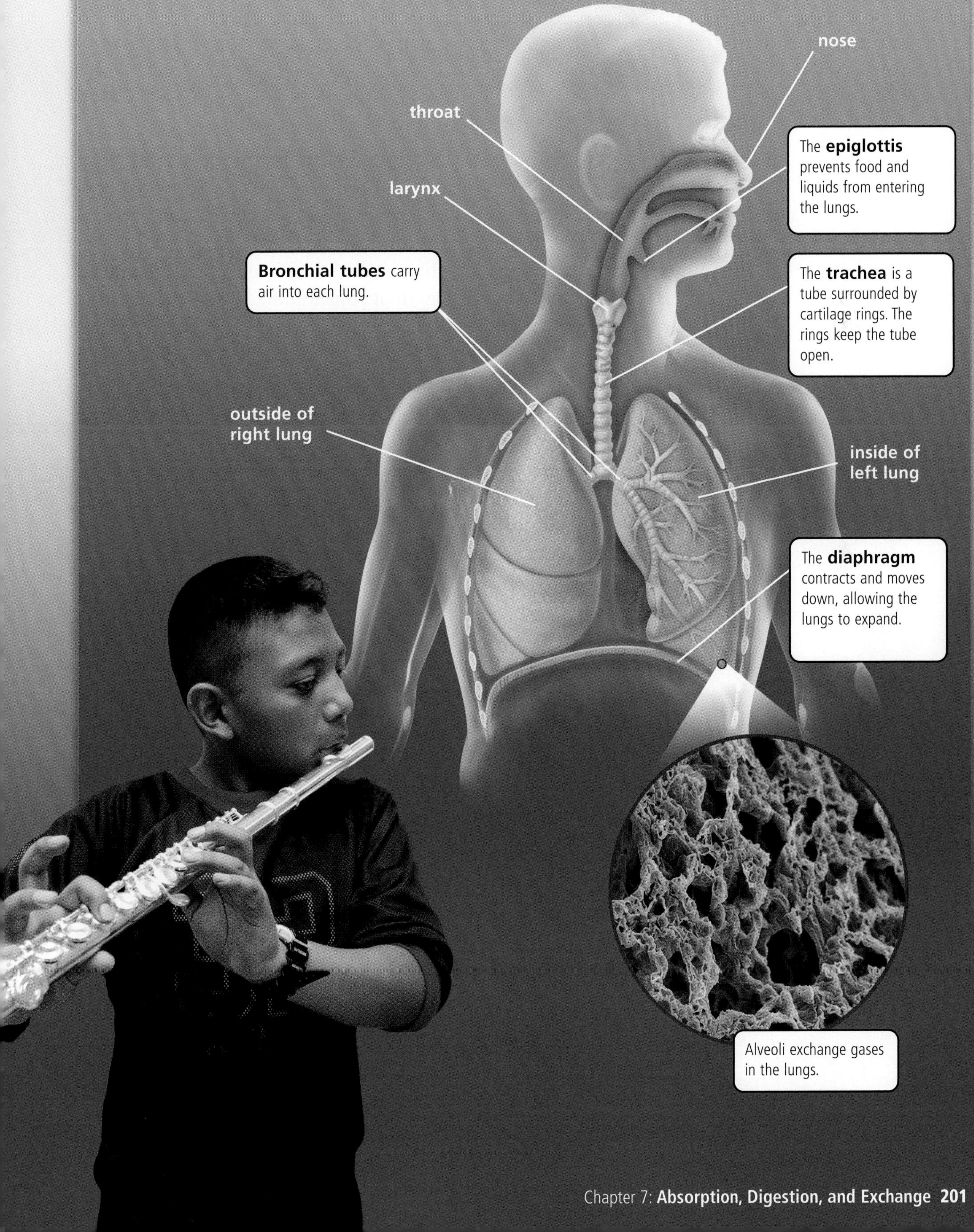

nose

throat

larynx

The **epiglottis** prevents food and liquids from entering the lungs.

Bronchial tubes carry air into each lung.

The **trachea** is a tube surrounded by cartilage rings. The rings keep the tube open.

outside of right lung

inside of left lung

The **diaphragm** contracts and moves down, allowing the lungs to expand.

Alveoli exchange gases in the lungs.

The respiratory system is also involved in other activities.

In addition to providing oxygen and removing carbon dioxide, the respiratory system is involved in other activities of the body. Speaking and singing, along with actions such as sneezing, can be explained in terms of how the parts of the respiratory system work together.

Speech and Other Respiratory Movements

If you place your hand on your throat and hum softly, you can feel your vocal cords vibrating. Air moving over your vocal cords allows you to produce sound, and the muscles in your throat, mouth, cheeks, and lips allow you to form sound into words. The vocal cords are folds of tissue in the larynx. The larynx, sometimes called the voice box, is a two-inch, tube-shaped organ about the length of your thumb, located in the neck, at the top of the trachea. When you speak, the vocal cords become tight, squeeze together, and force air from the lungs to move between them. The air causes the vocal cords to vibrate and produce sound.

How Speech Works

Sound is formed by structures in the respiratory system.

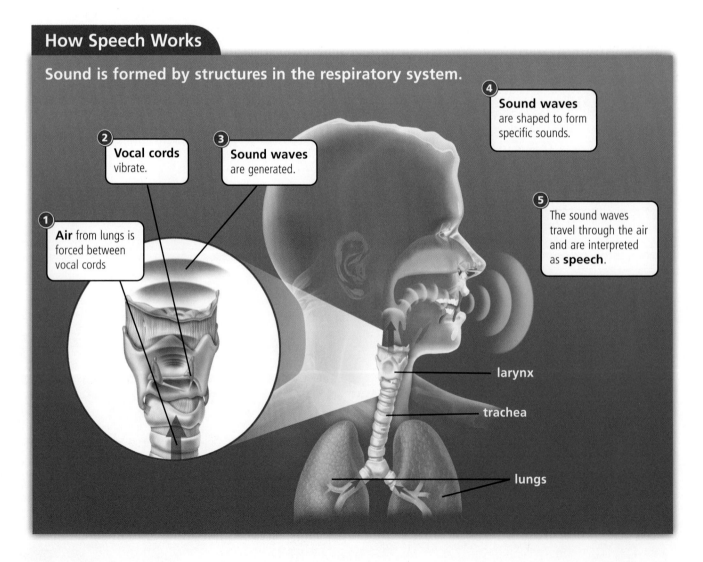

4 Sound waves are shaped to form specific sounds.

2 Vocal cords vibrate.

3 Sound waves are generated.

5 The sound waves travel through the air and are interpreted as **speech**.

1 Air from lungs is forced between vocal cords

larynx

trachea

lungs

Some movements of the respiratory system allow you to clear particles out of your nose and throat or to express emotion. The respiratory system is involved when you cough or sneeze. Sighing, yawning, laughing, and crying also involve the respiratory system.

Sighing and yawning both involve taking deep breaths. A sigh is a long breath followed by a shorter exhalation. A yawn is a long breath taken through a wide-open mouth. Laughing and crying are movements that are very similar to each other. In fact, sometimes it's difficult to see the difference between laughing and crying.

The respiratory system also allows you to hiccup. A hiccup is a sudden inhalation that makes the diaphragm contract. Several systems are involved when you hiccup. Air rushes into the throat, causing the diaphragm to contract. When the diaphragm contracts, the air passageway between the vocal cords closes. The closing of this passageway produces the sound of the hiccup. Hiccups can be caused by eating too fast, sudden temperature changes, and stress.

Water Removal

Hiccups, coughs, yawns, and all other respiratory movements, including speaking and breathing, release water from your body into the environment. Water is lost through sweat, urine, and exhalations of air. When it is cold enough outside, you can see your breath in the air. That is because the water vapor you exhale condenses into larger droplets when it moves from your warm body to the cold air.

Water leaves your body through your breath every time you exhale.

7.1 Review

KEY CONCEPTS

1. How is oxygen used by your body's cells?
2. What are the structures in the respiratory system and what do they do?
3. In addition to breathing, what functions does the respiratory system perform?

CRITICAL THINKING

4. **Sequence** List in order the steps that occur when you exhale.
5. **Compare and Contrast** How is the air you inhale different from the air you exhale?

⬤ CHALLENGE

6. **Hypothesize** Why do you think a person breathes more quickly when exercising?

YOGA INSTRUCTOR

Breathing and Yoga

If you're reading this, you must be breathing. Are you thinking about how you are breathing? Yoga instructors help their students learn deep, slow breathing. The practice of yoga uses an understanding of the respiratory system as a tool for healthy exercise.

nostrils

Nostril Breathing

An important aspect of breathing is removing wastes from the body:
- Yoga instructors teach students to inhale through the nostrils and exhale through the mouth.
- The nostrils filter dust and other particles, keeping dirt out of the lungs.
- The nostrils also warm the air as it enters the body.

Abdominal Breathing

Yoga instructors tell students to slowly expand and release the diaphragm:
- The diaphragm is a muscle below the lungs.
- When the muscle contracts, air enters into the lungs.
- When it relaxes, air is pushed out of the lungs.

lungs

diaphragm muscle

Full Lung Breathing

Yoga instructors help students breathe in slowly so that first the abdomen expands, then the rib cage area, and finally the upper chest by the shoulders. When students exhale, they collapse the diaphragm, then release the chest, and lastly relax the shoulders.

EXPLORE

1. **APPLY** Try one of the three breathing methods described. Start by taking a few slow deep breaths; then try the yoga breathing. Count to 4 as you inhale, and to 4 again breathing out. How do you feel after each breath?

2. **CHALLENGE** Choose one of the breathing methods above. Describe what happens to air each time you inhale and exhale. Draw or write your answer.

7.2 The digistive system breaks down food.

McDougal Littell Science

SOUTH CAROLINA

STANDARDS

7–3.2 Recall the major organs of the human body and their function within their particular body system.

7–3.3 Summarize the relationships of the major body systems (including the circulatory, respiratory, digestive, excretory, nervous, muscular, and skeletal systems).

VOCABULARY

nutrient p. 205
digestion p. 206
digestive system p. 206
peristalsis p. 206

◄ BEFORE, you learned

- The respiratory system takes in oxygen and expels waste
- Oxygen is necessary for cellular respiration
- The respiratory system is involved in speech and water removal

▶ NOW, you will learn

- About the role of digestion in providing energy and materials
- About the chemical and mechanical process of digestion
- How materials change as they move through the digestive system

---

EXPLORE Digestion

How does the digestive system break down fat?

PROCEDURE

① Using a dropper, place 5 mL of water into a test tube. Add 5 mL of vegetable oil. Seal the test tube with a screw-on top. Shake the test tube for 10 seconds, then place it in a test tube stand. Record your observations.

② Drop 5 mL of dish detergent into the test tube. Seal the tube. Shake the test tube for 10 seconds, then place in the stand. Observe the mixture for 2 minutes. Record your observations.

MATERIALS

- water
- graduated cylinders
- test tube with cap
- vegetable oil
- test tube stand
- liquid dish detergent

WHAT DO YOU THINK?

- What effect does detergent have on the mixture of oil and water?
- How do you think your digestive system might break down fat?

The body needs energy and materials.

After not eating for a while, have you ever noticed how little energy you have to do the simplest things? You need food to provide energy for your body. You also need materials from food. Most of what you need comes from nutrients within food. **Nutrients** are important substances that enable the body to move, grow, and maintain homeostasis. Proteins, carbohydrates, fats, and water are some of the nutrients your body needs.

You might not think of water as a nutrient, but it is necessary for all living things. More than half of your body is made up of water.

Protein is another essential nutrient; it is the material that the body uses for growth and repair. Cells in your body—such as those composing muscles, bones, and skin—are built of proteins. Carbohydrates are nutrients that provide cells with energy. Carbohydrates make up cellulose, which helps move materials through the digestive system. Another nutrient, fat, stores energy.

Before your body can use these nutrients, they must be broken into smaller substances. **Digestion** is the process of breaking down food into usable materials. Your digestive system transforms the energy and materials in food into forms your body can use.

The digestive system moves and breaks down food.

VISUALIZATION
CLASSZONE.COM

Observe the process of peristalsis.

Your **digestive system** performs the complex jobs of moving and breaking down food. Material is moved through the digestive system by wavelike contractions of smooth muscles. This muscular action is called **peristalsis** (PEHR-ih-STAWL-sihs). Mucous glands throughout the system keep the material moist so it can be moved easily, and the muscles contract to push the material along. The muscles move food along in much the same way as you move toothpaste from the bottom of the tube with your thumbs. The body has complicated ways of moving food, and it also has complicated ways of breaking down food. The digestive system processes food in two ways: physically and chemically.

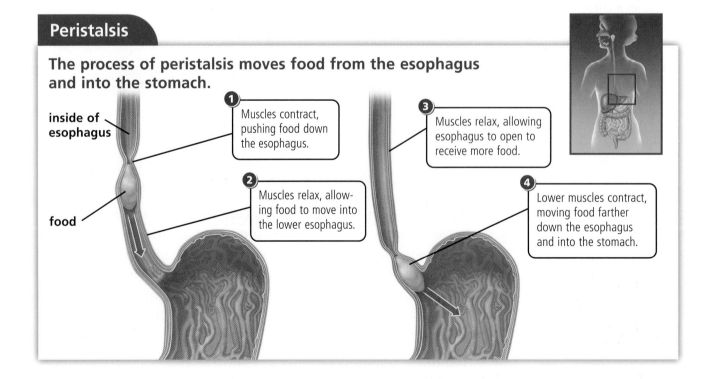

Peristalsis

The process of peristalsis moves food from the esophagus and into the stomach.

inside of esophagus

food

1 Muscles contract, pushing food down the esophagus.

2 Muscles relax, allowing food to move into the lower esophagus.

3 Muscles relax, allowing esophagus to open to receive more food.

4 Lower muscles contract, moving food farther down the esophagus and into the stomach.

INVESTIGATE Chemical Digestion

How does saliva affect starch?

PROCEDURE

(1) Cut two slices of the same thickness from the center of a potato. Lay the slices on a plate or tray.

(2) Using a dropper, add 15 drops of solution A to one potato slice. Add 15 drops of water to the other potato slice. Observe both potato slices for several minutes. Record your observations.

WHAT DO YOU THINK?

• What evidence did you see that starch is being broken down?

• How would you identify the substance left by the breakdown of starch?

• What is the purpose of the water in this activity?

CHALLENGE How could you change your experiment to model mechanical digestion? What structures in your mouth mechanically break down food?

SKILL FOCUS
Making Models

MATERIALS
• cooked potato slices
• droppers
• solution A
• water

TIME
25 minutes

Mechanical Digestion

Physical changes, which are sometimes called mechanical changes, break food into smaller pieces. You chew your food with your teeth so you are able to swallow it. Infants without teeth need an adult to cut up or mash food for them. They need soft food that they can swallow without chewing. Your stomach also breaks down food mechanically by mashing and pounding it during peristalsis.

Chemical Digestion

Chemical changes actually change food into different substances. For example, chewing a cracker produces a physical change—the cracker is broken into small pieces. At the same time, liquid in the mouth called saliva produces a chemical change—starches in the cracker are changed to sugars. If you chew a cracker, you may notice that after you have chewed it for a few seconds, it begins to taste sweet. The change in taste is a sign of a chemical reaction.

VOCABULARY
Don't forget to add magnet word diagrams for *digestion, digestive system,* and *peristalsis* to your notebook.

 CHECK YOUR READING What are the two types of changes that take place during digestion?

Materials are broken down as they move through the digestive tract.

The digestive system contains several organs. Food travels through organs in the digestive tract: the mouth, esophagus, stomach, small intestine, and large intestine. Other organs, such as the pancreas, liver, and gall bladder, release chemicals that are necessary for chemical digestion. The diagram on page 209 shows the major parts of the entire digestive system.

READING TiP

As you read about the digestive tract, look at the structures on page 209.

Mouth and Esophagus Both mechanical and chemical digestion begin in the mouth. The teeth break food into small pieces. The lips and tongue position food so that you can chew. When food is in your mouth, salivary glands in your mouth release saliva, which softens the food and begins chemical digestion. The tongue pushes the food to the back of the mouth and down the throat while swallowing.

 What part does the mouth play in digestion?

When you swallow, your tongue pushes food down into your throat. Food then travels down the esophagus to the stomach. The muscle contractions of peristalsis move solid food from the throat to the stomach in about eight seconds. Liquid foods take about two seconds.

Stomach Strong muscles in the stomach further mix and mash food particles. The stomach also uses chemicals to break down food. Some of the chemicals made by the stomach are acids. These acids are so strong that they could eat through the stomach itself. To prevent this, the cells of the stomach's lining are replaced about every three days, and the stomach lining is coated with mucus.

Small Intestine Partially digested food moves from the stomach to the small intestine. There, chemicals released by the pancreas, liver, and gallbladder break down nutrients. Most of the nutrients broken down in digestion are absorbed in the small intestine. Structures called villi are found throughout the small intestine. These structures contain folds that absorb nutrients from proteins, carbohydrates, and fats. Once absorbed by the villi, nutrients are transported by the circulatory system around the body. You will read more about the circulatory system in Chapter 8.

Large Intestine In the large intestine, water and some other nutrients are absorbed from the digested material. Most of the solid material then remaining is waste material, which is compacted and stored. Eventually it is eliminated through the rectum.

Villi allow broken-down nutrients to be absorbed into your bloodstream.

 Where in your digestive system does mechanical digestion occur?

Digestive System

As food moves through the digestive tract, structures of the digestive system break it down and absorb necessary materials.

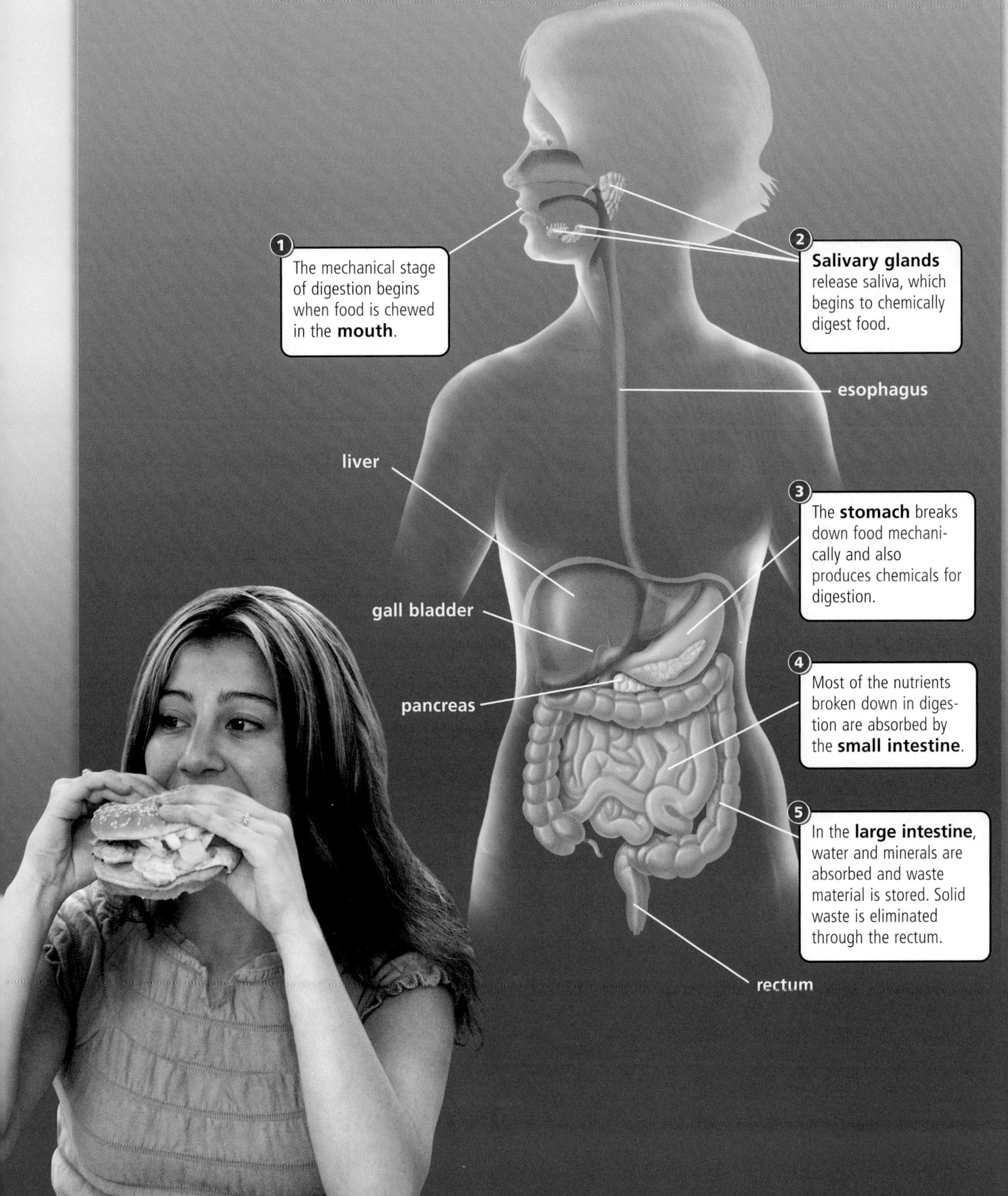

1 The mechanical stage of digestion begins when food is chewed in the **mouth**.

2 **Salivary glands** release saliva, which begins to chemically digest food.

esophagus

liver

3 The **stomach** breaks down food mechanically and also produces chemicals for digestion.

gall bladder

pancreas

4 Most of the nutrients broken down in digestion are absorbed by the **small intestine**.

5 In the **large intestine**, water and minerals are absorbed and waste material is stored. Solid waste is eliminated through the rectum.

rectum

Other organs aid digestion and absorption.

The digestive organs not in the digestive tract—the liver, gallbladder, and pancreas—also play crucial roles in your body. Although food does not move through them, all three of these organs aid in chemical digestion by producing or concentrating important chemicals.

Liver The liver—the largest internal organ of the body—is located in your abdomen, just above your stomach. Although you can survive losing a portion of your liver, it is an important organ. The liver filters blood, cleansing it of harmful substances, and stores unneeded nutrients for later use in the body. It produces a golden yellow substance called bile, which is able to break down fats, much like the way soap breaks down oils. The liver also breaks down medicines and produces important proteins, such as those that help clot blood if you get a cut.

Gallbladder The gallbladder is a tiny pear-shaped sac connected to the liver. Bile produced in the liver is stored and concentrated in the gallbladder. The bile is then secreted into the small intestine.

Pancreas Located between the stomach and the small intestine, the pancreas produces chemicals that are needed as materials move between the two. The pancreas quickly lowers the acidity in the small intestine and breaks down proteins, fats, and starch. The chemicals produced by the pancreas are extremely important for digesting and absorbing food substances. Without these chemicals, you could die of starvation, even with plenty of food in your system. Your body would not be able to process and use the food for energy without the pancreas.

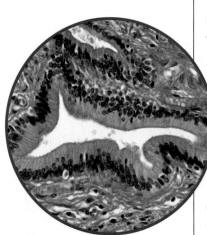

Bile is transferred from the liver to the gallbladder and small intestines through the bile duct.

 CHECK YOUR READING How does the pancreas aid in digestion?

7.2 Review

KEY CONCEPTS

1. List three of the functions of the digestive system.

2. Give one example each of mechanical digestion and chemical digestion.

3. How does your stomach process food?

CRITICAL THINKING

4. **Apply** Does an antacid deal with mechanical or chemical digestion?

5. **Apply** You have just swallowed a bite of apple. Describe what happens as the apple moves through your digestive system. Include information about what happens to the material in the apple.

CHALLENGE

6. **Compare and Contrast** Describe the roles of the large and the small intestines. How are they similar? How are they different?

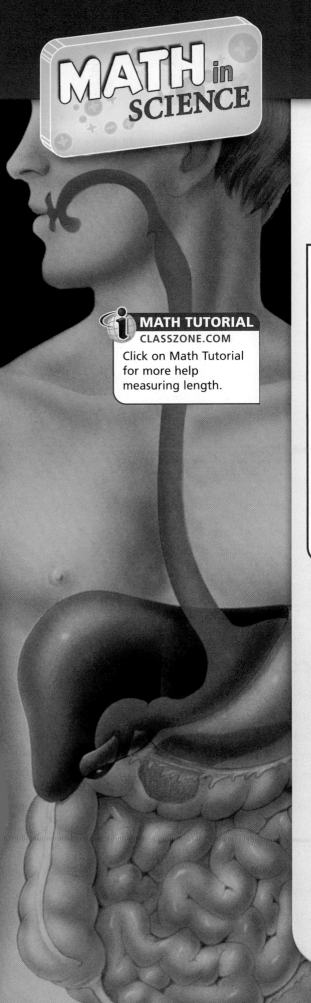

Internal Measurement

It wouldn't be useful if someone told you the length of your tongue in meters, or the length of a tooth in centimeters. To be meaningful, these measurements must be given in appropriate units.

MATH TUTORIAL
CLASSZONE.COM
Click on Math Tutorial for more help measuring length.

Example

Your esophagus is about the length of your forearm. Choose the appropriate units to measure its length. Would meters, centimeters, or millimeters be most appropriate?

(1) Look at your arm from your wrist to your elbow. It is about the same as a rolling pin. You don't need to measure your forearm to see that a meter would be too large a unit. One meter is about the height of a lab table.

(2) Look at the ruler in the picture. Compare your arm to the centimeters shown and the millimeters.

(3) You can measure your arm with either unit, but if you wiggle a bit, the count of millimeters is thrown off.

ANSWER Centimeters are the most appropriate units.

Answer the following questions.

1. If you uncoiled a human intestine, its length would be about equal to that of 2 cars parked end to end. What would be appropriate units to use to measure that?

2. What units would you use to measure the length of your tongue? The length of a tooth?

3. The large intestine is actually shorter than the small intestine. The small intestine is about the length of a small bus, and the large is about as long as a car's back seat. Tell the units you would choose for each. Explain why.

CHALLENGE Your stomach when empty is about the size of your clenched fist. To measure its volume (the space it takes up), what units would you use?

The ruler shows 20 centimeters (cm).
There are 10 millimeters (mm) in each centimeter.

1 cm

7.3 The urinary system removes waste materials.

BEFORE, you learned

- The digestive system breaks down food
- Organs in the digestive system have different roles

NOW, you will learn

- How different body systems remove different types of waste
- Why the kidneys are important organs
- About the role of the kidneys in homeostasis

STANDARDS

7–3.2 Recall the major organs of the human body and their function within their particular body system.

7–3.3 Summarize the relationships of the major body systems (including the circulatory, respiratory, digestive, excretory, nervous, muscular, and skeletal systems).

VOCABULARY

urinary system p. 213
urine p. 213

EXPLORE Waste Removal

How does the skin get rid of body waste?

PROCEDURE

① Place a plastic bag over the hand you do not use for writing and tape it loosely around your wrist.

② Leave the bag on for five minutes. Write down the changes you see in conditions within the bag.

WHAT DO YOU THINK?

- What do you see happen to the bag?
- How does what you observe help explain the body's method of waste removal?

MATERIALS

- plastic bag
- tape
- stopwatch

Life processes produce wastes.

You have read that the respiratory system and the digestive system provide the body with energy and materials necessary for important processes. During these processes, waste materials are produced. The removal of these wastes is essential for the continuing function of body systems. Several systems in your body remove wastes.

- The urinary system disposes of liquid waste products removed from the blood.
- The respiratory system disposes of water vapor and waste gases from the blood.
- The digestive system disposes of solid waste products from food.
- The skin releases wastes through sweat glands.

 CHECK YOUR READING What are four ways the body disposes of waste products?

The urinary system removes waste from the blood.

If you have observed an aquarium, you have seen a filter at work. Water moves through the filter, which removes waste materials from the water. Just as the filter in a fish tank removes wastes from the water, structures in your urinary system filter wastes from your blood.

As shown in the diagram, the **urinary system** contains several structures. The kidneys are two organs located high up and toward the rear of the abdomen, one on each side of the spine. Kidneys function much as the filter in the fish tank does. In fact, the kidneys are often called the body's filters. Materials travel in your blood to the kidneys. There, some substances are removed, and others are returned to the blood.

After the kidneys filter chemical waste from the blood, the liquid travels down two tubes called ureters (yu-REE-tuhrz). The ureters bring the waste to the bladder, a storage sac with a wall of smooth muscle. The lower neck of the bladder leads into the urethra, a tube that carries the liquid waste outside the body. Voluntary muscles at one end of the bladder allow a person to hold the urethra closed until he or she is ready to release the muscles. At that time, the bladder contracts and sends the liquid waste, or **urine,** out of the body.

VOCABULARY
Add a magnet diagram for *urinary system* to your notebook. Include in your diagram information about how kidneys function.

Urinary System

The urinary system transports wastes out of the body.

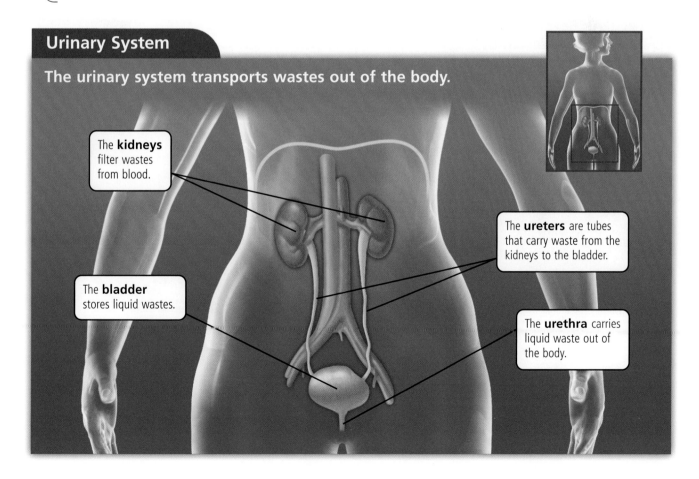

The **kidneys** filter wastes from blood.

The **ureters** are tubes that carry waste from the kidneys to the bladder.

The **bladder** stores liquid wastes.

The **urethra** carries liquid waste out of the body.

RESOURCE CENTER
CLASSZONE.COM

Find out more about the
urinary system.

The kidneys act as filters.

At any moment, about one quarter of the blood leaving your heart is headed toward your kidneys to be filtered. The kidneys, which are about as long as your index finger—only 10 centimeters (3.9 in.) long—filter all the blood in your body many times a day.

The Nephron

Inside each kidney are approximately one million looping tubes called nephrons. The nephron regulates the makeup of the blood.

1 Fluid is filtered from the blood into the nephron through a structure called the glomerulus (gloh-MEHR-yuh-luhs). Filtered blood leaves the glomerulus and circulates around the tubes that make up the nephron.

2 As the filtered fluid passes through the nephron, some nutrients are absorbed back into the blood surrounding the tubes. Some water is also filtered out in the glomerulus, but most water is returned to the blood.

3 Waste products travel to the end of the nephron into the collecting duct. The remaining liquid, now called urine, passes out of the kidney and into the ureters.

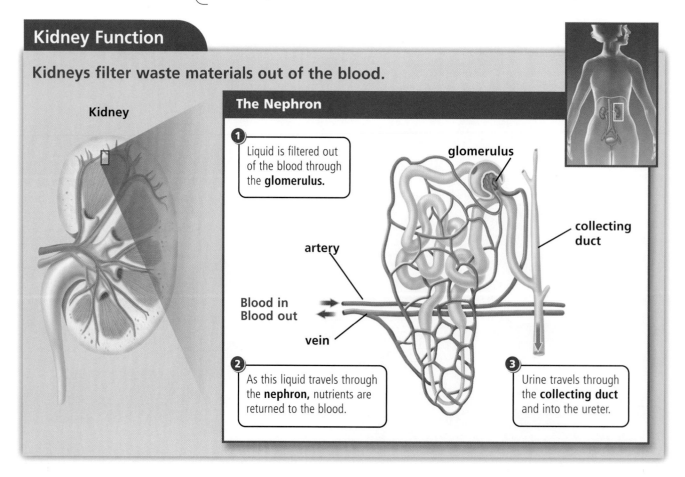

Kidney Function

Kidneys filter waste materials out of the blood.

Kidney

The Nephron

1 Liquid is filtered out of the blood through the **glomerulus.**

glomerulus

collecting duct

artery

Blood in
Blood out

vein

2 As this liquid travels through the **nephron,** nutrients are returned to the blood.

3 Urine travels through the **collecting duct** and into the ureter.

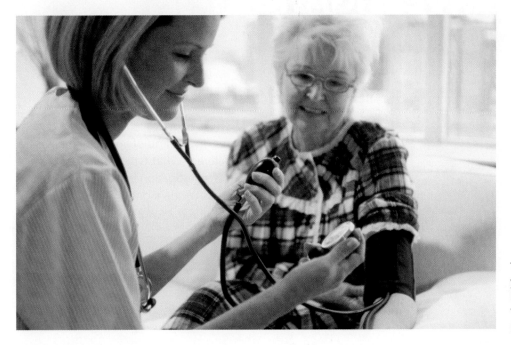

The amount of water in your body affects your blood pressure. Excess water increases blood pressure.

Water Balance

The kidneys not only remove wastes from blood, they also regulate the amount of water in the body. You read in Chapter 6 about the importance of homeostasis—a stable environment within your body. The amount of water in your cells affects homeostasis. If your body contains too much water, parts of your body may swell. Having too little water interferes with cell processes.

About one liter of water leaves the body every day. The kidneys control the amount of water that leaves the body in urine. Depending on how much water your body uses, the kidneys produce urine with more or less water.

 How do your kidneys regulate the amount of water in your body?

7.3 Review

KEY CONCEPTS

1. Describe the four organ systems that remove waste and explain how each removes waste.
2. Describe the function of four organs in the urinary system.
3. Describe homeostasis and explain why the kidneys are important to homeostasis.

CRITICAL THINKING

4. **Connect** Make a word web with the term *kidney* in the center. Add details about kidney function to the web.

CHALLENGE

5. **Synthesize** Explain why you may become thirsty on a hot day. Include the term *homeostasis* in your explanation.

CHAPTER INVESTIGATION

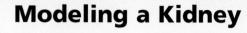

Modeling a Kidney

OVERVIEW AND PURPOSE Your kidneys are your body's filters. Every 20 to 30 minutes, every drop of your blood passes through the kidneys and is filtered. What types of materials are filtered by the kidneys? In this investigation you will
- model the filtering process of the kidneys
- determine what types of materials are filtered by your kidneys

▶ Problem

What types of materials can be removed from the blood by the kidneys?

▶ Hypothesize

Write a hypothesis to explain how substances are filtered out of the blood by the kidneys. Your hypothesis should take the form of an "If . . . , then . . . , because . . . " statement.

▶ Procedure

1. Make a data table like the one shown on the sample notebook page. Fold the filter paper as shown. Place the filter paper in the funnel, and place the funnel in the graduated cylinder.

2. Pour 20 mL of solution A into a beaker. Test the solution for salt concentration using a test strip for salinity. Record the results in your notebook. Slowly pour the solution into the funnel. Wait for it all to drip through the filter paper.

step 2

MATERIALS
- fine filter paper
- small funnel
- graduated cylinder
- 100 mL beaker
- solution A
- solution B
- solution C
- salinity test strips
- glucose test strips
- protein test strips

4 Test the filtered liquid for salt concentration again. Record the results.

5 Repeat steps 1, 2, and 3 for solution B using glucose test strips. Record the results in your notebook.

Repeat steps 1, 2, and 3 for solution C using protein test strips. Record the results in your notebook.

step 5

▶ Observe and Analyze

Write It Up

1. **RECORD** Be sure your data table is complete.

2. **OBSERVE** What substances were present in solutions A, B, and C?

3. **IDENTIFY VARIABLES** Identify the variables and constants in the experiment. List them in your notebook.

▶ Conclude

Write It Up

1. **COMPARE AND CONTRAST** In what ways does your model function like a kidney? How is your model not like a kidney?

2. **INTERPRET** Which materials were able to pass through the filter and which could not?

3. **INFER** What materials end up in the urine? How might materials be filtered out of the blood but not appear in the urine?

4. **APPLY** How could a filtering device be useful in your body?

▶ INVESTIGATE Further

CHALLENGE Your blood contains many chemicals. Some of these chemicals are waste products, but some are in the blood to be transported to different parts of the body. What other substances are filtered out of the blood by the kidneys? Which of the filtered substances are normally present in the urine? Use a variety of reference materials to research the chemicals found in urine. Revise your experiment to test the ability of your model kidney to filter other substances.

Modeling a Kidney

Table 1. Test-strip results

	Before filtering	After filtering
Solution A		
Solution B		
Solution C		

Chapter Review

the BIG idea

Systems in the body obtain and process materials and remove waste.

CONTENT REVIEW
CLASSZONE.COM

◄ **KEY CONCEPTS SUMMARY**

1 **The respiratory system gets oxygen and removes carbon dioxide.**

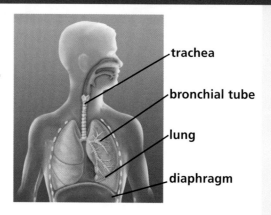

- trachea
- bronchial tube
- lung
- diaphragm

- Your body needs oxygen
- Structures in the respiratory system function together
- Your respiratory system is involved in other functions

VOCABULARY
respiratory system
p. 197
cellular respiration
p. 199

2 **The digestive system breaks down food.**

Structure	Function
Mouth	chemical and mechanical digestion
Esophagus	movement of food by peristalsis from mouth to stomach
Stomach	chemical and mechanical digestion; absorption of broken-down nutrients
Small intestine	chemical digestion; absorption of broken-down nutrients
Large intestine	absorption of water and broken-down nutrients, elimination of wastes

VOCABULARY
nutrient p. 205
digestion p. 206
digestive system
p. 206
peristalsis p. 206

3 **The urinary system removes waste materials.**

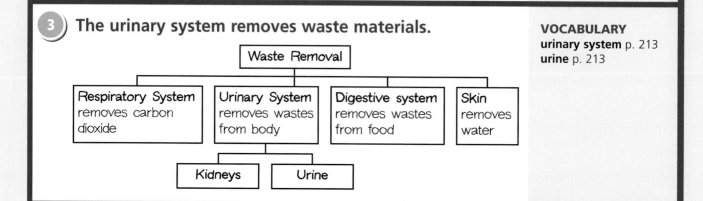

Waste Removal

| Respiratory System removes carbon dioxide | Urinary System removes wastes from body | Digestive system removes wastes from food | Skin removes water |

Kidneys — Urine

VOCABULARY
urinary system p. 213
urine p. 213

Copy the chart below and write the definition for each word. Use the meaning of the word's root to help you.

Word	Root Meaning	Definition
EXAMPLE: rib <u>cage</u>	to arch over	bones enclosing the internal organs of the body
1. <u>respir</u>ation	to breathe	
2. <u>nutri</u>ent	to nourish	
3. <u>dige</u>stion	to separate	
4. peristalsis	to wrap around	

Reviewing Key Concepts

Multiple Choice *Choose the letter of the best answer.*

5. Which system brings oxygen into your body and removes carbon dioxide?
   a. digestive system
   b. urinary system
   c. respiratory system
   d. muscular system

6. Which body structure in the throat keeps air from entering the stomach?
   a. trachea
   b. epiglottis
   c. lungs
   d. alveoli

7. Oxygen and carbon dioxide are exchanged through structures in the lungs called
   a. bronchial tubes
   b. alveoli
   c. cartilage
   d. villi

8. Carbon dioxide is a waste product that is formed during which process?
   a. cellular respiration
   b. peristalsis
   c. urination
   d. circulation

9. Carbohydrates are nutrients that
   a. make up most of the human body
   b. make up cell membranes
   c. enable cells to grow and repair themselves
   d. are broken down for energy

10. Which is *not* a function of the digestive system?
    a. absorb water from food
    b. absorb nutrients from food
    c. filter wastes from blood
    d. break down food

11. Which is an example of a physical change?
    a. teeth grind cracker into smaller pieces
    b. liquids in mouth change starches to sugars
    c. bile breaks down fats
    d. stomach breaks down proteins

12. Where in the digestive system is most water absorbed?
    a. kidneys
    b. stomach
    c. large intestine
    d. esophagus

13. Chemical waste is filtered from the blood in which structure?
    a. alveoli
    b. kidney
    c. stomach
    d. villi

14. The kidneys control the amount of
    a. oxygen that enters the blood
    b. blood cells that leave the body
    c. urine that is absorbed by the body
    d. water that leaves the body

Short Answer *Write a short answer to each question.*

15. Draw a sketch that shows how the thoracic cavity changes as the diaphragm contracts and pulls downward.

16. What are two products that are released into the body as a result of cellular respiration?

17. Through which organs does food pass as it travels through the digestive system?

18. What is the function of the urinary system?

Thinking Critically

19. SUMMARIZE Describe how gas exchange takes place inside the lungs.

20. SYNTHESIZE Summarize what happens during cellular respiration. Explain how the digestive system and the respiratory system are involved.

21. ANALYZE When there is a lot of dust or pollen in the air, people may cough and sneeze. What function of the respiratory system is involved?

22. INFER When you exhale onto a glass surface, the surface becomes cloudy with a thin film of moisture. Explain why this happens.

23. COMPARE AND CONTRAST Where does mechanical digestion take place? How is it different from chemical digestion?

24. PREDICT People with stomach disease often have their entire stomachs removed and are able to live normally. Explain how this is possible. Would a person be able to live normally without the small intestine? Explain your answer.

25. APPLY An athlete drinks a liter of water before a basketball game and continues to drink water during the game. Describe how the athlete's body is able to maintain homeostasis during the course of the game.

26. INTERPRET Use the diagram of the nephron shown below to describe what happens to the blood as it travels through the vessels surrounding the nephron.

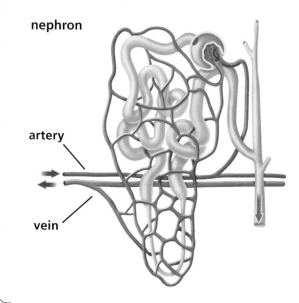

nephron

artery

vein

the **BIG** idea

27. INFER Look again at the picture on pages 194–195. Now that you have finished the chapter, how would you change or add details to your answer to the question on the photograph?

28. SYNTHESIZE Write a paragraph explaining how the respiratory system, the digestive system, and the urinary system work together with the circulatory system to eliminate waste materials from the body. Underline these terms in your paragraph.

UNIT PROJECTS

Check your schedule for your unit project. How are you doing? Be sure that you've placed data or notes from your research in your project folder.

Analyzing Data

The bar graph below shows respiration rates.

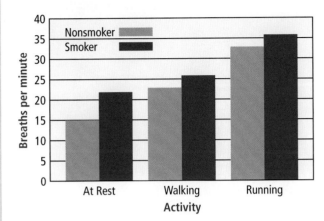

Use the graph to answer the questions below.

1. What is the best title for this graph?

a. Respiration Rates of Smokers and Nonsmokers

b. Cigarettes Smoked During Exercise

c. Activities Performed by Smokers and Nonsmokers

d. Blood Pressure Levels of Smokers and Nonsmokers.

2. How many breaths per minute were taken by a nonsmoker at rest?

a. 15 breaths per minute

b. 22 breaths per minute

c. 26 breaths per minute

d. 33 breaths per minute

3. For the nonsmokers, by how much did the respiration rate increase between resting and running?

a. 15 breaths per minute

b. 18 breaths per minute

c. 23 breaths per minute

d. 33 breaths per minute

4. Which statement is *not* true?

a. The nonsmoker at rest took more breaths per minute than the smoker at rest.

b. The nonsmoker took more breaths per minute running than walking.

c. The smoker took more breaths per minute than the nonsmoker while walking.

d. The nonsmoker took fewer breaths per minute than the smoker while running.

5. Which statement is the most logical conclusion to draw from the data in the chart?

a. Smoking has no effect on respiration rate.

b. Increased activity has no effect on respiration rate.

c. There is no difference in the respiration rates between the smoker and the nonsmoker.

d. Smoking and activity both cause an increase in respiration rate.

Extended Response

6. Tar, which is a harmful substance found in tobacco smoke, coats the lining of the lungs over time. Based on the information in the graph and what you know about the respiratory system, write a paragraph describing how smoking cigarettes affects the functioning of the respiratory system.

7. Ads for cigarettes and other tobacco products have been banned from television. However, they still appear in newspapers and magazines. These ads make tobacco use look glamorous and exciting. Using your knowledge of the respiratory system, design an ad that discourages the use of tobacco products. Create a slogan that will help people remember how tobacco affects the health of the respiratory system.

CHAPTER

8 Transport and Protection

the BIG idea

Systems function to transport materials and to defend and protect the body.

Key Concepts

SECTION

1 **The circulatory system transports materials.**
Learn how materials move through blood vessels.

SECTION

2 **The immune system defends the body.**
Learn about the body's defenses and responses to foreign materials.

SECTION

3 **The integumentary system shields the body.**
Learn about the structure of skin and how it protects the body.

 Internet Preview

CLASSZONE.COM

Chapter 8 online resources: Content Review, two Visualizations, four Resource Centers, Math Tutorial, Test Practice

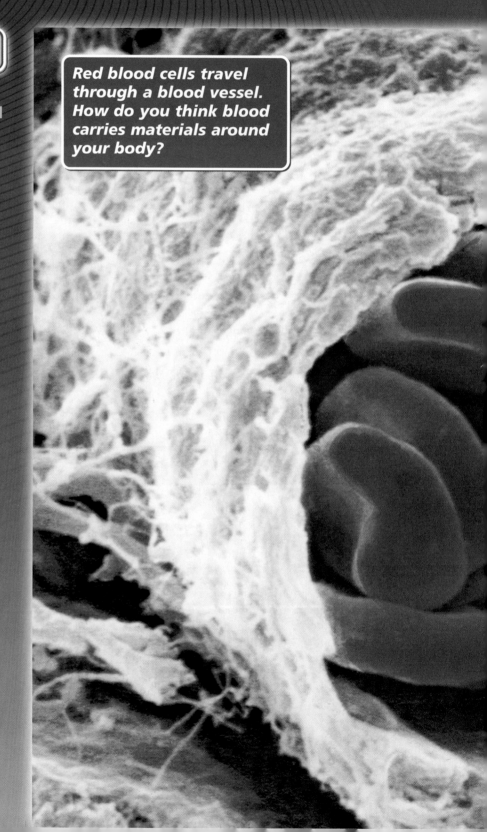

Red blood cells travel through a blood vessel. How do you think blood carries materials around your body?

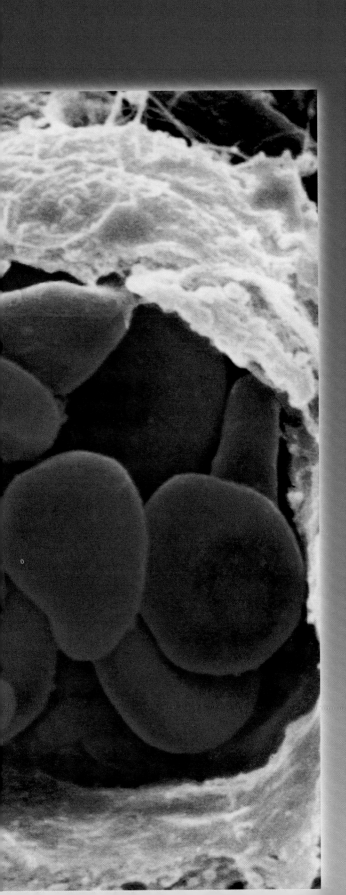

Blood Pressure

Fill a small, round balloon halfway full with air. Tie off the end. Gently squeeze the balloon in your hand. Release the pressure. Squeeze again.

Observe and Think As you squeeze your hand, what happens to the air in the balloon? What happens as you release the pressure?

Wet Fingers

Dip your finger into a cup of room-temperature water. Then hold the finger up in the air and note how it feels.

Observe and Think How does your finger feel now compared with the way it felt before you dipped it?

Internet Activity: Heart Pumping

Go to **ClassZone.com** to learn about how the heart pumps blood. See how the circulatory system interacts with the respiratory system.

Observe and Think Where does the blood go after it leaves the right side of the heart? the left side of the heart?

NSTA
scilinks.org

SCI**LINKS**

Immune System **Code: MDL046**

Getting Ready to Learn

◀ CONCEPT REVIEW

- The body's systems interact.
- The body's systems work to maintain internal conditions.
- The digestive system breaks down food.
- The respiratory system gets oxygen and removes carbon dioxide.

◀ VOCABULARY REVIEW

organ p. 171

organ system p. 172

homeostasis p. 172

nutrient p. 205

 **CONTENT REVIEW**
CLASSZONE.COM
Review concepts and vocabulary.

▶ TAKING NOTES

MAIN IDEA AND DETAIL NOTES

Make a two-column chart. Write the main ideas, such as those in the blue headings, in the column on the left. Write details about each of those main heads in the column on the right.

VOCABULARY STRATEGY

Write each new vocabulary term in the center of a **frame game** diagram. Decide what information to frame it with. Use examples, descriptions, parts, sentences that use the term in context, or pictures. You can change the frame to fit each term.

See the Note-Taking Handbook on pages R45–R51.

SCIENCE NOTEBOOK

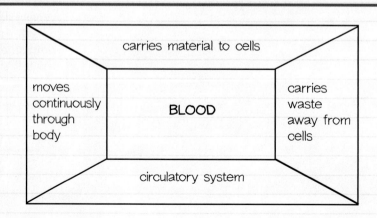

MAIN IDEAS	DETAIL NOTES
1. The circulatory system works with other body systems.	1. Transports materials from digestive and respiratory systems to cells 2. Blood is fluid that carries materials and wastes 3. Blood is always moving through the body 4. Blood delivers oxygen and takes away carbon dioxide

Frame game diagram:
carries material to cells / moves continuously through body / **BLOOD** / carries waste away from cells / circulatory system

8.1

KEY CONCEPT

The circulatory system transports materials.

BEFORE, you learned

- The urinary system removes waste
- The kidneys play a role in homeostasis

NOW, you will learn

- How different structures of the circulatory system work together
- About the structure and function of blood
- What blood pressure is and why it is important

STANDARDS

7–3.2 Recall the major organs of the human body and their function within their particular body system.

7–3.3 Summarize the relationships of the major body systems (including the circulatory, respiratory, digestive, excretory, nervous, muscular, and skeletal systems).

VOCABULARY

circulatory system p. 225
blood p. 225
red blood cell p. 227
artery p. 229
vein p. 229
capillary p. 229

EXPLORE The Circulatory System

How fast does your heart beat?

PROCEDURE

① Hold out your left hand with your palm facing up.

② Place the first two fingers of your right hand on your left wrist below your thumb. Move your fingertips slightly until you can feel your pulse.

③ Use the stopwatch to determine how many times your heart beats in one minute.

WHAT DO YOU THINK?

- How many times did your heart beat?
- What do you think you would find if you took your pulse after exercising?

MATERIALS
stopwatch

The circulatory system works with other body systems.

VOCABULARY
Add a frame game diagram for the term *circulatory system* to your notebook.

You have read that the systems in your body provide materials and energy. The digestive system breaks down food and nutrients, and the respiratory system provides the oxygen that cells need to release energy. Another system, called the **circulatory system,** transports materials from the digestive and the respiratory systems to the cells.

Materials and wastes are carried in a fluid called **blood.** Blood moves continuously through the body, delivering oxygen and other materials to cells and removing carbon dioxide and other wastes from cells.

Structures in the circulatory system function together.

In order to provide the essential nutrients and other materials that your cells need, your blood must keep moving through your body. The circulatory system, which is made up of the heart and blood vessels, allows blood to flow to all parts of the body. The circulatory system works with other systems to provide the body with this continuous flow of life-giving blood.

The Heart

The heart is the organ that pushes blood throughout the circulatory system. The human heart actually functions as two pumps—one pump on the right side and one on the left side. The right side of the heart pumps blood to the lungs to receive oxygen, and the left side pumps blood to the entire body. The lungs receive oxygen when you inhale and remove carbon dioxide when you exhale. Inside the lungs, the respiratory system interacts with the circulatory system.

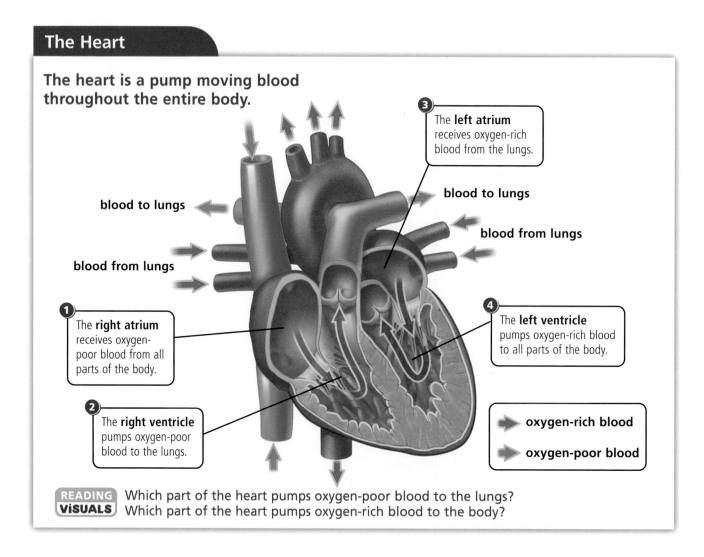

The Heart

The heart is a pump moving blood throughout the entire body.

3 The **left atrium** receives oxygen-rich blood from the lungs.

blood to lungs

blood from lungs

blood to lungs

blood from lungs

1 The **right atrium** receives oxygen-poor blood from all parts of the body.

4 The **left ventricle** pumps oxygen-rich blood to all parts of the body.

2 The **right ventricle** pumps oxygen-poor blood to the lungs.

oxygen-rich blood

oxygen-poor blood

READING VISUALS Which part of the heart pumps oxygen-poor blood to the lungs? Which part of the heart pumps oxygen-rich blood to the body?

Each side of the heart is divided into two areas called chambers. Oxygen-poor blood, which is blood from the body with less oxygen, flows to the right side of your heart, into a filling chamber called the right atrium. With each heartbeat, blood flows from the right atrium into a pumping chamber, the right ventricle, and then into the lungs. There the blood releases carbon dioxide waste and absorbs oxygen.

After picking up oxygen, blood is pushed back to the heart, filling another chamber, which is called the left atrium. Blood moves from the left atrium to the left ventricle, a pumping chamber, and again begins its trip out to the rest of the body. Both oxygen-poor blood and oxygen-rich blood are red. However, oxygen-rich blood is a much brighter and lighter shade of red than is oxygen-poor blood. The diagram on page 226 shows oxygen-poor blood in blue, so that you can tell where in the circulatory system oxygen-poor and oxygen-rich blood are found.

 Summarize the way blood moves through the heart. Remember, a summary contains only the most important information.

Blood

The oxygen that your cells need in order to release energy must be present in blood to travel through your body. Blood is a tissue made up of plasma, red blood cells, white blood cells, and platelets. About 60 percent of blood is plasma, a fluid that contains proteins, glucose, hormones, gases, and other substances dissolved in water.

White blood cells help your body fight infection by attacking disease-causing organisms. **Red blood cells** are more numerous than white blood cells and have a different function. They pick up oxygen in the lungs and transport it throughout the body. As red blood cells travel through the circulatory system, they deliver oxygen to other cells.

Platelets are large cell fragments that help form blood clots when a blood vessel is injured. You know what a blood clot is if you've observed a cut or a scrape. The scab that forms around a cut or scrape is made of clotted blood. After an injury such as a cut, platelets nearby begin to enlarge and become sticky. They stick to the injured area of the blood vessels and release chemicals that result in blood clotting. Blood clotting keeps blood vessels from losing too much blood.

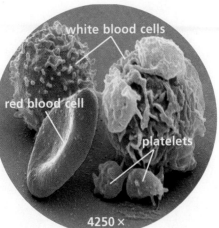

Blood is made mostly of plasma, which transports red blood cells, white blood cells, and platelets.

 What are the four components that make up blood?

Circulatory System

The circulatory system allows blood to flow continuously throughout the body. The runner depends on a constant flow of oxygen-rich blood to fuel his cells.

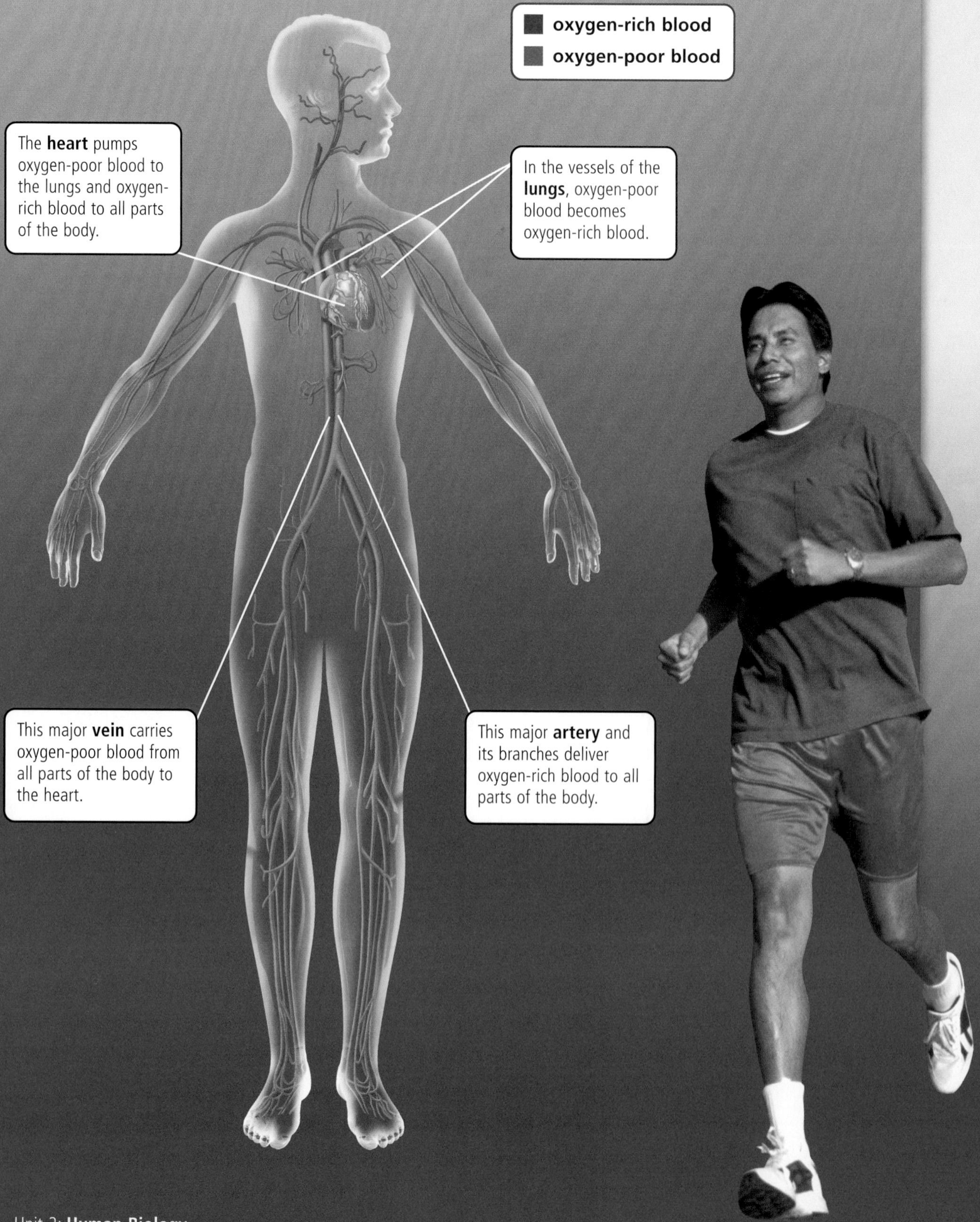

■ oxygen-rich blood
■ oxygen-poor blood

The **heart** pumps oxygen-poor blood to the lungs and oxygen-rich blood to all parts of the body.

In the vessels of the **lungs**, oxygen-poor blood becomes oxygen-rich blood.

This major **vein** carries oxygen-poor blood from all parts of the body to the heart.

This major **artery** and its branches deliver oxygen-rich blood to all parts of the body.

As blood travels through blood vessels, some fluid is lost. This fluid, called lymph, is collected in lymph vessels and returned to veins and arteries. As you will read in the next section, lymph and lymph vessels are associated with your immune system. Sometimes scientists refer to the lymph and lymph vessels as the lymphatic system. The lymphatic system helps you fight disease.

Blood Vessels

Blood moves through a network of structures called blood vessels. Blood vessels are tube-shaped structures that are similar to flexible drinking straws. The structure of blood vessels suits them for particular functions. **Arteries**, which are the vessels that take blood away from the heart, have strong walls. An artery wall is thick and elastic and can handle the tremendous force produced when the heart pumps. **Veins** are blood vessels that carry blood back to the heart. The walls of veins are thinner than those of arteries. However, veins are generally of greater diameter than are arteries.

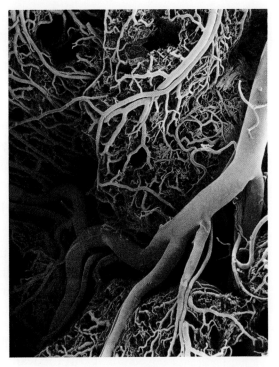

Arteries, capillaries, and veins form a complex web to carry blood to all the cells in the body (30×).

Most arteries carry oxygen-rich blood away from the heart, and most veins carry oxygen-poor blood back to the heart. However, the pulmonary blood vessels are exceptions. Oxygen-poor blood travels through the two pulmonary arteries, one of which goes to each lung. The two pulmonary veins carry oxygen-rich blood from the lungs to the heart.

Veins and arteries branch off into very narrow blood vessels called capillaries. **Capillaries** connect arteries with veins. Through capillaries materials are exchanged between blood and tissues. Oxygen and materials from nutrients move from the blood in the arteries to the body's tissues through tiny openings in the capillary walls. Waste materials and carbon dioxide move from the tissues' cells through the capillary walls and into the blood in the veins.

 Compare and contrast arteries, veins, and capillaries.

Blood exerts pressure on blood vessels.

As you have read, the contractions of the heart push blood through blood vessels. The force produced when the heart contracts travels through the blood, putting pressure on the blood vessels. This force is called blood pressure. Compare a vessel to a plastic bag filled with water.

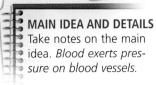

MAIN IDEA AND DETAILS
Take notes on the main idea. *Blood exerts pressure on blood vessels.*

If you push down at the center of the bag, you can see the water push out against the sides of the bag.

The heart pushes blood in a similar way, exerting pressure on the arteries, veins, and capillaries in the circulatory system. It is important to maintain healthy blood pressure so that materials in blood get to all parts of your body. If blood pressure is too low, some of the cells will not get oxygen and other materials. On the other hand, if blood pressure is too high, the force may weaken the blood vessels and require the heart to work harder to push blood through the blood vessels. High blood pressure is a serious medical condition, but it can be treated.

The circulatory system can be considered as two smaller systems: one, the pulmonary system, moves blood to the lungs; the other, the systemic system, moves blood to the rest of the body. Blood pressure is measured in the systemic part of the circulatory system.

You can think of blood pressure as the pressure that blood exerts on the walls of your arteries at all times. Health professionals measure blood pressure indirectly with a device called a sphygmomanometer (SFIHG-moh-muh-NAHM-ih-tuhr).

Blood pressure is expressed with two numbers—one number over another number. The first number refers to the pressure in the arteries when the heart contracts. The second number refers to the pressure in the arteries when the heart relaxes and receives blood from the veins.

Blood Pressure

Blood pressure allows materials to travel to all parts of your body.

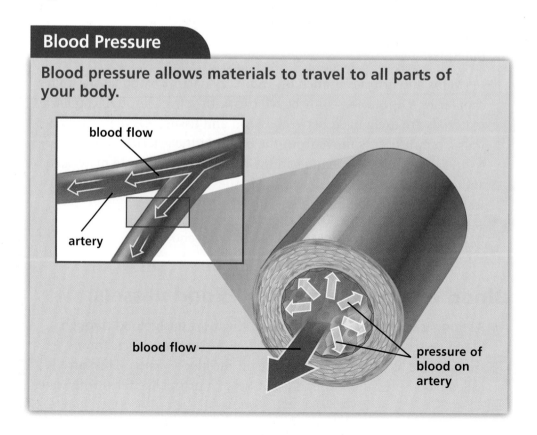

blood flow

artery

blood flow

pressure of blood on artery

There are four different blood types.

Each red blood cell has special proteins on its surface. One group of surface proteins determines blood type. There are two blood-type proteins, A and B. A person whose blood cells have the A proteins has type A blood. One with cells having B proteins has type B blood. Some people have both proteins—type AB blood. Other people have neither protein, a type of blood referred to as type O.

Maybe you, or someone you know, has had a blood transfusion, a procedure in which one person receives blood donated by another. Knowing blood type is important for transfusions. As you will learn in the next section, the body has structures that protect it from unknown substances. They are part of an immune system that recognizes and protects cells and molecules that are "self" from those that are unrecognized, or "nonself." The body attacks unrecognized substances, including those in donated blood.

The blood used for transfusions is usually the same type as the blood type of the receiver, but sometimes other blood types are used. The diagram shows which blood types are compatible. Because the cells in type O blood have neither protein, the immune system of someone with A, B, or AB blood will not attack O blood cells. A person with type O blood, however, cannot receive any other blood type because that person's immune system would attack A or B surface proteins.

Blood Type Compatibility		
Blood Type	**Can Donate Blood To**	**Can Receive Blood From**
A	A, AB	A, O
B	B, AB	B, O
AB	AB	A, B, AB, O
O	A, B, AB, O	O

People can donate blood to others.

 **RESOURCE CENTER** CLASSZONE.COM

Learn more about blood types.

 CHECK YOUR READING Why is it important to know your blood type?

8.1 Review

KEY CONCEPTS

1. What are the functions of the two sides of the heart?
2. What is the primary function of red blood cells?
3. Why can both high and low blood pressure be a problem?

CRITICAL THINKING

4. **Apply** List three examples of the circulatory system working with another system in your body.
5. **Compare and Contrast** Explain why blood pressure is expressed with two numbers.

CHALLENGE

6. **Identify Cause and Effect** You can feel the speed at which your heart is pumping by pressing two fingers to the inside of your wrist. This is your pulse. If you run for a few minutes, your pulse rate is faster for a little while, then it slows down again. Why did your pulse rate speed up and slow down?

CHAPTER INVESTIGATION

Heart Rate and Exercise

OVERVIEW AND PURPOSE In this activity, you will calculate your resting, maximum, and target heart rates. Then you will examine the effect of exercise on heart rate. Before you begin, read through the entire investigation.

▶ Procedure

1. Make a data table like the one shown on the sample notebook page.

2. Measure your resting heart rate. Find the pulse in the artery of your neck, just below and in front of the bottom of your ear, with the first two fingers of one hand. Do not use your thumb to measure pulse since the thumb has a pulse of its own. Once you have found the pulse, count the beats for 30 seconds and multiply the result by 2. The number you get is your resting heart rate in beats per minute. Record this number in your notebook.

step 2

3. Calculate your maximum heart rate by subtracting your age from 220. Record this number in your notebook. Your target heart rate should be 60 to 75 percent of your maximum heart rate. Calculate and record this range in your notebook.

4. Someone who is very athletic or has been exercising regularly for 6 months or more can safely exercise up to 85 percent of his or her maximum heart rate. Calculate and record this rate in your notebook.

5. Observe how quickly you reach your target heart rate during exercise. Begin by running in place at an intensity that makes you breathe harder but does not make you breathless. As with any exercise, remember that if you experience difficulty breathing, dizziness, or chest discomfort, stop exercising immediately.

step 5

MATERIALS
- notebook
- stopwatch
- calculator
- graph paper

6 Every 2 minutes, measure your heart rate for 10 seconds. Multiply this number by 6 to find your heart rate in beats per minute and record it in your notebook. Try to exercise for a total of 10 minutes. After you stop exercising, continue recording your heart rate every 2 minutes until it returns to the resting rate you measured in step 2.

▶ Observe and Analyze | Write It Up

1. **GRAPH DATA** Make a line graph of your heart rate during and after the exercise. Graph the values in beats per minute versus time in minutes. Your graph should start at your resting heart rate and continue until your heart rate has returned to its resting rate. Using a colored pencil, shade in the area that represents your target heart-rate range.

2. **ANALYZE DATA** How many minutes of exercising were needed for you to reach your target heart rate of 60 to 75 percent of maximum? Did your heart rate go over your target range?

3. **INTERPRET DATA** How many minutes after you stopped exercising did it take for your heart rate to return to its resting rate? Why do you think your heart rate did not return to its resting rate immediately after you stopped exercising?

▶ Conclude | Write It Up

1. **INFER** Why do you think that heart rate increases during exercise?

2. **IDENTIFY** What other body systems are affected when the heart rate increases?

3. **PREDICT** Why do you think that target heart rate changes with age?

4. **CLASSIFY** Create a table comparing the intensity of different types of exercise, such as walking, skating, bicycling, weight lifting, and any others you might enjoy.

▶ INVESTIGATE Further

CHALLENGE Determine how other exercises affect your heart rate. Repeat this investigation by performing one or two of the other exercises from your table. Present your data, with a graph, to the class.

Heart Rate and Exercise

Resting heart rate:

Maximum heart rate:

Target heart rate (60–75% of maximum):

Target heart rate (85% of maximum):

Table 1. Heart Rate During and After Exercise

Time (minutes)	0	2	4	6	8	10	12	14	16	18	20
Heart rate (beats per minute)											

8.2 The immune system defends the body.

McDougal Littell Science
SOUTH CAROLINA

STANDARDS

7–3.3 Summarize the relationships of the major body systems (including the circulatory, respiratory, digestive, excretory, nervous, muscular, and skeletal systems).

7–3.4 Explain the effects of disease on the major organs and body systems (including infectious diseases such as colds and flu, AIDS, and athlete's foot and noninfectious diseases such as diabetes, Parkinson's, and skin cancer).

VOCABULARY

pathogen p. 234
immune system p. 235
antibody p. 235
antigen p. 238
immunity p. 240
vaccine p. 240
antibiotic p. 241

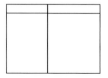

MAIN IDEA AND DETAILS
Add the main idea *Many systems defend the body from harmful materials* to your chart along with detail notes.

◀ BEFORE, you learned

- The circulatory system works with other systems to fuel the body cells
- Structures in the circulatory system work together
- Blood pressure allows materials to reach all parts of the body

▶ NOW, you will learn

- How foreign material enters the body
- How the immune system responds to foreign material
- Ways that the body can become immune to a disease

EXPLORE Membranes

How does the body keep foreign particles out?

PROCEDURE

① Place a white cloth into a sandwich bag and seal it. Fill a bowl with water and stir in several drops of food coloring.

② Submerge the sandwich bag in the water. After five minutes, remove the bag and note the condition of the cloth.

③ Puncture the bag with a pin. Put the bag back in the water for five minutes. Remove the bag and note the condition of the cloth.

WHAT DO YOU THINK?

- How does a puncture in the bag affect its ability to protect the cloth?

MATERIALS
- white cloth
- zippered sandwich bag
- large bowl
- water
- food coloring
- small pin

Many systems defend the body from harmful materials.

You might not realize it, but you come into contact with harmful substances constantly. Because your body has ways to defend itself, you don't even notice. One of the body's best defenses is to keep foreign materials from entering in the first place. The integumentary (ihn-TEHG-yu-MEHN-tuh-ree), respiratory, and digestive systems are the first line of defense against **pathogens,** or disease-causing agents. Pathogens can enter through your skin, the air you breathe, and even the food you eat or liquids you drink.

Which systems are your first line of defense against pathogens?

Integumentary System Defenses Most of the time, your skin functions as a barrier between you and the outside world. The physical barrier the skin forms is just one obstacle for pathogens and other foreign materials. The growth of pathogens on your eyes can be slowed by substances contained in tears. The millions of bacteria cells that live on the skin can also kill pathogens. A common way pathogens can enter the body is through a cut. The circulatory system is then able to help defend the body because blood contains cells that respond to foreign materials.

Respiratory System Defenses Sneezing and coughing are two ways the respiratory system defends the body from harmful substances. Cilia and mucus also protect the body. Cilia are tiny, hairlike protrusions in the nose and the lungs that trap dust particles present in the air. Mucus is a thick and slippery substance found in the nose, throat, and lungs. Like the cilia, mucus traps dirt and other particles. Mucus contains substances similar to those in tears that can slow the growth of pathogens.

Digestive System Defenses Some foreign materials manage to enter your digestive system, but many are destroyed by saliva, mucus, enzymes, and stomach acids. Saliva in your mouth helps kill bacteria. Mucus protects the digestive organs by coating them. Pathogens can also be destroyed by enzymes produced in the liver and pancreas or by the acids in the stomach.

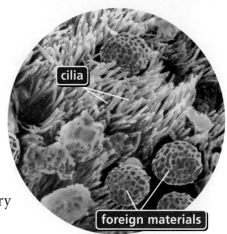

cilia

foreign materials

Cilia are hairlike protrusions that trap materials entering your respiratory system (600×).

The immune system has response structures.

Sometimes foreign materials manage to get past the first line of defense. When this happens, the body relies on the **immune system** to respond. This system functions in several ways:

- Tissues in the bone marrow, the thymus gland, the spleen, and the lymph nodes produce white blood cells, which are specialized cells that function to destroy foreign organisms.

- Some white blood cells produce a nonspecific response to injury or infection.

- Some white blood cells produce proteins called **antibodies,** which are part of a specific immune response to foreign materials.

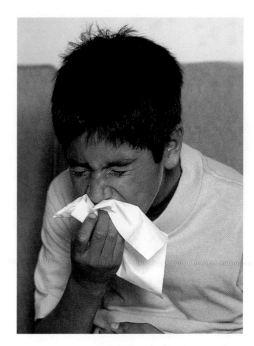

Sneezing helps to expel foreign substances from the body.

White Blood Cells

The immune system has specialized cells called white blood cells that recognize foreign materials in the body and respond. The number of white blood cells in the blood can increase during an immune response. These cells travel through the circulatory system and the lymphatic system to an injured or infected area of the body. White blood cells leave the blood vessels and travel into the damaged tissue, where the immune response takes place.

The Lymphatic System

RESOURCE CENTER
CLASSZONE.COM

Learn more about the lymphatic system.

The lymphatic system transports pathogen-fighting white blood cells throughout the body, much as the circulatory system does. The lymphatic system carries lymph, and the circulatory system carries blood. Both fluids transport similar materials, such as white blood cells.

Lymph is the fluid left in the tissues by the circulatory system. It moves through lymph vessels, which are similar to veins. However, the lymphatic system has no pump like the heart to move fluid. Lymph drifts through the lymph vessels when your skeletal muscles contract or when your body changes position. As it moves, it passes through lymph nodes, which filter out pathogens and store white blood cells and antibodies. Because lymph nodes filter out pathogens, infections are often fought in your lymph nodes, causing them to swell when you get sick.

CHECK YOUR READING How does the lymphatic system help the immune system?

The immune system responds to attack.

8750 ×

The mast cell above is an important part of the immune system.

Certain illnesses can cause symptoms such as coughing, sneezing, and fever. These symptoms make you uncomfortable when you are sick. But in fact, most symptoms are the result of the immune system's response to foreign materials in the body.

The immune system responds in two ways. The white blood cells that first respond to the site of injury or infection attack foreign materials in a nonspecific response. Some of these cells attack foreign materials and produce chemicals that help other white blood cells work better. The second part of the response is very specific to the types of pathogens invading the body. These white blood cells produce antibodies specific to each pathogen and provide your body with immunity.

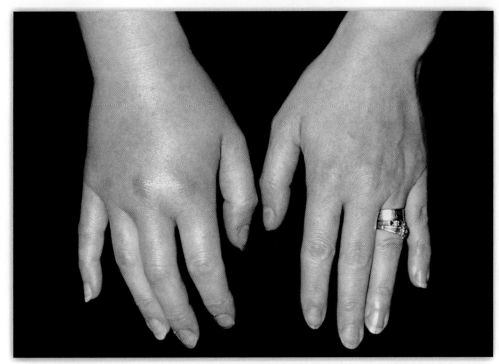

Wasp stings cause an immediate immune response. The area of the sting swells up and increases in temperature while your body battles the injury.

Nonspecific Response

Swelling, redness, and heat are some of the symptoms that tell you that a cut or scrape has become infected by foreign materials. They are all signs of inflammation, your body's first defense reaction against injuries and infections.

When tissue becomes irritated or damaged, it releases large amounts of histamine (HIHS-tuh-meen). Histamine raises the temperature of the tissues and increases blood flow to the area. Increased blood flow, which makes the injured area appear red, allows antibodies and white blood cells to arrive more quickly for battle. Higher temperatures improve the speed and power of white blood cells. Some pathogens cannot tolerate heat, so they grow weaker. The swelling caused by the production of histamine can be a small price to pay for this chemical's important work.

When a foreign material affects more than one area of your body, many tissues produce histamine. As a result, the temperature of your whole body rises. Any temperature above 37 degrees Celsius (98.6°F) is considered a fever, but only temperatures hot enough to damage tissues are dangerous. Trying to lower a high fever with medication is advisable in order to avoid tissue damage. When you have a small fever, lowering your body temperature might make you more comfortable, but it will not affect how long you stay sick.

 CHECK YOUR READING   What causes a fever when you are sick?

Specific Response

Specific immune responses differ from nonspecific responses in two ways. First, specific responses are triggered by antigens. An **antigen** is a chemical marker on a cell's surface that indicates whether the cell is from your body or is a foreign material. When the body detects a foreign antigen, specific immune responses occur. Second, a specific immune response provides protection from future exposure to the same material. Three major types of white blood cells—phagocytes, T cells, and B cells—function together in a specific response.

Phagocytes and T Cells Phagocytes ingest and break down foreign materials. Small pieces of the foreign materials are incorporated into the surface of the phagocyte's cell membrane. These foreign particles contain antigens that are detected as foreign by T cells. The T cells

Immune Response

When pathogens invade the body, several types of white blood cells function together to identify and attack foreign materials.

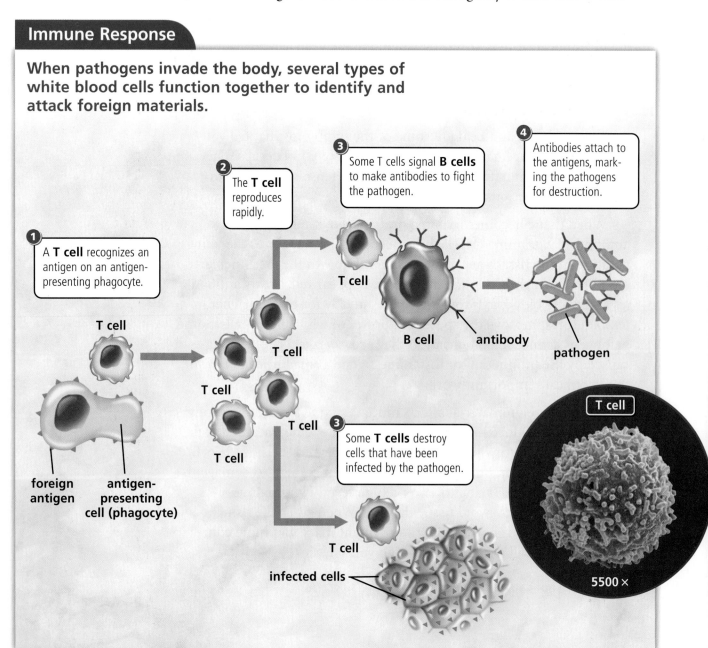

1 A **T cell** recognizes an antigen on an antigen-presenting phagocyte.

2 The **T cell** reproduces rapidly.

3 Some T cells signal **B cells** to make antibodies to fight the pathogen.

4 Antibodies attach to the antigens, marking the pathogens for destruction.

3 Some **T cells** destroy cells that have been infected by the pathogen.

T cell

T cell

T cell

T cell

T cell

T cell

T cell

T cell

B cell   antibody

pathogen

foreign antigen

antigen-presenting cell (phagocyte)

infected cells

T cell

5500×

INVESTIGATE Antibodies

How do antibodies stop pathogens from spreading?

PROCEDURE

① Your teacher will hand out plastic lids, each labeled with the name of a different pathogen. You will see plastic containers spread throughout the room. There is one container in the room with the same label as your lid.

② At the signal, find the plastic container with the pathogen that has the same label as your lid and wait in place for the teacher to tell you to stop. If you still haven't found the matching container when time is called, your model pathogen has spread.

③ If your pathogen has spread, write its name on the board.

WHAT DO YOU THINK?

- Which pathogens spread?
- What do you think the lid and container represent? Why?
- How do antibodies identify pathogens?

CHALLENGE Why do you think it is important for your body to identify pathogens?

SKILL FOCUS
Making models

MATERIALS
- plastic containers with lids
- masking tape

TIME
15 minutes

---

respond by dividing rapidly. Some types of T cells attack the materials with the foreign antigens, whereas others have different functions. Because antigens that differ from those on a person's cells and provoke an immune response are found on pathogens, the human immune system is necessary for survival in a germ-filled world.

B Cells After T cells divide, B cells that recognize the same foreign antigen are activated and divide rapidly. After several days, many of these B cells begin to produce antibodies that help destroy pathogens. Antibodies attach to the foreign antigens, marking the pathogens for killer T cells or other cells and chemicals that can destroy pathogens.

Some B cells do not make antibodies but remain in the body as a form of immune system memory. If the same pathogen enters the body again, the immune system can respond much more quickly. B cells that recognize the foreign antigen already exist, and antibodies will be produced more quickly.

 Why is it important for the body to store B cells?

Development of Immunity

After your body has destroyed a specific pathogen, B cells that fight that pathogen remain in your system. If the same pathogen were to enter your body again, your immune system would almost certainly destroy it before you became ill. This resistance to a sickness is called **immunity.**

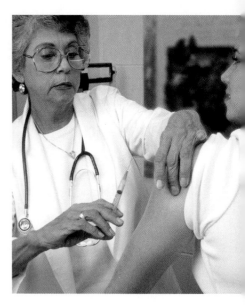

COMPARE A doctor gives a girl a vaccination. Is getting a vaccination an example of passive or active immunity?

Immunity takes two forms: passive and active. When babies are first born, they have only the immune defenses transferred to them by their mothers. They have not had the chance to develop antibodies of their own. This type of immunity is called passive immunity. Antibodies are not produced by the person's own body but given to the body from another source. Babies develop their own antibodies after a few months.

You have active immunity whenever your body makes its own antibodies. Your body will again fight against any specific pathogen you have developed antibodies against. For example, it is most unlikely that you will get chicken pox twice.

 What is the difference between active and passive immunity?

Most diseases can be prevented or treated.

Given enough time, your immune system will fight off most diseases. However, some infections can cause significant and lasting damage before they are defeated by the body's defenses. Other infections are so strong that the immune system cannot successfully fight them. Medical advances in the prevention and treatment of diseases have reduced the risks of many serious illnesses.

Vaccination

Another way to develop an immunity is to receive a **vaccine.** Vaccines contain small amounts of weakened or dead pathogens that stimulate an immune response. Your B cells are called into action to create antibodies as if you were fighting the real illness. The pathogens are usually weakened or dead so that you will not get sick, yet they still enable your body to develop an active immunity.

Today we have vaccines for many common pathogens. Most children who are vaccinated will not get many diseases that their great grandparents, grandparents, and even parents had. Vaccinations can be administered by injection or by mouth. Babies are not the only ones who get them, either. You can be vaccinated at any age.

 CHECK YOUR READING Why don't vaccinations usually make you sick?

Treatment

Not all diseases can be prevented, but many of them can be treated. In some cases, treatments can only reduce the symptoms of the disease while the immune system fights the disease-causing pathogens. Other treatments attack the pathogens directly.

In some cases, treatment can only prevent further damage to body tissues by a pathogen that cannot be cured or defeated by the immune system. The way in which a disease is treated depends on what pathogen causes it. Many bacterial infections can be treated with antibiotics. **Antibiotics** are medicines that block the growth and reproduction of bacteria. You may have taken antibiotics when you have had a disease such as strep throat or an ear infection. Other types of medicine can help fight infections caused by viruses, fungi, and parasites.

Types of Pathogens	
Disease	**Pathogen**
Colds, chicken pox, hepatitis, AIDS, influenza, mumps, measles, rabies	virus
Food poisoning, strep throat, tetanus, tuberculosis, acne, ulcers, Lyme disease	bacteria
Athlete's foot, thrush, ringworm	fungus
Malaria, parasitic pneumonia, pinworm, scabies	parasites

8.2 Review

KEY CONCEPTS

1. Make a chart showing three ways that foreign material enters the body and how the immune system defends against each type of attack.

2. What are white blood cells and what is their function in the body?

3. What are two ways to develop immunity?

CRITICAL THINKING

4. **Compare and Contrast** Make a chart comparing B cells and T cells. Include an explanation of the function of antibodies.

5. **Apply** Describe how your immune system responds when you scrape your knee.

CHALLENGE

6. **Hypothesize** Explain why, even if a person recovers from a cold, that person could get a cold again.

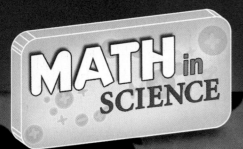

Pollen Counts

Every year, sometime between July and October, in nearly every state in the United States, the air will fill with ragweed pollen. For a person who has a pollen allergy, these months blur with tears. Linn County, Iowa, takes weekly counts of ragweed and non-ragweed pollen.

Weekly Pollen Counts, Linn County, Iowa										
	Jul. 29	Aug. 5	Aug. 12	Aug. 19	Aug. 26	Sept. 2	Sept. 9	Sept. 16	Sept. 23	Sept. 30	Oct. 7
Ragweed (Grain/m^3)	0	9	10	250	130	240	140	25	20	75	0
Non-Ragweed (Grain/m^3)	10	45	15	50	100	50	40	10	20	25	0

Example

A line graph of the data will show the pattern of increase and decrease of ragweed pollen in the air.

(1) Begin with a quadrant with horizontal and vertical axes.

(2) Mark the weekly dates at even intervals on the horizontal axis.

(3) Starting at 0 on the vertical axis, mark even intervals of 50 units.

(4) Graph each point. Connect the points with line segments.

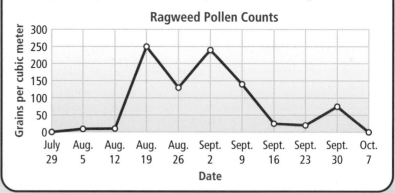

Complete and present your graph as directed below.

1. Use graph paper to make your own line graph of the non-ragweed pollen in Linn County.

2. Write some questions that can be answered by comparing the two graphs. Trade questions with a partner.

3. Which weeks have the highest pollen counts in Linn County?

CHALLENGE Try making a double line graph combining both sets of data in one graph.

MATH TUTORIAL
CLASSZONE.COM
Click on Math Tutorial for more help making line graphs.

The integumentary system shields the body.

McDougal Littell Science

SOUTH CAROLINA

STANDARDS

7–3.3 Summarize the relationships of the major body systems (including the circulatory, respiratory, digestive, excretory, nervous, muscular, and skeletal systems).

VOCABULARY

integumentary system p. 243

epidermis p. 244

dermis p. 244

 BEFORE, you learned

- The body is defended from harmful materials
- Response structures fight disease
- The immune system responds in many ways to illness

NOW, you will learn

- About the functions of the skin
- How the skin helps protect the body
- How the skin grows and heals

EXPLORE The Skin

What are the functions of skin?

PROCEDURE

① Using a vegetable peeler, remove the skin from an apple. Take notes on the characteristics of the apple's peeled surface. Include observations on its color, moisture level, and texture.

② Place the apple on a dry surface. After fifteen minutes, note any changes in its characteristics.

WHAT DO YOU THINK?

- What is the function of an apple's skin? What does it prevent?
- What does this experiment suggest about how skin might function in the human body?

MATERIALS
- vegetable peeler
- apple

Skin performs important functions.

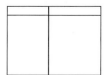

MAIN IDEA AND DETAILS
Start a two-column chart with the main idea *Skin performs important functions.* Add detail notes about those functions.

Just as an apple's skin protects the fruit inside, your skin protects the rest of your body. Made up of flat sheets of cells, your skin protects the inside of your body from harmful materials outside. The skin is part of your body's **integumentary system** (ihn-TEHG-yu-MEHN-tuh-ree), which also includes your hair and nails.

Your skin fulfills several vital functions:

- Skin repels water.
- Skin guards against infection.
- Skin helps maintain homeostasis.
- Skin senses the environment.

Skin Structure

When you look at your hand, you only see the outer layer of skin. The skin has many structures to protect your body.

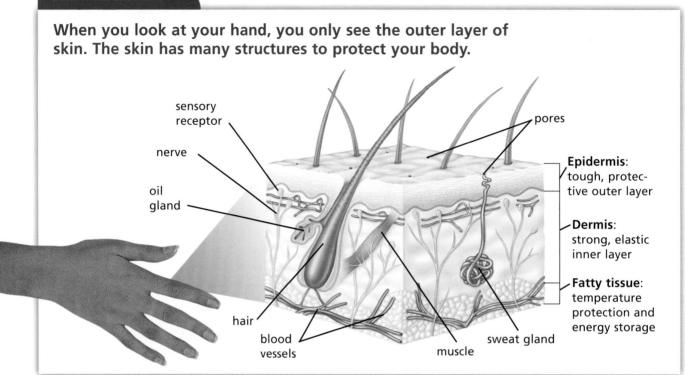

sensory receptor
nerve
oil gland
hair
blood vessels
muscle
sweat gland
pores

Epidermis: tough, protective outer layer

Dermis: strong, elastic inner layer

Fatty tissue: temperature protection and energy storage

The structure of skin is complex.

Have you ever looked closely at your skin? Your skin is more complex than it might at first seem. It does more than just cover your body. The skin is made up of many structures, which perform many different jobs.

Dermis and Epidermis

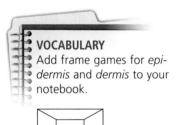

VOCABULARY
Add frame games for *epidermis* and *dermis* to your notebook.

As you can see in the diagram above, human skin is composed of two layers: an outer layer, called the **epidermis,** and an inner layer, called the **dermis.** The cells of the epidermis contain many protein fibers that give the skin tough, protective qualities. These cells are formed in the deepest part of the epidermis. Skin cells move upward slowly as new cells form below them. Above new cells, older cells rub off. The surface cells in the epidermis are dead but form a thick, waterproof layer about 30 cells deep.

The dermis, the inner layer of skin, is made of tissue that is strong and elastic. The structure of the dermis allows it to change shape instead of tear when it moves against surfaces. The dermis is rich in blood vessels, which supply oxygen and nutrients to the skin's living cells. Just beneath the dermis lies a layer of fatty tissue. This layer protects the body from extremes in temperature, and it stores energy for future use. Also in the dermis are structures that have special functions, including sweat and oil glands, hair, nails, and sensory receptors.

Sweat and Oil Glands

Deep within the dermis are structures that help maintain your body's internal environment. Sweat glands help control body temperature, and oil glands protect the skin by keeping it moist. Both types of glands open to the surface through tiny openings in the skin called pores. Pores allow important substances to pass to the skin's surface. Pores can become clogged with dirt and oil. Keeping the skin clean can prevent blockages.

Sweat glands, which are present almost everywhere on the body's surface, help maintain homeostasis. When you become too warm, the sweat glands secrete sweat, a fluid that is 99 percent water. This fluid travels from the sweat glands, through the pores, and onto the skin's surface. You probably know already about evaporation. Evaporation is the process by which a liquid becomes a gas. During evaporation, heat is released. Thus, sweating cools the skin's surface and the body.

Like sweat glands, oil glands are present almost everywhere on the body. They secrete an oil that moistens skin and hair and keeps them from becoming dry. Skin oils add flexibility and provide part, but not all, of the skin's waterproofing.

RESOURCE CENTER
CLASSZONE.COM
Explore the structure of skin.

 CHECK YOUR READING What are the functions of oil glands?

INVESTIGATE Skin Protection

How does oil protect your skin?

PROCEDURE

1. Rub a cotton ball dampened with alcohol across one of your palms. Alcohol removes the oil from the surface of your skin.

2. Drip a couple of drops of water onto the palm with alcohol. Observe what happens. Record your observations.

3. Drip a couple of drops of water onto your other palm. Observe what happens. Record your observations.

WHAT DO YOU THINK?

- Compare the observations for each palm.
- What does this investigation suggest about the importance of oil and oil glands?

CHALLENGE Predict what might happen to your skin if you removed every trace of oil several times a day.

SKILL FOCUS
Observing

MATERIALS
- cotton ball
- rubbing alcohol
- dropper
- water

TIME
10 minutes

Hair and Nails

In addition to your skin, your integumentary system includes your hair and nails. Many cells in your hair and nails are actually dead but continue to perform important functions.

The hair on your head helps your body in many ways. When you are outside, it shields your head from the Sun. In cold weather, it traps heat close to your head to keep you warmer. Your body hair works the same way, but it is much less effective at protecting your skin and keeping you warm.

Fingernails and toenails protect the tips of the fingers and toes from injury. Both are made of epidermal cells that are thick and tough. They grow from the nail bed, which continues to manufacture cells as the cells that form the nail bond together and grow.

CHECK YOUR READING What are the functions of hair and nails?

145 ×

Hair

220 ×

Nails

Your hair and nails are made of dead cells, which continue to protect you.

Sensory Receptors

How does your body know when you are touching something too hot or too cold? You get that information from sensory receptors attached to the nerves. These receptors are actually part of the nervous system, but they are located in your skin. Your skin contains receptors that sense heat, cold, pain, touch, and pressure. These sensors help protect the body. For example, temperature receptors sense when an object is hot. If it is too hot and you touch it, pain receptors send signals to your brain telling you that you have been burned.

CHECK YOUR READING What are the five types of sensory receptors in skin?

The skin grows and heals.

As a person grows, skin also grows. As you have noticed if you have ever had a bruise or a cut, your skin is capable of healing. Skin can often repair itself after injury or illness.

Growth

As your bones grow, you get taller. As your muscles develop, your arms and legs become thicker. Through all your body's growth and change, your skin has to grow, too.

Most of the growth of your skin occurs at the base of the epidermis, just above the dermis. The cells there grow and divide to form new cells, constantly replacing older epidermal cells as they die and are brushed off during daily activity. Cells are lost from the skin's surface all the time: every 2 to 4 weeks, your skin surface is entirely new. In fact, a percentage of household dust is actually dead skin cells.

Healing Skin

Small injuries to the skin heal by themselves over time.

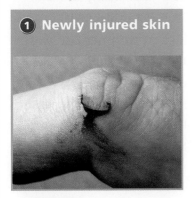
1 Newly injured skin

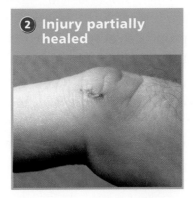
2 Injury partially healed

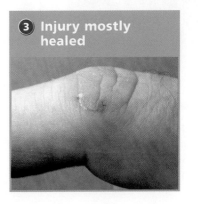
3 Injury mostly healed

READING VISUALS How do you think small injuries to the skin heal?

Injuries and Healing

You have probably experienced some injuries to your skin, such as blisters, burns, cuts, and bruises. Most such injuries result from the skin's contact with the outside world, such as a concrete sidewalk. In simple injuries, the skin can usually repair itself.

Burns can be serious injuries. They can be caused by heat, electricity, radiation, or certain chemicals. In mild cases—those of first-degree burns—skin merely becomes red, and the burn heals in a day or two. In severe cases—those of second-degree and third-degree burns—the body loses fluids, and death can result from fluid loss, infection, and other complications.

VISUALIZATION
CLASSZONE.COM
Explore how the skin heals.

Sunburns are usually minor first-degree burns, but that does not mean they cannot be serious. Rays from the Sun can burn and blister the skin much as a hot object can. Repeated burning can increase the chance of skin cancer. Specialized cells in the skin make a pigment that absorbs the Sun's ultraviolet rays and helps prevent tissue damage. These cells produce more of the skin pigment melanin when exposed to the Sun. The amount of melanin in your skin determines how dark your skin is.

Severe cold can damage skin as well. Skin exposed to cold weather can get frostbite, a condition in which the cells are damaged by freezing. Mild frostbite often heals just as well as a minor cut. In extreme cases, frostbitten limbs become diseased and have to be amputated.

 What types of weather can damage your skin?

Protection

Your skin is constantly losing old cells and gaining new cells. Although your skin is always changing, it is still important to take care of it.

- Good nutrition supplies materials the skin uses to maintain and repair itself. By drinking water, you help your body, and thus your skin, to remain moist and able to replace lost cells.

- Appropriate coverings, such as sunblock in summer and warm clothes in winter, can protect the skin from weather damage.

- Skin also needs to be kept clean. Many harmful bacteria cannot enter the body through healthy skin, but they should be washed off regularly. This prevents them from multiplying and then entering the body through small cuts or scrapes.

Wearing sunblock when you are outside protects your skin from harmful rays from the Sun.

8.3 Review

KEY CONCEPTS

1. List four functions of the skin.
2. How do the epidermis and dermis protect the body?
3. Make your own diagram with *How skin grows and repairs itself* at the center. Around the center, write at least five facts about skin growth and healing.

CRITICAL THINKING

4. **Apply** Give three examples from everyday life of sensory receptors in your skin reacting to changes in your environment.
5. **Connect** Describe a situation in which sensory receptors could be critical to survival.

CHALLENGE

6. **Infer** Exposure to sunlight may increase the number of freckles on a person's skin. Explain the connection between sunlight, melanin, and freckles.

Artificial Skin

Skin acts like a barrier, keeping our insides in and infections out. Nobody can survive without skin. But when a large amount of skin is severely damaged, the body cannot work fast enough to replace it. In some cases there isn't enough undamaged skin left on the body for transplanting. Using skin from another person risks introducing infections or rejection by the body. The answer? Artificial skin.

Here's the Skinny

To make artificial skin, scientists start with cells in a tiny skin sample. Cells from infants are used because infant skin-cell molecules are still developing, and scientists can manipulate the molecules to avoid transplant rejection. The cells from just one small sample of skin can be grown into enough artificial skin to cover 15 basketball courts. Before artificial skin, badly burned victims didn't have much chance to live. Today, 96 out of 100 burn victims survive.

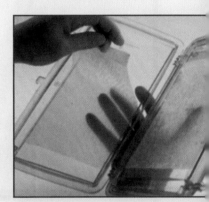

A surgeon lifts a layer of artificial skin. The skin is so thin, a newspaper could be read behind it.

What's Next?

- Scientists are hoping to be able to grow organs using this technology. Someday artificially grown livers, kidneys, and hearts may take the place of transplants and mechanical devices.

- A self-repairing plastic skin that knits itself back together when cracked has been developed. It may someday be used to create organs or even self-repairing rocket and spacecraft parts.

- Artificial polymer "skin" for robots is being developed to help robots do delicate work such as microsurgery or space exploration.

Robot designer David Hanson has developed the K-bot, a lifelike face that uses 24 motors to create expressions.

EXPLORE

1. **COMPARE AND CONTRAST** Detail the advantages and disadvantages of skin transplanted from another place on the body and artificial skin.

2. **CHALLENGE** Artificial skin is being considered for applications beyond those originally envisioned. Research and present a new potential application.

A spray-on polymer creates an artificial outer skin to help heal surface wounds on an arm.

Chapter Review

the BIG idea

Systems function to transport materials and to defend and protect the body.

CONTENT REVIEW
CLASSZONE.COM

◀ KEY CONCEPTS SUMMARY

1 **The circulatory system transports materials.**

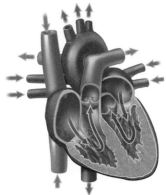

The heart, blood vessels, and blood of the circulatory system work together to transport materials from the digestive and respiratory systems to all cells. The blood exerts pressure on the walls of the blood vessels as the heart keeps the blood moving through the body.

VOCABULARY
circulatory system
  p. 225
blood p. 225
red blood cell p. 227
artery p. 229
vein p. 229
capillary p. 229

---

2 **The immune system defends the body.**

The immune system defends the body from pathogens. White blood cells identify and attack pathogens that find their way inside the body. The immune system responds to attack with inflammation, fever, and development of immunity.

Types of Pathogens	
Disease	**Pathogen**
colds, chicken pox, hepatitis, AIDS, influenza, mumps, measles, rabies	virus
food poisoning, strep throat, tetanus, tuberculosis, acne, ulcers, Lyme disease	bacteria
athlete's foot, thrush, ring worm	fungus
malaria, parasitic pneumonia, pinworm, scabies	parasites

VOCABULARY
pathogen p. 234
immune system p. 235
antibody p. 235
antigen p. 238
immunity p. 240
vaccine p. 240
antibiotic p. 241

---

3 **The integumentary system shields the body.**

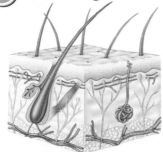

The skin protects the body from harmful materials in the environment, and allows you to sense temperature, pain, touch, and pressure. In most cases the skin is able to heal itself after injury.

VOCABULARY
integumentary system
  p. 243
epidermis p. 244
dermis p. 244

Reviewing Vocabulary

Draw a word triangle for each of the terms below. Write a term and its definition in the bottom section. In the middle section, write a sentence in which you use the term correctly. In the top section, draw a small picture to illustrate the term.

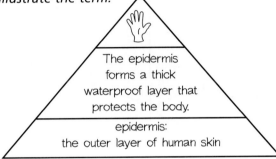

The epidermis forms a thick waterproof layer that protects the body.

epidermis: the outer layer of human skin

1. capillary

2. blood

3. dermis

4. antigen

Write a sentence describing the relationship between each pair of terms.

5. pathogen, antibody

6. artery, vein

7. immunity, vaccine

Reviewing Key Concepts

Multiple Choice *Choose the letter of the best answer.*

8. Which chamber of the heart pumps oxygen-poor blood into the lungs?
   a. right atrium
   b. right ventricle
   c. left atrium
   d. left ventricle

9. Which structures carry blood back to the heart?
   a. veins   c. arteries
   b. capillaries   d. platelets

10. The structures in the blood that carry oxygen to the cells of the body are the
    a. plasma   c. white blood cells
    b. platelets   d. red blood cells

11. High blood pressure is unhealthy because it
    a. does not exert enough pressure on your arteries
    b. causes your heart to work harder
    c. does not allow enough oxygen to get to the cells in your body
    d. causes your veins to collapse

12. Which category of pathogens causes strep throat?
    a. virus   c. fungus
    b. bacteria   d. parasite

13. Which of the following is a function of white blood cells?
    a. destroying foreign organisms
    b. providing your body with nutrients
    c. carrying oxygen to the body's cells
    d. forming a blood clot

14. Which makes up the integumentary system?
    a. a network of nerves
    b. white blood cells and antibodies
    c. the brain and spinal cord
    d. the skin, hair, and nails

15. Which structure is found in the epidermis layer of the skin?
    a. pores   c. hair follicles
    b. sweat glands d. oil glands

16. The layer of fatty tissue below the dermis protects the body from
    a. cold temperatures c. sunburn
    b. bacteria   d. infection

Short Answer *Write a short answer to each question.*

17. What are platelets? Where are they found?

18. What are antibodies? Where are they found?

19. What special structures are found in the dermis layer of the skin?

Thinking Critically

20. COMPARE AND CONTRAST How do the functions of the atria and ventricles of the heart differ? How are they alike? Use this diagram of the heart as a guide.

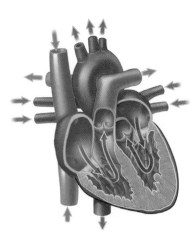

21. APPLY Veins have one-way valves that prevent the blood from flowing backwards. Most arteries do not have valves. Explain how these structures help the circulatory system function.

22. PROVIDE EXAMPLES Describe three structures in the body that help prevent harmful foreign substances from entering the body.

23. IDENTIFY CAUSE HIV is a virus that attacks and destroys the body's T cells. Why is a person who is infected with HIV more susceptible to infection and disease?

24. APPLY You fall and scrape your knee. How does the production of histamines aid the healing of this injury?

25. ANALYZE Describe how the structure of the epidermis helps protect the body from disease.

26. SYNTHESIZE Explain how sweat glands, oil glands, and hair help your body maintain homeostasis.

27. HYPOTHESIZE People with greater concentrations of melanin in their skin are less likely to get skin cancer than people who have lesser concentrations of melanin. Write a hypothesis explaining why this is so.

Answer the next six questions by listing the main structures and functions of the systems shown in the graphic organizer.

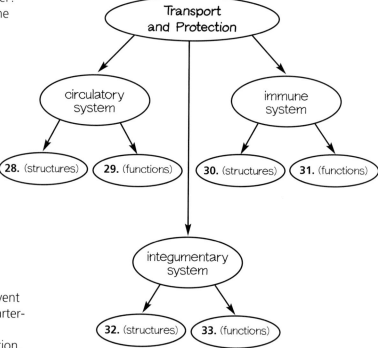

the BIG idea

34. INFER Look again at the picture on pages 222–223. Now that you have finished the chapter, how would you change or add details to your answer to the question on the photograph?

35. SYNTHESIZE Write a paragraph explaining how the integumentary system and the immune system work together to help your body maintain its homeostasis. Underline these terms in your paragraph.

UNIT PROJECTS

If you need to create graphs or other visuals for your project, be sure you have grid paper, poster board, markers, and other supplies.

Standardized Test Practice

Analyzing Data

Choose the letter of the best answer.

This chart shows the amount of time a person can stay in sunlight without burning, based on skin type and use of a sunscreen with the SPF shown.

Minimum Sun Protection Factors (SPF)					
Skin Type	1 hr	2 hr	3 hr	4 hr	5 hr
Very Fair/Sensitive	15	30	30	45	45
Fair/Sensitive	15	15	30	30	45
Fair	15	15	15	30	30
Medium	8	8	15	15	30
Dark	4	8	8	15	15

1. What is the least SPF that a person with very fair skin should use while exposed to the sun?

   a. 8
   b. 15
   c. 30
   d. 45

2. If a person with a medium skin type is exposed to sunlight for 5 hours, which SPF should be used?

   a. 4
   b. 8
   c. 15
   d. 30

3. Which skin type requires SPF 30 for three hours of sun exposure?

   a. fair/sensitive   **c.** medium
   b. fair   **d.** dark

4. Based on the data in the chart, which statement is a reasonable conclusion?

   a. People with a fair skin type are less prone to UV damage than those with a dark skin type.
   b. The darker the skin type, the more SPF protection a person needs.
   c. A person with a fair skin type does not need as much SPF protection as a person with a medium skin type.
   d. If exposure to sunlight is longer, then a person needs a higher SPF for protection.

5. If a person normally burns after 10 minutes with no protection, an SPF 2 would protect that person for 20 minutes. How long would the same person be protected with SPF 15?

   a. 1 hour
   b. $1\frac{1}{2}$ hours
   c. 2 hours
   d. $2\frac{1}{2}$ hours

Extended Response

6. UV index levels are often broadcast with daily weather reports. A UV index of 0 to 2 indicates that it would take an average person about 60 minutes to burn. A UV index level of 10 indicates that it would take the average person about 10 minutes to burn. Write a paragraph describing some variable conditions that would affect this rate. Include both environmental as well as conditions that would apply to an individual.

7. Sun protection factors are numbers on a scale that rate the effectiveness of sunscreen. Without the use of sunscreen, UV rays from the Sun can cause sunburns. People who spend time in sunlight without protection, or who get repeated burns are at a higher risk of developing deadly forms of skin cancer. Based on the information in the table and your knowledge of the layers of the skin, design a brochure encouraging people to protect their skin from sunlight. Include in your brochure the harmful effects on your skin and ways to protect your skin from harmful UV rays.

TIMELINES in Science

SEEING INSIDE *the Body*

What began as a chance accident in a darkened room was only the beginning. Today, technology allows people to produce clear and complete pictures of the human body. From X-rays to ultrasound to the latest computerized scans, accidental discoveries have enabled us to study and diagnose the inner workings of the human body.

Being able to see inside the body without cutting it open would have seemed unthinkable in the early 1890s. But within a year of the discovery of the X-ray in 1895, doctors were using technology to see through flesh to bones. In the time since then, techniques for making images have advanced to allow doctors to see soft tissue, muscle, and even to see how body systems work in real time. Many modern employ X-ray technology, while others employ sound waves or magnetic fields.

1895

Accidental X-Ray Shows Bones

Working alone in a darkened lab to study electric currents passing through vacuum tubes, William Conrad Roentgen sees a mysterious light. He puts his hand between the tubes and a screen, and an image appears on the screen—a skeletal hand! He names his discovery the X-ray, since the images are produced by rays behaving like none known before them. Roentgen uses photographic paper to take the first X-ray picture, his wife's hand.

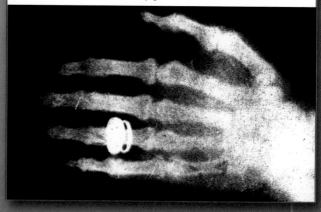

EVENTS

1880   1890

APPLICATIONS AND TECHNOLOGY

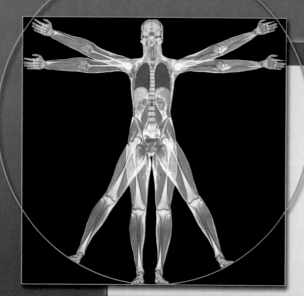

APPLICATION

Doctor Detectives

Within a year of Roentgen's discovery, X-rays were used in medicine for examining patients. By the 1920s, their use was wide-spread. Modern day X-ray tubes are based on the design of William Coolidge. Around 1913, Coolidge developed a new X-ray tube which, unlike the old gas tube, provides consistent exposure and quality. X-ray imaging changed the practice of medicine by allowing doctors to look inside the body without using surgery. Today, X-ray images, and other technologies, like the MRI used to produce the image at the left, show bones, organs, and tissues.

1914–1918

Radiologists in the Trenches

In World War I field hospitals, French physicians use X-ray technology to quickly diagnose war injuries. Marie Curie trains the majority of the female X-ray technicians. Following the war, doctors return to their practices with new expertise.

1898

Radioactivity

Building on the work of Henri Becquerel, who in 1897 discovers "rays" from uranium, physicist Marie Curie discovers radioactivity. She wins a Nobel Prize in Chemistry in 1911 for her work in radiology.

1955

See-Through Smile

X-ray images of the entire jaw and teeth allow dentist to check the roots of teeth and wisdom teeth growing below the gum line.

1900

1910

1950

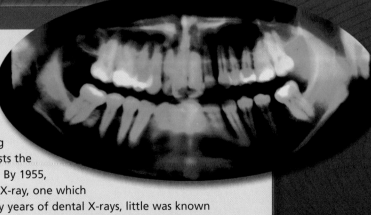

APPLICATION

Better Dental Work

Throughout the 1940s and 1950s dentists began to use X-rays. Photographing teeth with an X-ray allows cavities or decay to show up as dark spots on a white tooth. Photographing below the gum line shows dentists the pattern of growth of new teeth. By 1955, dentists could take a panoramic X-ray, one which shows the entire jaw. In the early years of dental X-rays, little was known about the dangers of radiation. Today, dentists cover a patient with a lead apron to protect them from harmful rays.

1976

New Scans Show Blood Vessels

The first computerized tomography (CT) systems scan only the head, but whole-body scanners follow by 1976. With the CT scan, doctors see clear details of blood vessels, bones, and soft organs. Instead of sending out a single X-ray, a CT scan sends several beams from different angles. Then a computer joins the images, as shown in this image of a heart.

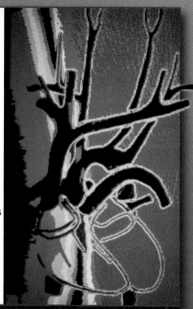

1977

Minus the X-ray

Doctors Raymond Damadian, Larry Minkoff, and Michael Goldsmith, develop the first magnetic resonance imaging (MRI). They nick-name the new machine "The Indomitable," as everyone told them it couldn't be done. MRI allows doctors to "see" soft tissue, like the knee below, in sharp detail without the use of X-rays.

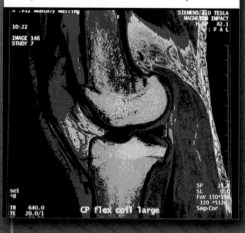

1973

PET Shows What's Working

The first positron emission tomography machine is called PET Scanner 1. It uses small doses of radioactive dye which travel through a patient's bloodstream. A PET scan then shows the distribution of the dye.

1960   1970   1980

TECHNOLOGY

Ultrasound: Moving Images in Real Time

Since the late 1950s, Ian Donald's team in Scotland had been viewing internal organs on a TV monitor using vibrations faster than sound. In 1961, while examining a female patient, Donald noticed a developing embryo. Following the discovery, ultrasound imaging became widely used to monitor the growth and health of fetuses. Ultrasound captures images in real-time, showing movement of internal tissues and organs. Ultrasound uses high frequency sound waves to create images of organs or structures inside the body. Sound waves are bounced back from organs, and a computer converts the sound waves into moving images on a television monitor.

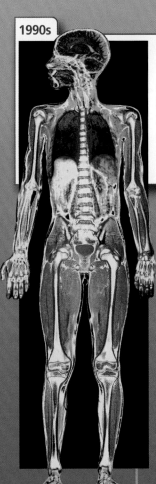

1990s

Filmless Images

With digital imaging, everything from X-rays to MRIs is now filmless. Data move directly into 3-D computer programs and shared databases.

2003

Multi-Slice CT

By 2003, 8- and 16-slice CT scanners offer detail and speed. A multi-slice scanner reduces exam time from 45 minutes to under 10 seconds.

 RESOURCE CENTER
CLASSZONE.COM

Find more on advances in medical imaging.

1990 **2000**

TECHNOLOGY

3-D Images and Brain Surgery

In operating rooms, surgeons are beginning to use another type of 3-D ultrasound known as interventional MRI. They watch 3-D images in real time and observe details of tissues while they operate. These integrated technologies now allow scientists to conduct entirely new types of studies. For example, 3-D brain images of many patients with one disease—can now be integrated into a composite image of a "typical" brain of someone with that disease.

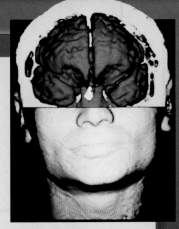

INTO THE FUTURE

Although discovered over 100 years ago X-rays are certain to remain a key tool of health workers for many years. What will be different in the future? Dentists have begun the trend to stop using film images, and rely on digital X-rays instead. In the future, all scans may be viewed and stored on computers. Going digital allows doctors across the globe to share images quickly by email.

Magnetic resonance imaging has only been in widespread use for about 20 years. Look for increased brain mapping—ability to scan the brain during a certain task. The greater the collective data on brain-mapping, the better scientists will understand how the brain works. To produce such an image requires thousands of patients and trillions of bytes of computer memory.

Also look for increased speed and mobile MRI scanners, which will be used in emergency rooms and doctor's offices to quickly assess internal damage after an accident or injury.

ACTIVITIES

Writing About Science: Brochure

Make a chart of the different types of medical imaging used to diagnose one body system. Include an explanation of how the technique works and list the pros and cons of using it.

Reliving History

X-rays use radioactivity which can be dangerous. You can use visible light to shine through thin materials that you don't normally see through. Try using a flashlight to illuminate a leaf. Discuss or draw what you see.

CHAPTER

Control and Reproduction

the BIG idea

The nervous and endocrine systems allow the body to respond to internal and external conditions.

Key Concepts

SECTION
1 **The nervous system responds and controls.**
Learn how the senses help the body get information about the environment.

SECTION
2 **The endocrine system helps regulate body conditions.**
Learn the functions of different hormones.

SECTION
3 **The reproductive system allows the production of offspring.**
Learn about the process of reproduction.

Internet Preview

CLASSZONE.COM
Chapter 9 online resources: Content Review, Visualization, three Resource Centers, Math Tutorial, Test Practice

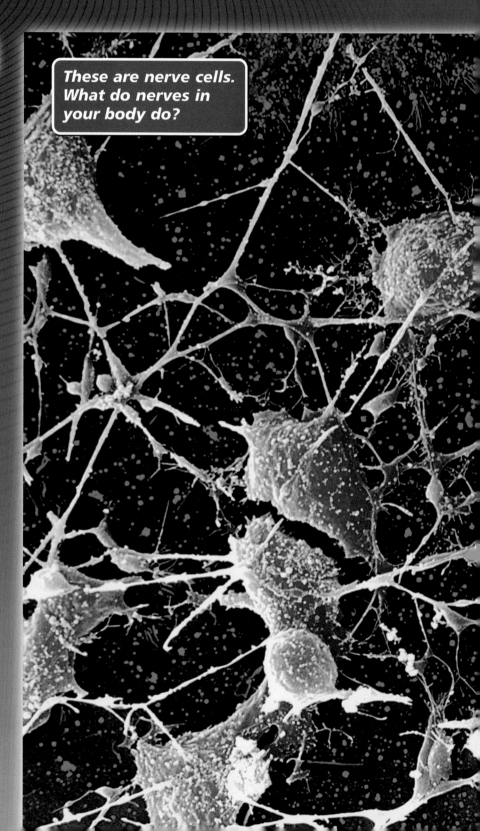

These are nerve cells. What do nerves in your body do?

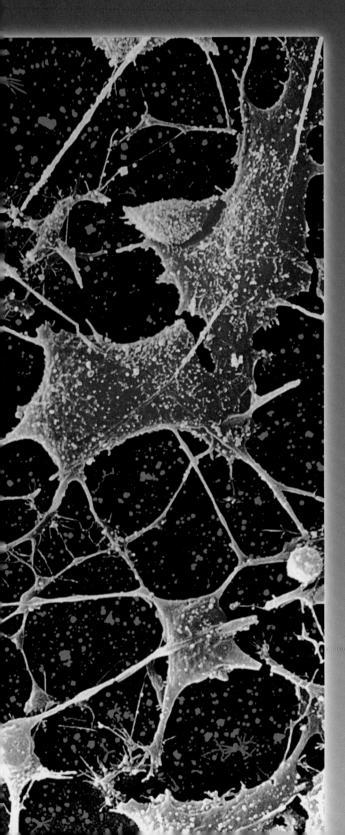

EXPLORE (the BIG idea)

Color Confusion

Make a list of six colors using a different color marker or colored pencil to write each one. Make sure not to write the color name with the same color marker or pencil. Read the list out loud as fast as you can. Now try quickly saying the color of each word out loud.

Observe and Think Did you notice a difference between reading the words in the list and saying the colors? If so, why do you think that is?

Eggs

Examine a raw chicken egg. Describe the appearance of the outside shell. Break it open into a small dish and note the different parts inside. Wash your hands when you have finished.

Observe and Think If this egg had been fertilized, which part do you think would have served as the food for the growing chicken embryo? Which part would protect the embryo from impact and serve to cushion it?

Internet Activity: The Senses

Go to **ClassZone.com** to learn how the senses allow the body to respond to external conditions. See how each sense sends specific information to the brain.

Observe and Think How do the different senses interact with one another?

NSTA
scilinks.org
SCLINKS

Reproductive System **Code: MDL047**

Getting Ready to Learn

CONCEPT REVIEW

- The circulatory system transports materials.
- The immune system responds to foreign materials.
- The integumentary system protects the body.

VOCABULARY REVIEW

homeostasis p. 172

circulatory system p. 225

immune system p. 235

integumentary system p. 243

 CONTENT REVIEW
CLASSZONE.COM
Review concepts and vocabulary.

TAKING NOTES

CHOOSE YOUR OWN STRATEGY

Take notes using one or more of the strategies from earlier chapters—**main idea webs, outlines,** or **main idea and detail notes.** You can also use other note-taking strategies that you might already know.

VOCABULARY STRATEGY

Place each vocabulary term at the center of a **description wheel** diagram. Write some words describing it on the spokes.

See the Note-Taking Handbook on pages R45–R51.

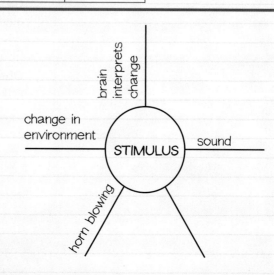

SCIENCE NOTEBOOK

Main Idea Web

Main Idea and Detail Notes

Outline
I. Main Idea
  A. Supporting idea
    1. Detail
    2. Detail
  B. Supporting idea

brain interprets change

change in environment

STIMULUS

sound

horn blowing

The nervous system responds and controls.

STANDARDS

7–3.2 Recall the major organs of the human body and their function within their particular body system.

7–3.3 Summarize the relationships of the major body systems (including the circulatory, respiratory, digestive, excretory, nervous, muscular, and skeletal systems).

VOCABULARY

stimulus p. 262
central nervous system p. 264
neuron p. 265
peripheral nervous system p. 266
autonomic nervous system p. 267
voluntary nervous system p. 267

◀ **BEFORE, you learned**

- The body can respond to the presence of foreign materials
- The body is defended from harmful materials
- The immune system responds to pathogens in many ways

▶ **NOW, you will learn**

- How the body's senses help monitor the environment
- How the sensory organs respond to stimuli
- How the nervous system works with other body systems

EXPLORE Smell

Can you name the scent?

PROCEDURE

① With a small group, take turns smelling the 3 mystery bags given to you by your teacher.

② In your notebook, write down what you think is inside each bag without showing the people in your group.

③ Compare your answers with those in your group and then look inside the bags.

WHAT DO YOU THINK?

- Did you know what was in the bags before looking inside? If so, how did you know?
- What are some objects that would require more than a sense of smell to identify?

MATERIALS
three small paper bags

Senses connect the human body to its environment.

CHOOSE YOUR OWN STRATEGY
Use a strategy from an earlier chapter to take notes on the main idea. *Senses connect the human body to its environment.*

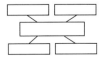

To maintain homeostasis and to survive, your body must constantly monitor the environment in which you live. This involves organs that interact so closely with the nervous system that they are often considered extensions of the nervous system. These are your sense organs. They give you the ability to see, smell, touch, hear, and taste.

Each of the senses can detect a specific type of change in the environment. For example, if you have begun to cross the street but suddenly hear a horn blowing, you may stop and step back onto the curb. Your sense of hearing allowed your brain to perceive that a car was coming and thus helped you to protect yourself.

The sound of the horn is a **stimulus.** A stimulus is a change in your environment that you react to, such as a smell, taste, sound, feeling, or sight. Your brain interprets any such change. If it did not, the information detected by the senses would be meaningless.

Sight

If you have ever tried to find your way in the dark, you know how important light is for seeing. Light is a stimulus. You are able to detect it because your eyes, the sense organs of sight, capture light and help turn it into an image, which is processed by the brain.

Light enters the eye through the lens, a structure made of transparent tissue. Muscles surrounding the lens change its shape so the lens focuses light. Other muscles control the amount of light that enters the eye by altering the size of the pupil, a dark circle in the center of the eye. To reduce the amount of light, the area around the pupil, called the iris, contracts, making the pupil smaller, thus allowing less light to enter. When the iris relaxes, more light can enter the eye.

At the back of the eye, the light strikes a layer called the retina. Among the many cells of the retina are two types of receptors, called rods and cones. Rods detect changes in brightness, while cones are sensitive to color.

Sight

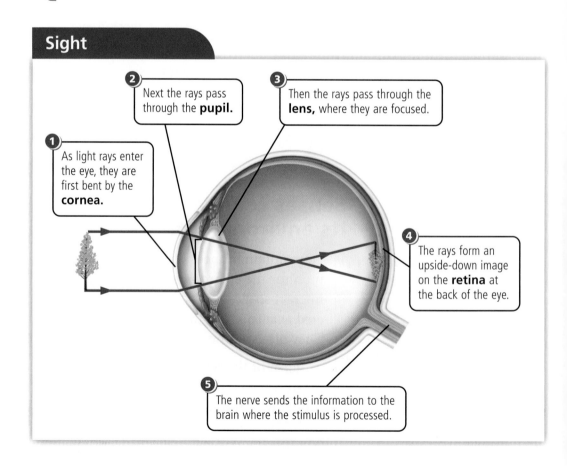

2 Next the rays pass through the **pupil.**

3 Then the rays pass through the **lens,** where they are focused.

1 As light rays enter the eye, they are first bent by the **cornea.**

4 The rays form an upside-down image on the **retina** at the back of the eye.

5 The nerve sends the information to the brain where the stimulus is processed.

Hearing

Your eyes perceive light waves, but your ears detect a different type of stimulus, sound waves. Sound waves are produced by vibrations. A reed on a clarinet vibrates, and so do your vocal cords. So does a bell after it has been hit by a mallet. The motion causes changes in the air that surrounds the bell. These changes can often be detected by the ear as sound, although many vibrations are too low or high to be heard by humans.

Sound waves enter the ear and are funneled into the auditory canal, a tube-shaped structure that ends at the eardrum. The eardrum vibrates when the sound waves strike it, and it transmits some of the vibrations to a tiny bone called the stirrup. Pressure caused by vibrations from the stirrup causes fluid in the ear to move. The movement of the fluid results in signals sent to the brain that are interpreted as sound.

 How are vibrations involved in hearing?

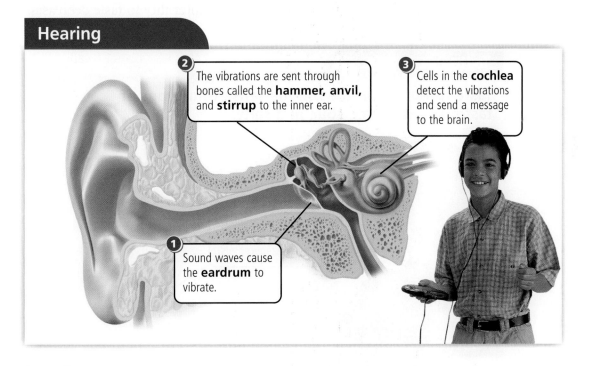

Hearing

② The vibrations are sent through bones called the **hammer, anvil, and stirrup** to the inner ear.

③ Cells in the **cochlea** detect the vibrations and send a message to the brain.

① Sound waves cause the **eardrum** to vibrate.

Touch

The sense of touch depends on tiny sensory receptors in the skin. Without these you wouldn't be able to feel pressure, temperature, or pain. Nerves near the top of the inner layer of your skin, or dermis, sense textures, like smooth glass or rough concrete. Nerves deeper in the dermis sense pressure. Other receptors in the dermis sense how hot or cold an object is and can thus help protect you from burning yourself. The sense of touch is important in alerting your brain to danger. Though you might wish that you couldn't feel pain, it serves a critical purpose. Without it, you could harm your body without realizing it.

Smell

Whereas sight, touch, and hearing involve processing physical information from the environment, the senses of smell and taste involve detecting chemical information. Much as taste receptors sense chemicals in food, scent receptors sense chemicals in the air. High in the back of your nose, a patch of tissue grows hairlike fibers covered in mucus. Molecules enter your nose, stick to the mucus, and then bind to receptors in the hairlike fibers. The receptors send an impulse to your brain, and you perceive the scent.

Taste

Your tongue is covered with small sensory structures called taste buds, which are also found in the throat and on the roof of the mouth. Each taste bud includes about 100 sensory cells. The receptors are specialized to detect four general tastes: sweet, sour, bitter, and salty. The thousands of tastes you experience are also partially due to sense organs in your nose. That is why when you have a cold, your ability to taste decreases.

Taste

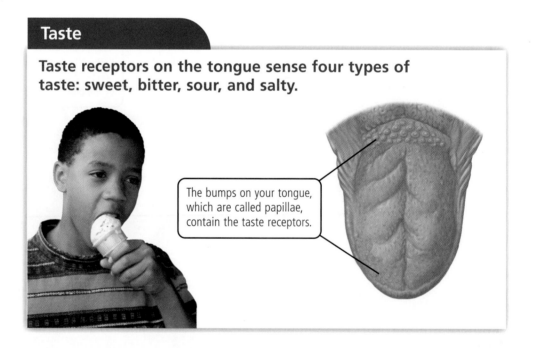

Taste receptors on the tongue sense four types of taste: sweet, bitter, sour, and salty.

The bumps on your tongue, which are called papillae, contain the taste receptors.

RESOURCE CENTER
CLASSZONE.COM

Explore the nervous system.

The central nervous system controls functions.

The **central nervous system** consists of the brain and spinal cord. The brain is located in and protected by the skull, and the spinal cord is located in and protected by the spine. The central nervous system communicates with the rest of the nervous system through electrical signals sent through nerve cells. Impulses travel very quickly, some as fast as 90 meters (295 ft) per second. That's like running almost the entire length of a soccer field in one second.

The Brain

Different areas of the brain control different functions.

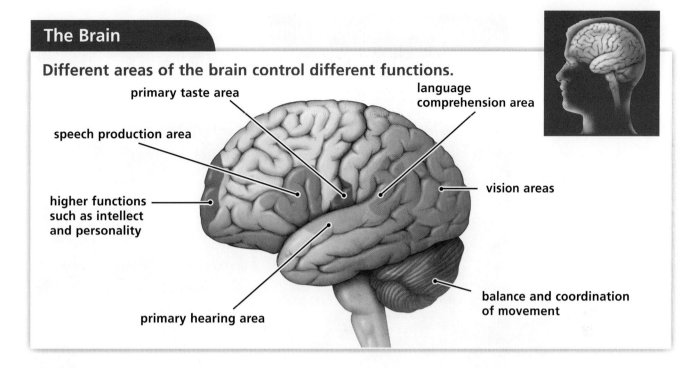

primary taste area

language comprehension area

speech production area

vision areas

higher functions such as intellect and personality

balance and coordination of movement

primary hearing area

Brain

The average adult brain contains nearly 100 billion nerve cells, called **neurons.** The brain directly controls voluntary behavior, such as walking and thinking. It also allows the body to control most involuntary responses such as heartbeat, blood pressure, fluid balance, and posture.

As you can see in the diagram, every area of the brain has a specific function, although many functions involve more than one area. For example, certain areas in the brain process and perceive senses, while other areas help you stand up straight. The lower part of the brain, called the brain stem, controls activities such as breathing and vomiting.

VOCABULARY
Be sure to make a description wheel for the term *neuron*.

Spinal Cord

The spinal cord is about 44 centimeters (17 in.) long and weighs about 35–40 grams (1.25–1.4 oz). It is the main pathway for information, connecting the brain and the nerves throughout your body. The spinal cord is protected and supported by the vertebral column, which is made up of small bones called vertebrae. The spinal cord itself looks like a double-layered tube with an outer layer of nerve fibers wrapped in tissue, an inner layer of nerve cell bodies, and a central canal that runs the entire length of the cord. Extending from the spinal cord are 31 pairs of nerves, which send sensory impulses into the spinal cord, which in turn sends them to the brain. In a similar way, spinal nerves send impulses to muscles and glands.

CHECK YOUR READING Describe the functions performed by the central nervous system.

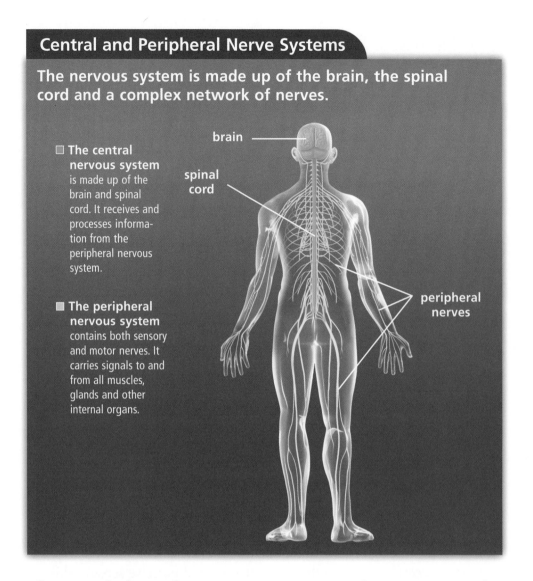

Central and Peripheral Nerve Systems

The nervous system is made up of the brain, the spinal cord and a complex network of nerves.

■ **The central nervous system** is made up of the brain and spinal cord. It receives and processes information from the peripheral nervous system.

■ **The peripheral nervous system** contains both sensory and motor nerves. It carries signals to and from all muscles, glands and other internal organs.

brain

spinal cord

peripheral nerves

The peripheral nervous system is a network of nerves.

Nerves, which are found throughout the body, are often referred to all together as the **peripheral nervous system.** Both sensory and motor nerves are parts of the peripheral nervous system. Sensory nerves receive information from the environment—such as heat or cold—and pass the information to the central nervous system. Motor nerves send signals to your muscles that allow you to move. The peripheral nervous system carries information for both voluntary and involuntary responses.

Involuntary responses of the body are necessary for your survival. In times of danger, there is no time to think. The body must respond immediately. In less stressful situations, the body maintains activities like breathing and digesting food. These functions go on without conscious thought. They are controlled by part of the peripheral nervous system called the autonomic (AW-tuh-NAHM-ihk) nervous system.

The **autonomic nervous system** controls the movement of the heart, the smooth muscles in the stomach, the intestines, and the glands. The autonomic nervous system has two distinct functions: to conserve and store energy and to respond quickly to changes. You can think of the autonomic nervous system as having a division that performs each of these two main functions.

Each division is controlled by different locations on the spinal cord, or within the brain and the brain stem. The cerebellum, which is located at the rear of the brain, coordinates balance and related muscle activity. The brain stem, which lies between the spinal cord and the rest of the brain, controls heartbeat, respiration, and the smooth muscles in the blood vessels.

When you are under stress, one part of the autonomic nervous system causes what is called the "fight or flight response." Rapid changes in your body prepare you either to fight the danger or to take flight and run away from the danger. The response of your nervous system is the same, whether the stress is a real danger, like falling off a skateboard, or a perceived danger, like being worried or embarrassed.

The **voluntary nervous system** monitors movement and functions that can be controlled consciously. Every movement you think about is voluntary. The voluntary nervous system controls the skeletal muscles of the arms, the legs, and the rest of the body. It also controls the muscles that are responsible for speech and the senses.

The autonomic nervous system responds quickly to changes in balance.

 CHECK YOUR READING What is the difference between the voluntary and the autonomic nervous systems?

9.1 Review

KEY CONCEPTS

1. Make a chart of five senses that includes a definition and a stimulus for each sense.

2. Explain the process by which you hear a sound.

3. What are two body systems with which the nervous system interacts? How do these interactions take place?

CRITICAL THINKING

4. **Classify** Determine if the following actions involve the autonomic or the voluntary nervous system: chewing, eye blinking, jumping at a loud noise, and riding a bike.

5. **Apply** Describe what messages are sent by the nervous system when you go outside wearing a sweater on a hot day.

○ CHALLENGE

6. **Hypothesize** When people lose their sense of smell, their sense of taste is often affected as well. Why do you think the ability to taste would be decreased by the loss of the ability to smell?

CHAPTER INVESTIGATION

Are You a Supertaster?

OVERVIEW AND PURPOSE Do you think broccoli tastes bitter? If so, you might be extra sensitive to bitter tastes. In this investigation you will

- examine the surface of your tongue to find a possible connection between the bumps you find there and your sensitivity to bitter flavors
- calculate the average number of papillae in your class

Make sure to do this investigation in the cafeteria since you will be placing food coloring on your tongue.

MATERIALS

- blue food coloring
- paper cup
- 1 cotton swab
- 1 reinforcement circle for ring-binder paper
- paper towel or napkin
- 1 sheet of white paper

▶ **Problem**

How can you tell if you are a supertaster?

▶ **Hypothesize**

Write a hypothesis to explain how you might tell if you are a supertaster. Your hypothesis should take the form of an "If . . . , then . . . , because . . ." statement.

▶ **Procedure**

1. Make a data table in your **Science Notebook** like the one shown on page 269.

2. Put a few drops of blue food coloring into a paper cup.

3. Use a paper towel or a napkin to pat your tongue thoroughly dry.

4. Dip the tip of a cotton swab into the blue food coloring, and use it to paint the first 2 centimeters of your tongue.

5 Press a piece of white paper firmly onto the painted surface of your tongue, and then place the paper on your desk.

step 5

6 Place a notebook reinforcement circle on the blue area.

7 You should see white circles in a field of blue. The white circles are the bumps on your tongue called fungiform papillae, which contain taste buds. Count the number of white circles inside the reinforcement circle. There may be many white circles crammed together that vary in size, or just a few. If there are just a few, they may be larger than the ones on someone who has many white circles close together. If there are too many to count, try to count the number in half of the circle and multiply this number by 2. Record your total count in your data table.

▶ Observe and Analyze
Write It Up

1. OBSERVE What did you observe while looking at the tongue print? Is the surface the same all over your tongue?

2. CALCULATE Record the number of papillae within the reinforcement circle of all the students in your class.

AVERAGE Calculate the average number of papillae counted in the class.

$$\text{average} = \frac{\text{sum of papillae in class}}{\text{number of students}}$$

▶ Conclude
Write It Up

1. INTERPRET How do the number of fungiform papillae on your tongue compare with the number your partner counted?

2. INFER Do you think there is a relationship between the number of fungiform papillae and taste? If so, what is it?

3. IDENTIFY What foods might a supertaster not like?

4. APPLY Do you think that there are other taste perceptions besides bitterness that might be influenced by the number of fungiform papillae that an individual has? Why do you think so?

▶ INVESTIGATE Further

CHALLENGE Calculate the area in square millimeters inside the reinforcement circle, and use this value to express each person's papillae count as a density (number of papillae per square millimeter).

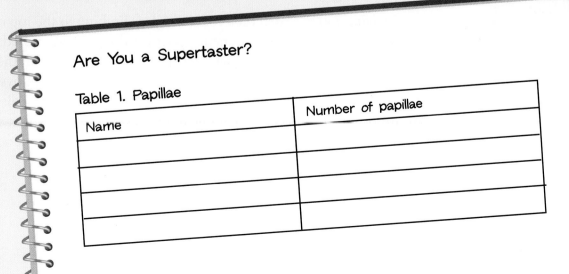

Are You a Supertaster?

Table 1. Papillae

Name	Number of papillae

The endocrine system helps regulate body conditions.

STANDARDS

7–3.2 Recall the major organs of the human body and their function within their particular body system.

7–3.3 Summarize the relationships of the major body systems (including the circulatory, respiratory, digestive, excretory, nervous, muscular, and skeletal systems).

VOCABULARY

endocrine system p. 270
hormone p. 271
gland p. 271

◀ BEFORE, you learned

- Many body systems function without conscious control
- The body systems work automatically to maintain homeostasis
- Homeostasis is important to an organism's survival

▶ NOW, you will learn

- About the role of hormones
- About the functions of glands
- How the body uses feedback mechanisms to help maintain homeostasis

THINK ABOUT

How does your body react to surprise?

In a small group, determine how your body responds to a surprising situation. Have one student in the group pretend he or she is responding to a surprise. The other group members should determine how the body reacts physically to that event. How do your respiratory system, digestive system, circulatory system, muscle system, and skeletal system react?

CHOOSE YOUR OWN STRATEGY

Begin taking notes on the main idea: *Hormones are the body's chemical messengers.* Use a strategy from an earlier chapter or one of your own. Include a definition of *hormone* in your notes.

Hormones are the body's chemical messengers.

Imagine you're seated on a roller coaster climbing to the top of a steep incline. In a matter of moments, your car drops one hundred feet. You might notice that your heart starts beating faster. You grab the seat and notice that your palms are sweaty. These are normal physical responses to scary situations. The **endocrine system** controls the conditions in your body by making and releasing chemicals that are transported thoughout the body. Most responses of the endocrine system are controlled by the autonomic nervous system.

Hormones are chemicals that are made in one organ, travel through the blood, and produce an effect in target cells. Target cells have structures that allow them to respond to the chemical. Many hormones, as you can see in the table below, affect all the cells in the body.

Because hormones are made at one location and function at another, they are often called chemical messengers. In order for a hormone to have an effect, it binds to receptors on the surface of or inside the cells. There the hormone begins the chemical changes that cause the target cells to function in a specific way. All of the functions of the endocrine system work automatically, without your conscious control.

Different types of hormones perform different jobs. Some of these jobs are to control the production of other hormones, to regulate the balance of chemicals such as glucose and salt in your blood, or to produce responses to changes in the environment. Some hormones are made only during specific times in a person's life. For example, hormones that control the development of sexual characteristics are not produced in significant amounts during childhood. During adolescence, high levels of these hormones cause major changes in a person's body.

The individuals on this roller coaster are experiencing a burst of the hormone adrenaline.

 How are hormones like messengers?

Hormones		
Name	**Where produced**	**Produces responses in**
Growth hormone	pituitary gland	all body cells
Antidiuretic hormone	pituitary gland	kidneys
Thyroxine	thyroid gland	all body cells
Cortisol	adrenal glands	all body cells
Adrenaline	adrenal glands	heart, lungs, stomach, intestines, glands
Insulin	pancreas	all body cells
Testosterone (males)	testes	all body cells
Estrogen (females)	ovaries	all body cells

Glands produce and release hormones.

The main structures of the endocrine system are groups of specialized cells called **glands.** Many glands in the body produce hormones and release them into your circulatory system. As you can see in the illustration on page 273, endocrine glands can be found in many parts of your body. However, all hormones move from the cells in which they are produced to cause effects in target cells.

RESOURCE CENTER
CLASSZONE.COM

Learn more about the endocrine system.

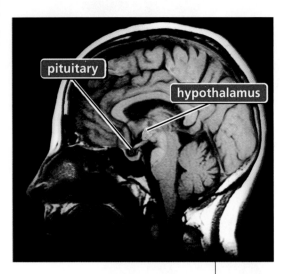

The hypothalamus and the pituitary are important endocrine glands.

Pituitary Gland The pituitary (pih-TOO-ih-TEHR-ee) gland can be thought of as the director of the endocrine system. The pituitary gland is the size of a pea and is located at the base of the brain—right above the roof of your mouth. Many important hormones are produced in the pituitary gland, including hormones that control growth, sexual development, and the absorption of water into the blood by the kidneys.

Hypothalamus The hypothalamus (HY-poh-THAL-uh-muhs) is attached to the pituitary gland and is the primary connection between the nervous and endocrine systems. All of the secretions of the pituitary gland are controlled by the hormones produced in the hypothalamus.

Pineal Gland The pineal (PIHN-ee-uhl) gland is a tiny organ about the size of a pea. It is buried deep in the brain. The pineal gland is sensitive to different levels of light and the hormone it produces is essential to rhythms such as sleep, body temperature, reproduction, and aging.

Thyroid Gland You can feel your thyroid gland if you place your hand on the part of your throat called the Adam's apple and swallow. What you feel is the cartilage surrounding your thyroid gland. The thyroid releases hormones necessary for growth and metabolism. The tissue of the thyroid is made of millions of tiny pouches, which store the thyroid hormones. The thyroid gland also produces the hormone calcitonin, which is involved in the regulation of calcium in the body.

Thymus The thymus is located in your chest. It is relatively large in the newborn baby and continues to grow until puberty. Following puberty, it gradually decreases in size. The thymus helps the body fight disease by controlling the production of white blood cells called T cells.

Adrenal Glands The adrenal glands are located on top of your kidneys. The adrenal glands secrete about 30 different hormones that regulate carbohydrate, protein, and fat metabolism and water and salt levels in your body. Some other hormones produced by the adrenal glands help you fight allergies. Roller coaster rides, loud noises, or stress can activate your adrenal glands to produce adrenaline, the hormone that makes your heart beat faster.

Pancreas The pancreas is part of both the digestive and the endocrine systems. The pancreas secretes two hormones, insulin and glucagon. These hormones regulate the level of glucose in your blood. The pancreas sits beneath the stomach and is connected to the small intestine.

Ovaries and Testes The ovaries and testes secrete hormones that control sexual development.

Other Organs Some organs that are not considered part of the
endocrine system do produce important hormones. The kidneys
secrete a hormone that regulates the production of red blood cells.
This hormone is secreted whenever the oxygen level in your blood
decreases. Once the hormone has stimulated the red bone marrow to
produce more red blood cells, the oxygen level of the blood increases.
The heart produces two hormones that help regulate blood pressure.
These hormones, secreted by one of the chambers of the heart,
stimulate the kidneys to remove more salt from the blood.

 Which glands and organs are part of the endocrine system?

Endocrine System

The endocrine system is made of a group of glands. These glands
produce and release hormones, or chemical messengers.

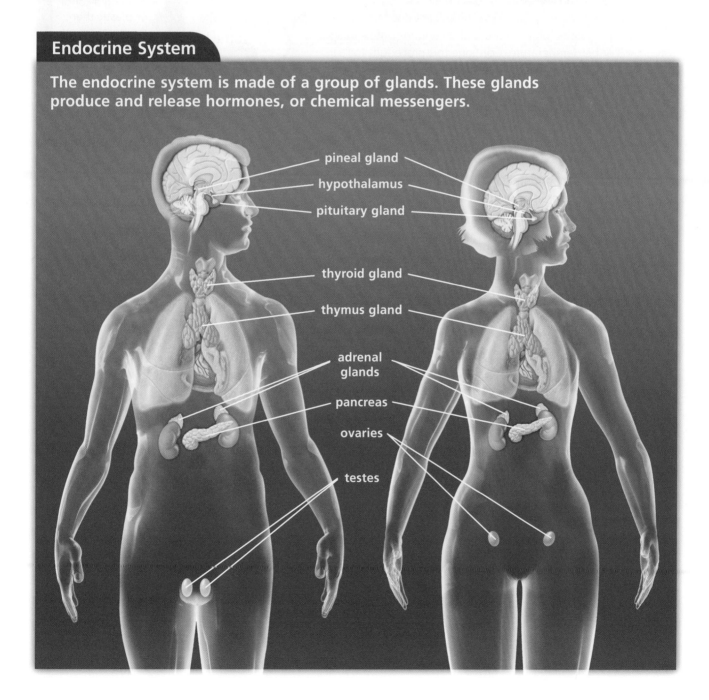

pineal gland
hypothalamus
pituitary gland

thyroid gland
thymus gland

adrenal
glands

pancreas

ovaries

testes

INVESTIGATE Response to Exercise

How does your body temperature change when you exercise?

PROCEDURE

1. Working in groups of two, read all the instructions in this activity first. Appoint one person to be the subject and one person to be the timer and note taker. Using a mercury-free thermometer, have the subject take his or her temperature. Record the temperature in your notebook.

2. While staying seated the subject begins to do sitting-down jumping jacks. The subject does the jumping jacks for 1 minute and then immediately takes his or her temperature. Continue this procedure for a total of 3 times, measuring the temperature after each minute of exercise.

WHAT DO YOU THINK?

- How did the subject's temperature change while exercising?
- What factors may contribute to the rate at which the temperature changed in each person?
- How did the subject's physical appearance change from the beginning of the activity to the end?

CHALLENGE Graph the results on a line graph, with temperature on the *x*-axis and time on the *y*-axis.

SKILL FOCUS
Observing

MATERIALS
- stopwatch or timing device
- notebook
- graph paper
- mercury-free thermometer
- rubbing alcohol or plastic thermometer covers

TIME
30 minutes

Control of the endocrine system includes feedback mechanisms.

As you might recall, the cells in the human body function best within a specific set of conditions. Homeostasis (HOH-mee-oh-STAY-sihs) is the process by which the body maintains these internal conditions, even though conditions outside the body may change. The endocrine system is very important in maintaining homeostasis.

 Why is homeostasis important?

Because hormones are powerful chemicals capable of producing dramatic changes, their levels in the body must be carefully regulated. The endocrine system has several levels of control. Most glands are regulated by the pituitary gland, which in turn is controlled by the hypothalamus, part of the brain. The endocrine system helps maintain homeostasis through the action of negative feedback mechanisms.

Negative Feedback

Most feedback mechanisms in the body are called negative mechanisms, because the final effect of the response is to turn off the response. An increase in the amount of a hormone in the body feeds back to inhibit the further production of that hormone.

The production of the hormone thyroxine by the thyroid gland is an example of a negative feedback mechanism. Thyroxine controls the body's metabolism, or the rate at which the cells in the body release energy by cellular respiration. When the body needs energy, the thyroid gland releases thyroxine into the blood to increase cellular respiration. However, the thyroid gland is controlled by the pituitary gland, which in turn is controlled by the hypothalamus. Increased levels of thyroxine in the blood inhibit the signals from the hypothalamus and the pituitary gland to the thyroid gland. Production of thyroxine in the thyroid gland decreases.

Negative and Positive Feedback

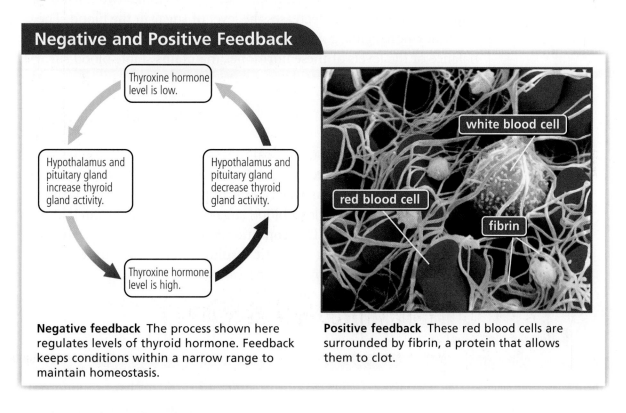

Thyroxine hormone level is low.

Hypothalamus and pituitary gland increase thyroid gland activity.

Hypothalamus and pituitary gland decrease thyroid gland activity.

Thyroxine hormone level is high.

white blood cell

red blood cell

fibrin

Negative feedback The process shown here regulates levels of thyroid hormone. Feedback keeps conditions within a narrow range to maintain homeostasis.

Positive feedback These red blood cells are surrounded by fibrin, a protein that allows them to clot.

Positive Feedback

Some responses of the endocrine system, as well as other body systems, are controlled by positive feedback. The outcome of a positive feedback mechanism is not to maintain homeostasis, but to produce a response that continues to increase. Most positive feedback mechanisms result in extreme responses that are necessary under extreme conditions.

For example, when you cut yourself, the bleeding is controlled by positive feedback. First, the damaged tissue releases a chemical signal.

The signal starts a series of chemical reactions that lead to the formation of threadlike proteins called fibrin. The fibrin causes the blood to clot, filling the injured area. Other examples of positive feedback include fever, the immune response, puberty, and the process of childbirth.

 READING What is the difference between negative and positive feedback?

Balanced Hormone Action

In the body, the action of one hormone is often balanced by the action of another. When you ride a bicycle, you are able to ride in a straight line, despite bumps and dips in the road, by making constant steering adjustments. If the bicycle is pulled to the right, you adjust the handlebars by turning a tiny bit to the left.

Some hormones maintain homeostasis in the same way that you steer your bicycle. The pancreas, for example, produces two hormones. One hormone, insulin, decreases the level of sugar in the blood. The other hormone, glucagon, increases sugar levels in the blood. The balance of the levels of these hormones maintains stable blood sugar between meals.

Hormone Imbalance

Because hormones regulate critical functions in the body, too little or too much of any hormone can cause serious disease. When the pancreas produces too little insulin, sugar levels in the blood can rise to dangerous levels. Very high levels of blood sugar can damage the circulatory system and the kidneys. This condition, known as diabetes mellitus, is often treated by injecting synthetic insulin into the body to replace the insulin not being made by the pancreas.

9.2 Review

KEY CONCEPTS

1. List three different jobs that hormones perform.

2. Draw an outline of the human body. Add the locations and functions of the pituitary, thyroid, adrenal, and pineal glands to your drawing.

3. What is the function of a negative feedback mechanism?

CRITICAL THINKING

4. **Analyze** Explain why hormones are called chemical messengers.

5. **Analyze** List two sets of hormones that have opposing actions. How do the actions of these hormones help maintain homeostasis?

CHALLENGE

6. **Connect** Copy the diagram below and add three more stimuli and the resulting feedback mechanisms.

CONNECTING SCIENCES

Heating and Cooling

The cells in our bodies can survive only within a limited temperature range. The body must maintain a constant core temperature at about 37°C (98.6°F). Body temperature is a measure of the average thermal energy in the body. To keep a constant temperature range, our bodies either lose or gain thermal energy.

Energy cannot be created or destroyed, but it can be transferred from one form or place to another. The major source of thermal energy in our bodies is food. When our bodies break down nutrients, some of the chemical energy is released as thermal energy that heats our bodies. Also, some of the kinetic energy from muscle movement is converted into thermal energy.

Body temperature is controlled by the hypothalamus region of the brain. The hypothalamus controls the rate of nutrient use. The hypothalamus also controls shivering and sweating.

Heat is the flow of energy from a warmer to a cooler object. Heat transfer between the body and its surroundings occurs in four ways.

1 Evaporation: When water evaporates, or changes from liquid to gas, energy is required. When perspiration evaporates from the surface of our skin, we lose thermal energy as heat.

2 Radiation: Heat transfer also occurs through waves that radiate out from a warm object or area. Sitting in the sunshine warms us because we gain thermal energy from the Sun's radiation. Our warm bodies can also radiate energy into cooler air.

3 Conduction: When two objects are in direct contact, heat flows by conduction from the warmer to the cooler object. If you stand barefoot on hot sand, heat quickly flows into your feet by conduction.

4 Convection: In convection, heat transfer occurs through the movement of particles in a gas or liquid. Your body loses some thermal energy because of convection in the air around you.

EXPLORE

1. **CONNECT** What are some behaviors that help you lose or gain thermal energy?

2. **CHALLENGE** Choose a behavior that either warms or cools your body. Draw a diagram and label it with the types of heat transfer that are occurring.

The reproductive system allows the production of offspring.

STANDARDS

7–3.3 Summarize the relationships of the major body systems (including the circulatory, respiratory, digestive, excretory, nervous, muscular, and skeletal systems).

VOCABULARY

menstruation p. 279
fertilization p. 281
embryo p. 281
fetus p. 282

 BEFORE, you learned

- Some hormones regulate sexual development
- Glands release hormones

NOW, you will learn

- About specialized cells and organs in male and female reproductive systems
- About fertilization
- About the development of the embryo and fetus during pregnancy

---

EXPLORE Reproduction

How are sperm and egg cells different?

PROCEDURE

1. From your teacher, gather slides of egg cells and sperm cells.
2. Put each slide under a microscope.
3. Draw a sketch of each cell.
4. With a partner, discuss the differences that you observed.

WHAT DO YOU THINK?

- What were the differences that you observed?
- What are the benefits of the different characteristics for each cell?

MATERIALS

- slides of egg and sperm cells
- microscope
- paper
- pencil

CHOOSE YOUR OWN STRATEGY
Begin taking notes on the idea that the reproductive system produces specialized cells. You might use an outline or another strategy of your choice.

The reproductive system produces specialized cells.

Like all living organisms, humans reproduce. The reproductive system allows adults to produce offspring. Although males and females have different reproductive systems, both systems share an important characteristic. They both make specialized cells. In any organism or any system, a specialized cell is a cell that takes on a special job.

In the female these specialized cells are called egg cells. In the male they are called sperm cells. In the reproductive system, each specialized cell provides genetic material. Genetic material contains the information that an organism needs to form, develop, and grow.

Both the male and female reproductive systems rely on hormones from the endocrine system. The hormones act as chemical messengers that signal the process of sexual development. Sexual development includes the growth of reproductive organs and the development of sexual characteristics. Once mature, the reproductive organs produce hormones to maintain secondary sexual characteristics.

The Female Reproductive System

The female reproductive system has two functions. The first is to produce egg cells, and the second is to protect and nourish the offspring until birth. The female has two reproductive organs called ovaries. Each ovary contains on average hundreds of egg cells. About every 28 days, the pituitary gland releases a hormone that stimulates some of the eggs to develop and grow. The ovaries then produce hormones that get the uterus ready to receive the egg.

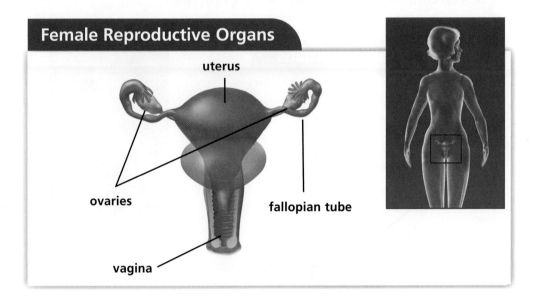

Female Reproductive Organs

uterus

ovaries

fallopian tube

vagina

Menstruation

After an egg cell develops fully, another hormone signals the ovary to release the egg. The egg moves from the ovary into a fallopian tube. Within ten to twelve hours, the egg cell may be fertilized by a sperm cell and move to the uterus. Once inside the thick lining of the uterus, the fertilized egg cell rapidly grows and divides.

However, if fertilization does not occur within 24 hours after the egg cell leaves the ovary, both the egg and the lining of the uterus begin to break down. The muscles in the uterus contract in a process called **menstruation.** Menstruation is the flow of blood and tissue from the body through a canal called the vagina over a period of about five days.

CHECK YOUR READING   Where does the egg travel after it leaves the ovary?

The Male Reproductive System

Testes The organs that produce sperm are called the testes (TEHS-teez). Inside the testes are tiny, coiled tubes hundreds of feet long. Sperm are produced inside these coiled tubes. The testes release a hormone that controls the development of sperm. This hormone is also responsible for the development of physical characteristics in men such as facial hair and a deep voice.

Sperm Sperm cells are the specialized cells of the male reproductive system. Males start producing sperm cells sometime during adolescence. The sperm is a single cell with a head and a tail. The sperm's head is filled with chromosomes, and the tail functions as a whip, making the sperm highly mobile. The sperm travel from the site of production, the testes, through several different structures of the reproductive system. While they travel, the sperm mix with fluids. This fluid is called semen and contains nutrients for the sperm cells. One drop of semen contains up to several million sperm cells.

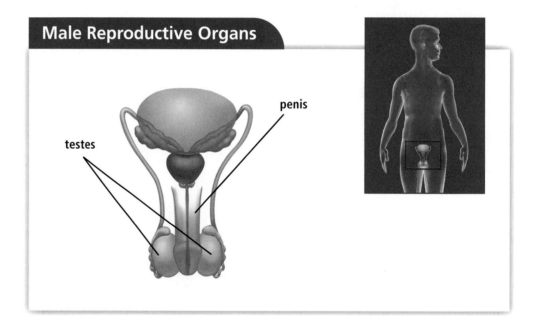

Male Reproductive Organs

testes

penis

The production of offspring includes fertilization, pregnancy, and birth.

VISUALIZATION
CLASSZONE.COM

Follow an egg from fertilization to implantation.

Each sperm cell, like each egg cell, has half of the genetic material needed for a human being to grow and develop. During sexual intercourse, millions of sperm cells leave the testes. The sperm cells exit the male's body through the urethra, a tube that leads out of the penis. The sperm cells enter the female's body through the vagina. Next they travel into the uterus and continue on to the fallopian tube.

Fertilization

Fertilization occurs when one sperm cell joins the egg cell. The fallopian tube is the site of fertilization. Immediately, chemical changes in the egg's surface prevent any more sperm from entering. Once inside the egg, the genetic material from the sperm combines with the genetic material of the egg cell. Fertilization is complete.

The fertilized egg cell then moves down the fallopian tube toward the uterus. You can trace the path of the egg cell in the diagram on this page. It divides into two cells. Each of those cells divides again, to form a total of four cells. Cell division continues, and a ball of cells forms, called an **embryo** (EM-bree-OH). Within a few days, the embryo attaches itself to the thickened, spongy lining of the uterus in a process called implantation.

VOCABULARY
Be sure to add the description wheels for the terms *fertilization* and *embryo* to your notebook.

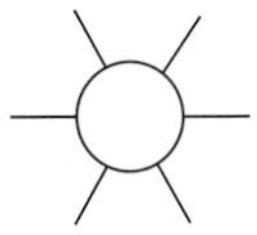

Fertilization

The egg moves down the fallopian tube following fertilization. Its final destination is the uterus.

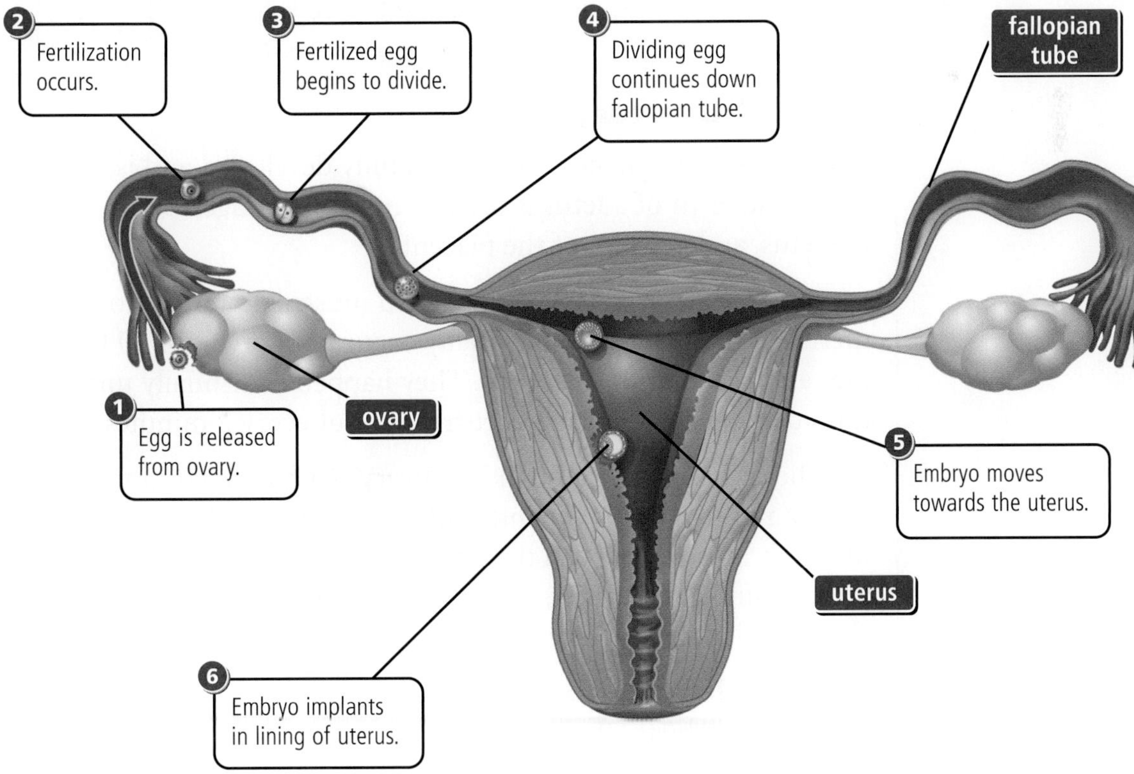

2 Fertilization occurs.

3 Fertilized egg begins to divide.

4 Dividing egg continues down fallopian tube.

fallopian tube

1 Egg is released from ovary.

ovary

5 Embryo moves towards the uterus.

uterus

6 Embryo implants in lining of uterus.

READING VISUALS Where does fertilization occur?

Pregnancy

The nine months of pregnancy can be divided into three periods of about the same length. Each period marks specific stages of development. In the first week following implantation, the embryo continues to grow rapidly. Both the embryo and the uterus contribute cells to a new, shared organ called the placenta. The placenta has blood vessels that lead from the mother's circulatory system to the embryo through a large tube called the umbilical cord. Oxygen and nutrients from the mother's body will move through the placenta and umbilical cord to the growing embryo.

Around the eighth week of pregnancy, the developing embryo is called a **fetus.** The fetus begins to have facial features, major organ systems, and the beginnings of a skeleton. The fetus develops the sexual traits that are either male or female. In the twelfth week, the fetus continues to grow and its bones develop further. In the last twelve weeks, the fetus and all of its organ systems develop fully.

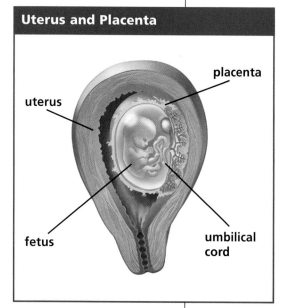

Uterus and Placenta

placenta

uterus

fetus

umbilical cord

 CHECK YOUR READING Describe the development of an embryo and fetus at two weeks, eight weeks, and twelve weeks.

Labor and Delivery

At the end of pregnancy, the fetus is fully developed and is ready to be born. The birth of a fetus is divided into three stages; labor, delivery of the fetus, and delivery of the placenta.

The first stage of birth begins with muscular contractions of the uterus. These contractions initially occur at intervals of 10 to 30 minutes and last about 40 seconds. They happen continually until the muscular contractions are occurring about every 2 minutes.

The second stage of birth is delivery. With each contraction, the opening to the uterus expands until it becomes wide enough for the mother's muscles to push the fetus out. During delivery the fetus is pushed out of the uterus, through the vagina, and out of the body. The fetus is still connected to the mother by the umbilical cord.

The umbilical cord is cut shortly after the fetus is delivered. Within minutes after birth, the placenta separates from the uterine wall and the mother pushes it out with more muscular contractions.

 CHECK YOUR READING What happens during each of the three stages of birth?

Growth of the Fetus

An embryo grows and develops from a cluster of cells to a fully formed fetus.

4-day blastula

magnification 620x

- Embryo has 16 cells
- Not yet implanted in the uterus

5-week embryo

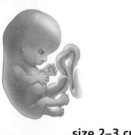

size < 1 cm

- Heart is beating
- Beginning of eyes, arms and legs are visible

8-week fetus

size 2–3 cm

- Embryo is now called a fetus
- Has all basic organs and systems

16-week fetus

size 12 cm

- Can move around in the womb
- Hair, eyelashes and eyebrows are growing

7–8 month fetus shown in this composite image is about 35–40 cm in length and weighs about 1.5–2.3 kg. The fetus usually gains at least 1 kg during the final month of pregnancy.

These twins provide an example of offspring born in a multiple birth.

Multiple Births

Do you have any friends who are twins or triplets? Perhaps you and your brothers or sisters are twins or triplets. The birth of more than one offspring is called a multiple birth. Multiple births are relatively uncommon in humans.

Identical twins are produced when a single fertilized egg divides in half early in embryo development. Each half then forms one complete organism, or twin. Such twins are always of the same sex, look alike, and have identical blood types. Approximately 1 in 29 of twin births, or 4 in every 1000 of all births, is a set of identical twins.

Twins that are not identical are called fraternal twins. Fraternal twins are produced when two eggs are released at the same time and are fertilized by two different sperm. Consequently, fraternal twins may be as similar or different from each other as siblings born at different times. Fraternal twins can be the same sex or different sexes.

 Why are some twins identical and some are not?

9.3 Review

KEY CONCEPTS

1. Describe the function of the male reproductive system and the two main functions of the female reproductive system.

2. Identify two roles hormones play in making egg cells available for fertilization.

3. How is an embryo different from a fetus?

CRITICAL THINKING

4. **Sequence** Describe the sequence of events that occurs between fertilization and the stage called implantation.

5. **Analyze** Detail two examples of hormones interacting with the reproductive system, one involving the male system and one involving the female system.

⬤ CHALLENGE

6. **Synthesize** Describe the interaction between the endocrine system and the reproductive system.

MATH in SCIENCE

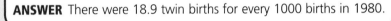

MATH TUTORIAL

Click on Math Tutorial for more help with solving proportions.

Twins and Triplets

Is the number of twins and triplets on the rise? Between 1980 and 1990, twin births in The United States rose from roughly 68,000 to about 105,000. In 1980, there were about 3,600,000 births total. To convert the data to birth rates, you can use proportions. A proportion is an equation. It shows two ratios that are equivalent.

Example

Find the birth rate of twins born in The United States for 1980. The rate is the number of twin births per 1000 births.

(1) Write the ratio of twin births to total births for that year.

$$\frac{68,000 \text{ twin births}}{3,600,000 \text{ total births}}$$

(2) Write a proportion, using x for the number you need to find.

$$\frac{68,000}{3,600,000} = \frac{x}{1000}$$

(3) In a proportion, the cross products are equal, so

$$68,000 \cdot 1000 = x \cdot 3,600,000$$

(4) Solve for x:

$$\frac{68,000,000}{3,600,000} = 18.9$$

ANSWER There were 18.9 twin births for every 1000 births in 1980.

Find the following birth rates.

1. In 1990, there were about 105,000 twin births and about 3,900,000 total births. What was the birth rate of twins?

2. In 1980, about 1,350 sets of triplets were born, and by 1990, this number had risen to about 6,750. What were the birth rates of triplets in 1980 and in 1990?

3. How much did the birth rate increase for twins between 1980 and 1990? for triplets?

4. Find the overall birth rate of twins and triplets in 1980.

5. Find the overall rate of twin and triplet births in 1990. How much did it increase between 1980 and 1990?

CHALLENGE In 1989, there were about 4 million total births, and the rate of triplets born per million births was about 700. How many triplets were born?

Chapter Review

the **BIG** idea

The nervous and endocrine systems allow the body to respond to internal and external conditions.

CONTENT REVIEW
CLASSZONE.COM

◀ KEY CONCEPTS SUMMARY

1 **The nervous system responds and controls.**

- The nervous system connects the body with its environment using different senses: sight, touch, hearing, smell, and taste. Central nervous system includes the brain, the control center, and the spinal cord.
- The peripheral nervous system includes the autonomic and voluntary systems

VOCABULARY
stimulus p. 262
central nervous system p. 264
neuron p. 265
peripheral nervous system p. 266
autonomic nervous system p. 267
voluntary nervous system p. 267

2 **The endocrine system helps regulate body conditions.**

The body has chemical messengers called **hormones** that are regulated by the **endocrine system. Glands** produce and release hormones. The endocrine system includes feedback systems that maintain homeostasis.

Thyroxine hormone level is low.

Hypothalamus and pituitary gland increase thyroid gland activity.

Hypothalamus and pituitary gland decrease thyroid gland activity.

Thyroxine hormone level is high.

VOCABULARY
endocrine system p. 270
hormone p. 271
gland p. 271

3 **The reproductive system allows the production of offspring.**

The female produces eggs, and the male produces sperm. Following **fertilization** the fetus develops over a period of about nine months.

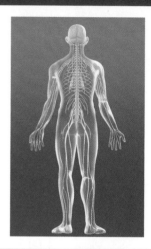

VOCABULARY
menstruation p. 279
fertilization p. 281
embryo p. 281
fetus p. 282

Reviewing Vocabulary

Make a frame for each of the vocabulary words listed. Write the word in the center. Decide what information to frame it with. Use definitions, examples, descriptions, parts, or pictures.

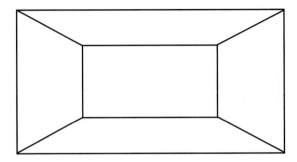

1. stimulus

2. neurons

3. hormones

4. fertilization

5. embryo

Reviewing Key Concepts

Multiple Choice *Choose the letter of the best answer.*

6. Which is a stimulus?
   a. a car horn blowing
   b. jumping at a loud noise
   c. taste buds on the tongue
   d. turning on a lamp

7. Light enters the eye through
   a. the lens
   b. the auditory canal
   c. the olfactory epithelium
   d. the taste buds

8. Which senses allow you to process chemical information?
   a. sight and smell
   b. taste and smell
   c. touch and hearing
   d. hearing and taste

9. What conserves energy and responds quickly to change?
   a. central nervous system
   b. spinal cord
   c. autonomic nervous system
   d. voluntary nervous system

10. Which is not regulated by hormones?
    a. production of white blood cells
    b. physical growth
    c. blood pressure
    d. sexual development

11. Which gland releases hormones that are necessary for growth and metabolism?
    a. thymus   c. pancreas
    b. pituitary gland d. pineal gland

12. Eggs develop in the female reproductive organ called
    a. an ovary   c. a uterus
    b. a fallopian tube d. a vagina

13. The joining of one sperm cell and one egg cell is an event called
    a. menstruation c. implantation
    b. fertilization d. birth

14. A cluster of cells that is formed by fertilization is called the
    a. testes   c. ovary
    b. urethra d. embryo

15. The period in which a fetus and all of its systems develop fully is the
    a. first three months
    b. second three months
    c. third three months
    d. pregnancy

Short Answer *Write a short answer to each question.*

16. List the parts of the body that are controlled by the autonomic nervous system.

17. What is a negative feedback mechanism? Give an example.

18. How are fertilization and menstruation related?

Thinking Critically

Use the diagram to answer the following two questions.

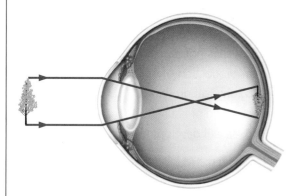

19. SUMMARIZE Use the diagram of the eye to describe how images are formed on the retina.

20. COMPARE AND CONTRAST How is the image that forms on the retina like the object? How is it different? Explain how the viewer interprets the image that forms on the retina.

21. APPLY A person steps on a sharp object with a bare foot and quickly pulls the foot back in pain. Describe the parts of the nervous system that are involved in this action.

22. ANALYZE Explain why positive feedback mechanisms do not help the body maintain homeostasis. Give an example.

23. CONNECT Copy the concept map and add the following terms to the correct box: brain, spinal cord, autonomic.

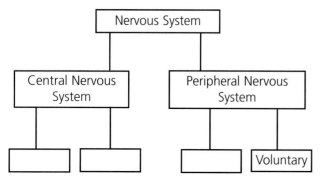

24. DRAW CONCLUSIONS A person who is normally very active begins to notice a significant decrease in energy level. After visiting a doctor, tests results show that one of the endocrine glands is not secreting enough of its hormone. Which gland could this be? Explain your answer.

25. SUMMARIZE Describe the events that occur during the female's 28-day menstrual cycle. Include in your answer how hormones are involved in the cycle.

26. COMPARE AND CONTRAST How are the functions of the ovaries and the testes alike? How are their functions different?

the BIG idea

27. INFER Look again at the picture on pages 258–259. Now that you have finished the chapter, how would you change or add details to your answer to the question on the photograph?

28. SYNTHESIZE How does the nervous system interact with the endocrine and reproductive systems? Give examples that support your answer.

UNIT PROJECTS

If you need to do an experiment for your unit project, gather the materials. Be sure to allow enough time to observe results before the project is due.

Analyzing Data

This chart shows some of the stages of development of a typical fetus.

Week of Pregnancy	Approximate Length of Fetus (cm)	Developmental Changes in the Fetus
6	1	Primitive heartbeat
10	3	Face, fingers, and toes are formed
14	8.5	Muscle and bone tissue have developed
18	14	Fetus makes active movements
24	30	Fingerprints and footprints forming
28	37.5	Rapid brain development
36	47.5	Increase in body fat
38	50	Fetus is considered full term

Use the chart to answer the questions below.

1. What is the approximate length of the fetus at 10 weeks?

   a. 1 cm   **c.** 3 cm

   b. 2 in.   **d.** 3 in.

2. At about which week of development does the fetus begin to make active movements?

   a. week 10   **c.** week 18

   b. week 14   **d.** week 24

3. At about which week of development does the fetus reach a length of about 30 cm?

   a. week 18   **c.** week 36

   b. week 24   **d.** week 38

4. Which statement is true?

   a. Between weeks 28 and 38, the fetus grows at an average of a little over a centimeter per week.

   b. The fetus begins to develop fingerprints at about week 28.

   c. During week 10, the length of the fetus is about 7.5 cm

   d. The fetus is about 12.5 cm long when muscle and bone tissue develop.

5. Between which two weeks of development does the greatest overall increase in length usually take place?

   a. weeks 6 and 10

   b. weeks 10 and 14

   c. weeks 14 and 18

   d. weeks 24 and 28

Extended Response

6. A pregnancy lasts about 42 weeks, roughly 9 months. The development of the fetus can be broken down into three stages, each 14 weeks long. These stages are referred to as trimesters. Briefly describe changes in length and development that occur during each of these stages.

7. The endocrine system and the nervous system have similar functions. Compare and contrast the two systems including the terms in the box. Underline each term in your answer.

homeostasis	autonomic system	hormones
feedback	smooth muscles	

CHAPTER

Growth, Development, and Health

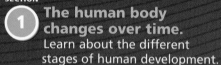

The body develops and maintains itself over time.

How do people change as they grow?

Key Concepts

SECTION

1 The human body changes over time.
Learn about the different stages of human development.

SECTION

2 Systems in the body function to maintain health.
Learn about what a body needs to be healthy.

SECTION

3 Science helps people prevent and treat disease.
Learn how to help prevent the spread of disease.

 Internet Preview

CLASSZONE.COM
Chapter 10 online resources: Content Review, Visualization, three Resource Centers, Math Tutorial, Test Practice

How Much Do You Exercise?

In your notebook, create a chart to keep track of your exercise for a week. Each time you exercise, write down the type of activity and the amount of time you spend. If possible, measure your heart rate during the activity.

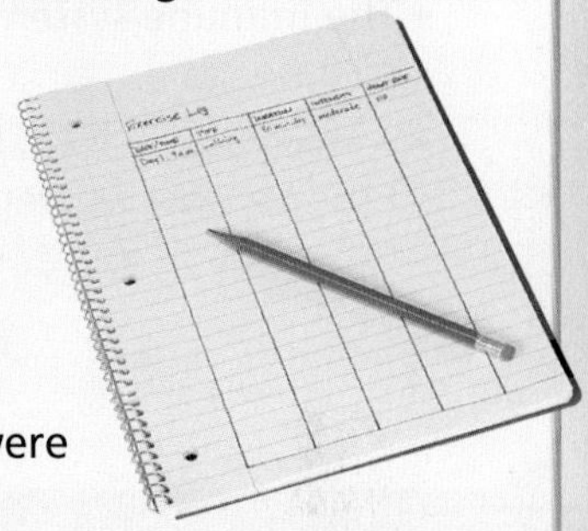

Observe and Think How does the exercise affect your heart rate? If you exercised regularly, what would be the effect on your heart rate while you were resting?

How Safe Is Your Food?

Almost all food that you buy in a store is dated for freshness. Look at the labels of various foods including cereal, juice, milk, eggs, cheese, and meats.

Observe and Think Why do you think some foods have a longer freshness period than others? What types of problems could you have from eating food that is past date?

Internet Activity: Human Development

Go to **ClassZone.com** to watch a movie of a person aging.

Observe and Think In what ways does a person's face change as he or she ages?

NSTA
scilinks.org
SCI LINKS

Human Development **Code: MDL048**

Getting Ready to Learn

◀ CONCEPT REVIEW

- The integumentary system protects the body.
- The immune system fights disease.
- A microscope is an instrument used to observe very small objects.

◀ VOCABULARY REVIEW

nutrient p. 205

pathogen p. 234

antibiotic p. 241

hormone p. 271

CONTENT REVIEW
CLASSZONE.COM
Review concepts and vocabulary.

▶ TAKING NOTES

CONTENT FRAME

Make a content frame for each main idea. Include the following columns: *Topic, Definition, Detail,* and *Connection.* In the first column, list topics about the title. In the second column, define the topic. In the third column, include a detail about the topic. In the fourth column, add a sentence that connects that topic to another topic in the chart.

SCIENCE NOTEBOOK

The human body develops and grows.

Topic	Definition	Detail	Connection
Childhood	Period after infancy and before sexual maturity.	Children depend on parents, but learn to do things for themselves, such as get dressed.	Adults do not have to depend on parents; they are independent and can care for others.

CHOOSE YOUR OWN STRATEGY

For each new vocabulary term, take notes by choosing a strategy from earlier chapters—**four square, magnet word, frame game,** or **description wheel.** Or, use a strategy of your own.

See the Note-Taking Handbook on pages R45–R51.

Four Square

Frame Game

Magnet Word

Description Wheel

The human body changes over time.

BEFORE, you learned

- Living things grow and develop
- The digestive system breaks down nutrients in food
- Organ systems interact to keep the body healthy

NOW, you will learn

- About four stages of human development
- About the changes that occur as the body develops
- How every body system interacts constantly with other systems to keep the body healthy

VOCABULARY

infancy p. 294
childhood p. 294
adolescence p. 295
adulthood p. 296

EXPLORE Growth

Are there patterns of growth?

PROCEDURE

① Measure the circumference of your wrist by using the measuring tape as shown. Record the length. Now measure the length from your elbow to the tip of your middle finger. Record the length.

② Create a table and enter all the data from each person in the class.

WHAT DO YOU THINK?

- How does the distance between the elbow and the fingertip compare with wrist circumference?
- Do you see a pattern between the size of one's wrist and the length of one's forearm?

MATERIALS
- flexible tape measure
- graph paper

CONTENT FRAME
Make a content frame for the first main idea: *The human body develops and grows.* List the red headings in this section in the topics column.

The human body develops and grows.

Have you noticed how rapidly your body has changed over the past few years? Only five years ago you were a young child in grade school. Today you are in middle school. How has your body changed? Growth is both physical and emotional. You are becoming more responsible and socially mature. What are some emotional changes that you have noticed?

Human development is a continuous process. Although humans develop at different rates, there are several stages of development common to human life. In this section we will describe some of the stages, including infancy, childhood, adolescence, and adulthood.

Infancy

The stage of life that begins at birth and ends when a baby begins to walk is called **infancy.** An infant's physical development is rapid. As the infant's body grows larger and stronger, it also learns physical skills. When you were first born, you could not hold up your head. But as your muscles developed, you gained the ability to hold up your head, to roll over, to sit, to crawl, to stand, and finally to walk. You also learned to use your hands to grasp and hold objects.

Infants also develop thinking skills and social skills. At first, they simply cry when they are uncomfortable. Over time, they learn that people respond to those cries. They begin to expect help when they cry. They learn to recognize the people who care for them. Smiling, cooing, and eventually saying a few words are all part of an infant's social development.

Nearly every body system changes and grows during infancy. For example, as the digestive system matures, an infant becomes able to process solid foods. Changes in the nervous system, including the brain, allow an infant to see more clearly and to better control parts of her or his body.

The Apgar score is used to evaluate the newborn's condition after delivery.

Apgar Score			
Quality	0 points	1 point	2 points
Appearance	Completely blue or pale	Good color in body, blue hands or feet	Completely pink or good color
Pulse	No heart rate	<100 beats per minute	>100 beats per minute
Grimace	No response to airway suction	Grimace during suctioning	Grimace, cough/ sneeze with suction
Activity	Limp	Some arm and leg movement	Active motion
Respiration	Not breathing	Weak cry	Good, strong cry

Childhood

The stage called **childhood** lasts for several years. Childhood is the period after infancy and before the beginning of sexual maturity. During childhood, children still depend very much upon their parents. As their bodies and body systems grow, children become more able to care for themselves. Although parents still provide food and other needs, children perform tasks such as eating and getting dressed. In addition, children are able to do more complex physical tasks such as running, jumping, and riding a bicycle.

Childhood is also a time of mental and social growth. During childhood a human being learns to talk, read, write, and communicate in other ways. Along with the ability to communicate come social skills such as cooperation and sharing. A child learns to interact with others.

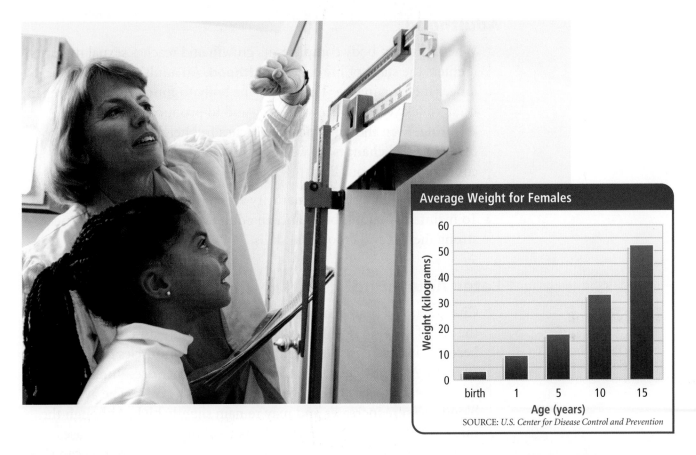

Average Weight for Females

SOURCE: *U.S. Center for Disease Control and Prevention*

Adolescence

The years from puberty to adulthood are called **adolescence** (AD-uhl-EHS-uhns). Childhood ends when the body begins to mature sexually. This process of physical change is called puberty. Not all people reach puberty at the same age. For girls, the changes usually start between ages eight and fourteen; for boys, puberty often begins between ages ten and sixteen.

The human body changes greatly during adolescence. As you learned in Chapter 9, the endocrine system produces chemicals called hormones. During adolescence, hormones signal parts of the reproductive system to mature. At this stage a person's sexual organs become ready for reproduction. These changes are accompanied by other changes. Adolescents develop secondary sexual characteristics. Boys may notice their voices changing. Girls begin developing breasts. Boys and girls both begin growing more body hair.

Probably the change that is the most obvious is a change in height. Boys and girls grow taller by an average of 10 centimeters (3.9 in.) per year during adolescence. Most adolescents eat more as they grow. Food provides materials necessary for growth.

VOCABULARY
Choose a strategy from earlier chapters or one of your own to take notes on the term *adolescence*.

CHECK YOUR READING What are some of the ways the body changes during adolescence?

Adulthood

When a human body completes its growth and reaches sexual maturity, it enters the stage of life called **adulthood.** An adult's body systems no longer increase in size. They allow the body to function fully, to repair itself, to take care of its own needs, and to produce and care for offspring. Even though a person reaches full height early in adulthood, other physical changes, as well as mental and social development, continue throughout life.

Mental and emotional maturity are important parts of adulthood. To maintain an adult body and an adult lifestyle, an individual needs strong mental and emotional skills.

Later Adulthood

READING TiP

You may find it helpful to review the information on the skeletal and muscular system in Chapter 6.

Changes in the body that you might think of as aging begin at about the age of 30. Skin begins to wrinkle and lose its elasticity. Eyesight becomes increasingly poor, hair loss begins, and muscles decrease in strength. After the age of 65, the rate of aging increases. Internal organs become less efficient. Blood vessels become less elastic. The average blood pressure increases and may remain slightly high. Although the rate of breathing usually does not change, lung function decreases slightly. Body temperature is harder to regulate. However, one can slow the process of aging by a lifestyle of exercise and healthy diet.

Systems interact to maintain the human body.

It's easy to observe the external changes to the body during growth and development. Inside the body, every system interacts constantly with other systems to keep the whole person healthy throughout his or her lifetime. For example, the respiratory system constantly sends oxygen to the blood cells of the circulatory system. The circulatory system transports hormones produced by the endocrine system.

Your body systems also interact with the environment outside your body. Your nervous system monitors the outside world through your senses of taste, smell, hearing, vision, and touch. It allows you to respond to your environment. For example, your nervous system allows you to squint if the sun is too bright or to move indoors if the weather is cold. Your endocrine system releases hormones that allow you to have an increased heart rate and send more blood to your muscles if you have to respond to an emergency.

INVESTIGATE Life Expectancy

How has life expectancy changed over time?

In this activity, you will look for trends in the changes in average life expectancy over the past 100 years.

SKILL FOCUS
Graphing

PROCEDURE

1. Using the following data, create a bar graph to chart changes in life expectancy in the U.S. over the last 100 years.

MATERIALS
- graph paper
- computer graphing program

TIME
30 minutes

Life Expectancy 1900–2000

Year	1900	1910	1920	1930	1940	1950	1960	1970	1980	1990	2000
Average Life Expectancy (years)	47.3	50.0	54.1	59.7	62.9	68.2	69.7	70.8	73.7	75.4	76.9

SOURCE: National Center for Health Statistics

2. Study the graph. Observe any trends that you see. Record them in your notebook.

WHAT DO YOU THINK?

- In general, what do these data demonstrate about life expectancy?
- Between which decades did average life expectancy increase the most?

CHALLENGE Using a computer program, create a table and bar graph to chart the data shown above.

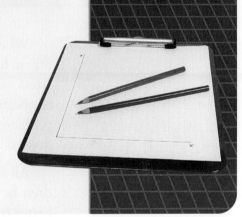

Every part of your daily life requires interactions among your body systems. Even during sleep body systems cooperate. When you sleep, your nervous system allows your muscular system to keep your heart pumping and your lungs breathing. The heart pumps blood through your circulatory system, which has received oxygen from your respiratory system. All this cooperation takes place even while you are sleeping. Your endocrine system releases growth hormone during your sleep, allowing your bones and muscles to grow. The activity of neurons in your brain changes when you fall asleep.

Keeping the body healthy is complex. The digestive and urinary systems eliminate solid and liquid wastes from the body. The circulatory and respiratory systems remove carbon dioxide gas. As you will learn in the next section, a healthy diet and regular exercise help the body to stay strong and function properly.

 CHECK YOUR READING Name three systems that interact as your body grows and maintains itself.

READING VISUALS **COMPARE AND CONTRAST** How do the interactions of your body system change when you are active and when you rest?

When body systems fail to work together, the body can become ill. Stress, for example, can affect all the body systems. Some types of stress, such as fear, can be a healthy response to danger. However, if the body experiences stress over long periods of time, serious health problems such as heart disease, headaches, muscle tension, and depression can arise.

All stages of life include different types of stress. Infants and children face stresses as they learn to become more independent and gain better control over their bodies. Adolescents can be challenged by school, by the changes of puberty, or by being socially accepted by their peers. Adults may encounter stress in their jobs or with their families. The stress of aging can be very difficult for some older adults.

10.1 Review

KEY CONCEPTS

1. Make a development timeline with four sections. Write the names of the stages in order under each section. Include a definition and two details.

2. List a physical characteristic of each stage of development.

3. Give an example of an activity that involves two or more body systems.

CRITICAL THINKING

4. **Compare and Contrast** Make a chart to compare and contrast the infancy and childhood stages of development.

5. **Identify Cause and Effect** How is the endocrine system involved in adolescence?

⬥ CHALLENGE

6. **Synthesis** How does each of the body systems described change as a human being develops from infancy to older adulthood?

SCIENCE on the JOB

Aging the Face

In a movie, characters may go through development stages of a whole lifetime in just over an hour. An actor playing such a role will need to look both older and younger than he or she really is. Makeup artists have a toolbox full of techniques to make the actor look the part.

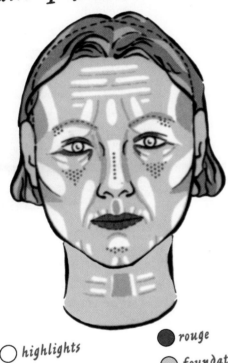

Makeup Guide for Aging

○ highlights
● shadows
● rouge
○ foundation

Hair

As humans go through adulthood, their hair may lose the pigments that make it dark. Makeup artists color hair with dyes or even talcum powder. Wigs and bald caps, made of latex rubber, cover an actor's real hair. Eyebrows can be colored or aged by rubbing them with makeup.

Features

For a bigger-looking nose or extra skin around the neck, makeup artists use foam rubber, or layers of liquid rubber, and, sometimes, wads of paper tissue to build up facial features. For example, building up the cheekbones with layers of latex makes the cheeks appear sharper, less rounded, and more hollow.

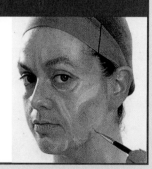

Skin

To make wrinkles or scars, makeup artists use light-colored makeup for the raised highlights and dark-colored makeup for lower shadows and spots.

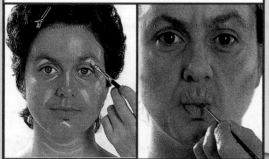

EXPLORE

1. **COMPARE** Look at photos of an older relative at three different stages of life, at about ten years apart. Describe how you might apply makeup to your own face if you were to portray this person's life in three movie scenes. What changes do you need to show?

2. **CHALLENGE** Research to find an image of a character portrayed in a movie by an actor who looked very different in real life. From the picture, describe how the effect was achieved.

10.2 Systems in the body function to maintain health.

McDougal Littell Science
SOUTH CAROLINA

STANDARDS

7–3 The student will demonstrate an understanding of the functions and interconnections of the major body systems, including the breakdown in structure or function that disease causes.

VOCABULARY

nutrition p. 300
addiction p. 306

◀ **BEFORE,** you learned

- Human development involves all the body systems
- The human body continues to develop throughout life
- Every body system interacts constantly with other systems to keep the body healthy

▶ **NOW,** you will learn

- About the role of nutrients in health
- Why exercise is needed to keep body systems healthy
- How drug abuse, eating disorders, and addiction can affect the body

THINK ABOUT

What is health?

If you went online and searched under the word *health*, you would find millions of links. Clearly, health is important to most people. You may be most aware of your health when you aren't feeling well. But you know that clean water, food, exercise, and sleep are all important for health. Preventing illness is also part of staying healthy. How would you define health? What are some ways that you protect your health?

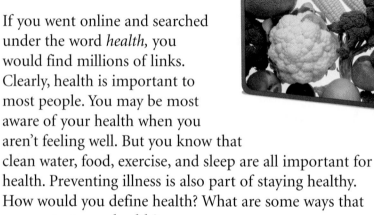

Diet affects the body's health.

VOCABULARY
Choose a strategy from an earlier chapter, such as a magnet word diagram, for taking notes on the term *nutrition*. Or use any strategy that you think works well.

What makes a meal healthy? The choices you make about what you eat are important. Nutrients from food are distributed to every cell in your body. You use those nutrients for energy and to maintain and build new body tissues. **Nutrition** is the study of the materials that nourish your body. It also refers to the process in which the different parts of food are used for maintenance, growth, and reproduction. When a vitamin or other nutrient is missing from your diet, illness can occur. Your body's systems can function only when they get the nutrients they need.

 How is nutrition important to health?

This family is enjoying a healthy meal that includes proteins, carbohydrates, and fats.

Getting Nutrients

RESOURCE CENTER
CLASSZONE.COM

Discover more about human health.

In order to eat a healthy diet, you must first understand what good nutrition is. There are six classes of nutrients: carbohydrates, proteins, fats, vitamins, minerals, and water. All of these nutrients are necessary for your body cells to carry out the chemical reactions that sustain life.

Proteins are molecules that build tissues used for growth and repair. Proteins provide the building blocks for many important hormones. Good sources of proteins are poultry, red meat, fish, eggs, nuts, beans, grains, soy, and milk. Protein should make up at least 20 percent of your diet.

Carbohydrates are the body's most important energy source and are found in starch, sugar, and fiber. Fiber provides little energy, but is important for regular elimination. Natural sugars such as those found in fruits and vegetables are the best kinds of sugars for your body. Carbohydrates are found in bread and pasta, fruits, and vegetables. Carbohydrates should make up about 40 to 50 percent of your diet.

Fats are essential for energy and should account for about 10 to 15 percent of your diet. Many people eliminate fats from their diet in order to lose weight. But a certain amount of fat is necessary. Fats made from plants have the greatest health benefits. For example, olive oil is better for you than the oil found in butter.

Vitamins and minerals are needed by your body in small amounts. Vitamins are small molecules that regulate body growth and development. Minerals help build body tissues. While some vitamins can be made by your body, most of them are supplied to the body in food.

Water is necessary for life. A human being could live for about a month without food, but only about one week without water. Water has several functions. Water helps regulate your body temperature through evaporation when you sweat and breathe. Without water, important materials such as vitamins and other nutrients could not be transported around the body. Water helps your body get rid of the waste products that move through the kidneys and pass out of the body in urine. Urine is composed mostly of water.

To make sure your body can function and maintain itself, you need to drink about two and one half liters, or about eight glasses, of water every day. You also get water when you eat foods with water in them, such as fresh fruit and vegetables.

Vitamins and Minerals	
Vitamin or Mineral	**Recommended Daily Allowance**
Vitamin A	0.3 to 1.3 mg
Niacin	6–18 mg
Vitamin B$_2$	0.5–1.6 mg
Vitamin B$_6$	0.5–2.0 mg
Vitamin C	15–120 mg
Vitamin E	6–19 mg
Calcium	500–1300 mg
Phosphorus	460–1250 mg
Potassium	1600–2000 mg
Zinc	3–13 mg
Magnesium	80–420 mg
Iron	7–27 mg

Source: National Institutes of Health

Understanding Nutrition

RESOURCE CENTER
CLASSZONE.COM

Examine the basic principles of nutrition.

Ever wonder what the word *lite* really means? What do labels saying that food is fresh or natural or organic mean? Not all advertising about nutrition is reliable. It is important to know what the labels on food really mean. Groups within the government, such as the United States Department of Agriculture, have defined terms that are used to describe food products. For example, if a food label says the food is "all natural," that means it does not contain any artificial flavor, color, or preservative.

Another example is the term *low-fat*. That label means that the food provides no more than 3 grams of fat per serving. The word *organic* means that the produce has been grown using no human-made fertilizers or chemicals that kill pests or weeds. It also means that live-stock has been raised on organic feed and has not been given antibiotics or growth hormones. It takes some effort and a lot of reading to stay informed, but the more you know, the better the choices you can make.

INVESTIGATE Food Labels

What are you eating?

PROCEDURE

① Gather nutrition labels from the following products: a carbonated soft drink, a bag of fresh carrots, canned spaghetti in sauce, potato chips, plain popcorn kernels, unsweetened applesauce, and fruit juice. Look at the percent of daily values of the major nutrients, as shown on the label for each food.

② Make a list of ways to evaluate a food for high nutritional value. Include such criteria as nutrient levels and calories per serving.

③ Examine the nutrition labels and compare them with your list. Decide which of these foods would make a healthy snack.

WHAT DO YOU THINK?

• How does serving size affect the way you evaluate a nutritional label?

• What are some ways to snack and get nutrients at the same time?

CHALLENGE Design a full day's food menu that will give you all the nutrients you need. Use snacks as some of the foods that contribute these nutrients.

SKILL FOCUS
Analyzing

MATERIALS
nutrition labels

TIME
30 minutes

Spaghetti
IN TOMATO SAUCE WITH CHEESE

Nutrition Facts
Serving Size: 1 cup (252g)
Servings Per Container: about 2

Amount Per Serving
Calories 210   Calories from Fat 20

	% Daily Value*
Total Fat 2g	
Saturated Fat 1g	3%
Cholesterol 5mg	5%
Sodium 1,020 mg	2%
Total Carbohydrate 41g	43%
Dietary Fiber 3g	14%
Sugars 14g	12%
Protein 7g	

Vitamin A 10%   Vitamin C 0%
Calcium 4%   Iron 10%

* Percent Daily Values are based on a 2,000 calorie diet. Your daily values may be higher or lower depending on your calorie needs.

Exercise is part of a healthy lifestyle.

Regular exercise allows all your body systems to stay strong and healthy. You learned that your lymphatic system doesn't include a structure like the heart to pump its fluid through the body. Instead, it relies on body movement and strong muscles to help it move antibodies and white blood cells. Exercise is good for the lymphatic system.

Exercise

When you exercise, you breathe harder and more quickly. You inhale and exhale more air, which exercises the muscles of your respiratory system and makes them stronger. Exercise also brings in extra oxygen. Oxygen is necessary for cellular respiration, which provides energy to other body systems. The circulatory system is strengthened by exercise. Your heart becomes stronger the more it is used. The skeletal system grows stronger with exercise as well. Studies show that older adults who lift weights have stronger bones than those who do not. In addition, physical activity can flush out skin pores by making you sweat, and it reduces the symptoms of depression.

By eating healthy meals and exercising, you help your body to grow and develop.

Lifestyle

The lifestyles of many people involve regular exercise. Some lifestyles, however, include more sitting still than moving. A lifestyle that is sedentary, associated mostly with sitting down, can harm a person's health. Muscles and bones that are not exercised regularly can begin to break down. Your body stores unused energy from food as fat. The extra weight of body fat can make it harder for you to exercise. Therefore, it is harder to use up energy or to strengthen your skeletal, muscular, and immune systems. Researchers have also made connections between excess body fat and heart disease and diabetes.

 How does lifestyle affect health?

CONTENT FRAME
Make a content frame for the main idea: *Drug abuse, addiction, and eating disorders cause serious health problems.*

Drug abuse, addiction, and eating disorders cause serious health problems.

Every day, you make choices that influence your health. Some choices can have more serious health risks, or possibilities for harm, than others. You have the option to make healthy choices for yourself. Making unhealthy decisions about what you put into your body can lead to drug abuse, addiction, or eating disorders.

Drug Abuse

A drug is any chemical substance that you take in to change your body's functions. Doctors use drugs to treat and prevent disease and illness. The use of a drug for any other reason is an abuse of that drug. Abuse can also include using too much of a substance that is not harmful in small amounts. People abuse different drugs for different reasons. Drugs often do allow an individual to feel better for the moment. But they can also cause serious harm to an individual's health.

Tobacco Nicotine, the drug in tobacco, increases heart rate and blood pressure and makes it seem as if the user has more energy. Nicotine is also a poison; in fact, some farmers use it to kill insects. Tobacco smoke contains thousands of chemicals. Tar and carbon monoxide are two harmful chemicals in smoke. Tar is a sticky substance that is commonly used to pave roads. Carbon monoxide is one of the gases that cars release in their exhaust. People who smoke or chew tobacco have a higher risk of cancer, and smokers are also at risk for heart disease.

Compounds Found in Unfiltered Tobacco Smoke		
Compound	Amount in First-Hand Smoke (mg per cigarette)	Amount in Second-Hand Smoke (mg per cigarette)
Nicotine	1–3	2.1–46
Tar	15–40	14–30
Carbon monoxide	14–23	27–61
Benzene	0.012–0.05	0.4
Formaldehyde	0.07–0.1	1.5
Hydrogen cyanide	0.4–0.5	0.014–11
Phenol	0.08–0.16	0.07–0.25

Source: U.S. Department of Health and Human Services

Alcohol Even a small amount of alcohol can affect a person's ability to think and reason. Alcohol can affect behavior and the ability to make decisions. Many people are killed every year, especially in automobile accidents, because of choices they made while drinking alcohol. Alcohol abuse damages the heart, the liver, the nervous system, and the digestive system.

Other Drugs Some drugs, such as cocaine and amphetamines, can make people feel more energetic and even powerful because they stimulate parts of the nervous system and speed up the heart. These drugs are very dangerous. They can cause heart attacks, and long-term use may cause brain damage.

Drugs called narcotics also affect the nervous system. Instead of stimulating it, however, they decrease its activity. Narcotics are prescribed by doctors to relieve pain and to help people sleep. Because narcotics work by decreasing the function of nerves in some brain regions, large amounts of these drugs can cause the heart and lungs to stop. Abuse of narcotics can also lead to addiction.

Students can be active in protesting drug abuse.

Addiction

Drug abuse can often lead to addiction. **Addiction** is an illness in which a person becomes dependent on a substance or behavior. Repeated use of drugs such as alcohol, tobacco, and narcotics can cause the body to become physically dependent. When a person is dependent on a drug, taking away that drug can cause withdrawal. If affected by withdrawal, a person may become physically ill, sometimes within a very short period of time. Symptoms of withdrawal from some types of drugs can include fever, muscle cramps, vomiting, and hallucinations.

Another type of addiction can result from the effect produced by a drug or even a behavior. Although physical dependency may not occur, a person can become emotionally dependent. Gambling, overeating, and risk-taking are some examples of addictive behaviors. Someone who suffers from an addiction can be treated and can work to live a healthy life, but most addictions never go away completely.

Eating Disorders

An eating disorder is a condition in which people continually eat too much or too little food. One example of an eating disorder is anorexia nervosa. People with this disorder eat so little and exercise so hard that they become unhealthy. No matter how thin they are, they believe they need to be thinner. People with anorexia do not receive necessary nutrients because they don't eat. When the energy used by the body exceeds the energy taken in from food, tissues in the body are broken down to provide fuel. Bones and muscles, including the heart, can be damaged, and the person can die.

10.2 Review

KEY CONCEPTS

1. How do nutrients affect health?

2. Explain the effects of exercise on the respiratory and circulatory systems.

3. Make a chart showing the effects of tobacco, alcohol, and other drugs on the body.

CRITICAL THINKING

4. **Explain** How would you define health? Write your own definition.

5. **Synthesize** Explain how water can be considered a nutrient. Include a definition of *nutrient* in your explanation.

⬥ CHALLENGE

6. **Apply** You have heard about a popular new diet. Most of the foods in the diet are fat-free, and the diet promises fast weight loss. How might this diet affect health? Explain your answer.

MATH TUTORIAL
CLASSZONE.COM

Click on Math Tutorial for more help with choosing a data display.

Pumping Up the Heart

Heart rates differ with age, level of activity, and fitness. To communicate the differences clearly, you need to display the data visually. Choosing the appropriate display is important.

Example

The fitness trainer at a gym wants to display the following data:

Maximum heart rate while exercising (beats per minute)		
Age 21	Men	197
	Women	194
Age 45	Men	178
	Women	177
Age 65	Men	162
	Women	164

Here are some different displays the trainer could use:

- A bar graph shows how different categories of data compare. Data can be broken into 2 or even 3 bars per category.
- A line graph shows how data changes over time.
- A circle graph represents data as parts of a whole.

ANSWER The fitness trainer wants to show heart rate according to both age and gender, so a double bar graph would be the clearest.

What would be an appropriate way to display data in the following situations?

1. A doctor wants to display how a child's average heart rate changes as the child grows.

2. A doctor wants to display data showing how a person's resting heart rate changes the more the person exercises.

3. A scientist is studying each type of diet that the people in an experiment follow. She will show what percentage of the people with each diet had heart disease.

CHALLENGE Describe a situation in which a double line graph is the most appropriate data display.

Science helps people prevent and treat disease.

 BEFORE, you learned

- Good nutrition and exercise help keep the body healthy
- Drug abuse can endanger health
- Eating disorders can affect the body's health

NOW, you will learn

- About some of the causes of disease
- How diseases can be treated
- How to help prevent the spread of disease

STANDARDS

7–3.4 Explain the effects of disease on the major organs and body systems (including infectious diseases such as colds and flu, AIDS, and athlete's foot and noninfectious diseases such as diabetes, Parkinson's, and skin cancer).

VOCABULARY

microorganism p. 308
bacteria p. 309
virus p. 309
resistance p. 313

EXPLORE The Immune System

How easily do germs spread?

PROCEDURE

1. Early in the day, place a small amount of glitter in the palm of one hand. Rub your hands together to spread the glitter to both palms. Go about your day normally.

2. At the end of the day, examine your environment, including the people around you. Where does the glitter show up?

WHAT DO YOU THINK?

- How easily did the glitter transfer to other people and objects?
- What do you think this might mean about how diseases might spread?

MATERIALS
glitter

VOCABULARY
Remember to choose a strategy from earlier chapters or one of your own to take notes on the term *microorganism.*

Scientific understanding helps people fight disease.

Disease is a change that disturbs the normal functioning of the body's systems. If you have ever had a cold, you have experienced a disease that affected your respiratory system. What are the causes of disease? Many diseases are classified as infectious diseases, or diseases that can be spread. Viruses, bacteria, and other pathogens cause infectious disease. The organisms that cause sickness are called **microorganisms.**

Before the invention of the microscope, people didn't know about microorganisms that cause disease. They observed that people who lived near each other sometimes caught the same illness, but they didn't understand why. Understanding disease has helped people prevent and treat many illnesses.

The germ theory describes some causes of disease.

In the 1800s, questions about the causes of some diseases were answered. Scientists showed through experiments that diseases could be caused by very small living things. In 1857, French chemist Louis Pasteur did experiments that showed that microorganisms caused food to decay. Later, Pasteur's work and the work of Robert Koch and Robert Lister contributed to the germ theory. Pasteur's germ theory states that some diseases, called infectious diseases, are caused by germs.

Bacteria and Viruses

Germs are the general name given to organisms that cause disease. **Bacteria** (bak-TEER-ee-uh) are single-celled organisms that live almost everywhere. Within your intestines, bacteria function to digest food. Some bacteria, however, cause disease. Pneumonia (nu-MOHN-yuh), ear infections (ihn-FEHK-shuhnz), and strep throat can be caused by bacteria.

Viruses do not fit all parts of the definition of living things. For example, they must enter and exist inside living cells in order to reproduce. Stomach flu, chicken pox, and colds are sicknesses caused by viruses. Both bacteria and viruses are examples of pathogens, agents that cause disease. The word *pathogen* comes from the Greek *pathos*, which means "suffering." Other pathogens include yeasts, fungi, and protists.

RESOURCE CENTER
CLASSZONE.COM
Explore ways to fight disease.

Treating Infectious Diseases

Diseases caused by bacteria can be treated with medicines that contain antibiotics. An antibiotic is a substance that can destroy bacteria. The first antibiotics were discovered in 1928 when a scientist named Alexander Fleming was performing experiments on bacteria. Fleming found mold growing on his bacteria samples. While most of the petri dish was covered with bacterial colonies, the area around the mold was clear. From this observation, Fleming concluded that a substance in the mold had killed the bacteria.

Fleming had not intended to grow mold in his laboratory, but the accident led to the discovery of penicillin. Since the discovery of penicillin, many antibiotics have been developed. Antibiotics have saved the lives of millions of people.

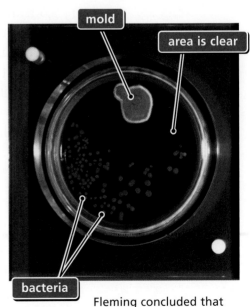

mold

area is clear

bacteria

Fleming concluded that something in the mold had killed the bacteria.

Infectious diseases spread in many ways.

READING **TiP**

As you read the text on this page, notice how each pathogen shown on p. 311 spreads.

SOUTH CAROLINA
Essentials

See the South Carolina Essentials, page 647, to read about different infectious and noninfectious diseases.

One of the best ways to protect your health is by being informed and by avoiding pathogens. Pathogens can be found in many places, including air, water, and on the surfaces of objects. By knowing how pathogens travel, people are able to limit the spreading of disease.

Food, Air, and Water

Sometimes people get sick when they breathe in pathogens from the air. The viruses that cause colds can travel through air. If you cover your mouth when you sneeze or cough, you can avoid sending pathogens through the air. Pathogens also enter the body in food or water. Washing fruits and vegetables and cooking meats and eggs kills bacteria. Most cities in the United States add substances, such as chlorine, to the supply of public water. These substances kill pathogens. Boiling water also kills pathogens. People sometimes boil water if their community loses power or experiences a flood. Campers need to boil or filter water taken from a stream before they use it.

Contact with Animals

Animals can also carry organisms that cause disease. The animal itself does not cause the illness, but you can become sick if you take in the pathogen that the animal carries. Lyme disease, for example, is caused by bacteria that inhabit ticks. The ticks are not the cause of illness, but if an infected tick bites you, you will get Lyme disease.

A deadly central nervous system infection called rabies can also come from animal contact. The virus that causes rabies is found in the saliva of an infected animal, such as a bat, raccoon, or opossum. If that animal bites you, you may get the disease. A veterinarian can give your pet an injection to prevent rabies. You can get other infections from pets. These infections include worms that enter through your mouth or nose and live in your intestines. You can also get a skin infection called ringworm, which is actually a fungus rather than a worm.

Person-to-Person Contact

Most of the illnesses you have had have probably been passed to you by another person. Even someone who does not feel sick can have pathogens on his or her skin. If you touch that person or if that person touches something and then you touch it, the pathogens will move to your skin. If the pathogens then enter your body through a cut or through your nose, mouth, or eyes, they can infect your body. The simplest way to avoid giving or receiving pathogens is to wash your hands often and well.

Pathogens and Disease

Infectious diseases are caused by microorganisms.

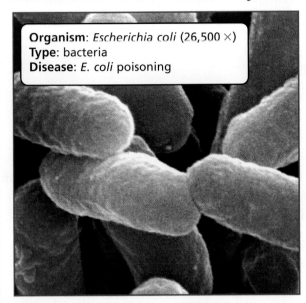

Organism: *Escherichia coli* (26,500 ×)
Type: bacteria
Disease: *E. coli* poisoning

Spread: contaminated food or water

Prevention: handwashing, thoroughly cooking meat, boiling contaminated water, washing fruits and vegetables, drinking only pasteurized milk, juice, or cider

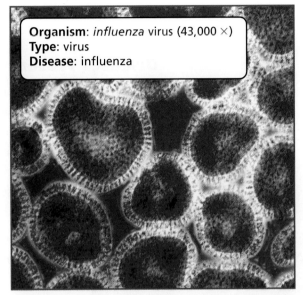

Organism: *influenza* virus (43,000 ×)
Type: virus
Disease: influenza

Spread: inhaling virus from sneezes or coughs of infected person

Prevention: vaccination

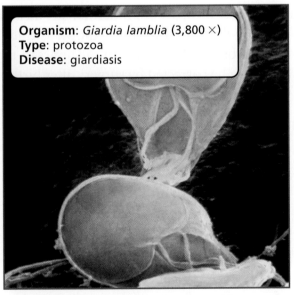

Organism: *Giardia lamblia* (3,800 ×)
Type: protozoa
Disease: giardiasis

Spread: contaminated food or water, close contact with infected person

Prevention: handwashing, thoroughly cooking meat, boiling contaminated water, washing fruits and vegetables, drinking only pasteurized milk, juice, or cider

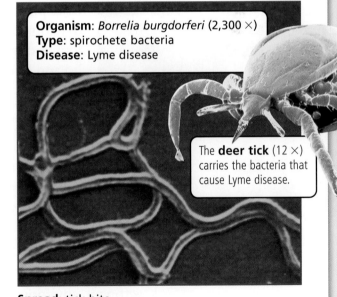

Organism: *Borrelia burgdorferi* (2,300 ×)
Type: spirochete bacteria
Disease: Lyme disease

The **deer tick** (12 ×) carries the bacteria that cause Lyme disease.

Spread: tick bite

Prevention: wear light-colored clothing, tuck pants into socks or shoes, check for ticks after outdoor activities, use repellents containing DEET

READING VISUALS How can people prevent each of these pathogens from spreading?

Noninfectious diseases are not contagious.

Noninfectious diseases are diseases that cannot be spread by pathogens. They are not contagious. People are born with some of these, and others can develop during life.

Diseases Present at Birth

Some diseases present at birth are inherited. Genes, which act as instructions for your cells, are inherited from your parents. Some forms of a gene produce cells that do not function properly. Most genetic disorders are due to recessive forms of a gene, which means that while both parents carry the defective form, neither one has the disorder. Cystic fibrosis and sickle cell disease are diseases inherited this way.

The symptoms of some genetic diseases may not be present immediately at birth. Huntington's disease, even though it is an inherited condition, does not begin to produce symptoms until a person reaches adulthood. Other genes can increase the chances of developing a disease later in life, such as cancer or diabetes, but the pattern of inheritance is complex.

The process of human development is complex. Some diseases present at birth may involve both inherited factors and development. Talipes, a disorder commonly known as club-foot, is due to the improper development of the bones of the leg and foot. Talipes can be corrected by surgery after birth.

Asthma is a noncontagious disease often present at birth.

Diseases in Later Life

Some diseases, including heart disease, certain forms of cancer, and many respiratory disorders, have much less to do with genetics and more to do with environment and lifestyle. You have learned about the ways in which you can lead a healthy lifestyle. Good nutrition, exercise, and avoiding substances that can damage the body systems not only increase the length of life, but also the quality of life.

While people with family histories of cancer are at higher risk of getting it, environmental factors can influence risk as well. Tar and other chemicals from cigarettes can damage the lungs, in addition to causing cancer. Much is still not known about the causes of cancer.

 CHECK YOUR READING Name a noninfectious disease that is present at birth and one that may occur later in life.

Scientists continue efforts to prevent and treat illness.

In spite of all that scientists have learned, disease is still a problem all over the world. Illnesses such as AIDS and cancer are better understood than they used to be, but researchers must still find ways to cure them.

Even though progress is sometimes slow, it does occur. Better education has led to better nutrition. The use of vaccines has made some diseases nearly extinct. However, new types of illness sometimes appear. AIDS was first identified in the 1980s and spread quickly before it was identified. More recently, the West Nile virus appeared in the United States. This virus is transmitted by infected mosquitoes and can cause the brain to become inflamed. Efforts to control the disease continue.

Scientists work hard to fight disease.

Antibiotics fight pathogens, but they can also lead to changes in them. When an antibiotic is used too often, bacteria can develop **resistance,** which means that the strain of bacteria is no longer affected by the drug. Once a strain of bacteria has developed resistance, the resistance will be passed on to new generations of the bacteria. This means that a particular antibiotic will not stop that particular bacterial infection.

 CHECK YOUR READING Describe the advantages and disadvantages of using an antibiotic when you are sick.

 **Review**

KEY CONCEPTS

1. Define microorganism and explain how microorganisms can affect health.
2. What is an antibiotic?
3. Make a chart showing ways that infectious diseases spread and ways to keep them from spreading.

CRITICAL THINKING

4. **Connect** Make a list of things you can do to avoid getting Lyme disease or the West Nile virus.
5. **Apply** How does washing your hands before eating help protect your health?

● CHALLENGE

6. **Synthesize** How can nutrition help in the prevention of disease? Use these terms in your answer: *nutrients, pathogens,* and *white blood cells.*

CHAPTER INVESTIGATION

Cleaning Your Hands

OVERVIEW AND PURPOSE Your skin cells produce oils that keep the skin moist. This same layer of oil provides a nutrient surface for bacteria to grow. When you wash your hands with soap, the soap dissolves the oil and the water carries it away, along with the bacteria. In this activity you will

- sample your hands for the presence of bacteria
- test the effectiveness of washing your hands with water compared with washing them with soap and water

▶ Problem

Is soap effective at removing bacteria?

▶ Hypothesize

Write a hypothesis explaining how using soap affects the amount of bacteria on your hands. Your hypothesis should take the form of an "If . . . , then . . . , because . . ." statement.

▶ Procedure

1. Make a data table in your **Science Notebook** like the one shown on page 315.

2. Obtain three agar petri dishes. Be careful not to open the dishes accidentally.

3. Remove the lid from one dish and gently press two fingers from your right hand onto the surface of the agar. Close the lid immediately. Tape the dish closed. Mark the tape with the letter *A*. Include your initials and the date.

step 3

MATERIALS
- 3 covered petri dishes with sterile nutrient agar
- soap
- marker
- tape
- hand lens

4 Wash your hands in water and let them air-dry. Open the second dish with your right hand and press two fingers of your left hand into the agar. Close the lid immediately. Tape and mark the dish *B*, as in step 3.

5 Wash your hands in soap and water and let them air-dry. Open the third dish with one hand and press two fingers of the other hand into the agar. Close the lid immediately. Tape and mark the dish *C*, as in step 3.

6 Place the agar plates upside down in a dark, warm place for two to three days. **Caution:** Do not open the dishes. Wash your hands.

▶ Observe and Analyze

Write It Up

1. **OBSERVE** Use a hand lens to observe the amounts of bacterial growth in each dish, and record your observations in Table 1. Which dish has the most bacterial growth? the least growth?

2. **OBSERVE** Is there anything you notice about the bacterial growth in each dish other than the amount of bacterial growth?

3. Return the petri dishes to your teacher for disposal. **Caution:** Do not open the dishes. Wash your hands thoroughly with warm water and soap when you have finished.

▶ Conclude

Write It Up

1. **INFER** Why is it necessary to air-dry your hands instead of using a towel?

2. **INFER** Why is it important to use your right hand in step 3 and your left hand in step 4?

3. **INTERPRET** Compare your results with your hypothesis. Do your observations support your hypothesis?

4. **EVALUATE** Is there much value in washing your hands simply in water?

5. **EVALUATE** How might the temperature of the water you used when you washed your hands affect the results of your experiment?

6. **EVALUATE** Given the setup of your experiment, could you have prepared a fourth sample, for example to test the effectiveness of antibacterial soap?

▶ INVESTIGATE Further

CHALLENGE It is hard to tell which products are best for washing hands without testing them. Design an experiment to determine which cleans your hands best: baby wipes, hand sanitizer, regular soap, or antibacterial soap.

Cleaning Your Hands

Table 1. Observations

Petri Dish	Source	Amount of Bacteria
A	hand	
B	hand washed with water	
C	hand washed with soap and water	

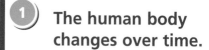

Chapter Review

the **BIG** idea

The body develops and maintains itself over time.

CONTENT REVIEW
CLASSZONE.COM

KEY CONCEPTS SUMMARY

1 The human body changes over time.

Your body changes through-out your entire life. Some changes are physical and some are emotional. The stages of life are infancy, childhood, adolescence, adulthood, and later adult-hood. All the different sys-tems in the body interact to maintain your health.

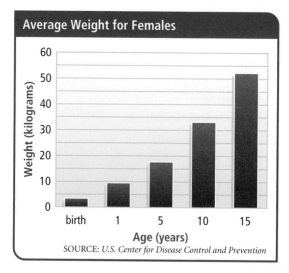

Average Weight for Females

Weight (kilograms): 0, 10, 20, 30, 40, 50, 60

Age (years): birth, 1, 5, 10, 15

SOURCE: *U.S. Center for Disease Control and Prevention*

VOCABULARY
infancy p. 294
childhood p. 294
adolescence p. 295
adulthood p. 296

2 Systems in the body function to maintain health.

Your diet affects your health. Important nutrients include proteins, carbohydrates, fats, vitamins, minerals, and water. Water is also essential to healthy living. Exercise is another ingredient to a healthy life. Problems that can interfere with a healthy life are drug abuse, addiction, and eating disorders.

Spaghetti
IN TOMATO SAUCE WITH CHEESE
Nutrition Facts
Serving Size: 1 cup (252g)
Servings Per Container: about 2

Amount Per Serving
Calories 210
Calories from Fat 20

	% Daily Value*
Total Fat 2g	
Saturated Fat 1g	3%
Cholesterol 5mg	5%

VOCABULARY
nutrition p. 300
addiction p. 306

3 Science helps people prevent and treat disease.

- Science helps people fight disease.
- Antibiotics are used to fight diseases caused by bacteria.
- Infectious disease can spread in many ways including food, air, water, insects, other animals, and person-to-person contact.
- Noninfectious diseases are not contagious. Some noninfectious diseases are present at birth and others occur in later life.

VOCABULARY
microorganism p. 308
bacteria p. 309
virus p. 309
resistance p. 313

Reviewing Vocabulary

Make a frame for each of the vocabulary words listed below. Write the word in the center. Decide what information to frame it with. Use definitions, examples, descriptions, parts, or pictures.

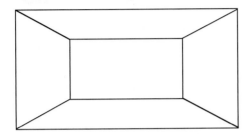

1. infancy
2. childhood
3. adolescence
4. adulthood

Reviewing Key Concepts

Multiple Choice *Choose the letter of the best answer.*

5. The stage of life known as infancy ends when an infant
   a. begins to cry
   b. learns to walk
   c. holds up his head
   d. sees more clearly

6. The process in which the body begins to mature sexually is called
   a. adolescence   c. nutrition
   b. adulthood   d. puberty

7. Which nutrients are the main sources of energy for the body?
   a. fats and carbohydrates
   b. water and protein
   c. fats and proteins
   d. water and carbohydrates

8. Which is *not* a benefit of regular exercise?
   a. flushed-out skin pores
   b. stronger skeletal system
   c. increased body fat
   d. strengthened heart

9. A sedentary life style is associated with
   a. a stronger immune system
   b. more sitting than moving
   c. regular exercise
   d. an eating disorder

10. The chemical found in tobacco that increases heart rate and blood pressure is
    a. cocaine   c. tar
    b. narcotics   d. nicotine

11. Which term includes all of the others?
    a. bacteria   c. virus
    b. fungus   d. pathogen

12. An example of a disease caused by bacteria is
    a. an ear infection
    b. stomach flu
    c. chicken pox
    d. a cold

13. Which statement about viruses is true?
    a. Viruses function to digest food.
    b. Viruses are one-celled organisms.
    c. Viruses need living cells to reproduce.
    d. Examples of viruses are fungi and yeasts.

14. A substance that can destroy bacteria is called
    a. a vitamin   c. an antibiotic
    b. a pathogen   d. a mold

15. Lyme disease is spread through
    a. drinking unfiltered water
    b. uncooked meats
    c. the bite of a dog
    d. the bite of a tick

Short Answer *Write a short answer to each question.*

16. In your own words, define *nutrition.*

17. What are pathogens? Give three examples.

18. Explain what happens if antibiotics are used too often.

Thinking Critically

19. **ANALYZE** Why do you think crying is an example of a social skill that develops during infancy?

20. **ANALYZE** Describe one physical, one mental, and one social change that a ten-year-old boy might experience over the next five years.

21. **EVALUATE** Explain why a diet that doesn't contain any fat would be unhealthy.

22. **APPLY** Explain why people who live sedentary lifestyles should get more exercise.

23. **SYNTHESIZE** Discuss why doctors recommend that women avoid alcohol and tobacco use during pregnancy.

24. **COMPARE AND CONTRAST** People who overeat and then quickly try to lose weight are bulimic. How is bulimia like anorexia? How does it differ?

25. **ANALYZE** Explain why Pasteur's work was important in the understanding of disease.

26. **HYPOTHESIZE** In 1854 a disease called cholera spread through the city of London. Most of the people who contracted the disease lived near the city's various water pumps. What might you hypothesize about the cause of the disease? How could you prevent people from contracting the disease in the future?

27. **PROVIDE EXAMPLES** What are some ways that a person can prevent noninfectious diseases such as cancer or diabetes?

the BIG idea

28. **INFER** Look again at the picture on pages 290–291. Now that you have finished the chapter, how would you change or add details to your answer to the question on the photograph?

29. **SUMMARIZE** Write one or more paragraphs explaining how lifestyle can lead to a healthy body and a longer life. Include these terms in your description.

nutrition	alcohol
exercise	infectious disease
germs	noninfectious disease
tobacco	

UNIT PROJECTS

Evaluate all the data, results, and information from your project folder. Prepare to present your project.

Ⓟ Pump   Ⓟ Contaminated pump   • Cholera death

Standardized Test Practice

Analyzing Data

The table below presents information about causes of death in the United States.

Leading Causes of Death in the United States

2000		1900	
Cause of Death	**Percent of Deaths**	**Cause of Death**	**Percent of Deaths**
heart disease	31%	pneumonia*	12%
cancer	23%	tuberculosis*	11%
stroke	9%	diarrhea*	11%
lung disease	5%	heart disease	6%
accident	4%	liver disease	5%
pneumonia*	4%	accident	4%
diabetes	3%	cancer	4%
kidney disease	1%	senility	2%
liver disease	1%	diphtheria*	2%

* infectious disease

Use the table to answer the questions below.

1. What was the leading cause of death in 1900?
 a. heart disease
 b. cancer
 c. pneumonia
 d. tuberculosis

2. Which infectious disease was a leading cause of death both in 1900 and 2000?
 a. tuberculosis
 b. diphtheria
 c. stroke
 d. pneumonia

3. Which was the leading noninfectious cause of death in both 1900 and 2000?
 a. pneumonia
 b. cancer
 c. heart disease
 d. accidents

4. Which cause of death showed the greatest increase between 1900 and 2000?
 a. heart disease
 b. cancer
 c. liver disease
 d. pneumonia

5. Which statement is true?
 a. The rate of infectious disease as a leading cause of death increased from 1900 to 2000.
 b. The rate of infectious disease as a leading cause of death decreased from 1900 to 2000.
 c. The rate of noninfectious disease as a leading cause of death decreased from 1900 to 2000.
 d. The rate of noninfectious disease as a leading cause of death remained the same.

6. The percent of deaths caused by heart disease in 2000 was how much greater than in 1900?
 a. 37%
 b. 31%
 c. 25%
 d. 6%

Extended Response

7. Write a paragraph explaining the change in the number of deaths due to infectious diseases from 1900 to 2000. Use the information in the data and what you know about infectious disease in your description. Use the vocabulary words in the box in your answer.

bacterium	virus	pathogen
antibiotic	resistance	microorganism

8. The spread of infectious disease can be controlled in many different ways. Write a paragraph describing how the spread of infectious disease may be limited. Give at least two examples and describe how these diseases can be prevented or contained.

UNIT 3

Ecology

symbiosis

Tickbird
(Buphagus erythrorhynchus)

Impala
(Aepyceros melampus)

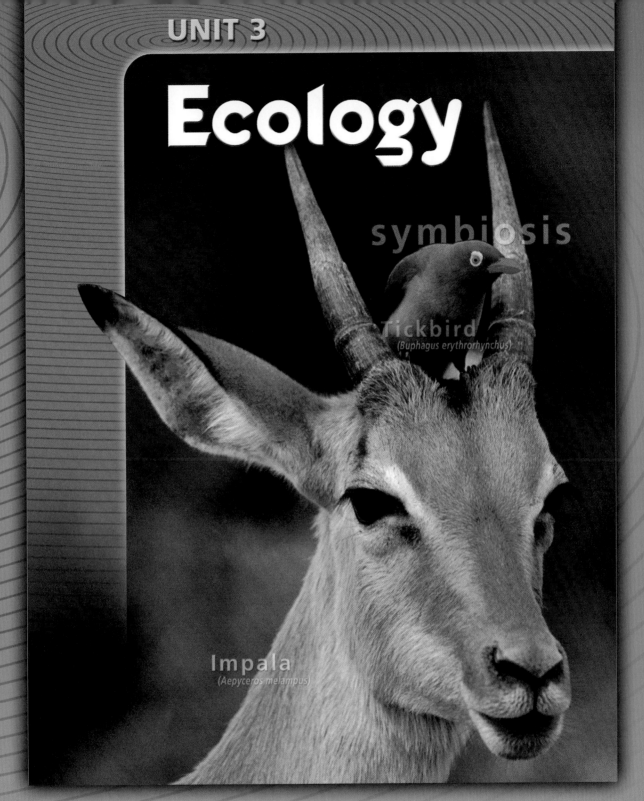

Contents Overview

Frontiers in Science
Ecosystems on FIre   322

Timelines in Science
Wilderness Conservation   394

Chapter 11 Ecosystems and Biomes 326

Chapter 12 Interactions Within
Ecosystems   362

Chapter 13 Human Impact on
Ecosystems   398

ECOSYSTEMS ON FIRE

It may seem strange to set fire to a wilderness preserve, but fire brings health to some ecosystems.

SCIENTIFIC AMERICAN FRONTIERS

View the video "Prairie Comeback" to learn about the restoration of a prairie ecosystem.

An astonishing variety of plants blooms in this prairie in Missouri.

Fire and Life

Intense heat, smoke, the crackling of burning grasses, the crashing of flaming trees—all these characteristics of fire seem threatening. In recent years, forest fires have burned huge areas of forest and have endangered people and property nearby. But even though fire can be destructive, it can also be an agent of life. In fact, scientists are actively using fire to manage ecosystems—areas that contain specific groups of living and nonliving things. Prairies, forests, and woodlands are examples of ecosystems.

The fear of fire has led people to limit fires that are a natural part of some ecosystems. Preventing or putting out smaller fires in a forest ecosystem can mean trouble. Occasional small fires burn small amounts of material and cause only limited damage. Without these smaller fires, burnable materials may build up and lead to the outbreak of a catastrophic fire.

The species of living things in some ecosystems have adaptations that allow them to thrive on fire. In North America trees such as lodgepole pine and jack pine depend upon flames to release seeds from their cones. Cape lilies lying under the forest floor blossom almost immediately after a forest fire. On prairies, flowers such as the rare coastal gayfeather in Texas or the fringed prairie orchid in Illinois benefit from prairie fires.

controlled burn

new growth

Seven months after a controlled burn, light shines on a new patch of wild hyacinth growing at the base of an oak tree.

Observing Patterns

Ecosystems include living things, such as plants and animals, and nonliving things, such as water and soil. Fires affect both the living and the nonliving. The photographs above show part of an oak woodland ecosystem. The photograph on the left shows a burn—a fire set deliberately by humans. The photograph on the right shows the same area seven months later.

Ashes left from fires add nutrients to the soil. Fire also opens space on the forest floor. Areas that were shaded by small trees, plants, and dead branches receive light. Over time, wild hyacinth and other new plants grow around the oak, and new insects and animals move into the area.

View the "Prairie Comeback" segment of your Scientific American Frontiers video to see how understanding ecosystems can help bring a prairie into bloom.

IN THIS SCENE FROM THE VIDEO ⏵ a bison grazes on new growth that appears after the prairie is burned.

BRINGING BACK THE PRAIRIE At one time natural events, such as lightning, along with human activity caused regular patterns of fire on the prairie. Bison grazed on tender young plants that grew up after fires, and the plants that weren't eaten by the bison had room to grow. In 1989, an organization called The Nature Conservancy turned the Chapman-Barnard Cattle Ranch in Northeast Oklahoma into the Tall Grass Prairie Restoration Preserve.

Scientists at the preserve are using controlled fire and reintroducing bison to the area. Today there are more than 750 species of plants and animals growing in the preserve.

In tall-grass prairie ecosystems, fire provides similar benefits. Fire burns away overgrown plants, enriches the soil, and clears the way for the growth of new plants. Bison prefer to graze on these new plants that appear after a fire.

A New Understanding

Although some of the benefits provided by ecosystems can't be measured, researchers are starting to measure the financial contributions of ecosystems. Ecosystems may help clean our water, balance gases in the atmosphere, and maintain temperature ranges.

Researchers today are studying these benefits. In fact, a new frontier in ecology, called ecosystem services, is emerging. This new study is gaining the attention of both scientists and economists.

Given our growing awareness of the importance of ecosystems, should humans deliberately set fire to areas in forests or prairies? The answer to this question requires an understanding of interactions among living and nonliving parts of ecosystems. Forest and prairie fires can be dangerous, but properly managed, they provide important benefits to society as well as to the natural world.

UNANSWERED Questions

Understanding the connections within ecosystems raises more questions. In the coming years, people will need to analyze the costs and benefits of ecosystem restoration.

- How will humans balance the need to feed the human population with the cost of destroying ecosystems such as the prairie?
- How can scientists and wildlife managers protect people and property near forests while maintaining forest ecosystems?
- How do ecosystems protect natural resources, such as soil and water?

UNIT PROJECTS

As you study this unit, work alone or with a group on one of the projects listed below. Use the bulleted steps to guide your project.

Build an Ecosystem

Use an aquarium or other container to build an ecosystem.

- Set up your ecosystem. Observe it daily, and record your observations.
- Bring your ecosystem into your classroom, or take photographs and make diagrams of it. Present the record of your observations along with the visual displays.

Conservation Campaign

Find out how much water, paper, and energy are used in a month at your school.

- Describe a plan for conserving resources.
- Present your plan. You might make posters, write announcements, or perform a short skit.

Design a Park

You are part of a group that is planning a park near your school. Your group wants the park to include plants that lived in the area twenty-five years ago.

- Collect information from local museums, park districts, or botanic gardens. You can also visit Web sites sponsored by those organizations.
- Prepare a report and drawing of your park design.

 **CAREER CENTER**
CLASSZONE.COM

Learn more about careers in ecology.

CHAPTER 11

Ecosystems and Biomes

the BIG idea

Matter and energy together support life within an environment.

> How many living and nonliving things can you identify in this photograph?

Key Concepts

SECTION
1 **Ecosystems support life.**
Learn about different factors that make up an ecosystem.

SECTION
2 **Matter cycles through ecosystems.**
Learn about the water, carbon, and nitrogen cycles.

SECTION
3 **Energy flows through ecosystems.**
Learn how energy moves through living things.

SECTION
4 **Biomes contain many ecosystems.**
Learn about different land and water biomes.

Internet Preview

CLASSZONE.COM
Chapter 11 online resources: Content Review, Simulation, Visualization, three Resource Centers, Math Tutorial, Test Practice

EXPLORE (the BIG idea)

How Do Plants React to Sunlight?

Move a potted plant so that the Sun shines on it from a different direction. Observe the plant each day for a week.

Observe and Think What change do you observe in the plant? What is it that plants get from the Sun?

What Is Soil?

Get a cupful of soil from outside and funnel it into a clear plastic bottle. Fill the bottle two-thirds full with water and place the bottle cap on tightly. Shake the bottle so that the soil and water mix completely. Place the bottle on a windowsill overnight. Wash your hands.

Observe and Think What has happened to the soil and water mixture? How many different types of material do you observe?

Internet Activity: A Prairie Ecosystem

Go to **ClassZone.com** to discover the types of plants and animals best adapted for tall-grass and short-grass prairies. Learn more about how to keep a prairie thriving.

Observe and Think What do all prairie plants have in common? How do prairie plants differ?

NSTA
scilinks.org
SCiLINKS

Food Chains and Food Webs **Code: MDL001**

Chapter 11: **Ecosystems and Biomes 327**

Getting Ready to Learn

◀ CONCEPT REVIEW

- The natural world that surrounds all living things is called the environment.
- Most living things need water, air, food, and living space.
- All living things need a source of energy to stay alive and grow.

◀ VOCABULARY REVIEW

See Glossary for definitions.

biology	nutrient
energy	photosynthesis
environment	respiration
matter	system

ⓘ CONTENT REVIEW
CLASSZONE.COM
Review concepts and vocabulary.

▶ TAKING NOTES

COMBINATION NOTES

To take notes about a new concept, first make an informal outline of the information. Then make a sketch of the concept and label it so you can study it later.

VOCABULARY STRATEGY

Write each new vocabulary term in the center of a **frame game** diagram. Decide what information to frame the term with. Use examples, descriptions, parts, sentences that use the term in context, or pictures. You can change the frame to fit each item.

See the Note-Taking Handbook on pages R45–R51.

SCIENCE NOTEBOOK

NOTES

Parts of an ecosystem:
- Animals
- Plants
- Soil
- Water
- Light
- Microorganisms

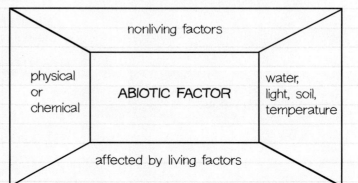

	nonliving factors	
physical or chemical	**ABIOTIC FACTOR**	water, light, soil, temperature
	affected by living factors	

KEY CONCEPT

Ecosystems support life.

STANDARDS

7–4.4 Explain the effects of soil quality on the characteristics of an ecosystem.

7–4.5 Summarize how the location and movement of water on Earth's surface through groundwater zones and surface-water drainage basins, called watersheds, are important to ecosystems and to human activities.

VOCABULARY

ecology p. 329
ecosystem p. 329
biotic factor p. 330
abiotic factor p. 330

◀ **BEFORE,** you learned

- Living things need to obtain matter and energy from the environment
- The Sun provides Earth with light and heat

▶ **NOW,** you will learn

- What factors define an ecosystem
- About living factors in an ecosystem
- About nonliving factors in an ecosystem

EXPLORE Your Environment

How much can temperature vary in one place?

PROCEDURE

① Choose three different locations inside your classroom where you can measure temperature.

② Place a thermometer at each location. Wait for at least two minutes. Record the temperatures in your notebook.

③ Compare the data you and your classmates have collected.

WHAT DO YOU THINK?

- Which location was the warmest, and which was the coldest?
- Describe what factors may have affected the temperature at each location.

MATERIALS
- thermometer
- stopwatch

Living things depend on the environment.

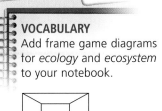

VOCABULARY
Add frame game diagrams for *ecology* and *ecosystem* to your notebook.

You wouldn't find a kangaroo in the Arctic and you won't see a polar bear in Australia. Each of these organisms is suited to a certain environment. The kangaroo and the polar bear are able to survive despite the harsh conditions of their surroundings. **Ecology** is the scientific study of how organisms interact with their environment and all the other organisms that live in that environment.

Scientists use the word **ecosystem** to describe a particular environment and all the living things that are supported by it. An ecosystem can be as small as a pond or as large as a desert. What is important in an ecosystem is how the living parts of the ecosystem relate to the nonliving parts.

Chapter 11: **Ecosystems and Biomes 329**

RESOURCE CENTER
CLASSZONE.COM

Learn more about
ecosystems.

Let's take a look at a pond. A pond ecosystem is more than just water and fish. Plants grow in and around the water, and animals feed on these plants. A variety of tiny microorganisms in the water are food for fish and for each other. These are just a few of the living parts, or **biotic factors** (by-AHT-ihk), of a pond ecosystem. The nonliving parts, or **abiotic factors** (AY-by-AHT-ihk), include the air that supplies oxygen and carbon dioxide, the soil that provides nutrients, the water in the pond, and the sunlight that plants need to grow.

CLASSIFY Name three living and three nonliving factors that are part of this pond ecosystem.

Biotic factors interact with an ecosystem.

Living things depend upon an ecosystem for food, air, and water, as well as other things they need for survival. In turn, living things have an impact on the ecosystem in which they live. Plants, as a biotic factor in land ecosystems, affect other biotic and abiotic parts of ecosystems. Plants are an important source of food. The types of plants found in a particular ecosystem will determine the types of animals that can live there. Plants can affect temperature by blocking sunlight. Plant roots hold soil in place. Even the atmosphere is affected by plants taking in carbon dioxide and releasing oxygen.

Animals, as biotic factors, also affect an ecosystem. A beaver that builds a dam changes the flow of a river and so affects the surrounding landscape. Large herds of cattle can overgraze a grassland ecosystem and cause the soil to erode. In an ocean biome, corals form giant reefs that provide food and shelter for marine organisms.

Many abiotic factors affect ecosystems.

Abiotic factors include both the physical and chemical parts of an ecosystem. Physical factors are factors that you can see or feel, such as the temperature or the amount of water or sunlight. Important chemical factors include the minerals and compounds found in the soil and whether the ecosystem's water is fresh or salty. It is the combination of different abiotic factors that determines the types of organisms that an ecosystem will support.

READING TIP
The word *biotic* means "living." The prefix *a-* in *abiotic* means "not," so *abiotic* means "not living."

 List four different abiotic factors that can affect an ecosystem.

Temperature

Temperature is an important abiotic factor in any ecosystem. In a land ecosystem, temperature affects the types of plants that will do well there. The types of plants available for food and shelter, in turn, determine the types of animals that can live there. For example, a tropical rain forest has not only a lot of rain but it has consistently warm temperatures. The wide variety of plants that grow in a tropical rain forest supports a wide variety of monkeys, birds, and other organisms.

Animals are as sensitive to temperature as plants are. Musk oxen with their thick coat of fur can survive in very cold environments, where temperatures of –40°C (–40°F) are normal. The water buffalo, with its light coat, is better suited to warm temperatures. The wild water buffalo lives where temperatures can reach 48°C (118°F).

This musk ox's thick fur keeps it warm in the cold temperatures of northern Canada.

A water buffalo cools itself in a shallow stream during a hot day in India.

 COMPARE AND CONTRAST How are these animals alike? How are they different?

Light

COMBINATION NOTES
Remember to make notes and diagrams to show how abiotic factors affect biotic factors in an ecosystem.

You can easily understand how abiotic factors work together when you think about sunlight and temperature. Sunlight warms Earth's surface and atmosphere. In addition, energy from sunlight supports all life on Earth. The Sun provides the energy that plants capture and use to produce food in a process called photosynthesis. The food produced by plants, and other photosynthetic organisms, feeds almost all the other living things found on Earth.

The strength of sunlight and the amount of sunlight available in a land ecosystem determine the types of plants in that ecosystem. A desert ecosystem will have plants like cacti, which can survive where sunlight is very strong. Meanwhile, mosses and ferns grow well on the forest floor, where much of the light is blocked by the trees above.

Light is a factor in ocean ecosystems as well. The deeper the water is, the less light there is available. In the shallow water near the shore, photosynthetic organisms can survive at the surface and on the ocean floor. In the open ocean, light is available for photosynthetic organisms only in the first hundred meters below the surface.

Soil

Soil, which is a mixture of small rock and mineral particles, is an important abiotic factor in land ecosystems. Organisms within the soil break down the remains of dead plants and animals. This process of decay provides important raw materials to the living plants and animals of an ecosystem.

The size of soil particles affects how much air and water the soil can hold.

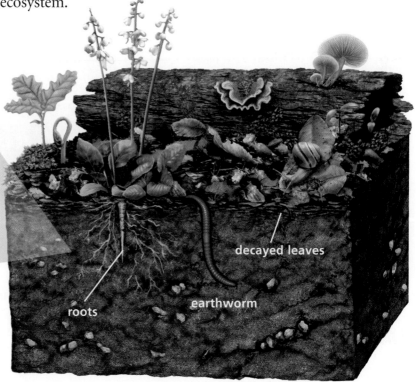

decayed leaves

earthworm

roots

Different ecosystems have different types of soil. The characteristics of the soil in an ecosystem affect plant growth. Soils that have a lot of decaying, or organic, matter can hold water well and allow air to reach the plant roots. Sandy soils usually do not hold water well because the water flows through too easily. Clay soil, which has small, tightly packed particles, will not allow water to move through easily at all. Minerals in the soil also affect plant growth.

SOUTH CAROLINA
Essentials
See the South Carolina Essentials, pages 648–650, to read about the characteristics of soil.

 CHECK YOUR READING   Explain how soil can affect plant life in an ecosystem.

Water

Another important abiotic factor in land ecosystems is the amount of water available to support life. All living things need water to carry out life processes. Plants need water as well as sunlight for photosynthesis. Animals need water to digest food and release the energy stored in the food. Look at the photograph to see the effect that an underground water source has on an otherwise dry, desert ecosystem. Trees could not survive there without a plentiful supply of water.

Ecosystems that have a lot of water can support a large number of different types of plants. These different types of plants can then support a large number of different types of animals. Tropical rain forests, the wettest of all ecosystems on land, are also the most diverse. Desert ecosystems, which are the driest land ecosystems, have far fewer types of plants and animals. The types and number of living things in a land ecosystem will always be related to the amount of fresh water available for its inhabitants.

INFER An oasis forms in the desert when underground water comes to the surface. How can you identify the boundary of this oasis?

11.1 Review

KEY CONCEPTS

1. Draw a diagram of an ecosystem near where you live. Label the factors "biotic" or "abiotic."

2. Give two examples of how plants and animals affect their environment.

3. Describe how temperature, light, and soil affect an ecosystem.

CRITICAL THINKING

4. **Predict** Think of a forest ecosystem. Now imagine that a large volcanic eruption throws large amounts of dust and ash into the air, blocking out sunlight. How might the forest ecosystem be affected if the sunlight is blocked for a day? For a year?

CHALLENGE

5. **Apply** Think of how you fit into your local environment. List ways in which you interact with biotic and abiotic factors within your ecosystem.

CHAPTER INVESTIGATION

Soil Samples

OVERVIEW AND PURPOSE Nonliving, or abiotic, factors all have an effect on soil. The quality of the soil affects how well plants grow in a particular environment. In this investigation, you will

- observe and record how water travels through three soil samples
- predict how different types of soil would affect plant growth

▶ Problem

How does soil type affect how water moves through soil?

▶ Hypothesize

You should complete steps 1–5 in the procedure before writing your hypothesis. Write a hypothesis to explain how water moves through certain types of soil. Your hypothesis should take the form of an "If . . . , then . . . , because . . ." statement.

▶ Procedure

1. Make a data table in your **Science Notebook** like the one shown on page 335.

2. Label three sheets of paper "Clay," "Sand," and "Loam." Carefully place a spoonful of each sample on the appropriately labeled paper.

3. Carefully examine each of the soils, with and without the hand lens. Describe the color of each, and record the information in your data table.

MATERIALS
- 3 pieces of paper
- spoon
- 50 mL each of clay, coarse sand, loam
- hand lens
- toothpick
- eyedropper
- water
- 3 pieces of filter paper
- 3 plastic funnels
- 3 large beakers
- small beaker
- stopwatch

4 Use a toothpick to separate the particles of each sample of soil. Record the size of the particles in the data table.

5 Put a small amount of each soil sample in the palm of your hand. Add a drop of water and mix the soil around with your finger. Write a description of the texture of each sample in your data table. Be sure to wash your hands after you finish. After you have recorded your observations, write your hypothesis.

6 Fold each piece of filter paper to form cones as shown in the diagram. Place one filter inside each funnel. Place one funnel in each large beaker. Measure 50 mL of each soil sample and place the sample in one of the funnels.

7 Measure 150 mL of water and pour it into the funnel containing the clay. Start the stopwatch when the water begins to drip out of the funnel. Stop the watch when the water stops dripping. Record the time in seconds in the data table.

8 Repeat step 7 for the sand and the loam. When you have finished with the activity, dispose of the materials according to your teacher's directions, and wash your hands.

▶ Observe and Analyze

1. **INTERPRET DATA** Through which soil sample did the water move the fastest? The slowest?

2. **OBSERVE** What type of changes occurred in the soil as the water was added?

▶ Conclude

1. **INTERPRET** Compare your results with your hypothesis. Does your data support your hypothesis?

2. **IDENTIFY LIMITS** What sources of error could have affected this investigation?

3. **EVALUATE** Based on your observations, what can account for the differences in the times recorded for the three soil samples?

4. **PREDICT** Based on your results, which of the soil samples would you expect to be the best type of soil in which to grow plants? Explain.

▶ INVESTIGATE Further

CHALLENGE Design an experiment in which you test which of the three soil samples is best for growing plants. Include a materials list, hypothesis, and procedure for your experiment.

Soil Samples
Table 1. Soil Characteristics

Characteristics	Clay	Sand	Loam
Color			
Particle size			
Texture			
Time for water to stop dripping (sec)			

KEY CONCEPT
11.2 Matter cycles through ecosystems.

STANDARDS

7–4.5 Summarize how the location and movement of water on Earth's surface through groundwater zones and surface-water drainage basins, called watersheds, are important to ecosystems and to human activities.

VOCABULARY

cycle p. 336
water cycle p. 337
carbon cycle p. 338
nitrogen cycle p. 339

◀ **BEFORE, you learned**

- Ecosystems support life
- Living and nonliving factors interact in an ecosystem
- Temperature, light, soil, and water are important nonliving factors in ecosystems

▶ **NOW, you will learn**

- How matter is exchanged between organisms and their environment
- About the water, carbon, and nitrogen cycles

EXPLORE The Water Cycle

Do plants release water?

PROCEDURE

① Cover a branch of the plant with a plastic bag. Tape the bag firmly around the stem.

② Water the plant and place it in a sunny window or under a lamp. Wash your hands.

③ Check the plant after ten minutes, at the end of class, and again the next day.

WHAT DO YOU THINK?
- What do you see inside the plastic bag?
- What purpose does the plastic bag serve?

MATERIALS
- 1 small potted plant
- 1 clear plastic bag
- tape
- water

CLASSZONE.COM

Explore cycles in nature.

All ecosystems need certain materials.

Living things depend on their environment to meet their needs. You can think of those needs in terms of the material, or matter, required by all living things. For example, all organisms take in water and food in order to survive. All of the materials an organism takes in are returned to the ecosystem, while the organism lives or after it dies.

The movement of matter through the living and nonliving parts of an ecosystem is a continuous process, a cycle. A **cycle** is a series of events that happens over and over again. Matter in an ecosystem may change form, but it never leaves the ecosystem, so the matter is said to cycle through the ecosystem. Three of the most important cycles in ecosystems involve water, carbon, and nitrogen.

Water Cycle

Different processes combine to move water through the environment.

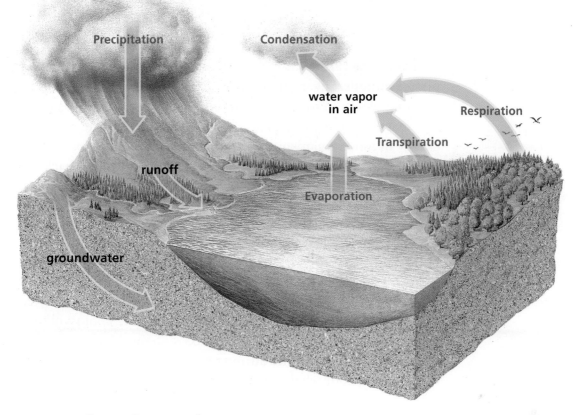

Precipitation

Condensation

water vapor in air

Respiration

Transpiration

runoff

Evaporation

groundwater

Water cycles through ecosystems.

Water is stored on Earth's surface in lakes, rivers, and oceans. Water is found underground, filling the spaces between soil particles and cracks in rocks. Large amounts of water are stored in glaciers and polar ice sheets. Water is also part of the bodies of living things. But water is not just stored, it is constantly moving. The movement of water through the environment is called the **water cycle.**

Water is made up of just two elements: oxygen and hydrogen. As water moves through an ecosystem, it changes in physical form, moving back and forth between gas, liquid, and solid. Water in the atmosphere is usually in gaseous form—water vapor. Water that falls to Earth's surface is referred to as precipitation. For precipitation to occur, water vapor must condense—it must change into a liquid or solid. This water can fall as rain, snow, sleet, mist, or hail.

CHECK YOUR READING What are the three physical forms of water in the water cycle?

Water returns to the atmosphere when heated, changing back into vapor, a process called evaporation. Living things also release water vapor. Animals release water vapor when they breathe, or respire. Plants release water vapor through a process called transpiration.

COMBINATION NOTES
Make notes and draw a diagram to show how water cycles through ecosystems.

SOUTH CAROLINA Essentials

See the South Carolina Essentials, pages 651–654, to read about groundwater zones and watersheds.

Carbon cycles through ecosystems.

Carbon is an element found in all living things. Carbon moves through Earth's ecosystems in a cycle referred to as the **carbon cycle.** It is through carbon dioxide gas found in Earth's atmosphere that carbon enters the living parts of an ecosystem.

Plants use carbon dioxide to produce sugar—a process called photosynthesis. Sugars are carbon compounds that are important building blocks in food and all living matter. Food supplies the energy and materials living things need to live and grow. To release the energy in food, organisms break down the carbon compounds—a process called respiration. Carbon is released and cycled back into the atmosphere as carbon dioxide. When living things die and decay, the rest of the carbon that makes up living matter is released.

READING TiP

Notice that photosynthesis is a process that brings carbon into living matter and respiration is a process that releases carbon.

 CHECK YOUR READING Name three ways that living things are part of the carbon cycle.

Earth's oceans contain far more carbon than the air does. In water ecosystems—lakes, rivers, and oceans—carbon dioxide is dissolved in water. Algae and certain types of bacteria are the photosynthetic organisms that produce food in these ecosystems. Marine organisms, too, release carbon dioxide during respiration. Carbon is also deposited on the ocean floor when organisms die.

Carbon Cycle

Different processes combine to move carbon through the environment.

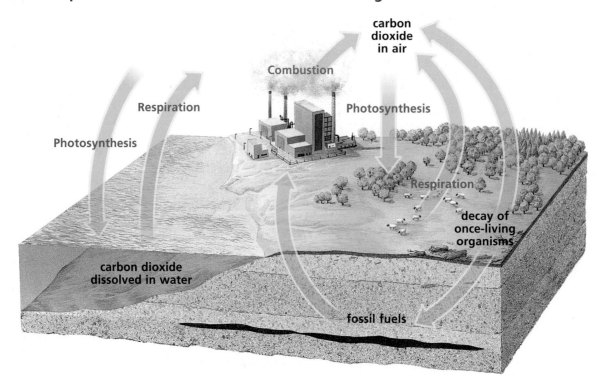

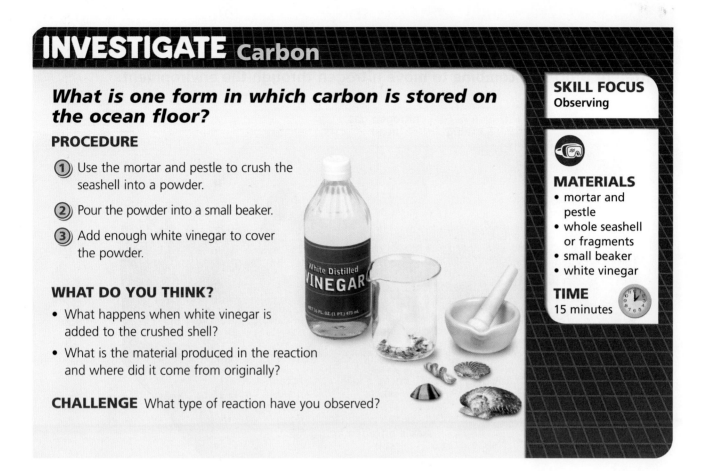

INVESTIGATE Carbon

What is one form in which carbon is stored on the ocean floor?

PROCEDURE

1. Use the mortar and pestle to crush the seashell into a powder.
2. Pour the powder into a small beaker.
3. Add enough white vinegar to cover the powder.

WHAT DO YOU THINK?

- What happens when white vinegar is added to the crushed shell?
- What is the material produced in the reaction and where did it come from originally?

CHALLENGE What type of reaction have you observed?

SKILL FOCUS
Observing

MATERIALS
- mortar and pestle
- whole seashell or fragments
- small beaker
- white vinegar

TIME
15 minutes

Large amounts of carbon are stored underground. The remains of plants and animals buried for millions of years decay slowly and change into fossil fuels, such as coal and oil. The carbon in fossil fuels returns to ecosystems in a process called combustion. As humans burn fossil fuels to release energy, dust particles and gases containing carbon are also released into the environment.

Nitrogen cycles through ecosystems.

Nitrogen is another element important to life that cycles through Earth in the **nitrogen cycle.** Almost four-fifths of the air you breathe is clear, colorless nitrogen gas. Yet, you cannot get the nitrogen you need to live from the air. All animals must get nitrogen from plants.

Plants cannot use pure nitrogen gas either. However, plants can absorb certain compounds of nitrogen. Plants take in these nitrogen compounds through their roots, along with water and other nutrients. So how does the nitrogen from the atmosphere get into the soil? One source is lightning. Every lightning strike breaks apart, or fixes, pure nitrogen, changing it into a form that plants can use. This form of nitrogen falls to the ground when it rains.

Nitrogen Cycle

Different processes combine to move nitrogen through the environment.

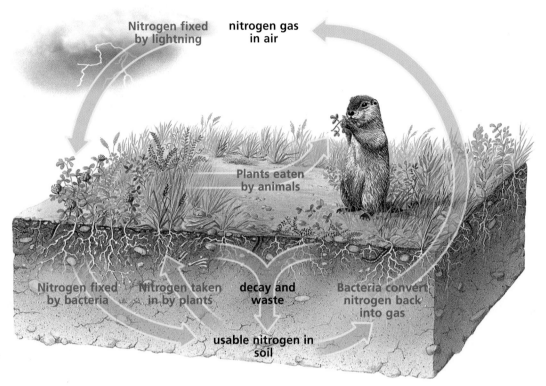

Nitrogen fixed by lightning

nitrogen gas in air

Plants eaten by animals

Nitrogen fixed by bacteria

Nitrogen taken in by plants

decay and waste

Bacteria convert nitrogen back into gas

usable nitrogen in soil

VISUALIZATION
CLASSZONE.COM

Watch the nitrogen cycle in action.

A far greater source of nitrogen is nitrogen-fixing bacteria. These bacteria live in the oceans as well as the soil. Some even attach themselves to the roots of certain plants, like alfalfa or soybeans. When organisms die, decomposers in the ocean or soil break them down. Nitrogen in the soil or water is used again by living things. A small amount is returned to the atmosphere by certain bacteria that can break down nitrogen compounds into nitrogen gas.

11.2 Review

KEY CONCEPTS

1. Draw a diagram of the water cycle. Show three ways in which water moves through the cycle.

2. Summarize the main parts of the carbon cycle.

3. Explain two ways that nitrogen gas in the atmosphere is changed into nitrogen compounds that plants can use.

CRITICAL THINKING

4. **Predict** When people burn fossil fuels, carbon dioxide gas is added to the atmosphere. How might increased carbon dioxide affect plant growth?

5. **Compare and Contrast** Review the nitrogen and carbon cycles. How are these two cycles similar and different?

● CHALLENGE

6. **Apply** Draw a cycle diagram that shows how water is used in your household. Include activities that use water, sources of water, and ways that water leaves your house.

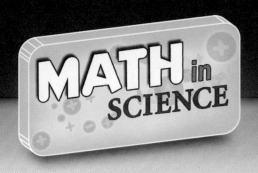

MATH in SCIENCE

 MATH TUTORIAL
CLASSZONE.COM

Click on Math Tutorial for more help with adding integers.

This iceberg is made up of fresh water, which freezes at 0°C. The surrounding ocean is salt water, which doesn't freeze at 0°C.

SKILL: ADDING INTEGERS

Temperature and the Water Cycle

Changes in temperature help water move through the environment. At freezing temperatures—below 32°F or 0°C for sea-level environments—water can begin to become solid ice. Ice starts to melt when the temperature rises above freezing, causing the water to become liquid again. Temperature change also causes water to become vapor, or gas, within the air.

Example

Suppose you are waiting for winter to come so you can skate on a small pond near your house. The weather turns cold. One day the temperature is 25°C, then the next day the air temperature drops by 35°C. What temperature is the air? If the air stays below 0°C, some of the water will begin to freeze.

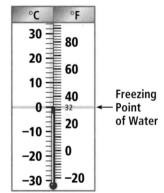

(1) Write a verbal model:
25 degrees + a 35-degree drop = what temperature?

(2) Write an equation. Use negative and positive integers:
$25 + (-35) = ?$

(3) Solve the equation:
$25 - 35 = -10$

ANSWER $-10°C$.

Answer the following questions.

1. A container of water is left out over night, when the temperature is $-18°C$. In the morning, the air temperature rises by 8°C. What temperature is the air? What will happen to the water?

2. An ice block sits in a field where the air is 0°C. The air temperature rises by 16°C, then it drops by 8°C. What temperature is the air in the field now? What will happen to the ice?

3. What happens to a block of ice after the temperature in the air follows this pattern: $-6 + 17 + 10 + 18 + (-5)$?
What temperature has the air reached?

CHALLENGE Use a thermometer to measure the temperature of the air outside and indoors in degrees Celsius. Write two addition equations that show the temperature change between the two locations. One equation should show a rise, and one should show a drop.

11.3

Energy flows through ecosystems.

STANDARDS

7–4.2 Illustrate energy flow in food chains, food webs, and energy pyramids.

VOCABULARY

producer p. 343
consumer p. 344
decomposer p. 345
food chain p. 346
food web p. 346
energy pyramid p. 348

◀ BEFORE, you learned

- Matter cycles continuously through an ecosystem
- Living things are part of the water, carbon, and nitrogen cycles

▶ NOW, you will learn

- How living things move energy through an ecosystem
- How feeding relationships are important in ecosystems
- How the amount of energy changes as it flows through an ecosystem

EXPLORE Energy

How can you observe energy changing form?

PROCEDURE

① Mark and cut a spiral pattern in a square piece of paper.

② Cut a 15-cm piece of thread and tape one end to the center of the spiral.

③ Adjust the lamp to shine straight at the ceiling. Turn the lamp on.

④ Hold the spiral by the thread and let it hang 10 cm above the light bulb. CAUTION: Don't let the paper touch the bulb!

WHAT DO YOU THINK?

- What do you see happen to the spiral?
- In what sense has the energy changed form?

MATERIALS
- paper
- marker
- scissors
- thread
- tape
- desk lamp

Living things capture and release energy.

Everything you do—running, reading, and working—requires energy. The energy you use is chemical energy, which comes from the food you eat. When you go for a run, you use up energy. Some of that energy is released to the environment as heat, as you sweat. Eventually, you will need to replace the energy you've used.

Energy is vital to all living things. Most of that energy comes either directly or indirectly from the Sun. To use the Sun's energy, living things must first capture that energy and store it in some usable form. Because energy is continuously used by the activities of living things, it must be continuously replaced in the ecosystem.

Producers

All of these producers capture energy from sunlight.

Plants

This tomato plant uses energy from the Sun to produce food.

The food is used as a source of energy and material for the plant and all the organisms that eat the plant.

READING VISUALS What process do all of these producers have in common?

Seaweed

Seaweed is a producer found in Earth's oceans and coastal zones.

Phytoplankton

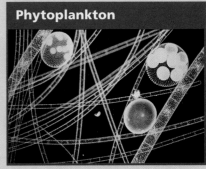

The most numerous producers are tiny organisms that live in water called phytoplankton.

Producers

A **producer** is an organism that captures energy and stores it in food as chemical energy. The producers of an ecosystem make energy available to all the other living parts of an ecosystem. Most energy enters ecosystems through photosynthesis. Plants, and other photosynthetic organisms, take water and carbon dioxide from their environment and use energy from the Sun to produce sugars. The chemical energy stored in sugars can be released when sugars are broken down.

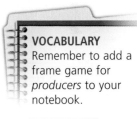

VOCABULARY
Remember to add a frame game for *producers* to your notebook.

CHECK YOUR READING How does energy enter into the living parts of an ecosystem?

Plants are the most common producers found in land ecosystems. In water ecosystems, most food is produced by photosynthetic bacteria and algae. A few examples of producers that use photosynthesis are shown in the photographs above.

The Sun provides most of the energy that is stored in food. One exception is the unusual case of a type of bacteria that lives in the deep ocean, where there is no sunlight. These bacteria produce food using heated chemicals released from underwater vents. This process is called chemosynthesis. Whether producers use photosynthesis or chemosynthesis, they do just as their name suggests—they produce food for themselves and for the rest of the ecosystem.

Consumers

A consumer is an organism that gets energy by eating producers or other consumers.

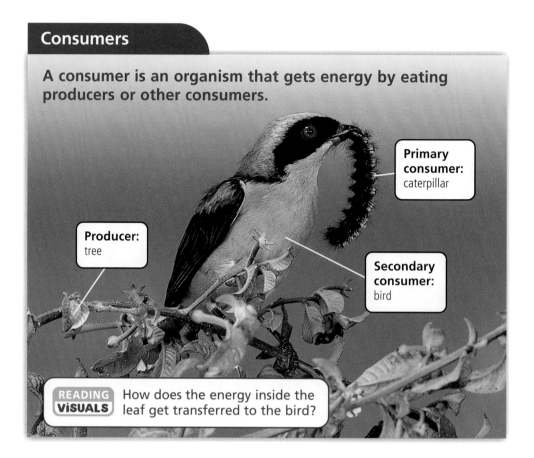

Producer: tree

Primary consumer: caterpillar

Secondary consumer: bird

 READING VISUALS How does the energy inside the leaf get transferred to the bird?

Consumers

Organisms that cannot produce their own food must get their food from other sources. **Consumers** are organisms that get their energy by eating, or consuming, other organisms. To understand how energy flows through an ecosystem, you have to study feeding relationships. A feeding relationship starts with a producer, followed by one and often many more consumers.

CHECK YOUR READING Describe the producer-consumer relationship in terms of energy.

READING **TiP**

Primary is a word that means "first in order," *secondary* means "second in order," and *tertiary* means "third in order."

Consumers are classified by their position in a feeding relationship. In a meadow ecosystem, animals such as antelopes and grasshoppers feed on grasses. They are primary consumers because they are the first link between the producers and the rest of the consumers in an ecosystem. The wolves that eat the antelopes and the meadowlarks that eat the grasshoppers are secondary consumers. There are also tertiary consumers, like the prairie falcon that eats the meadowlark. Ecosystems also have special consumers called scavengers, like the vulture, which is a consumer that feeds on dead animals.

In the photograph above, energy enters the ecosystem through the tree, which is the producer. The caterpillar that gets its energy by feeding on the leaves is the first, or primary, consumer. The bird that gets its energy by feeding on the caterpillar is a secondary consumer.

Decomposers

If you've been for a hike through a forest, or a walk through a park, you have seen the interaction of producers and consumers. Tall trees and leafy shrubs are home to many insects and the birds that feed upon the insects. Also important to the maintenance of an ecosystem are decomposers, a group of organisms that often go unseen. **Decomposers** are organisms that break down dead plant and animal matter into simpler compounds.

mushrooms

Fungi, such as these mushrooms, are decomposers.

You can think of decomposers as the clean-up crew of an ecosystem. In a forest, consumers such as deer and insects eat a tiny fraction of the leaves on trees and shrubs. The leaves that are left on the forest floor, as well as dead roots and branches, are eventually digested by fungi and bacteria living in the soil. Decomposers also break down animal remains, including waste materials. A pinch of soil may contain almost half a million fungi and billions of bacteria.

The energy within an ecosystem gets used up as it flows from organism to organism. Decomposers are the organisms that release the last bit of energy from once-living matter. Decomposers also return matter to soil or water where it may be used again and again.

INVESTIGATE Decomposers

Where do decomposers come from?

PROCEDURE

1. Carefully use scissors to cut an opening across the middle of the bottle.

2. Place a handful of stones in the bottom of the bottle for drainage, and add enough soil to make a layer 10 cm deep.

3. Place some leaves and fruit slices on top of the soil.

4. Seal the cut you made with tape. Mark the date on the tape.

5. Add water through the top of the bottle to moisten the soil, and put the cap on the bottle. Wash your hands.

6. Observe the fruit slices each day for two weeks. Record your observations. Keep the soil moist.

WHAT DO YOU THINK?

- What do you observe happening to the fruit slices?
- Where do the decomposers in your bottle come from?

CHALLENGE Predict what would happen if you used potting soil instead of soil from outside.

345

Models help explain feeding relationships.

COMBINATION NOTES
Remember to take notes and draw a diagram for *food chain* and *food web*.

You have learned how energy is captured by producers and moved through ecosystems by consumers and decomposers. Scientists use two different models to show the feeding relationships that transfer energy from organism to organism. These models are food chains and food webs.

Food Chain

A chain is made of links that are connected one by one. Scientists use the idea of links in a chain as a model for simple feeding relationships. A **food chain** describes the feeding relationship between a producer and a single chain of consumers in an ecosystem.

The illustration in the white box on page 347 shows a wetland food chain. The first link in the chain is a cattail, a primary producer that captures the Sun's energy and stores it in food. The second link is a caterpillar, a primary consumer of the cattail. The frog is the next link, a secondary consumer that eats the caterpillar. The final link is a heron, a tertiary consumer that eats the frog. Energy is captured and released at each link in the chain. The arrows represent the flow of energy from organism to organism. You can see that some of the energy captured by the cattail makes its way through a whole chain of other organisms in the ecosystem.

Food Web

A **food web** is a model of the feeding relationships between many different consumers and producers in an ecosystem. A food web is more like a spiderweb, with many overlapping and interconnected food chains. It is a better model for the complex feeding relationships in an ecosystem, which usually has many different producers, with many primary and secondary consumers.

READING TiP

Notice that the food chain described above is also a part of the food web described here. Follow the blue arrows in the diagram on page 347.

The illustration on page 347 also shows a wetland food web. You can see that the feeding relationships can go in several directions. For example, the food web shows that ruddy ducks eat bulrushes, which are producers. That makes ruddy ducks primary consumers. Ruddy ducks are also secondary consumers because they eat snails. A food web shows how one consumer can play several roles in an ecosystem.

CHECK YOUR READING What is the difference between a food chain and a food web?

Both food chains and food webs show how different organisms receive their energy. They also show how different organisms depend on one another. If one organism is removed from the food web or food chain, it may affect many other organisms in the ecosystem.

Energy Flows Through Ecosystems

Energy is transferred from one organism to the next as organisms eat or are eaten.

A Wetland Food Chain

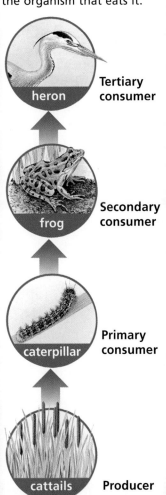

Flow of Energy
Energy flow starts at the bottom. Arrows represent energy moving from an organism that is eaten to the organism that eats it.

heron — **Tertiary consumer**

frog — **Secondary consumer**

caterpillar — **Primary consumer**

cattails — **Producer**

Decomposers
These tiny organisms recycle dead and decayed material.

A Wetland Food Web

heron

water snake

frog

blackbird

duck

beetle

caterpillar

snail

muskrat

bulrush

cattails

Available energy decreases as it moves through an ecosystem.

Another way to picture the flow of energy in an ecosystem is to use an energy pyramid. An **energy pyramid** is a model that shows the amount of energy available at each feeding level of an ecosystem. The first level includes the producers, the second level the primary consumers, and so on. Because usable energy decreases as it moves from producers to consumers, the bottom level is the largest. The available energy gets smaller and smaller the farther up the pyramid you go.

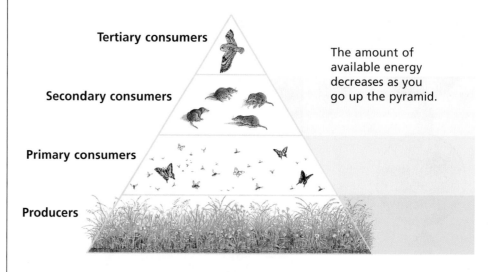

Tertiary consumers

Secondary consumers

Primary consumers

Producers

The amount of available energy decreases as you go up the pyramid.

READING TiP

Refer to the diagram above as you read the text. It is because available energy decreases at each level that the diagram takes the shape of a pyramid.

In the pyramid shown here, plants are the producers. They capture energy from sunlight, use some of it, then store the rest as food. The plants are eaten by insects, which also use some of the energy before being eaten by shrews. The shrews use energy before being eaten by the owl. You can see that it takes a lot of sunlight to support the producers and consumers in a food web that feeds an owl.

11.3 Review

KEY CONCEPTS

1. Describe the role of producers, consumers, and decomposers in an ecosystem.

2. Explain why a food web provides a better model of an ecosystem than a food chain does.

3. Explain how the amount of available energy changes as energy moves up a food chain.

CRITICAL THINKING

4. **Apply** Draw a food chain and a food web for an ecosystem near your home.

5. **Predict** Imagine that muskrats are removed from a wetland ecosystem. Predict what would happen both to producers and to secondary consumers.

⬥ CHALLENGE

6. **Synthesize** Explain how the carbon cycle is related to a food web. Describe how energy and matter move through the food web and the carbon cycle.

Biomagnification

Matter moves through living things in an ecosystem. Some of it is used up, some of it is stored. Sometimes, a toxic, or poisonous, material can get into a food chain and be stored. Biomagnification is the process by which matter becomes concentrated in living things.

Moving up the Food Chain

DDT provides one example of the effects of biomagnification in an ecosystem. DDT is a chemical that was widely used to kill plant-eating insects. Some chemicals break down over time, but DDT does not. DDT collected in water and soil, was absorbed by living things, and moved up the food chain. The diagram shows how DDT became magnified in a wetland ecosystem. It entered through tiny organisms called zooplankton, which absorbed DDT from the water.

1 The concentration of DDT in zooplankton was about 800 times greater than in the environment.

2 Minnows fed on zooplankton. DDT was magnified 31 times, so the concentration of DDT in minnows was 24,800 times greater than in the environment: $800 \times 31 = 24{,}800$.

3 Trout ate minnows. DDT was magnified 1.7 times, so the concentration of DDT in trout was 42,160 times greater than in the environment.

4 Gulls ate trout. DDT was magnified 4.8 times, so the concentration of DDT in gulls was over 200,000 times greater than in the environment.

DDT is especially harmful to large birds such as osprey and eagles. The chemical made the shells of the eggs of these large birds so thin that the eggs did not survive long enough to hatch.

Moving up the Food Chain

This diagram shows how DDT moved up a food chain in Long Island Sound. The color in each circle below represents a certain level of DDT.

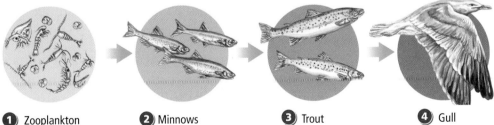

1 Zooplankton   **2** Minnows   **3** Trout   **4** Gull

CHALLENGE Even though DDT was effective, some insects were not harmed by DDT. Predict what might happen to the numbers of those insects as a result of DDT use.

KEY CONCEPT

Biomes contain many ecosystems.

<table>
<tr><td>◀ BEFORE, you learned</td><td>▶ NOW, you will learn</td></tr>
<tr><td>

• Feeding relationships describe how energy flows through ecosystems
• The amount of available energy decreases as it flows through ecosystems
</td><td>

• How biomes vary by region and by the plant life they support
• How different ecosystems make up a biome
• About the different land and water biomes on Earth
</td></tr>
</table>

VOCABULARY

biome p. 350
coniferous p. 352
deciduous p. 353
estuary p. 356

THINK ABOUT

What do this plant's characteristics suggest about its environment?

A plant's overall shape and form help it to survive in its environment. Look closely at this plant in the photograph. Describe its shape. Does it have leaves? a stem? flowers? Look at the surrounding area. What do your observations suggest about the environment in general?

Regions of Earth are classified into biomes.

COMBINATION NOTES
Remember to take notes and draw a diagram for each of the six land biomes described in the text.

If you could travel along the 30° latitude line, either north or south of the equator, you'd notice an interesting pattern. You would see deserts give way to grasslands and grasslands give way to forests. Across Earth, there are large geographic areas that are similar in climate and that have similar types of plants and animals. Each of these regions is classified as a **biome** (BY-OHM). There are six major land biomes on Earth, as shown on the map on page 351.

Climate is an important factor in land biomes. Climate describes the long-term weather patterns of a region, such as average yearly rainfall and temperature ranges. Climate also affects soil type. Available water, temperature, and soil are abiotic factors important in ecosystems. The fact that the abiotic factors of a particular biome are similar helps to explain why the ecosystems found in these biomes are similar. Biomes represent very large areas, which means that there will be many ecosystems within a biome.

Each land biome is characterized by a particular climate, the quality of the soil, and the plant life found there.

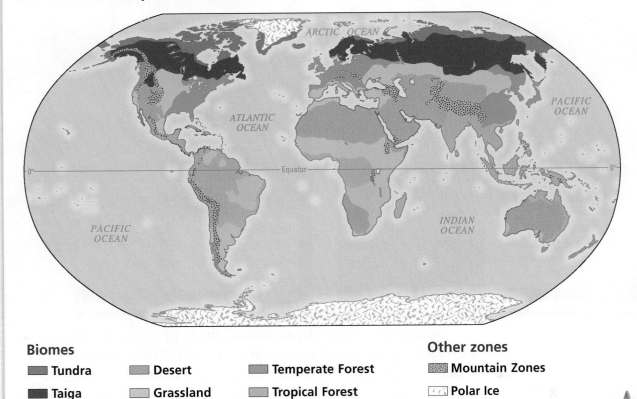

Biomes

- Tundra
- Taiga
- Desert
- Grassland
- Temperate Forest
- Tropical Forest

Other zones

- Mountain Zones
- Polar Ice

Taiga and Tundra

If you go to the northernmost regions of Earth, you will find two biomes—tundra and taiga—that are characterized by long cold winters and short cool summers. In the Arctic tundra, temperatures can go as low as –50°C, with a high of about 18°C. Temperature ranges in the taiga (TY-guh) are similar, –40°C to 20°C.

snowy owl

The tundra doesn't get much precipitation, less than 25 centimeters each year. Yet the area is wet because cold temperatures keep the water from evaporating. One of the important characteristics of tundra is permafrost, a deep layer of permanently frozen soil that lies just below the surface soil. Permafrost prevents trees from taking root in the tundra. Plants of the tundra are small and include mosses, grasses, and woody shrubs. Organisms called lichens also do well in the tundra.

The producers of tundra ecosystems support rodents, caribou, and musk oxen. Grizzly bears, white fox, and snowy owls are predators found there. Migrating birds come to nest in the tundra, feeding on insects that mature in summer.

Tundra Only small plants and lichens grow in the tundra because the soil below the surface is frozen.

Taiga Evergreen trees grow in the taiga, where the ground is cold but not frozen.

Even though the temperatures of the taiga are similar to those of the tundra, the taiga has more precipitation, 30 to 60 centimeters a year. The effect of this is that there is more snow on the ground, which insulates the soil below, keeping it from permanently freezing.

Taiga ecosystems are characterized by evergreen trees called **coniferous** (koh-NIHF-uhr-uhs) trees. These trees have needlelike leaves that produce food all year long. This is an advantage in taiga ecosystems because decomposers work slowly in the cold, so the soil is low in nutrients. The wood and leaves of these trees feed insects and their seeds feed birds and squirrels. Taiga ecosystems support deer, elk, snowshoe hares, and beavers. Predators include lynx, owls, bears, and wolves.

Desert and Grassland

collared lizard

Deserts and grasslands are biomes found toward the middle latitudes. You can see from the map on page 351 that a desert biome often leads into a grassland biome. What deserts and grasslands have in common is that they do not get enough precipitation to support trees.

Some deserts are cold and some deserts are hot, but all deserts are characterized by their dry soil. Less than 25 centimeters of rain falls each year in a desert. Desert plants, like the cactus, and desert animals, like the collared lizard, can get by on very little water. Small burrowing animals like the kangaroo rat and ground squirrel are part of desert ecosystems. Desert predators include snakes, owls, and foxes.

Grassland ecosystems develop in areas of moderate rainfall, generally from 50 to 90 centimeters each year. There is enough rain to support grasses, but too little rain to support forests. Periodic wildfires and droughts keep smaller shrubs and tree seedlings from growing. Summers in grassland ecosystems are warm, up to 30°C, but winters are cold.

Grasses do well in large open areas. The more rain a grassland ecosystem gets, the higher the grasses grow. These ecosystems support seed-eating rodents that make their burrows in the grassland soil. There are also large grazing animals, like bison, wild horses, gazelle, and zebra. Predators include wolves, tigers, and lions.

Desert Plants of the desert are adapted to survive in dry soil. Many must also survive high daytime temperatures.

Grassland Grasslands receive enough rain to support grasses. Wildfires keep shrubs and trees from growing.

Temperate Forest and Tropical Forest

Trees need more water than smaller plants, shrubs, and grasses. So forest biomes are usually located in regions where more water is available. The taiga is a forest biome. There the coniferous trees survive on smaller amounts of precipitation because the cold weather limits evaporation. Across the middle latitudes, temperate forests grow where winters are short and 75 to 150 centimeters of precipitation fall each year. Near the equator, there are no winters. There, tropical forests grow where 200 to 450 centimeters of rain fall each year.

Most temperate forests are made up of deciduous trees, sometimes referred to as broadleaf trees. **Deciduous** (dih-SIHJ-oo-uhs) trees drop their leaves as winter approaches and then grow new leaves in spring.

Temperate Forest
Temperate forests contain many trees with leaves that change color and fall as winter approaches.

Tropical Forest
Tropical forests are warm enough that trees stay green during the entire year.

The most common broadleaf trees in North American deciduous forests are oak, birch, beech, and maple. Temperate forests support a wide variety of animals. Animals like mice, chipmunks, squirrels, raccoons, and deer live off seeds, fruit, and insects. Predators include wolves, bobcats, foxes, and mountain lions.

Most temperate forests in North America are deciduous. However, the wet winters and dry summers in the Pacific Northwest support forests made up mostly of coniferous trees—redwoods, spruce, and fir. These forests are referred to as temperate rain forests. The largest trees in the United States are found in these temperate rain forests.

Tropical forests are located near the equator, where the weather is warm all year, around 25°C. The tropical rain forest is the wettest land biome, with a rainfall of 250 to 400 centimeters each year. The trees tend to have leaves year round. This provides an advantage because the soil is poor in nutrients. High temperatures cause materials to break down quickly, but there are so many plants the nutrients get used up just as quickly.

More types of animals, plants, and other organisms live in the tropical rain forest than anywhere else on Earth. The trees grow close together and support many tree-dwelling animals like monkeys, birds, insects, and snakes. There are even plants, like orchids and vines, that grow on top of the trees.

CHECK YOUR READING How does the variety of plants in a biome affect the variety of animals in a biome?

INVESTIGATE Climate

How can you graph climate data for your area?

PROCEDURE

1. Gather local data on the average monthly precipitation and the average monthly temperature for a 12-month period.

2. On graph paper, mark off 12 months along the *x*-axis. Make a *y*-axis for each side of the graph, marking one "Temperature (°C)" and the other "Precipitation (mm)."

3. Plot the average precipitation for each month as a bar graph.

4. Plot the average temperature for each month as a line graph.

WHAT DO YOU THINK?

- How much precipitation did the area receive overall?
- What is the temperature range for the area?

CHALLENGE Collect data for the same location, going back 10, 20, and 30 years ago. Graph the data for each of these and compare these graphs to your original graph. Has the climate in your area changed? How might severe changes in climate affect the plant and animal life in your area?

SKILL FOCUS
Graphing data

MATERIALS
- graph data
- 2 colored pencils

TIME
20 minutes

Water covers most of Earth's surface.

Close to three-quarters of Earth's surface is covered by water. Water, or aquatic, biomes can be divided into two broad categories: freshwater biomes and saltwater biomes. Plants have a role as producers in the water biomes that are closely surrounded by land—in ponds and streams and wetlands, and in coastal areas. The food chains of deepwater ecosystems depend on tiny photosynthetic microorganisms called phytoplankton.

leopard frog

Freshwater Biomes

The ecosystems of freshwater biomes are affected by the qualities of the landscape in which they are found. For example, the running water of streams and rivers results from differences in elevation. In shallow rivers, green algae and plants grow in from the banks, providing food for insects and snails that feed fish, salamanders, turtles, and frogs. Plants in a freshwater biome, like a stream or river, may take root in the soil under the water if the water is not too deep or moving too fast. Phytoplankton are not part of river ecosystems because of the moving water.

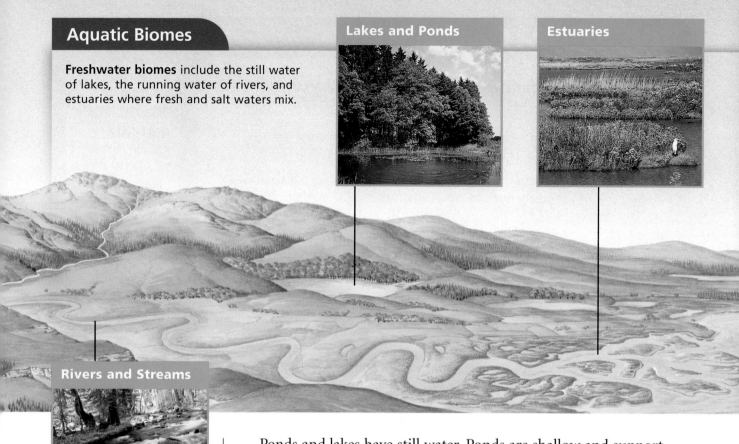

Aquatic Biomes

Freshwater biomes include the still water of lakes, the running water of rivers, and estuaries where fresh and salt waters mix.

Lakes and Ponds

Estuaries

Rivers and Streams

Ponds and lakes have still water. Ponds are shallow and support many plants as producers. The deeper lakes depend much more on phytoplankton. Ponds and lakes support many different insects, shellfish, snakes, fish, and the land animals that feed off them.

⬆ **CHECK YOUR READING** Name two types of freshwater biomes.

Estuaries are water ecosystems that mark a transition between freshwater and saltwater biomes. An **estuary** is the lower end of a river that feeds into the ocean, where fresh water and salt water mix. Marshes and wetlands are two types of estuaries. Estuaries are sometimes referred to as the nurseries of the sea because so many marine animals travel into the calm waters of an estuary to reproduce. Seaweed, marsh grasses, shellfish, and birds all thrive in estuaries.

Marine Biomes

Marine biomes are saltwater biomes. The three general marine biomes are coastal ocean, open ocean, and deep ocean. Beaches are part of the coastal ocean biome. Tidal pools also form along the coast as the tide comes in and goes out and the conditions constantly change. Organisms like crabs and clams are able to survive the ever-changing conditions to thrive in coastal areas.

Organisms in the open ocean receive less sunlight than in the coastal ocean, and the temperatures are colder. Many types of fish and

RESOURCE CENTER
CLASSZONE.COM
Find out more about land and aquatic biomes.

Coastal

Marine biomes include rocky and sandy shores as well as the open ocean and the deep waters below, where little or no light can reach.

Open Ocean

Deep Ocean

other marine animals and floating seaweed live in the upper ocean. There are no plants in the open ocean. The producers at the bottom of the food chain are different types of phytoplankton.

The deep-ocean regions are much colder and darker than the upper ocean. In the deep ocean there is no sunlight available for photosynthesis. The animals in the deep ocean either feed on each other or on material that falls down from upper levels of the ocean. Many organisms in deep ocean biomes can only be seen with a microscope.

11.4 Review

KEY CONCEPTS

1. In biomes located on land, abiotic factors are used to classify the different biome types. What are these abiotic factors?

2. Name a characteristic type of plant for each of the six land biomes.

3. Name six different aquatic biomes.

CRITICAL THINKING

4. **Predict** If an ecosystem in the grassland biome started to receive less and less rainfall every year, what new biome would be established?

5. **Infer** Name some abiotic factors that affect aquatic biomes and ecosystems.

⬤ CHALLENGE

6. **Apply** Use the map on page 351 to list the following four biomes in the order you would find them moving from the equator to the poles.

   • desert
   • taiga
   • tropical Forest
   • tundra

Chapter Review

the BIG idea

Matter and energy together support life within an environment.

CONTENT REVIEW
CLASSZONE.COM

KEY CONCEPTS SUMMARY

1 Ecosystems support life.

Ecosystems are made up of living things (biotic) and nonliving things (abiotic).

plants	animals	temperature	Sun	soil	water

Biotic Factors   **Abiotic Factors**

VOCABULARY
ecology p. 329
ecosystem p. 329
biotic factor p. 330
abiotic factor p. 330

2 Matter cycles through ecosystems.

Water, carbon, and nitrogen are materials that are necessary for life. They move through ecosystems in continuous cycles.

VOCABULARY
cycle p. 336
water cycle p. 337
carbon cycle p. 338
nitrogen cycle p. 339

3 Energy flows through ecosystems.

Producers are the basis of feeding relationships in ecosystems.

cattails   caterpillar   frog

Producer   **Primary consumer**   **Secondary consumer**

Food chains and food webs help show how energy moves through living things.

VOCABULARY
producer p. 343
consumer p. 344
decomposer p. 345
food chain p. 346
food web p. 346
energy pyramid p. 348

4 Biomes contain many ecosystems.

Ecosystems of land biomes
- are affected by climate
- are affected by conditions of the soil
- are characterized by types of plants

Ecosystems of water biomes
- can be freshwater or saltwater
- are affected by landscape if freshwater
- are affected by depth if marine

VOCABULARY
biome p. 350
coniferous p. 352
deciduous p. 353
estuary p. 356

Reviewing Vocabulary

Write a statement describing how the terms in each pair are similar and different.

1. biotic, abiotic

2. producer, consumer

3. food chain, food web

The table shows the meanings of word roots that are used in many science terms.

Root	Meaning
bio-	life
ecos-	house
-ogy	study of

Use the information in the table to write definitions for the following terms.

4. ecology

5. biome

6. ecosystem

Reviewing Key Concepts

Multiple Choice *Choose the letter of the best answer.*

7. Which best describes the components of an ecosystem?
- **a.** light, water, soil, and temperature
- **b.** autotrophs and heterotrophs
- **c.** biotic and abiotic factors
- **d.** producers, consumers, and decomposers

8. What is the primary source of energy for most ecosystems?
- **a.** water
- **b.** nitrogen
- **c.** soil
- **d.** sunlight

9. What is the process by which the water in rivers, lakes, and oceans is converted to a gas and moves into the atmosphere?
- **a.** precipitation
- **b.** evaporation
- **c.** condensation
- **d.** transpiration

10. The process called nitrogen fixation is essential for life on Earth. Which of the following is an example of nitrogen fixation?
- **a.** Plants take in nitrogen gas from the atmosphere.
- **b.** Animals take in nitrogen gas from the atmosphere.
- **c.** Water absorbs nitrogen.
- **d.** Bacteria convert nitrogen gas into a form that plants can use.

11. Which organism is a decomposer?
- **a.** vulture
- **b.** sunflower
- **c.** musk ox
- **d.** fungus

12. How are decomposers important in an ecosystem?
- **a.** They make atmospheric nitrogen available to plants in a usable form.
- **b.** They convert organic matter into more complex compounds.
- **c.** They are an important source of food for scavengers.
- **d.** They break down organic matter into simpler compounds.

13. What factor is least important in determining the plant life in a biome?
- **a.** average annual rainfall
- **b.** average annual temperature
- **c.** the type of soil
- **d.** the type of animals living there

Short Answer *Write a short answer to each question.*

14. Write a paragraph to describe how carbon dioxide gas in the atmosphere can become part of the carbon compounds found inside animals.

15. Write a paragraph to explain how the amount of available energy changes as you move from producers to consumers in a food web.

16. Write a paragraph to describe one important way in which the flow of energy through ecosystems is different from the cycling of matter.

Thinking Critically

Use the diagram to answer the next four questions.

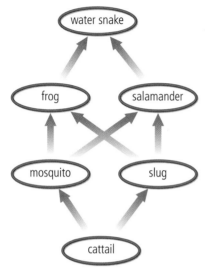

17. CONNECT What does the diagram above represent and how does it relate to energy in an ecosystem?

18. CLASSIFY Identify each of the animals in the diagram above as a producer, primary consumer, or secondary consumer or tertiary consumer.

19. APPLY Another animal that is found in many wetlands ecosystems is the shrew. The shrew eats salamanders and slugs and is eaten by water snakes. Copy the diagram above and show how you would add the shrew to the diagram.

20. CONNECT Use the diagram above to make an energy pyramid. If only one-tenth of the energy available at each level is passed on to the next higher level, how much of the energy in a cattail is transferred to a salamander?

21. SYNTHESIZE Why would it be difficult to show a decomposer as part of an energy pyramid?

22. RANK Arrange the following list of biomes according to the relative amounts of precipitation in each, going from the least amount to the most: grassland, desert, deciduous forest, taiga, tropical rain forest.

23. SYNTHESIZE Why are plants but not animals considered an important factor in classifying a land biome?

24. SUMMARIZE Draw a diagram that illustrates aquatic biomes. On your diagram label the following: freshwater river, freshwater lake, estuary, coastal zone, open ocean zone. How do abiotic factors differ among these biomes?

25. COMPARE AND CONTRAST In what ways is your home like an ecosystem? In what ways is it different?

26. APPLY Describe a change in an abiotic factor that affected living factors in an ecosystem near you.

the BIG idea

27. CLASSIFY Look again at the photograph on pages 326–327. Now that you have finished the chapter, how would you change or add details to your answer to the question on the photograph?

28. SYNTHESIZE Write one or more paragraphs describing how matter and energy together support life in an ecosystem. You may use examples from one specific ecosystem if you wish. In your description, use each of the following terms. Underline each term in your answer.

ecosystem	decomposer
food web	nitrogen cycle
producer	carbon cycle
primary consumer	secondary consumer

UNIT PROJECTS

If you are doing a unit project, make a folder for your project. Include in your folder a list of the resources you will need, the date on which the project is due, and a schedule to track your progress. Begin gathering data.

Standardized Test Practice

Interpreting Graphs

Choose the letter of the best response.

The graphs below show average monthly temperature and precipitation for one year in Staunton, Virginia, an area located in a temperate deciduous forest biome.

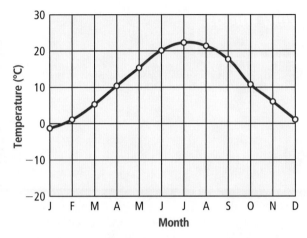

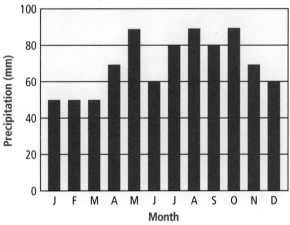

SOURCE: NASA

1. What was the average temperature during July?
   a. 20°
   b. 10°
   c. 23°
   d. 0°

2. Which months had the most precipitation?
   a. January, February, March
   b. May, August, October
   c. July, August, September
   d. December, January, February

3. What were conditions during May?
   a. warm and moist
   b. warm and dry
   c. cool and moist
   d. cool and dry

4. Which temperature is closest to the average temperature for the year shown?
   a. about 16°
   b. about 0°
   c. about 20°
   d. about 10°

5. How much precipitation would you estimate fell as snow in the year shown?
   a. less than 50 mm
   b. between 50 and 100 mm
   c. between 100 and 200 mm
   d. over 200 mm

Extended Response

6. Most of the United States is part of a temperate deciduous forest biome. The deciduous forest biome has four seasons. Trees in this biome lose their leaves yearly. Use this information, as well as the information in the graphs, to describe the seasons in the temperate deciduous forest biome.

7. Write a paragraph in which you describe a typical ecosystem in your city or town. In your answer include biotic factors such as plants, animals, and other organisms. Also include abiotic factors such as light, temperature, soil, and water. Finish your description by saying how you and other humans affect the ecosystem.

CHAPTER

12

Interactions Within Ecosystems

How do living things interact?

the **BIG** idea

Living things within an ecosystem interact with each other and the environment.

Key Concepts

SECTION

1 **Groups of living things interact within ecosystems.**
Learn about how different organisms share living areas, interact in larger communities, and show different patterns within those communities.

SECTION

2 **Organisms can interact in different ways.**
Learn about the different types of interactions in an ecosystem, including competition, cooperation, and symbiosis.

SECTION

3 **Ecosystems are always changing.**
Learn about the limits and boundaries of organisms within an ecosystem and how ecosystems may change over time.

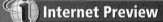

Internet Preview

CLASSZONE.COM

Chapter 12 online resources: Content Review, Simulation, two Resource Centers, Math Tutorial, Test Practice

How Do Living Things Interact Where You Live?

Take your notebook outside. Observe how different living things interact. Record your observations.

Observe and Think Do the interactions you see benefit both living things or just one? Do they involve just animals or plants and animals?

How Many Roles Can a Living Thing Have in an Ecosystem?

While you are outside, choose an organism within your view and think about how it fits into the ecosystem.

Observe and Think In what way does the organism fit into feeding relationships in the ecosystem? What are some other roles the organism plays?

Internet Activity: Carrying Capacity

Go to **ClassZone.com** to simulate the carrying capacity of an area for a population of deer.

Observe and Think What factors other than available food might affect the carrying capacity for a popuation of deer?

NSTA
scilinks.org
SCiLINKS

Populations and Communities **Code: MDL002**

Getting Ready to Learn

◀ CONCEPT REVIEW

- Ecosystems support life.
- Different ecosystems make up a biome.

◀ VOCABULARY REVIEW

producer p. 343

consumer p. 344

food chain p. 346

food web p. 346

interaction *See Glossary.*

 CONTENT REVIEW
CLASSZONE.COM
Review concepts and vocabulary.

▶ TAKING NOTES

OUTLINE

As you read, copy the headings on your paper in the form of an outline. Then add notes in your own words that summarize what you read.

VOCABULARY STRATEGY

Write each new vocabulary term in the center of a **four square** diagram. Write notes in the squares around each term. Include definition, some characteristics, and some examples of the term. If possible, write some things that are not examples of the terms.

See the Note-Taking Handbook on pages R45–R51.

SCIENCE NOTEBOOK

I. Groups of living things interact within ecosystems.
  A. Organisms occupy specific living areas.
    1. populations: same species in one area
    2. habitat and niche: place where organisms live; role of organisms
    3. community: several populations living together

Definition	Characteristics
where something lives	supplies shelter and food
HABITAT	
Examples	Nonexamples
a tree is a habitat for a bird	(you won't always use this square)

12.1

Groups of living things interact within ecosystems.

STANDARDS

7–4.1 Summarize the characteristics of the levels of organization within ecosystems (including populations, communities, habitats, niches, and biomes).

VOCABULARY

species p. 365
population p. 366
habitat p. 366
niche p. 367
community p. 368

◀ **BEFORE, you learned**

- Abiotic and biotic factors interact in an ecosystem
- Matter and energy necessary for life move through the environment

▶ **NOW, you will learn**

- How groups of organisms interact in an ecosystem
- About levels of organization in an ecosystem
- About living patterns of different groups of organisms

EXPLORE Counting Animals

How can you use a grid to estimate the number of animals in an area?

PROCEDURE

① Mark off an area on the graph paper as shown. Count the number of large squares in that area.

② Use a handful of rice to represent a group of animals. Spread the rice evenly within the area you marked. Count the number of "animals" inside one large square.

③ Use a calculator to multiply the counts from steps 1 and 2. This will give you an estimate of the total number of "animals." Check your answer by counting all the grains of rice.

WHAT DO YOU THINK?
- How close was your estimate to the actual number?
- What would prevent a scientist from making an actual count of animals in an area?

MATERIALS
- handful of rice
- large-grid graph paper
- marker
- calculator

Organisms occupy specific living areas.

On a walk through the woods, you may see many different plants and animals. These organisms, like all living things, depend on their environment to meet their needs. The particular types of living things you see will depend on the characteristics of the area you are visiting.

Scientists group living things according to their shared characteristics. The smallest grouping is the species. Scientists consider organisms to be members of the same **species** (SPEE-sheez) if the organisms are so similar that they can produce offspring that can also produce offspring. Members of a species can successfully reproduce.

READING TiP

The terms *species, specific,* and *special* come from the same Latin root meaning "kind." A species is a kind, or type, of organism.

Galápagos Island Populations

A population is a group of the same organisms that live in the same area.

Cacti	Crabs	Iguanas

VOCABULARY
Add a four square for *population* to your notebook. Include the word *habitat* in your diagram.

Populations

Scientists use the term **population** to mean a group of organisms of the same species that live in a particular area. In a way, this is similar to the population of people who live in a particular city or town. You can then think of those people who live in different cities or towns as belonging to different populations. It is the boundary of an area that defines a population. In the study of ecology, members of the same species that live in different areas belong to different populations.

A biological population can be a group of animals or a group of plants. It can be a group of bacteria or fungi or any other living thing. Populations of many different species will be found living in the same area. For example, the photographs above show different populations of organisms that all live in the same place—on one of the Galápagos Islands. The island has a population of cacti, a population of crabs, and a population of iguanas.

 CHECK YOUR READING   What is the difference between a species and a population?

Habitats and Niches

The Galápagos Islands are a small group of volcanic islands, off the coast of South America, that are famous for their unusual plant and animal life. These islands are the **habitat**—the physical location—where these plants and animals live. Island habitats have certain physical characteristics that describe them, including the amount of precipitation, a range of temperatures, and the quality of the soil. Different habitats have different characteristics.

Galápagos Island Habitat

This island habitat is home to many different populations.

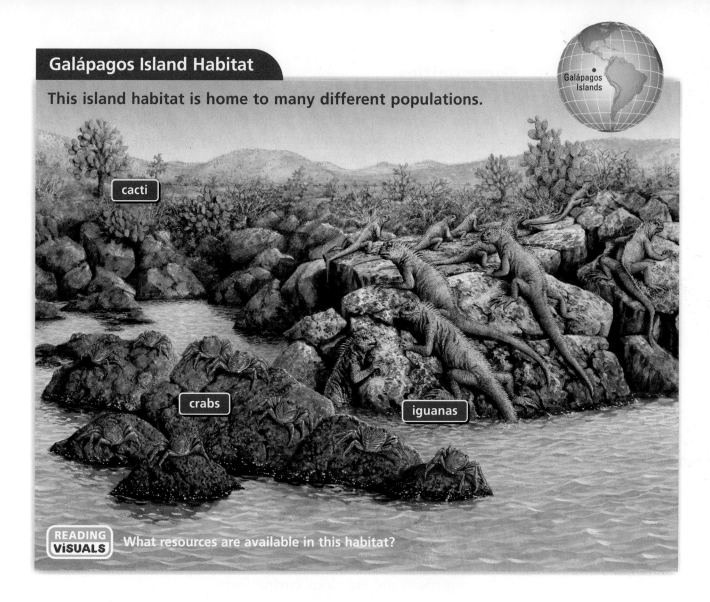

Galápagos Islands

cacti

crabs

iguanas

READING VISUALS What resources are available in this habitat?

A habitat is filled with different species, each of which depends on the habitat's resources to meet its needs. The characteristics of a habitat determine the species of plants that can grow there. The species of plants found in a habitat, in turn, determine the species of animals and other organisms that will do well there.

Different populations within a habitat interact. They are part of the flow of energy and matter through an ecosystem. For example, in the Galápagos Island scene above, the cacti capture the Sun's energy and store fresh water. They also provide food for the iguana, who eats the cactus leaves. The cactus is a producer and the iguana is a primary consumer. The crabs of the Galápagos are secondary consumers that feed on other shellfish. Each of these organisms has a role to play in the habitat, a role which is referred to as its **niche** (nihch).

The niche an organism fills in a habitat is not limited to its place in a food web. Plants provide nesting sites as well as food. The droppings left behind by animals fertilize soil and often spread seed. Generally, no two species will fill exactly the same niche in a habitat.

Communities

Take a mental tour of your school. Note that you share space with people who do many different things—students, teachers, custodians, librarians, counselors, and many others. They all work together and help each other. We often say that a school is a community.

Scientists use the term *community* in a slightly different way. A biological **community** is a group of populations that live in a particular area and interact with one another. Cacti, iguanas, and crabs are part of the Galápagos Island community. This community also includes populations of tortoises, finches, fleas, bacteria, and many other species.

 How is a school community similar to a community of living things?

The environment can be organized into five levels.

OUTLINE
Add the different levels of the environment to your outline. Make sure to explain each term in the supporting details.

The five terms—biome, ecosystem, community, population, and organism—describe the environment at different levels.

1 Biome A biome describes in very general terms the climate and types of plants that are found in similar places around the world.

2 Ecosystem Within each biome are many ecosystems. Inside an ecosystem, living and nonliving factors interact to form a stable system. An ecosystem is smaller than a biome and includes only organisms and their local environment.

3 Community A community is made up of the living components of the ecosystem. In a community, different plants, animals, and other organisms interact with each other.

4 Population A population is a group of organisms of the same species that live in the same area.

5 Organism An organism is a single individual animal, plant, fungus, or other living thing. As the picture on page 369 shows, an organism plays a part in each level of the environment.

Patterns exist in populations.

Members of a population settle themselves into the available living space in different ways, forming a pattern. Populations may be crowded together, be spread far apart, or live in small groups. A population may also show a pattern over time. The number of individuals in the population may rise and fall, depending on the season or other conditions, or as a result of interactions with other organisms.

Levels in the Environment

Organisms living in an African savannah illustrate the different levels of the environment.

Grassland

1 Biome
The African savannah is part of a grassland biome.

2 Ecosystem
The community of organisms, along with water, soil, and other abiotic factors, make up an ecosystem.

3 Community
Populations of wildebeests, gazelles, lions, and grasses share the same living areas and resources. These and other populations form a savannah community.

4 Population
Gazelles travel together in herds looking for areas to graze in. The total number of gazelles in an ecosystem is called a population of gazelles.

5 Organism
The gazelle lives in various grassland habitats in eastern Africa and fills a particular niche.

READING VISUALS Describe the gazelle's place in each level of the environment.

Patterns in Living Space

The patterns formed by a population often show how the population meets its needs. For example, in California's Mojave desert the pale soil is dotted with dark-green shrubs called creosote bushes. A surprising thing about the bushes is their even spacing. No human shaped this habitat, however. The bushes are the same distance from each other because the roots of each bush release a toxin, a type of poison, that prevents the roots of other bushes from growing.

The distribution of animals in a habitat is often influenced by how they meet their needs. Animals must be able to reach their food supply and have places to raise their young. If you put up bird houses for bluebirds on your property, they must be spaced at least a hundred meters apart. Bluebirds need a large area of their own around their nest in order to collect enough insects to feed their young.

Sometimes, the particular pattern of individuals in a living space helps a population survive. Herring swim in schools, with the individual fish spaced close together. Wildebeests roam African grasslands in closely packed herds. These animals rely on the group for their safety. Even if one member of the group is attacked, many more will survive.

READING TiP

As you read this paragraph, note the pattern of wildebeests and elephants in the photograph.

CHECK YOUR READING What are some reasons for the spacing patterns observed in different populations?

elephant

wildebeest

READING VISUALS COMPARE AND CONTRAST How would you describe the spacing of these elephants and wildebeests?

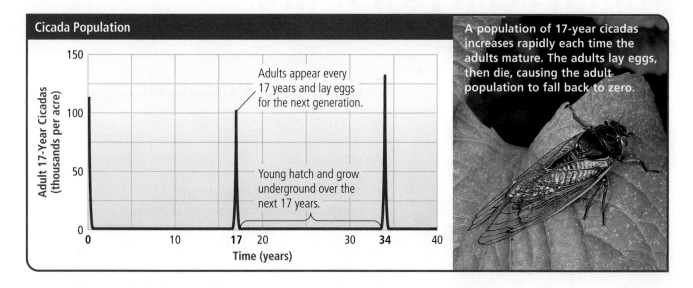

Cicada Population

Adult 17-Year Cicadas (thousands per acre)

150
100
50
0

Time (years)

0 10 17 20 30 34 40

Adults appear every 17 years and lay eggs for the next generation.

Young hatch and grow underground over the next 17 years.

A population of 17-year cicadas increases rapidly each time the adults mature. The adults lay eggs, then die, causing the adult population to fall back to zero.

Patterns in Time

At a spring picnic, you would rarely see the wasps called yellow jackets. At a fall picnic, however, they swarm to the food. This is an example of a population whose size changes with time. In spring, the queen wasp lays eggs and new wasps hatch. She continues to lay eggs all summer and the population grows. When winter comes, all the wasps except the queen die, and the population decreases.

Many birds that nest in North America in summer fly south to Central and South America in winter. There they find enough food and good nesting sites. In North America, this seasonal pattern leads to small bird populations in winter and large ones in summer.

The graph above shows an unusual pattern of population growth. Certain species of cicadas appear only every 17 years. Because no other species can rely on these insects as their main source of food, the cicadas survive long enough to lay eggs when they do appear.

12.1 Review

KEY CONCEPTS

1. What are two characteristics of a population?

2. Order these terms from the simplest to the most complex: biome, community, ecosystem, organism, population.

3. How do the terms *habitat* and *niche* relate to each other?

CRITICAL THINKING

4. **Apply** Choose a biological community in your region. Describe some of the populations that make up that community.

5. **Infer** How might the seasonal patterns of insect populations relate to the seasonal patterns of bird populations?

CHALLENGE

6. **Apply** The Explore activity on page 365 shows one way in which scientists sample a population to determine its total size. Would this method work for estimating the size of a population of 17-year cicadas? Why or why not?

CHAPTER INVESTIGATION

Estimating Populations

OVERVIEW AND PURPOSE The number of animals in a wild population cannot be easily counted. Wildlife biologists have developed a formula that can estimate a population's size by using small samples. This method is referred to as mark and recapture. In this investigation you will
- use the mark-recapture method to estimate population size
- test the effectiveness of the mark-recapture method by simulating an outbreak of disease in a population

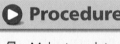

▶ Problem

How effective is the mark-recapture method in estimating population size?

▶ Hypothesize

Write a hypothesis to explain how you will use a sudden change in population size to determine the effectiveness of the mark-recapture method. Your hypothesis should take the form of an "If . . . , then . . . , because . . ." statement.

▶ Procedure

MATERIALS
- paper bag
- white kidney beans
- 2 colored markers
- calculator

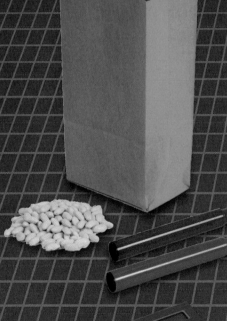

1. Make two data tables in your **Science Notebook,** like the ones shown on page 373.

2. From your teacher, obtain a paper bag containing a "population" of white kidney beans.

step 3

3. Remove a small handful of beans. Count the sample and record the count in Table 1, under First Capture Total.

4. Use a colored marker to mark your sample population. Return the beans to the bag, and gently shake the bag to mix all the beans.

5. Remove and count a second sample of beans. Record the count in Table 1, under Recapture Total.

6. Count the number of beans from this sample that were marked from the first capture. Record this number in Table 1, under Recapture Marked. Return all the beans to the bag.

7 Use a calculator and the following formula to estimate the population size. Record the estimate in Table 1 as the Calculated Population Estimate.

$$\frac{\text{First Capture Total} \times \text{Recapture Total}}{\text{Recapture Marked}} = \begin{array}{l}\text{Population}\\\text{Estimate}\end{array}$$

8 Disease strikes. Remove a small handful of beans from the bag. Count the beans, and record this count in Table 2, under Killed by Disease. Set these beans aside.

9 Repeat steps 3–7 to mark and recapture your survivor population. This time use a different colored marker to mark your sample population, and only include the beans marked in the second color in your counts.

10 Fill in Data Table 2 for the survivor population. Use the formula from step 7 to calculate your estimate of the survivor population.

11 Once you have calculated your estimate of survivors, dump out the paper bag and count all the beans that were inside. Record this count in Table 2, under Actual Survivors Total.

▶ Observe and Analyze

Write It Up

1. CALCULATE From Table 2 add together the number of actual survivors and the number killed by disease. Put this in Table 1, under Actual Population Total.

2. CALCULATE Find the percentage of the population affected by disease using the following formula:

$$\frac{\text{Killed by disease} \times 100}{\text{Actual Population Total}} = \text{Percentage affected}$$

▶ Conclude

Write It Up

1. INFER How did the estimated number of beans compare with the actual number?

2. IDENTIFY LIMITS What aspects of this investigation most likely would not be possible in a natural habitat? Why not?

3. EVALUATE Compare your results with your hypothesis. Do your data support your hypothesis?

▶ INVESTIGATE Further

CHALLENGE Determine if using larger samples of a population gives better population estimates. Get another bag of unmarked beans from your teacher. Use a spreadsheet program, if available, to record your data and calculate the results.

Estimating Populations
Table 1. Population sampling before disease

First Capture Total	Recapture Total	Recapture Marked	Calculated Population Estimate	Actual Population Total

Table 2. Population sampling after disease

Survivors First Capture Total	Survivors Recapture Total	Survivors Recapture Marked	Calculated Survivors Estimate	Killed by Disease	Actual Survivors Total

12.2 Organisms can interact in different ways.

BEFORE, you learned

- Different populations live together in a habitat
- Different species fill different niches in a habitat
- There are patterns in the ways organisms interact with each other and their environment

NOW, you will learn

- About different types of interactions in an ecosystem
- How some species benefit from interactions
- How some species are harmed by interactions

VOCABULARY

predator p. 375
prey p. 375
competition p. 375
cooperation p. 377
symbiosis p. 378
mutualism p. 378
commensalism p. 379
parasitism p. 379

THINK ABOUT

What are some of the ways people interact?

People in a community interact with each other in many ways. An interaction is the way a person behaves toward or responds to another person. This photograph shows groups of people at a soccer game. There are players from two teams and fans who are watching the game. How would you describe the interactions among the people in this photograph?

Organisms interact in different ways.

The photograph above shows how members of a human community both compete and cooperate. Different members of the populations of a biological community also compete and cooperate. They not only share a habitat, but they also share the resources in that habitat. How different organisms interact depends on their relationship to each other.

A robin in a meadow finds a caterpillar and swallows it. This is one obvious way organisms in an ecosystem interact—one eats, and the other gets eaten. Organisms also compete. The robin may have to compete with a flicker to get the caterpillar. And organisms can cooperate. Ants work together to build a nest, collect food, and defend their colony.

 CHECK YOUR READING   Name three ways organisms may interact with each other in an ecosystem.

Predator and Prey

Many interactions between organisms in an ecosystem involve food. A food chain shows the feeding relationships between different species. There are producers and consumers. Another way to look at a food chain is through the interactions of predators and prey. The **predator** is an animal that eats another. The **prey** is an animal that is eaten by a predator. In a food chain, an organism can be both predator and prey. A meadowlark that feeds on a grasshopper is, in turn, eaten by a prairie falcon.

Predators can affect how members of their prey populations are distributed. Herring move together in a school and wildebeests travel in herds to protect themselves. It is the sick or older members of the population that will most likely be eaten by predators. Species of prey may also have adaptations that relate to the behavior of predators. This is true of cicadas and their long reproductive cycles.

Prey populations, in turn, affect the location and number of predator populations. For example some birds are predators feeding on insects. One factor that may affect movement of birds from one location to another is the availability of insects.

REMINDER

A *producer* is an organism that makes its own food; a *consumer* is an organism that eats another organism for food.

Competition

In a team game, two teams compete against each other with the same goal in mind—to win the game. In a biological community, competition is for resources, not wins. **Competition** is the struggle between individuals or different populations for a limited resource.

In an ecosystem, competition may occur within the same species. Individual plants compete with each other for light, space, and nutrients. For example, creosote bushes compete with other creosote bushes for the same water supply. The toxins produced by the roots of one creosote bush prevent other creosote bushes from growing.

Competition also occurs between members of different species. In the tropical rain forests of Indonesia, vines called strangler figs compete with trees for water, light, and nutrients. The vine attaches itself to a host tree. As it grows, the vine surrounds and eventually kills the tree by blocking out sunlight and using up available water and nutrients.

INFER Do you think a strangler fig could survive on its own?

host tree

strangler fig

Competition

Competition between species
Two different species, hyenas and vultures, compete for the remains of a dead animal.

Competition within species Two male deer lock horns as they battle over territory.

Competition occurs between species and within species. For example, vultures and hyenas will compete over the food left in the remains of a dead animal. Wolves will compete with one another over territory. A wolf will mark its territory by urinating on trees and so warn off other wolves. Animals also compete over territory by fighting, using threatening sounds, and putting on aggressive displays.

Competition within species often occurs during the mating season. Male birds use mating songs and displays of feathers to compete for the attention of females. Male hippopotamuses fight to attract female hippopotamuses. Male crickets chirp to attract female crickets.

CHECK YOUR READING What sorts of resources do plants and animals compete for?

READING TIP

Compare and contrast the meanings of *competition* and *coexistence*.

Competition does not occur between all populations that share the same resources. Many populations can coexist in a habitat—different species can live together without causing harm to one another. Many different populations of plants coexist in a forest. Maple trees, beech trees, and birch trees can live side by side and still have enough water, nutrients, and sunlight to meet their needs.

INVESTIGATE Species Interactions

How do predator-prey populations interact?

Use these rules for predator-prey interaction for each round. If a predator card touches three or more prey cards, remove the prey cards touched. If the predator card does not touch at least three prey cards, remove the predator card and leave the prey cards. Predator cards are large, prey cards are small.

PROCEDURE

1. Use masking tape to mark a boundary on a table top.

2. Scatter five prey cards into the area. Take a predator card and toss it, trying to get it to land on the prey.

3. According to the rules above, remove the predators and prey that have "died." Record the number of predators and prey that have "survived." This represents one generation.

4. Double the populations of predators and prey—they have "reproduced."

5. Scatter the prey cards into the area and then toss the predator cards as before. Repeat steps 3 and 4 for a total of 15 rounds (generations).

WHAT DO YOU THINK?

- How does the size of the prey population affect the predator population?
- How might the size of a habitat affect the interaction of predators and prey?

CHALLENGE Use graph paper and colored pencils to make a graph of your results. Or use a spreadsheet program if one is available to you.

MATERIALS
- 20 10 × 10 cm cardboard squares—predators
- 200 3 × 3 cm paper squares—prey
- masking tape
  for Challenge:
- graph paper
- 2 colored pencils

TIME
30 minutes

predator

prey

Cooperation

Not all interactions in an ecosystem involve competition. **Cooperation** is an interaction in which organisms work in a way that benefits them all. Some predators cooperate when they hunt. Although individual lions may hunt on their own, they also hunt in packs to kill large prey.

Killer whales also cooperate when they hunt. The whales swim in packs called pods. The pod swims in circles around a school of fish, forcing the fish close together so they are easier to catch. Pod members may also take turns chasing a seal until it gets tired and is easily killed. The pod may even work together to attack larger species of whales.

Ants, bees, and termites are social insects. Members of a colony belong to different groups, called castes, and have different responsibilities. Some groups gather food while others defend the colony. Other animals, like apes and monkeys, live in family groups. Members of the family cooperate to care for their young.

Cooperation
Driver ants work together to bring food to their nest.

The survival of one species might depend on another species.

OUTLINE

Add a sentence about *symbiosis* to your outline and define the three types of symbiosis in the supporting details.

You have learned that many different organisms live together in a habitat. The fact that organisms live together forces them to interact in different ways. For example, an organism preys upon another for food. Or perhaps there is competition among organisms over resources such as food, water, and territory.

The actions of different organisms can be so closely related that the survival of one species depends on the action or presence of another. In such a relationship, at least one of the species is getting a resource that it needs to survive. Benefits of the relationship may include food, reproductive help, or protection.

The relationship between individuals of two different species who live together in a close relationship is called **symbiosis** (SIHM-bee-OH-sihs). This word means "living together." A symbiotic relationship may affect the partners in different ways.

- Both species benefit from the relationship.
- One species benefits while the other is not affected.
- One species benefits while the other is harmed.

Here are some examples for each of the three types of symbiosis.

Both Species Benefit

Mutualism The interaction between the hummingbird and the flower benefits both.

Stroll through a garden on a sunny day and notice the bees buzzing from flower to flower. Look closely at a single bee and you may see yellow pollen grains sticking to its hairy body. The relationship between the flower and the bee is an example of **mutualism** (MYOO-choo-uh-LIHZ-uhm)—an interaction between two species that benefits both. The bees get food in the form of nectar, and the flowers get pollen from other flowers, which they need to make seeds.

Many plants rely on mutualism to reproduce. The pollen needed to make seeds must be spread from flower to flower. The birds and insects that feed on the nectar in these flowers transfer pollen from one flower to the next. The seeds produced are then moved to new ground by animals that eat the seeds or the fruits that hold the seeds. This form of mutualism doesn't benefit the individual flower but instead ensures the survival of the species.

In some cases, mutualism is necessary for the survival of the organisms themselves. For example, termites are able to live off a food that most animals cannot digest: wood. The termites, in fact, can't digest wood either. However, they have living in their guts tiny single-celled organisms, protozoans, that can break the wood down into digestible components. The protozoans get a safe place to live, and the termites can take advantage of a plentiful food source.

RESOURCE CENTER
CLASSZONE.COM
Explore symbiotic relationships.

CHECK YOUR READING Describe how a bee and a flower benefit from a symbiotic relationship.

One Species Benefits

Commensalism (kuh-MEHN-suh-LIHZ-uhm) is a relationship between two species in which one species benefits while the other is not affected. Orchids and mosses are plants that can have a commensal relationship with trees. The plants grow on the trunks or branches of trees. They get the light they need as well as nutrients that run down along the tree. As long as these plants do not grow too heavy, the tree is not affected.

Commensal relationships are very common in ocean ecosystems. Small fish called remoras use a type of built-in suction cup to stick to a shark's skin and hitch a ride. When the shark makes a kill, the remora eats the scraps. The shark makes no attempt to attack the remora. The remora benefits greatly from this commensal relationship; the shark is barely affected.

Not all commensal relationships involve food. Some fish protect themselves by swimming among the stinging tentacles of a moon jellyfish. The fish benefit from the relationship because the tentacles keep them safe from predators. The jellyfish is not helped or hurt by the presence of the fish. As in this example, it is common in commensal relationships for the species that benefits to be smaller than the species it partners with.

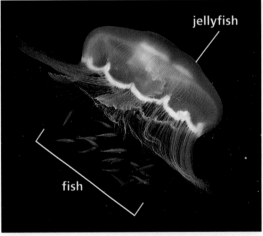

Commensalism The interaction between the jellyfish and the fish benefits the fish only.

One Species Is Harmed

There is one symbiotic relationship in which a small partner can harm a much larger host. **Parasitism** (PAR-uh-suh-TIHZ-uhm) is a relationship between two species in which one species benefits while the species it depends on, its host, is harmed. Parasites are often tiny organisms that feed off, and weaken, their hosts. Ticks, lice, and mites are external parasites that live on or attach to their host's skin. Other parasites, like tapeworms and ringworms, are internal parasites that live inside their hosts.

Symbiotic Relationships

Mutualism
Both species benefit from the relationship.

Commensalism
One species benefits while the other is not affected.

Parasitism
One species benefits while the other is harmed.

Parasitism
Mistletoe is a plant that takes nourishment from a tree, causing damage to the tree.

Mutualism
Aphids are insects that provide ants with a sweet liquid. Ants live alongside the aphids, protecting them from predators.

Commensalism
Lichens benefit from living on a tree, but the tree is not harmed.

Parasitism
Ticks are animals that attach to their hosts, feeding on the host's blood.

Mutualism
Nitrogen-fixing bacteria get their nourishment from the roots of certain plants, providing the plants with nitrogen in return.

Commensalism
Mice do well living near humans, living off the food scraps humans leave behind.

The relationship between cowbirds and warblers is an unusual type of association called nest or brood parasitism. Female cowbirds never build their own nests or rear their own young. Instead, they lay their eggs in warbler nests. Although nest parasitism does not harm the host warbler, it does harm the warbler species because either warblers eggs do not hatch, or the chicks do not survive. The warbler species is often harmed because cowbirds push most warbler eggs from the nest in order to make room for their own eggs. Once the cowbird chicks hatch, their larger size helps them to outcompete the smaller warbler chicks for food, so that the host's chicks starve.

Parasitism The larger cowbird chick is cared for by a warbler at the expense of the smaller warbler chick.

 How is parasitism different from commensalism?

Interactions in an ecosystem are complex.

Different types of symbiosis occur throughout an ecosystem and often overlap. They may occur in the same locations, and the same species might be involved in more than one symbiotic relationship. The illustration on page 380 shows different symbiotic relationships that may occur in a backyard.

Symbiosis is just one of many interactions that take place in an ecosystem. The yard may have a garden, with individual tomato plants competing for water and nutrients; it may have ants cooperating to maintain a successful colony. An ecosystem is more than just a collection of biotic and abiotic factors. Interactions within an ecosystem help explain how resources are shared and used up and how energy flows through the system.

12.2 Review

KEY CONCEPTS

1. Name two ways in which members of the same species interact.

2. In what ways do members of different species interact?

3. Give an example of each type of symbiotic relationship: mutualism, commensalism, and parasitism.

CRITICAL THINKING

4. **Apply** Think of a biological community near you, and give an example of how one population has affected another.

5. **Compare and Contrast** Explain how symbiotic relationships are similar to and different from predator-prey interactions.

○ CHALLENGE

6. **Synthesize** Mutualism is more common in tropical ecosystems such as rain forests and coral reefs than in other ecosystems. Why do you think this is so?

Think SCIENCE

Where Are the Salamanders?

At the Cottonwood Lake Study Area in rural Stutsman County, North Dakota, U.S. Fish and Wildlife Service biologists have been studying wetland ecosystems for more than 30 years. Salamanders are one of the most abundant species in these wetlands. But in May 2000, the researchers started noticing sick salamanders in one wetland. By July, most salamanders had died. What killed them?

▶ Observations

a. In the past, cold winter weather and food shortages have killed salamanders at Cottonwood Lake.

b. The sick salamanders had discolored skin and enlarged livers.

c. The previous year, leopard frogs in a nearby wetland were found dying from a contagious fungal infection.

d. A viral disease has killed tiger salamanders elsewhere in the West.

e. Both large, well-fed salamanders and small, poorly nourished salamanders died.

This barred tiger salamander can be found in many wetlands in the Great Plains.

▶ Inferences

The following statements are possible inferences:

a. A food shortage caused salamanders to starve.

b. The fungal disease that killed leopard frogs also killed the salamanders

c. Salamanders were killed by a viral disease.

▶ Evaluate Inferences

On Your Own Which of the inferences are supported by the observations? Write the observations that support each of the inferences you identify.

As a Group Discuss your decisions. Come up with a list of reasonable inferences.

CHALLENGE What further observations would you make to test any of these inferences?

12.3

KEY CONCEPT
Ecosystems are always changing.

◀ BEFORE, you learned

- Populations in an ecosystem interact in different ways
- Organisms can benefit from interactions in an ecosystem
- Organisms can be harmed by interactions in an ecosystem

▶ NOW, you will learn

- How different factors affect the size of a population
- How biological communities get established
- How biological communities change over time

STANDARDS

7–4.3 Explain the interaction among changes in the environment due to natural hazards (including landslides, wildfires, and floods), changes in populations, and limiting factors (including climate and the availability of food and water, space, and shelter).

VOCABULARY

limiting factor p. 384
carrying capacity p. 385
succession p. 386
pioneer species p. 386

EXPLORE Population Growth

How does sugar affect the growth of yeast?

PROCEDURE

1. Use a marker to label the cups A, B, C. Pour 150 mL of warm water into each cup. Mark the water level with the marker.

2. Add 1/2 teaspoon of dry yeast to each plastic cup and stir.

3. Add 1/4 teaspoon of sugar to cup B. Add 1 teaspoon of sugar to cup C. Stir.

4. Wait 15 minutes. Measure the height of the foam layer that forms in each cup.

WHAT DO YOU THINK?

- Which cup had the most foam, which cup had the least?
- Describe the effect of sugar on a population of yeast.

MATERIALS

- 3 clear plastic cups
- warm water
- sugar
- dry yeast
- measuring spoons
- measuring cup
- stirring rod
- marker
- ruler

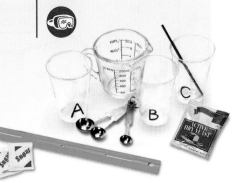

REMINDER

A *population* is a group of organisms of the same species that live together in the same habitat.

Populations change over time.

You may have a strong memory of a park you visited as a little child. You remember collecting pine cones, listening to woodpeckers, and catching frogs. Then you visit again, years later, and the park has changed. Maybe more land has been added, there are more birds and trees. Or maybe the area around the park has been developed. There seem to be fewer woodpeckers, and you can't find any frogs. The community has changed. There are a lot of factors that affect the populations within a biological community. Some have to do with the organisms themselves. Others relate to the habitat.

Chapter 12: **Interactions Within Ecosystems** 383

Population Growth and Decline

One factor that obviously affects population size is how often organisms reproduce. Birth rate is a measure of the number of births in an animal population. It can also be a measure of the stability of an ecosystem. For example, black bears reproduce once every two years. If there is not enough food available, however, the female bear's reproductive cycle is delayed, and the bear population does not grow.

Predator-prey interactions also affect population size. The graphs show how an increase in the moose population—the prey—in Isle Royale National Park was followed by an increase in the island's population of wolves—the predators. The wolves preyed upon the moose, the moose population decreased, then the wolf population decreased.

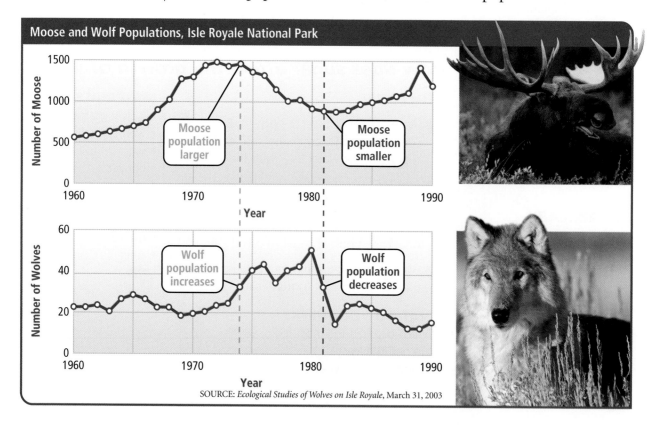

Moose and Wolf Populations, Isle Royale National Park

Moose population larger

Moose population smaller

Wolf population increases

Wolf population decreases

SOURCE: *Ecological Studies of Wolves on Isle Royale*, March 31, 2003

READING TiP

Note in the graphs above that it can take some time for the size of one population to affect the size of the other.

Any factor or condition that limits the growth of a population in an ecosystem is called a **limiting factor.** A large population of predators will limit the population of prey; a small population of prey will limit the population of predators. Too much or too little of any biotic or abiotic factor—like food, water, or light—makes an ecosystem unstable and brings about change.

A lack of nutrients in the soil is a limiting factor for plants. That is why farmers fertilize their crops. That same fertilizer, if it runs off into a lake, can increase the population of algae, another photosynthetic organism. A large population of algae can cover a lake with scum and use up oxygen needed by fish. This then limits the fish population.

INVESTIGATE Limiting Factors

What effect does spacing have upon a population of plants?

DESIGN —YOUR OWN— EXPERIMENT

Using the materials listed, design an experiment to test this hypothesis: "If plants grow too close together, the health of the population will be affected because the individual plants do not get enough of the nutrients and water that they need."

PROCEDURE

① Decide how to use the seeds, cups, and soil to test the hypothesis.

② Write up your experimental procedure. Include safety tips.

WHAT DO YOU THINK?

• What are the variables in your experiment?

• What evidence would you expect to see if your hypothesis is true?

CHALLENGE Conduct your experiment. Note that seeds must be planted near the top of the soil. A good measure for this is the tip of a pencil. Measure and record the growth of the seedlings. Allow the seedlings to grow for two weeks before drawing your conclusions.

SKILL FOCUS
Designing experiments

MATERIALS
• paper cups
• potting soil
• radish seeds
• water
• pencil
• ruler

TIME
20 minutes

Maintaining a Balance

Living things have certain minimum requirements for food, water, and living space. When a population reaches a state where it can no longer grow, the population has reached its **carrying capacity,** the maximum number of individuals that an ecosystem can support. You can see on page 384 that the graph for the moose population does appear to peak around 1500. Even if there were no wolves on the island of Isle Royale, the population of moose would still be limited because there is only so much food and space available.

 CHECK YOUR READING Explain the term *carrying capacity.*

An ecosystem's carrying capacity is different for each population. A meadow ecosystem will support many more bees and ants than bluebirds, for example. Isle Royale supports many more moose than wolves. The moose is a primary consumer of plants. It is at a lower level of the energy pyramid than the wolf, a secondary consumer.

Biotic factors can be limiting factors. These factors include the interactions between populations, such as competition, predation, and parasitism. Abiotic factors, such as temperature, availability of water or minerals, and exposure to wind, are also limiting.

VOCABULARY
Remember to make a four square diagram for *carrying capacity* in your notebook. Try to use *limiting factor* in your diagram.

Ecosystems change over time.

Take a walk in a New Hampshire woods and you may see the remains of old stone walls scattered about. A hundred years ago this land was mostly farmland. The farms were abandoned. And now, new trees have grown where farm animals once grazed.

Succession (suhk-SEHSH-uhn) is the gradual change in an ecosystem in which one biological community is replaced by another. The change from field to forest is an example of succession. Over time the grasses of open farmland are slowly replaced by small plants and shrubs, then trees.

Primary Succession

READING TiP

Succeed and *succession* come from the same Latin root word, *succedere*, meaning to go up or to follow after.

Very few places on Earth are without some form of life. Even when a lava flow covers an area or a glacier retreats and leaves behind an empty and barren environment, plants will move into the area and bring it back to life. These are examples of primary succession, the establishment of a new biological community.

Pioneer species are the first living things to move into a barren environment. In the illustration below, moss and lichen move in after a glacier retreats. There is little or no topsoil. Moss and lichen are common pioneers because they have tiny rootlike structures that can take hold on exposed rock.

Primary Succession

Primary succession can occur after a glacier retreats, when little topsoil is present.

1. Moss and lichen grow on rock with little or no soil. These pioneer species break apart the surface rock.

2. Over time, the rock breaks down further, forming soil. Larger plants take root. These support populations of animals.

3. Coniferous trees take root in a deep layer of soil. A diversity of plants and animals are supported in this habitat.

As the pioneers grow, they gradually weaken the rock surface. The rock breaks down and weathers over time. Decaying plant matter adds nutrients, forming soil. Now a variety of small plants and shrubs can take root. These plants, in turn, support insects, birds, and small rodents. Eventually there is enough soil to support coniferous trees. Forests grow, providing a stable habitat for larger animals.

 RESOURCE CENTER
CLASSZONE.COM

Learn more about succession.

Secondary Succession

Secondary succession takes place after a major disturbance to the biological community in a stable ecosystem. Despite the disturbance, the soil remains. A community can be disturbed by a natural event, like fire or flood, or it can be disturbed by human activity. A forest cleared or farmland abandoned can lead to secondary succession.

The illustration below shows secondary succession following a forest fire. The damage, as bad as it is, is surface damage. Below the surface, seeds and plant roots survive. After a time, grasses and small shrubs grow up among the decaying remains of the original plants. Birds, insects, and rodents return. Alder trees take root—alders are trees that put nutrients into the soil. Over time, a variety of trees and plants grow, providing food for a variety of animals.

 CHECK YOUR READING   What is the difference between primary and secondary succession?

Secondary Succession

Secondary succession occurs if soil remains after a disturbance, such as a forest fire.

① Plants at the surface are burned; however, below the surface seeds and some plant roots survive.

② Grasses and small shrubs sprout among the charred trees and vegetation. Smaller animals return.

③ Deciduous trees like elm and maple grow and mature. A forest habitat is reestablished. More animals are supported.

Patterns of Change

All types of ecosystems go through succession. Succession can establish a forest community, a wetland community, a coastal community, or even an ocean community. Succession can happen over tens or hundreds of years. The pattern is the same, however. First a community of producers is established. These are followed by decomposers and consumers, then more producers, then more decomposers and consumers. Over time, a stable biological community develops.

In a way, the establishment of a biological community is like planting a garden. You first prepare the soil. Perhaps you add compost. This adds organic matter and nutrients to the soil, which helps the soil hold water. With the right preparation, your vegetables and flowers should grow well.

Pioneer species can function in one of two ways in an ecological succession. They can help other species to grow or they can prevent species from getting established.

READING TiP

As you read about the two ways plant species function in succession, think in terms of cooperation and competition.

- Some plant species function a bit like gardeners. Trees such as alders have nitrogen-fixing bacteria on their roots that improve the nutrient content of the soil and allow other tree seedlings to grow. Pioneering species may also stabilize the soil, shade the soil surface, or add nutrients to the soil when they die and decay.

- Other plant species produce conditions that keep out other plants. The plants may release chemicals that keep other plants from taking root. Or a new species may outcompete other species by using up resources or better resisting a disease.

Such interactions between living things help to determine succession in an ecosystem.

12.3 Review

KEY CONCEPTS

1. Describe three factors that could limit the size of a population in a habitat.

2. List two natural disturbances and two human-made disturbances that can lead to succession.

3. What role do pioneer species play in succession?

CRITICAL THINKING

4. **Infer** How and why would secondary succession in a tundra habitat differ from secondary succession in a rainforest habitat?

5. **Predict** Suppose you are clearing an area in your yard to construct a small pond. Sketch the stages of succession that would follow this disturbance.

○ CHALLENGE

6. **Synthesize** Imagine you are the wildlife manager for a forest preserve that supports both moose and wolves. What types of information should you collect to determine the carrying capacity for each species?

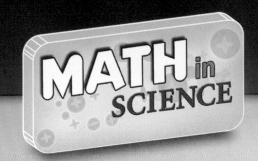

MATH TUTORIAL
CLASSZONE.COM

Click on Math Tutorial for more help with multiplying fractions and whole numbers.

SKILL: MULTIPLYING A FRACTION BY A WHOLE NUMBER

Birth Rates and Populations

Ecologists pay careful attention to the yearly birth rates of endangered species. A birth rate is usually expressed as a fraction. It is the number of births divided by the number of adult females. A 2/5 birth rate for a population means that there are 2 births for every 5 adult females.

Example

Suppose at a national park in Borneo, there is a 2/5 birth rate among orangutans. There are 150 adult females in the park. Estimate how many young will be born. To find out, multiply the fraction by the number of adult females.

(1) Multiply the numerator of the fraction by the whole number.

$$150 \text{ females} \times \frac{2 \text{ births}}{5 \text{ females}} = \frac{150 \times 2}{5} = \frac{300}{5}$$

(2) Divide by the denominator.

$$\frac{300}{5} = 300 \div 5 = 60$$

ANSWER 60 young

Answer the following questions.

1. In 2001, there were about 72 adult female right whales. Scientists observing the whales reported a 1/3 birth rate. About how many right whales were born in 2001?

2. Giant pandas are severely endangered. Currently about 140 giant pandas live in captivity, in zoos and parks. About 3/5 of these were born in captivity. How many is that?

3. The orangutan population of the world has decreased sharply. At one time there were over 100,000 ranging across Asia. Now there may be 21,000, of which, 2/3 live in Borneo. About how many orangutans live in Borneo?

CHALLENGE Suppose 1/1 is given as the desired birth rate to save an endangered population. If the population is currently at 4 births per 20 adult females, by how many times does the rate need to increase to reach the desired rate?

the BIG idea

Living things within an ecosystem interact with each other and the environment.

CONTENT REVIEW
CLASSZONE.COM

◀ KEY CONCEPTS SUMMARY

1 **Groups of living things interact within ecosystems.**

- Members of the same species form a population within a habitat.

- Each species has a distinct role within a habitat. This is its niche.

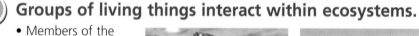

Population of Crabs   **Island Habitat for Crabs**

VOCABULARY
species p. 365
population p. 366
habitat p. 366
niche p. 367
community p. 368

---

2 **Organisms can interact in different ways.**

Organisms within a community interact with each other in many ways. Some are predators, some are prey. Some compete with one another, some cooperate. Some species form symbiotic relationships with other species:

Mutualism
benefits both

Commensalism
benefits one, other unaffected

Parasitism
benefits one, harms other

VOCABULARY
predator p. 375
prey p. 375
competition p. 375
cooperation p. 377
symbiosis p. 378
mutualism p. 378
commensalism p. 379
parasitism p. 379

---

3 **Ecosystems are always changing.**

Primary Succession

In a barren area, a new community is established with pioneer species, like mosses, that do well with little or no soil. Mosses eventually give way to coniferous trees.

Secondary Succession

When a disturbance damages a community but soil remains, the community gets reestablished from seeds and roots left behind. Grasses grow, then small shrubs, and eventually trees.

VOCABULARY
limiting factor p. 384
carrying capacity p. 385
succession p. 386
pioneer species p. 386

Reviewing Vocabulary

Draw a Venn diagram for each pair of terms. Put shared characteristics in the overlap area, put differences to the outside. A sample diagram is provided.

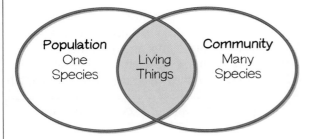

1. habitat, niche

2. mutualism, commensalism

3. mutualism, parasitism

4. competition, cooperation

5. primary succession, secondary succession

Reviewing Key Concepts

Multiple Choice *Choose the letter of the best answer.*

6. What is carrying capacity?
   a. the largest population an ecosystem can support
   b. the smallest population an ecosystem can support
   c. the number of species an ecosystem can support
   d. the number of habitats in an ecosystem

7. A new species of bird moves into a habitat. The birds feed on a particular caterpillar, so that the resulting population of butterflies is small. What can be said of the relationship between the birds and the butterflies?
   a. The birds and the butterflies have a commensal relationship.
   b. The birds and butterflies compete.
   c. The birds are a limiting factor for the butterflies.
   d. The birds and butterflies cooperate.

8. Certain types of worms live in the mud at the bottom of lakes. What does the mud represent for the worm?
   a. an ecosystem   c. a community
   b. a niche   d. a habitat

9. What is a pioneer species?
   a. a species that travels within an ecosystem
   b. a species that is among the first to move into an area after a natural disaster
   c. a species that depends upon animal life
   d. a species that cannot return after a natural disaster

10. Which is an example of competition within the same species?
    a. whales in a pod
    b. wildebeests in a herd
    c. creosote bushes in a desert
    d. birds that fly south

11. Which is an example of parasitism?
    a. dog and tick
    b. termite and protozoans
    c. shark and remora
    d. flower and hummingbird

12. Which is an example of secondary succession?
    a. succession after a forest fire
    b. succession after a large volcanic lava flow devastates an area
    c. succession after a glacier retreats, leaving bare rock
    d. succession after a hurricane washes away all the sand from a beach

Short Answer *Write a short answer to each question.*

13. Put the terms in order, starting with the term that includes the largest number of individuals and ending with the group containing the fewest individuals: community, population, ecosystem, biome.

14. List four ways in which members of the same species can cooperate with each other.

15. Describe three different types of symbiosis.

Thinking Critically

The data in the table below come from the records of a Canadian trading company that, in the late 1800s, bought lynx and hare pelts from hunters and trappers. The Canadian lynx and varying hare share the same habitat. The lynx relies on the hare as a food source. Use the table to answer the next three questions.

Year	Lynx	Hare
1	2	30
2	15	55
3	65	90
4	75	160
5	100	200
6	95	140
7	75	80
8	40	35
9	20	3
10	3	4
11	30	40
12	55	95

16. **ANALYZE** How would you describe the pattern that emerges between the two populations in years 1–7? How does the pattern change in years 8–10?

17. **EVALUATE** The data on the lynx and hare pelts have been used to suggest the sizes of the lynx and hare populations. Is this a reasonable approach to take? Why or why not?

18. **ANALYZE** Scientists have observed that hare populations will go through cycles of increasing and decreasing populations even when the lynx is not part of the habitat. How would you explain this observation?

19. **APPLY** A forest has pine trees, along with oak trees and birch trees. All the trees provide shelter and food for different animals in the habitat. Do these trees occupy the same niche? Explain.

20. **INFER** Explain why low-growing plants like mosses are eventually replaced by shrubs, and shrubs replaced by trees, in both primary and secondary successions.

21. **PROVIDE EXAMPLES** List three human activities that could lead to secondary succession.

22. **ANALYZE** Creosote bushes in the Mojave desert are spread out, so that each plant is about an equal distance from another. Write a short paragraph to describe the interaction of the creosote bushes, using the terms from the table.

competition	population pattern
limiting factor	community

23. **APPLY** How might building homes in a wooded area affect carrying capacity of different populations in the area?

the **BIG** idea

24. **SUMMARIZE** Look again at the photograph on pages 362–363. How would you change or add details to your answer to the question on the photograph?

25. **APPLY** Imagine that you are an ecologist from another galaxy who arrives on Earth. Describe a human community using the terms that an Earth ecologist would use to describe a natural community. Your description should include at least three examples of interactions between individuals (whether the same or different species). Identify the biotic or abiotic factors that serve as limiting factors to human population growth. Also state whether you think the human population is at or below its carrying capacity—and why.

UNIT PROJECTS

By now you should have completed the following items for your unit project.

- questions that you have asked about the topic
- schedule showing when you will complete each step of your project
- list of resources including Web sites, print resources, and materials

Standardized Test Practice

Understanding Symbiosis

Read the following description of the strangler fig and the relationship it has with other species in a rain forest. Then answer the questions that follow.

Strangler figs are part of many symbiotic relationships in a rain-forest ecosystem. In some cases, the symbiotic relationship benefits both the fig and an animal. Fig wasps lay their eggs in the fruit of the strangler fig and, in turn, pollinate it. Many birds feed on the fruit of the strangler fig and, in doing so, spread the seeds of the plant. The fig does not benefit from its interactions with all species. For example, certain butterflies feed on juice from the fruit without affecting the tree in any way.

The symbiotic relationship that gives the strangler fig its name is that between the strangler fig and its host tree. Birds drop seeds onto the top of a tree, and vines of the fig grow downward. Eventually, the vines of the strangler fig touch the ground and join with the roots of the host tree. The host tree is harmed because the leaves of the strangler fig block sunlight and its vines take root, using up nutrients the host tree needs.

1. Which feeding relationship is a form of mutualism in which both species benefit?
   a. the strangler fig and its host tree
   b. the strangler fig and the butterflies
   c. the strangler fig and the birds
   d. the strangler fig and the fig wasp

2. Which symbiotic relationship is a form of parasitism in which one species benefits and the other is harmed?
   a. the strangler fig and its host tree
   b. the strangler fig and the butterflies
   c. the strangler fig and the birds
   d. the strangler fig and the fig wasp

3. Which symbiotic relationship is a commensal relationship in which one species benefits without affecting the other?
   a. the strangler fig and its host tree
   b. the strangler fig and the butterflies
   c. the strangler fig and the birds
   d. the strangler fig and the fig wasp

4. Which word best describes the interaction between the strangler fig and its host?
   a. coexistence
   b. cooperation
   c. competition
   d. community

Extended Response

5. Strangler figs attach to trees that are sometimes cut for lumber. Write a paragraph that describes how removal of the host trees would affect these populations.
   • butterflies
   • birds
   • wasps
   • strangler figs

6. Write a paragraph describing some of the different roles played by a strangler fig in the rain forest. Use the vocabulary terms listed below in your answer.

habitat	niche	populations
community	ecosystem	

TIMELINES in Science

WILDERNESS CONSERVATION

The idea of wilderness conservation would have seemed strange to anyone living before the 1800s. The wilderness was vast and much of the wildlife in it dangerous to humans.

In the late 1800s, as smoke from railroads and factories rose in American skies, scientists, artists, even presidents began the work of setting aside land as parks and reservations to protect natural landscapes. Forestry, unpracticed in the U.S. before the 1890s, became a priority of the federal government as the new century dawned. Industries learned to harvest and nurture forests rather than clearing them. Next came the protection of animal species along with a call to control the pollution and depletion caused by human activity.

1872

National Parks Protect Resources

On March 1, 1872, President Ulysses S. Grant signs a law declaring Yellowstone's 2 million acres in northwest Wyoming as the country's first national park. Yellowstone serves as a model, and by 1887, about 45 million acres of forest have been set aside.

EVENTS

1870

APPLICATIONS and TECHNOLOGY

TECHNOLOGY

Seeing the Wilderness

Developments in photography in 1839, and its spread during the Civil War, led to adventurous mobile photographers in the late 1800s. In the early 1860s Mathew Brady and other photographers took mobile studios to the battlefields to bring war news to the public. By the late 1860s and early 1870s the wagonload shrank to a pack load. In 1871, William Henry Jackson balanced his tripod in Yellowstone, as the official photographer of the region's first U.S. Geological Survey.

1898
U.S. Division of Forestry Formed

Gifford Pinchot becomes the first chief of the Division of Forestry. Pinchot warns lumberers to abandon clear-cutting, urging them to practice forestry, a more scientific approach. Pinchot instructs lumberers "to have trees harvested when they are ripe."

1892
Sierra Club Founded

The Sierra Club is formed to help people explore and enjoy the mountains of the Pacific region. The Club's goal, with John Muir the unanimous choice for President, is to help people and government preserve the forests of the Sierra Nevada.

1916
National Park Service (NPS) Founded

The system of protected forests grows so big that a federal agency is formed to oversee it. Stephen Mather serves as its first director. Today the NPS employs 20,000 staff; has 90,000 volunteers; and oversees 83.6 million acres.

1880   **1890**   **1900**   **1910**

APPLICATION
Protecting Animal Species

Fashions of the 1890s used feathers, furs, even whole birds. Out of concern for the extinction of many birds, including the Carolina parakeet and the heath hen, a movement to stop wearing rare feathers began at small tea parties. The U.S. Congress enacted the Lacey Act in 1900 to restore endangered species of game and wild birds. The landmark act became the first in a century of laws protecting animals. The Migratory Bird Treaty of 1918, the Bald Eagle Act of 1940, and the Endangered Species Act of 1973 set animal conservation as a national priority. The Endangered Species Act met its strongest test in protecting the northern spotted owl, whose entire range—in California, Oregon, Washington, and Canada—is protected.

1951
Nature Conservancy Established

The Nature Conservancy is formed to preserve plants, animals, and natural communities that represent Earth's biological diversity.

1963
Glen Canyon Destroyed

Completion of the Glen Canyon dam causes flooding in Glen Canyon, an immense area north of the Grand Canyon. Many groups fight to close the dam, but it is too late. The canyon is destroyed as Lake Powell forms.

1962
Silent Spring *Breaks Silence*

Biologist and science writer Rachel Carson publishes *Silent Spring.* Chemical pesticides have been widely used and publicized, but Carson uses scientific evidence to show that many of these chemicals harm people and the environment.

1968
Grand Canyon Dam Plans Squashed

Plans to dam the Grand Canyon are withdrawn as a result of public outcry. Recalling what happened to Glen Canyon, organizers ran national newspaper ads in 1966 making the public aware of plans to dam the Canyon.

1950   **1960**   **1970**

TECHNOLOGY

Maps to Save the Wilderness

Land and wildlife conservation has benefited from computer-based mapping technology called global information systems (GIS). GIS compiles satellite photographs, temperature readings, and other information into a central set of data. Scientists enter distributions of animals and overlay these data on existing maps. The resulting GIS maps show the gap in an animal's range and the quality of its habitat. Government efforts to restore the habitat of the endangered San Joaquin Kit Fox relied on GIS maps.

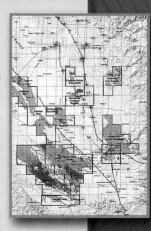

1980 to present

Reservation vs. Resource

In 1980, Congress expands the Arctic National Wildlife Refuge (ANWR) to more than twice its 1960 size. In 2001, President George W. Bush proposes limited oil drilling within the range. Today, debate continues over how to manage its resources and wildlife.

 RESOURCE CENTER
CLASSZONE.COM

Read more about current conservation efforts.

1990   2000

APPLICATION

Selling a Service

In New York City in 1996, the water department spent $1.5 billion to protect natural watersheds rather than build a $6 billion water treatment plant. In 2001, a group of scientists met to promote the value that ecosystems bring to society—benefits that include pest control, air purification, and water treatment. For example, dragonflies can eat 300 mosquitoes in a single day. Toads and bats can eat a thousand or more mosquitoes in a single day or night.

INTO THE FUTURE

Society has long put a price on natural resources—minerals, water, timber, and so on. But how much is an ecosystem worth? Communities have begun to look at the dollar values of "ecosystem services," the ongoing activities in nature that keep our environment healthy. Data is needed on ecosystem processes. Such data can be compared to the services of human-made treatment plants and agriculture.

Other questions arise with protecting species. Many species, such as wild turkeys and bald eagles, once endangered have come back in great numbers. When a protected species thrives it may endanger another species or bump up against the human landscape and human activity. How can managers of resources set priorities?

ACTIVITIES

Ecosystem Services Proposal

What services to the human population are provided by your local ecosystem? Choose one service and describe how natural processes and interactions within the ecosystem provide the benefits you've identified. What processes are involved?

Write a proposal for protecting the ecosystem. Include a comparison of the estimated cost of protecting the ecosystem and the cost of human services that provide a similar benefit.

Writing Project: The Story Behind the News

Research one of the events described on the timeline. Then write the story behind that event.

CHAPTER

Human Impact on Ecosystems

the **BIG** idea

Humans and human population growth affect the environment.

Key Concepts

SECTION

1 **Human population growth presents challenges.**
Learn how the increasing human population must share land and resources and dispose of its wastes.

SECTION

2 **Human activities affect the environment.**
Learn how humans may affect natural resources, air and water quality, and biodiversity.

SECTION

3 **People are working to protect ecosystems.**
Learn about federal, local, and scientific efforts to improve resource use and protect ecosystems.

Internet Preview

CLASSZONE.COM

Chapter 13 online resources: Content Review, Visualization, four Resource Centers, Math Tutorial, Test Practice

How have humans affected this landscape?

EXPLORE (the BIG idea)

How Many Is Six Billion?

Use a piece of paper, scissors, and some tape to make a box that measures 1 cm by 1 cm by 1 cm. Fill the box with rice. Use the number of grains of rice in 1 cm^3 to calculate the volume of 6,000,000,000 grains of rice.

Observe and Think How many grains of rice are in a cubic centimeter? Do 6 billion grains take up more or less space than you expected?

How Easily Does Polluted Water Move Through Plants?

Place a few drops of food coloring in a half cup of water. Take a leafy stalk of celery and make a fresh cut across the bottom. Place the celery in the water overnight.

Observe and Think What do you observe about the celery and its leaves? What do your observations suggest about plants growing near polluted water?

Internet Activity: The Environment

Go to **ClassZone.com** to explore the effects of human activities on the environment.

Observe and Think How are people working to protect the environment?

Population Growth **Code: MDL003**

Getting Ready to Learn

◀ CONCEPT REVIEW

- Both living and nonliving factors affect ecosystems.
- Populations can grow or decline over time.
- Matter and energy move through the environment.

◀ VOCABULARY REVIEW

species p. 365

habitat p. 366

See Glossary for definitions.

diversity, urban

ⓘ CONTENT REVIEW
CLASSZONE.COM

Review concepts and vocabulary.

▶ TAKING NOTES

SUPPORTING MAIN IDEAS

Make a chart to show main ideas and the information that supports them. Copy each blue heading; then add supporting information, such as reasons, explanations, and examples.

VOCABULARY STRATEGY

Think about a vocabulary term as a **magnet word** diagram. Write the other terms or ideas related to that term around it.

See the Note-Taking Handbook on pages R45–R51.

SCIENCE NOTEBOOK

Human populations can put pressure on ecosystems.

→ Humans produce waste that must be disposed of.

→ Resources must be shared among a growing human population.

→ Human population centers are expanding.

diversity   BIODIVERSITY   habitats

populations   variety

life   species

13.1
KEY CONCEPT
Human population growth presents challenges.

McDougal Littell Science
SOUTH CAROLINA

STANDARDS

Introduction to 7–4.6 Classify resources as renewable or nonrenewable and explain the implications of their depletion and the importance of conservation.

VOCABULARY

natural resource p. 404
population density p. 406

◀ **BEFORE,** you learned

- Populations have boundaries and are affected by limiting factors
- Living things form communities

▶ **NOW,** you will learn

- How a growing human population puts pressure on ecosystems
- How sharing resources can be difficult

EXPLORE Sharing Resources

How can you model resource distribution?

PROCEDURE

① You will work in a group of several classmates. One member of your group gets a bag of objects from your teacher.

② Each object in the bag represents a necessary resource. Divide the objects so that each member of the group gets the resources he or she needs.

③ After 10 minutes, you may trade resources with other groups.

WHAT DO YOU THINK?

- Did you get a fair share of your group's objects?
- How does the number of people in each group affect the outcome?
- Was the job made easier when trading occurred across groups?

MATERIALS
bag containing an assortment of objects

SUPPORTING MAIN IDEAS
Make a chart to show information that supports the first main idea presented: *The human population is increasing.*

The human population is increasing.

According to the United Nations, on October 12, 1999, Earth's human population reached 6 billion. Until 300 years ago, it had never grown beyond a few hundred million people. Only 200 years ago, the population reached 1 billion. So the increase to 6 billion people has occurred in a very short time. About one-third of all humans alive today are 14 years old or younger. Partly for this reason, experts predict Earth's population will keep growing—to 9 billion or more by the year 2050.

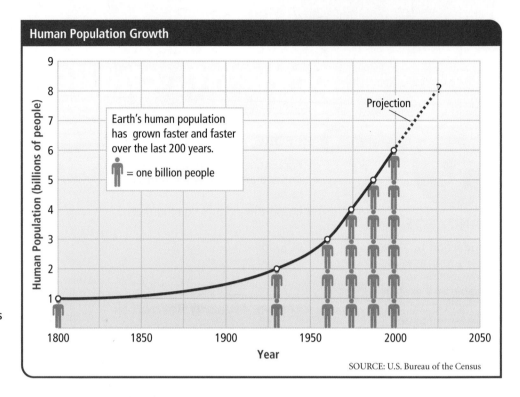

Human Population Growth

Human Population (billions of people)

Earth's human population has grown faster and faster over the last 200 years.

 = one billion people

Projection

Year

SOURCE: U.S. Bureau of the Census

PREDICT The graph shows actual population growth through 2000. Predict how the population will grow in the future.

The graph above shows how the human population has grown in the last 200 years. You can see from the way the graph gets noticeably steeper after 1950 how quickly the population has increased in just the last 50 years. It is not just the number of babies being born that contributes to Earth's large human population. People are living longer as a result of improving health care and nutrition.

The dotted line on the graph shows a projection, which helps us predict what the population would be if it continues to grow at the rate it is growing today. However, remember that an ecosystem has a carrying capacity for any given population. At some point, Earth will reach its carrying capacity for the human population. Today, many people think that our planet is close to—if not already at—its carrying capacity for humans.

CHECK YOUR READING How might Earth's carrying capacity affect human population growth?

Human populations can put pressure on ecosystems.

VISUALIZATION
CLASSZONE.COM

Examine how the human population has grown.

If your family has guests for the weekend, you may find that you run out of hot water for showers or do not have enough milk for everyone's breakfast. The resources that would ordinarily be enough for your family are no longer enough.

You read in Chapter 12 that resources such as food, water, and space can be limiting factors for biological populations. These same resources limit Earth's human population. As the human population grows, it uses more resources—just as your weekend visitors used more of your home's resources. The activities of the growing human population are putting pressure on Earth's ecosystems.

▼ REMINDER

A *limiting factor* is something that prevents a population from continuing to grow.

Pressures of Waste Disposal

As Earth's human population grows, so does the amount of waste produced by humans. Humans, like all living things, produce natural waste. Often, the water that carries this waste is treated to remove harmful chemicals before being cycled back to the environment. However, some of these materials still make it into lakes, rivers, and oceans, harming these ecosystems.

Much of the waste material produced by humans is the result of human activity. Some of this waste is garbage, or food waste. The rest of it is trash, or nonfood waste. In the United States, huge amounts of trash are thrown out each year. Most garbage and trash ends up in landfills.

Landfills take up a lot of space. The Fresh Kills Landfill in Staten Island, New York, is 60 meters (197 ft) high and covers an area as big as 2200 football fields. Decomposing trash and garbage can release dangerous gases into the air as well as harmful chemicals into the ground. Liners, which are layers of plastic or packed clay, are used to keep chemicals from leaking into surrounding land and water.

Waste is deposited in one area at a time.

Each layer is covered with soil and clay.

Liners at the base of the landfill keep harmful materials from leaking.

clay

groundwater

Another way to get rid of trash and garbage is to incinerate it—burn it. The problem with incineration is that it releases harmful gases and chemicals into the air. To prevent the release of these harmful substances, incinerator smokestacks have filters. To prevent further environmental contamination, used filters must be disposed of safely.

Pressures on Resources

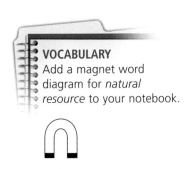

VOCABULARY
Add a magnet word diagram for *natural resource* to your notebook.

You have seen that a growing human population puts pressure on ecosystems by the amount of waste it leaves behind. Human populations also put pressure on ecosystems by what they take away. Humans depend on the environment for resources. A **natural resource** is any type of material or energy that humans use to meet their needs. Natural resources that humans take from their environment include water, food, wood, stone, metal, and minerals.

Clean fresh water is an important resource. Only 3 percent of Earth's water supply is fresh water—and two-thirds of that small amount is locked up in polar ice caps, glaciers, and permanent snow. As the human population grows, sharing this important resource will become more difficult.

INVESTIGATE Resources

How does your community meet its needs?

PROCEDURE

① Obtain a recent map of your county, city, or town.

② Using the map, try to identify where your community gets its electricity and water and how it disposes of trash and garbage.

③ Identify locations where food is grown.

WHAT DO YOU THINK?

- How much does your community rely on other communities for resources?

- What resources does your community share with other communities?

- Where does your community dispose of its own waste materials?

CHALLENGE Draw a grid on a piece of tracing paper and place it on top of the map. Use your grid to estimate what percentage of land in your city or town is used for housing and what percentage is used for governmental, agricultural, and commercial purposes.

SKILL FOCUS
Interpreting

MATERIALS
- map of your county, city, or town
For Challenge:
- tracing paper
- pencil
- ruler

TIME
30 minutes

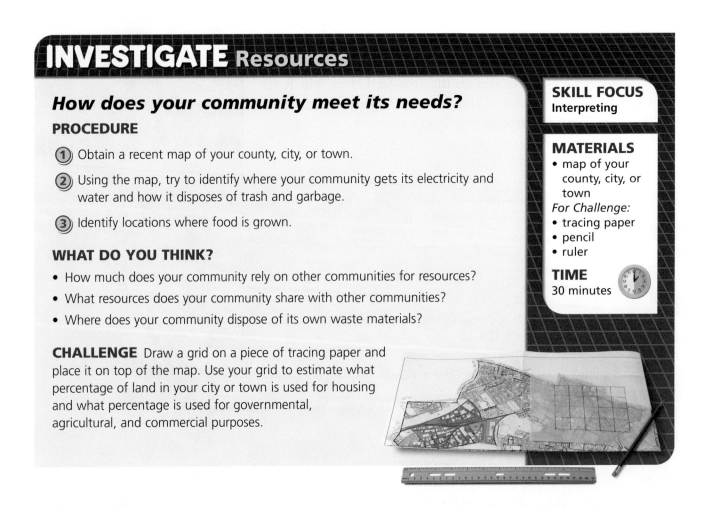

Case Study: The Colorado River

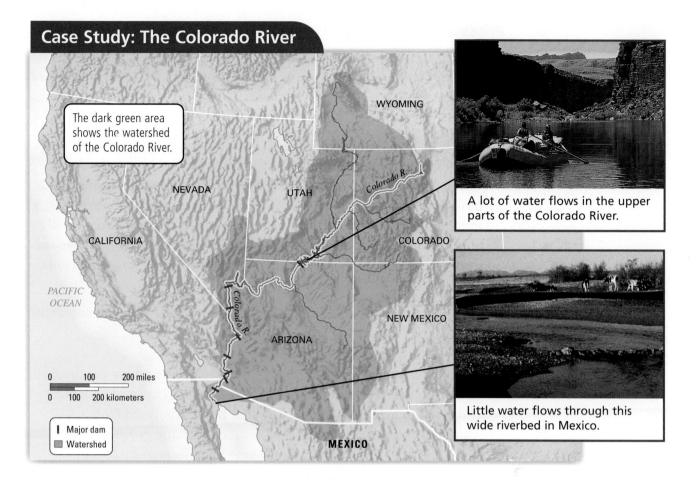

The dark green area shows the watershed of the Colorado River.

WYOMING

NEVADA

UTAH

Colorado R.

CALIFORNIA

COLORADO

PACIFIC OCEAN

Colorado R.

NEW MEXICO

ARIZONA

0   100   200 miles
0   100   200 kilometers

| Major dam
▪ Watershed

MEXICO

A lot of water flows in the upper parts of the Colorado River.

Little water flows through this wide riverbed in Mexico.

A case study that involves the Colorado River shows how a growing human population puts pressures on natural resources. This example also shows that sharing resources isn't easy. The watershed of this major Western river extends into seven U.S. states and parts of Mexico. The watershed includes all the smaller rivers and streams that flow into the Colorado River. In a region where little rain falls each year, these streams and rivers are an important source of water for drinking and agriculture.

As the West was settled, people in the downstream states of California, Arizona, and Nevada worried that the people in the upstream states of Colorado, Utah, Wyoming, and New Mexico would drain too much water from the river. In 1922 the seven states signed an agreement that divided the water between the two groups.

Problems with this agreement soon became apparent. First, the needs of Native American and Mexican populations were not considered. Second, the dams and channels built to prevent floods and transport water harmed river ecosystems. And third, the seven states planned to use more water than the river usually holds. As a result, the river often runs nearly dry at its mouth, in Mexico.

READING TiP

As you read about the Colorado River, refer to the map above to see where the river flows and the states that use the Colorado River's water.

 CHECK YOUR READING   List three problems that developed after people made a plan to share Colorado River water.

Pressures of Urban Growth

RESOURCE CENTER
CLASSZONE.COM

Learn more about urban expansion.

Until recently, the majority of Earth's population was spread out, so the population density was low. **Population density** is the measure of the number of people in a given area. Generally, the lower the population density, the less pressure there is on the environment.

Today, about half of the world's population lives in urban, or city, areas. People are attracted to these areas to live and to work. Over time, suburban areas around a city develop as more and more people look for a place to live. In cities, buildings are spaced close together, so the population density is high. A large number of people in a small area changes the landscape. The local environment can no longer support the number of people living there, and so resources must come from outside.

CHECK YOUR READING How does population density in a city differ from the population density of a suburb?

In recent years, some people have raised concern over the dramatic growth in and around urban areas. Los Angeles; Houston; Atlanta; and Washington, D.C. are all cities that have rapidly expanded. Another urban area that has experienced dramatic growth is Las Vegas, Nevada. The images below show the effects of increasing

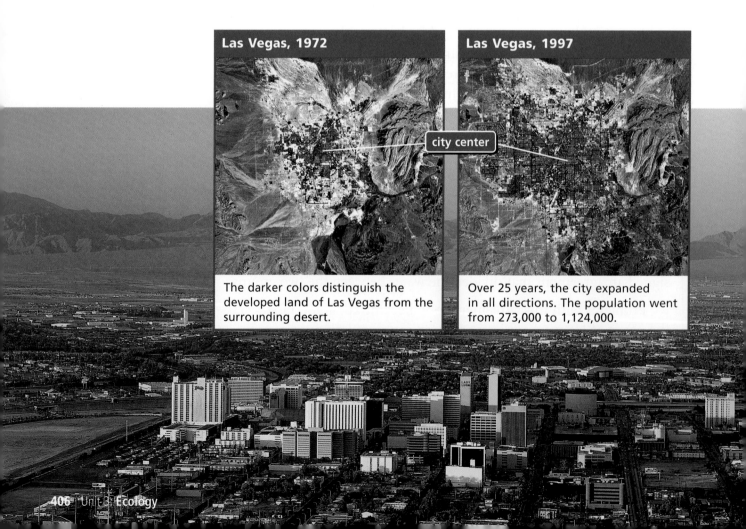

Las Vegas, 1972

The darker colors distinguish the developed land of Las Vegas from the surrounding desert.

Las Vegas, 1997

city center

Over 25 years, the city expanded in all directions. The population went from 273,000 to 1,124,000.

population density around the city between 1972 and 1997. Located in the middle of the desert, Las Vegas depends upon the Colorado River for water and electrical energy. As the population grows, so does the need for natural resources.

Pressures of Expanding Land Use

An increasing demand for resources in a particular area is one consequence of urban growth. But as communities around cities expand onto surrounding land, the environment is affected. Natural habitats, such as forests, are destroyed. Because forests cycle carbon through the environment, cutting down trees affects the carbon cycle. Soil that was held in place by tree roots may wash into lakes and rivers.

Another consequence of widespread development is the loss of productive farmland. Development replaces more than 2.5 million acres of farmland each year in the United States. This means less land is available locally to produce food for the growing population. The result is that food is often transported great distances.

Unlike compact city development, widespread suburban development also increases the need for residents to have cars. This is because most people in suburban areas live farther from where they work, shop, or go to school. A greater number of cars decreases the air quality in communities and requires additional road construction, which can interrupt natural habitats and endanger wildlife.

INFER What do you think this ecosystem looked like a hundred years ago? two hundred years ago?

 CHECK YOUR READING Describe some ways that development harms natural ecosystems.

13.1 Review

KEY CONCEPTS

1. Identify four pressures placed on ecosystems by an increasing human population.

2. Give an example that shows how resources can be difficult to share.

CRITICAL THINKING

3. **Apply** Describe an example of sharing resources that occurs in your home.

4. **Infer** How would a city's population density change if the city increased in area and the number of people in it remained the same?

○ CHALLENGE

5. **Evaluate** Imagine that you lived along the Colorado River. What information would you need if you wanted to evaluate a water-sharing agreement?

Ecology in Urban Planning

Urban planners design and locate buildings, transportation systems, and green spaces in cities. One important thing they consider is how their proposal for development will affect the ecosystem. With the help of ecology, urban planners can balance the needs of humans and the environment.

1 GATHERING DATA Urban planners use maps to gather information about the layout of a city, where populations of plants and animals exist, and where water and land resources are located.

2 ANALYZING DATA Scientists help urban planners determine how the location and density of buildings, roads, or parks can affect natural habitats.

3 APPLYING DATA By understanding the ecosystem, urban planners can develop areas to support different needs.

This habitat is left untouched because it supports rare migrating birds. Development would disturb the ecosystem and put the birds at risk.

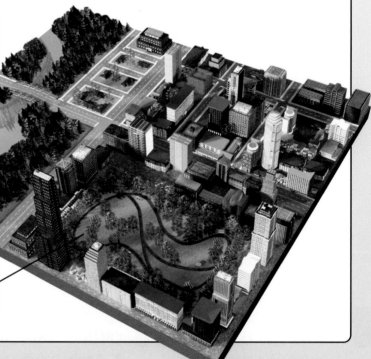

This area has a stable population of native species. Park benches and trails encourage human recreation in well defined areas.

EXPLORE

1. **APPLY** Both ecologists and urban planners have to understand the ways that biotic and abiotic factors are interconnected. List some biotic and abiotic factors in a human community.

2. **CHALLENGE** Use the Internet to find out more about the planning board or planning office in your community. Is your community growing? In what ways? What are some decisions that planners are helping to make?

13.2

Human activities affect the environment.

STANDARDS

7–4.6 Classify resources as renewable or nonrenewable and explain the implications of their depletion and the importance of conservation.

VOCABULARY

pollution p. 411
biodiversity p. 411

◀ **BEFORE, you learned**

• Human populations are increasing
• Human population growth causes problems

▶ **NOW, you will learn**

• How natural resources are classified
• How pollution affects the environment
• How a loss of diversity affects the environment

THINK ABOUT

How do you use water?

Think of the number of times you use water every day. Like all living things, you need water. In fact, more than half of the material that makes up your body is water.

No matter where you live, most of the time you can turn on a faucet and clean water flows out the spout. You use water when you take a shower, fix a snack, or wash a dish. If you've ever lost water service to your home, you've probably been reminded how much you depend upon it. No doubt about it, our need for water is serious.

SUPPORTING MAIN IDEAS
Make a chart to show information that supports the main idea: *Humans use many resources.*

Humans use many resources.

Throughout history, people around the world have relied on natural resources for survival. Ancient civilizations used stone to create tools and weapons. And wood was an important fuel for cooking and keeping warm. Today, humans continue to rely on the environment and have discovered additional resources to meet their needs. In Section 13.1 you read about sharing natural resources. Scientists classify these resources into two categories:

• renewable resources
• nonrenewable resources

RESOURCE CENTER
CLASSZONE.COM

Find out more about
natural resources.

Renewable Resources

Two hundred years ago, most small towns in the Northeastern part of the United States included farm fields, pasture, and woods. The wooded areas that weren't farmed were used as wood lots. The wood from these lots supplied firewood for towns and was often exported for income.

Trees are an example of a renewable resource—a resource that can be used over and over again. Energy from sunlight is another important renewable resource. Because the Sun is expected to supply energy for another five billion years, energy from sunlight is considered essentially unlimited. As you read earlier in your study of the water cycle, water can be classified as a renewable resource. Renewable resources can be replaced naturally or by humans in a short amount of time, but they may run out if they are overused or managed poorly.

CHECK YOUR READING Give three examples of renewable resources. Explain why each one is considered renewable.

Nonrenewable Resources

Nonrenewable resources are resources that cannot be replaced. In some cases, they may be replenished by natural processes, but not quickly enough for human purposes. Nonrenewable resources are often underground, making them more difficult to reach. But technology has enabled humans to locate and remove nonrenewable resources from places that used to be impossible to reach.

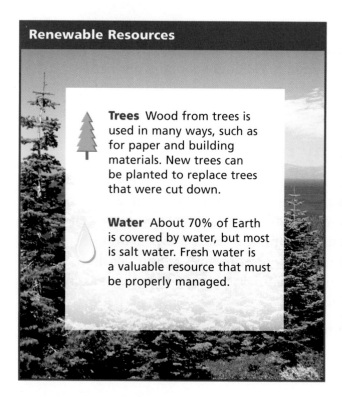

Renewable Resources

Trees Wood from trees is used in many ways, such as for paper and building materials. New trees can be planted to replace trees that were cut down.

Water About 70% of Earth is covered by water, but most is salt water. Fresh water is a valuable resource that must be properly managed.

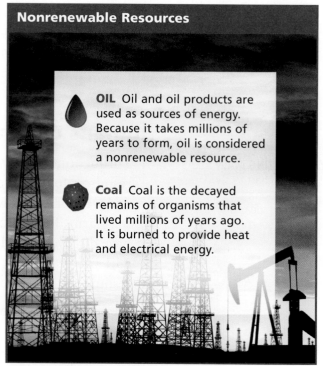

Nonrenewable Resources

OIL Oil and oil products are used as sources of energy. Because it takes millions of years to form, oil is considered a nonrenewable resource.

Coal Coal is the decayed remains of organisms that lived millions of years ago. It is burned to provide heat and electrical energy.

Coal, petroleum, and natural gas are nonrenewable resources that are removed from underground by mining or drilling. Also called fossil fuels, they are the main energy source for heating, industry, and transportation and are used to make many products. Many minerals, like copper and gold, are also considered nonrenewable resources.

Pollution endangers biodiversity.

As you walk along a city street, you may smell exhaust or see litter. These are examples of pollution. **Pollution** is the addition of harmful substances to the environment. Many of the ways humans use natural resources cause pollution to be released into the soil, air, and water. Pollutants include chemicals, bacteria, and dirt. Even materials that are ordinarily not harmful can cause pollution when they build up in one location.

As pollution becomes common in an ecosystem, living things may be threatened. Plant and animal populations may decrease and biodiversity may decline. **Biodiversity** is the number and variety of life forms within an ecosystem. Healthy ecosystems support a variety of species. An ecosystem with a variety of organisms can recover more easily from disturbances than an ecosystem that has fewer species.

VOCABULARY
Don't forget to add magnet diagrams for the words *pollution* and *biodiversity*.

INVESTIGATE Particles in the Air

Where do you find air pollution?

PROCEDURE

1. Use a hole punch to make holes at the ends of two index cards. Cut two pieces of string 30 cm long and tie one string to each card.

2. Choose a different location for each card. Mark the card with its location and the date.

3. Spread a thin film of petroleum jelly on a 3 cm^2 area on each card and hang each card at the location you've chosen.

4. Collect the cards in one week and examine them with the hand lens.

WHAT DO YOU THINK?

- Identify the types of particles collected at each location.
- Do you think of all of the particles collected as pollution?
- Which location had the most pollution?

CHALLENGE Hypothesize why certain locations have more particles in the air than others.

SKILL FOCUS
Observing

MATERIALS
- 2 index cards
- marker
- hole punch
- string
- scissors
- petroleum jelly
- hand lens

TIME
30 minutes

Air Quality

Air quality affects entire ecosystems. For example, in 1980, Mount St. Helens erupted on the West Coast of the United States. Hot ash was blown 15 miles up into the air. Three days later some of that ash reached the East Coast. Although natural events occasionally release air pollutants, human activities pollute every day.

READING TiP

Pollute and *pollutant* are in the same word family as *pollution*.

Today in the United States, motor vehicles, factories, and power plants are the main sources of air pollution. The fossil fuels they burn release sulfur dioxide, nitrogen dioxide, and carbon monoxide into the air. These pollutants affect humans and animals and are the main cause of acid rain, a serious problem affecting ecosystems.

CHECK YOUR READING What air pollutants contribute to acid rain problems in the United States?

Acid rain occurs when air pollutants such as sulfur dioxide and nitrogen dioxide mix with water in the atmosphere to form acid droplets of rain, ice, snow, or mist. Just as the wind carried ash from Mount St. Helens, wind can carry these droplets for very long distances before they fall as rain.

Acid rain has been very harmful in areas without rich soil to help correct the rain's acidity. In New York's Adirondack Mountains, acid rain has killed all the fish in some lakes. The photograph below shows the impact of acid rain on trees in the Adirondacks. Where acid rain falls, it damages leaves and soil. This damage destroys both habitats and food sources for many animals, eventually reducing biodiversity.

Acid-Rain Damage

A close look at the branch reveals that some of the needles are turning brown.

Air Quality Spruce trees in the Adirondacks show damage caused when pollutants in the air mix with rain.

Water Quality

SOUTH CAROLINA Essentials
See the South Carolina Essentials, pages 651–654, to read more about how human activities affect water quality.

Water quality is another factor that affects biodiversity in ecosystems. Forty years ago, newspaper headlines announced that Lake Erie was "dead" because of pollution. Almost every living thing in the lake had died. Lake Erie suffered for years from pollution by neighborhoods, industries, and farms along its banks. Rivers that emptied into the lake also carried pollution with them.

The pollution found in Lake Erie is common in communities across the United States. Chemicals or waste that drain off of farm fields, animal feedlots, and landfills all cause water pollution. So do oil spills, soil erosion, and the discharging of wastewater from towns and industries.

 CHECK YOUR READING Name four different sources of water pollution.

Like air pollution, water pollution affects entire ecosystems. One river that suffers from heavy pollution is the Duwamish River in Washington. Over 600 million gallons of untreated waste and storm water drain off the land into the river. As a result, large amounts of bacteria and harmful chemicals contaminate the water, killing fish and putting humans at risk.

When fish and amphibians in aquatic ecosystems are exposed to pollution, the entire food web is affected. If fish become scarce, some birds may no longer find enough food. The bird population may decrease as birds die or move to a new habitat. The result is that biodiversity in the ecosystem decreases.

Water Quality A scientist tests the water of the Duwamish River after chemicals were released into the river.

Chemical Pollution

Pollution that flows into aquatic ecosystems can harm—even kill—organisms like these fish.

Pollution Across Systems

As you have learned, pollution can be spread among ecosystems by abiotic factors. For example, wind carried ash from Mount St. Helens to different ecosystems. Wind also carries acid rain to forest ecosystems. Pollution can also move between air and water. For example, some chemical pollutants can run off land and into a body of water. These pollutants, like the water itself, can evaporate from the water's surface and cycle into the air, moving into the atmosphere.

① Runoff containing harmful chemicals flows into this pond.

② The chemicals evaporate into the air from the surface of the water.

Habitat loss endangers biodiversity.

Scientists know that an ecosystem with many different species of plants and animals can withstand the effects of flooding, drought, and disease more effectively than an ecosystem with fewer species. But for biodiversity to be maintained, a habitat must be able to support a large number of different species. If living space is limited or a food source is removed, then the number of species in a biological community will be reduced.

Removing Habitat

One way human activities affect habitats is by reducing the amounts of natural resources available to living things. When this occurs, populations that rely on those resources are less likely to survive. For example, if you trim all the dead branches off the trees in your yard and remove them, insects that live in rotting wood will not settle in your yard. As a result, woodpeckers that may have nested in the area will lose their source of food. By removing this food source, you might affect the biodiversity in your backyard.

Now consider altering an ecosystem much larger than your backyard. Instead of removing a single resource, imagine removing a large area of land that is a habitat to many different species. Disturbing habitats removes not only food but space, shelter, and protection for living things.

Removing Habitat

A clear-cut forest provides a dramatic example of habitat loss.

Forest Habitat The forest provides food and shelter for many organisms.

Deforestation Removing all the trees from an area removes habitat that other species depend on.

Because of land development, forests that once stretched for hundreds of miles have been fragmented, or broken apart into small patches. Organisms that depend on trees cannot live in woods that have large areas that have been clear-cut. Their habitat is removed or reduced so there is a greater risk of attack by predators. Skunks, raccoons, and crows, which eat the eggs of forest songbirds, will not travel deep into large forests. However, they can reach nests more easily when forests are broken into small areas.

 CHECK YOUR READING Why is biodiversity important and how can human activities affect it?

Changing Habitat

Another kind of habitat loss occurs when humans move species into new habitats, either on purpose or by accident. Some species, when released in a new place, successfully compete against the native species, crowding them out. Over time, these species, called invasive species, may replace the native species.

One example of an invasive plant is purple loosestrife. In the 1800s loosestrife from Europe was brought to the United States to use as a garden plant and medicinal herb. One loosestrife plant can make about 2 million seeds a year. These seeds are carried long distances by wind, water, animals, and humans. Loosestrife sprouts in wetlands, where it can fill in open-water habitat or replace native plants such as goldenrod. Most ducks and fish do not feed on purple loosestrife.

Changing Habitat

Habitat loss occurs when purple loosestrife fills in open water or crowds out goldenrod.

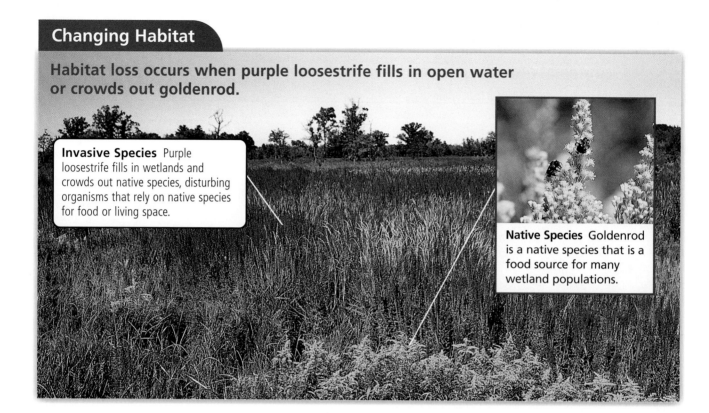

Invasive Species Purple loosestrife fills in wetlands and crowds out native species, disturbing organisms that rely on native species for food or living space.

Native Species Goldenrod is a native species that is a food source for many wetland populations.

When the native plants that wetland animals depend on are crowded out by loosestrife, the animals disappear, too.

Scientists estimate that Earth supports more than 10 million different species. They also estimate that thousands of species are threatened, and over a hundred species of plants and animals become extinct every year. By protecting biodiversity we can help ecosystems thrive and even recover more quickly after a natural disturbance such as a hurricane. And biodiversity directly benefits humans. For example, many medications are based on natural compounds from plants that only grow in certain types of ecosystems.

13.2 Review

KEY CONCEPTS

1. List some renewable and nonrenewable resources that you need to survive.

2. Describe two ways in which pollution can move through ecosystems.

3. Explain what scientists mean by *biodiversity*.

CRITICAL THINKING

4. **Explain** Under some circumstances, valuable natural resources can be considered pollutants. Explain this statement, giving two examples.

5. **Compare** Identify two natural habitats in your area, one with high biodiversity and one with low biodiversity. Describe the biodiversity of each.

⬤ CHALLENGE

6. **Hypothesize** When lakes are polluted by acid rain, the water appears to become clearer, not cloudier. Why do you think this is the case?

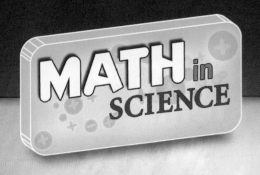

MATH in SCIENCE

MATH TUTORIAL
CLASSZONE.COM

Click on Math Tutorial for more help with finding the volume of a rectangular prism.

SKILL: FINDING VOLUMES

How Much Water?

When you take a 10-minute shower, you are using about 190 liters of water. How much is that? Liters are a metric unit of capacity—the amount of liquid that can fit into a container of a certain size. The liter is based on a metric unit of volume. One liter is equal to 1000 cubic centimeters.

Example

A rectangular tank holds the amount of water used for a 10-minute shower. The dimensions of the tank are 250 cm × 40 cm × 19 cm. What is the volume of the tank?

Volume = **length** × **width** × **height**

$V = l \times w \times h$

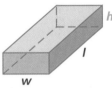

(1) Use the formula for volume.
Replace variables with actual dimensions.

$V = 250 \text{ cm} \times 40 \text{ cm} \times 19 \text{ cm}$

(2) Calculate by multiplying.

$(250 \times 40) \times 19$

$10{,}000 \qquad \times 19 = 190{,}000$

(3) Check units:
cm × cm × cm = cm³ (cubic centimeters)

ANSWER 250 cm × 40 cm × 19 cm = 190,000 cm³

Find the following volumes or dimensions.

1. Brushing your teeth with the water running uses the water in a tank 14 cm by 45 cm by 12 cm. Sketch an aquarium that holds exactly this amount. Label the dimensions. What is the volume?

2. If you turn off the water while you brush, you use only about half as much water. Sketch a rectangular tank that holds this volume. Label the dimensions. What is the volume?

3. A typical toilet flush uses the water in a 50 cm by 20 cm by 20 cm space. Find the volume in cubic centimeters. Sketch a model of this volume.

CHALLENGE An Olympic swimming pool is 50 m by 25 m by 3 m. What is its volume? There are approximately 5678 cubic meters of water in the water tower shown. How many Olympic pools of water would it take to fill the tower?

13.3 People are working to protect ecosystems.

STANDARDS

7–4.6 Classify resources as renewable or nonrenewable and explain the implications of their depletion and the importance of conservation.

VOCABULARY

conservation p. 419
sustainable p. 422

 BEFORE, you learned

- Human activities produce pollutants
- Human activity is depleting some natural resources

▶ **NOW, you will learn**

- About some of the laws that have been passed to help protect the environment
- About efforts that are being made to conserve natural resources

---

EXPLORE Environmental Impacts

What happens when soil is compressed?

PROCEDURE

① Fill two pots with 1 cup each of potting soil.

② Compress the soil in the second pot by pushing down hard upon it with your hand.

③ Pour 1 cup of water into the first pot. Start the stopwatch as soon as you start pouring. Stop the watch as soon as all the water has been absorbed. Record the time.

④ Pour 1 cup of water into the second pot and again record how long it takes for the water to be absorbed. Wash your hands.

MATERIALS

- 2 plant pots with trays
- measuring cups
- potting soil
- water
- stopwatch

WHAT DO YOU THINK?

- What effect does compressing the soil have upon how quickly the water is absorbed?
- What might happen to water that is not absorbed quickly by soil?

Environmental awareness is growing.

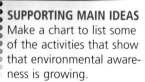

 SUPPORTING MAIN IDEAS
Make a chart to list some of the activities that show that environmental awareness is growing.

As people moved westward across grassy plains and steep mountain ranges of the United States, many believed our nation's resources were endless. Midwestern prairies were converted to farmland. Forests were clear-cut for lumber. Land was mined for coal.

By the 1800s, foresters and naturalists began to take interest in preserving the wild areas they saw rapidly disappearing. In 1872 our nation's outlook started to change when Yellowstone, the world's first national park, was established. It wasn't long before conservation of wild places became a goal. **Conservation** is the process of saving or protecting a natural resource.

RESOURCE CENTER
CLASSZONE.COM

Discover how people help ecosystems recover.

The movement to protect our environment grew rapidly in the 1960s. *Silent Spring,* a book that raised public awareness of the effect of harmful chemicals in the environment, sparked debate about serious pollution problems. As local efforts for environmental protection grew, the United States government responded. Throughout the 1970s important laws were passed to preserve and protect the environment. Today small groups of citizens, along with local and national government efforts, protect America's natural resources.

 List three events in the history of the environmental movement in the United States.

Volunteers work to clean up a stream.

Local Efforts

Maybe you have heard the expression "Think globally, act locally." It urges people to consider the health of the entire planet and to take action in their own communities. Long before federal and state agencies began enforcing environmental laws, individuals were coming together to protect habitats and the organisms that depend on them. These efforts are often referred to as grassroots efforts. They occur on a local level and are primarily run by volunteers.

Often the efforts of a few citizens gather the support and interest of so many people that they form a larger organization. These groups work to bring about change by communicating with politicians, publishing articles, or talking to the news media. Some groups purchase land and set it aside for preservation.

Federal Efforts

You have probably heard of the Endangered Species Act or the Clean Air Act. You might wonder, though, exactly what these laws do. The United States government works with scientists to write laws that ensure that companies and individuals work together to conserve natural resources and maintain healthy ecosystems.

In the late 1960s the National Environmental Policy Act, known as NEPA, made the protection of natural ecosystems a national goal. Several important laws followed. For example, the Clean Air Act and Clean Water Act improved the control of different kinds and amounts of pollutants that can be put into the air and water. The Environmental Protection Agency (EPA) enforces all federal environmental laws.

 CHECK YOUR READING   Identify two federal environmental laws.

Over the past decades, chemical waste from factories has piled up in landfills and polluted water sources. These wastes can threaten ecosystems and human health. In 1980, citizen awareness of the dangers led to the Superfund Program. The goal of the program is to identify dangerous areas and to clean up the worst sites.

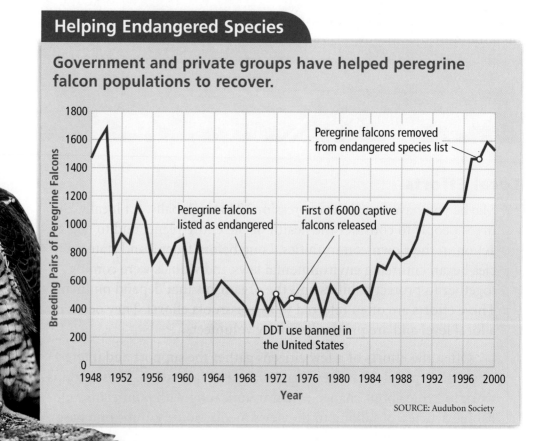

Helping Endangered Species

Government and private groups have helped peregrine falcon populations to recover.

Peregrine falcons removed from endangered species list

Peregrine falcons listed as endangered

First of 6000 captive falcons released

DDT use banned in the United States

Breeding Pairs of Peregrine Falcons

Year

SOURCE: Audubon Society

Ecosystem Recovery

A growing awareness of the importance of healthy ecosystems is inspiring restoration projects.

Wetland

Restoration efforts in Galveston Bay, Texas, focus on bringing back the sea-grass meadows near the coast.

Volunteers help replant sea grass around Galveston Island State Park. Sea grass is a major habitat for birds, fish, and crabs and helps prevent erosion by holding bottom sediments in place.

Desert

Members of a restoration group work to restore desert plants and soil in Red Rock Canyon State Park, California.

① A power auger is used to break up severely compacted soil and prepare it for planting.

② Seedlings of native species, like the saltbush, are grown off site. Once they reach a more mature size, they are brought in to be planted.

③ Plastic cones are used to protect plants from being disturbed by severe weather or predators.

Federal agencies oversee the Superfund Program and other environmental laws. In addition to federal laws protecting the environment, there are state laws. Companies must follow all the laws that apply in each state where they do business. The same company may need to follow different laws in different states.

The United States is just one of many countries learning to deal with the effects of their human population on the environment. Dozens of countries have already met to discuss concerns about clear-cutting, water pollution, and endangered species. At this international level, the United Nations Environment Programme encourages sound environmental practices worldwide.

INFER At this Superfund site, the chemical cadmium pollutes the soil. Why does this worker need to wear a face mask?

Conserving resources protects ecosystems.

Around the world, individuals and companies are expressing more interest in **sustainable** practices—ways of living and doing business that use natural resources without using them up. Sustainable development allows people to enjoy a high quality of life while limiting harm to ecosystems. Developing new technologies, reducing resource use, and creating less waste are three ways to practice sustainability.

 What are sustainable practices?

Improving Resource Use

As you read in Chapter 12, many different interactions take place in ecosystems. Some organisms form close relationships with one other and their environment. Humans are like other organisms. We depend on the environment to help meet our requirements for life. Because many of the resources we rely on are limited, businesses and governments are changing the way they manage farms, forests, and energy resources. They are adopting sustainable practices.

Some farmers are practicing sustainable methods that protect land and provide nutritious food. Nearly one-third of U.S. farms practice conservation tillage, a method that involves planting seeds without plowing the soil. This technique can cut soil erosion by more than 90 percent. Organic farmers reject fertilizers and pesticides made from fossil fuels. Instead they use natural fertilizers, like compost, and natural pest controls, like ladybugs, which eat aphids.

Forestry practices are also changing. Cutting selectively instead of clear-cutting reduces soil erosion and encourages rapid regrowth. The U.S. Forest Service has adopted an ecosystem-management approach that tries to balance the need for timber with the need to conserve soil and water and preserve wildlife and biodiversity.

⬤ CHECK YOUR READING Give two examples of sustainable practices.

Energy companies are also promoting sustainability by developing alternative energy sources that do not come from fossil fuels. By the time you buy your first car, it may run on fuel cells, and the electricity in your house may be generated by a solar power plant.

Commercial geothermal power plants are a renewable energy source that uses the heat of molten rock in the Earth's interior. Geothermal power already supplies electricity to households in New Zealand, Japan, the United States, and elsewhere.

The energy of falling or flowing water can also be used to generate electricity in a hydropower plant. Commercial hydropower plants generate over half of the alternative energy used in the United States. Like solar and geothermal power, hydropower releases no pollutants. But hydropower often requires dams, which are expensive to build and can flood wildlife habitats and interfere with fish migration.

Wind is another source of energy that is clean and renewable. Large open areas with relatively constant winds are used as wind farms. Wind turbines are spread across these farms and convert the energy of moving air into electricity. Wind-generating capacity has increased steadily around the world in just the last ten years.

Solar Energy These mirrors collect and concentrate sunlight, which will be used to generate electricity.

INFER What benefits do people get from using mass transit? Why might some people be reluctant to use mass transit?

READING TIP

The prefix *re–* means *again*, so to *recycle* a resource is to use it again.

Reducing Waste and Pollution

Perhaps you are one of the many students who take a bus to school. Buses and trains are examples of mass transit, which move large groups of people at the same time. When you travel by mass transit, you are working to reduce waste and pollution. The photograph to the left shows a light rail train that carries commuters from downtown Portland, Oregon, into suburbs an hour away. In Portland, mass transit like this light rail helps reduce traffic congestion, air pollution, and noise pollution.

Another way to reduce pollution is by carpooling. Many states encourage carpools by reducing tolls or reserving highway lanes for cars carrying more than one person. Traffic is also reduced when workers telecommute, or work from home, using computers and telephones. Of course a telecommuter uses energy at home. But there are many ways to reduce home energy use. You can install compact fluorescent light bulbs, which use less electricity than a regular light bulb. And you can choose energy-efficient appliances.

CHECK YOUR READING How does mass transit benefit the environment?

Most homes are heated with oil or natural gas, two nonrenewable resources. To use less of these resources, you lower your thermostat in winter or add insulation around doors and windows to keep heat inside. Many power companies offer a free energy audit, to show how you can use less energy at home.

Recycling is a fairly new idea in human communities, but if you think about it, it's what biological communities have always done to reduce waste and pollution. Resources are used again and again as they move through the water, nitrogen, and carbon cycles. Materials

These students are participating in a local recycling program.

that people now commonly recycle include glass, aluminum, certain types of plastic, office paper, newspaper, and cardboard.

Sometimes materials are recycled into the same product. Cans and glass bottles are melted down to make new cans and bottles. Materials can also be recycled into new products. Your warm fleece jacket might be made from recycled soda bottles. The cereal box on your breakfast table might be made from recycled paper.

 CHECK YOUR READING Name three things people can do at home that reduce waste and pollution.

Think globally, act locally.

Visitors to an ocean beach may find signs like the one on the right. Such signs remind people that small actions—like protecting the nests of sandpipers—make a difference in the preservation of ecosystems.

The challenges facing society are great. Providing Earth's growing population with clean water and air and with energy for warmth and transportation are only some of the many tasks. Scientists continue to learn about the interactions in ecosystems and how important ecosystems are to humans. As you have read about the interactions in ecosystems, you have probably realized that humans—including you—have a large effect on the natural world.

In the coming years, protection of ecosystems will remain a major challenge. By thinking globally, you will be able to understand the effects of society's decisions about resources, development, and transportation. By acting locally you can become involved in efforts to reduce the use of limited resources and to restore ecosystems.

BIRDS ONLY
Beyond
This
Sign

13.3 Review

KEY CONCEPTS

1. List at least five ways that you can reduce your use of natural resources.
2. Describe three ways that resources can be managed in a sustainable way.

CRITICAL THINKING

3. **Infer** Controlling air and water pollution and protecting endangered species usually require the involvement of the federal government. Why can't state or local governments do this on their own?

⬤ CHALLENGE

4. **Apply** Explain how efforts to protect endangered species relate to restoration of ecosystems.

CHAPTER INVESTIGATION

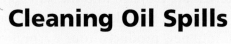

Cleaning Oil Spills

OVERVIEW AND PURPOSE

One example of a harmful effect of human activity is an oil spill. You've probably heard about oil spills in the news. Damage to an oil-carrying ship or barge can cause thick black oil to spill into the water. The oil floats on the water, and waves can carry the oil to shore. Oil gets caught on sand and living things that are part of a coastal ecosystem. These spills are especially difficult to clean up. In this investigation you will

- simulate an oil spill and test the effectiveness of various materials used to remove oil
- evaluate materials and processes used to clean up oil spills

Problem

What materials are effective at removing oil spilled near a coastal ecosystem?

Hypothesize

Write a hypothesis to propose a material or materials that might best remove oil from a coastal area. Your hypothesis should take the form of an "If . . . , then . . . , because . . ." statement.

Procedure

1. Measure out 40 mL of vegetable oil in a small beaker. Stir in turmeric to make the oil yellow.

2. Pour sand into one end of the pan as shown to model a beach.

3. Carefully pour enough water into the pan so that it forms a model ocean at least 2 cm deep. Try not to disturb the sand pile.

4. Use the yellow-colored oil to model an oil spill. Pour the oil onto the slope of the sand so that it runs off into the water.

step 4

MATERIALS

- small beaker
- 40 mL vegetable oil
- turmeric
- spoon
- aluminum baking pan
- sand
- large beaker
- water
- sponge
- dish soap
- rubbing alcohol
- paper towels
- cotton balls
- cotton rag
- cornstarch
- yarn
- feather
- seaweed

Observe and Analyze
Write It Up

1. **RECORD** Write up your procedure for cleaning oil from sand and water. You may want to include a diagram.

2. **EVALUATE** What, if any, difficulties did you encounter in carrying out this experiment?

Conclude
Write It Up

1. **INTERPRET** How do your results compare with your hypothesis? Answer the problem statement.

2. **EVALUATE** Which materials were most useful for cleaning the water? Were they the same materials that were most useful for cleaning the sand?

3. **EVALUATE** Suppose you are trying to clean oil off of living things, such as a bird or seaweed. What process would you use?

4. **IDENTIFY LIMITS** In which ways did this demonstration fail to model a real oil spill?

INVESTIGATE Further

CHALLENGE Explain how the observations you made in this investigation might be useful in designing treatments for an actual oil spill.

5. Test the materials for effectiveness in removing the oil from the sand and the water.

6. Place the feather and the seaweed on the beach or in the water, where the oil is. Test materials for effectiveness in removing oil from the feather and seaweed.

7. Make a table in your **Science Notebook** like the one below. Record your observations on the effectiveness of each material.

8. Using your observations from step 7, design a process for removing oil from sand and water. This process may involve several materials and require a series of steps.

Cleaning Oil Spills
Problem What material or method is most effective in containing or cleaning up oil spills?

Hypothesis

Observations

	water	sand	feather	seaweed
paper towel				
cotton				

the BIG idea

Humans and human population growth affect the environment.

CONTENT REVIEW
CLASSZONE.COM

◀ KEY CONCEPTS SUMMARY

① Human population growth presents challenges.

As the population continues to grow, there is a greater demand for natural resources. Cities and countries share many resources. Increasing populations put pressure on ecosystems.

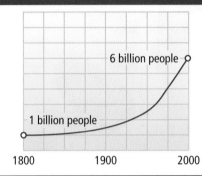

6 billion people

1 billion people

1800   1900   2000

VOCABULARY
natural resource p. 404
population
 density p. 406

② Human activities affect the environment.

Pollution and habitat loss make it difficult for plants and animals to survive. Without the necessary resources, biodiversity of living things decreases, and ecosystems become less stable.

Pollution

Habitat Loss

VOCABULARY
pollution p. 411
biodiversity p. 411

③ Humans are working to protect ecosystems.

Working at local and governmental levels, humans are helping ecosystems recover.

Laws protect endangered species.

Researchers are investigating alternative resources.

VOCABULARY
conservation p. 419
sustainable p. 422

Place each vocabulary term at the center of a description wheel diagram. Write some words describing it on the spokes.

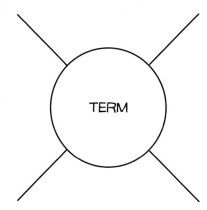

TERM

1. population density

2. natural resources

3. pollution

4. biodiversity

5. sustainable

6. conservation

Reviewing Key Concepts

Multiple Choice *Choose the letter of the best answer.*

7. In 2000, how big was Earth's human population?
- **a.** 1 billion
- **c.** 6 billion
- **b.** 3 billion
- **d.** 9 billion

8. Experts predict that by the year 2050, Earth's population will reach what number?
- **a.** 3 billion
- **c.** 9 billion
- **b.** 6 billion
- **d.** 12 billion

9. Which statement best explains why Earth's population has grown very rapidly in the last 100 years?
- **a.** On average, women are having children at an older age.
- **b.** People live longer because of improved health care and nutrition.
- **c.** Global warming has enabled farmers to grow more food.
- **d.** More land has been developed for housing.

10. Which of the four natural resources listed is likely to be used up the soonest?
- **a.** petroleum
- **c.** sunlight
- **b.** water
- **d.** wood

11. Which of the following is an example of increasing biodiversity?
- **a.** A forest is clear-cut for its wood, leaving land available for new uses.
- **b.** New species of animals and plants appear in a wildlife preserve.
- **c.** A new species of plant outcompetes all of the others around a lake.
- **d.** A cleared rain forest results in a change to a habitat.

12. Which represents a sustainable practice?
- **a.** conservation tillage and use of natural fertilizers
- **b.** more efficient removal of oil
- **c.** allowing unlimited use of water for higher fees
- **d.** restocking a lake with fish every year

13. What environmental problem does the Superfund Program address?
- **a.** habitat loss
- **b.** land development
- **c.** biodiversity
- **d.** pollution

Short Answer *Write a short answer to each question.*

14. List four ways increased human population density affects ecosystems.

15. Three ways that humans dispose of waste are landfills, incineration, and wastewater treatment plants. List one advantage and one disadvantage of each.

16. Write a paragraph to describe how an increase in population density affects land development.

Thinking Critically

Use the graph to answer the next three questions.

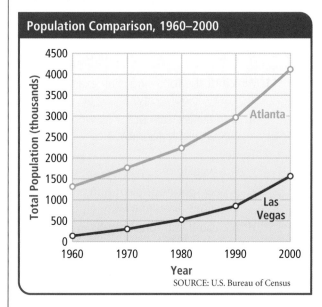

Population Comparison, 1960–2000

Total Population (thousands) vs. Year

Atlanta

Las Vegas

SOURCE: U.S. Bureau of Census

17. COMPARE AND CONTRAST Describe the population size and rate of growth for the cities of Atlanta and Las Vegas. Would you expect the population of Las Vegas to ever get bigger than that of Atlanta based on the data supplied?

18. EVALUATE Is it possible to determine from the data shown whether the population density is higher in Atlanta than Las Vegas? What other information would you need?

19. CONNECT Atlanta is located in a temperate-forest biome and Las Vegas is located in a desert biome. How might the characteristics of these biomes affect the carrying capacity of the human populations in these cities?

20. PREDICT If states in the U.S. used less water from the Colorado River, how would the depth of the river in Mexico be affected?

21. COMPARE AND CONTRAST Explain why trees are generally considered a renewable resource. Now describe circumstances under which they could be considered a nonrenewable resource.

22. CLASSIFY Sort the resources below into the correct categories:

Resource	Renewable	Nonrenewable
Water		
Coal		
Soil		
Wood		
Copper		
Petroleum		
Aluminum		
Sunlight		

23. CALCULATE A compact fluorescent bulb uses less energy than a regular bulb. It is estimated that a coal-burning power plant would release 72 kilograms more carbon dioxide (CO_2) a year to power one regular bulb than it would to power one fluorescent bulb. If you replace five regular bulbs with five compact bulbs, how much less CO_2 would be released in a 10-year period?

the BIG idea

24. PROVIDE EXAMPLES Look again at the photograph on pages 398–399. How would you change or add details to your answer to the question on the photograph?

25. APPLY You are on the town council of a community located on a small island. The council has decided to make a brochure for the town's citizens. In your brochure, describe the island habitat. Include information about natural resources, such as water and soil. List the plants and animals that live there. Establish four rules that the community should follow to preserve the local habitat.

UNIT PROJECTS

Evaluate the materials in your project folder. Finish your project and get ready to present it to your class.

Analyzing Data

Nowhere is the impact of human population growth more obvious than in the growth of urbanized areas. Buildings, parking lots, and roads are replacing forests, farmland, and wetlands. The table below shows the growth of urbanized areas around 10 cities in the United States during a 20-year period.

1. What patterns can you see in the way information is presented from the top of the table to the bottom?
   a. Cities are arranged alphabetically.
   b. Cities are arranged by growth in population over 20 years.
   c. Cities are arranged by the growth in land area over 20 years.
   d. Cities are arranged by size of urban area.

2. How would you describe the change in the land around Atlanta between 1970 and 1990?
   a. In 1990, more land was used for farming.
   b. The number of buildings and roads increased.
   c. The urbanized area decreased.
   d. Natural habitats for birds increased.

3. Which type of graph would be best for displaying the data in the table?
   a. a bar graph
   b. a circle graph
   c. a line graph
   d. a double bar graph

4. How many square kilometers around Philadelphia were affected by urbanization between 1970 and 1990?
   a. 1116 km^2 c. 1068 km^2
   b. 1166 km^2 d. 1020 km^2

Growth in land area, 1970-1990

Location	Growth in Land Area (Km^2)
Atlanta, GA	1816
Houston, TX	1654
New York City-N.E. New Jersey	1402
Washington, D.C.-MD-VA	1166
Philadelphia, PA	1068
Los Angeles, CA	1020
Dallas-Fort Worth, TX	964
Tampa-St. Petersburg-Clearwater, FL	929
Phoenix, AZ	916
Minneapolis-Saint Paul, MN	885

SOURCE: U.S. Bureau of Census data on Urbanized Areas

Extended Response

5. Write a paragraph to describe how a rural area would change if the land were developed and the area became more urban. Use the vocabulary words listed below in your answer.

population density	biodiversity
renewable resources	nonrenewable resources

6. If you were an urban designer working for a small city that expected to expand rapidly in the next 10 years, what recommendations would you make to the city council on how the land should be developed?

UNIT 4

Matter

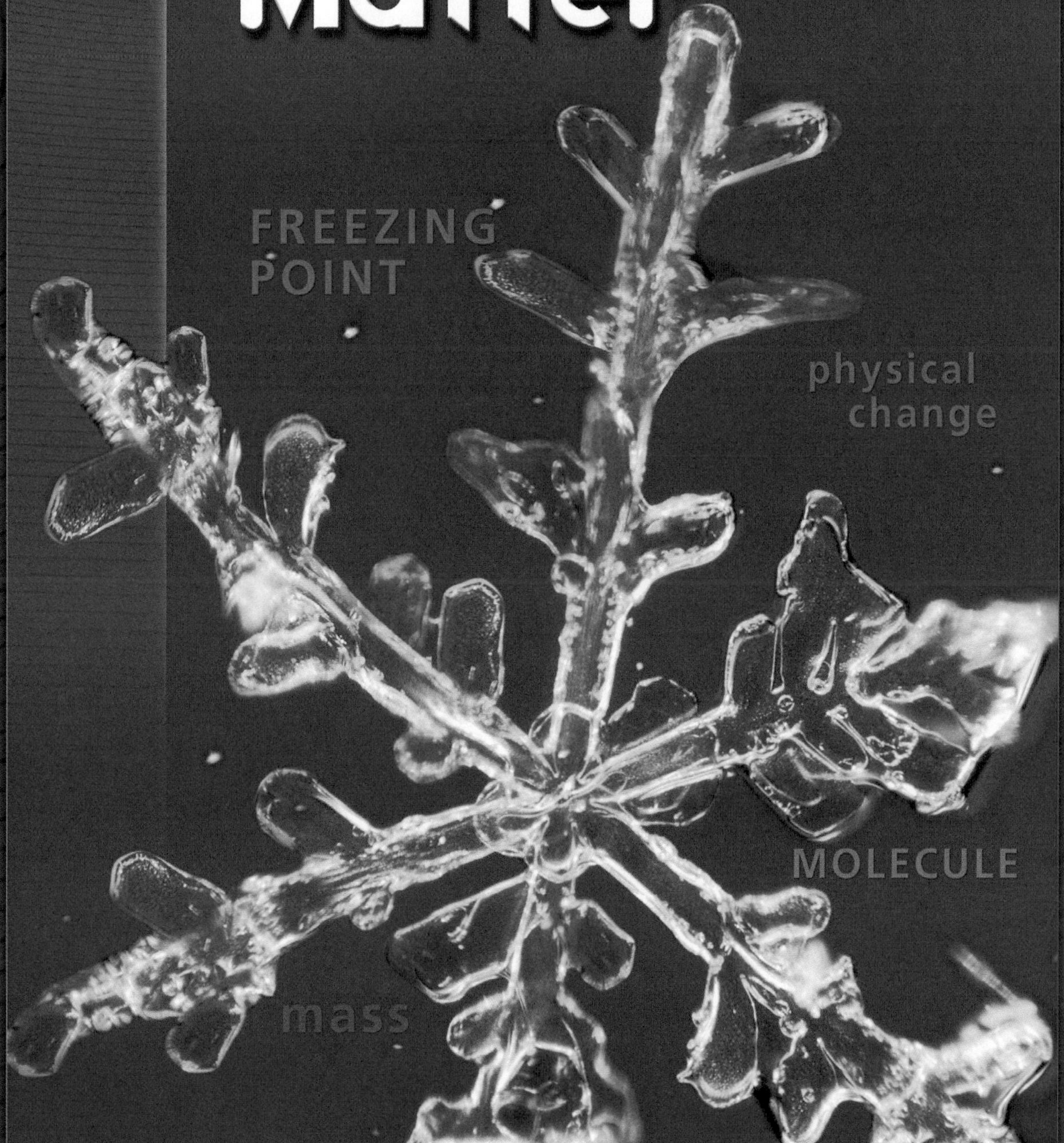
FREEZING POINT
physical change
MOLECULE
mass

Contents Overview

Frontiers in Science
Exploring the Water Planet 434

Chapter 14 Introduction to Matter 438

Chapter 15 Properties of Matter 470

Exploring the Water Planet

Technology allows scientists to see far below the ocean's surface, making exploration easier than ever before.

View the video segment "Into the Deep" to learn how scientists explore mid-ocean ridges and deep-sea vents.

A crab encounters a research submersible.

Earth's Least-Known Region

What is the least-explored region on Earth? You might guess it's a small area where few things live, perhaps in a vast desert or in high mountains. But this region covers more than 50 percent of the planet and contains almost 98 percent of its living space. It is the deep sea, the part of the ocean sunlight cannot reach, where no plants grow. The deep sea was once thought to be of little interest. Now researchers are studying the organisms living in the deep sea and mapping the resources of the sea floor. Other parts of the ocean are getting more attention, too. For example, researchers are studying how surface water carries nutrients to new areas and how the ocean affects Earth's climate.

As people explore the ocean more thoroughly, they frequently discover new organisms. Many of these organisms are being found in the deep sea. Some, though, are being found in water that is only a few meters deep. One octopus that lives in shallow tropical water was first described in 1998. This brown octopus avoids being eaten by predators by mimicking the appearances and colors of poisonous organisms. For example, the octopus slips six of its arms and much of its body into a hole on the sea floor. Then it waves its other two arms in opposite directions, which makes it look like a banded sea snake. The octopus's colors change to yellow and black, matching the snake's bands. Another organism the octopus mimics is a multicolored lionfish with its poisonous fins spread out.

An octopus (above) changes its colors and hides most of its body and all but two arms to mimic a poisonous sea snake (right).

These scale worms, first described in 1988, live only around deep-sea vents and are thought to feed on the larger tubeworms.

Exploring Deep-Sea Vents

Deep-sea vents support astonishing life forms. These organisms depend on materials dissolved in scalding hot vent water, not on sunlight, for their ultimate source of energy. The superheated vent water contains many dissolved minerals. The minerals become solid as the vent water mixes with cold ocean water. Earth's richest deposits of minerals like copper, silver, and gold may be

around some of these vents. To study the minerals that lie beneath thousands of meters of water, researchers use remotely operated devices to collect data and samples.

Exploring the Ocean and Climate

The ocean moves large amounts of heat energy between areas of Earth, affecting the atmosphere and climate. Consider that even though some parts of Alaska and Great Britain are equally close to the North Pole, Great Britain is warmer. Air over the Atlantic Ocean gains heat energy from a warm ocean current, and winds carry this warmth toward Great Britain. In addition to moving across the surface, water also mixes vertically in the ocean. The ocean contains many layers of water, with the warmest generally at the top. But the middle layers of the ocean may now be heating up quickly. Researchers are working to understand how the mixing of water in the ocean affects Earth's atmosphere and climate.

View the "Into the Deep" segment of your *Scientific American Frontiers* video to learn how scientists are exploring the deep sea.

IN THIS SCENE FROM THE VIDEO ◉ a deep-sea vent spews out superheated water that is rich in dissolved minerals.

helped prove that the mountains in a mid-ocean ridge are volcanoes.

While exploring a valley that runs along the top of a mid-ocean ridge, Ballard discovered deep-sea vents. Water that flows out of the vents is very hot and rich in minerals. Ballard was also one of the first scientists to see the giant clams, tube-

THE DEEPEST DIVES Robert Ballard has made dozens of expeditions in *Alvin*, a three-person submarine. This small vessel can dive deep below the surface to underwater mountain ranges called mid-ocean ridges. Ballard's photographs

worms, and other animals that live around the vents. Such life forms are unusual because they depend on energy from within Earth instead of energy from the Sun.

Exploring Ocean Nutrients

Some water masses move in circular or spiral patterns, as you can see in the photograph below. These spinning water masses are called eddies. Water in eddies mixes slowly with the surrounding water. An eddy that contains nutrient-rich water can drift great distances, mixing with nutrient-poor water over a long time, sometimes years. The added nutrients allow populations of tiny plantlike organisms to grow quickly. These organisms are the base of the ocean food chain, and almost all other ocean organisms depend on them. Researchers are studying how changes in the sizes and numbers of eddies affect ocean organisms. Nutrient-rich eddies may be important to fish, such as salmon, that many people eat.

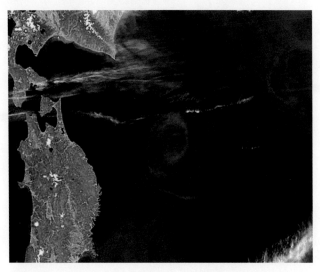

Eddies are mixing seawater from the coast of Japan with water farther from shore.

UNANSWERED Questions

Scientists who study the ocean know that much of it is yet to be explored and that many questions remain.

• How many, and what types of, ocean organisms will be discovered in the next decades?

• How do changes in ocean surface temperatures affect weather?

• What is the best way to maintain populations of fish that people depend on for food?

UNIT PROJECTS

As you study this unit, work alone or with a group on one of the projects listed below.

Track a Drop of Water

Suppose you could follow a drop of surface water as it journeys from your hometown to the ocean.

• Find out which rivers and lakes the drop would travel through, and which ocean it would join.

• Present your findings. You might make a travelogue, a map, or both.

Life in the Water

Investigate the different life forms that live in the water in your area.

• Collect water samples from different sources, such as indoor taps, fountains, puddles, marshes, lakes, and streams.

• Examine a drop from each sample under a microscope. Sketch any living organisms you see.

• Write a lab report to present your findings about the water samples.

Ocean News Report

Imagine that you are part of a news group assigned to report on major discoveries made about the world's oceans over the past 25 years.

• Research the most important or unusual facts uncovered about the oceans. Note what technology was used to gather the data.

• Prepare a special TV or Web-site report about your investigation. Where possible, include photographs or illustrations.

CAREER CENTER
CLASSZONE.COM

Learn more about careers in oceanography.

CHAPTER

14

Introduction to Matter

the BIG idea

Everything that has mass and takes up space is matter.

Key Concepts

SECTION

1 Matter has mass and volume.
Learn what mass and volume are and how to measure them.

SECTION

2 Matter is made of atoms.
Learn about the movement of atoms and molecules.

SECTION

3 Matter combines to form different substances.
Learn how atoms form compounds and mixtures.

SECTION

4 Matter exists in different physical states.
Learn how different states of matter behave.

Internet Preview

CLASSZONE.COM

Chapter 14 online resources: Content Review, two Simulations, four Resource Centers, Math Tutorial, Test Practice

What matter can you identify in this photograph?

EXPLORE the BIG idea

What Has Changed?

Blow up a balloon. Observe it. Let the air out of the balloon slowly. Observe it again.

Observe and Think Did the amount of material that makes up the balloon change? Did the amount of air inside the balloon change? How did the amount of air inside the balloon affect the size of the balloon?

Where Does the Sugar Go?

Stir some sugar into a glass of water. Observe what happens.

Observe and Think What happened to the sugar as you stirred? Do you think you would be able to separate the sugar from the water? If so, how?

Internet Activity: Scale

Go to **ClassZone.com** to explore the smallest units of matter. Start with a faraway view of an object. Then try closer and closer views until you see that object at the atomic level.

Observe and Think Are all objects seen at faraway views made up of the same parts at an atomic level? Explain your answer.

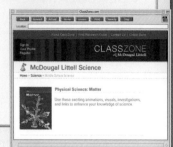

NSTA
scilinks.org
SCiLINKS

Solids, Liquids, and Gases **Code: MDL061**

Getting Ready to Learn

◀ CONCEPT REVIEW

- Matter is made of particles too small to see.
- Energy and matter change from one form to another.
- Energy cannot be created or destroyed.

◀ VOCABULARY REVIEW

See Glossary for definitions.

particle

substance

CONTENT REVIEW

CLASSZONE.COM

Review concepts and vocabulary.

▶ TAKING NOTES

MAIN IDEA AND DETAIL NOTES

Make a two-column chart. Write the main ideas, such as those in the blue headings, in the column on the left. Write details about each of those main ideas in the column on the right.

VOCABULARY STRATEGY

Write each new vocabulary term in the center of a **four square** diagram. Write notes in the squares around each term. Include a definition, some characteristics, and some examples of the term. If possible, write some things that are not examples of the term.

See the Note-Taking Handbook on pages R45–R51.

SCIENCE NOTEBOOK

MAIN IDEAS	DETAIL NOTES
1. All objects are made of matter.	1. All objects and living organisms are matter.
	1. Light and sound are not matter.
2. Mass is a measure of the amount of matter.	2. A balance can be used to compare masses.
	2. Standard unit of mass is kilogram (kg).

Definition	Characteristics
the downward pull on an object due to gravity	• standard unit is newton (N) • is measured by using a scale

WEIGHT

Examples	Nonexamples
On Earth, a 1 kg object has a weight of 9.8 N.	not the same as mass, which is a measure of how much matter an object contains

KEY CONCEPT
Matter has mass and volume.

 BEFORE, you learned

- Scientists study the world by asking questions and collecting data
- Scientists use tools such as microscopes, thermometers, and computers

 NOW, you will learn

- What matter is
- How to measure the mass of matter
- How to measure the volume of matter

VOCABULARY

matter p. 441
mass p. 442
weight p. 443
volume p. 443

EXPLORE Similar Objects

How can two similar objects differ?

PROCEDURE

① Look at the two balls but do not pick them up. Compare their sizes and shapes. Record your observations.

② Pick up each ball. Compare the way the balls feel in your hands. Record your observations.

WHAT DO YOU THINK?
How would your observation be different if the larger ball were made of foam?

MATERIALS
2 balls of different sizes

VOCABULARY
Make four square diagrams for *matter* and for *mass* in your notebook to help you understand their relationship.

All objects are made of matter.

Suppose your class takes a field trip to a museum. During the course of the day you see mammoth bones, sparkling crystals, hot-air balloons, and an astronaut's space suit. All of these things are matter.

Matter is what makes up all of the objects and living organisms in the universe. As you will see, **matter** is anything that has mass and takes up space. Your body is matter. The air that you breathe and the water that you drink are also matter. Matter makes up the materials around you. Matter is made of particles called atoms, which are too small to see. You will learn more about atoms in the next section.

Not everything is matter. Light and sound, for example, are not matter. Light does not take up space or have mass in the same way that a table does. Although air is made of atoms, a sound traveling through air is not.

 What is matter? How can you tell if something is matter?

Mass is a measure of the amount of matter.

MAIN IDEA AND DETAILS
As you read, write the blue headings on the left side of a two-column chart. Add details in the other column.

Different objects contain different amounts of matter. **Mass** is a measure of how much matter an object contains. A metal teaspoon, for example, contains more matter than a plastic teaspoon. Therefore, a metal teaspoon has a greater mass than a plastic teaspoon. An elephant has more mass than a mouse.

🔺 **CHECK YOUR READING** How are matter and mass related?

Measuring Mass

When you measure mass, you compare the mass of the object with a standard amount, or unit, of mass. The standard unit of mass is the kilogram (kg). A large grapefruit has a mass of about one-half kilogram. Smaller masses are often measured in grams (g). There are 1000 grams in a kilogram. A penny has a mass of between two and three grams.

How can you compare the masses of two objects? One way is to use a pan balance, as shown below. If two objects balance each other on a pan balance, then they contain the same amount of matter. If a basketball balances a metal block, for example, then the basketball and the block have the same mass. Beam balances work in a similar way, but instead of comparing the masses of two objects, you compare the mass of an object with a standard mass on the beam.

A bowling ball and a basketball are about the same size, but a bowling ball has more mass.

Measuring Weight

When you hold an object such as a backpack full of books, you feel it pulling down on your hands. This is because Earth's gravity pulls the backpack toward the ground. Gravity is the force that pulls two masses toward each other. In this example, the two masses are Earth and the backpack. **Weight** is the downward pull on an object due to gravity. If the pull of the backpack is strong, you would say that the backpack weighs a lot.

Weight is measured by using a scale, such as a spring scale like the one shown on the right, that tells how hard an object is pushing or pulling on it. The standard scientific unit for weight is the newton (N). A common unit for weight is the pound (lb).

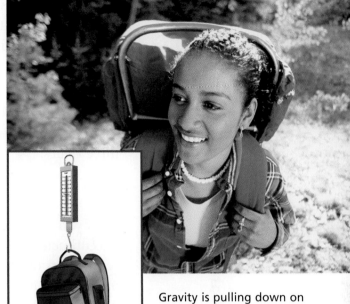

Gravity is pulling down on both the girl and the backpack. The heavier the backpack is, the stronger the pull of gravity is on it.

Mass and weight are closely related, but they are not the same. Mass describes the amount of matter an object has, and weight describes how strongly gravity is pulling on that matter. On Earth, a one-kilogram object has a weight of 9.8 newtons (2.2 lb). When a person says that one kilogram is equal to 2.2 pounds, he or she is really saying that one kilogram has a weight of 2.2 pounds on Earth. On the Moon, however, gravity is one-sixth as strong as it is on Earth. On the Moon, the one-kilogram object would have a weight of 1.6 newtons (0.36 lb). The amount of matter in the object, or its mass, is the same on Earth as it is on the Moon, but the pull of gravity is different.

SIMULATION
CLASSZONE.COM

Compare weights on different planets.

 CHECK YOUR READING What is the difference between mass and weight?

Volume is a measure of the space matter occupies.

Matter takes up space. A bricklayer stacks bricks on top of each other to build a wall. No two bricks can occupy the same place because the matter in each brick takes up space.

The amount of space that matter in an object occupies is called the object's **volume.** The bowling ball and the basketball shown on page 442 take up approximately the same amount of space. Therefore, the two balls have about the same volume. Although the basketball is hollow, it is not empty. Air fills up the space inside the basketball. Air and other gases take up space and have volume.

Determining Volume by Formula

RESOURCE CENTER
CLASSZONE.COM

Find out more about volume.

There are different ways to find the volume of an object. For objects that have well-defined shapes, such as a brick or a ball, you can take a few measurements of the object and calculate the volume by substituting these values into a formula.

A rectangular box, for example, has a length, a width, and a height that can be measured. To find the volume of the box, multiply the three values.

$$\text{Volume} = \text{length} \cdot \text{width} \cdot \text{height}$$
$$V = lwh$$

If you measure the length, the width, and the height of the box in centimeters (cm), the volume has a unit of centimeters times centimeters times centimeters, or centimeters cubed (cm^3). If the measurements are meters, the unit of volume is meters cubed (m^3). All measurements must be in the same unit to calculate volume.

Other regular solids, such as spheres and cylinders, also have formulas for calculating volumes. All formulas for volume require multiplying three dimensions. Units for volume are often expressed in terms of a length unit cubed, that is, a length to the third power.

Calculating Volume

▶ Sample Problem

What is the volume of a pizza box that is 8 cm high, 38 cm wide, and 38 cm long?

What do you know?	length = 38 cm, width = 38 cm, height = 8 cm
What do you want to find out?	Volume
Write the formula:	$V = lwh$
Substitute into the formula:	$V = 38 \text{ cm} \cdot 38 \text{ cm} \cdot 8 \text{ cm}$
Calculate and simplify:	$11{,}552 \text{ cm} \cdot \text{cm} \cdot \text{cm} = 11{,}552 \text{ cm}^3$
Check that your units agree:	Unit is cm^3. Unit of volume is cm^3. Units agree.
Answer:	$11{,}552 \text{ cm}^3$

▶ Practice the Math

1. A bar of gold is 10 cm long, 5 cm wide, and 7 cm high. What is its volume?
2. What is the volume of a large block of wood that is 1 m long, 0.5 m high, and 50 cm wide?

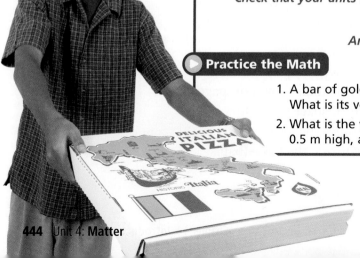

Measuring Volume by Displacement

Although a box has a regular shape, a rock does not. There is no simple formula for calculating the volume of something with an irregular shape. Instead, you can make use of the fact that two objects cannot be in the same place at the same time. This method of measuring is called displacement.

1 Add water to a graduated cylinder. Note the volume of the water by reading the water level on the cylinder.

2 Submerge the irregular object in the water. Because the object and the water cannot share the same space, the water is displaced, or moved upward. Note the new volume of the water with the object in it.

3 Subtract the volume of the water before you added the object from the volume of the water and the object together. The result is the volume of the object. The object displaces a volume of water equal to the volume of the object.

You measure the volume of a liquid by measuring how much space it takes up in a container. The volume of a liquid usually is measured in liters (L) or milliliters (mL). One liter is equal to 1000 milliliters. Milliliters and cubic centimeters are equivalent. This can be written as $1 \text{ mL} = 1 \text{ cm}^3$. If you had a box with a volume of one cubic centimeter and you filled it with water, you would have one milliliter of water.

In the first photograph, the graduated cylinder contains 50 mL of water. Placing a rock in the cylinder causes the water level to rise from 50 mL to 55 mL. The difference is 5 mL; therefore, the volume of the rock is 5 cm^3.

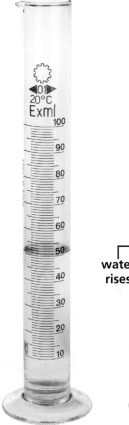

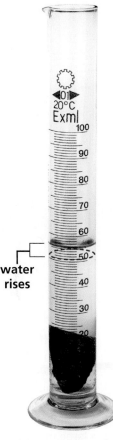

water rises

Measure the volume of water without the rock.

Measure the volume of water with the rock in it.

14.1 Review

KEY CONCEPTS

1. Give three examples of matter.
2. What do weight and mass measure?
3. How can you measure the volume of an object that has an irregular shape?

CRITICAL THINKING

4. **Calculate** What is the volume of a box that is 12 cm long, 6 cm wide, and 4 cm high?
5. **Synthesize** What is the relationship between the units of measurement for the volume of a liquid and of a solid object?

⚠ CHALLENGE

6. **Infer** Why might a small increase in the dimensions of an object cause a large change in its volume?

CHAPTER INVESTIGATION

Mass and Volume

OVERVIEW AND PURPOSE In order for scientists around the world to communicate with one another about calculations in their research, they use a common system of measurement called the metric system. Scientists use the same tools and methods for the measurement of length, mass, and volume. In this investigation you will

- use a ruler, a graduated cylinder, and a balance to measure the mass and the volume of different objects
- determine which method is best for measuring the volume of the objects

▶ Procedure

1. Make a data table like the one shown on the sample notebook page.

2. Measure the mass of each object: rock, pennies, sponge, and tissue box. Record each mass.

step 2

3. For each object, conduct three trials for mass. Average the trials to find a final mass measurement.

4. Decide how you will find the volume of each object.

   For rectangular objects, you will use the following formula:

   Volume = length • width • height

   For irregular objects, you will use the displacement method and the following formula:

   Volume of object = volume of water with object – volume of water without object

MATERIALS
- small rock
- 5 pennies
- rectangular sponge
- tissue box
- beam balance
- large graduated cylinder
- water
- ruler

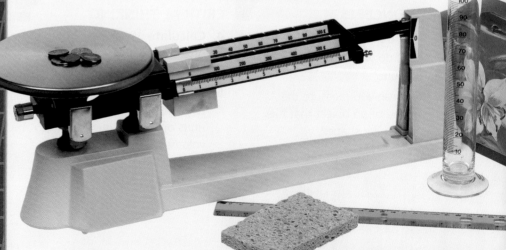

5 For each object, you will conduct three trials for measuring volume. Average the trials to find a final volume measurement.

6 For rectangular objects, use metric units for measuring the length, width, and height. Record the measurements in your data table.

step 6

7 For irregular objects, fill the graduated cylinder about half full with water. Record the exact volume of water in the cylinder. **Note:** The surface of the liquid will be curved in the graduated cylinder. Read the volume of the liquid at the bottom of the curve called the meniscus.

step 7

8 Carefully place the object you are measuring into the cylinder. The object must be completely under the water. Record the exact volume of water in the cylinder containing the object by reading the meniscus.

Observe and Analyze
Write It Up

1. **RECORD OBSERVATIONS** Make sure you have filled out your data table completely.

2. **INTERPRET** For each object, explain why you chose a particular method for measuring the volume.

1. **IDENTIFY LIMITS** Which sources of error might have affected your measurements?

2. **APPLY** Doctors need to know the mass of a patient before deciding how much of a medication to prescribe. Why is it important to measure each patient's mass before prescribing medicine?

3. **APPLY** Scientists in the United States work closely with scientists in other countries to develop new technology. What are the advantages of having a single system of measurement?

INVESTIGATE Further

CHALLENGE Measuring cups and spoons used in cooking often include both customary and metric units. Convert the measurements in a favorite recipe into metric units. Convert the amounts of solid ingredients to grams, and liquid ingredients to milliliters or liters. If possible, use the new measurements to follow the recipe and prepare the food. Were your conversions accurate?

Mass and Volume

Observe and Analyze

Table 1. Masses of Various Objects

Object	Mass (g)			Average
	Trial 1	Trial 2	Trial 3	
rock				
5 pennies				
sponge				
tissue box				

Table 2. Volumes of Various Objects

Object	Method Used	Volume (cm³ or mL)			
		Trial 1	Trial 2	Trial 3	Average
rock					
5 pennies					
sponge					
tissue box					

Matter is made of atoms.

STANDARDS

7–5.1 Recognize that matter is composed of extremely small particles called atoms.

VOCABULARY

atom p. 448
molecule p. 450

◀ **BEFORE,** you learned

- Matter has mass
- Matter has volume

▶ **NOW,** you will learn

- About the smallest particles of matter
- How atoms combine into molecules
- How atoms and molecules move

THINK ABOUT

How small is an atom?

All matter is made up of very tiny particles called atoms. It is hard to imagine exactly how small these particles are. Suppose that each of the particles making up the pin shown in the photograph on the right were actually the size of the round head on the pin. How large would the pin be in that case? If you could stick such a pin in the ground, it would cover about 90 square miles—about one-seventh the area of London, England. It would also be about 80 miles high—almost 15 times the height of Mount Everest.

Atoms are extremely small.

VOCABULARY
Make a four square diagram for *atom* that includes details that will help you remember the term.

How small can things get? If you break a stone wall into smaller and smaller pieces, you would have a pile of smaller stones. If you could break the smaller stones into the smallest pieces possible, you would have a pile of atoms. An **atom** is the smallest basic unit of matter.

The idea that all matter is made of extremely tiny particles dates back to the fifth century B.C., when Greek philosophers proposed the first atomic theory of matter. All matter, they said, was made of only a few different types of tiny particles called atoms. The different arrangements of atoms explained the differences among the substances that make up the world. Although the modern view of the atom is different from the ancient view, the idea of atoms as basic building blocks has been confirmed. Today scientists have identified more than 100 different types of atoms.

CHECK YOUR READING What are atoms? How are they like building blocks?

Atoms

It is hard to imagine that visible matter is composed of particles too tiny to see. Although you cannot see an individual atom, you are constantly seeing large collections of them. You are a collection of atoms. So are your textbook, a desk, and all the other matter around you. Matter is not something that contains atoms; matter is atoms. A desk, for example, is a collection of atoms and the empty space between those atoms. Without the atoms, there would be no desk—just empty space.

Atoms are so small that they cannot be seen even with very strong optical microscopes. Try to imagine the size of an atom by considering that a single teaspoonful of water contains approximately 500,000,000,000,000,000,000,000 atoms. Although atoms are extremely small, they do have a mass. The mass of a single teaspoonful of water is about 5 grams. This mass is equal to the mass of all the atoms that the water is made of added together.

READING TiP

The word *atom* comes from the Greek word *atomos*, meaning "indivisible," or "cannot be divided."

INVESTIGATE Mass

How do you measure the mass of an atom?

PROCEDURE

1. Find the mass of the empty beaker. Record your result.

2. Place 10 pennies into the beaker. Find the mass of the beaker with the pennies in it. Record your result.

3. Subtract the mass of the empty beaker from the mass of the beaker with the pennies. Record your result.

4. Divide the difference in mass by 10. Record your result.

WHAT DO YOU THINK?

• What is the mass of one penny? What assumptions do you make when you answer this question?

• How might scientists use a similar process to find the mass of a single atom?

CHALLENGE All pennies may not be the same. After years of use, some pennies may have had some of their metal rubbed away. Also, the materials that make up pennies have changed. Find the individual mass of several pennies and compare the masses. Do all pennies have exactly the same mass?

SKILL FOCUS
Modeling

MATERIALS
• beam balance
• beaker
• 10 pennies

TIME
20 minutes

Molecules

When two or more atoms bond together, or combine, they make a particle called a **molecule.** A molecule can be made of atoms that are different or atoms that are alike. A molecule of water, for example, is a combination of different atoms—two hydrogen atoms and one oxygen atom (also written as H_2O). Hydrogen gas molecules are made of the same atom—two hydrogen atoms bonded together.

A molecule is the smallest amount of a substance made of combined atoms that is considered to be that substance. Think about what would happen if you tried to divide water to find its smallest part. Ultimately you would reach a single molecule of water. What would you have if you divided this molecule into its individual atoms of hydrogen and oxygen? If you break up a water molecule, it is no longer water. Instead, you would have hydrogen and oxygen, two different substances.

CHECK YOUR READING How is a molecule related to an atom?

The droplets of water in this spider web are made of water molecules. Each molecule contains two hydrogen atoms (shown in white) and one oxygen atom (shown in red).

hydrogen
oxygen
water

Molecules can be made up of different numbers of atoms. For example, carbon monoxide is a molecule that is composed of one carbon atom and one oxygen atom. Molecules also can be composed of a large number of atoms. The most common type of vitamin E molecule, for example, contains 29 carbon atoms, 50 hydrogen atoms, and 2 oxygen atoms.

Molecules made of different numbers of the same atom are different substances. For example, an oxygen gas molecule is made of two oxygen atoms bonded together. Ozone is also composed of oxygen atoms, but an ozone molecule is three oxygen atoms bonded together. The extra oxygen atom gives ozone properties that are different from those of oxygen gas.

oxygen   **ozone**

This photograph shows the interior of Grand Central Terminal in New York City. Light from the window reflects off dust particles that are being moved by the motion of the molecules in air.

Atoms and molecules are always in motion.

If you have ever looked at a bright beam of sunlight, you may have seen dust particles floating in the air. If you were to watch carefully, you might notice that the dust does not fall toward the floor but instead seems to dart about in all different directions. Molecules in air are constantly moving and hitting the dust particles. Because the molecules are moving in many directions, they collide with the dust particles from different directions. This action causes the darting motion of the dust that you observe.

Atoms and molecules are always in motion. Sometimes this motion is easy to observe, such as when you see evidence of molecules in air bouncing dust particles around. Water molecules move too. When you place a drop of food coloring into water, the motion of the water molecules eventually causes the food coloring to spread throughout the water.

The motion of individual atoms and molecules is hard to observe in solid objects, such as a table. The atoms and molecules in a table cannot move about freely like the ones in water and air. However, the atoms and molecules in a table are constantly moving—by shaking back and forth, or by twisting—even if they stay in the same place.

14.2 Review

KEY CONCEPTS

1. What are atoms?
2. What is the smallest particle of a substance that is still considered to be that substance?
3. Why do dust particles in the air appear to be moving in different directions?

CRITICAL THINKING

4. **Apply** How does tea flavor spread from a tea bag throughout a cup of hot water?
5. **Infer** If a water molecule (H_2O) has two hydrogen atoms and one oxygen atom, how would you describe the make-up of a carbon dioxide molecule (CO_2)?

⬥ CHALLENGE

6. **Synthesize** Assume that a water balloon has the same number of water molecules as a helium balloon has helium atoms. If the mass of the water is 4.5 times greater than the mass of the helium, how does the mass of a water molecule compare with the mass of a helium atom?

Particles Too Small to See

Atoms are so small that you cannot see them through an ordinary microscope. In fact, millions of them could fit in the period at the end of this sentence. Scientists can make images of atoms, however, using an instrument called a scanning tunneling microscope (STM).

Bumps on a Surface

The needle of the scanning tunneling microscope has a very sharp tip that is only one atom wide. The tip is brought close to the surface of the material being observed, and an electric current is applied to the tip. The microscope measures the interaction between the electrically charged needle tip and the nearest atom on the surface of the material. An image of the surface is created by moving the needle just above the surface. The image appears as a series of bumps that shows where the atoms are located. The result is similar to a contour map.

Moving Atoms

Scientists also can use the tip of the STM needle to move atoms on a surface. The large image at left is an STM image of a structure made by pushing individual atoms into place on a very smooth metal surface. This structure was designed as a corral to trap individual atoms inside.

Scientists can manipulate individual atoms to build structures, such as this one made of iron atoms.

Tiny Pieces of Matter

- Images of atoms did not exist until 1970.

- Atoms are so small that a single raindrop contains more than 500 billion trillion atoms.

- If each atom were the size of a pea, your fingerprint would be larger than Alaska.

- In the space between stars, matter is so spread out that a volume of one liter contains only about 1000 atoms.

needle
material
tip of needle
atoms of material

An STM maps the position of atoms using a needle with a tip that is one atom wide.

EXPLORE

1. **INFER** Why must the tip of a scanning tunneling microscope be only one atom wide to make an image of atoms on a surface?

2. **CHALLENGE** Find out more about images of atoms on the Internet. How are STM images used in research to design better materials?

RESOURCE CENTER
CLASSZONE.COM
Find more images from scanning tunneling microscopes.

14.3

KEY CONCEPT
Matter combines to form different substances.

McDougal Littell Science
SOUTH CAROLINA

STANDARDS

7–5.2 Classify matter as element, compound, or mixture on the basis of its composition.

VOCABULARY

element p. 454
compound p. 455
mixture p. 455

◀ BEFORE, you learned	▶ NOW, you will learn
• Matter is made of tiny particles called atoms • Atoms combine to form molecules	• How pure matter and mixed matter are different • How atoms and elements are related • How atoms form compounds

---

EXPLORE Mixed Substances

What happens when substances are mixed?

PROCEDURE

① Observe and describe a teaspoon of cornstarch and a teaspoon of water.

② Mix the two substances together in the cup. Observe and describe the result.

WHAT DO YOU THINK?

• After you mixed the substances, could you still see each substance?
• How was the new substance different from the original substances?

MATERIALS
• cornstarch
• water
• small cup
• spoon

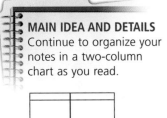

MAIN IDEA AND DETAILS
Continue to organize your notes in a two-column chart as you read.

Matter can be pure or mixed.

Matter can be pure, or it can be two or more substances mixed together. Most of the substances you see around you are mixed, although you can't always tell that by looking at them. For example, the air you breathe is a combination of several substances. Wood, paper, steel, and lemonade are all mixed substances.

You might think that the water that you drink from a bottle or from the tap is a pure substance. However, drinking water has minerals dissolved in it and chemicals added to it that you cannot see. Often the difference between pure and mixed substances is apparent only on the atomic or molecular level.

A pure substance has only one type of component. For example, pure water contains only water molecules. Pure silver contains only silver atoms. Coins and jewelry that look like silver are often made of silver in combination with other metals.

REMINDER

A molecule consists of two or more atoms that are bonded together.

If you could look at the atoms in a bar of pure gold, you would find only gold atoms. If you looked at the atoms in a container of pure water, you would find water molecules, which are a combination of hydrogen and oxygen atoms. Does the presence of two types of atoms mean that water is not really a pure substance after all?

A substance is considered pure if it contains only a single type of atom, such as gold, or a single combination of atoms that are bonded together, such as a water molecule. Because the hydrogen and oxygen atoms are bonded together as molecules, water that has nothing else in it is considered a pure substance.

Elements

One type of pure substance is an element. An **element** is a substance that contains only a single type of atom. The number of atoms is not important as long as all the atoms are of the same type. You cannot separate an element into other substances.

You are probably familiar with many elements, such as silver, oxygen, hydrogen, helium, and aluminum. There are as many elements as there are types of atoms—more than 100. You can see the orderly arrangement of atoms in the element gold, on the left below.

CHECK YOUR READING   Why is an element considered to be a pure substance?

Element: Gold

The atoms in gold are all the same type of atom. Therefore, gold is an element.

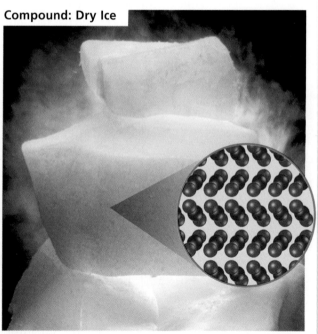

Compound: Dry Ice

Dry ice is frozen carbon dioxide, a compound. Each molecule is made of one carbon atom and two oxygen atoms.

Compounds

A **compound** is a substance that consists of two or more different types of atoms bonded together. A large variety of substances can be made by combining different types of atoms to make different compounds. Some types of compounds are made of molecules, such as water and carbon dioxide, shown on page 454. Other compounds are made of atoms that are bonded together in a different way. Table salt is an example.

A compound can have very different properties from the individual elements that make up that compound. Pure table salt is a common compound that is a combination of sodium and chlorine. Although table salt is safe to eat, the individual elements that go into making it—sodium and chlorine—are poisonous.

 What is the relationship between atoms and a compound?

Mixtures

Most of the matter around you is a mixture of different substances. Seawater, for instance, contains water, salt, and other minerals mixed together. Your blood is a mixture of blood cells and plasma. Plasma is also a mixture, made up of water, sugar, fat, protein, salts, and minerals.

A **mixture** is a combination of different substances that remain the same individual substances and can be separated by physical means. For example, if you mix apples, oranges, and bananas to make a fruit salad, you do not change the different fruits into a new kind of fruit. Mixtures do not always contain the same amount of the various substances. For example, depending on how the salad is made, the amount of each type of fruit it contains will vary.

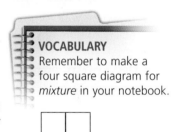

VOCABULARY
Remember to make a four square diagram for *mixture* in your notebook.

APPLY In what ways can a city population be considered a mixture?

How well do oil and water mix?

PROCEDURE

① Add a few drops of food coloring to the water in the beaker. Swirl the water around in the beaker until the water is evenly colored throughout.

② Pour the colored water from the beaker into the jar until the jar is about one-fourth full.

③ Add the same amount of vegetable oil to the jar. Screw the lid tightly on the jar.

④ Carefully shake the jar several times with your hand over the cover, and then set it on the table. Observe and record what happens to the liquids in the jar.

⑤ Turn the jar upside down and hold it that way. Observe what happens to the liquids and record your observations.

WHAT DO YOU THINK?

- Does water mix with food coloring? What evidence supports your answer?
- Do water and oil mix? What evidence supports your answer?
- What happened when you turned the jar upside down?
- Based on your observations, what can you infer about the ability of different liquids to mix?

CHALLENGE To clean greasy dishes, you add soap to the dishwater. Try adding soap to your mixture. What does the soap do?

SKILL FOCUS
Inferring

MATERIALS
- food coloring
- beaker of water
- jar with lid
- vegetable oil
for Challenge:
- dish soap

TIME
20 minutes

Comparing Mixtures and Compounds

RESOURCE CENTER
CLASSZONE.COM

Find out more about mixtures.

Although mixtures and compounds may seem similar, they are very different. Consider how mixtures and compounds compare with each other.

- The substances in mixtures remain the same substances. Compounds are new substances formed by atoms that bond together.

- Mixtures can be separated by physical means. Compounds can be separated only by breaking the bonds between atoms.

- The proportions of different substances in a mixture can vary throughout the mixture or from mixture to mixture. The proportions of different substances in a compound are fixed because the type and number of atoms that make up a basic unit of the compound are always the same.

CHECK YOUR READING How is a mixture different from a compound?

Parts of mixtures can be the same or different throughout.

It is obvious that something is a mixture when you can see the different substances in it. For example, if you scoop up a handful of soil, you might see that it contains dirt, small rocks, leaves, and even insects. You can separate the soil into its different parts.

Exactly what you see depends on what part of the soil you scoop up. One handful of soil might have more pebbles or insects in it than another handful would. There are many mixtures, such as soil, that have different properties in different areas of the mixture. Such a mixture is called a hetero-geneous (HEHT-uhr-uh-JEE-nee-uhs) mixture.

In some types of mixtures, however, you cannot see the individual substances. For example, if you mix sugar into a cup of water and stir it well, the sugar seems to disappear. You can tell that the sugar is still there because the water tastes sweet, but you cannot see the sugar or easily separate it out again.

When substances are evenly spread throughout a mixture, you cannot tell one part of the mixture from another part. For instance, one drop of sugar water will be almost exactly like any other drop. Such a mixture is called a homogeneous (HOH-muh-JEE-nee-uhs) mixture. Homogenized milk is processed so that it becomes a homogeneous mixture of water and milk fat. Milk that has not been homogenized will separate—most of the milk fat will float to the top as cream while leaving the rest of the milk low in fat.

READING TIP

The prefix *hetero* means "different," and the prefix *homo* means "same." The Greek root *genos* means "kind."

14.3 Review

KEY CONCEPTS

1. What is the difference between pure and mixed matter?
2. How are atoms and elements related?
3. How are compounds different from mixtures?

CRITICAL THINKING

4. **Infer** What can you infer about the size of sugar particles that are dissolved in a mixture of sugar and water?
5. **Infer** Why is it easier to remove the ice cubes from cold lemonade than it is to remove the sugar?

⬥ CHALLENGE

6. **Apply** A unit of sulfuric acid is a molecule of 2 atoms of hydrogen, 1 atom of sulfur, and 4 atoms of oxygen. How many of each type of atom are there in 2 molecules of sulfuric acid?

MATH in SCIENCE

MATH TUTORIAL
CLASSZONE.COM
Click on Math Tutorial for more help with circle graphs.

A Mixture of Spices

Two different mixtures of spices may contain the exact same ingredients but have very different flavors. For example, a mixture of cumin, nutmeg, and ginger powder can be made using more cumin than ginger, or it can be made using more ginger than cumin.

One way to show how much of each substance a mixture contains is to use a circle graph. A circle graph is a visual way to show how a quantity is divided into different parts. A circle graph represents quantities as parts of a whole.

Example

Make a circle graph to represent a spice mixture that is 1/2 cumin, 1/3 nutmeg, and 1/6 ginger.

(1) To find the angle measure for each sector of the circle graph, multiply each fraction in your mixture by 360°.

Cumin: $\frac{1}{2} \cdot 360° = 180°$

Nutmeg: $\frac{1}{3} \cdot 360° = 120°$

Ginger: $\frac{1}{6} \cdot 360° = 60°$

(2) Use a compass to draw a circle. Use a protractor to draw the angle for each sector.

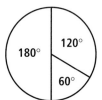

(3) Label each sector and give your graph a title.

ANSWER

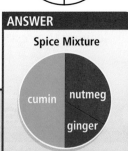

Spice Mixture

Answer the following questions.

1. Draw a circle graph representing a spice mixture that is 1/2 ginger, 1/4 cumin, and 1/4 crushed red pepper.

2. A jeweler creates a ring that is 3/4 gold, 3/16 silver, and 1/16 copper. Draw a circle graph representing the mixture of metals in the ring.

3. Draw a circle graph representing a mixture that is 1/5 sand, 2/5 water, and 2/5 salt.

CHALLENGE Dry air is a mixture of about 78 percent nitrogen, 21 percent oxygen, and 1 percent other elements. Create a circle graph representing the elements found in air.

KEY CONCEPT
Matter exists in different physical states.

SOUTH CAROLINA
McDougal Littell Science

STANDARDS

7–5.10 Compare physical changes (including changes in size, shape, and state) to chemical changes that are the result of chemical reactions (including changes in color or temperature and formation of a precipitate or gas).

VOCABULARY

states of matter p. 459
solid p. 460
liquid p. 460
gas p. 460

◀ **BEFORE, you learned**

- Matter has mass
- Matter is made of atoms
- Atoms and molecules in matter are always moving

▶ **NOW, you will learn**

- About the different states of matter
- How the different states of matter behave

EXPLORE Solids and Liquids

How do solids and liquids compare?

PROCEDURE

① Observe the water, ice, and marble. Pick them up and feel them. Can you change their shape? their volume?

② Record your observations. Compare and contrast each object with the other two.

WHAT DO YOU THINK?

- How are the ice and the water in the cup similar? How are they different?
- How are the ice and the marble similar? How are they different?

MATERIALS
- water in a cup
- ice cube
- marble
- pie tin

Particle arrangement and motion determine the state of matter.

When you put water in a freezer, the water freezes into a solid (ice). When you place an ice cube on a warm plate, the ice melts into liquid water again. If you leave the plate in the sun, the water becomes water vapor. Ice, water, and water vapor are made of exactly the same type of molecule—a molecule of two hydrogen atoms and one oxygen atom. What, then, makes them different?

Ice, water, and water vapor are different states of water. **States of matter** are the different forms in which matter can exist. The three familiar states are solid, liquid, and gas. When a substance changes from one state to another, the molecules in the substance do not change. However, the arrangement of the molecules does change, giving each state of matter its own characteristics.

Solid, liquid, and gas are common states of matter.

MAIN IDEA AND DETAILS
Remember to organize your notes in a two-column chart as you read.

A substance can exist as a solid, a liquid, or a gas. The state of a substance depends on the space between its particles and on the way in which the particles move. The illustration on page 461 shows how particles are arranged in the three different states.

① A **solid** is a substance that has a fixed volume and a fixed shape. In a solid, the particles are close together and usually form a regular pattern. Particles in a solid can vibrate but are fixed in one place. Because each particle is attached to several others, individual particles cannot move from one location to another, and the solid is rigid.

② A **liquid** has a fixed volume but does not have a fixed shape. Liquids take on the shape of the container they are in. The particles in a liquid are attracted to one another and are close together. However, particles in a liquid are not fixed in place and can move from one place to another.

③ A **gas** has no fixed volume or shape. A gas can take on both the shape and the volume of a container. Gas particles are not close to one another and can move easily in any direction. There is much more space between gas particles than there is between particles in a liquid or a solid. The space between gas particles can increase or decrease with changes in temperature and pressure.

 CHECK YOUR READING Describe two differences between a solid and a gas.

The particles in a solid are usually closer together than the particles in a liquid. For example, the particles in solid steel are closer together than the particles in molten—or melted—steel. However, water is an important exception. The molecules that make up ice actually have more space between them than the molecules in liquid water do.

The fact that the molecules in ice are farther apart than the molecules in liquid water has important consequences for life on Earth. Because there is more space between its molecules, ice floats on liquid water. By contrast, a piece of solid steel would not float in molten steel but would sink to the bottom.

Because ice floats, it remains on the surface of rivers and lakes when they freeze. The ice layer helps insulate the water and slow down the freezing process. Animals living in rivers and lakes can survive in the liquid water layer below the ice layer.

States of Matter

Matter can exist in different states. The state of matter depends on the arrangement and motion of the particles.

① Solid

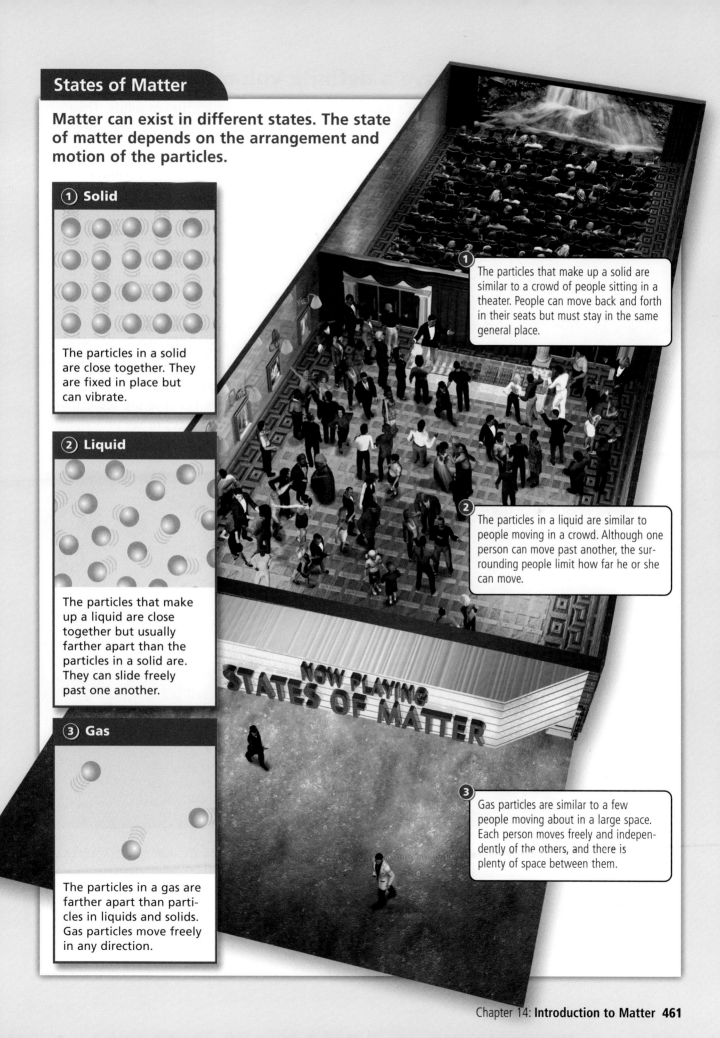

The particles in a solid are close together. They are fixed in place but can vibrate.

② Liquid

The particles that make up a liquid are close together but usually farther apart than the particles in a solid are. They can slide freely past one another.

③ Gas

The particles in a gas are farther apart than particles in liquids and solids. Gas particles move freely in any direction.

① The particles that make up a solid are similar to a crowd of people sitting in a theater. People can move back and forth in their seats but must stay in the same general place.

② The particles in a liquid are similar to people moving in a crowd. Although one person can move past another, the surrounding people limit how far he or she can move.

③ Gas particles are similar to a few people moving about in a large space. Each person moves freely and independently of the others, and there is plenty of space between them.

NOW PLAYING
STATES OF MATTER

Solids have a definite volume and shape.

REMINDER

Volume is the amount of space that an object occupies.

A piece of ice, a block of wood, and a ceramic cup are solids. They have shapes that do not change and volumes that can be measured. Any matter that is a solid has a definite shape and a definite volume.

The molecules in a solid are in fixed positions and are close together. Although the molecules can still vibrate, they cannot move from one part of the solid to another part. As a result, a solid does not easily change its shape or its volume. If you force the molecules apart, you can change the shape and the volume of a solid by breaking it into pieces. However, each of those pieces will still be a solid and have its own particular shape and volume.

The particles in some solids, such as ice or table salt, occur in a very regular pattern. The pattern of the water molecules in ice, for example, can be seen when you look at a snowflake like the one shown below. The water molecules in a snowflake are arranged in hexagonal shapes that are layered on top of one another. Because the molecular pattern has six sides, snowflakes form with six sides or six points. Salt also has a regular structure, although it takes a different shape.

The particles in many solids, such as the water molecules in this snowflake, have a regular pattern.

Not all solids have regular shapes in the same way that ice and salt do, however. Some solids, such as plastic or glass, have particles that are not arranged in a regular pattern.

 CHECK YOUR READING What two characteristics are needed for a substance to be a solid?

Liquids have a definite volume but no definite shape.

Water, milk, and oil are liquids. A liquid has a definite volume but does not have a definite shape. The volume of a certain amount of oil can be measured, but the shape that the oil takes depends on what container it is in. If the oil is in a tall, thin container, it has a tall, thin shape. If it is in a short, wide container, it has a short, wide shape. Liquids take the shape of their containers.

The molecules in a liquid are close together, but they are not tightly attached to one another as the molecules in a solid are. Instead, molecules in liquids can move independently. As a result, liquids can flow. Instead of having a rigid form, the molecules in a liquid move and fill the bottom of the container they are in.

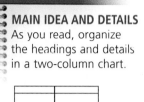

MAIN IDEA AND DETAILS
As you read, organize the headings and details in a two-column chart.

 How is a liquid different from a solid?

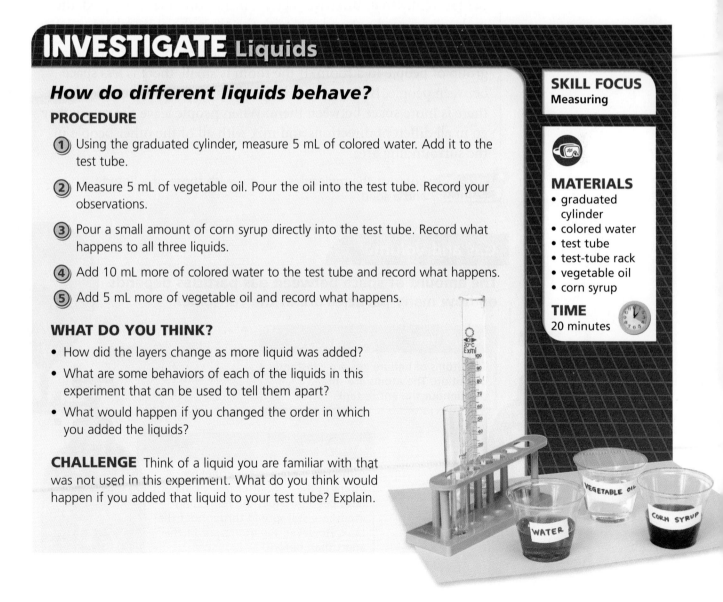

INVESTIGATE Liquids

How do different liquids behave?

PROCEDURE

1. Using the graduated cylinder, measure 5 mL of colored water. Add it to the test tube.

2. Measure 5 mL of vegetable oil. Pour the oil into the test tube. Record your observations.

3. Pour a small amount of corn syrup directly into the test tube. Record what happens to all three liquids.

4. Add 10 mL more of colored water to the test tube and record what happens.

5. Add 5 mL more of vegetable oil and record what happens.

WHAT DO YOU THINK?

- How did the layers change as more liquid was added?
- What are some behaviors of each of the liquids in this experiment that can be used to tell them apart?
- What would happen if you changed the order in which you added the liquids?

CHALLENGE Think of a liquid you are familiar with that was not used in this experiment. What do you think would happen if you added that liquid to your test tube? Explain.

SKILL FOCUS
Measuring

MATERIALS
- graduated cylinder
- colored water
- test tube
- test-tube rack
- vegetable oil
- corn syrup

TIME
20 minutes

Gases have no definite volume or shape.

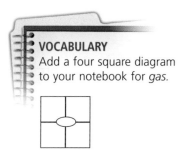
The air that you breathe, the helium in a balloon, and the neon inside the tube in a neon light are gases. A gas is a substance with no definite volume and no definite shape. Solids and liquids have volumes that do not change easily. If you have a container filled with one liter of a liquid that you pour into a two-liter container, the liquid will occupy only half of the new container. A gas, on the other hand, has a volume that changes to match the volume of its container.

Gas Composition

The molecules in a gas are very far apart compared with the molecules in a solid or a liquid. The amount of space between the molecules in a gas can change easily. If a rigid container—one that cannot change its shape—has a certain amount of air and more air is pumped in, the volume of the gas does not change. However, there is less space between the molecules than there was before. If the container is opened, the molecules spread out and mix with the air in the atmosphere.

As you saw, gas molecules in a container can be compared to a group of people in a room. If the room is small, there is less space between people. If the room is large, people can spread out so that there is more space between them. When people leave the room, they go in all different directions and mix with all of the other people in the surrounding area.

 CHECK YOUR READING   Contrast the molecules in a gas with those of a liquid and a solid.

Gas and Volume

The amount of space between gas particles depends on how many particles are in the container.

Before Use

The atoms of helium gas are constantly in motion. The atoms are spread throughout the entire tank.

After Use

Although there are fewer helium atoms in the tank after many balloons have been inflated, the remaining atoms are still spread throughout the tank. However, the atoms are farther apart than before.

Gas Behavior

Because gas molecules are always in motion, they are continually hitting one another and the sides of any container they may be in. As the molecules bounce off one another and the surfaces of the container, they apply a pressure against the container. You can feel the effects of gas pressure if you pump air into a bicycle tire. The more air you put into the tire, the harder it feels because more gas molecules are pressing the tire outward.

SIMULATION
CLASSZONE.COM

Explore the behavior of a gas.

The speed at which gas molecules move depends on the temperature of the gas. Gas molecules move faster at higher temperatures than at lower temperatures. The volume, pressure, and temperature of a gas are related to one another, and changing one can change the others.

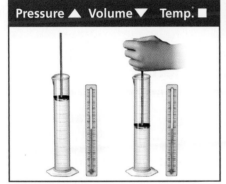

Pressure ▲ Volume ▼ Temp. ■

If the temperature of a gas stays the same, increasing the pressure of the gas decreases its volume.

Pressure ▲ Volume ■ Temp. ▲

If the volume of a gas stays the same, increasing the temperature of the gas also increases the pressure.

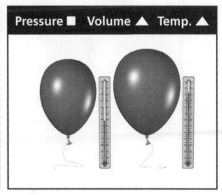

Pressure ■ Volume ▲ Temp. ▲

If the pressure of a gas stays the same, increasing the temperature of the gas also increases the volume.

In nature, volume, pressure, and temperature may all be changing at the same time. By studying how gas behaves when one property is kept constant, scientists can predict how gas will behave when all three properties change.

14.4 Review

KEY CONCEPTS

1. What are the characteristics of the three familiar states of matter?

2. How can you change the shape and volume of a liquid?

3. How does gas behave inside a closed container?

CRITICAL THINKING

4. **Infer** What happens to a liquid that is not in a container?

5. **Synthesize** What is the relationship between the temperature and the volume of a gas?

⚠ CHALLENGE

6. **Synthesize** Can an oxygen canister ever be half empty? Explain.

14 Chapter Review

the BIG idea

Everything that has mass and takes up space is matter.

CONTENT REVIEW
CLASSZONE.COM

KEY CONCEPTS SUMMARY

1 **Matter has mass and volume.**

Mass is a measure of how much matter an object contains.

Volume is the measure of the amount of space matter occupies.

VOCABULARY
matter p. 441
mass p. 442
weight p. 443
volume p. 443

---

2 **Matter is made of atoms.**

 An atom is the smallest basic unit of matter. Two or more atoms bonded together form a molecule. Atoms and molecules are always in motion.

VOCABULARY
atom p. 448
molecule p. 450

---

3 **Matter combines to form different substances.**

Matter can be pure, such as an element (gold), or a compound (water).

Matter can be a mixture. Mixtures contain two or more pure substances.

VOCABULARY
element p. 454
compound p. 455
mixture p. 455

---

4 **Matter exists in different physical states.**

 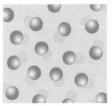 

Solids have a fixed volume and a fixed shape.

Liquids have a fixed volume but no fixed shape.

Gases have no fixed volume and no fixed shape.

VOCABULARY
states of matter p. 459
solid p. 460
liquid p. 460
gas p. 460

Reviewing Vocabulary

Copy and complete the chart below. If the right column is blank, give a brief description or definition. If the left column is blank, give the correct term.

Term	Description
1.	the downward pull of gravity on an object
2. liquid	
3.	the smallest basic unit of matter
4. solid	
5.	state of matter with no fixed volume and no fixed shape
6.	a combination of different substances that remain individual substances
7. matter	
8.	a measure of how much matter an object contains
9. element	
10.	a particle made of two or more atoms bonded together
11. compound	

Reviewing Key Concepts

Multiple Choice *Choose the letter of the best answer.*

12. The standard unit for measuring mass is the
    a. kilogram
    b. gram per cubic centimeter
    c. milliliter
    d. milliliter per cubic centimeter

13. A unit for measuring the volume of a liquid is the
    a. kilogram
    b. gram per cubic centimeter
    c. milliliter
    d. milliliter per cubic centimeter

14. The weight of an object is measured by using a scale that
    a. compares the mass of the object with a standard unit of mass
    b. shows the amount of space the object occupies
    c. indicates how much water is displaced by the object
    d. tells how hard the object is pushing or pulling on it

15. To find the volume of a rectangular box,
    a. divide the length by the height
    b. multiply the length, width, and height
    c. subtract the mass from the weight
    d. multiply one atom's mass by the total

16. Compounds can be separated only by
    a. breaking the atoms into smaller pieces
    b. breaking the bonds between the atoms
    c. using a magnet to attract certain atoms
    d. evaporating the liquid that contains the atoms

17. Whether a substance is a solid, a liquid, or a gas depends on how close its atoms are to one another and
    a. the volume of each atom
    b. how much matter the atoms have
    c. how free the atoms are to move
    d. the size of the container

18. A liquid has
    a. a fixed volume and a fixed shape
    b. no fixed volume and a fixed shape
    c. a fixed volume and no fixed shape
    d. no fixed volume and no fixed shape

Short Answer *Answer each of the following questions in a sentence or two.*

19. Describe the movement of particles in a solid, a liquid, and a gas.

20. In bright sunlight, dust particles in the air appear to dart about. What causes this effect?

21. Why is the volume of a rectangular object measured in cubic units?

22. Describe how the molecules in the air behave when you pump air into a bicycle tire.

Thinking Critically

23. CLASSIFY Write the headings *Matter* and *Not Matter* on your paper. Place each of these terms in the correct category: wood, water, metal, air, light, sound.

24. INFER If you could break up a carbon dioxide molecule, would you still have carbon dioxide? Explain your answer.

25. MODEL In what ways is sand in a bowl like a liquid? In what ways is it different?

26. INFER If you cut a hole in a basketball, what happens to the gas inside?

27. COMPARE AND CONTRAST Create a Venn diagram that shows how mixtures and compounds are alike and different.

28. ANALYZE If you place a solid rubber ball into a box, why doesn't the ball change its shape to fit the container?

29. CALCULATE What is the volume of an aquarium that is 120 cm long, 60 cm wide, and 100 cm high?

30. CALCULATE A truck whose bed is 2.5 m long, 1.5 m wide, and 1 m high is delivering sand for a sand-sculpture competition. How many trips must the truck make to deliver 7 cubic meters of sand?

Use the information in the photograph below to answer the next three questions.

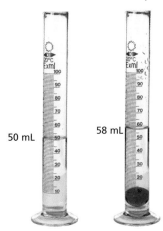

50 mL   58 mL

31. INFER One way to find the volume of a marble is by displacement. To determine a marble's volume, add 50 mL of water to a graduated cylinder and place the marble in the cylinder. Why does the water level change when you put the marble in the cylinder?

32. CALCULATE What is the volume of the marble?

33. PREDICT If you carefully removed the marble and let all of the water on it drain back into the cylinder, what would the volume of the water be? Explain.

the BIG idea

34. SYNTHESIZE Look back at the photograph on pages 438–439. Describe the picture in terms of states of matter.

35. WRITE Make a list of all the matter in a two-meter radius around you. Classify each as a solid, liquid, or gas.

UNIT PROJECTS

If you are doing a unit project, make a folder for your project. Include in your folder a list of the resources you will need, the date on which the project is due, and a schedule to track your progress. Begin gathering data.

Interpreting Graphs

The graph below shows the changing volume of a gas as it was slowly heated, with the pressure held constant.

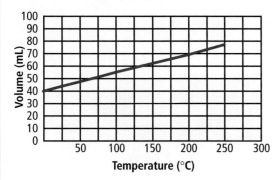

Use the graph to answer the questions.

1. As the temperature of the gas rises, what happens to its volume?

   a. It increases.

   b. It stays the same.

   c. It decreases.

   d. It changes without pattern.

2. What is the volume of the gas at 250°C as compared with the volume at 0°C?

   a. about three times greater

   b. about double

   c. about one-half

   d. about the same

3. What happens to a gas as it is cooled below 0°C?

   a. The volume would increase.

   b. The volume would continue to decrease.

   c. The volume would remain at 40 mL.

   d. A gas cannot be cooled below 0°C.

4. If you raised the temperature of this gas to 300°C, what would be its approximate volume?

   a. 70 mL   **c.** 80 mL

   b. 75 mL   **d.** 85 mL

5. If the volume of the gas at 0°C was 80 mL instead of 40 mL, what would you expect the volume to be at 200°C?

   a. 35 mL   **c.** 80 mL

   b. 70 mL   **d.** 140 mL

Extended Response

Answer the two questions below in detail. Include some of the terms from the word box. Underline each term you use in your answer.

gravity	mass	molecule
states of matter	weight	

6. An astronaut's helmet, measured on a balance, has the same number of kilograms on both Earth and the Moon. On a spring scale, though, it registers more newtons on Earth than on the Moon. Why?

7. Explain how water changes as it moves from a solid to a liquid and then to a gas.

CHAPTER

Properties of Matter

the **BIG** idea

Matter has properties that can be changed by physical and chemical processes.

Key Concepts

SECTION
Matter has observable properties.
Learn how to recognize physical and chemical properties.

SECTION
Changes of state are physical changes.
Learn how energy is related to changes of state.

SECTION
Properties are used to identify substances.
Learn how the properties of substances can be used to identify them and to separate mixtures.

Internet Preview

CLASSZONE.COM

Chapter 15 online resources: Content Review, Simulation, three Resource Centers, Math Tutorial, Test Practice

What properties could help you identify this sculpture as sugar?

EXPLORE (the BIG idea)

Float or Sink

Form a piece of clay into a solid ball or cube. Place it in a bowl of water. Notice if it floats or sinks. Then mold the clay into a boatlike shape. Notice if this new object floats or sinks.

Observe and Think
What did you change about the clay? What didn't you change? What would happen if you filled the boat with water?

Hot Chocolate

Place two candy-coated chocolates on a paper towel. Place two more in your hand and close your hand. Wait three minutes. Break open the candies and examine the chocolate.

Observe and Think What happened to the chocolate in your hand? on the towel? What do you think accounts for any differences you see?

Internet Activity: Physical and Chemical Changes

Go to **ClassZone.com** to see how materials can go through physical and chemical changes.

Observe and Think
Think about each change. What can you infer about the difference between a physical change and a chemical change?

NSTA
scilinks.org
SCI LINKS

Physical Properties of Matter **Code: MDL062**

Getting Ready to Learn

◀ CONCEPT REVIEW

- Everything is made of matter.
- Matter has mass and volume.
- Atoms combine to form molecules.

◀ VOCABULARY REVIEW

mass p. 442

volume p. 443

molecule p. 450

states of matter p. 459

CONTENT REVIEW
CLASSZONE.COM
Review concepts and vocabulary.

▶ TAKING NOTES

MAIN IDEA WEB

Write each new blue heading in a box. Then write notes in boxes around the center box that give important terms and details about that heading.

VOCABULARY STRATEGY

Think about a vocabulary term as a **magnet word** diagram. Write related terms and ideas in boxes around it.

See the Note-Taking Handbook on pages R45–R51.

SCIENCE NOTEBOOK

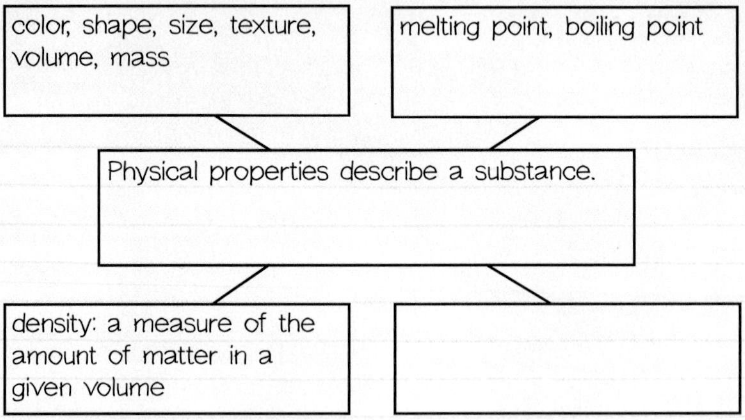

color, shape, size, texture, volume, mass	melting point, boiling point

Physical properties describe a substance.

density: a measure of the amount of matter in a given volume	

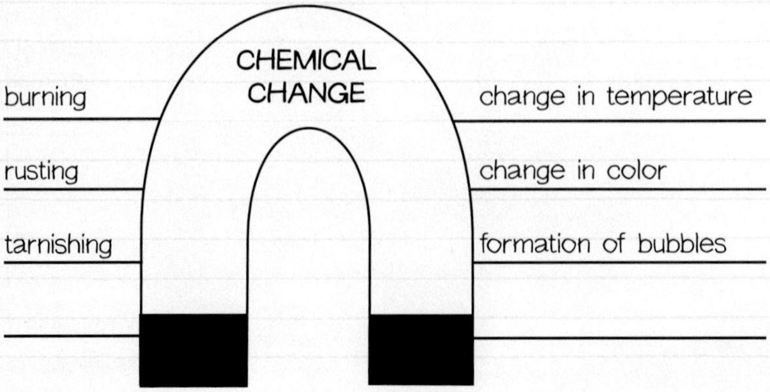

CHEMICAL CHANGE

burning

rusting

tarnishing

change in temperature

change in color

formation of bubbles

KEY CONCEPT

Matter has observable properties.

STANDARDS

7–5.9 Compare physical properties of matter (including melting or boiling point, density, and color) to the chemical property of reactivity with a certain substance (including the ability to burn or rust).

7–5.10 Compare physical changes (including changes in size, shape, and state) to chemical changes that are the result of chemical reactions (including changes in color or temperature and formation of a precipitate or gas).

VOCABULARY

physical property p. 473
density p. 475
physical change p. 476
chemical property p. 478
chemical change p. 478

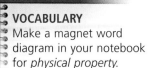

VOCABULARY
Make a magnet word diagram in your notebook for *physical property*.

◀ **BEFORE, you learned**

• Matter has mass and volume
• Matter is made of atoms
• Matter exists in different states

▶ **NOW, you will learn**

• About physical and chemical properties
• About physical changes
• About chemical changes

EXPLORE Physical Properties

How can a substance be changed?

PROCEDURE

MATERIAL
rectangular piece of clay

① Observe the clay. Note its physical characteristics, such as color, shape, texture, and size.

② Change the shape of the clay. Note which characteristics changed and which ones stayed the same.

WHAT DO YOU THINK?
• How did reshaping the clay change its physical characteristics?
• How were the mass and the volume of the clay affected?

Physical properties describe a substance.

What words would you use to describe a table? a chair? the sandwich you ate for lunch? You would probably say something about the shape, color, and size of each item. Next you might consider whether it is hard or soft, smooth or rough to the touch. Normally, when describing an object, you identify the characteristics of the object that you can observe without changing the identity of the object.

The characteristics of a substance that can be observed without changing the identity of the substance are called **physical properties.** In science, observation can include measuring and handling a substance. All of your senses can be used to detect physical properties. Color, shape, size, texture, volume, and mass are a few of the physical properties you probably have encountered.

 CHECK YOUR READING Describe some of the physical properties of your desk.

Physical Properties

How do you know which characteristics are physical properties? Just ask yourself whether observing the property involves changing the substance to a different substance. For example, you can stretch a rubber band. Does stretching the rubber band change what it is made of? No. The rubber band is still a rubber band before and after it is stretched. It may look a little different, but it is still a rubber band.

Mass and volume are two physical properties. Measuring these properties does not change the identity of a substance. For example, a lump of clay might have a mass of 200 grams (g) and a volume of 100 cubic centimeters (cm^3). If you were to break the clay in half, you would have two 100 g pieces of clay, each with a volume of 50 cm^3. You can bend and shape the clay too. Even if you were to mold a realistic model of a car out of the clay, it still would be a piece of clay. Although you have changed some of the properties of the object, such as its shape and volume, you have not changed the fact that the substance you are observing is clay.

REMINDER

Because all formulas for volume involve the multiplication of three measurements, volume has a unit that is cubed (such as cm^3).

CHECK YOUR READING Which physical properties listed above are found by taking measurements? Which are not?

Physical Properties

Physical properties of clay—such as volume, mass, color, texture, and shape—can be observed without changing the fact that the substance is clay.

Block of Clay

Shaped Clay

READING VISUALS COMPARE AND CONTRAST Which physical properties do the two pieces of clay have in common? Which are different?

Density

The relationship between the mass and the volume of a substance is another important physical property. For any substance, the amount of mass in a unit of volume is constant. For different substances, the amount of mass in a unit of volume may differ. This relationship explains why you can easily lift a shoebox full of feathers but not one filled with pennies, even though both are the same size. A volume of pennies contains more mass than an equal volume of feathers. The relationship between mass and volume is called density.

Density is a measure of the amount of matter present in a given volume of a substance. Density is normally expressed in units of grams per cubic centimeter (g/cm^3). In other words, density is the mass in grams divided by the volume in cubic centimeters.

$$\text{Density} = \frac{\text{mass}}{\text{Volume}} \qquad D = \frac{m}{V}$$

How would you find the density of 200 g of clay with a volume of 100 cm^3? You calculate that the clay has a density of 200 g divided by 100 cm^3, or 2 g/cm^3. If you divide the clay in half and find the density of one piece of clay, it will be 100 g/50 cm^3, or 2 g/cm^3—the same as the original piece. Notice that density is a property of a substance that remains the same no matter how much of the substance you have.

READING TIP

The density of solids is usually measured in grams per cubic centimeter (g/cm^3). The density of liquids is usually measured in grams per milliliter (g/mL). Recall that 1 mL = 1 cm^3.

Calculating Density

▶ Sample Problem

A glass marble has a volume of 5 cm^3 and a mass of 13 g. What is the density of glass?

What do you know?	Volume = 5 cm^3, mass = 13 g
What do you want to find out?	Density
Write the formula:	$D = \dfrac{m}{V}$
Substitute into the formula:	$D = \dfrac{13\ g}{5\ cm^3}$
Calculate and simplify:	$D = 2.6\ g/cm^3$
Check that your units agree:	Unit is g/cm^3. Unit of density is g/cm^3. Units agree.
Answer:	$D = 2.6\ g/cm^3$

▶ Practice the Math

1. A lead sinker has a mass of 227 g and a volume of 20 cm^3. What is the density of lead?

2. A glass of milk has a volume of 100 mL. If the milk has a mass of 103 g, what is the density of milk?

Physical Changes

MAIN IDEA WEB
As you read, organize your notes in a web.

You have read that a physical property is any property that can be observed without changing the identity of the substance. What then would be a physical change? A **physical change** is a change in any physical property of a substance, not in the substance itself. Breaking a piece of clay in half is a physical change because it changes only the size and shape of the clay. Stretching a rubber band is a physical change because the size of the rubber band changes. The color of the rubber band sometimes can change as well when it is stretched. However, the material that the rubber band is made of does not change. The rubber band is still rubber.

What happens when water changes from a liquid into water vapor or ice? Is this a physical change? Remember to ask yourself what has changed about the material. Ice is a solid and water is a liquid, but both are the same substance—both are composed of H_2O molecules. As you will read in more detail in the next section, a change in a substance's state of matter is a physical change.

CHECK YOUR READING How is a physical change related to a substance's physical properties?

A substance can go through many different physical changes and still remain the same substance. Consider, for example, the changes that happen to the wool that ultimately becomes a sweater.

1 Wool is sheared from the sheep. The wool is then cleaned and placed into a machine that separates the wool fibers from one another. Shearing and separating the fibers are physical changes that change the shape, volume, and texture of the wool.

2 The wool fibers are spun into yarn. Again, the shape and volume of the wool change. The fibers are twisted so that they are packed more closely together and are intertwined with one another.

3 The yarn is dyed. The dye changes the color of the wool, but it does not change the wool into another substance. This type of color change is a physical change.

4 Knitting the yarn into a sweater also does not change the wool into another substance. A wool sweater is still wool, even though it no longer resembles the wool on a sheep.

It can be difficult to determine if a specific change is a physical change or not. Some changes, such as a change in color, also can occur when new substances are formed during the change. When deciding whether a change is a physical change or not, ask yourself whether you have the same substance you started with. If the substance is the same, then the changes it underwent were all physical changes.

Physical Changes

The process of turning wool into a sweater requires that the wool undergo physical changes. Changes in shape, volume, texture, and color occur as raw wool is turned into a colorful sweater.

① Shearing

Preparing the wool produces physical changes. The wool is removed from the sheep and then cleaned before the wool fibers are separated.

② Spinning

Further physical changes occur as a machine twists the wool fibers into a long, thin rope of yarn.

③ Dyeing

Dyeing produces color changes but does not change the basic substance of the wool.

④ The final product, a wool sweater, is still wool.

READING VISUALS How does the yarn in the sweater differ from the wool on the sheep?

Chemical properties describe how substances form new substances.

RESOURCE CENTER
CLASSZONE.COM

Learn about the chemical properties of matter.

If you wanted to keep a campfire burning, would you add a piece of wood or a piece of iron? You would add wood, of course, because you know that wood burns but iron does not. Is the ability to burn a physical property of the wood? The ability to burn seems to be quite different from physical properties such as color, density, and shape. More important, after the wood burns, all that is left is a pile of ashes and some new substances in the air. The wood has obviously changed into something else. The ability to burn, therefore, must describe another kind of property that substances have—not a physical property but a chemical property.

Chemical Properties and Changes

Chemical properties describe how substances can form new substances. Combustibility, for example, describes how well an object can burn. Wood burns well and turns into ashes and other substances. Can you think of a chemical property for the metal iron? Especially when left outdoors in wet weather, iron rusts. The ability to rust is a chemical property of iron. The metal silver does not rust, but eventually a darker substance called tarnish forms on its surface. You may have noticed a layer of tarnish on some silver spoons or jewelry.

INFER The bust of Abraham Lincoln is made of bronze. Why is the nose a different color from the rest of the head?

The chemical properties of copper cause it to become a blue-green color when it is exposed to air. A famous example of tarnished copper is the Statue of Liberty. The chemical properties of bronze are different. Some bronze objects tarnish to a dark brown color, like the bust of Abraham Lincoln in the photograph on the left.

Chemical properties can be identified by the changes they produce. The change of one substance into another substance is called a **chemical change.** A piece of wood burning, an iron fence rusting, and a silver spoon tarnishing are all examples of chemical changes. A chemical change affects the substances involved in the change. During a chemical change, combinations of atoms in the original substances are rearranged to make new substances. For example, when rust forms on iron, the iron atoms combine with oxygen atoms in the air to form a new substance that is made of both iron and oxygen.

A chemical change is also involved when an antacid tablet is dropped into a glass of water. As the tablet dissolves, bubbles of gas appear. The water and the substances in the tablet react to form new substances. One of these substances is carbon dioxide gas, which forms the bubbles that you see.

Not all chemical changes are as destructive as burning, rusting, or tarnishing. Chemical changes are also involved in cooking. When you boil an egg, for example, the substances in the raw egg change into new substances as energy is added to the egg. When you eat the egg, further chemical changes take place as your body digests the egg. The process forms new molecules that your body then can use to function.

 CHECK YOUR READING Give three examples of chemical changes.

The only true indication of a chemical change is that a new substance has been formed. Sometimes, however, it is difficult to tell whether new substances have been formed or not. In many cases you have to judge which type of change has occurred only on the basis of your observations of the change and your previous experience. However, some common signs can suggest that a chemical change has occurred. You can use these signs to guide you as you try to classify a change that you are observing.

INVESTIGATE Chemical Changes

What are some signs of a chemical change?

PROCEDURE

1. Measure 80 mL of water and pour it into one of the cups.

2. Add 3 full droppers of iodine solution. Record your observations.

3. Add 1 spoonful of cornstarch to the iodine solution and stir. Record your observations.

4. Measure 50 mL of water and pour it into the second cup.

5. Using a clean eyedropper, add 4 full droppers of the iodine/cornstarch solution to the second cup.

6. Drop a vitamin C tablet into the second cup and stir the liquid with a clean spoon until the tablet is dissolved. Record your observations.

WHAT DO YOU THINK?

- What changes did you observe in the first cup? in the second cup?

- Do you think that chemical changes occurred? Why or why not?

- What are some characteristics of chemical changes?

CHALLENGE Describe some chemical changes that you have seen take place in your home or school.

SKILL FOCUS
Measuring

MATERIALS
- graduated cylinder
- water
- 2 clear plastic cups
- 2 eyedroppers
- iodine solution
- cornstarch
- spoon
- vitamin C tablet

TIME
15 minutes

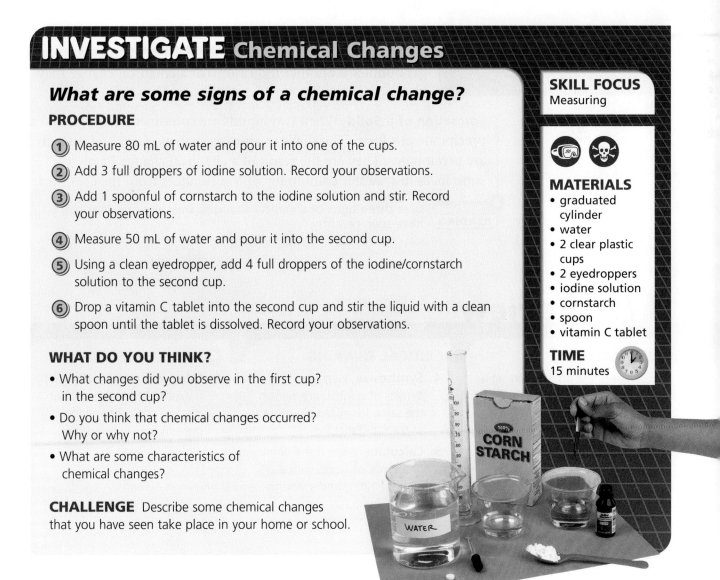

Signs of a Chemical Change

Carbon dioxide bubbles form as substances in the tablet react with water.

You may not be able to see that any new substances have formed during a change. Below are some signs that a chemical change may have occurred. If you observe two or more of these signs during a change, you most likely are observing a chemical change.

Production of an Odor Some chemical changes produce new smells. The chemical change that occurs when an egg is rotting produces the smell of sulfur. If you go outdoors after a thunderstorm, you may detect an unusual odor in the air. The odor is an indication that lightning has caused a chemical change in the air.

Change in Temperature Chemical changes often are accompanied by a change in temperature. You may have noticed that the temperature is higher near logs burning in a campfire.

Change in Color A change in color is often an indication of a chemical change. For example, fruit may change color when it ripens.

Formation of Bubbles When an antacid tablet makes contact with water, it begins to bubble. The formation of gas bubbles is another indicator that a chemical change may have occurred.

Formation of a Solid When two liquids are combined, a solid called a precipitate can form. The shells of animals such as clams and mussels are precipitates. They are the result of a chemical change involving substances in seawater combining with substances from the creatures.

CHECK YOUR READING Give three signs of chemical changes. Describe one that you have seen recently.

15.1 Review

KEY CONCEPTS

1. What effect does observing a substance's physical properties have on the substance?

2. Describe how a physical property such as mass or texture can change without causing a change in the substance.

3. Explain why burning is a chemical change in wood.

CRITICAL THINKING

4. **Synthesize** Why does the density of a substance remain the same for different amounts of the substance?

5. **Calculate** What is the density of a block of wood with a mass of 120 g and a volume of 200 cm^3?

CHALLENGE

6. **Infer** Iron can rust when it is exposed to oxygen. What method could be used to prevent iron from rusting?

MATH TUTORIAL
CLASSZONE.COM

Click on Math Tutorial for more help with solving proportions.

Density of Materials

Two statues are made of the same type of marble. One is larger than the other. However, they both have the same density because they are made of the same material. Recall the formula for density.

$$\text{Density} = \frac{\text{mass}}{\text{Volume}}$$

Because the density is the same, you know that the mass of one statue divided by its volume is the same as the mass of the other statue divided by its volume. You can set this up and solve it as a proportion.

Example

A small marble statue has a mass of 2.5 kg and a volume of 1000 cm^3. A large marble statue with the same density has a mass of 10 kg. What is the volume of the large statue?

(1) Write the information as an equation showing the proportion.

$$\frac{\text{mass of small statue}}{\text{volume of small statue}} = \frac{\text{mass of large statue}}{\text{volume of large statue}}$$

(2) Insert the known values into your equation.

$$\frac{2.5 \text{ kg}}{1000 \text{ cm}^3} = \frac{10 \text{ kg}}{\text{volume of large statue}}$$

(3) Compare the numerators: 10 kg is 4 times greater than 2.5 kg.

(4) The denominators of the fractions are related in the same way. Therefore, the volume of the large statue is 4 times the volume of the small one.

volume of large statue = 4 • 1000 cm^3 = 4000 cm^3

ANSWER The volume of the large statue is 4000 cm^3.

Answer the following questions.

1. A lump of gold has a volume of 10 cm^3 and a mass of 193 g. Another lump of gold has a mass of 96.5 g. What is the volume of the second lump of gold?

2. A carpenter saws a wooden beam into two pieces. One piece has a mass of 600 g and a volume of 1000 cm^3. What is the mass of the second piece if its volume is 250 cm^3?

3. A 200 mL bottle is completely filled with cooking oil. The oil has a mass of 180 g. If 150 mL of the oil is poured into a pot, what is the mass of the poured oil?

CHALLENGE You have two spheres made of the same material. One has a diameter that is twice as large as the other. How do their masses compare?

If the marble statue and the marble bust both have the same density, their masses are proportional to their volumes.

KEY CONCEPT

15.2 Changes of state are physical changes.

STANDARDS

7–5.10 Compare physical changes (including changes in size, shape, and state) to chemical changes that are the result of chemical reactions (including changes in color or temperature and formation of a precipitate or gas).

VOCABULARY

melting p. 483
melting point p. 483
freezing p. 484
freezing point p. 484
evaporation p. 485
sublimation p. 485
boiling p. 486
boiling point p. 486
condensation p. 487

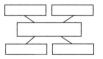

MAIN IDEA WEB
Remember to place each blue heading in a box. Add details around it to form a web.

◁ BEFORE, you learned

- Substances have physical and chemical properties
- Physical changes do not change a substance into a new substance
- Chemical changes result in new substances

▷ NOW, you will learn

- How liquids can become solids, and solids can become liquids
- How liquids can become gases, and gases can become liquids
- How energy is related to changes of state

THINK ABOUT

Where does dew come from?

On a cool morning, droplets of dew cover the grass. Where does this water come from? You might think it had rained recently. However, dew forms even if it has not rained. Air is made of a mixture of different gases, including water vapor. Some of the water vapor condenses—or becomes a liquid—on the cool grass and forms drops of liquid water.

Matter can change from one state to another.

Matter is commonly found in three states: solid, liquid, and gas. A solid has a fixed volume and a fixed shape. A liquid also has a fixed volume but takes the shape of its container. A gas has neither a fixed volume nor a fixed shape. Matter always exists in one of these states, but it can change from one state to another.

When matter changes from one state to another, the substance itself does not change. Water, ice, and water vapor are all the same basic substance. As water turns into ice or water vapor, the water molecules themselves do not change. What changes are the arrangement of the molecules and the amount of space between them. Changes in state are physical changes because changes in state do not change the basic substance.

 CHECK YOUR READING Why is a change in state a physical change rather than a chemical change?

Solids can become liquids, and liquids can become solids.

If you leave an ice cube on a kitchen counter, it changes to the liquid form of water. Water changes to the solid form of water, ice, when it is placed in a freezer. In a similar way, if a bar of iron is heated to a high enough temperature, it will become liquid iron. As the liquid iron cools, it becomes solid iron again.

Melting

Melting is the process by which a solid becomes a liquid. Different solids melt at different temperatures. The lowest temperature at which a substance begins to melt is called its **melting point.** Although the melting point of ice is 0°C (32°F), iron must be heated to a much higher temperature before it will melt.

Remember that particles are always in motion, even in a solid. Because the particles in a solid are bound together, they do not move from place to place—but they do vibrate. As a solid heats up, its particles gain energy and vibrate faster. If the vibrations are fast enough, the particles break loose and slide past one another. In other words, the solid melts and becomes a liquid.

Some substances have a well-defined melting point. If you are melting ice, for example, you can predict that when the temperature reaches 0°C, the ice will start to melt. Substances with an orderly structure start melting when they reach a specific temperature.

VOCABULARY
Add magnet word diagrams for *melting* and *melting point* to your notebook.

Melting a Solid

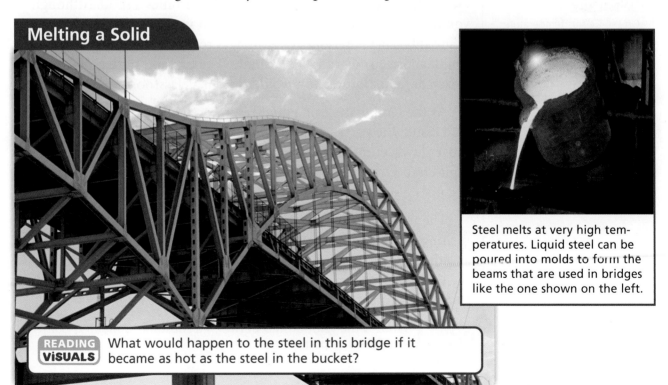

Steel melts at very high temperatures. Liquid steel can be poured into molds to form the beams that are used in bridges like the one shown on the left.

READING VISUALS What would happen to the steel in this bridge if it became as hot as the steel in the bucket?

Other substances, such as plastic and chocolate, do not have a well-defined melting point. Chocolate becomes soft when the temperature is high enough, but it still maintains its shape. Eventually, the chocolate becomes a liquid, but there is no specific temperature at which you can say the change happened. Instead, the melting happens gradually over a range of temperatures.

CHECK YOUR READING Describe the movement of molecules in a substance that is at its melting point.

Icicles grow as water drips down them, freezes, and sticks to the ice that is already there. On a warm day, the frozen icicles melt again.

Freezing

READING TiP

On the Celsius temperature scale, under normal conditions, water freezes at 0°C and boils at 100°C. On the Fahrenheit scale, water freezes at 32°F and boils at 212°F.

Freezing is the process by which a liquid becomes a solid. Although you may think of cold temperatures when you hear the word *freezing*, many substances are solid, or frozen, at room temperature and above. Think about a soda can and a candle. The can and the candle are frozen at temperatures you would find in a classroom.

As the temperature of a liquid is lowered, its particles lose energy. As a result, the particles move more slowly. Eventually, the particles move slowly enough that the attractions among them cause the liquid to become a solid. The temperature at which a specific liquid becomes a solid is called the **freezing point** of the substance.

The freezing point of a substance is the same as that substance's melting point. At this particular temperature, the substance can exist as either a solid or a liquid. At temperatures below the freezing/melting point, the substance is a solid. At temperatures above the freezing/melting point, the substance is a liquid.

CHECK YOUR READING What is the relationship between a substance's melting point and freezing point?

Liquids can become gases, and gases can become liquids.

Suppose you spill water on a picnic table on a warm day. You might notice that the water eventually disappears from the table. What has happened to the water molecules? The liquid water has become water vapor, a gas. The water vapor mixes with the surrounding air. At the same picnic, you might also notice that a cold can of soda has beads of water forming on it. The water vapor in the air has become the liquid water found on the soda can.

Evaporation

Evaporation is a process by which a liquid becomes a gas. It usually occurs at the surface of a liquid. Although all particles in a liquid move, they do not all move at the same speed. Some particles move faster than others. The fastest moving particles at the surface of the liquid can break away from the liquid and escape to become gas particles.

READING TiP

The root of the word *evaporation* is *vapor,* a Latin word meaning "steam."

As the temperature increases, the energy in the liquid increases. More particles can escape from the surface of the liquid. As a result, the liquid evaporates more quickly. This is why spilled water will evaporate faster in hot weather than in cold weather.

CHECK YOUR READING Describe the movement of particles in a liquid as it evaporates.

It is interesting to note that under certain conditions, solids can lose particles through a process similar to evaporation. When a solid changes directly to a gas, the process is called **sublimation.** You may have seen dry ice being used in a cooler to keep foods cold. Dry ice is frozen carbon dioxide that sublimates in normal atmospheric conditions.

Evaporation

During evaporation, fast-moving particles escape from the surface of a liquid and become gas particles.

Boiling

RESOURCE CENTER
CLASSZONE.COM

Explore melting points
and boiling points.

Boiling is another process by which a liquid becomes a gas. Unlike evaporation, boiling produces bubbles. If you heat a pot of water on the stove, you will notice that after a while tiny bubbles begin to form. These bubbles contain dissolved air that is escaping from the liquid. As you continue to heat the water, large bubbles suddenly form and rise to the surface. These bubbles contain energetic water molecules that have escaped from the liquid water to form a gas. This process is boiling.

Boiling can occur only when the liquid reaches a certain temperature, called the **boiling point** of the liquid. Liquids evaporate over a wide range of temperatures. Boiling, however, occurs at a specific temperature for each liquid. Water, for example, has a boiling point of 100°C (212°F) at normal atmospheric pressure.

In the mountains, water boils at a temperature lower than 100°C. For example, in Leadville, Colorado, which has an elevation of 3094 m (10,152 ft) above sea level, water boils at 89°C (192°F). This happens because at high elevations the air pressure is much lower than at sea level. Because less pressure is pushing down on the surface of the water, bubbles can form inside the liquid at a lower temperature. Less energetic water molecules are needed to expand the bubbles under these conditions. The lower boiling point of water means that foods cooked in water, such as pasta, require a longer time to prepare.

Different substances boil at different temperatures. Helium, which is a gas at room temperature, boils at –270°C (–454°F). Aluminum, on the other hand, boils at 2519°C (4566°F). This fact explains why some substances usually are found as gases but others are not.

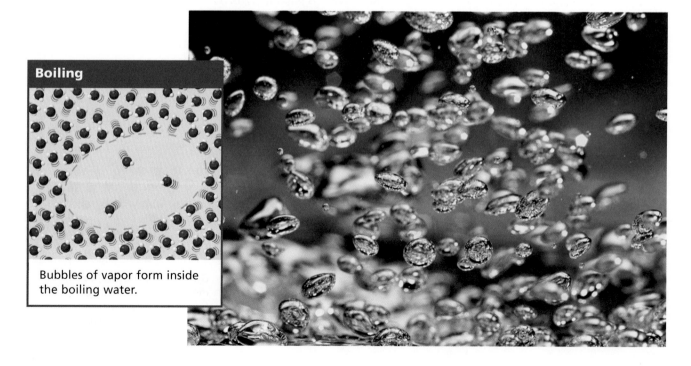

Boiling

Bubbles of vapor form inside the boiling water.

Tiny droplets of water form on a window as water vapor from the air condenses into liquid water.

Condensation

The process by which a gas changes its state to become a liquid is called **condensation.** You probably have seen an example of condensation when you enjoyed a cold drink on a warm day. The beads of water that formed on the glass or can were water vapor that condensed from the surrounding air.

The cold can or glass cooled the air surrounding it. When you cool a gas, it loses energy. As the particles move more slowly, the attractions among them cause droplets of liquid to form. Condensed water often forms when warm air containing water vapor comes into contact with a cold surface, such as a glass of ice or ground that has cooled during the night.

As with evaporation, condensation can occur over a wide range of temperatures. Like the particles in liquids, the individual particles in a gas are moving at many different speeds. Slowly moving particles near the cool surface condense as they lose energy. The faster moving particles also slow down but continue to move too fast to stick to the other particles in the liquid that is forming. However, if you cool a gas to a temperature below its boiling point, almost all of the gas will condense.

READING TiP

The root of the word *condensation* is *condense,* which comes from a Latin word meaning "to thicken."

15.2 Review

KEY CONCEPTS

1. Describe three ways in which matter can change from one state to another.

2. Compare and contrast the processes of evaporation and condensation.

3. How does adding energy to matter by heating it affect the energy of its particles?

CRITICAL THINKING

4. **Synthesize** Explain how water can exist as both a solid and a liquid at 0°C.

5. **Apply** Explain how a pat of butter at room temperature can be considered to be frozen.

⬥ **CHALLENGE**

6. **Infer** You know that water vapor condenses from air when the air temperature is lowered. Should it be possible to condense oxygen from air? What would have to happen?

CHAPTER INVESTIGATION

Freezing Point

OVERVIEW AND PURPOSE Stearic acid is a substance used in making candles. In this experiment you will
- observe melted stearic acid as it changes from a liquid to a solid
- record the freezing point of stearic acid

▶ Problem

What is the freezing point of stearic acid?

▶ Procedure

1. Make a data table like the one shown on the sample notebook page.

2. Use the test-tube tongs to take the test tube of melted stearic acid and place it in the test-tube rack. Keep the test tube in the rack for the entire experiment.

3. Use the wire-loop stirrer and stir the liquid to make sure that it is the same temperature throughout.

4. Place the thermometer into the stearic acid to take a reading. Hold the thermometer so that it does not touch the sides or bottom of the test tube. Wait until the temperature stops rising. Then record the temperature on your data table. Also note whether the stearic acid is a liquid or a solid—or whether both states are present.

5. Take the temperature of the stearic acid every minute, stirring the stearic acid with the stirrer before each reading. To get an accurate reading, place the loop of the stirrer around the thermometer and use an up-and-down motion.

6. Continue taking temperature readings until two minutes after the acid has become totally solid or you are no longer able to stir it.

MATERIALS
- large test tube
- stearic acid
- test-tube tongs
- test-tube rack
- wire-loop stirrer
- thermometer

7 Make a note of the temperature on your data table when the first signs of a solid formation appear.

8 Make a note of the temperature on your data table when the stearic acid is completely solid.

9 Leave the thermometer and stirrer in the test tube and carry it carefully in the test-tube rack to your teacher.

▶ Observe and Analyze   [Write It Up]

1. **RECORD OBSERVATIONS** Make a line graph showing the freezing curve of stearic acid. Label the vertical axis **Temperature** and the horizontal axis **Time**.

2. **RECORD OBSERVATIONS** Label your graph to show when the stearic acid was a liquid, when it was a solid, and when it was present in both states.

3. **ANALYZE** Explain how your graph tells you the freezing point of stearic acid.

▶ Conclude   [Write It Up]

1. **INTERPRET** Answer the question in the problem.

2. **IDENTIFY** How does the freezing point of stearic acid compare with the freezing point of water?

3. **INFER** What happened to the energy of the molecules as the stearic acid changed from a liquid to a solid?

4. **INFER** From your observations, infer the melting point of stearic acid. How is the melting point of stearic acid related to its freezing point?

5. **APPLY** Why do you think stearic acid is used as an ingredient in bar soaps but not in liquid soaps?

▶ INVESTIGATE Further

CHALLENGE What do you think would happen if you mixed in another substance with the stearic acid? How would that affect the freezing point? What experiment would you perform to find the answer?

Freezing Point

Problem What is the freezing point of stearic acid?

Observe and Analyze

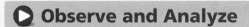

Table 1. Freezing Point of Stearic Acid

Time (min)	Temperature (°C)	Liquid	Solid	Both
0.0				
1.0				
2.0				
3.0				
4.0				
5.0				
6.0				
7.0				

KEY CONCEPT

15.3 Properties are used to identify substances.

 BEFORE, you learned

- Matter can change from one state to another
- Changes in state require energy changes

 NOW, you will learn

- How properties can help you identify substances
- How properties of substances can be used to separate substances

---

EXPLORE Identifying Substances

How can properties help you identify a substance?

PROCEDURE

MATERIALS
- substance A
- substance B
- 2 cups
- water

1. Place some of substance A into one cup and some of substance B into the other cup. Label the cups.

2. Carefully add some water to each cup. Observe and record what happens.

WHAT DO YOU THINK?

- Which result was a physical change? a chemical change? Explain.
- The substances are baking soda and baking powder. Baking powder and water produce carbon dioxide gas. Which substance is baking powder?

Substances have characteristic properties.

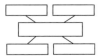

MAIN IDEA WEB
As you read, place each blue heading in a box. Add details around it to form a web.

You often use the properties of a substance to identify it. For example, when you reach into your pocket, you can tell the difference between a ticket stub and a folded piece of tissue because one is stiff and smooth and the other is soft. You can identify nickels, dimes, and quarters without looking at them by feeling their shapes and comparing their sizes. To tell the difference between a nickel and a subway token, however, you might have to use another property, such as color. Texture, shape, and color are physical properties that you use all the time to identify and sort objects.

 How can physical properties be used to identify a substance?

Identifying Unknown Substances

Suppose you have a glass of an unknown liquid that you want to identify. It looks like milk, but you cannot be sure. How could you determine what it is? Of course, you would not taste an unknown substance, but there are many properties other than taste that you could use to identify the substance safely.

To proceed scientifically, you could measure several properties of the unknown liquid and compare them with the properties of known substances. You might observe and measure such properties as color, odor, texture, density, boiling point, and freezing point. A few of these properties might be enough to tell you that your white liquid is glue rather than milk.

To determine the difference among several colorless liquids, scientists would use additional tests. Their tests, however, would rely on the same idea of measuring and comparing the properties of an unknown with something that is already known.

Properties Used for Identifying Substances

You are already familiar with the most common physical properties of matter. Some of these properties, such as mass and volume, depend upon the specific object in question. You cannot use mass to tell one substance from another because two very different objects can have the same mass—a kilogram of feathers has the same mass as a kilogram of peanut butter, for example.

aerogel

Other properties, such as density, can be used to identify substances. They do not vary from one sample of the same substance to another. For example, you could see a difference between a kilogram of liquid soap and a kilogram of honey by measuring their densities.

The physical properties described below can be used to identify a substance.

Aerogel, an extremely lightweight material used in the space program, has such a low density that it can float on soap bubbles.

Density The densities of wood, plastic, and steel are all different. Scientists already have determined the densities of many substances. As a result, you can conveniently compare the density of an unknown substance with the densities of known substances. Finding any matching densities will give you information about the possible identity of the unknown substance. However, it is possible for two different substances to have the same density. In that case, in order to identify the substance positively, you would need additional data.

 Why can't you identify a substance on the basis of density alone?

These fibers act as heat insulators to keep the inside of the sleeping bag warm.

READING TiP

The root of the word *solubility* is the Latin word *solvere,* which means "to loosen."

Iron filings are attracted by the magnet. The wood chips, however, are not.

Heating Properties Substances respond to heating in different ways. Some warm up very quickly, and others take a long while to increase in temperature. This property is important in selecting materials for different uses. Aluminum and iron are good materials for making pots and pans because they conduct heat well. Various materials used in household insulation are poor heat conductors. Therefore, these insulators are used to keep warm air inside a home on a cold day. You can measure the rate at which a substance conducts heat and compare that rate with the heat conduction rates of other substances.

Solubility Solubility is a measure of how much of a substance dissolves in a given volume of a liquid. Sugar and dirt, for instance, have very different solubilities in water. If you put a spoonful of sugar into a cup of water and stir, the sugar dissolves in the water very rapidly. If you put a spoonful of dirt into water and stir, most of the dirt settles to the bottom as soon as you stop stirring.

Electric Properties Some substances conduct electricity better than others. This means that they allow electric charge to move through them easily. Copper wire is used to carry electricity because it is a good conductor. Materials that do not conduct easily, such as rubber and plastics, are used to block the flow of charge. With the proper equipment, scientists can test the electric conductivity of an unknown substance.

Magnetic Properties Some substances are attracted to magnets, but others are not. You can use a magnet to pick up a paper clip but not a plastic button or a wooden match. The elements iron, cobalt, and nickel are magnetic—meaning they respond to magnets—but copper, aluminum, and zinc are not. Steel, which contains iron, is also magnetic.

Mixtures can be separated by using the properties of the substances in them.

Suppose you have a bag of cans that you want to recycle. The recycling center accepts only aluminum cans. You know that some of your cans contain steel. You would probably find it difficult to tell aluminum cans from steel ones just by looking at them. How could you separate the cans? Aluminum and steel may look similar, but they have different magnetic properties. You could use a magnet to test each can. If the magnet sticks to the can, the can contains steel. Recycling centers often use magnets to separate aluminum cans from steel cans.

Some mixtures contain solids mixed with liquids. A filter can be used to separate the solid from the liquid. One example of this is a tea bag. The paper filter allows the liquid water to mix with the tea, because water molecules are small enough to pass through the filter. The large pieces of tea, however, cannot pass through the filter and remain inside the tea bag.

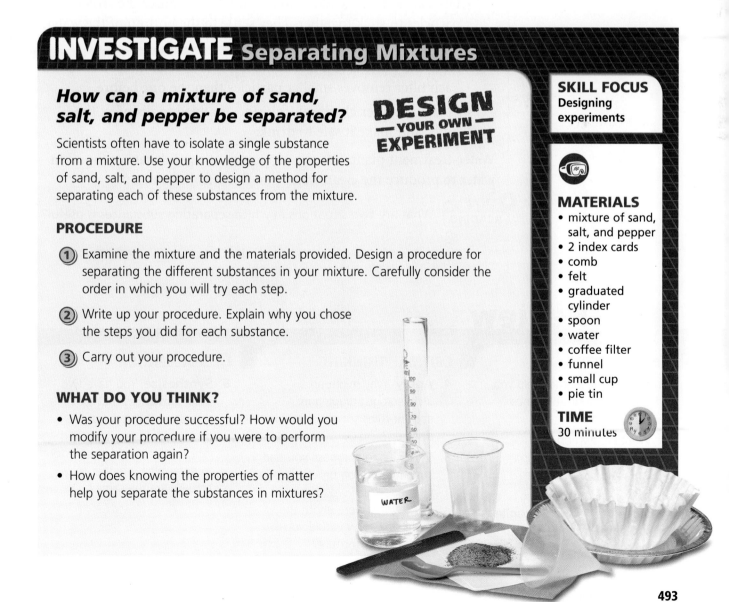

INVESTIGATE Separating Mixtures

How can a mixture of sand, salt, and pepper be separated?

DESIGN
— YOUR OWN —
EXPERIMENT

Scientists often have to isolate a single substance from a mixture. Use your knowledge of the properties of sand, salt, and pepper to design a method for separating each of these substances from the mixture.

PROCEDURE

1. Examine the mixture and the materials provided. Design a procedure for separating the different substances in your mixture. Carefully consider the order in which you will try each step.

2. Write up your procedure. Explain why you chose the steps you did for each substance.

3. Carry out your procedure.

WHAT DO YOU THINK?

- Was your procedure successful? How would you modify your procedure if you were to perform the separation again?

- How does knowing the properties of matter help you separate the substances in mixtures?

SKILL FOCUS
Designing experiments

MATERIALS
- mixture of sand, salt, and pepper
- 2 index cards
- comb
- felt
- graduated cylinder
- spoon
- water
- coffee filter
- funnel
- small cup
- pie tin

TIME
30 minutes

WATER

493

This water-treatment plant separates harmful substances from the water.

Some mixtures are more difficult to separate than others. For example, if you stir sugar into water, the sugar dissolves and breaks up into individual molecules that are too tiny to filter out. In this case, you can take advantage of the fact that water is a liquid and will evaporate from an open dish. Sugar, however, does not evaporate. The mixture can be heated to speed the evaporation of the water, leaving the sugar behind.

There are many important reasons for separating substances. One reason is to make a substance safe to consume, such as drinking water. In order to produce drinking water, workers at a water-treatment plant must separate many of the substances that are mixed in with the water.

The process in water-treatment plants generally includes these steps:

- First, a chemical is added to the water that causes the larger particles to stick together. They settle to the bottom of the water, where they can be removed.
- Next, the water is run through a series of special molecular filters. Each filter removes smaller particles than the one before.
- Finally, another chemical, chlorine, is added to disinfect the water and make it safe to drink.

Water-treatment plants use the properties of the substances found in water to produce the clean water that flows from your tap.

 CHECK YOUR READING   What are two situations in which separating substances is useful?

15.3 Review

KEY CONCEPTS

1. How can properties help you distinguish one substance from another?
2. What are two physical properties that can help you identify a substance?
3. How can understanding properties help you separate substances from a mixture?

CRITICAL THINKING

4. **Apply** Why might an archaeologist digging in ancient ruins sift dirt through a screen?
5. **Synthesize** Suppose you had a mixture of iron pellets, pebbles, and small wood spheres, all of which were about the same size. How would you separate this mixture?

CHALLENGE

6. **Synthesize** You have two solid substances that look the same. What measurements would you take and which tests would you perform to determine whether they actually are the same?

CONNECTING SCIENCES

Workers can identify garnets in a mine because their physical properties are different from the physical properties of their surroundings.

Separating Minerals

A few minerals, such as rock salt, occur in large deposits that can be mined in a form that is ready to use. Most minerals, however, are combined with other materials, so they need to be separated from the mixtures of which they are a part. Scientists and miners use the differences in physical properties to analyze samples and to separate the materials removed from a mine.

Appearance

Gemstones are prized because of their obvious physical properties, such as color, shininess, and hardness. Particularly valuable minerals, such as diamonds and emeralds, are often located by digging underground and noting the differences between the gemstone and the surrounding dirt and rock.

Density

When gold deposits wash into a streambed, tiny particles of gold mix with the sand. It is hard to separate them by appearance because the pieces are so small. In the 1800s, as prospectors swirled this sand around in a pan, the lighter particles of sand washed away with the water. The denser gold particles collected in the bottom of the pan. Some modern gold mines use the same principle in machines that handle tons of material, washing away the lighter dirt and rock to leave bits of gold.

Magnetism

Machines called magnetic separators divide a mixture into magnetic and nonmagnetic materials. In order to separate iron from other materials, rocks are crushed and carried past a strong magnet. Particles that contain iron are drawn toward the magnet and fall into one bin, while the nonmagnetic materials fall into another bin.

Melting Point

Thousands of years ago, people discovered that when some minerals are placed in a very hot fire, metals—such as copper, tin, and zinc—can be separated from the rock around them. When the ores reach a certain temperature, the metal melts and can be collected as a liquid.

EXPLORE

1. **INFER** At a copper ore mine in Chile, one of the world's largest magnets is used to remove pieces of iron from the ore. What can you infer about the copper ore?

2. **CHALLENGE** Electrostatic precipitators are important tools for protecting the environment from pollution. Use the Internet to learn how they are used in power plants and other factories that burn fuels.

 **RESOURCE CENTER** Find out more about separating
CLASSZONE.COM materials from mixtures.

the BIG idea

Matter has properties that can be changed by physical and chemical processes.

◀ **KEY CONCEPTS SUMMARY**

1 Matter has observable properties.

- Physical properties can be observed without changing the substance.

- Physical changes can change some physical properties but do not change the substance.

- Chemical properties describe how substances form new substances.

- Chemical changes create new substances.

VOCABULARY
physical property p. 473
density p. 475
physical change p. 476
chemical property p. 478
chemical change p. 478

2 Changes of states are physical changes.
Matter is commonly found in three states: solid, liquid, and gas.

freezing

Solid ← → Liquid

melting →

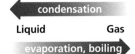

condensation

Liquid ← → Gas

evaporation, boiling →

VOCABULARY
melting p. 483
melting point p. 483
freezing p. 484
freezing point p. 484
evaporation p. 485
sublimation p. 485
boiling p. 486
boiling point p. 486
condensation p. 487

3 Properties are used to identify substances.
Physical properties that can be used to identify substances include:

- density
- heating properties
- solubility
- electric properties
- magnetic properties

Mixtures can be separated by using the properties of the substances they contain.

Reviewing Vocabulary

Describe how the terms in the following sets of terms are related.

1. physical property, physical change

2. chemical property, chemical change

3. density, matter

4. melting, melting point, freezing point

5. boiling, boiling point, liquid

6. evaporation, condensation

7. sublimation, solid

Reviewing Key Concepts

Multiple Choice *Choose the letter of the best answer.*

8. Color, shape, size, and texture are
   a. physical properties
   b. chemical properties
   c. physical changes
   d. chemical changes

9. Density describes the relationship between a substance's
   a. matter and mass
   b. mass and volume
   c. volume and area
   d. temperature and mass

10. Dissolving sugar in water is an example of a
    a. physical change
    b. chemical change
    c. change in state
    d. pressure change

11. An electric current can be used to decompose, or break down, water into oxygen gas and hydrogen gas. This is an example of a
    a. physical change
    b. chemical change
    c. change in state
    d. pressure change

12. The formation of rust on iron is a chemical change because
    a. the color and shape have changed
    b. the mass and volume have changed
    c. the substance remains the same
    d. a new substance has been formed

13. The process by which a solid becomes a liquid is called
    a. boiling
    b. freezing
    c. melting
    d. evaporating

14. The process by which a liquid becomes a solid is called
    a. boiling
    b. freezing
    c. melting
    d. evaporating

15. Two processes by which a liquid can become a gas are
    a. evaporation and boiling
    b. melting and freezing
    c. sublimation and condensation
    d. evaporation and condensation

Short Answer *Answer each of the following questions in a sentence or two.*

16. When a sculptor shapes marble to make a statue, is this a physical or a chemical change? Explain your answer.

17. Describe and identify various physical changes that water can undergo.

18. Why does dew often form on grass on a cool morning, even if there has been no rain?

19. Describe the difference between evaporation and boiling in terms of the movement of the liquid's particles in each case.

20. What effect does altitude have on the boiling point of water?

Thinking Critically

21. **ANALYZE** Whole milk is a mixture. When bacteria in the milk digest part of the mixture, changes occur. Lactic acid is produced, and the milk tastes sour. Explain why this process is a chemical change.

22. **INFER** Sharpening a pencil leaves behind pencil shavings. Why is sharpening a pencil a physical change instead of a chemical change?

23. **ANALYZE** Dumping cooked spaghetti and water into a colander separates the two substances because the liquid water can run through the holes in the colander but the solid spaghetti cannot. Explain how this is an example of separating a mixture based on the physical properties of its components.

24. **INFER** The density of water is 1.0 g/mL. Anything with a density less than 1.0 g/mL will float in water. The density of a fresh egg is about 1.2 g/mL. The density of a spoiled egg is about 0.9 g/mL. If you place an egg in water and it floats, what does that tell you about the egg?

Use the photograph below to answer the next three questions.

25. **COMPARE** Which physical properties of the puddle change as the water evaporates? Which physical properties remain the same?

26. **ANALYZE** Can water evaporate from this puddle on a cold day? Explain your answer.

27. **PREDICT** What would happen to any minerals and salts in the water if the water completely evaporated?

Use the chart below to answer the next two questions.

Densities Measured at 20°C

Material	Density (g/cm^3)
gold	19.3
lead	11.3
silver	10.5
copper	9.0
iron	7.9

28. **PREDICT** Suppose you measure the mass and the volume of a shiny metal object and find that its density is 10.5 g/mL. Could you make a reasonable guess as to what material the object is made of? What factor or factors might affect your guess?

29. **CALCULATE** A solid nickel bar has a mass of 2.75 kg and a volume of 308.71 cm^3. Between which two materials would nickel fall on the chart?

the **BIG** idea

30. **PREDICT** Look again at the photograph on pages 470–471. The chef has melted sugar to make a sculpture. Describe how the sugar has changed in terms of its physical and chemical properties. Predict what will happen to the sculpture over time.

31. **RESEARCH** Think of a question you have about the properties of matter that is still unanswered. For example, there may be a specific type of matter about which you are curious. What information do you need in order to answer your question? How might you find the information?

UNIT PROJECTS

Evaluate all the data, results, and information from your project folder. Prepare to present your project.

Standardized Test Practice

For practice on your
state test, go to . . .
TEST PRACTICE
CLASSZONE.COM

Analyzing Experiments

Read the following description of an experiment together with the chart.
Then answer the questions that follow.

Archimedes was a Greek mathematician and scientist who lived in
the third century B.C. He figured out that any object placed in a liquid
displaced a volume of that liquid equal to its own volume. He used this
knowledge to solve a problem.

The king of Syracuse had been given a crown of gold. But he was not
sure whether the crown was pure gold. Archimedes solved the king's
problem by testing the crown's density.

He immersed the crown in water and measured the volume of water
it displaced. Archimedes compared the amount of water displaced by the
crown with the amount of water displaced by a bar of pure gold with the
same mass. The comparison told him whether the crown was all gold or
a mixture of gold and another element.

Element	Density (g/cm³)
copper	8.96
gold	19.30
iron	7.86
lead	11.34
silver	10.50
tin	7.31

1. Which problem was Archimedes trying to solve?
   a. what the density of gold was
   b. what the crown was made of
   c. what the mass of the crown was
   d. how much water the crown displaced

2. Archimedes used the method that he did because
a crown has an irregular shape and the volume of
such an object cannot be measured in any other
way. Which one of the following objects would
also require this method?
   a. a square wooden box
   b. a cylindrical tin can
   c. a small bronze statue
   d. a rectangular piece of glass

3. Suppose Archimedes found that the crown had a
mass of 772 grams and displaced 40 milliliters of
water. Using the formula $D = m/V$, what would you
determine the crown to be made of?
   a. pure gold
   b. half gold and half another element
   c. some other element with gold plating
   d. cannot be determined from the data

4. Using the formula, compare how much water a gold
crown would displace if it had a mass of 579 grams.
   a. 10 mL   **c.** 30 mL
   b. 20 mL   **d.** 193 mL

5. If you had crowns made of each element in the chart
that were the same mass, which would displace
more water than a gold crown of that mass?
   a. all   **c.** tin only
   b. lead only   **d.** none

Extended Response

Answer the two questions below in detail.

6. What is the difference between a physical change
and a chemical change? Include examples of each
type in your explanation.

7. Why does someone cooking spaghetti at a high
elevation need to boil it longer than someone
cooking spaghetti at a lower elevation?

Chemical Interactions

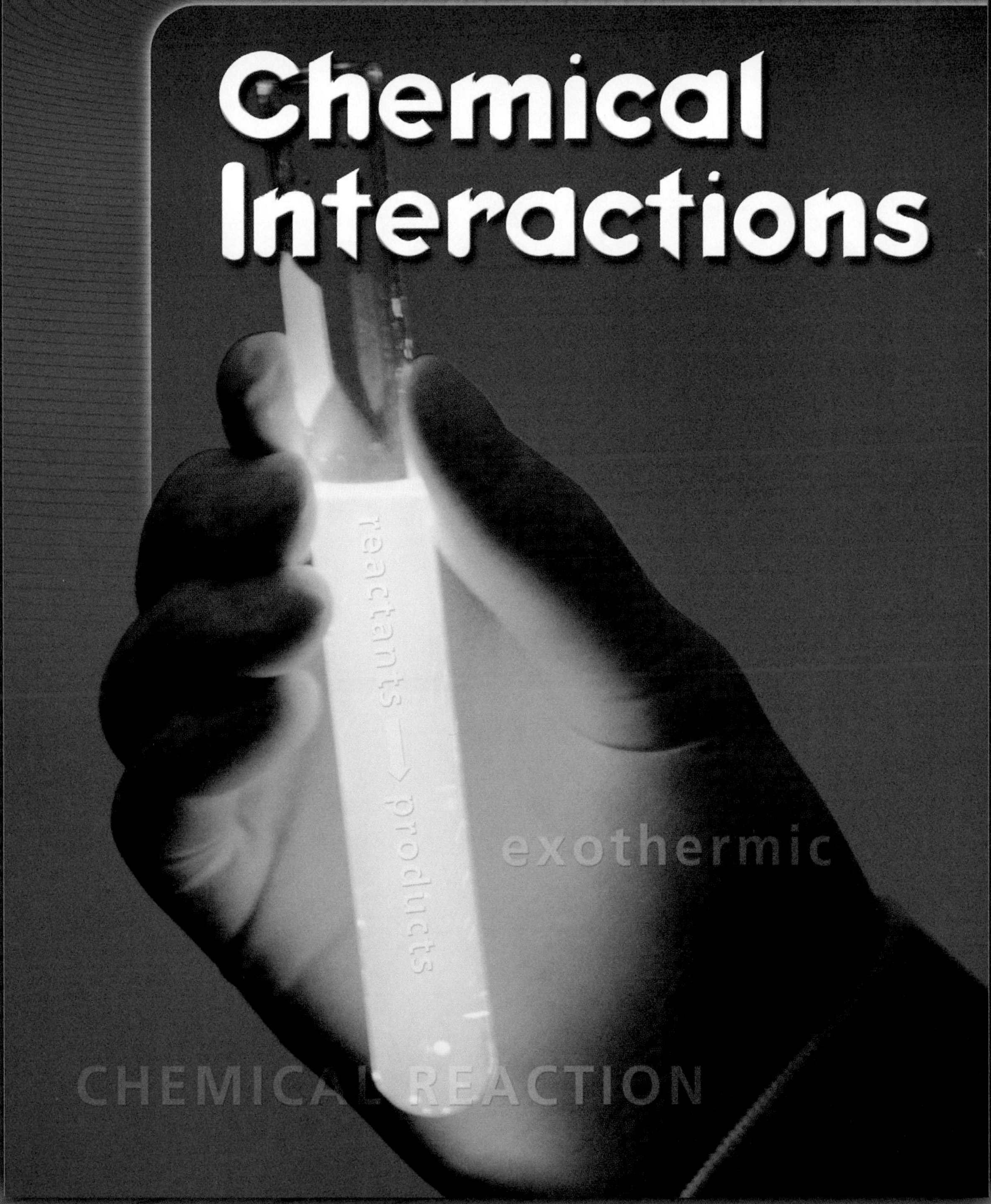

reactants → products

exothermic

CHEMICAL REACTION

Contents Overview

Frontiers in Science
  Medicines from Nature   502

Timelines in Science
  The Story of Atomic Structure   604

Chapter 16 Atomic Structure and
               the Periodic Table   506

Chapter 17 Chemical Bonds and
               Compounds   538

Chapter 18 Chemical Reactions   566

Chapter 19 Solutions   608

Medicines

from Nature

Where have people found medicines?

SCIENTIFIC AMERICAN FRONTIERS

View the "Endangered Wonder Drug" segment of your Scientific American Frontiers video to see how chemicals found in nature can improve the health of people.

In Brazil, extracts from plants are used to treat everything from Parkinson's Disease to arthritis.

Finding Natural Remedies

In the 1960s, people were searching desperately for new cancer-fighting agents. Scientists tested over 35,000 compounds, some of which came from the bark of the Pacific yew tree, long known to have strong effects on the body. The tests indicated that something in the bark stopped the growth of cancerous tumors. Scientists eventually derived the drug Taxol from the compounds found in the yew tree.

Natural medicines are much more than simple folk cures, like the sapi karta leaves that the Kuna people of Panama believe increase creativity. Many powerful medicines are based on compounds found in nature. But even though these natural compounds may be very effective at treating diseases, they can be limited in supply and can have harmful side effects. Organic chemists must find ways to make these compounds safer and produce them in greater amounts.

Modeling the Molecule

To make a compound, a chemist must know what its molecule looks like, atom by atom. Many useful drugs have structures that contain many atoms arranged in complicated ways. The chemist must know exactly how many atoms of each kind are in the molecule and how they are arranged. One atom in the wrong place might mean that the drug won't work the way it should.

To study the structures of molecules, chemists use a method called spectroscopy. Spectroscopy is a process that shows how the molecules of a compound respond to certain forms of radiation. Three important types of spectroscopy are

- NMR (nuclear magnetic resonance) spectroscopy, which allows chemists to identify small groups of atoms within larger molecules

- IR (infrared) spectroscopy, which shows the presence of certain types of bonds in molecules

- X-ray studies, which show details such as how much space there is between atoms and what the overall physical shapes of molecules are

Chemists put all this information together to determine the structure of a molecule. They might even build a model of the molecule.

Assembling the Puzzle

Once chemists know the structure of the molecule, they must figure out the starting reactants and the specific sequence of chemical reactions that will produce that molecule as a final product. It is a lot like doing a jigsaw puzzle when you know what the final picture looks like but still have to fit together all the pieces. Only in this case, the chemists may not even be sure what the little pieces look like.

Organic chemists often prefer to complete the process backward. They look at a model of the complete molecule and then figure out how they might build one just like it. How do chemists know what kinds of reactions might produce a certain molecule? Chemists have classified chemical reactions into different types. They determine how combinations of reactions will put the various kinds of atoms into their correct places in the molecule. Chemists may need to combine dozens of reactions to get the desired molecule.

Testing the Medicine

Once chemists have produced the desired drug molecule, the synthetic compound must be carefully tested to make sure it works like the natural substance does. The sequence of reactions must also be tested to make sure they produce the same compound when larger amounts of chemicals are used.

View the "Endangered Wonder Drug" segment of your *Scientific American Frontiers* video to see how modern medicines can be developed from chemical compounds found in nature.

IN THIS SCENE FROM THE VIDEO ▶

A researcher works with a substance found in bark.

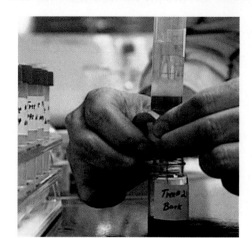

SAVING LIVES THROUGH NATURE AND CHEMISTRY
Medicines from plants and other natural sources have been used by different cultures around the world for thousands of years. The ephedra plant contains the raw material for many decongestants, which help shrink swollen nasal passages. It was used by the Chinese more than 5000 years ago. Today, the bark of the Pacific yew tree is being used as the source of the anticancer drug Taxol. A large amount of bark from the tree, however, is needed to make just one dose of the drug, and very few Pacific yew trees are available. Chemists, therefore, are trying to make this medicine in the laboratory.

Once a potential new drug is found in nature, it may take several years, or even decades, to figure out how to produce the drug synthetically and test it for safety. Only a small percentage of drugs tested ever goes to market, because the drugs must undergo several stages of testing on both animals and humans. Today, chemists routinely search the seas and the forests for marine organisms and rare plants that might have the power to fight cancer, heart disease, or viruses.

Chemists often use computers to make models of drug molecules. Computers allow the chemists to see how the drug molecules will interact with other molecules.

UNANSWERED Questions

The search for new chemical compounds that can be used to treat human illnesses raises many questions. Scientists need to find ways to investigate, produce, and test new, more powerful drugs.

- How might scientists more quickly test the safety and effectiveness of new medicines?
- Can easily synthesized compounds be just as effective as natural medicines?
- Might the processes that produce these drugs in nature be duplicated in a lab?
- Can we discover other new sources of medicines in the natural world?

UNIT PROJECTS

As you study this unit, work alone or with a group on one of these projects.

Medicines Around You

Present a report about a plant in your region that has medicinal properties.

- Collect samples of a plant that has medicinal properties.
- Bring your plant samples into your classroom. Prepare and present a report about the plant and the way it is used in medicine.

Model Medicine

Build a scale model of a molecule that is used to treat a certain illness.

- Using the Internet or an encyclopedia, determine the structure of a compound that interests you.
- Using foam balls, toothpicks, water colors, string, and other materials, construct a model of the molecule. Describe your model to the class.

Remedies

Write a news report about a popular herbal remedy, such as Saint John's Wort.

- To learn more about the herbal remedy, try interviewing a personal fitness trainer or an employee of a health-food store.
- Deliver a news report to the class telling of the advantages of the remedy and warning of its potential dangers.

CAREER CENTER
CLASSZONE.COM

Learn more about careers in chemistry.

Atomic Structure and the Periodic Table

the **BIG** idea

A substance's atomic structure determines its physical and chemical properties.

> You can't zoom in any closer than this! The picture is an extremely close-up view of nickel. How do things look different the closer you get to them?

Key Concepts

SECTION
Atoms are the smallest form of elements.
Learn about the structure of atoms and how each element's atoms are different.

SECTION
Elements make up the periodic table.
Learn how the periodic table of the elements is organized.

SECTION
The periodic table is a map of the elements.
Learn more about the groups of elements in the periodic table.

Internet Preview

CLASSZONE.COM

Chapter 16 online resources: Content Review, Simulation, Visualization, three Resource Centers, Math Tutorial, Test Practice

EXPLORE (the BIG idea)

That's Far!

Place a baseball in the middle of a large field. Hold a dime and count off the number of steps from the baseball to the edge of the field. If the baseball were an atom's nucleus and the dime an electron, you would need to go about 6000 steps to walk the distance between the nucleus and the electrons.

Observe and Think How far were you able to go? How much farther would you need to go to model the proportion of an atom? What does this tell you about atomic structure?

Element Safari

Locate the following products in your home or in a grocery store: baking soda, vinegar, cereal flakes, and antacid tablets. You may examine other products if you wish. Look at the labels on the products. Can you recognize the names of any elements? Use your periodic table as a reference.

Observe and Think Which element names did you find?

Internet Activity: Periodic Table

Go to **ClassZone.com** to explore the periodic table. See different ways to set up the table and learn more about the listed elements.

Observe and Think How do atomic number and mass change as you move across the periodic table?

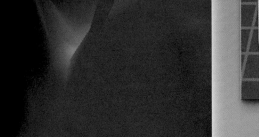

NSTA
scilinks.org

SCi
LINKS

Atomic Theory **Code: MDL022**

Getting Ready to Learn

CONCEPT REVIEW

- Matter is made of particles called atoms that are too small to see with the eyes.
- Matter can be an element, a compound, or a mixture.
- Matter can undergo physical and chemical changes.

VOCABULARY REVIEW

See Glossary for definitions.

atom

compound

element

CONTENT REVIEW
CLASSZONE.COM
Review concepts and vocabulary.

TAKING NOTES

MAIN IDEA WEB

Write each new blue heading in a box. Then write notes in boxes around the center box that give important terms and details about that blue heading.

VOCABULARY STRATEGY

Write each new vocabulary term in the center of a **frame game** diagram. Decide what information to frame it with. Use examples, descriptions, parts, sentences that use the term in context, or pictures. You can change the frame to fit each term.

See the Note-Taking Handbook on pages R45–R51.

SCIENCE NOTEBOOK

Atoms are made of protons, neutrons, and electrons.	The atomic number is the number of protons in the nucleus.

Each element is made of a different atom.

Every element has a certain number of protons in its nucleus.	

Central part of atom

Contains most of an atom's mass

NUCLEUS

Electrons move about it

Is made of protons and neutrons

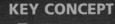

KEY CONCEPT

16.1 Atoms are the smallest form of elements.

STANDARDS

7–5.1 Recognize that matter is composed of extremely small particles called atoms.

7–5.2 Classify matter as element, compound, or mixture on the basis of its composition.

VOCABULARY

proton p. 511
neutron p. 511
nucleus p. 511
electron p. 511
atomic number p. 512
atomic mass number p. 512
isotope p. 512
ion p. 514

 BEFORE, you learned

• All matter is made of atoms
• Elements are the simplest substances

NOW, you will learn

• Where atoms are found and how they are named
• About the structure of atoms
• How ions are formed from atoms

EXPLORE The Size of Atoms

How small can you cut paper?

PROCEDURE

① Cut the strip of paper in half. Cut one of these halves in half.

② Continue cutting one piece of paper in half as many times as you can.

WHAT DO YOU THINK?
• How many cuts were you able to make?
• Do you think you could keep cutting the paper forever? Why or why not?

MATERIALS
• strip of paper about 30 centimeters long
• scissors

All matter is made of atoms.

Think of all the substances you see and touch every day. Are all of these substances the same? Obviously, the substances that make up this book you're reading are quite different from the substances in the air around you. So how many different substances can there be? This is a question people have been asking for thousands of years.

About 2400 years ago, Greek philosophers proposed that everything on Earth was made of only four basic substances—air, water, fire, and earth. Everything else contained a mixture of these four substances. As time went on, chemists came to realize that there had to be more than four basic substances. Today chemists know that about 100 basic substances, or elements, account for everything we see and touch. Sometimes these elements appear by themselves. Most often, however, these elements appear in combination with other elements to make new substances. In this section, you'll learn about the atoms of the elements that make up the world and how these atoms differ from one another.

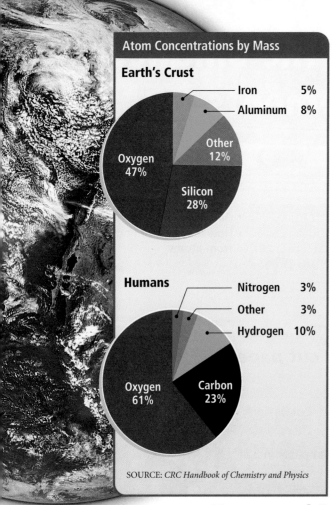

Atom Concentrations by Mass

Earth's Crust

Iron 5%
Aluminum 8%
Other 12%
Oxygen 47%
Silicon 28%

Humans

Nitrogen 3%
Other 3%
Hydrogen 10%
Oxygen 61%
Carbon 23%

SOURCE: *CRC Handbook of Chemistry and Physics*

Types of Atoms in Earth's Crust and Living Things

Atoms of the element hydrogen account for about 90 percent of the total mass of the universe. Hydrogen atoms make up only about 1 percent of Earth's crust, however, and most of those hydrogen atoms are combined with oxygen atoms in the form of water. The graph on the left shows the types of atoms in approximately the top 100 kilometers of Earth's crust.

The distribution of the atoms of the elements in living things is very different from what it is in Earth's crust. Living things contain at least 25 types of atoms. Although the amounts of these atoms vary somewhat, all living things—animals, plants, and bacteria—are composed primarily of atoms of oxygen, carbon, hydrogen, and nitrogen. As you can see in the lower graph on the left, oxygen atoms account for more than half your body's mass.

 CHECK YOUR READING What is the most common element in the universe?

Names and Symbols of Elements

Elements get their names in many different ways. Magnesium, for example, was named for the region in Greece known as Magnesia. Lithium comes from the Greek word *lithos,* which means "stone." Neptunium was named after the planet Neptune. The elements einsteinium and fermium were named after scientists Albert Einstein and Enrico Fermi.

Each element has its own unique symbol. For some elements, the symbol is simply the first letter of its name.

hydrogen (H)   sulfur (S)   carbon (C)

The symbols for other elements use the first letter plus one other letter of the element's name. Notice that the first letter is capitalized but the second letter is not.

aluminum (Al)   platinum (Pt)   cadmium (Cd)   zinc (Zn)

The origins of some symbols, however, are less obvious. The symbol for gold (Au), for example, doesn't seem to have anything to do with the element's name. The symbol refers instead to gold's name in Latin, *aurum.* Lead (Pb), iron (Fe), and copper (Cu) are a few other elements whose symbols come from Latin names.

Each element is made of a different atom.

In the early 1800s British scientist John Dalton proposed that each element is made of tiny particles called atoms. Dalton stated that all of the atoms of a particular element are identical but are different from atoms of all other elements. Every atom of silver, for example, is similar to every other atom of silver but different from an atom of iron.

Dalton's theory also assumed that atoms could not be divided into anything simpler. Scientists later discovered that this was not exactly true. They found that atoms are made of even smaller particles.

RESOURCE CENTER
CLASSZONE.COM
Learn more about the atom.

The Structure of an Atom

A key discovery leading to the current model of the atom was that atoms contain charged particles. The charge on a particle can be either positive or negative. Particles with the same type of charge repel each other—they are pushed apart. Particles with different charges attract each other—they are drawn toward each other.

Atoms are composed of three types of particles—electrons, protons, and neutrons. A **proton** is a positively charged particle, and a **neutron** is an uncharged particle. The neutron has approximately the same mass as a proton. The protons and neutrons of an atom are grouped together in the atom's center. This combination of protons and neutrons is called the **nucleus** of the atom. Because it contains protons, the nucleus has a positive charge. **Electrons** are negatively charged particles that move around outside the nucleus.

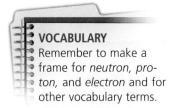

VOCABULARY
Remember to make a frame for *neutron, proton,* and *electron* and for other vocabulary terms.

The Atomic Model

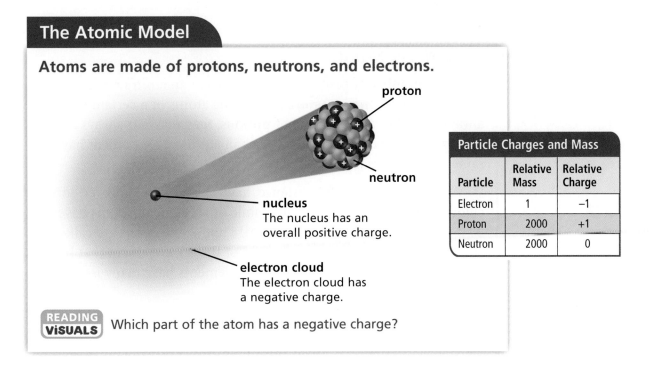

Atoms are made of protons, neutrons, and electrons.

proton

neutron

nucleus
The nucleus has an overall positive charge.

electron cloud
The electron cloud has a negative charge.

Particle Charges and Mass		
Particle	Relative Mass	Relative Charge
Electron	1	–1
Proton	2000	+1
Neutron	2000	0

READING VISUALS Which part of the atom has a negative charge?

Atoms are extremely small, about 10^{-10} meters in diameter. This means that you could fit millions of atoms in the period at the end of this sentence. The diagram on page 511, picturing the basic structure of the atom, is not drawn to scale. In an atom the electron cloud is about 10,000 times the diameter of the nucleus.

Electrons are much smaller than protons or neutrons—about 2000 times smaller. Electrons also move about the nucleus very quickly. Scientists have found that it is not possible to determine their exact positions with any certainty. This is why we picture the electrons as being in a cloud around the nucleus.

The negative electrons remain associated with the nucleus because they are attracted to the positively charged protons. Also, because electrical charges that are alike (such as two negative charges) repel each other, electrons remain spread out in the electron cloud. Neutral atoms have no overall electrical charge because they have an equal number of protons and electrons.

Atom Size

Millions of atoms could fit in a space the size of this dot. It would take you 500 years to count the number of atoms in a grain of salt.

Atomic Numbers

If all atoms are composed of the same particles, how can there be more than 100 different elements? The identity of an atom is determined by the number of protons in its nucleus, called the **atomic number.** Every hydrogen atom—atomic number 1—has exactly one proton in its nucleus. Every gold atom has 79 protons, which means the atomic number of gold is 79.

Gold has 79 protons and 79 electrons.

Atomic Mass Numbers

The total number of protons and neutrons in an atom's nucleus is called its **atomic mass number.** While the atoms of a certain element always have the same number of protons, they may not always have the same number of neutrons, so not all atoms of an element have the same atomic mass number.

All chlorine atoms, for instance, have 17 protons. However, some chlorine atoms have 18 neutrons, while other chlorine atoms have 20 neutrons. Atoms of chlorine with 18 and 20 neutrons are called chlorine isotopes. **Isotopes** are atoms of the same element that have a different number of neutrons. Some elements have many isotopes, while other elements have just a few.

READING TiP

The *iso-* in *isotope* is from the Greek language, and it means "equal."

 How is atomic mass number different from atomic number?

Isotopes

Isotopes have different numbers of neutrons.

Chlorine-35
atomic mass number = 35

17 protons
18 neutrons

nucleus   17 electrons

Chlorine-37
atomic mass number = 37

17 protons
20 neutrons

nucleus   17 electrons

A particular isotope is designated by the name of the element and the total number of its protons and neutrons. You can find the number of neutrons in a particular isotope by subtracting the atomic number from the atomic mass number. For example, chlorine-35 indicates the isotope of chlorine that has 18 neutrons. Chlorine-37 has 20 neutrons. Every atom of a given element always has the same atomic number because it has the same number of protons. However, the atomic mass number varies depending on the number of neutrons.

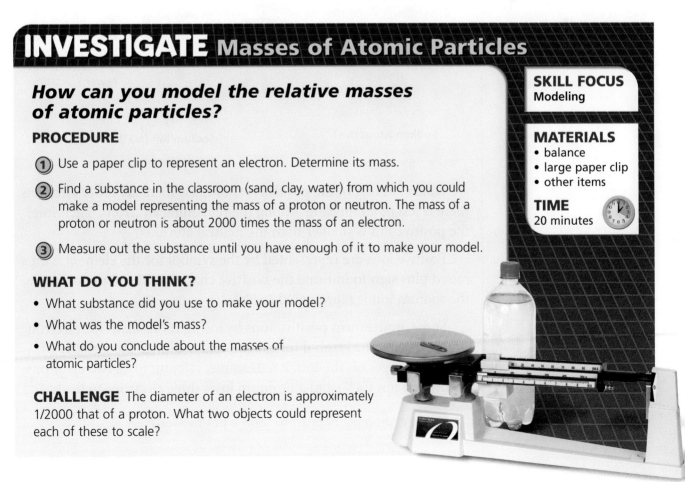

INVESTIGATE Masses of Atomic Particles

How can you model the relative masses of atomic particles?

PROCEDURE

1. Use a paper clip to represent an electron. Determine its mass.

2. Find a substance in the classroom (sand, clay, water) from which you could make a model representing the mass of a proton or neutron. The mass of a proton or neutron is about 2000 times the mass of an electron.

3. Measure out the substance until you have enough of it to make your model.

WHAT DO YOU THINK?

- What substance did you use to make your model?
- What was the model's mass?
- What do you conclude about the masses of atomic particles?

CHALLENGE The diameter of an electron is approximately 1/2000 that of a proton. What two objects could represent each of these to scale?

SKILL FOCUS
Modeling

MATERIALS
- balance
- large paper clip
- other items

TIME
20 minutes

MAIN IDEA WEB
Make a main idea web to organize what you know about ions.

Atoms form ions.

An atom has an equal number of electrons and protons. Since each electron has one negative charge and each proton has one positive charge, atoms have no overall electrical charge. An **ion** is formed when an atom loses or gains one or more electrons. Because the number of electrons in an ion is different from the number of protons, an ion does have an overall electric charge.

Formation of Positive Ions

Consider how a positive ion can be formed from an atom. The left side of the illustration below represents a sodium (Na) atom. Its nucleus contains 11 protons and some neutrons. Because the electron cloud surrounding the nucleus consists of 11 electrons, there is no overall charge on the atom. If the atom loses one electron, however, the charges are no longer balanced. There is now one more proton than there are electrons. The ion formed, therefore, has a positive charge.

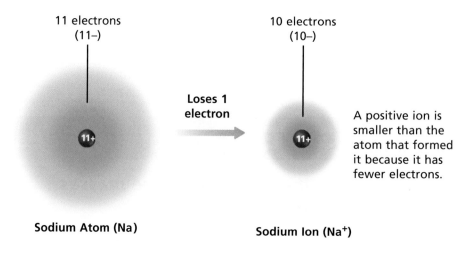

11 electrons
(11–)

10 electrons
(10–)

Loses 1 electron

A positive ion is smaller than the atom that formed it because it has fewer electrons.

Sodium Atom (Na)

Sodium Ion (Na⁺)

Notice the size of the positive ion. Because there are fewer electrons, there is less of a repulsion among the remaining electrons. Therefore, the positive ion is smaller than the neutral atom.

Positive ions are represented by the symbol for the element with a raised plus sign to indicate the positive charge. In the above example, the sodium ion is represented as Na^+.

Some atoms form positive ions by losing more than one electron. In those cases, the symbol for the ion also indicates the number of positive charges on the ion. For example, calcium loses two electrons to form an ion Ca^{2+}, and aluminum loses three electrons to form Al^{3+}.

CHECK YOUR READING   What must happen to form a positive ion?

Formation of Negative Ions

The illustration below shows how a negative ion is formed. In this case the atom is chlorine (Cl). The nucleus of a chlorine atom contains 17 protons and some neutrons. The electron cloud has 17 electrons, so the atom has no overall charge. When an electron is added to the chlorine atom, a negatively charged ion is formed. Notice that a negative ion is larger than the neutral atom that formed it. The extra electron increases the repulsion within the cloud, causing it to expand.

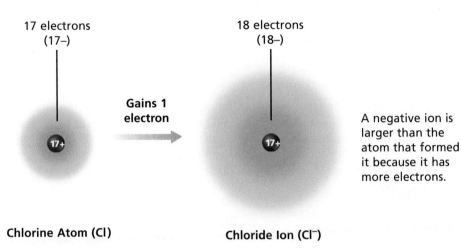

17 electrons
(17–)

Gains 1
electron

18 electrons
(18–)

17+

17+

A negative ion is larger than the atom that formed it because it has more electrons.

Chlorine Atom (Cl)

Chloride Ion (Cl⁻)

Negative ions are represented by placing a minus sign to the right and slightly above the element's symbol. The negative chloride ion in the example, therefore, would be written as Cl^-. If an ion has gained more than one electron, the number of added electrons is indicated by a number in front of the minus sign. Oxygen (O), for example, gains two electrons when it forms an ion. Its symbol is O^{2-}.

 **16.1 Review**

KEY CONCEPTS

1. Which two atoms are most common in Earth's crust? in the human body?

2. What are the particles that make up an atom?

3. What happens when an atom forms an ion?

CRITICAL THINKING

4. **Infer** Magnesium and sodium atoms are about the same size. How does the size of a magnesium ion with a 2+ charge compare with that of a sodium ion with a single + charge?

5. **Compare** The atomic number of potassium is 19. How does potassium-39 differ from potassium-41?

⬤ CHALLENGE

6. **Analyze** When determining the mass of an atom, the electrons are not considered. Why can scientists disregard the electrons?

PHYSICAL SCIENCE AND LIFE SCIENCE

Elements of Life

There are more than 25 different types of atoms in the cells of your body. The table below shows the amount of atoms of some of the elements in a 50-kilogram human. Atoms of the element oxygen account for about 61 percent of a person's mass. Atoms of carbon account for about 23 percent of a person's mass. Although the atoms of some elements are present only in very small amounts, they play an important role in the chemical processes that occur in your cells.

Blood and Other Fluids

Iron ions are part of the hemoglobin that gives your blood its red color and carries oxygen to cells throughout your body. Sodium and potassium ions help regulate the amount and location of the water in your body. Sodium and potassium ions also make up part of the sweat your body produces to regulate temperature.

Bones and Teeth

The sturdier structures of your body get their strength from calcium, magnesium, and phosphorus. You have less than a kilogram of calcium in your body, almost all of which is in your bones and teeth. Fluoride ions make up part of the hard coating on your teeth. This is why you'll often find fluoride ions added to toothpaste.

Elements to Avoid

In some way, the atoms of every element in the periodic table play a role in human lives. Many of them, however, can be hazardous if handled improperly. For example, arsenic and mercury are poisonous.

Mass of Elements in 50 kg Human	
Element	**Amount (kg)**
Oxygen (O)	30.5
Carbon (C)	11.5
Hydrogen (H)	5.0
Nitrogen (N)	1.3
Calcium (Ca)	0.7
Phosphorus (P)	0.6
Potassium (K)	0.1
Sodium (Na)	> 0.1
Chlorine (Cl)	> 0.1

Other elements are in the body in very small amounts.

SOURCE: *CRC Handbook of Chemistry and Physics*

EXPLORE

1. **CALCULATE** What percentage of your body is made up of oxygen, carbon, hydrogen, and nitrogen?

2. **CHALLENGE** Salt, made of sodium ions and chloride ions, is an essential part of your diet. However, too much salt can cause health problems. Use the Internet to find out about the problems caused by too much or too little salt in your diet.

 **RESOURCE CENTER**
CLASSZONE.COM   Find out more about the elements important to life.

This photo shows a false color X-ray of the human skull. X-rays show the bones in the human body. Bones contain calcium.

516 Unit 5: **Chemical Interactions**

16.2

KEY CONCEPT
Elements make up the periodic table.

STANDARDS

7–5.4 Use the periodic table to identify the basic organization of elements and groups of elements (including metals, nonmetals, and families).

VOCABULARY

atomic mass p. 517
periodic table p. 518
group p. 522
period p. 522

> **BEFORE, you learned**
>
> • Atoms have a structure
> • Every element is made from a different type of atom

> **NOW, you will learn**
>
> • How the periodic table is organized
> • How properties of elements are shown by the periodic table

---

EXPLORE Similarities and Differences of Objects

How can different objects be organized?

PROCEDURE

1. With several classmates, organize the buttons into three or more groups.

2. Compare your team's organization of the buttons with another team's organization.

WHAT DO YOU THINK?

• What characteristics did you use to organize the buttons?
• In what other ways could you have organized the buttons?

MATERIALS
buttons

Elements can be organized by similarities.

One way of organizing elements is by the masses of their atoms. Finding the masses of atoms was a difficult task for the chemists of the past. They could not place an atom on a pan balance. All they could do was find the mass of a very large number of atoms of a certain element and then infer the mass of a single one of them.

Remember that not all the atoms of an element have the same atomic mass number. Elements have isotopes. When chemists attempt to measure the mass of an atom, therefore, they are actually finding the average mass of all its isotopes. The **atomic mass** of the atoms of an element is the average mass of all the element's isotopes. Even before chemists knew how the atoms of different elements could be different, they knew atoms had different atomic masses.

Mendeleev's Periodic Table

In the early 1800s several scientists proposed systems to organize the elements based on their properties. None of these suggested methods worked very well until a Russian chemist named Dmitri Mendeleev (MENH-duh-LAY-uhf) decided to work on the problem.

In the 1860s, Mendeleev began thinking about how he could organize the elements based on their physical and chemical properties. He made a set of element cards. Each card contained the atomic mass of an atom of an element as well as any information about the element's properties. Mendeleev spent hours arranging the cards in various ways, looking for a relationship between properties and atomic mass.

The exercise led Mendeleev to think of listing the elements in a chart. In the rows of the chart, he placed those elements showing similar chemical properties. He arranged the rows so the atomic masses increased as one moved down each vertical column. It took Mendeleev quite a bit of thinking and rethinking to get all the relationships correct, but in 1869 he produced the first **periodic table** of the elements. We call it the periodic table because it shows a periodic, or repeating, pattern of properties of the elements. In the reproduction of Mendeleev's first table shown below, notice how he placed carbon (C) and silicon (Si), two elements known for their similarities, in the same row.

△ CHECK YOUR READING   What organizing method did Mendeleev use?

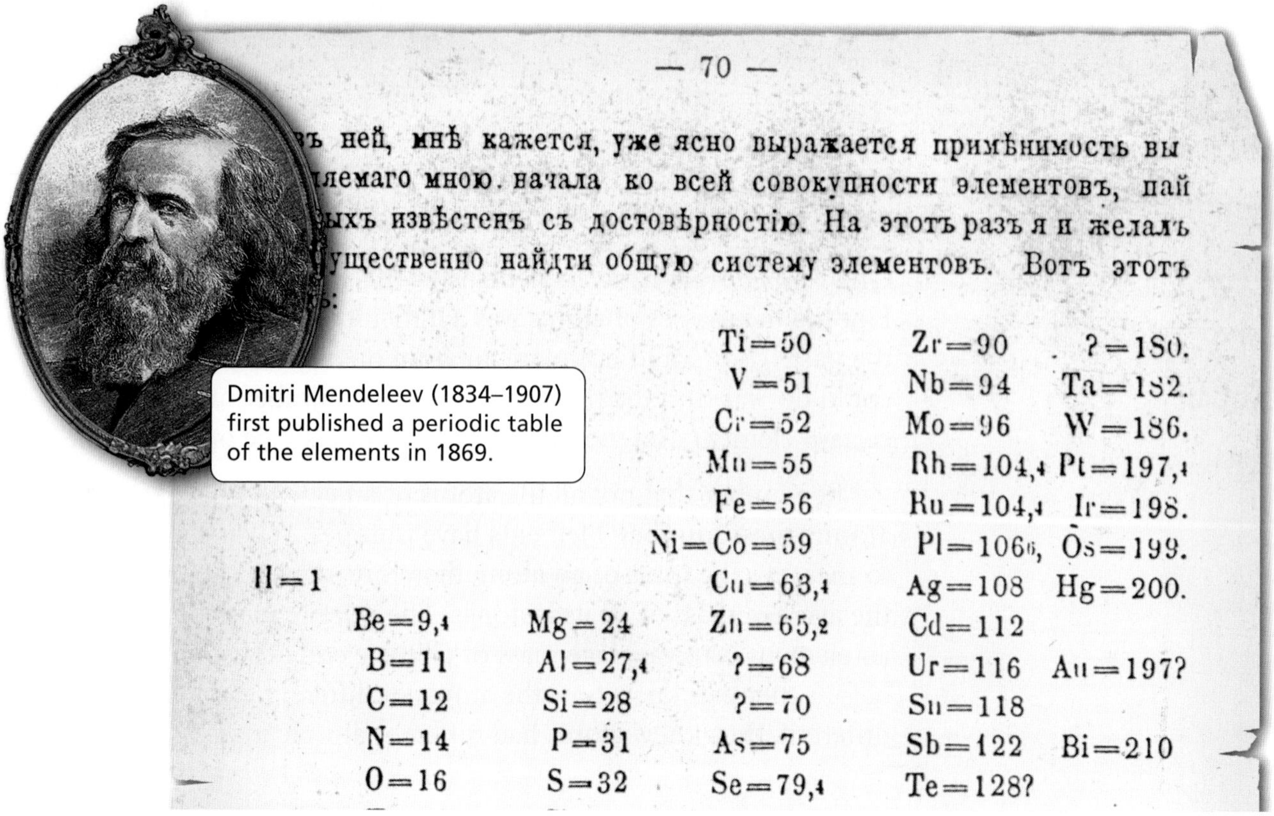

— 70 —

ъ ней, мнѣ кажется, уже ясно выражается примѣнимость вы
лемаго мною. начала ко всей совокупности элементовъ, пай
ыхъ извѣстенъ съ достовѣрностію. На этотъ разъ я и желалъ
ущественно найдти общую систему элементовъ. Вотъ этотъ

			Ti=50	Zr=90	?=180.
			V=51	Nb=94	Ta=182.
			Cr=52	Mo=96	W=186.
			Mn=55	Rh=104,4	Pt=197,4
			Fe=56	Ru=104,4	Ir=198.
		Ni=Co=59		Pl=106,6,	Os=199.
H=1			Cu=63,4	Ag=108	Hg=200.
	Be=9,4	Mg=24	Zn=65,2	Cd=112	
	B=11	Al=27,4	?=68	Ur=116	Au=197?
	C=12	Si=28	?=70	Sn=118	
	N=14	P=31	As=75	Sb=122	Bi=210
	O=16	S=32	Se=79,4	Te=128?	

Dmitri Mendeleev (1834–1907) first published a periodic table of the elements in 1869.

Predicting New Elements

When Mendeleev constructed his table, he left some empty spaces where no known elements fit the pattern. He predicted that new elements that would complete the chart would eventually be discovered. He even described some of the properties of these unknown elements.

At the start, many chemists found it hard to accept Mendeleev's predictions of unknown elements. Only six years after he published the table, however, the first of these elements—represented by the question mark after aluminum (Al) on his table—was discovered. This element was given the name gallium, after the country France (Gaul) where it was discovered. In the next 20 years, two other elements Mendeleev predicted would be discovered.

The periodic table organizes the atoms of the elements by properties and atomic number.

MAIN IDEA WEB
Make a main idea web to summarize the information you can learn from the periodic table.

The modern periodic table on pages 520 and 521 differs from Mendeleev's table in several ways. For one thing, elements with similar properties are found in columns, not rows. More important, the elements are not arranged by atomic mass but by atomic number.

Reading the Periodic Table

Each square of the periodic table gives particular information about the atoms of an element.

❶ The number at the top of the square is the atomic number, which is the number of protons in the nucleus of an atom of that element.

❷ The chemical symbol is an abbreviation for the element's name. It contains one or two letters. Some elements that have not yet been named are designated by temporary three-letter symbols.

❸ The name of the element is written below the symbol.

❹ The number below the name indicates the average atomic mass of all the isotopes of the element.

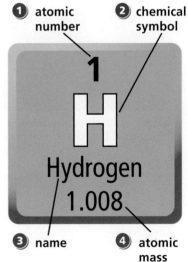

The color of the element's symbol indicates the physical state of the element at room temperature. White letters—such as the *H* for hydrogen in the box to the right—indicate a gas. Blue letters indicate a liquid, and black letters indicate a solid. The background colors of the squares indicate whether the element is a metal, nonmetal, or metalloid. These terms will be explained in the next section.

1

1								
1								
H								
Hydrogen								
1.008								

2

Period

Each row of the periodic table is called a **period**. As read from left to right, one proton and one electron are added from one element to the next.

2	3	4
2	**3** Li Lithium 6.941	**4** Be Beryllium 9.012
3	**11** Na Sodium 22.990	**12** Mg Magnesium 24.305

		3	**4**	**5**	**6**	**7**	**8**	**9**
4	**19** K Potassium 39.098	**20** Ca Calcium 40.078	**21** Sc Scandium 44.956	**22** Ti Titanium 47.87	**23** V Vanadium 50.942	**24** Cr Chromium 51.996	**25** Mn Manganese 54.938	**26** Fe Iron 55.845	**27** Co Cobalt 58.933
5	**37** Rb Rubidium 85.468	**38** Sr Strontium 87.62	**39** Y Yttrium 88.906	**40** Zr Zirconium 91.224	**41** Nb Niobium 92.906	**42** Mo Molybdenum 95.94	**43** Tc Technetium (98)	**44** Ru Ruthenium 101.07	**45** Rh Rhodium 102.906
6	**55** Cs Cesium 132.905	**56** Ba Barium 137.327	**57** La Lanthanum 138.906	**72** Hf Hafnium 178.49	**73** Ta Tantalum 180.95	**74** W Tungsten 183.84	**75** Re Rhenium 186.207	**76** Os Osmium 190.23	**77** Ir Iridium 192.217
7	**87** Fr Francium (223)	**88** Ra Radium (226)	**89** Ac Actinium (227)	**104** Rf Rutherfordium (261)	**105** Db Dubnium (262)	**106** Sg Seaborgium (266)	**107** Bh Bohrium (264)	**108** Hs Hassium (269)	**109** Mt Meitnerium (268)

Group

Each column of the table is called a **group**. Elements in a group share similar properties. Groups are read from top to bottom.

58 Ce Cerium 140.116	**59** Pr Praseodymium 140.908	**60** Nd Neodymium 144.24	**61** Pm Promethium (145)	**62** Sm Samarium 150.36
90 Th Thorium 232.038	**91** Pa Protactinium 231.036	**92** U Uranium 238.029	**93** Np Neptunium (237)	**94** Pu Plutonium (244)

 Metal   Metalloid   Nonmetal 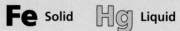 **Fe** Solid   Hg Liquid   O Gas

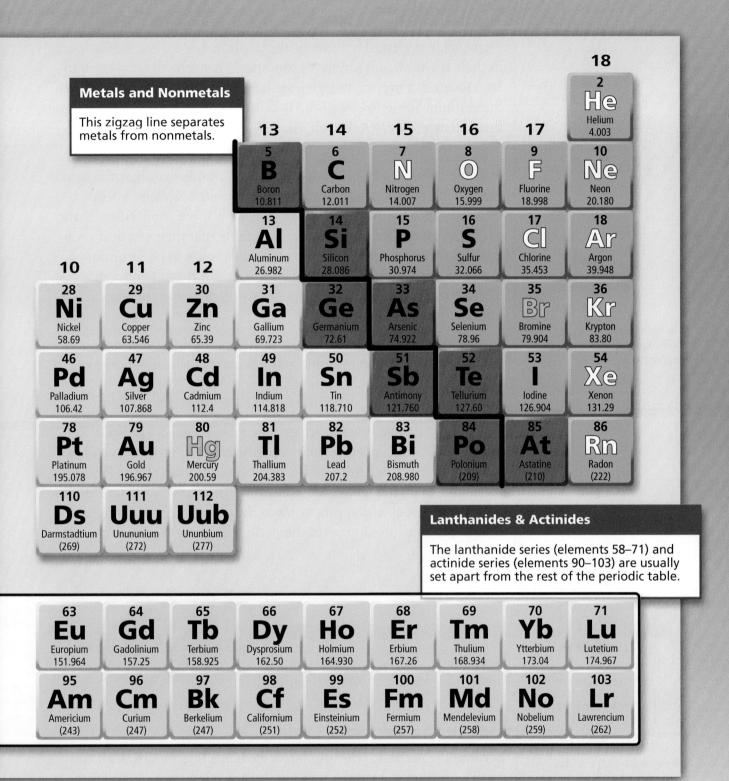

Metals and Nonmetals

This zigzag line separates metals from nonmetals.

18

| 2 | **He** | Helium | 4.003 |

13 | **14** | **15** | **16** | **17**

5	**B**	Boron	10.811
6	**C**	Carbon	12.011
7	**N**	Nitrogen	14.007
8	**O**	Oxygen	15.999
9	**F**	Fluorine	18.998
10	**Ne**	Neon	20.180

13	**Al**	Aluminum	26.982
14	**Si**	Silicon	28.086
15	**P**	Phosphorus	30.974
16	**S**	Sulfur	32.066
17	**Cl**	Chlorine	35.453
18	**Ar**	Argon	39.948

10 | **11** | **12**

28	**Ni**	Nickel	58.69
29	**Cu**	Copper	63.546
30	**Zn**	Zinc	65.39
31	**Ga**	Gallium	69.723
32	**Ge**	Germanium	72.61
33	**As**	Arsenic	74.922
34	**Se**	Selenium	78.96
35	**Br**	Bromine	79.904
36	**Kr**	Krypton	83.80

46	**Pd**	Palladium	106.42
47	**Ag**	Silver	107.868
48	**Cd**	Cadmium	112.4
49	**In**	Indium	114.818
50	**Sn**	Tin	118.710
51	**Sb**	Antimony	121.760
52	**Te**	Tellurium	127.60
53	**I**	Iodine	126.904
54	**Xe**	Xenon	131.29

78	**Pt**	Platinum	195.078
79	**Au**	Gold	196.967
80	**Hg**	Mercury	200.59
81	**Tl**	Thallium	204.383
82	**Pb**	Lead	207.2
83	**Bi**	Bismuth	208.980
84	**Po**	Polonium	(209)
85	**At**	Astatine	(210)
86	**Rn**	Radon	(222)

110	**Ds**	Darmstadtium	(269)
111	**Uuu**	Unununium	(272)
112	**Uub**	Ununbium	(277)

Lanthanides & Actinides

The lanthanide series (elements 58–71) and actinide series (elements 90–103) are usually set apart from the rest of the periodic table.

63	**Eu**	Europium	151.964
64	**Gd**	Gadolinium	157.25
65	**Tb**	Terbium	158.925
66	**Dy**	Dysprosium	162.50
67	**Ho**	Holmium	164.930
68	**Er**	Erbium	167.26
69	**Tm**	Thulium	168.934
70	**Yb**	Ytterbium	173.04
71	**Lu**	Lutetium	174.967

95	**Am**	Americium	(243)
96	**Cm**	Curium	(247)
97	**Bk**	Berkelium	(247)
98	**Cf**	Californium	(251)
99	**Es**	Einsteinium	(252)
100	**Fm**	Fermium	(257)
101	**Md**	Mendelevium	(258)
102	**No**	Nobelium	(259)
103	**Lr**	Lawrencium	(262)

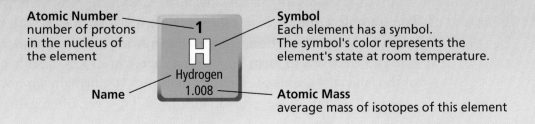

Atomic Number number of protons in the nucleus of the element

Name

1

H

Hydrogen 1.008

Symbol Each element has a symbol. The symbol's color represents the element's state at room temperature.

Atomic Mass average mass of isotopes of this element

Groups and Periods

Elements in a vertical column of the periodic table show similarities in their chemical and physical properties. The elements in a column are known as a **group**, and they are labeled by a number at the top of the column. Sometimes a group is called a family of elements, because these elements seem to be related.

The illustration at the left shows Group 17, commonly referred to as the halogen group. Halogens tend to combine easily with many other elements and compounds, especially with the elements in Groups 1 and 2. Although the halogens have some similarities to one another, you can see from the periodic table that their physical properties are not the same. Fluorine and chlorine are gases, bromine is a liquid, and iodine and astatine are solids at room temperature. Remember that the members of a family of elements are related but not identical.

Metals like copper can be used to make containers for water. Some metals—such as lithium, sodium, and potassium—however, react violently if they come in contact with water. They are all in the same group, the vertical column labeled 1 on the table.

Each horizontal row in the periodic table is called a **period.** Properties of elements change in a predictable way from one end of a period to the other. In the illustration below, which shows Period 3, the elements on the far left are metals and the ones on the far right are nonmetals. The chemical properties of the elements show a progression; similar progressions appear in the periods above and below this one.

The elements in Group 17, the halogens, show many similarities.

Period 3 contains elements with a wide range of properties. Aluminum (Al) is used to make drink cans, while argon (Ar) is a gas used in light bulbs.

Trends in the Periodic Table

Because the periodic table organizes elements by properties, an element's position in the table can give information about the element. Remember that atoms form ions by gaining or losing electrons. Atoms of elements on the left side of the table form positive ions easily. For example, Group 1 atoms lose an electron to form ions with one positive charge (1+). Atoms of the elements in Group 2, likewise, can lose two electrons to form ions with a charge of 2+. At the other side of the table, the atoms of elements in Group 18 normally do not form ions at all. Atoms of elements in Group 17, however, often gain one electron to form a negative ion (1–). Similarly, the atoms of elements in Group 16 can gain two electrons to form a 2– ion. The atoms of the elements in Groups 3 to 12 all form positive ions, but the charge can vary.

Other information about atoms can be determined by their position in the table. The illustration to the right shows how the sizes of atoms vary across periods and within groups. An atom's size is important because it affects how the atom will react with another atom.

The densities of elements also follow a pattern. Density generally increases from the top of a group to the bottom. Within a period, however, the elements at the left and right sides of the table are the least dense, and the elements in the middle are the most dense. The element osmium (Os) has the highest known density, and it is located at the center of the table.

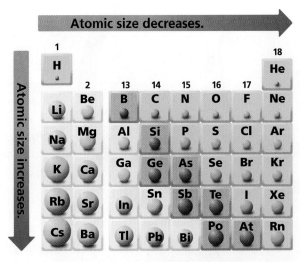

Atomic size is one property that changes in a predictable way across, up, and down the periodic table.

Chemists cannot predict the exact size or density of an atom of one element based on that of another. These trends, nonetheless, are a valuable tool in predicting the properties of different substances. The fact that the trends appeared after the periodic table was organized by atomic number was a victory for all of the scientists like Mendeleev who went looking for them all those years before.

 CHECK YOUR READING   What are some properties that can be related to position on the periodic table?

 **Review**

KEY CONCEPTS

1. How is the modern periodic table organized?

2. What information about an atom's properties can you read from the periodic table?

3. How are the relationships of elements in a group different from the relationships of elements in a period?

CRITICAL THINKING

4. **Infer** Would you expect strontium (Sr) to be more like potassium (K) or bromine (Br)? Why?

5. **Predict** Barium (Ba) is in Group 2. Recall that atoms in Group 1 lose one electron to form ions with a 1+ charge. What type of ion does barium form?

CHALLENGE

6. **Analyze** Explain how chemists can state with certainty that no one will discover an element between sulfur (S) and chlorine (Cl).

CHAPTER INVESTIGATION

Modeling Atomic Masses

OVERVIEW AND PURPOSE Atoms are extremely small. They are so small, in fact, that a single drop of water contains more atoms than you could count in a lifetime! Measuring the masses of atoms to discover the patterns in the periodic table was not an easy task for scientists in the past. This investigation will give you some sense of how scientists determined the mass of atoms. You will

- compare the masses of different film can "atoms"
- predict the number of washers in each film can "atom"

▶ Procedure

1. Create a data table similar to the one shown on the sample notebook page.

2. Find the mass of one empty film can. Record this mass in the second row of the table.

3. Collect the four film cans labeled A, B, C, and D in advance by your teacher. Each can contains a different number of washers and represents a different atom. The washers represent the protons and neutrons in an atom's nucleus.

4. Measure the mass of each of the four film cans. Record the masses of the film can atoms in the first row of your data table.

5. Subtract the mass of an empty film can from the mass of each film can atom. Record the differences in the correct spaces in your data table. These masses represent the masses of the washers in your film can atoms. Think of these masses as the masses of the nuclei.

6. Divide the mass of the washers in can B by the mass of the washers in can A. Record the value under the mass of the washers in can B.

MATERIALS
- empty film can
- balance
- 4 filled film cans

7 Repeat step 6 for film can atoms A, C, and D. Record the value under the masses of the washers in each can.

8 Round the values you obtained in steps 6 and 7 to the nearest whole number. Record the rounded figures in the next row of the table.

▶ Observe and Analyze

1. **RECORD OBSERVATIONS** Be sure your data table and calculations are complete. Double-check your arithmetic.

2. **ANALYZE DATA** Examine your data table. Do you notice any patterns in how the masses increase? Given that all the washers in the film can atoms have identical masses, what might the ratio of the mass of the washers to the smallest mass tell you?

3. **PREDICT** Assume there is only one washer in can A. Estimate the number of washers in the other cans and record your estimates in the last row of the table.

4. **GRAPH DATA** On a sheet of graph paper, plot the masses (in grams) of the washers in the film can atoms on the y-axis and the number of washers in each can on the x-axis. Connect the points on the graph.

5. **INTERPRET DATA** Compare the masses of your film can atoms with the masses of the first four atoms on the periodic table. Which represents which?

▶ Conclude

1. **IDENTIFY LIMITS** What can't this activity tell you about the identity of your film can atoms? (**Hint:** Protons and neutrons in real atoms have about the same mass.)

2. **INFER** Hydrogen has only a single proton in its nucleus. If your film can atoms represent the first four elements in the periodic table, what are the numbers of protons and neutrons in each atom?

3. **APPLY** Single atoms are far too small to place on a balance. How do you think scientists determine the masses of real atoms?

▶ INVESTIGATE Further

CHALLENGE Use a periodic table to find the masses of the next two atoms (boron and carbon). How many washers would you need to make film can atom models for each?

Modeling Atomic Masses

Observe and Analyze

Table 1. Masses of Film Can Atoms

	A	B	C	D
Mass of film can atom (g)				
Mass of empty film can (g)				
Mass of washers (g)				
Mass of washers divided by can A				
Value rounded to nearest whole number				
Estimated number of washers in each can				

16.3 The periodic table is a map of the elements.

SOUTH CAROLINA

STANDARDS

7–5.3 Compare the physical properties of metals and nonmetals.

VOCABULARY

reactive p. 526
metal p. 527
nonmetal p. 529
metalloid p. 530
radioactivity p. 530
half-life p. 532

BEFORE, you learned

- The periodic table is organized into groups of elements with similar characteristics
- The periodic table organizes elements according to their properties

NOW, you will learn

- How elements are classified as metals, nonmetals, and metalloids
- About different groups of elements
- About radioactive elements

THINK ABOUT

How are elements different?

The photograph shows common uses of the elements copper, aluminum, and argon: copper in a penny, aluminum in a pie plate, and argon in a light bulb. Each element is located in a different part of the periodic table, and each has a very different use. Find these elements on the periodic table. What other elements are near these?

The periodic table has distinct regions.

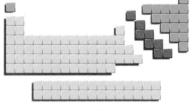

☐ metal ■ metalloid ■ nonmetal

The periodic table is a kind of map of the elements. Just as a country's location on the globe gives you information about its climate, an atom's position on the periodic table indicates the properties of its element. The periodic table has three main regions—metals on the left, nonmetals (except hydrogen) on the right, and metalloids in between. The periodic table on pages 520 and 521 indicates these regions with different colors. A yellow box indicates a metal; green, a nonmetal; and purple, a metalloid.

An element's position in the table also indicates how reactive it is. The term **reactive** indicates how likely an element is to undergo a chemical change. Most elements are somewhat reactive and combine with other materials. The atoms of the elements in Groups 1 and 17 are the most reactive. The elements of Group 18 are the least reactive of all the elements.

CHECK YOUR
READING   How does the periodic table resemble a map?

Most elements are metals.

When you look at the periodic table, it is obvious from the color that most of the elements are metals. In general, **metals** are elements that conduct electricity and heat well and have a shiny appearance. Metals can be shaped easily by pounding, bending, or being drawn into a long wire. Except for mercury, which is a liquid, metals are solids at room temperature.

Sodium is a metal that is so soft it can be cut with a knife at room temperature.

You probably can name many uses for the metal **copper.**

Aluminum is often used for devices that must be strong and light.

Reactive Metals

The metals in Group 1 of the periodic table, the alkali metals, are very reactive. Sodium and potassium are often stored in oil to keep them away from air. When exposed to air, these elements react rapidly with oxygen and water vapor. The ions of these metals, Na^+ and K^+, are important for life, and play an essential role in the functioning of living cells.

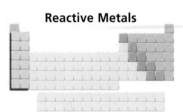

Reactive Metals

The metals in Group 2, the alkaline earth metals, are less reactive than the alkali metals. They are still more reactive than most other metals, however. Calcium ions are an essential part of your diet. Your bones and teeth contain calcium ions. Magnesium is a light, inexpensive metal that is often combined with other metals when a lightweight material is needed, such as for airplane frames.

Transition Metals

The elements in Groups 3–12 are called the transition metals. Among these metals are some of the earliest known elements, such as copper, gold, silver, and iron. Transition metals are generally less reactive than most other metals. Because gold and silver are easily shaped and do not react easily, they have been used for thousands of years to make jewelry and coins. Ancient artifacts made from transition metals can be found in many museums and remain relatively unchanged since the time they were made. Today, dimes and quarters are made of copper and nickel, and pennies are made of zinc with a coating of copper. Transition metal ions even are found in the foods you eat.

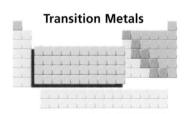

Transition Metals

The properties of the transition metals make them particularly important to industry. Iron is the main part of steel, a material used for bridges and buildings. Most electric wires and many other electrical devices are made of copper. Copper is also used to make water pipes. Indeed, it would be hard to think of an industry that doesn't make use of transition metals.

Although other transition metals may be less familiar, many of them are important for modern technology. The tiny coil of wire inside incandescent light bulbs is made of tungsten. Platinum is in the catalytic converters that reduce pollution from automobile engines.

For many applications, two or more metals are combined to form an alloy. Alloys can be stronger, less likely to corrode, or easier to shape than pure metals. Steel, which is stronger than the pure iron it contains, often includes other transition metals, such as nickel, chromium, or manganese. Brass, an alloy of copper and zinc, is stronger than either metal alone. Jewelry is often made of an alloy of silver and copper, which is stronger than pure silver.

Rare Earth Elements

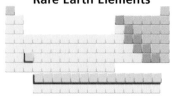

Rare Earth Elements

The rare earth elements are the elements in the top row of the two rows of metals that are usually shown outside the main body of the periodic table. Taking these elements out of the main body of the table makes the table more compact. The rare earth elements are often referred to as lanthanides because they follow the element lanthanum (La) on the table. They are called rare earth elements because scientists once thought that these elements were available only in tiny amounts in Earth's crust. As mining methods improved, scientists learned that the rare earths were actually not so rare at all—only hard to isolate in pure form.

More and more uses are being found for the rare earth elements. Europium (Eu), for example, is used as a coating for some television tubes. Praseodymium (Pr) provides a protective coating against harmful radiation in the welder's helmet in the photograph on the right.

Nonmetals and metalloids have a wide range of properties.

The elements to the right side of the periodic table are called **nonmetals.** As the name implies, the properties of nonmetals tend to be the opposite of those of metals. The properties of nonmetals also tend to vary more from element to element than the properties of the metals do. Many of them are gases at room temperature, and one—bromine—is a liquid. The solid nonmetals often have dull surfaces and cannot be shaped by hammering or drawing into wires. Nonmetals are generally poor conductors of heat and electric current.

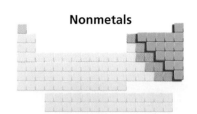

Nonmetals

The main components of the air that you breathe are the nonmetal elements nitrogen and oxygen. Nitrogen is a fairly unreactive element, but oxygen reacts easily to form compounds with many other elements. Burning and rusting are two familiar types of reactions involving oxygen. Compounds containing carbon are essential to living things. Two forms of the element carbon are graphite, which is a soft, slippery black material, and diamond, a hard crystal. Sulfur is a bright yellow powder that can be mined from deposits of the pure element.

Halogens

The elements in Group 17 are commonly known as halogens, from Greek words meaning "forming salts." Halogens are very reactive non-metals that easily form compounds called salts with many metals. Because they are so reactive, halogens are often used to kill harmful microorganisms. For example, the halogen chlorine is used to clean drinking water and to prevent the growth of algae in swimming pools. Solutions containing iodine are often used in hospitals and doctors' offices to kill germs on skin.

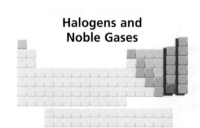

Halogens and Noble Gases

Noble Gases

Group 18 elements are called the noble, or inert, gases because they almost never react with other elements. Argon gas makes up about one percent of the atmosphere. The other noble gases are found in the atmosphere in smaller amounts. Colorful lights, such as those in the photograph on the right, are made by passing an electric current through tubes filled with neon, krypton, xenon, or argon gas. Argon gas also is placed in tungsten filament light bulbs, because it will not react with the hot filament.

Noble gases produce the light for many signs.

CHECK YOUR READING Where on Earth can you find noble gases?

Metalloids

Metalloids

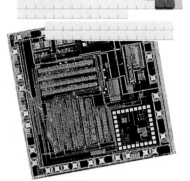

The metalloid silicon is found in sand and in computer microchips.

Metalloids are elements that have properties of both metals and nonmetals. In the periodic table, they lie on either side of a zigzag line separating metals from nonmetals. The most common metalloid is silicon. Silicon atoms are the second most common atoms in Earth's crust.

Metalloids often make up the semiconductors found in electronic devices. Semiconductors are special materials that conduct electricity under some conditions and not under others. Silicon, gallium, and germanium are three semiconductors used in computer chips.

Some atoms can change their identity.

The identity of an element is determined by the number of protons in its nucleus. Chemical changes do not affect the nucleus, so chemical changes don't change one type of atom into another. There are, however, conditions under which the number of protons in a nucleus can change and so change the identity of an atom.

Radioactive Elements

Recall that the nucleus of an atom contains protons and neutrons. Attractive forces between protons and neutrons hold the nucleus together even though protons repel one another. We say an atomic nucleus is stable when these attractive forces keep it together.

Each element has isotopes with different numbers of neutrons. The stability of a nucleus depends on the right balance of protons and neutrons. If there are too few or too many neutrons, the nucleus may become unstable. When this happens, particles are produced from the nucleus of the atom to restore the balance. This change is accompanied by a release of energy.

If the production of particles changes the number of protons, the atom is transformed into an atom of a different element. In the early 1900s, physicist Marie Curie named the process by which atoms produce energy and particles **radioactivity.** Curie was the first person to isolate polonium and radium, two radioactive elements.

An isotope is radioactive if the nucleus has too many or too few neutrons. Most elements have radioactive isotopes, although these isotopes are rare for small atoms. For the heaviest of elements—those beyond bismuth (Bi)—all of the isotopes are radioactive.

Scientists study radioactivity with a device called a Geiger counter. The Geiger counter detects the particles from the breakup of the atomic nucleus with audible clicks. More clicks indicate that more particles are being produced.

 CHECK YOUR READING How can an atom of one element change into an atom of a different element?

Uses of Radioactivity in Medicine

The radiation produced from unstable nuclei is used in hospitals to diagnose and treat patients. Some forms of radiation from nuclei are used to destroy harmful tumors inside a person's body without performing an operation. Another medical use of radiation is to monitor the activity of certain organs in the body. A patient is injected with a solution containing a radioactive isotope. Isotopes of a given atom move through the body in the same way whether or not they are radioactive. Doctors detect the particles produced by the radioactive isotopes to determine where and how the body is using the substance.

Although radiation has its benefits, in large doses it is harmful to living things and should be avoided. Radiation can damage or kill cells, and the energy from its particles can burn the skin. Prolonged exposure to radiation has been linked to cancer and other health problems.

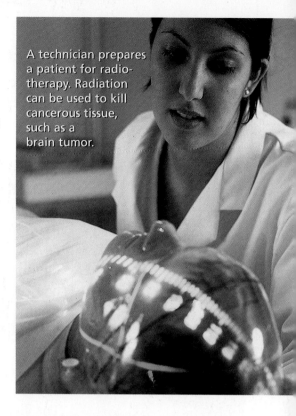

A technician prepares a patient for radiotherapy. Radiation can be used to kill cancerous tissue, such as a brain tumor.

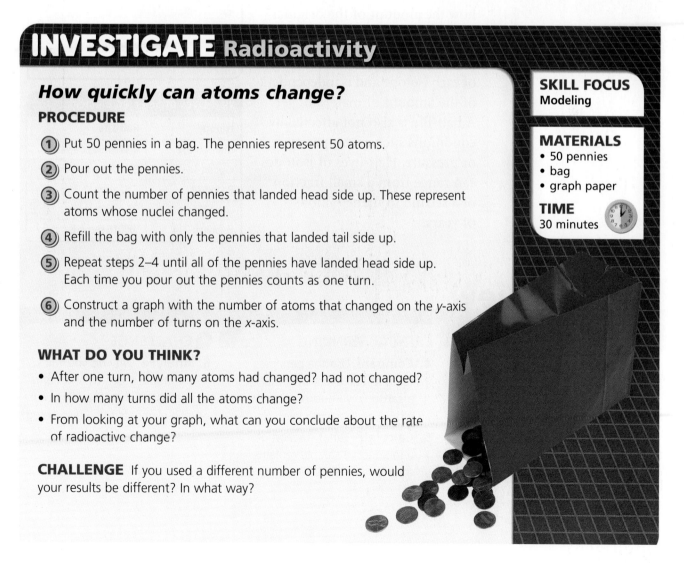

INVESTIGATE Radioactivity

How quickly can atoms change?

PROCEDURE

1. Put 50 pennies in a bag. The pennies represent 50 atoms.

2. Pour out the pennies.

3. Count the number of pennies that landed head side up. These represent atoms whose nuclei changed.

4. Refill the bag with only the pennies that landed tail side up.

5. Repeat steps 2–4 until all of the pennies have landed head side up. Each time you pour out the pennies counts as one turn.

6. Construct a graph with the number of atoms that changed on the y-axis and the number of turns on the x-axis.

WHAT DO YOU THINK?

- After one turn, how many atoms had changed? had not changed?
- In how many turns did all the atoms change?
- From looking at your graph, what can you conclude about the rate of radioactive change?

CHALLENGE If you used a different number of pennies, would your results be different? In what way?

SKILL FOCUS
Modeling

MATERIALS
- 50 pennies
- bag
- graph paper

TIME
30 minutes

Radioactive Decay

VISUALIZATION
CLASSZONE.COM

Watch how a radioactive element decays over time.

Radioactive atoms produce energy and particles from their nuclei. The identity of these atoms changes because the number of protons changes. This process is known as radioactive decay. Over time, all of the atoms of a radioactive isotope will change into atoms of another element.

Radioactive decay occurs at a steady rate that is characteristic of the particular isotope. The amount of time that it takes for one-half of the atoms in a particular sample to decay is called the **half-life** of the isotope. For example, if you had 1000 atoms of a radioactive isotope with a half-life of 1 year, 500 of the atoms would change into another element over the course of a year. In the next year, 250 more atoms would decay. The illustration to the right shows how the amount of the original isotope would decrease over time.

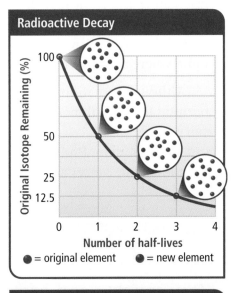

The half-life is a characteristic of each isotope and is independent of the amount of material. A half-life is also not affected by conditions such as temperature or pressure. Half-lives of isotopes can range from a small fraction of a second to many billions of years.

Half-Lives of Selected Elements	
Isotope	Half-Life
Uranium-238	4,510,000,000 years
Carbon-14	5,730 years
Radon-222	3.82 days
Lead-214	27 minutes
Polonium-214	.00016 seconds

16.3 Review

KEY CONCEPTS

1. What are the three main classes of elements in the periodic table?

2. What are the major characteristics of metals?

3. How can an atom of one element change to an atom of another element?

CRITICAL THINKING

4. **Compare** Use the periodic table to determine whether a carbon or a fluorine atom would be more reactive.

5. **Calculate** What fraction of a radioactive sample remains after three half-lives?

○ CHALLENGE

6. **Analyze** Why do you think the noble gases were among the last of the naturally occurring elements to be discovered?

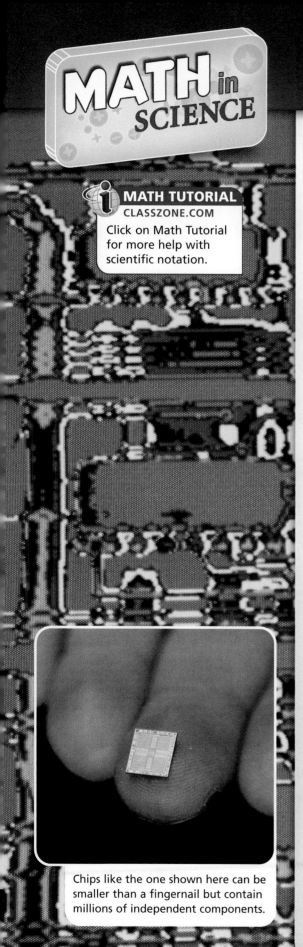

MATH TUTORIAL
CLASSZONE.COM
Click on Math Tutorial for more help with scientific notation.

Numbers with Many Zeros

Semiconductor devices are at the heart of the modern personal computer. Today tiny chips can contain more than 42,000,000 connections and perform about 3,000,000,000 calculations per second. Computers have little problem working with such large numbers. Scientists, however, use a scientific notation as a short-hand way to write large numbers. Scientific notation expresses a very large or very small number as the product of a number between 1 and 10 and a power of 10.

Example

Large Number How would you express the number 6,400,000,000—the approximate population of the world—in scientific notation?

(1) Look at the number and count how many spaces you would need to move the decimal point to get a number between 1 and 10.

$$6,\ 4\ 0\ 0,\ 0\ 0\ 0,\ 0\ 0\ 0$$
$$9\ 8\ 7\ 6\ 5\ 4\ 3\ 2\ 1$$

(2) Place the decimal point in the space and multiply the number by the appropriate power of 10. The power of 10 will be equivalent to the number of spaces you moved the decimal point.

ANSWER 6.4×10^9

Small Number How would you express 0.0000023 in scientific notation?

(1) Count the number of places you need to move the decimal point to get a number between 1 and 10. This time you move the decimal point to the right, not the left.

$$0.\ 0\ 0\ 0\ 0\ 0\ 2\ 3$$
$$1\ 2\ 3\ 4\ 5\ 6$$

(2) The power of 10 you need to multiply this number by is still equal to the number of places you moved the decimal point. Place a negative sign in front of it to indicate that you moved the decimal point to the right.

ANSWER 2.3×10^{-6}

Chips like the one shown here can be smaller than a fingernail but contain millions of independent components.

Answer the following questions.

1. Express the following numbers in scientific notation:
   (a) 75,000   (b) 54,000,000,000   (c) 0.0000064

2. Express these numbers in decimal form:
   (a) 6.0×10^{24} (b) 7.4×10^{22} (c) 5.7×10^{-10}

CHALLENGE What is 2.2×10^{22} subtracted from 4.6×10^{22}?

the **BIG** idea

A substance's atomic structure determines its physical and chemical properties.

CONTENT REVIEW
CLASSZONE.COM

KEY CONCEPTS SUMMARY

1 Atoms are the smallest form of elements.

- All matter is made of the atoms of approximately 100 elements.

- Atoms are made of protons, neutrons, and electrons.

- Different elements are made of different atoms.

- Atoms form ions by gaining or losing electrons.

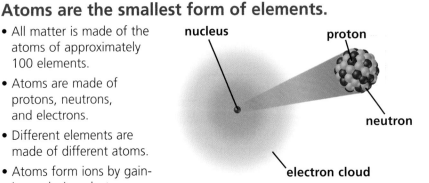

nucleus

proton

neutron

electron cloud

VOCABULARY
proton p. 511
neutron p. 511
nucleus p. 511
electron p. 511
atomic number p. 512
atomic mass number p. 512
isotope p. 512
ion p. 514

2 Elements make up the periodic table.

- Elements can be organized by similarities.

- The periodic table organizes the atoms of the elements by properties and atomic number.

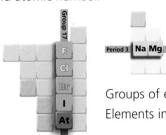

Groups of elements have similar properties.
Elements in a period have varying properties.

VOCABULARY
atomic mass p. 517
periodic table p. 518
group p. 522
period p. 522

3 The periodic table is a map of the elements.

- The periodic table has distinct regions.

- Most elements are metals.

- Nonmetals and metalloids have a wide range of properties.

- Some atoms can change their identity through radioactive decay.

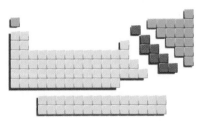

metal   metalloid   nonmetal

VOCABULARY
reactive p. 526
metal p. 527
nonmetal p. 529
metalloid p. 530
radioactivity p. 530
half-life p. 532

Reviewing Vocabulary

Describe how the vocabulary terms in the following pairs are related to each other. Explain the relationship in a one- or two-sentence answer. Underline each vocabulary term in your answer.

1. isotope, nucleus

2. atomic mass, atomic number

3. electron, proton

4. atomic number, atomic mass number

5. group, period

6. metals, nonmetals

7. radioactivity, half-life

Reviewing Key Concepts

Multiple Choice *Choose the letter of the best answer.*

8. The central part of an atom is called the
   a. electron
   c. proton
   b. nucleus
   d. neutron

9. The electric charge on a proton is
   a. positive
   c. neutral
   b. negative
   d. changing

10. The number of protons in the nucleus is the
    a. atomic mass
    c. atomic number
    b. isotope
    d. half-life

11. Nitrogen has atomic number 7. An isotope of nitrogen containing seven neutrons would be
    a. nitrogen-13
    c. nitrogen-15
    b. nitrogen-14
    d. nitrogen-16

12. How does the size of a negative ion compare to the size of the atom that formed it?
    a. It's smaller.
    b. It's larger.
    c. It's the same size.
    d. It varies.

13. The modern periodic table is organized by
    a. size of atom
    b. atomic mass
    c. number of neutrons
    d. atomic number

14. Elements in a group have
    a. a wide range of chemical properties
    b. the same atomic radius
    c. similar chemical properties
    d. the same number of protons

15. Elements in a period have
    a. a wide range of chemical properties
    b. the same atomic radius
    c. similar chemical properties
    d. the same number of protons

16. From left to right in a period, the size of atoms
    a. increases
    c. remains the same
    b. decreases
    d. shows no pattern

17. The elements in Group 1 of the periodic table are commonly called the
    a. alkali metals
    c. alkaline earth metals
    b. transition metals
    d. rare earth metals

18. The isotope nitrogen-13 has a half-life of 10 minutes. If you start with 40 grams of this isotope, how many grams will you have left after 20 minutes?
    a. 10
    c. 20
    b. 15
    d. 30

Short Answer *Write a short answer to each question. You may need to consult a periodic table.*

19. Rubidium forms the positive ion Rb^+. Is this ion larger or smaller than the neutral atom? Explain.

20. How can you find the number of neutrons in the isotope nitrogen-16?

21. Explain how density varies across and up and down the periodic table.

22. Place these elements in order from least reactive to most reactive: nickel (Ni), xenon (Xe), lithium (Li). How did you determine the order?

Thinking Critically

The table below lists some properties of six elements. Use the information and your knowledge of the properties of elements to answer the next three questions.

Element	Appearance	Density (g/cm³)	Conducts Electricity
A	dark purple crystals	4.93	no
B	shiny silvery solid	0.97	yes
C	shiny silvery solid	22.65	yes
D	yellow powder	2.07	no
E	shiny gray solid	5.32	semiconductor
F	shiny bluish solid	8.91	yes

23. **ANALYZE** Based on the listed properties, identify each of the elements as a metal, nonmetal, or metalloid.

24. **APPLY** Which would weigh more: a cube of element A or a same-sized cube of element D?

25. **HYPOTHESIZE** Which element(s) do you think you might find in electronic devices? Why?

26. **HYPOTHESIZE** The thyroid gland, located in your throat, secretes hormones. In 1924 iodine was added to table salt. As more and more Americans used iodized salt, the number of cases of thyroid diseases decreased. Write a hypothesis that explains the observed decrease in thyroid-related diseases.

27. **INFER** How does the size of a beryllium (Be) atom compare with the size of an oxygen (O) atom?

28. **PREDICT** Although noble gases do not naturally react with other elements, xenon and krypton have been made to react with halogens such as chlorine in laboratories. Why are the halogens most likely to react with the noble gases?

Below is an element square from the periodic table. Use it to answer the next two questions.

29. **CALCULATE** One of the more common isotopes of mercury is mercury-200. How many protons and neutrons are in the nucleus of mercury-200?

30. **INFER** Cadmium occupies the square directly above mercury on the periodic table. Is a cadium atom larger or smaller than a mercury atom?

31. **CALCULATE** An isotope has a half-life of 40 minutes. How much of a 100-gram sample would remain unchanged after two hours?

32. **APPLY** When a uranium atom with 92 protons and 146 neutrons undergoes radioactive decay, it produces a particle that consists of two protons and two neutrons from its nucleus. Into which element is the uranium atom transformed?

the BIG idea

33. **ANALYZE** Look again at the photograph on pages 506–507. Answer the question again, using what you have learned in the chapter.

34. **DRAW CONCLUSIONS** Suppose you've been given the ability to take apart and assemble atoms. How could you turn lead into gold?

35. **ANALYZE** Explain how the structure of an atom determines its place in the periodic table.

UNIT PROJECTS

If you are doing a unit project, make a folder for your project. Include in your folder a list of the resources you will need, the date on which the project is due, and a schedule to track your progress. Begin gathering data.

Interpreting Tables

The table below shows part of the periodic table of elements.

Group

Period	1	2	13	14	15	16	17	18
1	1 H	2						2 He
2	3 Li	4 Be	5 B	6 C	7 N	8 O	9 F	10 Ne
3	11 Na	12 Mg	13 Al	14 Si	15 P	16 S	17 Cl	18 Ar
4	19 K	20 Ca	31 Ga	32 Ge	33 As	34 Se	35 Br	36 Kr

Answer the questions based on the information given in the table.

1. What does the number above the symbol for each element represent?

  a. Its number of isotopes

  b. Its atomic number

  c. Its number of neutrons

  d. Its atomic mass

2. The atom of what element is in Period 4, Group 13?

  a. Na   **c.** Al

  b. Ga   **d.** K

3. What do the elements on the far right of the table (He, Ne, Ar, and Kr) have in common?

  a. They do not generally react with other elements.

  b. They are in liquids under normal conditions.

  c. They are metals that rust easily.

  d. They are very reactive gases.

4. How many electrons does a neutral chlorine (Cl) atom contain?

  a. 16   **c.** 18

  b. 17   **d.** 19

5. If a sodium (Na) atom loses one electron to form a positive ion, how many electrons would lithium (Li) lose to form a positive ion?

  a. 0   **c.** 2

  b. 1   **d.** 3

6. If a fluorine (F) atom gains one electron to form a negative ion, how many electrons would bromine (Br) gain to form a negative ion?

  a. 0   **c.** 2

  b. 1   **d.** 3

Extended Response

Answer the following two questions in detail. Include some of the terms shown in the word box at right. Underline each term you use in your answer.

electron	nucleus	proton
isotope	neutron	radioactivity

7. Democritus was an ancient Greek philosopher who claimed that all matter was made of tiny particles he called atoms. Democritus said that all atoms were made of the same material. The objects of the world differed because each was made of atoms of different sizes and shapes. How does the modern view of atoms differ from this ancient view? How is it similar?

8. Half-life is a measure of the time it takes half of the radioactive atoms in a substance to decay into other atoms. If you know how much radioactive material an object had to begin with, how could you use half-life to determine its age now?

CHAPTER

Chemical Bonds and Compounds

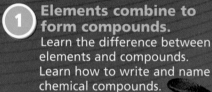

The properties of compounds depend on their atoms and chemical bonds.

How do these skydivers stay together? How is this similar to the way atoms stay together?

Key Concepts

SECTION

1 **Elements combine to form compounds.**
Learn the difference between elements and compounds. Learn how to write and name chemical compounds.

SECTION

2 **Chemical bonds hold compounds together.**
Learn about the different types of chemical bonds.

SECTION

3 **Substances' properties depend on their bonds.**
Learn how bonds give compounds certain properties.

Internet Preview

CLASSZONE.COM

Chapter 17 online resources: Content Review, two Visualizations, two Resource Centers, Math Tutorial, Test Practice

EXPLORE (the BIG idea)

Mixing It Up

Get some red and yellow modeling compound. Make three red and two yellow balls, each about the diameter of a nickel. Blend one red and one yellow ball together. Blend one yellow and two red balls together.

Observe and Think How different do your combinations look from the original? from each other?

The Shape of Things

Pour some salt onto dark paper. Look at the grains through a hand lens. Try to observe a single grain.

Observe and Think What do you notice about the salt grains? What do you think might affect the way the grains look?

Internet Activity: Bonding

Go to **ClassZone.com** and watch the animation showing ionic and covalent bonding. Observe the differences in the two types of bonding.

Observe and Think What's the difference between an ionic and a covalent bond? Explain how covalent bonding can have different characteristics.

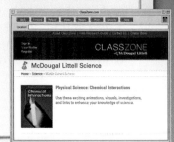

NSTA
scilinks.org
SCiLINKS

Compounds **Code: MDL023**

Getting Ready to Learn

◄ CONCEPT REVIEW

- Electrons occupy a cloud around an atom's nucleus.
- Atoms form ions by losing or gaining electrons.

◄ VOCABULARY REVIEW

electron p. 511
element *See Glossary.*

CONTENT REVIEW
CLASSZONE.COM
Review concepts and vocabulary.

▶ TAKING NOTES

MAIN IDEA AND DETAIL NOTES

Make a two-column chart. Write the main ideas, such as those in the blue headings, in the column on the left. Write details about each of those main ideas in the column on the right.

VOCABULARY STRATEGY

Place each vocabulary term at the center of a **description wheel** diagram. Write some words describing it on the spokes.

See the Note-Taking Handbook on pages R45–R51.

SCIENCE NOTEBOOK

MAIN IDEAS	DETAIL NOTES
Atoms combine in predictable numbers.	• Each compound has a specific ratio of atoms. • A ratio is a comparison between two quantities.
Writing chemical formulas	• Find symbols on the periodic table. • Note ratio of atoms with subscripts.

indicates number of atoms per molecule

written to the right of a symbol

SUBSCRIPT

slightly below the symbol

17.1

KEY CONCEPT

Elements combine to form compounds.

BEFORE, you learned

- Atoms make up everything on Earth
- Atoms react with different atoms to form compounds

NOW, you will learn

- How compounds differ from the elements that make them
- How a chemical formula represents the ratio of atoms in a compound
- How the same atoms can form different compounds

STANDARDS

7–5.2 Classify matter as element, compound, or mixture on the basis of its composition.

7–5.5 Translate chemical symbols and the chemical formulas of common substances to show the component parts of the substances (including NaCl [table salt], H_2O [water], $C_6H_{12}O_6$ [simple sugar], O_2 [oxygen gas], CO_2 [carbon dioxide], and N_2 [nitrogen gas]).

VOCABULARY

chemical formula p. 543
subscript p. 543

EXPLORE Compounds

How are compounds different from elements?

PROCEDURE

1. Examine the lump of carbon, the beaker of water, and the sugar. Record your observations of each.

2. Light the candle. Pour some sugar into a test tube and heat it over the candle for several minutes. Record your observations.

WHAT DO YOU THINK?

- The sugar is made up of atoms of the same elements that are in the carbon and water. How are sugar, carbon, and water different from one another?
- Does heating the sugar give you any clue that sugar contains more than one element?

MATERIALS

- carbon
- water
- sugar
- test tube
- test-tube holder
- candle
- matches

Compounds have different properties from the elements that make them.

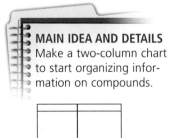

MAIN IDEA AND DETAILS
Make a two-column chart to start organizing information on compounds.

If you think about all of the different substances around you, it is clear that they cannot all be elements. In fact, while there are just over 100 elements, there are millions of different substances. Most substances are compounds. A compound is a substance made of atoms of two or more different elements. Just as the 26 letters in the alphabet can form thousands of words, the elements in the periodic table can form millions of compounds.

The atoms of different elements are held together in compounds by chemical bonds. Chemical bonds can hold atoms together in large networks or in small groups. Bonds help determine the properties of a compound.

The properties of a compound depend not only on which atoms the compound contains, but also on how the atoms are arranged. Atoms of carbon and hydrogen, for example, can combine to form many thousands of different compounds. These compounds include natural gas, components of automobile gasoline, the hard waxes in candles, and many plastics. Each of these compounds has a certain number of carbon and hydrogen atoms arranged in a specific way.

The properties of compounds are often very different from the properties of the elements that make them. For example, water is made from two atoms of hydrogen bonded to one atom of oxygen. At room temperature, hydrogen and oxygen are both colorless, odorless gases, and they remain gases down to extremely low temperatures. Water, however, is a liquid at temperatures up to 100°C (212°F) and a solid below 0°C (32°F). Sugar is a compound composed of atoms of carbon, hydrogen, and oxygen. Its properties, however, are unlike those of carbon, hydrogen, or oxygen.

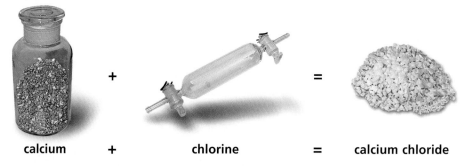

calcium   **+**   chlorine   **=**   calcium chloride

The picture above shows what happens when the elements calcium and chlorine combine to form the compound calcium chloride. Calcium is a soft, silvery metallic solid. Chlorine is a greenish-yellow gas that is extremely reactive and poisonous to humans. Calcium chloride, however, is a nonpoisonous white solid. People who live in cold climates often use calcium chloride to melt the ice that forms on streets in the wintertime.

 CHECK YOUR READING How do the properties of a compound compare with the properties of the elements that make it?

Atoms combine in predictable numbers.

A given compound always contains atoms of elements in a specific ratio. For example, the compound ammonia always has three hydrogen atoms for every nitrogen atom—a 3 to 1 ratio of hydrogen to nitrogen. This same 3:1 ratio holds for every sample of ammonia, under all physical conditions. A substance with a different ratio of hydrogen to nitrogen atoms is not ammonia. For example, hydrazoic acid also contains atoms of hydrogen and nitrogen but in a ratio of one hydrogen atom to three nitrogen atoms, or 1:3.

INVESTIGATE Element Ratios

How can you model a compound?

PROCEDURE

① Collect a number of nuts and bolts. The nuts represent hydrogen atoms. The bolts represent carbon atoms.

② Connect the nuts to the bolts to model the compound methane. Methane contains four hydrogen atoms attached to one carbon atom. Make as many of these models as you can.

③ Count the nuts and bolts left over.

WHAT DO YOU THINK?

• What ratio of nuts to bolts did you use to make a model of a methane atom?

• How many methane models did you make? Why couldn't you make more?

CHALLENGE The compound ammonia has one nitrogen atom and three hydrogen atoms. How would you use the nuts and bolts to model this compound?

Chemical Formulas

Remember that atoms of elements can be represented by their chemical symbols, as given in the periodic table. A **chemical formula** uses these chemical symbols to represent the atoms of the elements and their ratios in a chemical compound.

Carbon dioxide is a compound consisting of one atom of carbon attached by chemical bonds to two atoms of oxygen. Here is how you would write the chemical formula for carbon dioxide:

• Find the symbols for carbon (C) and oxygen (O) on the periodic table. Write these symbols side by side.

• To indicate that there are two oxygen atoms for every carbon atom, place the subscript *2* to the right of the oxygen atom's symbol. A **subscript** is a number written to the right of a chemical symbol and slightly below it.

• Because there is only one atom of carbon in carbon dioxide, you need no subscript for carbon. The subscript 1 is never used. The chemical formula for carbon dioxide is, therefore,

$$CO_2$$

The chemical formula shows one carbon atom bonded to two oxygen atoms.

Chemical Formulas

Chemical formulas show the ratios of atoms in a chemical compound.

Compound Name	Atoms	Atomic Ratio	Chemical Formula
Hydrogen chloride	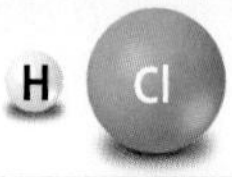 H Cl	1:1	HCl
Water	 H H O	2:1	H_2O
Ammonia	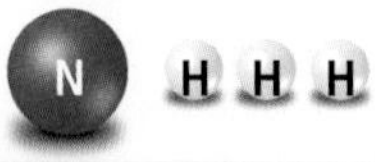 N H H H	1:3	NH_3
Methane	 C H H H H	1:4	CH_4
Propane	 C C C H H H H / H H H H	3:8	C_3H_8

READING VISUALS How many more hydrogen atoms does propane have than methane?

RESOURCE CENTER
CLASSZONE.COM

Find out more about chemical formulas.

The chart above shows the names, atoms, ratios, and chemical formulas for several chemical compounds. The subscripts for each compound indicate the number of atoms that combine to make that compound. Notice how hydrogen combines with different atoms in different ratios. Notice in particular that methane and propane are made of atoms of the same elements, carbon and hydrogen, only in different ratios. This example shows why it's important to pay attention to ratios when writing chemical formulas.

CHECK YOUR READING Why is the ratio of atoms in a chemical formula so important?

Same Elements, Different Compounds

Even before chemists devised a way to write chemical formulas, they realized that different compounds could be composed of atoms of the same elements. Nitrogen and oxygen, for example, form several compounds. One compound consists of one atom of nitrogen attached to one atom of oxygen. This compound's formula is NO. A second compound has one atom of nitrogen attached to two atoms of oxygen, so its formula is NO_2. A third compound has two nitrogen atoms attached to one oxygen atom; its formula is N_2O. The properties of these compounds are different, even though they are made of atoms of the same elements.

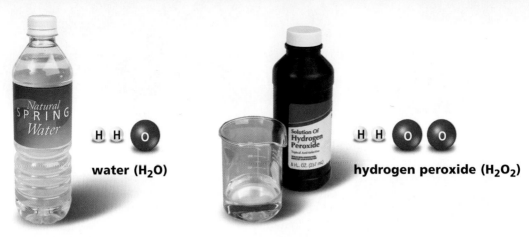

water (H₂O)   hydrogen peroxide (H₂O₂)

There are many other examples of atoms of the same elements forming different compounds. The photographs above show two bottles filled with clear, colorless liquids. You might use the liquid in the first bottle to cool off after a soccer game. The bottle contains water, which is a compound made from two atoms of hydrogen and one atom of oxygen (H_2O). You could not survive for long without water.

You definitely would not want to drink the liquid in the second bottle, although this liquid resembles water. This bottle also contains a compound of hydrogen and oxygen, hydrogen peroxide, but hydrogen peroxide has two hydrogen and two oxygen atoms (H_2O_2). Hydrogen peroxide is commonly used to kill bacteria on skin. One way to tell these two compounds apart is to test them using a potato. A drop of hydrogen peroxide on a raw potato will bubble; a drop of water on the potato will not.

The difference between the two compounds is greater than the labels or their appearance would indicate. The hydrogen peroxide that you buy at a drugstore is a mixture of hydrogen peroxide and water. In its concentrated form, hydrogen peroxide is a thick, syrupy liquid that boils at 150°C (302°F). Hydrogen peroxide can even be used as a fuel.

 What are the chemical formulas for water and hydrogen peroxide?

17.1 Review

KEY CONCEPTS

1. How do the properties of compounds often compare with the properties of the elements that make them?

2. How many atoms are in the compound represented by the formula $C_{12}H_{22}O_{11}$?

3. How can millions of compounds be made from the atoms of about 100 elements?

CRITICAL THINKING

4. **Apply** If a chemical formula has no subscripts, what can you conclude about the ratio of the atoms in it?

5. **Infer** How might you distinguish between hydrogen peroxide and water?

⬥ CHALLENGE

6. **Analyze** A chemist analyzes two compounds and finds that they both contain only carbon and oxygen. The two compounds, however, have different properties. How can two compounds made from the same elements be different?

MATH TUTORIAL
CLASSZONE.COM
Click on Math
Tutorial for more
help with ratios.

A good strikeout-to-walk ratio for a baseball pitcher is 2:1. This means that for every two strikeouts achieved, the pitcher only allows one walk.

SKILL: CALCULATING RATIOS

Regarding Ratios

No pitcher gets a batter out every time. Sometimes even the worst pitchers have spectacular games. If you're a fan of professional baseball, you've probably seen the quality of certain players rated by using a ratio. A ratio is a comparison of two quantities. For a major league baseball pitcher, for example, one ratio you might hear reported is the number of strikeouts to the number of walks during a season. Chemical formulas are also ratios—ratios that compare the numbers of atoms in a compound.

Example

Consider the chemical formula for the compound glucose:

$$C_6H_{12}O_6$$

From this formula you can write several ratios. To find the ratio of carbon atoms to hydrogen atoms, for instance, do the following:

(1) Find the number of each kind of atom by noting the subscripts.

6 carbon, 12 hydrogen

(2) Write the first number on the left and the second on the right, and place a colon between them.

6:12

(3) Reduce the ratio by dividing each side by the largest number that goes into each evenly, in this case 6.

1:2

ANSWER The ratio of carbon to hydrogen in glucose is 1:2.

Use the table below to answer the following questions.

Compounds and Formulas	
Compound Name	**Chemical Formula**
Carbon dioxide	CO_2
Methane	CH_4
Sulfuric acid	H_2SO_4
Glucose	$C_6H_{12}O_6$
Formic acid	CH_2O_2

1. In carbon dioxide, what is the ratio of carbon to oxygen?

2. What is the ratio of carbon to hydrogen in methane?

3. In sulfuric acid, what is the ratio of hydrogen to sulfur? the ratio of sulfur to oxygen?

CHALLENGE What two chemical compounds in the table have the same ratio of carbon atoms to oxygen atoms?

KEY CONCEPT
Chemical bonds hold compounds together.

South Carolina
McDougal Littell Science

STANDARDS

7–5.5 Translate chemical symbols and the chemical formulas of common substances to show the component parts of the substances (including NaCl [table salt], H_2O [water], $C_6H_{12}O_6$ [simple sugar], O_2 [oxygen gas], CO_2 [carbon dioxide], and N_2 [nitrogen gas]).

VOCABULARY

ionic bond p. 548
covalent bond p. 550
molecule p. 551
polar covalent bond
  p. 551

MAIN IDEA AND DETAILS
Make a two-column chart to organize information on chemical bonds.

▶ **BEFORE,** you learned

- Elements combine to form compounds
- Electrons are located in a cloud around the nucleus
- Atoms can lose or gain electrons to form ions

▶ **NOW,** you will learn

- How electrons are involved in chemical bonding
- About the different types of chemical bonds
- How chemical bonds affect structure

THINK ABOUT

How do you keep things together?

Think about the different ways the workers at this construction site connect materials. They may use nails, screws, or even glue, depending on the materials they wish to keep together. Why would they choose the method they do? What factors do you consider when you join two objects?

Chemical bonds between atoms involve electrons.

Water is a compound of hydrogen and oxygen. The air you breathe, however, contains oxygen gas, a small amount of hydrogen gas, as well as some water vapor. How can hydrogen and oxygen be water sometimes and at other times not? The answer is by forming chemical bonds.

Chemical bonds are the "glue" that holds the atoms of elements together in compounds. Chemical bonds are what make compounds more than just mixtures of atoms.

Remember that an atom has a positively charged nucleus surrounded by a cloud of electrons. Chemical bonds form when the electrons in the electron clouds around two atoms interact. How the electron clouds interact determines the kind of chemical bond that is formed. Chemical bonds have a great effect on the chemical and physical properties of compounds. Chemical bonds also influence how different substances interact. You'll learn more about how substances interact in a later chapter.

Atoms can transfer electrons.

Remember that elements in columns show similar chemical properties.

Ions are formed when atoms gain or lose electrons. Gaining electrons changes an atom into a negative ion. Losing electrons changes an atom into a positive ion. Individual atoms do not form ions by themselves. Instead, ions typically form in pairs when one atom transfers one or more electrons to another atom.

An element's location on the periodic table can give a clue as to the type of ions the atoms of that element will form. The illustration to the left shows the characteristic ions formed by several groups. Notice that all metals lose electrons to form positive ions. Group 1 metals commonly lose only one electron to form ions with a single positive charge. Group 2 metals commonly lose two electrons to form ions with two positive charges. Other metals, like the transition metals, also always form positive ions, but the number of electrons they may lose varies.

Nonmetals form ions by gaining electrons. Group 17 nonmetals, for example, gain one electron to form ions with a 1– charge. The nonmetals in Group 16 gain two electrons to form ions with a 2– charge. The noble gases do not normally gain or lose electrons and so do not normally form ions.

CHECK YOUR READING — What type of ions do metals form?

Ionic Bonds

What happens when an atom of an element from Group 1, like sodium, meets an atom of an element from Group 17, like chlorine? Sodium is likely to lose an electron to form a positive ion. Chlorine is likely to gain an electron to form a negative ion. An electron, therefore, moves from the sodium atom to the chlorine atom.

sodium atom (Na)   chlorine atom (Cl)   sodium ion (Na⁺)   chloride ion (Cl⁻)

Remember that particles with opposite electrical charges attract one another. When the ions are created, therefore, they are drawn toward one another by electrical attraction. This force of attraction between positive and negative ions is called an **ionic bond.**

Electrical forces act in all directions. Each ion, therefore, attracts all other nearby ions with the opposite charge. The next illustration shows how this all-around attraction produces a network of sodium and chloride ions known as a sodium chloride crystal.

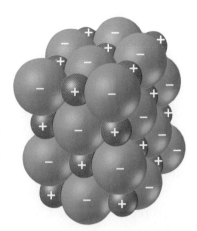

Notice how each positive ion is surrounded by six negative ions, and each negative ion is surrounded by six positive ions. This regular arrangement gives the sodium chloride crystal its characteristic cubic shape. You can see this distinctive crystal shape when you look at table salt crystals through a magnifying glass.

Ionic bonds form between all nearby ions of opposite charge. These interactions make ionic compounds very stable and their crystals very strong. Although sodium chloride crystals have a cubic shape, other ionic compounds form crystals with different regular patterns. The shape of the crystals of an ionic compound depends, in part, on the ratio of positive and negative ions and the sizes of the ions.

The cubic shape of sodium chloride crystals is a result of how the ions form crystals.

Names of Ionic Compounds

The name of an ionic compound is based on the names of the ions it is made of. The name for a positive ion is the same as the name of the atom from which it is formed. The name of a negative ion is formed by dropping the last part of the name of the atom and adding the suffix -ide. To name an ionic compound, the name of the positive ion is placed first, followed by the name of the negative ion. For example, the chemical name for table salt is sodium chloride. *Sodium* is the positive sodium ion and *chloride* is the negative ion formed from chlorine.

Therefore, to name the compound with the chemical formula BaI_2

- First, take the name of the positive metal element: barium.
- Second, take the name of the negative, nonmetal element, iodine, and give it the ending -ide: iodide.
- Third, combine the two names: barium iodide.

Similarly, the name for KBr is potassium bromide, and the name for MgF_2 is magnesium fluoride.

Atoms can share electrons.

In general, an ionic bond forms between atoms that lose electrons easily to form positive ions, such as metals, and atoms that gain electrons easily to form negative ions, such as nonmetals. Another way in which atoms can bond together is by sharing electrons. Nonmetal atoms usually form bonds with each other by sharing electrons.

Covalent Bonds

VOCABULARY
Make a description wheel for *covalent bond* and other vocabulary words.

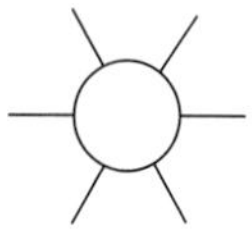

A pair of shared electrons between two atoms is called a **covalent bond.** In forming a covalent bond, neither atom gains or loses an electron, so no ions are formed. The shared electrons are attracted to both positively charged nuclei. The illustrations below show a covalent bond between two iodine atoms. In the first illustration, notice how the electron clouds overlap. A covalent bond is also often represented as a line between the two atoms, as in the second illustration.

Iodine (I_2)

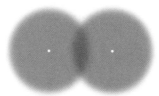

electron cloud model   ball-and-stick model

READING TiP

To help yourself remember that a covalent bond involves a sharing of electrons, remember that the prefix *co-* means "partner."

The number of covalent bonds that an atom can form depends on the number of electrons that it has available for sharing. For example, atoms of the halogen group and hydrogen can contribute only one electron to a covalent bond. These atoms, therefore, can form only one covalent bond. Atoms of Group 16 elements can form two covalent bonds. Atoms of the elements of Group 15 can form three bonds. Carbon and silicon in Group 14 can form four bonds. For example, in methane (CH_4), carbon forms four covalent bonds with four hydrogen atoms, as shown below.

Methane (CH_4)

ball-and-stick model    space-filling model

We don't always show the lines representing the covalent bonds between the atoms. The space-filling model still shows the general shape of the bonded atoms, but occupies far less space on the page.

Each carbon-hydrogen bond in methane is a single bond because one pair of electrons is shared between the atoms. Sometimes atoms may share more than one pair of electrons with another atom. For example, the carbon atom in carbon dioxide (CO_2) forms double bonds with each of the oxygen atoms. A double bond consists of four (two pairs of) shared electrons. Two nitrogen atoms form a triple bond, meaning that they share six (three pairs of) electrons.

Carbon Dioxide (CO₂)

Nitrogen (N₂)

READING TIP

Remember that each line in the model stands for a covalent bond—one shared pair of electrons.

A group of atoms held together by covalent bonds is called a **molecule.** A molecule can contain from two to many thousand atoms. Most molecules contain the atoms of two or more elements. For example, water (H_2O), ammonia (NH_3), and methane (CH_4) are all compounds made up of molecules. However, some molecules contain atoms of only one element. The following elements exist as two-atom molecules: H_2, N_2, O_2, F_2, Cl_2, Br_2, and I_2.

 What is a molecule?

Polar Covalent Bonds

In an iodine molecule, both atoms are exactly the same. The shared electrons therefore are attracted equally to both nuclei. If the two atoms involved in a covalent bond are very different, however, the electrons have a stronger attraction to one nucleus than to the other and spend more time near that nucleus. A covalent bond in which the electrons are shared unequally is called a **polar covalent bond.** The word *polar* refers to anything that has two extremes, like a magnet with its two opposite poles.

READING TIP

To remind yourself that polar covalent bonds have opposite partial charges, remember that Earth has both a North Pole and a South Pole.

Water (H₂O)

ball-and-stick model

space-filling model

VISUALIZATION
CLASSZONE.COM

Examine how electrons move in a polar covalent molecule.

In a water molecule (H_2O), the oxygen atom attracts electrons far more strongly than the hydrogen atoms do. The oxygen nucleus has eight protons, and the hydrogen nucleus has only one proton. The oxygen atom pulls the shared electrons more strongly toward it. In a water molecule, therefore, the oxygen side has a slightly negative charge, and the hydrogen side has a slightly positive charge.

Comparing Bonds

In Salar de Uyuni, Bolivia, salt is mined in great quantities from salt water. The salt is harvested as the water evaporates into the air, leaving the salt behind. All types of chemical bonds are involved.

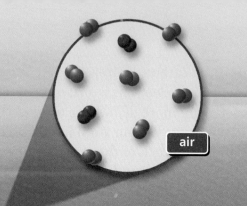

air

salt

water

Ionic Bonds (salt)

Sodium Chloride (NaCl)
A complete transfer of electrons produces the ionic bonds that hold sodium chloride (table salt) crystals together.

Covalent Bonds (air)

Nitrogen (N_2) and Oxygen (O_2)
Some molecules in air contain multiple covalent bonds. Nitrogen has triple bonds. Oxygen has double bonds.

Polar Covalent Bonds (water)

Water (H_2O)
The covalent bonds in water are very polar because oxygen attracts electrons far more strongly than hydrogen does.

READING VISUALS Atoms of which element are shown both in the air and in the water?

Chemical bonds give all materials their structures.

The substances around you have many different properties. The structure of the crystals and molecules that make up these substances are responsible for many of these properties. For example, crystals bend rays of light, metals shine, and medications attack certain diseases in the body because their atoms are arranged in specific ways.

Ionic Compounds

Most ionic compounds have a regular crystal structure. Remember how the size, shape, and ratio of the sodium ions and chloride ions give the sodium chloride crystal its shape. Other ionic compounds, such as calcium chloride, have different but equally regular structures that depend upon the ratio and sizes of the ions. One consequence of such rigid structures is that, when enough force is applied to the crystal, it shatters rather than bends.

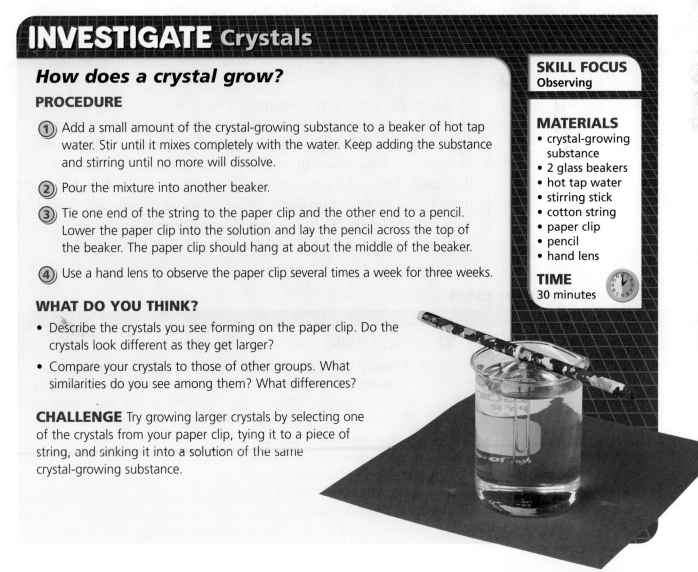

INVESTIGATE Crystals

How does a crystal grow?

SKILL FOCUS
Observing

PROCEDURE

1. Add a small amount of the crystal-growing substance to a beaker of hot tap water. Stir until it mixes completely with the water. Keep adding the substance and stirring until no more will dissolve.

2. Pour the mixture into another beaker.

3. Tie one end of the string to the paper clip and the other end to a pencil. Lower the paper clip into the solution and lay the pencil across the top of the beaker. The paper clip should hang at about the middle of the beaker.

4. Use a hand lens to observe the paper clip several times a week for three weeks.

MATERIALS
- crystal-growing substance
- 2 glass beakers
- hot tap water
- stirring stick
- cotton string
- paper clip
- pencil
- hand lens

TIME
30 minutes

WHAT DO YOU THINK?

- Describe the crystals you see forming on the paper clip. Do the crystals look different as they get larger?

- Compare your crystals to those of other groups. What similarities do you see among them? What differences?

CHALLENGE Try growing larger crystals by selecting one of the crystals from your paper clip, tying it to a piece of string, and sinking it into a solution of the same crystal-growing substance.

Covalent Compounds

Unlike ionic compounds, covalent compounds exist as individual molecules. Chemical bonds give each molecule a specific, three-dimensional shape called its molecular structure. Molecular structure can influence everything from how a specific substance feels to the touch to how well it interacts with other substances.

READING TiP

To help yourself appreciate the differences among these structures, try making three-dimensional models of them.

A few basic molecular structures are shown below. Molecules can have a simple linear shape, like iodine (I_2), or they can be bent, like a water molecule (H_2O). The atoms in an ammonia molecule (NH_3) form a pyramid, and methane (CH_4) molecules even have a slightly more complex shape. The shape of a molecule depends on the atoms it contains and the bonds holding it together.

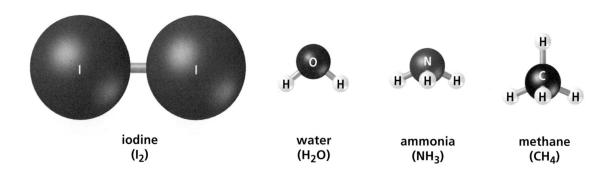

iodine
(I_2)

water
(H_2O)

ammonia
(NH_3)

methane
(CH_4)

Molecular shape can affect many properties of compounds. For example, there is some evidence to indicate that we detect scents because molecules with certain shapes fit into certain smell receptors in the nose. Molecules with similar shapes, therefore, should have similar smells. Molecular structure also plays an essential role in how our bodies respond to certain drugs. Some drugs work because molecules with certain shapes can fit into specific receptors in body cells.

17.2 Review

KEY CONCEPTS

1. What part of an atom is involved in chemical bonding?

2. How are ionic bonds and covalent bonds different?

3. Describe two ways that crystal and molecular structures affect the properties of ionic and covalent compounds.

CRITICAL THINKING

4. **Analyze** Would you expect the bonds in ammonia to be polar covalent? Why or why not?

5. **Infer** What kind of bond would you expect atoms of strontium and iodine to form? Why? Write the formula and name the compound.

CHALLENGE

6. **Conclude** Is the element silicon likely to form ionic or covalent bonds? Explain.

Think SCIENCE

Stick to It

Glues join objects by forming something like chemical bonds between their surfaces. While glue manufacturers try to make glues as strong as possible, simply being strong does not mean that a glue will join all surfaces equally well. For example, a glue that will hold two pieces of wood together very well may not be able to form a lasting bond between two pieces of plastic piping or two metal sheets.

Variables

When testing a new glue, a scientist wants to know exactly how that glue will perform under all conditions. In any test, however, there are a number of variables that could affect the quality of the bonds formed by the glue. The scientist needs to discover exactly which of these variables most affects the glue's ability to form lasting bonds. Identifying these variables and the effects each has on the glue's strength and lifetime enables glue makers to recommend the best uses for the glue. Following are a few of the variables a glue maker may consider when testing a glue.

- What surfaces the glue is being used to join
- How much glue is used in a test
- How evenly the glue is applied to the surface
- How much force the glue can withstand
- Over how long a time the force is applied
- The environment the glue is used in (wet, dry, or dusty)

The glue on the back of a postage stamp must be activated somehow. This scanning electron microscope photo shows postage stamp glue before (green) and after (blue) it has been activated by moisture.

This highly magnified photograph shows the attachment formed by a colorless, waterproof wood glue.

Variables to Test

On Your Own You are a scientist at a glue company. You have developed a new type of glue and need to know how specific conditions will affect its ability to hold surfaces together. First, select one variable you wish to test. Next, outline how you would ensure that only that variable will differ in each test. You might start out by listing all the variables you can think of and then put a check by each one and describe how you are controlling it.

As a Group Discuss the outlines of your tests with others. Are there any variables you haven't accounted for?

CHALLENGE Adhesive tapes come in many different types. Outline how you would test how well a certain tape holds in a wet environment and in a dry environment.

17.3 Substances' properties depend on their bonds.

BEFORE, you learned	NOW, you will learn
• Chemical bonds hold the atoms of compounds together • Chemical bonds involve the transfer or sharing of electrons • Molecules have a structure	• How metal atoms form chemical bonds with one another • How ionic and covalent bonds influence substances' properties

VOCABULARY

metallic bond p. 556

EXPLORE Bonds in Metals

What objects conduct electricity?

PROCEDURE

① Tape one end of a copper wire to one terminal of the battery. Attach the other end of the copper wire to the light bulb holder. Attach a second wire to the holder. Tape a third wire to the other terminal of the battery.

② Touch the ends of both wires to objects around the classroom. Notice if the bulb lights or not.

WHAT DO YOU THINK?
• Which objects make the bulb light?
• How are these objects similar?

MATERIALS
• masking tape
• 3 pieces of copper wire (15 cm)
• D cell (battery)
• light bulb and holder
• objects to test

Metals have unique bonds.

Metal atoms bond together by sharing their electrons with one another. The atoms share the electrons equally in all directions. The equal sharing allows the electrons to move easily among the atoms of the metal. This special type of bond is called a **metallic bond.**

▼ REMINDER

Chemical bonds involve the sharing of or transfer of electrons.

The properties of metals are determined by metallic bonds. One common property of metals is that they are good conductors of electric current. The electrons in a metal flow through the material, carrying the electric current. The free movement of electrons among metal atoms also means that metals are good conductors of heat. Metals also typically have high melting points. Except for mercury, all metals are solids at room temperature.

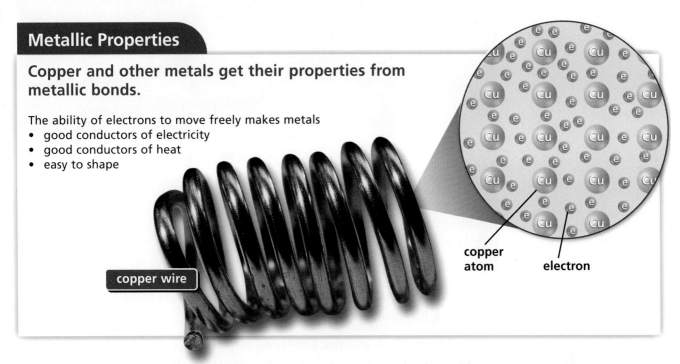

Metallic Properties

Copper and other metals get their properties from metallic bonds.

The ability of electrons to move freely makes metals
- good conductors of electricity
- good conductors of heat
- easy to shape

copper wire

copper atom

electron

Two other properties of metals are that they are easily shaped by pounding and can be drawn into a wire. These properties are also explained by the nature of the metallic bond. In metallic compounds, atoms can slide past one another. It is as if the atoms are swimming in a pool of surrounding electrons. Pounding the metal simply moves these atoms into other positions. This property makes metals ideal for making coins.

 CHECK YOUR READING What three properties do metals have because of metallic bonds?

SOUTH CAROLINA Essentials

See the South Carolina Essentials, page 655, to read about the properties of metals and nonmetals.

Ionic and covalent bonds give compounds certain properties.

The properties of a compound depend on the chemical bonds that hold its atoms together. For example, you can be pretty certain an ionic compound will be a solid at room temperature. Ionic compounds, in fact, usually have extremely high melting and boiling points because it takes a lot of energy to break all the bonds among all the ions in the crystal. The rigid crystal network also makes ionic compounds hard, brittle, and poor conductors of electricity. No moving electrical charges means no current will flow.

Ionic compounds, however, often dissolve easily in water, separating into positive ions and negative ions. The separated ions can move freely, making solutions of ionic compounds good conductors of electricity. Your body, in fact, uses ionic solutions to help transmit impulses between nerve and muscle cells. Exercise can rapidly deplete these ionic solutions in the body, so sports drinks contain ionic compounds.

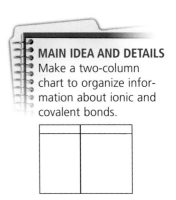

MAIN IDEA AND DETAILS Make a two-column chart to organize information about ionic and covalent bonds.

A hot pool in Yellowstone Park's Upper Geyser Basin. These pools are often characterized by their striking colors.

RESOURCE CENTER
CLASSZONE.COM

Find out more about the properties of ionic and covalent compounds.

These compounds, such as potassium chloride, replace the ions lost during physical activity.

Mineral hot springs, like those found in Yellowstone National Park, are another example of ionic solutions. Many of the ionic compounds dissolved in these hot springs contain the element sulfur, which can have an unpleasant odor. Evidence of these ionic compounds can be seen in the white deposits around the pool's rim.

Covalent compounds have almost the exact opposite properties of ionic compounds. Since the atoms are organized as individual molecules, melting or boiling a covalent compound does not require breaking chemical bonds. Therefore, covalent compounds often melt and boil at lower temperatures than ionic compounds. Unlike ionic compounds, molecules stay together when dissolved in water, which means covalent compounds are poor conductors of electricity. Table sugar, for example, does not conduct an electric current when in solution.

Bonds can make the same element look different.

Covalent bonds do not always form small individual molecules. This explains how the element carbon can exist in three very different forms—diamond, graphite, and fullerene. The properties of each form depend on how the carbon atoms are bonded to each other.

Diamond is the hardest natural substance. This property makes diamond useful for cutting other substances. Diamonds are made entirely of carbon. Each carbon atom forms covalent bonds with four other carbon atoms. The pattern of linked atoms extends throughout the entire volume of a diamond crystal. This three-dimensional structure of carbon atoms gives diamonds their strength—diamond bonds do not break easily.

Another form of carbon is graphite. Graphite is the dark, slippery component of pencil "lead." Graphite has a different structure from diamond, although both are networks of interconnected atoms. Each carbon atom in graphite forms covalent bonds with three other atoms to form two-dimensional layers. These layers stack on top of one another like sheets of paper. The layers can slide past one another easily. Graphite feels slippery and is used as a lubricant to reduce friction between metal parts of machines.

graphite

diamond

A third form of carbon, fullerene, contains large molecules. One type of fullerene, called buckminsterfullerene, has molecules shaped like a soccer ball. In 1985 chemists made a fullerene molecule consisting of 60 carbon atoms. Since then, many similar molecules have been made, ranging from 20 to more than 100 atoms per molecule.

buckminsterfullerene

17.3 Review

KEY CONCEPTS

1. How do metal atoms bond together?

2. Why do ionic compounds have high melting points?

3. What are three forms of the element carbon?

CRITICAL THINKING

4. **Apply** A compound known as cubic boron nitride has a structure similar to that of a diamond. What properties would you expect it to have?

5. **Infer** Sterling silver is a combination of silver and copper. How are the silver and copper atoms held together?

◆ CHALLENGE

6. **Infer** Why might the water in mineral springs be a better conductor of electricity than drinking water?

CHAPTER INVESTIGATION

Chemical Bonds

OVERVIEW AND PURPOSE Chemists can identify the type of bonds in a substance by examining its properties. In this investigation you will examine the properties of different substances and use what you have learned about chemical bonds to identify the type of bond each substance contains. You will

- observe the structure of substances with a hand lens
- test the conductivity of substances
- determine the melting point of substances

▶ Problem

How can you determine the type of chemical bond a substance has?

▶ Hypothesize

Write three hypotheses in "if . . . , then . . . , because . . ." form to answer the problem question for each bond type—ionic, covalent, and metallic.

▶ Procedure

1. Create a data table similar to the one shown on the sample notebook page.

2. To build the conductivity tester, connect the first wire to one terminal of the battery and to one of the metal strips. Attach the second wire to the other terminal and to the lamp socket. Finally, connect the lamp socket to the third wire, and connect the other end of this wire to the second metal strip.

3. To make sure your tester works properly, touch the tips of the metal strips together. If the bulb lights, the tester is working properly. If not, check the connections carefully.

4. Get the following test compounds from your teacher: Epsom salts (MgSO$_4$), sugar (C$_{12}$H$_{22}$O$_{11}$), and iron filings (Fe). For each substance, put about 20 grams in a cup and label it.

MATERIALS

- 3 wire leads with alligator clips
- battery
- zinc and copper strips
- light bulb and socket
- test compounds
- 3 plastic cups
- distilled water
- beaker
- construction paper
- hand lens
- plastic spoon
- 3 test tubes
- test-tube rack
- candle
- wire test-tube holder

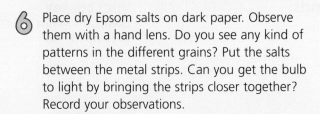

5 Test the conductivity of distilled water. Fill the beaker with 30 mL of water. Place the two metal strips into the water. Does the bulb light? Record your observations. Dry the strips completely.

6 Place dry Epsom salts on dark paper. Observe them with a hand lens. Do you see any kind of patterns in the different grains? Put the salts between the metal strips. Can you get the bulb to light by bringing the strips closer together? Record your observations.

7 Add all but a small amount of the Epsom salts to the beaker of water. Stir well. Repeat the conductivity test. What happens when you put the metal strips into the solution? Record your results.

8 Rinse and dry the beaker. Repeat steps 6–7 with other test substances. Record your results.

9 Put the remainder of each test substance into its own clean, dry test tube. Label the tubes. Light the candle. Use a test tube holder to hold each compound over the candle flame for 2 minutes. Do you notice any signs of melting? Record your observations.

▶ Observe and Analyze
Write It Up

1. **RECORD OBSERVATIONS** Be sure you have entered all your observations in your data table.

2. **CLASSIFY** Using the periodic table, find the elements these compounds contain. How might consulting the periodic table help you determine what type of bond exists in the compound?

▶ Conclude
Write It Up

1. **INTERPRET** Review your recorded observations. Classify the compounds as having ionic, covalent, or metallic bonds. Fill in the last row of the data table with your conclusions.

2. **INFER** Compare your results with your hypotheses. Did your results support your hypotheses?

3. **EVALUATE** Describe possible limitations, errors, or places where errors might have occurred.

4. **APPLY** Electrocardiograms are graphs that show the electrical activity of the heart. When an electrocardiogram is made, a paste of sodium chloride is used to hold small metal discs on the patient's skin. What property of ionic compounds does this medical test make use of?

▶ INVESTIGATE Further

CHALLENGE To grow crystals, put about 60 grams of Epsom salts into a baby-food jar that is half full of hot water. Do the same using a second jar containing about 60 grams of sugar. Cover and shake the jars for a count of 60. Line two clean jar lids with dark paper. Brush or spoon a thin coating of each liquid over the paper. Let them stand in a warm place. After several days, observe the crystals that form, using a hand lens.

Chemical Bonds
Problem How can you determine the type of chemical bond a substance has?

Hypothesize

Observe and Analyze

Table 1: Properties of Bonds

Property	Epsom Salts ($MgSO_4$)	Sugar ($C_{12}H_{22}O_{11}$)	Iron Filings (Fe)
Crystal structure			
Conductivity of solid			
Conductivity in water			
Melting			
Bond type			

Conclude

Chapter Review

the BIG idea

The properties of compounds depend on their atoms and chemical bonds.

CONTENT REVIEW
CLASSZONE.COM

KEY CONCEPTS SUMMARY

1 **Elements combine to form compounds.**

- Compounds have different properties from the elements that made them.
- Atoms combine in predictable numbers.

calcium (Ca)   +   chlorine (Cl₂)   =   calcium chloride (CaCl₂)

VOCABULARY
chemical formula p. 543
subscript p. 543

2 **Chemical bonds hold compounds together.**

- Chemical bonds between atoms involve electrons.
- Atoms can transfer electrons.
- Atoms can share electrons.
- Chemical bonds give all materials their structure.

ionic bond

covalent bond

VOCABULARY
ionic bond p. 548
covalent bond p. 550
molecule p. 551
polar covalent bond p. 551

3 **Substances' properties depend on their bonds.**

- Metals have unique bonds.
- Ionic and covalent bonds give compounds certain properties.
- Bonds can make the same element look different.

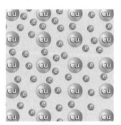

copper

diamond fragment

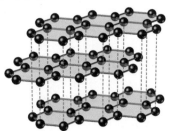

graphite fragment

VOCABULARY
metallic bond p. 556

Reviewing Vocabulary

Copy and complete the table below. Under each bond type, describe
* *how electrons are distributed*
* *how the compound is structured*
* *one of the properties of the compound containing this type of bond*

Some of the table has been filled out for you.

Ionic Bonds	Covalent Bonds	Metallic Bonds
1.	shared electron pair	2.
3.	4.	close-packed atoms in sea of electrons
have high melting points	5.	6.

Reviewing Key Concepts

Multiple Choice *Choose the letter of the best answer.*

7. Most substances are
  a. elements   **c.** metals
  b. compounds **d.** nonmetals

8. All compounds are made of
  a. atoms of two or more elements
  b. two or more atoms of the same element
  c. atoms arranged in a crystal
  d. atoms joined by covalent bonds

9. The chemical formula for a compound having one barium (Ba) ion and two chloride (Cl) ions is
  a. BCl   **c.** $BaCl_2$
  b. BaCl   **d.** Ba_2Cl_2

10. The 4 in the chemical formula CH_4 means there are
  a. four carbon atoms to one hydrogen atom
  b. four carbon and four hydrogen atoms
  c. four hydrogen atoms to one carbon atom
  d. four total carbon CH combinations

11. The compound KBr has the name
  a. potassium bromide
  b. potassium bromine
  c. bromide potassium
  d. bromine potassium

12. An atom becomes a positive ion when it
  a. is attracted to all nearby atoms
  b. gains an electron from another atom
  c. loses an electron to another atom
  d. shares an electron with another atom

13. A polar covalent bond forms when two atoms
  a. share one electron equally
  b. share two electrons equally
  c. share one electron unequally
  d. share two electrons unequally

14. Metallic bonds make many metals
  a. poor conductors of heat
  b. liquid at room temperature
  c. difficult to shape
  d. good conductors of electricity

15. Three forms of carbon are
  a. diamond, graphite, and salt
  b. diamond, graphite, and fullerene
  c. graphite, salt, and carbonate
  d. diamond, salt, and fullerene

Short Answer *Write a short answer to each question.*

16. Why does a mixture of sodium chloride and water conduct electricity but a sodium chloride crystal does not?

17. Describe what makes diamond and graphite, two forms of the element carbon, so different.

Thinking Critically

Use the illustration above to answer the next two questions.

18. **IDENTIFY** Write the chemical formula for the molecule pictured above.

19. **ANALYZE** The nitrogen atom has a far greater attraction for electrons than hydrogen atoms. Copy the molecule pictured above and indicate which parts of the molecule have a slightly positive charge and which parts have a slightly negative charge.

20. **PREDICT** The chemical formula for calcium chloride is $CaCl_2$. What would you predict the formula for magnesium chloride to be? [**Hint:** Find magnesium on the periodic table.]

21. **INFER** When scientists make artificial diamonds, they sometimes subject graphite to very high temperatures and pressures. What do you think happens to change the graphite into diamond?

22. **SYNTHESIZE** Why would seawater be a better conductor of electricity than river water?

23. **ANALYZE** How does the nature of the metallic bond explain the observation that most metals can be drawn into a wire?

24. **EVALUATE** Do you think the types of bonds you've studied occur on the planet Mars? Explain.

25. **INFER** Why don't we use the term *ionic molecule?*

Use the chemical formulas below and a periodic table to answer the next three questions.

Compound
I. K_2SO_4
II. CF_4
III. C_4H_{10}
IV. KCl

26. **APPLY** Name compound IV. Does this compound have ionic or covalent bonds?

27. **ANALYZE** Name the elements in each compound. Tell how many atoms are in each compound.

28. **CALCULATE** Express the ratio of atoms in compounds II, III, and IV. For compound I, express all three ratios.

29. **APPLY** By 1800 Alessandro Volta had made the first electric battery. He placed pieces of cardboard soaked in saltwater in between alternating zinc and silver discs. What properties of the metals and the saltwater made them good materials for a battery?

30. **PREDICT** What is the maximum number of covalent bonds that a hydrogen atom can form? Explain your answer.

the **BIG** idea

31. **DRAW CONCLUSIONS** Look at the photograph on pages 538–539 again. Can you now recognize any similarities between how the skydivers stay together and how atoms stay together?

32. **APPLY** Phosphorus can be a strange element. Pure phosphorus is sometimes white, black, or red. What can account for the differences in appearance?

UNIT PROJECTS

If you need to create graphs or other visuals for your project, be sure you have graph paper, poster board, markers, or other supplies.

Interpreting Tables

The table below lists some of the characteristics of substances that contain different types of bonds. Use the table to answer the questions.

Bond Type	Usually Forms Between	Electrons	Properties	Examples
Ionic	an atom of a metal and an atom of a nonmetal	transferred between atoms	• high melting points • conducts electricity when in water	BaS, $BaBr_2$, Ca_3N_2, LiCl, ZnO
Covalent	atoms of nonmetallic elements	shared between atoms but often not equally	• low melting points • does not conduct electricity	C_2H_6, C, Cl_2, H_2, $AsCl_3$
Metallic	atoms of metallic elements	freely moving about the atoms	• high melting points • conducts electricity at all times • easily shaped	Ca, Fe, Na, Cu, Zn

1. Which of these compounds would you expect to have the highest melting point?

  a. C_2H_6 **c.** $AsCl_3$

  b. Cl_2 **d.** $BaBr_2$

2. Which substance is likely to be easily shaped?

  a. $BaBr_2$ **c.** Na

  b. LiCl   **d.** C

3. In the compound LiCl, electrons are

  a. shared equally

  b. shared but not equally

  c. transferred between atoms to form ions

  d. freely moving among the atoms

4. Which of the following is an ionic compound?

  a. C_2H_6 **c.** $AsCl_3$

  b. Cl_2 **d.** ZnO

5. Which of the following compounds has a low melting point?

  a. Cl_2 **c.** Cu

  b. ZnO   **d.** $BaBr_2$

6. A solid mass of which substance would conduct electricity?

  a. Ca_3N_2 **c.** Cu

  b. LiCl   **d.** $AsCl_3$

Extended Response

Answer the next two questions in detail.
Include some of the terms from the list in the box.
Underline each term you use in your answer.

share electron	transfer electron
freely moving electrons	charge
compound	chemical formula

7. Compare how electrons are involved in making the three main types of bonds: ionic, covalent, and metallic.

8. Just about 100 elements occur naturally. There are, however, millions of different materials. How can so few basic substances make so many different materials?

Chemical Reactions

the **BIG** idea

Chemical reactions form new substances by breaking and making chemical bonds.

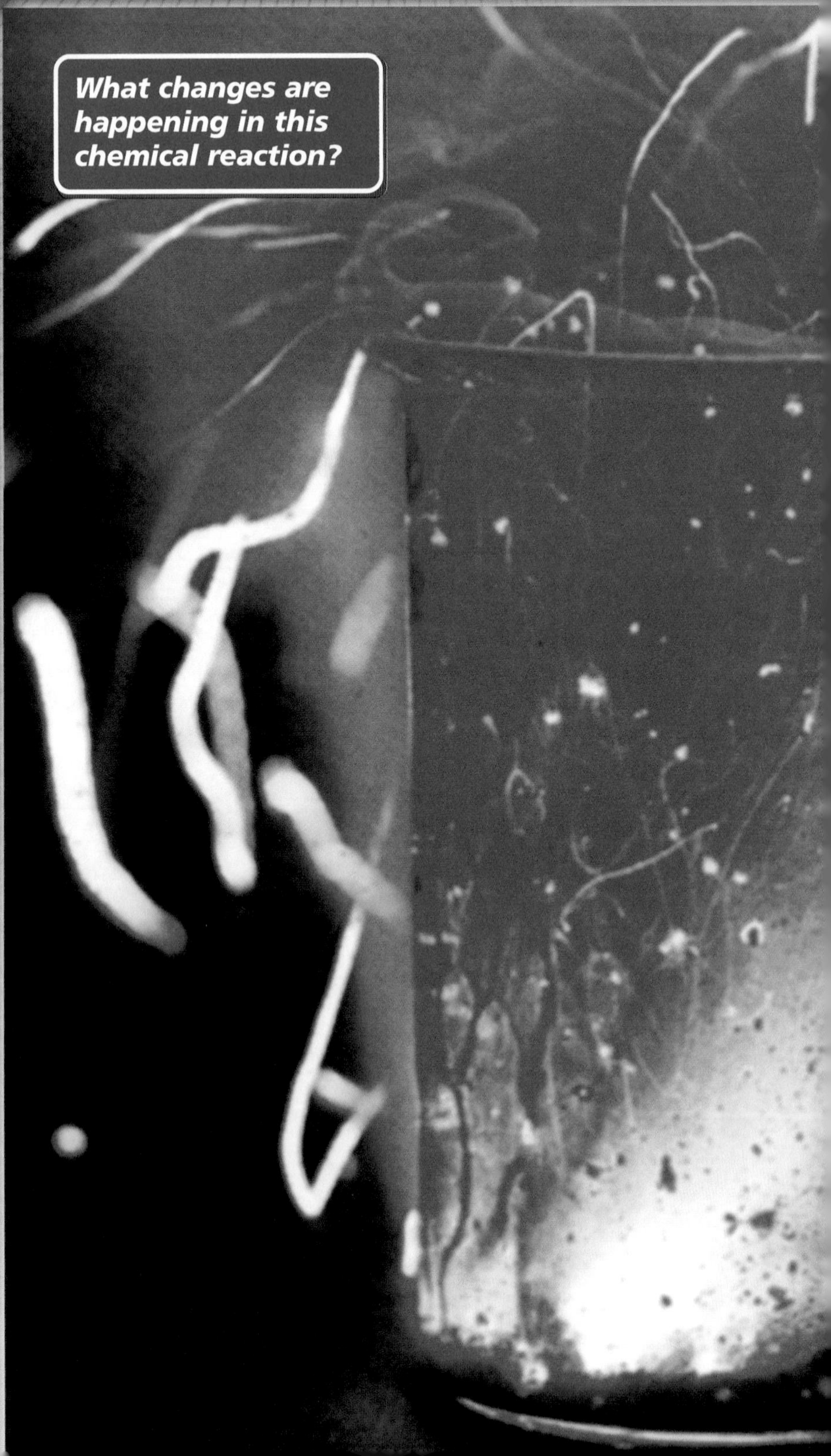

> **What changes are happening in this chemical reaction?**

Key Concepts

SECTION

1 **Chemical reactions alter arrangements of atoms.**
Learn how chemical reactions are identified and controlled.

SECTION

2 **The masses of reactants and products are equal.**
Learn how chemical equations show the conservation of mass.

SECTION

3 **Chemical reactions involve energy changes.**
Learn how energy is absorbed or released by chemical reactions.

SECTION

4 **Life and industry depend on chemical reactions.**
Learn about some chemical reactions in everyday life.

Internet Preview

CLASSZONE.COM
Chapter 18 online resources: Content Review, two Visualizations, two Resource Centers, Math Tutorial, Test Practice

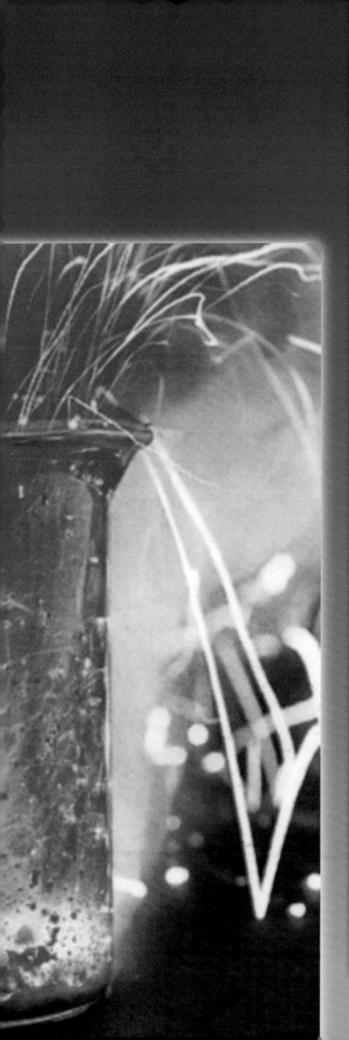

EXPLORE (the BIG idea)

Changing Steel Wool

Place a small lump of steel wool in a cup.
Pour in enough vinegar to cover the steel
wool. After five minutes, take the steel
wool out of the vinegar. Shake the steel
wool to remove any excess vinegar.
Place the steel wool in a small plastic
bottle, and cover the mouth of the
bottle with a balloon. Observe the
steel wool and balloon after one hour.

Observe and Think What happened
to the steel wool and balloon? What
might have caused this to occur?

A Different Rate

Half fill one cup with hot tap
water and a second cup with
cold tap water. Drop a seltzer
tablet into each cup at the
same time. Time how long
it takes for each tablet to
stop fizzing.

Observe and Think
Which tablet fizzed for a
longer period of time? How
might you explain any differences?

Internet Activity: Reactions

Go to **ClassZone.com** to explore chemical
reactions and chemical
equations. Learn how a
chemical equation can be
balanced.

Observe and Think How
do chemical equations
show what happens during
a chemical reaction?

NSTA
scilinks.org
SCiLINKS

Chemical Reactions **Code: MDL024**

Getting Ready to Learn

◀ CONCEPT REVIEW

- Atoms combine to form compounds.
- Atoms gain or lose electrons when they form ionic bonds.
- Atoms share electrons in covalent bonds.

◀ VOCABULARY REVIEW

electron p. 511
ionic bond p. 548
covalent bond p. 550
See Glossary for definitions.
atom, chemical change

 CONTENT REVIEW
CLASSZONE.COM
Review concepts and vocabulary.

▶ TAKING NOTES

COMBINATION NOTES

To take notes about a new concept, first make an informal outline of the information. Then make a sketch of the concept and label it so you can study it later.

VOCABULARY STRATEGY

Write each new vocabulary term in the center of a **four square** diagram. Write notes in the squares around each term. Include a definition, some characteristics, and some examples of the term. If possible, write some things that are not examples of the term.

See the Note-Taking Handbook on pages R45–R51.

SCIENCE NOTEBOOK

NOTES

Chemical reactions
- cause chemical changes
- make new substances
- change reactants into products

Evidence of Chemical Reactions

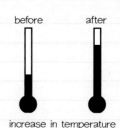

before   after

increase in temperature

Definition	Characteristics
substance present before a chemical reaction occurs	its bonds are broken during a reaction
REACTANT	
Examples	
oxygen in a combustion reaction	Nonexample carbon dioxide in a combustion reaction

18.1

Chemical reactions alter arrangements of atoms.

STANDARDS

7–5.7 Identify the reactants and products in chemical equations.

VOCABULARY

chemical reaction p. 569
reactant p. 571
product p. 571
precipitate p. 572
catalyst p. 576

◀ **BEFORE, you learned**

- Atoms of one element differ from atoms of all other elements
- Chemical bonds hold compounds together
- Chemical bonds may be ionic or covalent

▶ **NOW, you will learn**

- About chemical changes and how they occur
- About three types of chemical reactions
- How the rate of a chemical reaction can be changed

EXPLORE Chemical Changes

How can you identify a chemical change?

PROCEDURE

① Pour about 3 cm (1 in.) of vinegar into the bowl. Add a spoonful of salt. Stir until the salt dissolves.

② Put the pennies into the bowl. Wait two minutes, and then put the nail into the bowl.

③ Observe the nail after five minutes and record your observations.

WHAT DO YOU THINK?

- What did you see on the nail? Where do you think it came from?
- Did a new substance form? What evidence supports your conclusion?

MATERIALS

- vinegar
- clear bowl
- plastic spoon
- table salt
- 20 pennies
- large iron nail

Atoms interact in chemical reactions.

COMBINATION NOTES
Use combination notes to organize information about how atoms interact during chemical reactions.

You see substances change every day. Some changes are physical, such as when liquid water changes to water vapor during boiling. Other changes are chemical, such as when wood burns to form smoke and ash, or when rust forms on iron. During a chemical change, substances change into one or more different substances.

A **chemical reaction** produces new substances by changing the way in which atoms are arranged. In a chemical reaction, bonds between atoms are broken and new bonds form between different atoms. This breaking and forming of bonds takes place when particles of the original materials collide with one another. After a chemical reaction, the new arrangements of atoms form different substances.

Physical Changes

A change in the state of a substance is an example of a physical change. The substance may have some different properties after a physical change, but it is still the same substance. For example, you know that water can exist in three different physical states: the solid state (ice), the liquid state (water), and the gas state (water vapor). However, regardless of what state water is in, it still remains water, that is, H_2O molecules. As ice melts, the molecules of water move around more quickly, but the molecules do not change. As water vapor condenses, the molecules of water move more slowly, but they are still the same molecules.

Substances can undergo different kinds of physical changes. For example, sugar dissolves in water but still tastes sweet because the molecules that make up sugar do not change when it dissolves. The pressure of helium changes when it is pumped from a high-pressure tank into a balloon, but the gas still remains helium.

CHECK YOUR READING What happens to a substance when it undergoes a physical change?

When water changes from a liquid to a solid, it undergoes a physical change.

Ice is composed of water molecules that are locked together.

Liquid water is composed of molecules that move freely past each other.

Chemical Changes

Water can also undergo a chemical change. Water molecules can be broken down into hydrogen and oxygen molecules by a chemical reaction called electrolysis. When an electric current is passed through liquid water (H_2O), it changes the water into two gases—hydrogen and oxygen. The molecules of water break apart into individual atoms, which then recombine into hydrogen molecules (H_2) and oxygen molecules (O_2). The original material (water) changes into different substances through a chemical reaction.

Hydrogen and oxygen are used as rocket fuel for the space shuttle. During liftoff, liquid hydrogen and liquid oxygen are combined in a reaction that is the opposite of electrolysis. This reaction produces water and a large amount of energy that helps push the shuttle into orbit.

 How does a chemical change differ from a physical change?

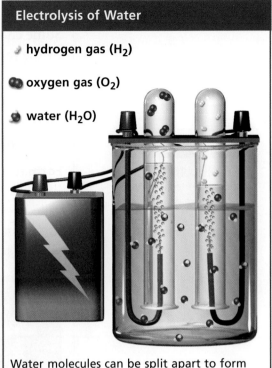

Electrolysis of Water

- hydrogen gas (H_2)
- oxygen gas (O_2)
- water (H_2O)

Water molecules can be split apart to form separate hydrogen and oxygen molecules.

Reactants and Products

Reactants are the substances present at the beginning of a chemical reaction. In the burning of natural gas, for example, methane (CH_4) and oxygen (O_2) are the reactants in the chemical reaction. **Products** are the substances formed by a chemical reaction. In the burning of natural gas, carbon dioxide (CO_2) and water (H_2O) are the products formed by the reaction. Reactants and products can be elements or compounds, depending on the reaction taking place.

During a chemical reaction, bonds between atoms in the reactants are broken and new bonds are formed in the products. When natural gas is burned, bonds between the carbon and hydrogen atoms in methane are broken, as are the bonds between the oxygen atoms in oxygen molecules. New bonds are formed between carbon and oxygen in carbon dioxide gas and between hydrogen and oxygen in water vapor.

Reactants—bonds broken		Products—new bonds formed	
methane + (CH₄)	oxygen (O₂)	carbon dioxide (CO₂)	+ water (H₂O)

 What must happen for reactants to be changed into products?

Evidence of Chemical Reactions

Some chemical changes are easy to observe—the products formed by the rearrangement of atoms look different than the reactants. Other changes are not easy to see but can be detected in other ways.

Color Change Substances often change color during a chemical reaction. For example, when gray iron rusts, the product that forms is brown, as shown in the photograph below.

Formation of a Precipitate Many chemical reactions form products that exist in a different physical state from the reactants. A solid product called a **precipitate** may form when chemicals in two liquids react, as shown in the photograph below. Seashells are often formed this way when a sea creature releases a liquid that reacts with seawater.

VOCABULARY
Remember to use a four square diagram for *precipitate* and other vocabulary terms.

Color Change

Formation of a Precipitate

Formation of a Gas Chemical reactions may produce a gas, like that often formed when antacid pills are mixed with excess stomach acid. The photograph below shows an example in which carbon dioxide gas is produced by a chemical reaction.

Temperature Change Most chemical reactions involve a temperature change. Sometimes this change can be inferred from the observation of a flame, as in the burning of the metal magnesium in the photograph below. Other temperature changes are not immediately obvious. If you have touched concrete before it hardens, you may have noticed that it felt warm. This warmth is due to a chemical reaction.

Formation of a Gas

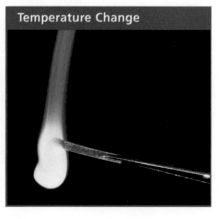

Temperature Change

Chemical reactions can be classified.

Scientists classify chemical reactions in several ways to help make the different types of reactions easier to understand. All reactions form new products, but the ways in which products are made can differ.

Synthesis In a synthesis reaction, a new compound is formed by the combination of simpler reactants. For example, nitrogen dioxide (NO_2), a component of smog, forms when nitrogen and oxygen combine in the air.

READING **TiP**

Synthesis means "making a substance from simpler substances."

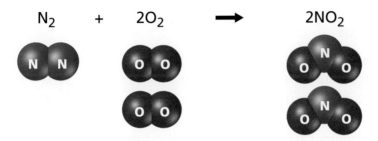

Decomposition In a decomposition reaction, a reactant breaks down into simpler products, which could be elements or other compounds. Decomposition reactions can be thought of as being the reverse of synthesis reactions. For example, water can be decomposed into its elements—hydrogen and oxygen.

READING **TiP**

Decomposition means "separation into parts."

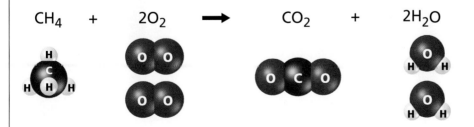

Combustion In a combustion reaction, one reactant is always oxygen and another reactant often contains carbon and hydrogen. The carbon and hydrogen atoms combine with oxygen, producing carbon dioxide and water. The burning of methane is a combustion reaction.

READING **TiP**

Combustion is the process of burning with oxygen.

CHECK YOUR READING How are synthesis reactions different from decomposition reactions?

The rates of chemical reactions can vary.

Most chemical reactions take place when particles of reactants collide with enough force to react. Chemical reactions can occur at different rates. Striking a match causes a very quick chemical reaction, while the rusting of an iron nail may take months. However, the rate of a reaction can be changed. For instance, a nail can be made to rust more quickly. Three physical factors—concentration, surface area, and temperature—and a chemical factor—a catalyst—can greatly affect the rate of a chemical reaction.

Concentration

VISUALIZATION
CLASSZONE.COM

Observe how changing the concentration of a reactant can change the rate of a reaction.

Concentration measures the number of particles present in a certain volume. A high concentration of reactants means that there is a large number of particles that can collide and react. Turning the valve on a gas stove to increase the flow of gas increases the concentration of methane molecules that can combine with oxygen in the air. The result is a bigger flame and a faster combustion reaction.

Surface Area

Suppose one of the reactants in a chemical reaction is present as a single large piece of material. Particles of the second reactant cannot get inside the large piece, so they can react only with particles on the surface. To make the reaction go faster, the large piece of material could be broken into smaller pieces before the reaction starts.

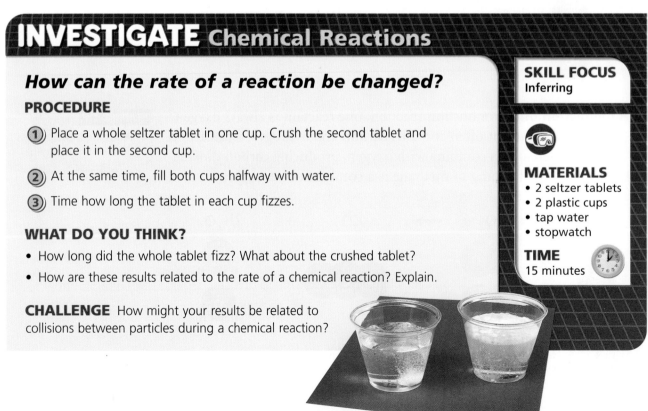

INVESTIGATE Chemical Reactions

How can the rate of a reaction be changed?

PROCEDURE

1. Place a whole seltzer tablet in one cup. Crush the second tablet and place it in the second cup.
2. At the same time, fill both cups halfway with water.
3. Time how long the tablet in each cup fizzes.

WHAT DO YOU THINK?

- How long did the whole tablet fizz? What about the crushed tablet?
- How are these results related to the rate of a chemical reaction? Explain.

CHALLENGE How might your results be related to collisions between particles during a chemical reaction?

SKILL FOCUS
Inferring

MATERIALS
- 2 seltzer tablets
- 2 plastic cups
- tap water
- stopwatch

TIME
15 minutes

Breaking a large piece of material into smaller parts increases the surface area of the material. All of the inner material has no surface when it is inside a larger piece. Each time the large piece is broken, however, more surfaces are exposed. The amount of material does not change, but breaking it into smaller parts increases its surface area. Increasing the surface area increases the rate of the reaction.

 CHECK YOUR READING Why does a reaction proceed faster when the reactants have greater surface areas?

Temperature

The rate of a reaction can be increased by making the particles move faster. The result is that more collisions take place per second and occur with greater force. The most common way to make the particles move faster is to add energy to the reactants, which will raise their temperature.

Many chemical reactions during cooking go very slowly, or do not take place at all, unless energy is added to the reactants. Too much heat can make a reaction go too fast, and food ends up burned. Chemical reactions can also be slowed or stopped by decreasing the temperature of the reactants. Again, think about cooking. The reactions that take place during cooking can be stopped by removing the food from the heat source.

▼ REMINDER

Temperature is the average amount of kinetic energy of the particles in a substance.

Particles and Reaction Rates		
Changes in Reactants	**Normal Reaction Rate**	**Increased Reaction Rate**
Concentration An increase in concentration of the reactants increases the number of particles that can interact.		
Surface area An increase in the surface area of the reactants increases the number of particles that can interact.		
Temperature Adding energy makes particles move faster and increases temperature. The increase in motion allows reactants to collide and react more frequently.		

Catalysts

RESOURCE CENTER
CLASSZONE.COM

Learn more about catalysts and how they work in living things.

The rate of a reaction can be changed chemically by adding a catalyst. A **catalyst** is a substance that increases the rate of a chemical reaction but is not itself consumed in the reaction. This means that after the reaction is complete, the catalyst remains unchanged. Catalysts are very important for many industrial and biological reactions. In fact, many chemical reactions would proceed slowly or not take place at all without catalysts.

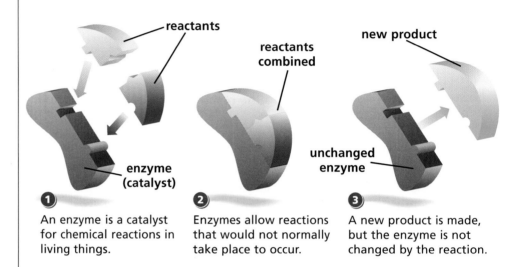

1 An enzyme is a catalyst for chemical reactions in living things.

2 Enzymes allow reactions that would not normally take place to occur.

3 A new product is made, but the enzyme is not changed by the reaction.

In living things, catalysts called enzymes are absolutely necessary for life. Without them, many important reactions could not take place under the conditions within your body. In fact, in 2003, scientists reported that they had discovered the slowest known chemical reaction in living things. This reaction would normally take one trillion years. Enzymes, though, allow the reaction to occur in 0.01 seconds.

CHECK YOUR READING Why are catalysts important in chemical reactions?

 Review

KEY CONCEPTS

1. How do physical changes differ from chemical changes? Explain.

2. Describe four types of evidence of a chemical reaction.

3. Describe the ways in which the rate of a chemical reaction can be changed.

CRITICAL THINKING

4. **Synthesize** What evidence shows that the burning of methane is a chemical reaction?

5. **Compare** What about combustion reactions makes them different from either synthesis or decomposition reactions?

● CHALLENGE

6. **Apply** How might the chewing of food be related to the rate of a chemical reaction—digestion—that occurs in your body? Explain.

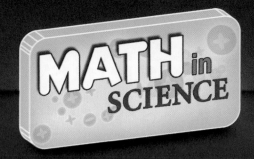

MATH in SCIENCE

 MATH TUTORIAL

Click on Math Tutorial for more help with interpreting line graphs.

Before   After

The reactants in the iodine clock reaction produce a sudden color change several seconds after the reactants are mixed.

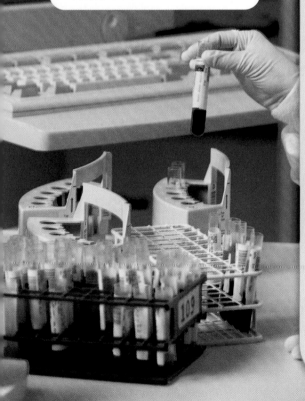

The Iodine Clock

Can a chemical reaction be timed? In the iodine clock reaction, a sudden color change indicates that the reaction has occurred. The length of time that passes before the color changes depends on the concentration ratios of the reactants. As shown in the graph below, the greater the concentration of the reactants, the faster the reaction.

Example

Suppose you are given an unknown iodine concentration to test in the iodine clock reaction. What is the concentration ratio of the iodine if it takes 40 seconds for the color change to occur?

(1) Find 40 seconds on the *x*-axis of the graph below and follow the vertical line up to the plotted data.

(2) Draw a horizontal line from that point on the curve to the *y*-axis to find the iodine concentration ratio in your sample.

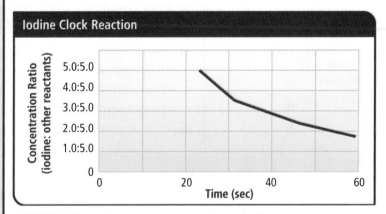

Iodine Clock Reaction

ANSWER The unknown concentration ratio is approximately 3.0:5.0.

Answer the following questions using the information in the graph above.

1. Approximately how long will it take for the reaction to occur if the concentration ratio is 4.0:5.0? 2.0:5.0?

2. Suppose you could extend the curve on the graph. If the reaction took 70 seconds to occur, what would be the approximate iodine concentration ratio?

CHALLENGE Using the following concentration ratios and times for another reactant, draw a reaction rate graph similar to the one shown above.

Concentration Ratios = 5.0:5.0, 4.0:5.0, 3.0:5.0, 2.0:5.0

Times = 24 sec, 25 sec, 43 sec, 68 sec

KEY CONCEPT

18.2 The masses of reactants and products are equal.

STANDARDS

7–5.7 Identify the reactants and products in chemical equations.

7–5.8 Explain how a balanced chemical equation supports the law of conservation of matter.

VOCABULARY

law of conservation of mass p. 579
coefficient p. 582

◀ **BEFORE,** you learned

- Chemical reactions turn reactants into products by rearranging atoms
- Chemical reactions can be observed and identified
- The rate of chemical reactions can be changed

▶ **NOW,** you will learn

- About the law of conservation of mass
- How a chemical equation represents a chemical reaction
- How to balance a simple chemical equation

THINK ABOUT

What happens to burning matter?

You have probably watched a fire burn in a fireplace, a campfire, or a candle flame. It looks as if the wood or candle disappears over time, leaving a small pile of ashes or wax when the fire has finished burning. But does matter really disappear? Combustion is a chemical reaction, and chemical reactions involve rearrangements of atoms. The atoms do not disappear, so where do they go?

Careful observations led to the discovery of the conservation of mass.

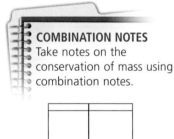

COMBINATION NOTES
Take notes on the conservation of mass using combination notes.

The ashes left over from a wood fire contain less mass than the wood. In many other chemical reactions, mass also appears to decrease. That is, the mass of the products appears to be less than the mass of the reactants. In other reactions, the products appear to gain mass. For example, plants grow through a complex series of reactions, but where does their extra mass come from? At one time, scientists thought that chemical reactions could create or destroy matter.

During the 1780s the French chemist Antoine Lavoisier (luh-VWAH-zee-ay) showed that matter can never be created or destroyed in a chemical reaction. Lavoisier emphasized the importance of making very careful measurements in his experiments. Because of his methods, he was able to show that reactions that seem to gain mass or lose mass actually involve reactions with gases in the air. These gases could not be seen, but their masses could be measured.

An example of Lavoisier's work is his study of the reaction of the metal mercury when heated in air. In this reaction, the reddish-orange product formed has more mass than the original metal. Lavoisier placed some mercury in a jar, sealed the jar, and recorded the total mass of the setup. After the mercury had been heated in the jar, the total mass of the jar and its contents had not changed.

Lavoisier showed that the air left in the jar would no longer support burning—a candle flame was snuffed out by this air. He concluded that a gas in the air, which he called oxygen, had combined with the mercury to form the new product.

Lavoisier conducted many experiments of this type and found in all cases that the mass of the reactants is equal to the mass of the products. This conclusion, called the **law of conservation of mass,** states that in a chemical reaction atoms are neither created nor destroyed. All atoms present in the reactants are also present in the products.

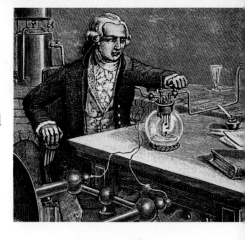

Lavoisier carefully measured both the reactants and the products of chemical reactions.

 How did Lavoisier investigate the conservation of mass?

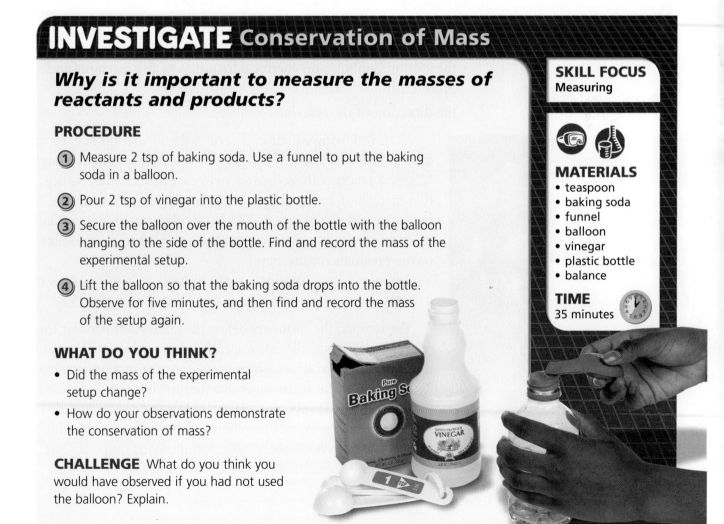

INVESTIGATE Conservation of Mass

Why is it important to measure the masses of reactants and products?

PROCEDURE

1. Measure 2 tsp of baking soda. Use a funnel to put the baking soda in a balloon.

2. Pour 2 tsp of vinegar into the plastic bottle.

3. Secure the balloon over the mouth of the bottle with the balloon hanging to the side of the bottle. Find and record the mass of the experimental setup.

4. Lift the balloon so that the baking soda drops into the bottle. Observe for five minutes, and then find and record the mass of the setup again.

WHAT DO YOU THINK?

- Did the mass of the experimental setup change?

- How do your observations demonstrate the conservation of mass?

CHALLENGE What do you think you would have observed if you had not used the balloon? Explain.

SKILL FOCUS
Measuring

MATERIALS
- teaspoon
- baking soda
- funnel
- balloon
- vinegar
- plastic bottle
- balance

TIME
35 minutes

Chemical reactions can be described by chemical equations.

The law of conservation of mass states that in a chemical reaction, the total mass of reactants is equal to the total mass of products. For example, the mass of sodium plus the mass of chlorine that reacts with the sodium equals the mass of the product sodium chloride. Because atoms are rearranged in a chemical reaction, there must be the same number of sodium atoms and chlorine atoms in both the reactants and products.

Chemical equations represent how atoms are rearranged in a chemical reaction. The atoms in the reactants are shown on the left side of the equation. The atoms in the products are shown on the right side of the equation. Because atoms are rearranged and not created or destroyed, the number of atoms of each different element must be the same on each side of the equation.

 CHECK YOUR READING How does a chemical equation show the conservation of mass?

In order to write a chemical equation, the information that you need to know is

- the reactants and products in the reaction
- the atomic symbols and chemical formulas of the reactants and products in the reaction
- the direction of the reaction

Carbon dioxide is a gas that animals exhale.

The following equation describes the formation of carbon dioxide from carbon and oxygen. In words, this equation says "Carbon reacts with oxygen to yield carbon dioxide." Notice that instead of an equal sign, an arrow appears between the reactants and the products. The arrow shows which way the reaction proceeds—from reactants on the left to the product or the products on the right.

reactants	direction of reaction	product
$C + O_2$	$\longrightarrow$	CO_2

Remember, the numbers below the chemical formulas for oxygen and carbon dioxide are called subscripts. A subscript indicates the number of atoms of an element in a molecule. You can see in the equation above that the oxygen molecule has two oxygen atoms, and the carbon dioxide molecule also has two oxygen atoms. If the chemical formula of a reactant or product does not have a subscript, it means that only one atom of each element is present in the molecule.

Chemical equations must be balanced.

Remember, chemical reactions follow the law of conservation of mass. Chemical equations show this conservation, or equality, in terms of atoms. The same number of atoms of each element must appear on both sides of a chemical equation. However, simply writing down the chemical formulas of reactants and products does not always result in equal numbers of atoms. You have to balance the equation to make the number of atoms equal on each side of an equation.

Balancing Chemical Equations

To learn how to balance an equation, look at the example of the combustion of natural gas, which is mostly methane (CH_4). The reactants are methane and oxygen. The products are carbon dioxide and water. You can write this reaction as the following equation.

▼ **REMINDER**

Oxygen is always a reactant in a combustion reaction.

Unbalanced Equation

This equation is not balanced. There is one C on each side of the equation, so C is balanced. However, on the left side, H has a subscript of 4, which means there are four hydrogen atoms. On the right side, H has a subscript of 2, which means there are two hydrogen atoms. Also, there are two oxygen atoms on the left and three oxygen atoms on the right. Because of the conservation of mass, you know that hydrogen atoms do not disappear and oxygen atoms do not suddenly appear.

You can balance a chemical equation by changing the amounts of reactants or products represented.

- To balance H first, add another H_2O molecule on the right. Now, both C and H are balanced.

- There are now two oxygen atoms on the left side and four oxygen atoms on the right side. To balance O, add another O_2 molecule on the left.

READING TiP

As you read how to balance the equation, look at the illustrations and count the atoms. The number of each type of atom is shown below the formula.

Balanced Equation

Using Coefficients to Balance Equations

The balanced equation for the combustion of methane shows that one molecule of methane reacts with two molecules of oxygen to produce one molecule of carbon dioxide and two molecules of water. The equation can be simplified by writing $2O_2$ instead of $O_2 + O_2$, and $2H_2O$ instead of $H_2O + H_2O$.

The numbers in front of the chemical formulas are called coefficients. **Coefficients** indicate how many molecules take part in the reaction. If there is no coefficient, then only one molecule of that type takes part in the reaction. The balanced equation, with coefficients, for the combustion of methane is shown below.

Balanced Equation with Coefficients

$$CH_4 \quad + \quad 2O_2 \quad \longrightarrow \quad CO_2 \quad + \quad 2H_2O$$

coefficient   subscript

Chemical formulas can have both coefficients and subscripts. In these cases, multiply the two numbers together to find the number of atoms involved in the reaction. For example, two water molecules ($2H_2O$) contain $2 \cdot 2 = 4$ hydrogen atoms and $2 \cdot 1 = 2$ oxygen atoms. Remember, coefficients in a chemical equation indicate how many molecules of each type take part in the reaction.

Only coefficients can be changed in order to balance a chemical equation. Subscripts are part of the chemical formula for reactants or products and cannot be changed to balance an equation. Changing a subscript changes the substance represented by the formula.

For example, the equation for the combustion of methane cannot be balanced by changing the formula CO_2 to CO. The formula CO_2 represents carbon dioxide gas, which animals exhale when they breathe. The formula CO represents carbon monoxide gas, which is a very different compound from CO_2. Carbon monoxide gas is poisonous, and breathing too much of it can be fatal.

REMINDER

A subscript shows the number of atoms in a molecule. If a subscript is changed, the molecule represented by the formula is changed.

 CHECK YOUR READING Why are coefficients used to balance equations?

The combustion of methane (CH_4) is used to melt glass.

Balancing Equations with Coefficients

The steps below show how to balance the equation for the synthesis reaction between nitrogen (N_2) and hydrogen (H_2), which produces ammonia (NH_3).

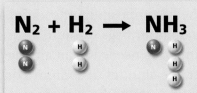

$$N_2 + H_2 \longrightarrow NH_3$$

1 **Count the atoms.** Neither N nor H is balanced. The reactants contain two atoms each of N and H, but the product contains one N atom and three H atoms.

$N_2 + H_2 \longrightarrow NH_3$	
N = 2	N = 1
H = 2	H = 3

Tip: Listing the number of atoms of each element makes it easy to see which elements must be balanced.

2 **Use a coefficient to add atoms to one side of the equation.** A coefficient of 2 on NH_3 balances the number of N atoms.

$N_2 + H_2 \longrightarrow 2\,NH_3$	
N = 2	N = 2
H = 2	H = 6

Tip: When adding coefficients, start with the reactant or product that contains the greatest number of different elements.

3 **Add a coefficient to another reactant or product.** Adding a coefficient of 3 to H_2 on the left side of the equation balances the number of H atoms on both sides. Now the equation is balanced.

$N_2 + 3\,H_2 \longrightarrow 2NH_3$	
N = 2	N = 2
H = 6	H = 6

Tip: Make sure that the coefficients in your balanced equation are the smallest whole numbers possible—that is, they have no common factor other than 1.

$$N_2 + 3H_2 \longrightarrow 2NH_3$$

APPLY
Balance the following equations.
1. $Hg + O_2 \longrightarrow HgO$
2. $Zn + HCl \longrightarrow ZnCl_2 + H_2$

The decomposition of sodium azide is used to inflate air bags in automobiles.

Using the Conservation of Mass

A balanced chemical equation shows that no matter how atoms are rearranged during a chemical reaction, the same number of atoms must be present before and after the reaction. The following example demonstrates the usefulness of chemical equations and the conservation of mass.

The decomposition of sodium azide (NaN_3) is used to inflate automobile air bags. Sodium azide is a solid, and the amount of sodium azide needed in an air bag fills only a small amount of space. In fact, the amount of sodium azide used in air bags is only about 130 grams—an amount that would fit in a large spoon. An inflated air bag, though, takes up much more space even though it contains the same number of atoms that entered the reaction. The reason is illustrated by the chemical equation for this reaction.

Balanced Equation

$$2NaN_3 \longrightarrow 2Na + 3N_2$$

According to the balanced equation shown above, three molecules of nitrogen gas are formed for every two molecules of sodium azide that decompose. Because the nitrogen is a gas, it fills a much greater volume than the original sodium azide. In fact, 67 liters of nitrogen gas are produced by the 130 grams of sodium azide in the reaction. This amount of nitrogen is enough to quickly inflate the air bag during a collision—the decomposition of sodium azide to sodium and nitrogen takes 0.03 seconds.

CHECK YOUR READING Why must chemical equations be balanced?

18.2 Review

KEY CONCEPTS

1. State the law of conservation of mass.

2. Write the chemical equation that shows sodium (Na) and chlorine (Cl_2) combining to form table salt (NaCl).

3. Is the following equation balanced? Why or why not?

$$CO \longrightarrow C + O_2$$

CRITICAL THINKING

4. **Communicate** Describe Lavoisier's experiment with mercury. How does this experiment show the law of conservation of mass?

5. **Synthesize** Suppose a log's mass is 5 kg. After burning, the mass of the ash is 1 kg. Explain what may have happened to the other 4 kg of mass.

CHALLENGE

6. **Synthesize** Suppose a container holds 1000 hydrogen molecules (H_2) and 1000 oxygen molecules (O_2) that react to form water. How many water molecules will be in the container? Will anything else be in the container? If so, what?

SCIENCE on the JOB

FIREFIGHTER

Chemistry in Firefighting

A firefighter's job may seem simple: to put out fires. However, a firefighter needs to know about chemicals and chemical reactions. A fire is a combustion reaction that requires oxygen as a reactant. Without oxygen, a fire will normally burn itself out, so firefighters try to prevent oxygen from reaching the burning substances. Firefighters often use water or carbon dioxide for this purpose, but these materials make some types of fires more dangerous.

Grease Fires

Some fires can be extinguished by a chemical reaction. In kitchen grease fires, the chemicals that are used to fight the fire react with the grease. The reaction produces a foam that puts out the fire.

Metal Fires

Some fires involve metals such as magnesium. This metal burns at a very high temperature and reacts violently with water. Firefighters try to smother metal fires with a material such as sand.

Hazardous Reactions

Chemicals may react with water to form poisonous gases or acids. Firefighters might use a foam that extinguishes the fire, cools the area around the fire, and traps gases released by the fire. The symbols shown on the left are among several that show firefighters what chemical dangers may be present.

EXPLORE

Build a carbon dioxide fire extinguisher.

1. Put 3 tsp of baking soda on a tissue and roll it into a tube. Tie the ends and middle of the tube with thread. Leave extra thread at one end of the tube.
2. Mold clay tightly around a straw.
3. Pour some vinegar into a bottle.
4. Hold the thread to suspend the tissue tube above the vinegar. Place the straw inside the bottle. Use the clay molded around the straw to hold the thread in place. Be sure that the straw is not touching the vinegar.
5. Shake and observe the fire extinguisher.

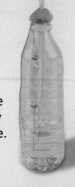

The fire shown above is a magnesium fire in Chicago in 1998. Firefighters used water to protect surrounding buildings, but dumped road salt on the burning magnesium.

18.3 Chemical reactions involve energy changes.

STANDARDS

7–5.8 Explain how a balanced chemical equation supports the law of conservation of matter.

VOCABULARY

bond energy p. 586
exothermic reaction p. 587
endothermic reaction p. 587
photosynthesis p. 590

◀ **BEFORE,** you learned

- Bonds are broken and made during chemical reactions
- Mass is conserved in all chemical reactions
- Chemical reactions are represented by balanced chemical equations

▶ **NOW,** you will learn

- About the energy in chemical bonds between atoms
- Why some chemical reactions release energy
- Why some chemical reactions absorb energy

EXPLORE Energy Changes

How can you identify a transfer of energy?

PROCEDURE

① Pour 50 mL of hot tap water into the cup and place the thermometer in the cup.

② Wait 30 seconds, then record the temperature of the water.

③ Measure 5 tsp of Epsom salts. Add the Epsom salts to the cup and immediately record the temperature while stirring the contents of the cup.

④ Continue to record the temperature every 30 seconds for 2 minutes.

WHAT DO YOU THINK?

- What happened to the temperature after you added the Epsom salts?
- What do you think caused this change to occur?

MATERIALS

- graduated cylinder
- hot tap water
- plastic cup
- thermometer
- stopwatch
- plastic spoon
- Epsom salts

WATER

Chemical reactions release or absorb energy.

COMBINATION NOTES
Use combination notes to organize information on how chemical reactions absorb or release energy.

Chemical reactions involve breaking bonds in reactants and forming new bonds in products. Breaking bonds requires energy, and forming bonds releases energy. The energy associated with bonds is called **bond energy.** What happens to this energy during a chemical reaction?

Chemists have determined the bond energy for bonds between atoms. Breaking a bond between carbon and hydrogen requires a certain amount of energy. This amount of energy is different from the amount of energy needed to break a bond between carbon and oxygen, or between hydrogen and oxygen.

Energy is needed to break bonds in reactant molecules. Energy is released when bonds are formed in product molecules. By adding up the bond energies in the reactants and products, you can determine whether energy will be released or absorbed.

If more energy is released when the products form than is needed to break the bonds in the reactants, then energy is released during the reaction. A reaction in which energy is released is called an **exothermic reaction.**

If more energy is required to break the bonds in the reactants than is released when the products form, then energy must be added to the reaction. That is, the reaction absorbs energy. A reaction in which energy is absorbed is called an **endothermic reaction.**

These types of energy changes can also be observed in different physical changes such as dissolving or changing state. The state change from a liquid to a solid, or freezing, releases energy—this is an exothermic process. The state change from a solid to a liquid, or melting, absorbs energy—this is an endothermic process.

 How are exothermic and endothermic reactions different?

Exothermic reactions release energy.

Exothermic chemical reactions often produce an increase in temperature. In exothermic reactions, the bond energies of the reactants are less than the bond energies of the products. As a result, less energy is needed to break the bonds in the reactants than is released during the formation of the products. This energy difference between reactants and products is often released as heat. The release of heat causes a change in the temperature of the reaction mixture.

Even though energy is released by exothermic reactions, some energy must first be added to break bonds in the reactants. In exothermic reactions, the formation of bonds in the products releases more energy. Overall, more energy is released than is added.

Some reactions are highly exothermic. These reactions produce a great deal of heat and significantly raise the temperature of their surroundings. One example is the reaction of powdered aluminum metal with a type of iron oxide, a reaction known as the thermite reaction. The equation for this reaction is

$$2Al + Fe_2O_3 \longrightarrow Al_2O_3 + 2Fe$$

This reaction releases enough heat to melt the iron that is produced. In fact, this reaction is used to weld iron rails together.

 What is evidence for an exothermic chemical reaction?

The white clouds of water vapor are formed by the exothermic reaction between hydrogen and oxygen.

$$2H_2 + O_2 \longrightarrow 2H_2O$$

The thermite reaction releases enough heat to weld pieces of iron together.

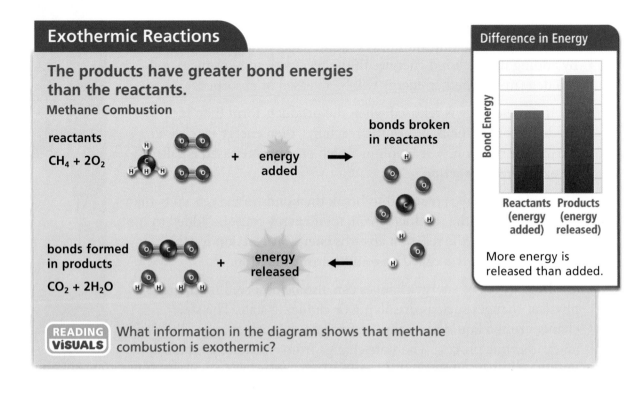

Exothermic Reactions

The products have greater bond energies than the reactants.

Methane Combustion

reactants

$CH_4 + 2O_2$

+ energy added →

bonds broken in reactants

bonds formed in products

$CO_2 + 2H_2O$

+ energy released ←

Difference in Energy

Bond Energy

Reactants (energy added)   Products (energy released)

More energy is released than added.

READING VISUALS What information in the diagram shows that methane combustion is exothermic?

All common combustion reactions, such as the combustion of methane, are exothermic. To determine how energy changes in this reaction, the bond energies in the reactants—oxygen and methane—and in the products—carbon dioxide and water—can be added and compared. This process is illustrated by the diagram shown above. The difference in energy is released to the surrounding air as heat.

Some chemical reactions release excess energy as light instead of heat. For example, glow sticks work by a chemical reaction that releases energy as light. One of the reactants, a solution of hydrogen peroxide, is contained in a thin glass tube within the plastic stick. The rest of the stick is filled with a second chemical and a brightly colored dye. When you bend the stick, the glass tube inside it breaks and the two solutions mix. The result is a bright glow of light.

These cup coral polyps glow because of exothermic chemical reactions.

Exothermic chemical reactions also occur in living things. Some of these reactions release energy as heat, and others release energy as light. Fireflies light up due to a reaction that takes place between oxygen and a chemical called luciferin. This type of exothermic reaction is not unique to fireflies. In fact, similar reactions are found in several different species of fish, squid, jellyfish, and shrimp.

CHECK YOUR READING In which ways might an exothermic reaction release energy?

The bombardier beetle, shown in the photograph on the right, uses natural exothermic reactions to defend itself. Although several chemical reactions are involved, the end result is the production of a hot, toxic spray. The most important reaction in the process is the decomposition of hydrogen peroxide into water and oxygen.

$$2H_2O_2 \longrightarrow 2H_2O + O_2$$

When the hydrogen peroxide rapidly breaks down, the hot, toxic mixture made by the series of reactions is pressurized by the oxygen gas from the reaction in the equation above. After enough pressure builds up, the beetle can spray the mixture.

Endothermic reactions absorb energy.

Endothermic reactions often produce a decrease in temperature. In endothermic reactions, the bond energies of the reactants are greater than the bond energies of the products. As a result, more energy is needed to break the bonds in the reactants than is released during the formation of the products. The difference in energy is usually absorbed from the surroundings as heat. This often causes a decrease in the temperature of the reaction mixture.

All endothermic reactions absorb energy. However, they do not all absorb energy as heat. One example of an endothermic reaction of this type is the decomposition of water by electrolysis. In this case, the energy that is absorbed is in the form of electrical energy. When the electric current is turned off, the reaction stops. The change in energy that occurs in this reaction is shown below.

READING TiP
The prefix *endo-* means "inside."

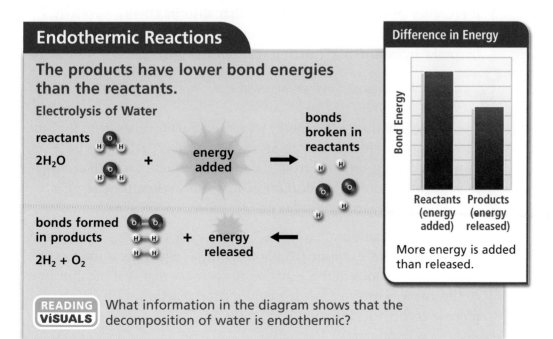

Endothermic Reactions

The products have lower bond energies than the reactants.

Electrolysis of Water

reactants

$2H_2O$ + energy added → bonds broken in reactants

bonds formed in products + energy released ←

$2H_2 + O_2$

Difference in Energy

Bond Energy

Reactants (energy added) Products (energy released)

More energy is added than released.

READING VISUALS What information in the diagram shows that the decomposition of water is endothermic?

Probably the most important series of endothermic reactions on Earth is photosynthesis. Many steps occur in the process, but the overall chemical reaction is

$$6CO_2 + 6H_2O \longrightarrow C_6H_{12}O_6 + 6O_2$$

Unlike many other endothermic reactions, photosynthesis does not absorb energy as heat. Instead, during **photosynthesis,** plants absorb energy from sunlight to turn carbon dioxide and water into oxygen and glucose, which is a type of sugar molecule. The energy is stored in the glucose molecules, ready to be used when needed.

 How can you determine if a reaction is endothermic?

Exothermic and endothermic reactions work together to supply energy.

When thinking about exothermic and endothermic reactions, it is often useful to consider energy as part of the reaction. An exothermic reaction releases energy, so energy is on the product side of the chemical equation. An endothermic reaction absorbs energy, so energy is on the reactant side of the chemical equation.

Exothermic Reaction
Reactants ⟶ Products + Energy

Endothermic Reaction
Reactants + Energy ⟶ Products

As you can see in the general reactions above, exothermic and endothermic reactions have opposite energy changes. This means that if an exothermic chemical reaction proceeds in the opposite direction, it becomes an endothermic reaction that absorbs energy. Similarly, if an endothermic reaction proceeds in the opposite direction, it becomes an exothermic reaction that releases energy.

 What happens when an exothermic reaction is reversed?

A large amount of the energy we use on Earth comes from the Sun. This energy includes energy in fossil fuels such as coal and petroleum, as well as energy obtained from food. In all of these cases, the energy in sunlight is stored by endothermic reactions. When the energy is needed, it is released by exothermic reactions.

This combination of reactions forms a cycle of energy storage and use. For example, examine the photosynthesis equation at the top of the page. If you look at this equation in reverse—that is, if the direction of the arrow is reversed—it is a combustion reaction, with oxygen and glucose as the reactants, and it is exothermic.

VISUALIZATION
CLASSZONE.COM

View examples of endothermic and exothermic reactions.

Plants store energy through the endothermic reactions of photosynthesis. Living things can release this energy through a series of exothermic reactions that will be described in the next section.

The energy stored in plants through photosynthesis can also be released in other ways. Consider energy from fossil fuels. Fossil fuels include petroleum, natural gas, and coal. These substances formed from fossilized materials, mainly plants, that had been under high pressures and temperatures for millions of years. When these plants were alive, they used photosynthesis to produce glucose and other molecules from carbon dioxide and water.

The energy stored in the bonds of these molecules remains, even though the molecules have changed over time. The burning of gasoline in a car releases this energy, enabling the car's engine to work. Similarly, the burning of coal in a power plant, or the burning of natural gas in a stove, releases the energy originally stored by the endothermic series of photosynthesis reactions.

Plants such as trees store energy through photosynthesis. Cars and trucks release this energy through combustion.

CHECK YOUR READING How can endothermic and exothermic reactions work together?

18.3 Review

KEY CONCEPTS

1. What are the differences between exothermic and endothermic reactions?

2. Is the combustion of methane an exothermic or endothermic reaction? Explain.

3. Is photosynthesis an exothermic or endothermic reaction? Explain.

CRITICAL THINKING

4. **Synthesize** Describe the connections between the processes of photosynthesis and combustion.

5. **Communicate** Explain how most energy used on Earth can be traced back to the Sun.

◆ CHALLENGE

6. **Synthesize** Electrolysis of water is endothermic. What does this indicate about the bond energy in the reactants and products? What happens when this reaction is reversed?

CHAPTER INVESTIGATION

Exothermic or Endothermic?

OVERVIEW AND PURPOSE A clue that a chemical reaction has taken place is a transfer of energy, often in the form of heat or light. The chemical reaction used to demolish an old building, as shown in the photograph to the left, is a dramatic example of energy release by a reaction. In this investigation, you will use what you have learned about chemical reactions to
- measure and record temperature changes in two processes
- compare temperature changes during the processes in order to classify them as exothermic or endothermic

▶ Procedure

1 Make a data table like the one shown on the sample notebook page.

2 Work with a partner. One should keep track of time. The other should observe the thermometer and report the temperature.

PART 1

3 Pour 30 mL of hydrogen peroxide into a beaker. Put a thermometer into the beaker. Wait 2 minutes to allow the thermometer to reach the temperature of the hydrogen peroxide. During the time you are waiting, measure 1 g of yeast with the balance.

4 Record the starting temperature. Add the yeast to the beaker and immediately record the temperature while gently stirring the contents of the beaker. Continue to record the temperature every 30 seconds as you observe the process for 5 minutes.

MATERIALS
- graduated cylinder
- hydrogen peroxide
- 2 beakers
- 2 thermometers
- stopwatch
- measuring spoons
- yeast
- balance
- plastic spoon
- large plastic cup
- hot tap water
- vinegar
- baking soda

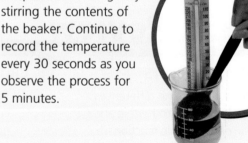

step 4

PART 2

5 Make a hot water bath by filling a large plastic cup halfway with hot tap water.

6 Measure and pour 30 mL of vinegar into a small beaker. Set this beaker in the hot water bath and place a thermometer in the vinegar. Wait until the temperature of the vinegar rises to between 32 and 38°C (90 to 100°F). While waiting for the vinegar's temperature to increase, measure 1 g of baking soda.

step 6

7 Remove the beaker from the hot water bath. Record the starting temperature.

8 Add the baking soda to the vinegar and immediately record the temperature as you swirl the contents of the beaker. Continue to record the temperature every 30 seconds as you observe the reaction for 5 minutes.

▶ Observe and Analyze

Write It Up

1. **RECORD OBSERVATIONS** Remember to complete your data table.

2. **GRAPH** Use the information from your data table to graph your results. Make a double-line graph, plotting your data in a different color for each part of the investigation. Plot temperature in degrees Celsius on the vertical, or *y*-axis. Plot the time in minutes on the horizontal, or *x*-axis.

3. **ANALYZE DATA** Examine the graph. When did the temperature change the most in each part of the investigation? When did it change the least? Compare the temperature at the start of each process with the temperature after 5 minutes. How do the temperature changes compare?

▶ Conclude

Write It Up

1. **CLASSIFY** Is the mixture of hydrogen peroxide and yeast endothermic or exothermic? Is the reaction between vinegar and baking soda endothermic or exothermic? Provide evidence for your answers.

2. **EVALUATE** Did you have any difficulties obtaining accurate measurements? Describe possible limitations or sources of error.

3. **APPLY** What does the reaction between baking soda and vinegar tell you about their bond energies?

▶ INVESTIGATE Further

CHALLENGE Repeat Part 2, but instead of using the hot water bath, add the hot water directly to the vinegar before pouring in the baking soda. Does this change in procedure change the results of the experiment? Why might your observations have changed? Explain your answers.

Exothermic or Endothermic?

Observe and Analyze

Table 1. Temperature Measurements

Time (min)	Hydrogen Peroxide and Yeast Temperature (°C)	Vinegar and Baking Soda Temperature (°C)
0		
0.5		
1.0		
....		
5.0		

Conclude

18.4 Life and industry depend on chemical reactions.

 BEFORE, you learned

- Chemical reactions turn reactants into products by rearranging atoms
- Mass is conserved during chemical reactions
- Chemical reactions involve energy changes

 NOW, you will learn

- About the importance of chemical reactions in living things
- How chemistry has helped the development of new technology

VOCABULARY

respiration p. 594

THINK ABOUT

How is a glow stick like a firefly?

When a firefly glows in the dark, a chemical reaction that emits light is taking place. Similarly, when you activate a glow stick, a chemical reaction that causes the glow stick to emit light occurs. Many reactions in modern life and technology adapt chemical reactions found in nature. Can you think of other examples?

Living things require chemical reactions.

In section 3, you saw that photosynthesis stores energy from the Sun in forms that can be used later. These forms of stored energy include fossil fuels and the sugar glucose. The glucose molecules produced by photosynthesis make up the basic food used for energy by almost all living things. For example, animals obtain glucose molecules by eating plants or eating other animals that have eaten plants.

Living cells obtain energy from glucose molecules through the process of **respiration,** which is the "combustion" of glucose to obtain energy. This series of chemical reactions is, in general, the reverse of photosynthesis. It produces carbon dioxide and water from oxygen and glucose. The overall reactions for both photosynthesis and respiration are shown on the top of page 595. From a chemical point of view, respiration is the same as any other combustion reaction.

VOCABULARY
Remember to make a four square diagram for *respiration*.

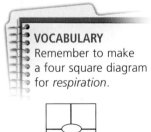

Photosynthesis

$$6CO_2 + 6H_2O + energy \longrightarrow C_6H_{12}O_6 + 6O_2$$

Respiration

$$C_6H_{12}O_6 + 6O_2 \longrightarrow 6CO_2 + 6H_2O + energy$$

The energy released by respiration can be used for growth of new cells, movement, or any other life function. Suppose that you are late for school and have to run to get to class on time. Your body needs to activate nerves and muscles right away, without waiting for you to first eat some food as a source of energy. The glucose molecules in food are stored in your body until you need energy. Then, respiration consumes them in a process that includes several steps.

To make these steps go quickly, the body uses catalysts—enzymes—for each step. Some enzymes break the glucose molecules into smaller pieces, while other enzymes break bonds within each piece. Still other enzymes help form the reaction products—carbon dioxide and water. With the help of enzymes, these reactions take place quickly and automatically. You do not have to think about breaking down glucose when you run—you just start to run and the energy is there.

 CHECK YOUR READING How are photosynthesis and respiration opposites?

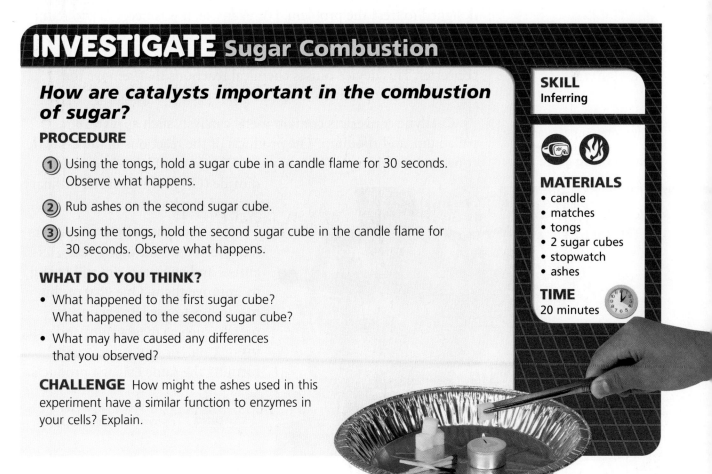

INVESTIGATE Sugar Combustion

How are catalysts important in the combustion of sugar?

PROCEDURE

① Using the tongs, hold a sugar cube in a candle flame for 30 seconds. Observe what happens.

② Rub ashes on the second sugar cube.

③ Using the tongs, hold the second sugar cube in the candle flame for 30 seconds. Observe what happens.

WHAT DO YOU THINK?

• What happened to the first sugar cube? What happened to the second sugar cube?

• What may have caused any differences that you observed?

CHALLENGE How might the ashes used in this experiment have a similar function to enzymes in your cells? Explain.

SKILL
Inferring

MATERIALS
• candle
• matches
• tongs
• 2 sugar cubes
• stopwatch
• ashes

TIME
20 minutes

Chemical reactions are used in technology.

Every time your cells need energy, they essentially complete respiration—the "combustion" of glucose. The series of chemical reactions in respiration involves enzymes, which are catalysts. Every time someone drives a car, another combustion reaction occurs—the combustion of gasoline. While the combustion of gasoline does not require a catalyst, the chemical reactions that change a car's exhaust gases do use a catalyst.

No chemical reaction is ever completely efficient. It does not matter what the reaction is or how the reaction conditions are set up. There are always some reactants that do not change completely into products. Sometimes a chemical reaction makes unwanted waste products.

In the case of gasoline combustion, some of the original carbon compounds, called hydrocarbons, do not burn completely, and carbon monoxide gas (CO) is produced. Also, nitrogen in the air reacts with oxygen in a car's engine to produce compounds of nitrogen and oxygen, including nitric oxide (NO). The production of these gases lowers the overall efficiency of combustion. More importantly, these gases can react with water vapor in the air to form smog and acid rain.

Sometimes, as you can see with gasoline combustion, chemical technology causes a problem. Then, new chemical technology is designed to treat the problem. For example, it was necessary to reduce carbon monoxide and nitric oxide emissions from car exhaust. As a result, engineers in the 1970s developed a device called a catalytic converter. This device causes chemical reactions that remove the unwanted waste products from the combustion of gasoline.

Catalytic converters contain metal catalysts such as platinum, palladium, and rhodium. The products of the reactions in the catalytic converter are nitrogen (N_2), oxygen (O_2), water (H_2O), and carbon dioxide (CO_2), which are all ordinary parts of Earth's atmosphere.

Even though catalytic converters have been used for many years, scientists and engineers are still trying to improve them. One goal of this research is to use less expensive metals, such as magnesium and zinc, inside catalytic converters, while forming the same exhaust products.

Many states inspect vehicles to test the pollutants in their exhaust gases.

CHECK YOUR READING Why were catalytic converters developed?

Chemical Reactions in Catalytic Converters

The combustion of gasoline makes harmful waste products. Chemical reactions in catalytic converters make these waste products less harmful.

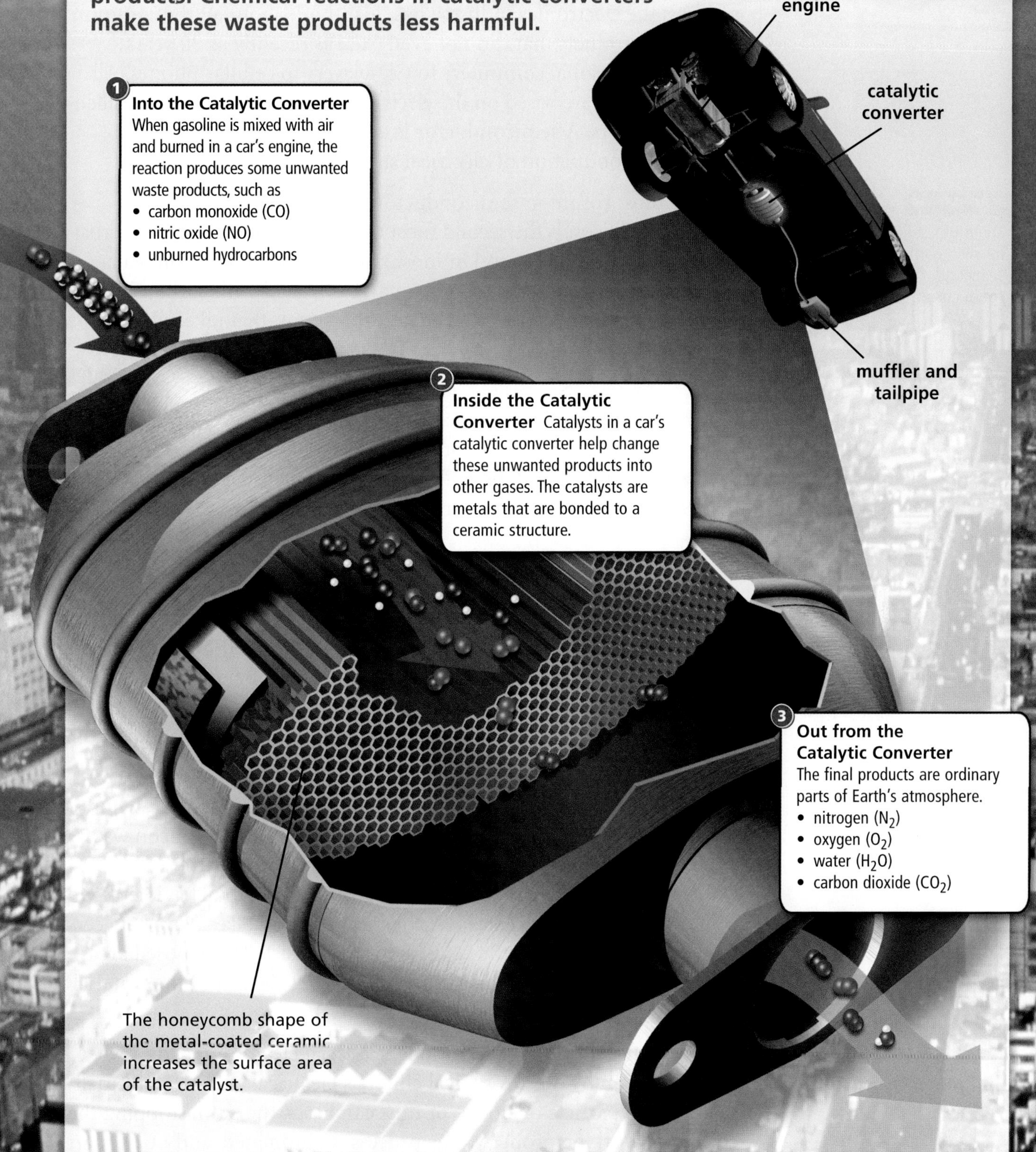

engine

catalytic converter

muffler and tailpipe

1 Into the Catalytic Converter When gasoline is mixed with air and burned in a car's engine, the reaction produces some unwanted waste products, such as
- carbon monoxide (CO)
- nitric oxide (NO)
- unburned hydrocarbons

2 Inside the Catalytic Converter Catalysts in a car's catalytic converter help change these unwanted products into other gases. The catalysts are metals that are bonded to a ceramic structure.

3 Out from the Catalytic Converter The final products are ordinary parts of Earth's atmosphere.
- nitrogen (N_2)
- oxygen (O_2)
- water (H_2O)
- carbon dioxide (CO_2)

The honeycomb shape of the metal-coated ceramic increases the surface area of the catalyst.

READING VISUALS What are CO and NO changed into by a catalytic converter?

Industry uses chemical reactions to make useful products.

No area of science and technology has changed today's society as much as the electronics industry has. Just think about all the common electronic products that did not even exist as recently as 30 years ago—from personal computers to CD players to cellular phones. All of these devices are based on the electrical properties of materials called semiconductors. A semiconductor is a material that can precisely control the conduction of electrical signals.

READING **TiP**

The prefix *semi-* means "partial," so a semiconductor partially conducts electricity.

The most common semiconductor material is the element silicon (Si). Silicon is the second most common element in Earth's crust after oxygen, and it is found in most rocks and sand. Pure silicon is obtained from quartz (SiO_2). The quartz is heated with carbon in an electric furnace at 3000°C. The chemical reaction that takes place is

$$SiO_2 + 2C \longrightarrow Si + 2CO$$

This reaction produces silicon that is about 98 percent pure. However, this silicon is still not pure enough to be used in electronics. Several other refining steps must be used to make silicon that is more than 99.999999999 percent pure.

 CHECK YOUR READING | **What property makes silicon useful in electronic devices?**

Quartz (SiO_2) is the source of silicon for chips.

Early electronic devices had to be large enough to fit various types of glass tubes and connecting wires inside. In the 1950s, however, engineers figured out how to replace all of these different tubes and wires with thin layers of material placed on a piece of silicon. The resulting circuits are often called microchips, or simply chips.

In order to make these chips, another reaction is used. This reaction involves a material called photoresist (FOH-toh-rih-ZIST), whose properties change when it is exposed to ultraviolet light. Silicon wafers are first coated with photoresist. A stencil is placed over the surface, which allows some areas of the wafer to be exposed to ultraviolet light while other areas are protected. A chemical reaction takes place between the ultraviolet light and the coating of photoresist. The exposed areas of photoresist remain on the silicon surface after the rest of the material is washed away.

The entire process is carried out in special clean rooms to prevent contamination by dust. A typical chip has electrical pathways so small that a single particle of smoke or dust can block the path, stopping the chip from working properly. The process is automated, and no human hand ever touches a chip.

From Quartz to Microchips

A chemical reaction makes the tiny circuits that are used to run electronic devices such as cellular phones.

① After silicon is sliced into very thin wafers, it is coated with photoresist. The silicon is covered with a stencil and exposed to ultraviolet light, which reacts with the photoresist.

② The entire process takes place in clean rooms, where workers wear special clothing to prevent dust from reaching the chips.

③ The areas of the chip that were exposed to ultraviolet light form tiny circuits used in electronic devices.

The reaction of photoresist with ultraviolet light is an important chemical reaction. The same type of material is used in the printing of books and newspapers. A similar reaction occurs in photocopiers and laser printers. This is an example of how one type of chemical reaction has helped change industry and society in important ways.

One of the many uses of silicon chips is in cellular phones.

 Describe how chemical reactions are important in industry.

18.4 Review

KEY CONCEPTS

1. Explain how respiration and photosynthesis are chemically opposite from each other.

2. Provide an example of how catalysts are used in technology.

3. Describe two chemical reactions used in making silicon chips.

CRITICAL THINKING

4. **Compare and Contrast** How are respiration and the combustion of gasoline similar? How are they different?

5. **Analyze** In microchip manufacture, what would happen if the clean rooms had outside windows? Explain.

◇ CHALLENGE

6. **Infer** The gases released from a catalytic converter include N_2, O_2, H_2O, and CO_2. The original reactants must contain atoms of which elements?

18 Chapter Review

the **BIG** idea

Chemical reactions form new substances by breaking and making chemical bonds.

CONTENT REVIEW
CLASSZONE.COM

◄ KEY CONCEPTS SUMMARY

 Chemical reactions alter arrangements of atoms.

- Chemical changes occur through chemical reactions.
- Evidence of a chemical reaction includes a color change, the formation of a precipitate, the formation of a gas, and a change in temperature.
- Chemical reactions change reactants into products.

VOCABULARY
chemical reaction p. 569
reactant p. 571
product p. 571
precipitate p. 572
catalyst p. 576

 The masses of reactants and products are equal.

- Mass is conserved in chemical reactions.
- Chemical equations summarize chemical reactions.
- Balanced chemical equations show the conservation of mass.

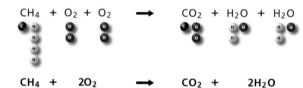

$$CH_4 + O_2 + O_2 \longrightarrow CO_2 + H_2O + H_2O$$

$$CH_4 + 2O_2 \longrightarrow CO_2 + 2H_2O$$

VOCABULARY
law of conservation of mass p. 579
coefficient p. 582

---

3 **Chemical reactions involve energy changes.**

- Different bonds contain different amounts of energy.
- In an exothermic reaction, more energy is released than added.
- In an endothermic reaction, more energy is added than released.

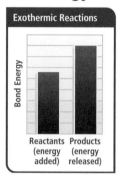

Exothermic Reactions

Bond Energy

Reactants (energy added)   Products (energy released)

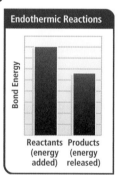

Endothermic Reactions

Bond Energy

Reactants (energy added)   Products (energy released)

VOCABULARY
bond energy p. 586
exothermic reaction p. 587
endothermic reaction p. 587
photosynthesis p. 590

 Life and industry depend on chemical reactions.

- Living things rely on chemical reactions that release energy from molecules.
- Different parts of modern society rely on chemical reactions.

VOCABULARY
respiration p. 594

Describe how the vocabulary terms in the following pairs are related to each other. Explain the relationship in a one- or two-sentence answer.

1. reactant, product

2. law of conservation of mass, chemical reaction

3. endothermic, exothermic

4. respiration, photosynthesis

Reviewing Key Concepts

Multiple Choice *Choose the letter of the best answer.*

5. During a chemical reaction, reactants always
   a. become more complex
   b. require catalysts
   c. lose mass
   d. form products

6. The splitting of water molecules into hydrogen and oxygen molecules is an example of a
   a. combination reaction
   b. chemical change
   c. synthesis reaction
   d. physical change

7. Combustion reactions
   a. destroy atoms   c. form precipitates
   b. require glucose   d. require oxygen

8. Which of the following will increase the rate of a reaction?
   a. breaking solid reactants into smaller pieces
   b. removing a catalyst
   c. decreasing the temperature
   d. decreasing the concentration

9. What does a catalyst do in a chemical reaction?
   a. It slows the reaction down.
   b. It speeds the reaction up.
   c. It becomes a product.
   d. It is a reactant.

10. During a chemical reaction, the total amount of mass present
    a. increases
    b. decreases
    c. may increase or decrease
    d. does not change

11. Chemical equations show summaries of
    a. physical changes
    b. changes of state
    c. chemical reactions
    d. changes in temperature

12. A chemical equation must
    a. show energy   c. use subscripts
    b. be balanced   d. use coefficients

13. What type of reaction occurs if the reactants have a greater total bond energy than the products?
    a. an endothermic reaction
    b. a synthesis reaction
    c. an exothermic reaction
    d. a decomposition reaction

14. Endothermic reactions always
    a. absorb energy
    b. make more complex products
    c. release energy
    d. make less complex products

Short Answer *Write a short answer to each question.*

15. Describe the differences between physical and chemical changes. How can each be identified?

16. Compare and contrast the overall chemical reactions of photosynthesis and respiration. How can these reactions be described in terms of bond energy in the reactants and products?

17. Describe an example of an advance in technology that makes use of a chemical reaction.

18. When you balance a chemical equation, why can you change coefficients of reactants or products, but not subscripts?

Thinking Critically

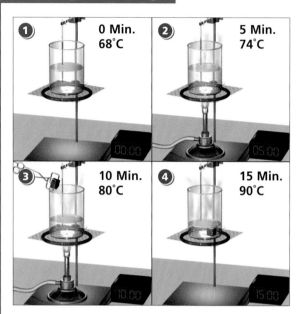

| ❶ 0 Min. 68°C | ❷ 5 Min. 74°C |
| ❸ 10 Min. 80°C | ❹ 15 Min. 90°C |

The series of illustrations above shows a chemical reaction at five-minute intervals. Use the information in the illustrations to answer the following six questions.

19. OBSERVE What happened to the temperature of the substance in the beaker from the beginning to the end of each five-minute interval?

20. ANALYZE Does the reaction appear to continue in step 4? What evidence tells you?

21. CLASSIFY Is this an endothermic or exothermic reaction? Explain.

22. INFER Suppose the metal cube placed in the beaker in step 3 is a catalyst. What effect did the metal have on the reaction? Why?

23. PREDICT If the metal cube is a catalyst, how much of the metal cube will be left in the beaker when the reaction is completed? Explain.

24. SYNTHESIZE Assume that the reaction shown is a decomposition reaction. Describe what happens to the reactants.

Using Math Skills in Science

Answer the following ten questions based on the equations below.

Equation 1—$HgO \longrightarrow Hg + O_2$

Equation 2—$Al + O_2 \longrightarrow Al_2O_3$

Equation 3—$S_8 + O_2 \longrightarrow SO_3$

25. Copy and balance equation 1.

26. What coefficients, if any, did you add to equation 1 to balance it?

27. How many Hg atoms take part in the reaction represented by equation 1 when it is balanced?

28. Copy and balance equation 2.

29. What coefficients, if any, did you add to equation 2 to balance it?

30. How many O atoms take part in the reaction represented by equation 2 when it is balanced?

31. Copy and balance equation 3.

32. What coefficients, if any, did you add to equation 3 to balance it?

33. How many S atoms take part in the reaction represented by equation 3 when it is balanced?

34. How many O atoms take part in the reaction represented by equation 3 when it is balanced?

the BIG idea

35. DRAW CONCLUSIONS Describe three ways in which chemical reactions are important in your life.

36. ANALYZE Look back at the photograph and question on pages 566 and 567. Answer the question in terms of the chapter's Big Idea.

UNIT PROJECTS

Check your schedule for your unit project. How are you doing? Be sure that you have placed data or notes from your research in your project folder.

Standardized Test Practice

For practice on your
state test, go to . . .
TEST PRACTICE
CLASSZONE.COM

Analyzing Theories

Answer the questions based on the information in the following passage.

During the 1700s, scientists thought that matter contained a substance called phlogiston. According to this theory, wood was made of phlogiston and ash. When wood burned, the phlogiston was released and the ash was left behind.

The ash that remained had less mass than the original wood. This decrease in mass was explained by the release of phlogiston. However, when substances such as phosphorus and mercury burned, the material that remained had more mass than the original substances. This increase in mass did not make sense to some scientists.

The scientists who supported the phlogiston theory said that the phlogiston in some substances had negative mass. So, when the substances burned, they released phlogiston and gained mass. Other scientists disagreed, and their research led to the discovery of a scientific law. Antoine Lavoisier carried out several experiments by burning metals in sealed containers. He showed that mass is never lost or gained in a chemical reaction.

1. What did the phlogiston theory successfully explain?
   a. the presence of ash in unburned wood
   b. the apparent gain of mass in some reactions
   c. the chemical makeup of the air
   d. the apparent decrease in mass in some situations

2. Why did some scientists disagree with the phlogiston theory?
   a. Burning a substance always produced an increase in mass.
   b. Burning a substance always produced a decrease in mass.
   c. Burning could produce either an increase or decrease in mass.
   d. Burning wood produced ash and phlogiston.

3. What law did Lavoisier's work establish?
   a. conservation of energy
   b. conservation of mass
   c. conservation of momentum
   d. conservation of resources

4. To carry out his experiments, what kind of equipment did Lavoisier need?
   a. devices to separate the different elements in the air
   b. machines that could separate wood from ash
   c. microscopes that could be used to study rust and ash
   d. balances that could measure mass very accurately

Extended Response

Answer the following questions in detail.
Include some of the terms from the list on the right.
Underline each term you use in your answers.

catalyst	coefficient	concentration
temperature	reaction	subscript
surface area		

5. Suppose you wanted to change the rate of a chemical reaction. What might you change in the reaction? Explain each factor.

6. Is the chemical equation shown below balanced? Why or why not? How are balanced chemical equations related to conservation of mass?

$$6CO_2 + 6H_2O \longrightarrow C_6H_{12}O_6 + O_2$$

TIMELINES in Science

THE STORY OF
ATOMIC STRUCTURE

About 2500 years ago, certain Greek thinkers proposed that all matter consisted of extremely tiny particles called atoms. The sizes and shapes of different atoms, they reasoned, was what determined the properties of a substance. This early atomic theory, however, was not widely accepted. Many at the time found these tiny, invisible particles difficult to accept.

What everyone could observe was that all substances were liquid, solid, or gas, light or heavy, hot or cold. Everything, they thought, must then be made of only a few basic substances or elements. They reasoned these elements must be water, air, fire, and earth. Different substances contained different amounts of each of these four substances.

The timeline shows a few of the major events that led scientists to accept the idea that matter is made of atoms and agree on the basic structure of atoms. With the revised atomic theory, scientists were able to explain how elements could be basic but different.

1661

Boyle Challenges Concept of the Four Elements
British chemist Robert Boyle proposes that more than four basic substances exist. Boyle also concludes that all matter is made of very tiny particles he calls corpuscles.

EVENTS

| 1600 | 1620 | 1640 | 1660 |

APPLICATIONS AND TECHNOLOGY

TECHNOLOGY

Collecting and Studying Gases
Throughout the 1600s, scientists tried to study gases but had difficulty collecting them. English biologist Stephen Hales designed an apparatus to collect gases. The "pneumatic trough" was a breakthrough in chemistry because it allowed scientists to collect and study gases for the first time. The pneumatic trough was later used by such chemists as Joseph Black, Henry Cavendish, and Joseph Priestley to study the gases that make up the air we breathe. The work of these scientists showed that air was made of more than a single gas.

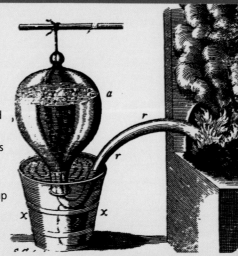

1808
John Dalton Says: "Bring Back the Atom"
English chemist John Dalton revives the ancient Greek idea that all matter is made of atoms. Dalton claims that each element has its own type of atom and that the atoms combine in fixed and predictable ratios with one another in different substances.

1897
It's Smaller Than the Atom!
English physicist Joseph John Thomson discovers the electron—the first subatomic particle to be identified. Thomson concludes that these tiny particles have a negative charge. Thomson will later propose that atoms are made of a great many of these negative particles floating in a sea of positive charge. Thomson suggests that each atom resembles a dish of pudding with raisins in it. The electrons are the raisins and the pudding the positive charge in which they float.

1808
Humphrey Davy Shocks Chemistry
English chemist Humphrey Davy applies an electric current to different materials. He discovers that many materials once thought to be elements break apart into even simpler materials. Davy succeeds in isolating the elements sodium, calcium, strontium, and barium.

| 1800 | 1820 | 1840 | 1860 | 1880 |

TECHNOLOGY
Chemistry and Electric Charge
In 1800 Italian physicist Alessandro Volta announced that he had produced an electric current from a pile, or battery, of alternating zinc and silver discs. Volta's invention was important for the study of atoms and elements in two ways. First, the fact that the contact of two different metals could produce an electric current suggested that electric charge must be part of matter. Second, the powerful electric current produced by the batteries enabled chemists to break apart many other substances, showing that there were more elements than previously thought.

1903
Atoms Release Energy
Polish-born French physicist Marie Curie and her husband, Pierre, have won the Nobel Prize for their isolation of the elements polonium and radium. These elements are unique because they release energy. Marie Curie names this trait "radioactivity." They share the award with Henri Becquerel, who previously observed this trait with the element uranium.

1911
Atoms Have a Center
By aiming a stream of particles at a piece of gold foil, New Zealand-born physicist Ernest Rutherford finds that atoms are not like a dish of pudding filled with raisins, as J. J. Thomson had suggested. Atoms must have a positive center because many of the particles bounce back. He calls the atom's center its nucleus.

1913
Bohr Puts Electrons into Orbit
Building on the work of Rutherford, Danish physicist Niels Bohr claims that electrons move about the nucleus only in certain, well-defined orbits. Bohr also says that electrons can jump to different orbits and emit or absorb energy when doing so.

1919
Atoms Share a Common Bond
U.S. chemists G.N. Lewis and Irving Langmuir suggest that atoms of many elements form bonds by sharing pairs of electrons. The idea that atoms could share electrons leads to a greater understanding of how molecules are structured.

1900   1905   1910   1915   1920   1940

APPLICATION

The Chemistry of Communication
The discovery of the electron resulted in more than a greater understanding of the atom. It also opened new ways of communicating. In 1906, U.S. inventor Lee De Forest invented a device for detecting and amplifying radio signals that he called the audion. The audion worked by producing a beam of electrons inside a vacuum tube. The beam was then made to respond to radio signals that it received from an antenna. The audion helped pave the way for later devices such as the transistor.

1960s
Smaller Particles Discovered

By smashing atoms into one another, scientists discover that protons and neutrons are themselves composed of even smaller particles. In a bit of scientific humor, these smaller particles are named "quarks," a nonsense word taken from a novel. Scientists detect these particles by observing the tracks they make in special detectors.

1980s
Tunneling to the Atomic Level

Scanning tunneling microscopes (STMs) allow scientists to interact with matter at the atomic level. Electrons on the tiny tip of an STM "tunnel" through the gap between the tip and target surface. By recording changes in the tunneling current, researchers get an accurate picture.

RESOURCE CENTER
CLASSZONE.COM
Explore advances in atomic research.

1960　　　　**1980**　　　　**2000**

TECHNOLOGY

Particle Accelerators

Particle accelerators speed up charged particles by passing them through an electric field. By smashing subatomic particles into one another, scientists are able to learn what these particles are made of as well as the forces holding them together. The H1 particle detector in Hamburg, Germany, can accelerate protons to 800 billion volts and is used to study the quarks that make up protons.

INTO THE FUTURE

Humans have gone from hypothesizing atoms exist to being able to see and move them. People once considered only four substances to be true elements; today we understand how there are more than a hundred simple substances. Not only have scientists learned atoms contain electric charges, they have also learned how to use these charges.

As scientists learn more and more about the atom, it is difficult to say what they will find next. Is there something smaller than a quark? Is there one type of particle from which all other particles are made? Will we one day be able to move and connect atoms in any way we want? Are there other kinds of atoms to discover? Maybe one day we will find answers to these questions.

ACTIVITIES

Explore a Model Atom

The discovery of the nucleus was one of the most important discoveries in human history. Rutherford's experiment, however, was a simple one that you can model. Take an aluminum pie plate and place a table tennis ball-sized piece of clay at its center. The clay represents a nucleus. Place the end of a grooved ruler at the edge of the plate. Hold the other end up to form a ramp. Roll a marble down the groove toward the clay. Move the ruler to different angles with each roll. Roll the marble 20 times. How many rolls out of 20 hit the clay ball? How do you think the results would be different if the atoms looked like pudding with raisins in it, as Thomson suggested?

Writing About Science

Suppose you are an atom. Choose one of the events on the timeline and describe it from the atom's point of view.

CHAPTER 19 Solutions

the **BIG** idea

When substances dissolve to form a solution, the properties of the mixture change.

Key Concepts

SECTION 1
A solution is a type of mixture.
Learn how solutions differ from other types of mixtures.

SECTION 2
The amount of solute that dissolves can vary.
Learn how solutions can contain different amounts of dissolved substances.

SECTION 3
Solutions can be acidic, basic, or neutral.
Learn about acids and bases and where they are found.

SECTION 4
Metal alloys are solid mixtures.
Learn about alloys and how they are used.

Internet Preview

CLASSZONE.COM
Chapter 19 online resources: Content Review, Simulation, Visualization, three Resource Centers, Math Tutorial, Test Practice

Why might some substances dissolve in the seawater in this photograph, but others do not?

EXPLORE the BIG idea

Does It Dissolve?

Pour water into four small clear cups. Add a teaspoon of each of the following: in cup 1, powdered drink mix; in cup 2, vinegar; in cup 3, milk; in cup 4, sand. Stir briefly. Observe the contents of all four cups for five minutes.

Observe and Think Do all of the substances dissolve in water? How can you tell?

Acid Test

Rub a radish on three blank index cards until the marks on the cards become dark pink. Use cotton swabs to wipe lemon juice onto the mark on the first card, tap water onto the mark on the second card, and soda water onto the mark on the third card. Observe the color of the radish mark on each index card.

Observe and Think What happened to the color on each index card? How might the three liquids that you tested differ?

Internet Activity: Alloys

Go to **ClassZone.com** to investigate alloys. Explore the production of different varieties of an alloy by changing the percentages of the metals used to make them. Find out how different alloys have different properties.

Observe and Think How does changing the composition of an alloy change its properties? Why?

NSTA
scilinks.org

SCiLINKS

Solutions Code: MDL025

Getting Ready to Learn

◀ CONCEPT REVIEW

- Matter can change from one physical state to another.
- A mixture is a blend of substances that do not react chemically.
- Particles can have electrical charges.

◀ VOCABULARY REVIEW

proton p. 511

ion p. 514

molecule p. 551

chemical reaction p. 569

mixture *See Glossary.*

ⓘ CONTENT REVIEW
CLASSZONE.COM
Review concepts and vocabulary.

▶ TAKING NOTES

MIND MAP

Write each main idea, or blue heading, in an oval; then write details that relate to each other and to the main idea. Organize the details so that each line of the map has a note about one part of the main idea.

CHOOSE YOUR OWN STRATEGY

For each new vocabulary term, take notes by choosing one of the strategies from earlier chapters—**frame game**, **description wheel**, or **four square** diagram. You can also use other vocabulary strategies that you might already know.

See the Note-Taking Handbook on pages R45–R51.

SCIENCE NOTEBOOK

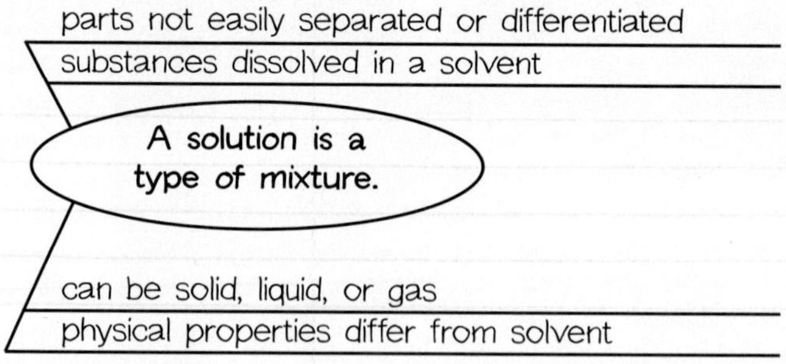

parts not easily separated or differentiated

substances dissolved in a solvent

A solution is a type *of* mixture.

can be solid, liquid, or gas

physical properties differ from solvent

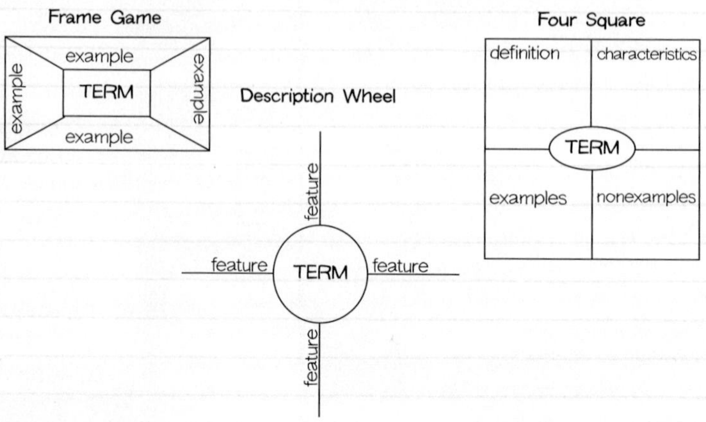

Frame Game

example
example | TERM | example
example

Description Wheel

feature
feature | TERM | feature
feature

Four Square

definition	characteristics
	TERM	
examples	nonexamples

19.1

KEY CONCEPT

A solution is a type of mixture.

◀ BEFORE, you learned

- Ionic or covalent bonds hold a compound together
- Chemical reactions produce chemical changes
- Chemical reactions alter the arrangements of atoms

▶ NOW, you will learn

- How a solution differs from other types of mixtures
- About the parts of a solution
- How properties of solutions differ from properties of their separate components

STANDARDS

7–5.2 Classify matter as element, compound, or mixture on the basis of its composition.

VOCABULARY

solution p. 611
solute p. 612
solvent p. 612
suspension p. 613

EXPLORE Mixtures

Which substances dissolve in water?

PROCEDURE

① Pour equal amounts of water into each cup.

② Pour one spoonful of table salt into one of the cups. Stir.

③ Pour one spoonful of flour into the other cup. Stir.

④ Record your observations.

WHAT DO YOU THINK?

- Did the salt dissolve? Did the flour dissolve?
- How can you tell?

MATERIALS

- tap water
- 2 clear plastic cups
- plastic spoon
- table salt
- flour

The parts of a solution are mixed evenly.

> **VOCABULARY**
> Remember to use the strategy of your choice. You might use a four square diagram for *solution*.

A mixture is a combination of substances, such as a fruit salad. The ingredients of any mixture can be physically separated from each other because they are not chemically changed—they are still the same substances. Sometimes, however, a mixture is so completely blended that its ingredients cannot be identified as different substances. A **solution** is a type of mixture, called a homogeneous mixture, that is the same throughout. A solution can be physically separated, but all portions of a solution have the same properties.

If you stir sand into a glass of water, you can identify the sand as a separate substance that falls to the bottom of the glass. Sand in water is a mixture that is not a solution. If you stir sugar into a glass of water, you cannot identify the sugar as a separate substance. Sugar in water is a common solution, as are examples such as seawater, gasoline, and the liquid part of your blood.

Solutes and Solvents

READING TIP

The words *solute* and *solvent* are both related to the Latin word *solvere,* which means "to loosen."

Like other mixtures, a solution has definite components. A **solute** (SAHL-yoot) is a substance that is dissolved to make a solution. When a solute dissolves, it separates into individual particles. A **solvent** is a substance that dissolves a solute. Because a solute dissolves into individual particles in a solvent, it is not possible to identify the solute and solvent as different substances when they form a solution.

In a solution of table salt and water, the salt is the solute and the water is the solvent. In the cells of your body, substances such as calcium ions and sugar are solutes, and water is the solvent. Water is the most common and important solvent, but other substances can also be solvents. For example, if you have ever used an oil-based paint you know that water will not clean the paintbrushes. Instead, a solvent like turpentine must be used.

 CHECK YOUR READING What is the difference between a solute and a solvent?

Types of Solutions

Many solutions are made of solids dissolved in liquids. However, solutes, solvents, and solutions can be gases, liquids, or solids. For example, oxygen, a gas, is dissolved in seawater. The bubbles in carbonated drinks come from the release of carbon dioxide gas that was dissolved in the drink.

In some solutions, both the solute and the solvent are in the same physical state. Vinegar, for example, is a solution of acetic acid in water. In a solution of different liquids, it may be difficult to say which substance is the solute and which is the solvent. In general, the substance present in the greater amount is the solvent. Since there is more water than acetic acid in vinegar, water is the solvent and acetic acid is the solute.

Although you may usually think of a solution as a liquid, solid solutions also exist. For example, bronze is a solid solution in which tin is the solute and copper is the solvent. Solid solutions are not formed as solids. Instead, the solvent metal is heated until it melts and becomes a liquid. Then the solute is added, and the substances are thoroughly mixed together. When the mixture cools, it is a solid solution.

Solutions made of combinations of gases are also common. The air you breathe is a solution. Because nitrogen makes up the largest portion of air, it is the solvent. Other gases present, such as oxygen and carbon dioxide, are solutes.

 CHECK YOUR READING When substances in a solution are in the same physical state, which is the solvent?

Gas Solution
Air is oxygen and other gases dissolved in nitrogen.

Solid Solution
Bronze consists of tin dissolved in copper.

Liquid Solution
Water often contains many dissolved substances.

INVESTIGATE Solutions

How can you separate the parts of a solution?

PROCEDURE

1. Draw a solid black circular region 6 cm in diameter around the point of the filter.

2. Place the filter, point up, over the top of the bottle.

3. Squeeze several drops of water onto the point of the filter.

4. Observe the filter once every minute for 10 minutes. Record your observations.

WHAT DO YOU THINK?

- What happened to the ink on the filter?
- Identify, in general, the solutes and the solution in this investigation.

CHALLENGE Relate your observations of the ink and water on the coffee filter to the properties of solutions.

MATERIALS
- black marker
- coffee filter
- plastic bottle
- eyedropper
- tap water
- stopwatch

TIME
15 minutes

Suspensions

When you add flour to water, the mixture turns cloudy, and you cannot see through it. This mixture is not a solution but a suspension. In a **suspension,** the particles are larger than those found in a solution. Instead of dissolving, these larger particles turn the liquid cloudy. Sometimes you can separate the components of a suspension by filtering the mixture.

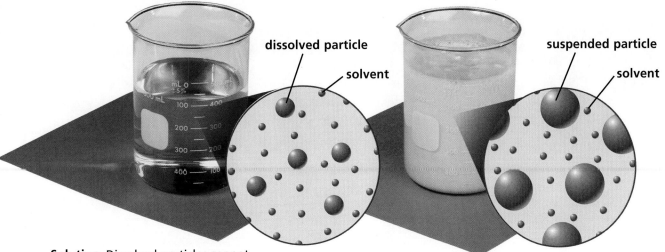

dissolved particle

solvent

suspended particle

solvent

Solution Dissolved particles cannot be identified as a substance different from the solvent.

Suspension Particles that do not dissolve make a suspension look cloudy.

Solvent and solute particles interact.

The parts of a solution—that is, the solute and the solvent—can be physically separated because they are not changed into new substances. However, individual particles of solute and solvent do interact. When a solid dissolves in a liquid, the particles of the solute are surrounded by particles of the liquid. The solute particles become evenly distributed throughout the solvent.

The way in which a solid compound dissolves in a liquid depends on the type of bonds in the compound. Ionic compounds, such as table salt (NaCl), split apart into individual ions. When table salt dissolves in water, the sodium and chloride ions separate, and each ion is surrounded by water molecules. When a covalent compound, such as table sugar ($C_{12}H_{22}O_{11}$), dissolves, each molecule stays together and is surrounded by solvent molecules. The general processes that take place when ionic compounds dissolve and when covalent compounds dissolve are shown below.

How Solutes Dissolve

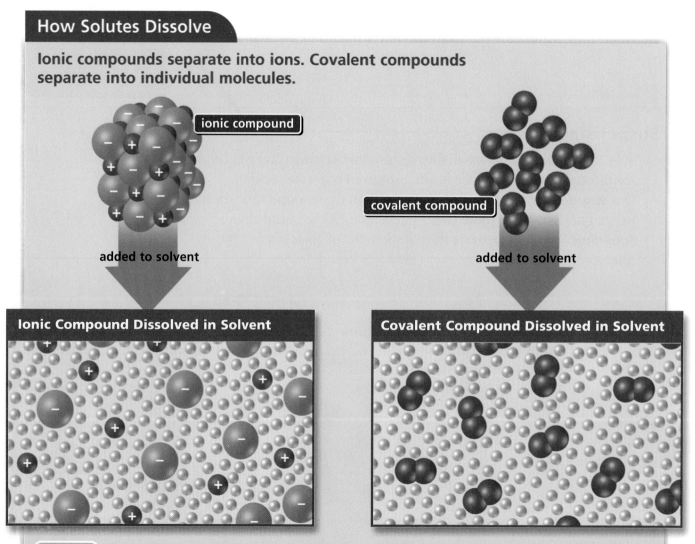

Ionic compounds separate into ions. Covalent compounds separate into individual molecules.

ionic compound

covalent compound

added to solvent

added to solvent

Ionic Compound Dissolved in Solvent

Covalent Compound Dissolved in Solvent

READING VISUALS   What difference between the two illustrations tells you whether a compound is ionic or covalent?

Properties of solvents change in solutions.

In every solution—solid, liquid, and gas—solutes change the physical properties of a solvent. Therefore, a solution's physical properties differ from the physical properties of the pure solvent. The amount of solute in the solution determines how much the physical properties of the solvent are changed.

Lowering the Freezing Point

Recall that the freezing point is the temperature at which a liquid becomes a solid. The freezing point of a liquid solvent decreases—becomes lower—when a solute is dissolved in it. For example, pure water freezes at 0°C (32°F) under normal conditions. When a solute is dissolved in water, the resulting solution has a freezing point below 0°C.

Lowering the freezing point of water can be very useful in winter. Road crews spread salt on streets and highways during snowstorms because salt lowers the freezing point of water. When snow mixes with salt on the roads, a saltwater solution that does not freeze at 0°C is formed. The more salt that is used, the lower the freezing point of the solution.

Since salt dissolves in the small amount of water usually present on the surface of ice, it helps to melt any ice already present on the roads. However, there is a limit to salt's effectiveness because there is a limit to how much will dissolve. No matter how much salt is used, once the temperature goes below –21°C (–6°F), the melted ice will freeze again.

> **CHECK YOUR READING** How does the freezing point of a solvent change when a solute is dissolved in it?

Making ice cream also depends on lowering the freezing point of a solvent. Most hand-cranked ice cream makers hold the liquid ice cream ingredients in a canister surrounded by a mixture of salt and ice. The salt added to the ice lowers the freezing point of this mixture. This causes the ice to melt—absorbing heat from its surroundings, including the ice cream ingredients. The ice cream mix is chilled while its ingredients are constantly stirred. As a result, tiny ice crystals form all at once in the ice cream mixture instead of a few crystals forming and growing larger as the mix freezes. This whole process helps to make ice cream that is smooth and creamy.

> **REMINDER**
> In temperature measurements, *C* stands for "Celsius" and *F* stands for "Fahrenheit."

Adding salt to lower the freezing point of ice helps to make ice cream.

615

Raising the Boiling Point

The boiling point of a liquid is the temperature at which the liquid forms bubbles in its interior and becomes a gas. Under normal conditions, a substance cannot exist as a liquid at a temperature greater than its boiling point. However, the boiling point of a solution is higher than the boiling point of the pure solvent. Therefore, a solution can remain a liquid at a higher temperature than its pure solvent.

For example, the boiling point of pure water is 100°C (212°F) under normal conditions. Saltwater, however, can be a liquid at temperatures above 100°C because salt raises the boiling point of water. The amount of salt in the water determines how much the boiling point is increased. The more solute that is dissolved in a solution, the greater the increase in boiling point.

APPLY Why might the addition of antifreeze to the water in this car's radiator have prevented the car from overheating?

○ CHECK YOUR READING How does the boiling point of a solution depend on the amount of solute in it?

A solute lowers the freezing point and raises the boiling point of the solvent in the solution. The result is that the solute extends the temperature range in which the solvent remains a liquid. One way in which both a decrease in freezing point and an increase in boiling point can be useful in the same solution involves a car's radiator. Antifreeze, which is mostly a chemical called ethylene glycol, is often added to the water in the radiator. This solution prevents the water from freezing in the winter and also keeps it from boiling in the summer.

19.1 Review

KEY CONCEPTS

1. How is a solution different from other mixtures?

2. Describe the two parts of a solution. How can you tell them apart?

3. How does the boiling point of a solvent change when a solute is dissolved in it? How does the freezing point change?

CRITICAL THINKING

4. **Contrast** Contrast the way in which an ionic compound, such as table salt, dissolves with the way in which a covalent compound, such as sugar, dissolves.

5. **Infer** Pure water freezes at 0°C and boils at 100°C. Would tap water likely freeze and boil at those exact temperatures? Why or why not?

○ CHALLENGE

6. **Synthesize** People often sprinkle salt on icy driveways and sidewalks. Would a substance like flour have a similar effect on the ice? Explain.

19.2 The amount of solute that dissolves can vary.

◀ **BEFORE, you learned**

- Solutions are a type of mixture
- A solution is made when a solute is dissolved in a solvent
- Solutes change the properties of solvents

▶ **NOW, you will learn**

- About the concentration of a solution
- How a solute's solubility can be changed
- How solubility depends on molecular structure

VOCABULARY

concentration p. 617
dilute p. 618
saturated p. 618
solubility p. 619

EXPLORE Solutions and Temperature

How does temperature affect a solution?

PROCEDURE

① Pour cold soda water into one cup and warm soda water into another cup. Record your observations.

② After 5 minutes, observe both cups of soda water. Record your observations.

WHAT DO YOU THINK?

- Which solution bubbled more at first?
- Which solution bubbled for a longer period of time?

MATERIALS
- soda water
- 2 clear plastic cups

A solution with a high concentration contains a large amount of solute.

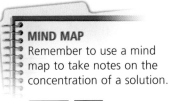

MIND MAP
Remember to use a mind map to take notes on the concentration of a solution.

Think of water from the ocean and drinking water from a well. Water from the ocean tastes salty, but water from a well does not. The well water does contain salt, but in a concentration so low that you cannot taste it. A solution's **concentration** depends on the amount of solute dissolved in a solvent at a particular temperature. A solution with only a small amount of dissolved solute, such as the salt dissolved in well water, is said to have a low concentration. As more solute is dissolved, the concentration gets higher.

If you have ever used a powdered mix to make lemonade, you probably know that you can change the concentration of the drink by varying the amount of mix you put into a certain amount of water. Two scoops of mix in a pitcher of water makes the lemonade stronger than just one scoop. The lemonade with two scoops of mix has a higher concentration of the mix than the lemonade made with one scoop.

Degrees of Concentration

READING TiP

The word *dilute* can be used as either an adjective or a verb. A dilute solution has a low concentration of solute. To dilute a solution is to add more solvent to it, thus lowering the concentration of the solution.

A solution that has a low concentration of solute is called a **dilute** solution. Salt dissolved in the drinking water from a well is a dilute solution. The concentration of a solution can be even further reduced, or diluted, by adding more solvent. On the other hand, as more solute is added to a solution, the solution becomes more concentrated. A concentrated solution has a large amount of solute.

Less solute is dissolved in a dilute solution.

More solute is dissolved in a concentrated solution.

Have you ever wondered how much sugar can be dissolved in a glass of iced tea? If you keep adding sugar to the tea, eventually no more sugar will dissolve. The tea will contain as much dissolved sugar as it can hold at that temperature. Such a solution is called a **saturated** solution because it contains the maximum amount of solute that can be dissolved in the solvent at a given temperature. If a solution contains less solute than this maximum amount, it is an unsaturated solution.

CHECK YOUR READING How are the terms *dilute* and *saturated* related to the concept of concentration?

Supersaturated Solutions

VISUALIZATION
CLASSZONE.COM

Explore supersaturated solutions and precipitation.

Sometimes, a solution contains more dissolved solute than is normally possible. This type of solution is said to be supersaturated. A saturated solution can become supersaturated if more solute is added while the temperature is raised. Then if this solution is slowly cooled, the solute can remain dissolved. This type of solution is very unstable, though. If the solution is disturbed, or more solute is added in the form of a crystal, the excess solute will quickly solidify and form a precipitate. This process is shown in the photographs on the top of page 619.

A supersaturated solution contains more dissolved solute than is normally possible.

After a crystal of solute is added, or the solution is disturbed, a precipitate forms.

REMINDER

A precipitate is a solid substance that comes out of a solution.

One example of a supersaturated solution is a chemical heat pack that contains sodium acetate and water. The pack contains more sodium acetate than can normally dissolve at room temperature, but when the pack is heated in a microwave oven, all of the sodium acetate dissolves. The solution inside the pack is supersaturated. The heat pack is activated by bending it. This disturbs the solution, solidifying the sodium acetate and releasing a large amount of heat over a long period of time.

Solubility

The **solubility** (SAHL-yuh-BIHL-ih-tee) of a substance is the amount of that substance that will dissolve in a certain amount of solvent at a given temperature. For example, consider household ammonia used for cleaning. This ammonia is not pure ammonia—it is a solution of ammonia in water.

Because a large amount of ammonia can dissolve in water, ammonia is said to have a high solubility in water. However, other substances do not dissolve in such large amounts in water. Only a small amount of carbon dioxide will dissolve in water, so carbon dioxide has a low solubility in water. Oils do not dissolve at all in water, so oils are said to be insoluble in water.

The amount of solute needed to make a saturated solution depends on the solubility of a solute in a particular solvent.

- If the solute is highly soluble, a saturated solution will be very concentrated.
- If the solute has a low solubility, the saturated solution will be dilute.

In other words, a saturated solution can be either dilute or concentrated, depending on the solubility of a solute in a particular solvent.

READING TIP

The word *solubility* is related to the words *solute* and *solvent*, and means "ability to be dissolved." A substance that is insoluble will not dissolve.

CHECK YOUR READING How does solubility affect a solution?

The solubility of a solute can be changed.

The solubility of a solute can be changed in two ways. Raising the temperature is one way to change the solubility of the solute, because most solids are more soluble at higher temperatures. Another way to change solubility when the solute is a gas is to change the pressure. The solubility of gases in a liquid solvent increases at high pressure.

Temperature and Solubility

REMINDER

An increase in temperature means an increase in particle movement.

An increase in temperature has two effects on most solid solutes—they dissolve more quickly, and a greater amount of the solid dissolves in a given amount of solvent. In general, solids are more soluble at higher temperatures, and they dissolve faster.

The opposite is true of all gases—an increase in temperature makes a gas less soluble in water. You can see this by warming tap water in a pan. As the water approaches its boiling point, any air that is dissolved in the water comes out of solution. The air forms tiny bubbles that rise to the surface.

CHECK YOUR READING What effect does temperature have on most solid solutes? on gaseous solutes?

INVESTIGATE Solubility

How can you change solubility?

Use what you know about solubility to design an experiment that shows how a change in temperature can change the amount of table salt that will dissolve in water.

DESIGN — YOUR OWN — EXPERIMENT

PROCEDURE

① Use the materials in the list to identify the relationship between temperature and solubility.

② Write your procedure, identifying the constants and variables.

③ Perform your experiment and record your results.

WHAT DO YOU THINK?

• Which variable did you change? What were your constants? Why?

• How do your results demonstrate the effect of temperature on solubility?

SKILL FOCUS
Designing experiments

MATERIALS
• clear plastic cups
• thermometer
• tap water
• table salt
• balance
• plastic spoon
• hot-water bath
• cold-water bath

TIME
20 minutes

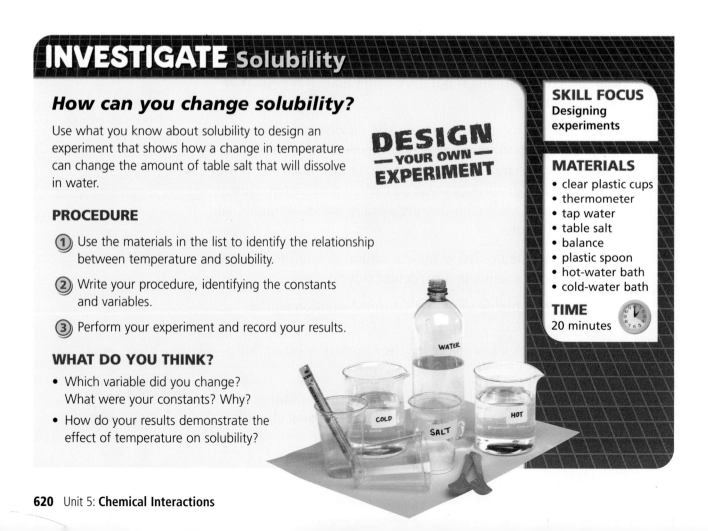

Think back to the earlier discussion of supersaturated solutions. One way in which a solution can become supersaturated is through a change in temperature. For example, suppose that a solution is saturated at 50°C (122°F), and is then allowed to cool slowly. The solid is less soluble in the cooler solution, but the excess solute may not form a precipitate. As a result, the solution contains more of the dissolved solute than would be possible under normal conditions because of the change in temperature.

Temperature and Solubility		
Solute	Increased Temperature	Decreased Temperature
Solid	increase in solubility	decrease in solubility
Gas	decrease in solubility	increase in solubility

A change in temperature can produce changes in solutions in the environment. For example, a factory located on the shore of a lake may use the lake water as a coolant and then return heated water to the lake. This increase in temperature decreases the solubility of oxygen in the lake water. As a result, less oxygen will remain dissolved in the water. A decrease in the oxygen concentration can harm plant and animal life in the lake.

Changing Temperature Changes Solubility

More sugar dissolves in hot water than in cold water.

Solubility of Table Sugar (in 100 g H$_2$O)

The solubility of most solids increases with a rise in temperature.

READING VISUALS About how much sugar will dissolve in 100 g of water at 70°C?

Pressure and Solubility

A change in pressure does not usually change the solubility of solid or liquid solutes. However, the solubility of any gas increases at higher pressures and decreases at lower pressures.

When manufacturers make carbonated beverages, such as soda, they add carbon dioxide gas at a pressure slightly greater than normal air pressure. When you open the can or bottle, the pressure decreases and the carbon dioxide bubbles out of solution with a fizz.

Another example is shown in the photograph on the left. When a diver's tank contains regular air, about 79 percent of the air is nitrogen. People breathe air like this all the time without any problem, but the pressure underwater is much greater than on Earth's surface. The higher pressure increases the solubility of nitrogen in the diver's blood.

When a diver heads up to the surface too fast, the pressure decreases, and so does the solubility of the nitrogen. The nitrogen comes out of solution, forming bubbles in the diver's blood vessels. These bubbles can cause a painful and sometimes fatal condition called the bends.

Divers can avoid the bends in two ways. They can rise to the surface very slowly, so that nitrogen bubbles stay small and pass through the bloodstream more easily. They can also breathe a different mixture of gases. Some professional divers breathe a mixture of oxygen and nitrogen that contains only about 66 percent nitrogen. For very deep dives, the mixture can also include helium because helium is less soluble in blood than nitrogen.

 CHECK YOUR READING How does pressure affect the solubility of solids? of gases?

INFER If these divers are breathing regular air, why might they be looking at their depth gauges?

Pressure and Solubility

Solute	Increased Pressure	Decreased Pressure
Solid	no effect on solubility	no effect on solubility
Gas	increase in solubility	decrease in solubility

Solubility depends on molecular structure.

Everyone knows that oil and water do not mix. When a tanker spills oil near shore, the oil floats on the water and pollutes the beaches. Why do oil and water not mix? The answer involves their different molecular structures.

When a substance dissolves, its molecules or ions separate from one another and become evenly mixed with molecules of the solvent. Recall that water contains polar covalent bonds. As a result, water molecules have a negative region and a positive region. Water molecules are said to be polar. The molecules of an oil are nonpolar—the molecules do not have positive and negative regions. This difference makes oil insoluble in water.

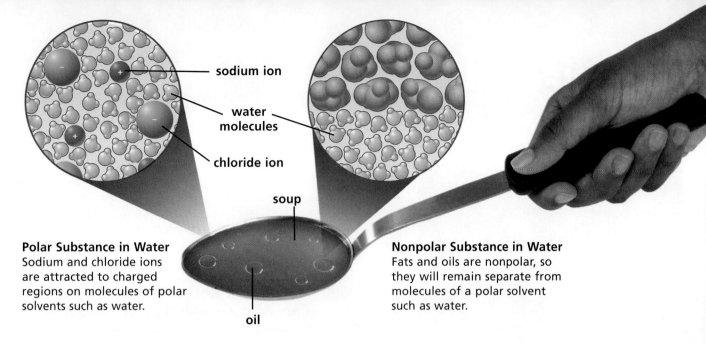

Polar Substance in Water
Sodium and chloride ions are attracted to charged regions on molecules of polar solvents such as water.

sodium ion

water molecules

chloride ion

soup

oil

Nonpolar Substance in Water
Fats and oils are nonpolar, so they will remain separate from molecules of a polar solvent such as water.

Because water is polar and oil is nonpolar, their molecules are not attracted to each other. The molecules of a polar solvent like water are attracted to other polar molecules, such as those of sugar. This explains why sugar has such a high solubility in water. Ionic compounds, such as sodium chloride, are also highly soluble in water. Because water molecules are polar, they interact with the sodium and chloride ions. In general, polar solvents dissolve polar solutes, and nonpolar solvents dissolve nonpolar solutes. This concept is often expressed as "Like dissolves like."

So many substances dissolve in water that it is sometimes called the universal solvent. Water is considered to be essential for life because it can carry so many different ions and molecules—just about anything the body needs or needs to get rid of—through the body.

 Why will a nonpolar substance not dissolve in a polar substance?

19.2 Review

KEY CONCEPTS

1. How can a solution be made more concentrated? less concentrated?

2. What two factors can change the solubility of a gas?

3. Are nonpolar compounds highly soluble in water? Why or why not?

CRITICAL THINKING

4. **Predict** Suppose you stir sugar into ice water. Some sugar remains on the bottom of the glass. After the glass sits out for an hour, you stir it again. What will happen? Why?

5. **Infer** A powder dissolves easily in water but not in oil. Are the molecules in the powder probably polar or nonpolar? Explain.

⬥ CHALLENGE

6. **Synthesize** If mixing a substance with water forms a suspension, does the substance have a high or a low solubility in water? Explain.

Cool, Clear Water

Water that looks clear, clean, and pure may not be. The water you drink every day contains many dissolved substances.

The drinking water that comes out of a tap is a solution. Many minerals, chemicals, and even gases are dissolved in it. Some drinking water comes from rivers, lakes, or reservoirs, but about half of the drinking water in the United States is pumped from wells. Well water comes from underground aquifers. The water in aquifers flows through gaps in broken or porous rocks.

Filtering Impurities

The water in a puddle is not pure water. It contains suspended dirt and dissolved chemicals. This water can be cleaned underground. As the solution flows through soil and rocks, the soil and rocks filter and trap particles. Some chemicals in the water are removed from the solution by clay particles in the soil. Other chemicals, such as acids from acid rain, are neutralized by limestone and other rocks.

Adding Minerals

The rocks surrounding aquifers do not just remove chemicals from water. As water flows underground, minerals dissolve in the water. The solutes include compounds of calcium, magnesium, and iron. These compounds do not harm the quality of drinking water because they are necessary parts of your diet. Water with a high concentration of dissolved minerals is called hard water.

Copying Earth

Aquifer Layer

Water that has been used by people must be cleaned before it is returned to the environment. Waste treatment plants copy some of the natural cleansing processes of Earth. Wastewater solutions may contain many dissolved impurities and harmful chemicals, but the water can be filtered through beds of sand and gravel. Water must be treated after it is used because so many substances dissolve in it.

EXPLORE

1. **INFER** A white solid often forms around a tiny leak in a water pipe. Where does the white solid come from?

2. **CHALLENGE** Use the Internet or call your local water company to find out the source of your drinking water. Find out whether you have hard or soft water and what dissolved chemicals are in your drinking water.

RESOURCE CENTER
CLASSZONE.COM

Learn more about aquifers and water purification.

19.3

KEY CONCEPT
Solutions can be acidic, basic, or neutral.

STANDARDS

7–5.6 Distinguish between acids and bases and use indicators (including litmus paper, pH paper, and phenol-phthalein) to determine their relative pH.

VOCABULARY

acid p. 626
base p. 626
pH p. 629
neutral p. 629

◀ **BEFORE, you learned**

- Substances dissolved in solutions can break apart into ions
- Concentration is the amount of a substance dissolved in a solution
- Water is a common solvent

▶ **NOW, you will learn**

- What acids and bases are
- How to determine if a solution is acidic or basic
- How acids and bases react with each other

EXPLORE Acids and Bases

What happens when an antacid mixes with an acid?

PROCEDURE

1. Fill the cup halfway with vinegar.
2. Observe the vinegar in the cup. Record your observations.
3. Crush two antacid tablets and place them in the vinegar.
4. Observe the contents of the cup for 5 minutes. Record your observations.

WHAT DO YOU THINK?
- What did you observe before adding the antacid tablets?
- What happened after you added the tablets?

MATERIALS
- clear plastic cup
- vinegar
- 2 antacid tablets

Acids and bases have distinct properties.

Many solutions have certain properties that make us call them acids or bases. Acids are found in many foods, such as orange juice, tomatoes, and vinegar. They taste slightly sour when dissolved in water and produce a burning or itchy feeling on the skin. Strong acids should never be tasted or touched—these solutions are used in manufacturing and are dangerous chemicals.

Bases are the chemical opposite of acids. They tend to taste bitter rather than sour and often feel slippery to the touch. Bases are also found in common products around the home, including soap, ammonia, and antacids. Strong bases, like the lye used for unclogging drains, are also dangerous chemicals.

 READING TiP

The prefix *ant-* means "against," so an antacid is a substance that works against an acid.

RESOURCE CENTER
CLASSZONE.COM

Find out more about acids and bases.

Acids, Bases, and Ions

Generally, a compound that is an acid or a base acts as an acid or a base only when it is dissolved in water. In a water-based solution, these compounds produce ions. Recall that an ion is a charged particle. For example, if a hydrogen atom, which consists of one proton and one electron, loses its electron, it becomes a hydrogen ion. The hydrogen ion is simply a proton and has a positive charge.

An **acid** can be defined as a substance that can donate a hydrogen ion—that is, a proton—to another substance. The diagram below shows what happens when the compound hydrogen chloride (HCl) is dissolved in water. The compound separates into hydrogen ions (H^+) and chloride ions (Cl^-). Hydrogen ions are free to react with other substances, so the solution is an acid. When hydrogen chloride is dissolved in water, the solution is called hydrochloric acid.

READING TIP

The H_2O above the arrow means the substance on the left is added to water and the substances on the right are dissolved in the water.

Acid

$$HCl \xrightarrow{H_2O} H^+ + Cl^-$$

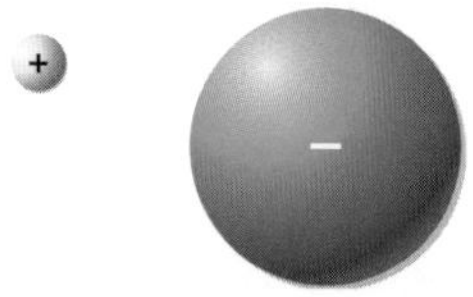

In water, acids release a proton (H^+) into the solution.

A **base** can be defined as a substance that can accept a hydrogen ion from another substance. The diagram below shows what happens when the compound sodium hydroxide (NaOH) is dissolved in water. The compound separates into sodium ions (Na^+) and hydroxide ions (OH^-). The hydroxide ions are free to accept protons from other substances, so the solution is a base. The solution that results when NaOH is dissolved in water is called sodium hydroxide.

Base

$$NaOH \xrightarrow{H_2O} Na^+ + OH^-$$

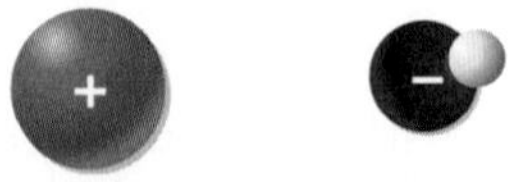

In water, many bases release a hydroxide ion (OH^-), which can accept a proton.

On the atomic level, the difference between acids and bases is that acids donate protons and bases accept protons. When a proton—a hydrogen ion—from an acid is accepted by a hydroxide ion from a base, the two ions join together and form a molecule of water. This simple transfer of protons between substances is involved in a great many useful and important chemical reactions.

CHECK YOUR READING How are protons related to acids and bases?

Characteristics of Acids

As you read earlier, acids in foods taste sour and produce a burning or prickling feeling on the skin. However, since tasting or touching an unknown chemical is extremely dangerous, other methods are needed to tell whether a solution is an acid.

One safe way to test for an acid is to place a few drops of a solution on a compound that contains a carbonate (CO_3). For example, limestone is a rock that contains calcium carbonate ($CaCO_3$). When an acid touches a piece of limestone, a reaction occurs that produces carbon dioxide gas.

Acids also react with most metals. The reaction produces hydrogen gas, which you can see as bubbles in the photograph on the right. Such a reaction is characteristic of acids.

The feature of acids most often used to identify them is their ability to change the colors of certain compounds known as acid-base indicators. One common indicator is litmus, which is often prepared on slips of paper. When a drop of an acid is placed on litmus paper, the paper turns red.

Acids react with some metals, such as zinc, and release hydrogen gas.

$$2HCl + Zn \longrightarrow H_2 + ZnCl_2$$

CHECK YOUR READING What are three safe methods to test for an acid?

Characteristics of Bases

Bases also have certain common characteristics. Mild bases in foods taste bitter and feel slippery, but as with acids, tasting and touching are not safe ways of testing whether a solution is a base. In fact, some strong bases can burn the skin as badly as strong acids.

Bases feel soapy or slippery because they react with acidic molecules in your skin called fatty acids. In fact, this is exactly how soap is made. Mixing a base—usually sodium hydroxide—with fatty acids produces soap. So, when a base touches your skin, the combination of the base with your own fatty acids actually makes a small amount of soap.

Like acids, bases change the colors of acid-base indicators, but the colors they produce are different. Bases turn litmus paper blue. A base will counteract the effect that an acid has on an acid-base indicator. You might put a few drops of acid on litmus paper to make it turn red. If you put a few drops of a base on the red litmus paper, the litmus paper will change colors again.

CHECK YOUR READING How do the characteristics of bases differ from those of acids?

Bases are found in many cleaning agents, including soap.

The strengths of acids and bases can be measured.

MIND MAP
Remember to use a mind map to take notes about acid and base strength.

Battery fluid and many juices contain acids. Many people drink some type of juice every morning, but you would not want to drink, or even touch, the liquid in a car battery. Similarly, you probably wash your hands with soap several times a day, but you would not want to touch the liquid used to unclog drains. Both soap and drain cleaners are bases. Clearly, some acids and bases are stronger than others.

Acid and Base Strength

Strong acids break apart completely into ions. For example, when hydrogen chloride (HCl) dissolves in water to form hydrochloric acid, it breaks down into hydrogen ions and chloride ions. No hydrogen chloride remains in the solution. Because all of the hydrogen chloride forms separate ions, hydrochloric acid is a strong acid.

A weak acid does not form many ions in solution. When acetic acid ($HC_2H_3O_2$), which is the acid in vinegar, dissolves in water, only about 1 percent of the acetic acid breaks up into hydrogen ions and acetate ions. The other 99 percent of the acetic acid remains unchanged. Therefore, acetic acid is a weak acid.

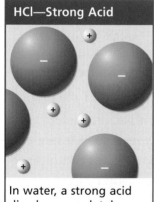

HCl—Strong Acid

In water, a strong acid dissolves completely into ions.

$HC_2H_3O_2$—Weak Acid

In water, a weak acid forms only a small number of ions.

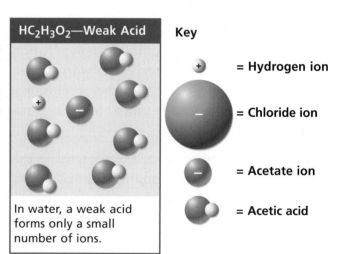

Key

+ = Hydrogen ion

− = Chloride ion

− = Acetate ion

= Acetic acid

Bases also can be strong or weak. When sodium hydroxide (NaOH) dissolves in water, it forms sodium ions (Na^+) and hydroxide ions (OH^-). None of the original NaOH remains in the solution, so sodium hydroxide is a strong base. However, when ammonia (NH_3) dissolves in water, only about 1 percent of the ammonia reacts with water to form OH^- ions.

$$NH_3 + H_2O \longrightarrow NH_4^+ + OH^-$$

The other 99 percent of the ammonia remains unchanged, so ammonia is a weak base. The ions formed when NaOH or NH_3 is dissolved in water are shown on the top of page 629.

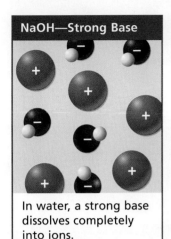

NaOH—Strong Base

In water, a strong base dissolves completely into ions.

NH₃—Weak Base

In water, a weak base forms only a small number of ions.

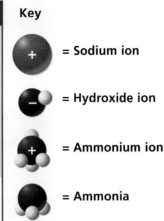

Key

= Sodium ion

= Hydroxide ion

= Ammonium ion

= Ammonia

READING TiP

Look at the reaction on the bottom of page 628 for help with the illustration of NH_3 in water.

Note that the strength of an acid or base is not the same as its concentration. Dilute hydrochloric acid is still strong and can burn holes in your clothing, whereas acetic acid cannot. The strengths of acids and bases depend on the percentage of the substance that forms ions.

 CHECK YOUR READING   What determines acid and base strength?

Measuring Acidity

The acidity of a solution depends on the concentration of H^+ ions in the solution. This concentration is often measured on the **pH** scale. In this scale, a high H^+ concentration is indicated by a low number, and a low H^+ concentration is indicated by a high number. The numbers of the pH scale usually range from 0 to 14, but numbers outside this range are possible. The middle number, 7, represents a neutral solution. A **neutral** substance is neither an acid nor a base. Pure water has a pH of 7.

The strip of universal indicator paper in the bottom front of the photograph shows a nearly neutral pH.

Numbers below 7 indicate acidic solutions. A concentrated strong acid has a low pH value—the pH of concentrated hydrochloric acid, for example, is less than 0. Numbers above 7 indicate a basic solution. A concentrated strong base has a high pH value—the pH of concentrated sodium hydroxide, for example, is greater than 14. The illustration on page 630 shows the pH values of some common acids and bases.

Today, electronic pH meters are commonly used to measure pH. A probe is placed in a solution, and the pH value is indicated by the meter. An older method of measuring pH is to use an acid-base indicator. You read earlier that acids turn litmus paper red and bases turn litmus paper blue. Other acid-base indicators, such as a universal pH indicator, show a variety of colors at different pH values.

 CHECK YOUR READING   Is the pH of a base higher or lower than the pH of an acid?

Common Acids and Bases

Dilute acids and bases are found in many common products.

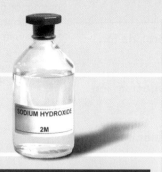

sodium hydroxide (NaOH)—pH > 14

Concentrated NaOH has a pH greater than 14 because it has a very low H^+ concentration. Drain openers usually contain concentrated NaOH.

milk—pH 6.5

Milk contains molecules called fatty acids, which make milk slightly acidic.

lemon—pH 2

Lemons and other types of citrus fruit contain citric acid.

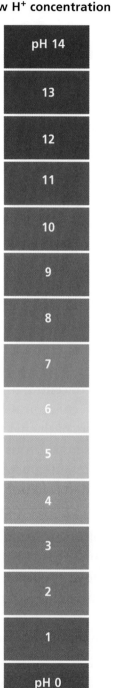

low H^+ concentration

pH 14
13
12
11
10
9
8
7
6
5
4
3
2
1
pH 0

high H^+ concentration

soap—pH 10

Soap is commonly made by mixing fats with NaOH. There is a relatively low concentration of NaOH in soap.

pure water (H₂O)—pH 7

In pure water, the H^+ concentration is equal to the OH^- concentration. Pure water has a pH of 7 and is neutral.

hydrochloric acid (HCl)—pH < 0

Concentrated HCl has a pH lower than 0 because it has a very high H^+ concentration. HCl is used in many processes, including refining sugar from sugar cane.

READING VISUALS Where are the strong acids on the chart? Where are the strong bases? How does the concentration of hydrogen ions change?

Acids and bases neutralize each other.

Acids donate hydrogen ions, and bases accept hydrogen ions. Therefore, it is not surprising that acids and bases react when they come into contact with each other. Recall that when a hydrogen ion (H^+) from an acid collides with a hydroxide ion (OH^-) from a base, the two ions join to form a molecule of water (H_2O).

The negative ion of an acid (Cl^-) joins with the positive ion of a base (Na^+) to form a substance called a salt. Since both the salt and water are neutral, an acid-base reaction is called a neutralization (NOO-truh-lih-ZAY-shuhn) reaction. The reactants are an acid and a base, and the products are a salt and water.

READING TIP

The salt produced by a neutralization reaction is not necessarily table salt.

A common example of a neutralization reaction occurs when you swallow an antacid tablet to relieve an upset stomach. The acid in your stomach has a pH of about 1.5, due mostly to hydrochloric acid produced by the stomach lining. If your stomach produces more acid than is needed, you may feel a burning sensation. An antacid tablet contains a base, such as sodium bicarbonate, magnesium hydroxide, or calcium carbonate. The base reacts with the stomach acid and produces a salt and water. This reaction lowers the acidity—and raises the pH—to its normal value.

Acid rain forms when certain gases in the atmosphere dissolve in water vapor, forming acidic solutions. During rainstorms these acids fall to Earth. They can harm forests by making soil acidic and harm aquatic life by making lakes acidic. Acid rain can also dissolve marble and limestone in buildings and statues, because both marble and limestone contain calcium carbonate, which is a base.

CHECK YOUR READING How is neutralization an example of a chemical reaction?

19.3 Review

KEY CONCEPTS

1. Use the concept of ions to explain the difference between an acid and a base.

2. How do the properties of an acid differ from the properties of a base?

3. What happens when an acid and a base react with each other?

CRITICAL THINKING

4. **Infer** When an acid reacts with a metal, such as zinc, what is released? Where does that product come from?

5. **Infer** Suppose that you have 1 L of an acid solution with a pH of 2. You add 1 L of pure water. What happens to the pH of the solution? Explain.

⬤ CHALLENGE

6. **Synthesize** Suppose that equal amounts of solutions of HCl and NaOH with the same concentration are mixed together. What will the pH of the new solution be? What are the products of this reaction?

CHAPTER INVESTIGATION

Acids and Bases

OVERVIEW AND PURPOSE Acids and bases are very common. For example, the limestone formations in the cave shown on the left are made of a substance that is a base when it is dissolved in water. In this activity you will use what you have learned about solutions, acids, and bases to

- test various household substances and place them in categories according to their pH values
- investigate the properties of common acids and bases

▶ Procedure

1. Make a data table like the one shown on the sample notebook page.

2. Set out 7 cups in your work area. Collect the substances that you will be testing: baking soda, fruit juice, shampoo, soda water, table salt, laundry detergent, and vinegar.

3. Label each cup. Be sure to wear goggles when pouring the substances that you will be testing. Pour 30 mL of each liquid substance into a separate cup. Dissolve 1 tsp of each solid substance in 30 mL of distilled water in a separate cup. To avoid contaminating the test solutions, wash and dry your measuring tools and hands between measurements.

MATERIALS
- plastic cups
- baking soda
- fruit juice
- shampoo
- soda water
- table salt
- detergent powder
- vinegar
- masking tape
- marking pen
- measuring spoons
- graduated cylinder
- distilled water
- paper towels
- pH indicator paper

FRUIT JUICE

BAKING SODA

DETERGENT

SHAMPOO

4 Dip a piece of indicator paper into each solution. Compare the color of the test strip with the colors in the chart included in the package. Record the indicator color and the approximate pH number for each solution.

Step 4

5 After you have tested all of the solutions, arrange the cups in order of their pH values.

▶ Observe and Analyze
Write It Up

1. **RECORD DATA** Check to be sure that your data table is complete.

2. **ANALYZE DATA** What color range did the substances show when tested with the indicator paper? What do your results tell you about the pH of each substance you tested?

3. **CLASSIFY** Look for patterns in the pH values. Use your test results to place each household substance in one of three groups—acids, bases, or neutral.

4. **MODEL** Draw a diagram of the pH scale from 0 to 14. Use arrows and labels to show where the substances you tested fall on this scale.

SALT

SODA WATER

▶ Conclude
Write It Up

1. **GENERALIZE** What general conclusions can you draw about the hydrogen ion concentration in many acids and bases found in the home? Are the hydrogen ion concentrations very high or very low? How do you know?

2. **EVALUATE** What limitations or difficulties did you experience in interpreting the results of your tests or other observations?

3. **APPLY** Antacid tablets react with stomach acid containing hydrochloric acid. What is this type of reaction called? What are the products of this type of reaction?

▶ INVESTIGATE Further

CHALLENGE Repeat the experiment, changing one variable. You might change the concentrations of the solutions you are testing or see what happens when you mix an acidic solution with a basic solution. Get your teacher's approval of your plan before proceeding. How does changing one particular variable affect the pH of the solutions?

Acids and Bases
Observe and Analyze
Table 1. Acid-Base Test Results

Substance	Indicator Color	pH	Group
baking soda			
juice			
shampoo			
soda water			
table salt			

Conclude

19.4 Metal alloys are solid mixtures.

STANDARDS

7–5.2 Classify matter as element, compound, or mixture on the basis of its composition.

VOCABULARY

alloy p. 634

◀ **BEFORE**, you learned

- A solution can be a solid
- Solutes change the properties of solvents
- The concentration of a solution can vary

▶ **NOW**, you will learn

- How metal alloys are made
- How a variety of alloys are used in modern society
- Why different alloys have different uses

THINK ABOUT

If gold jewelry is not pure gold, what is it?

People have prized gold since ancient times—archaeologists have found gold jewelry that was made thousands of years ago. Gold is a very soft metal, and jewelry made of pure gold bends very easily. Today, most gold jewelry is about 75 percent gold and 25 percent other metals. Why might these metals be mixed in?

Humans have made alloys for thousands of years.

VOCABULARY
Remember to use the strategy of your choice. You might use a description wheel diagram for *alloy*.

The gold used in jewelry is an example of an alloy. An **alloy** is a mixture of a metal and one or more other elements, usually metals as well. The gold alloys used in jewelry contain silver and copper in various amounts.

Many alloys are made by melting the metals and mixing them in the liquid state to form a solution. For example, bronze is made by melting and mixing copper and tin and then letting the solution cool. Bronze is not difficult to make, because both copper and tin melt at relatively low temperatures. Bronze was probably the first alloy made in ancient times—historians say it was discovered about 3800 B.C.

 How is an alloy usually made?

Recall that the addition of a solute changes the properties of a solvent. The alloy bronze is harder than either copper or tin alone. This hardness made bronze a better material than stones or animal bones for making tools. The transition from the Stone Age to the Bronze Age, when humans first began to use metals, was an important period in human history.

Even though alloys have been made for thousands of years, new alloys with new properties are still being developed. One alloy with a very interesting property is nitinol, which is made of nickel and titanium. Nitinol is called a memory alloy because it can be given a particular shape and then reshaped. What makes nitinol unusual is that it will return to its original shape after being heated. Because of this property, nitinol is used in several common products, including eyeglass frames.

A short list of useful alloys is given in the table below. The percentages shown in the table are those for only one type of each alloy.

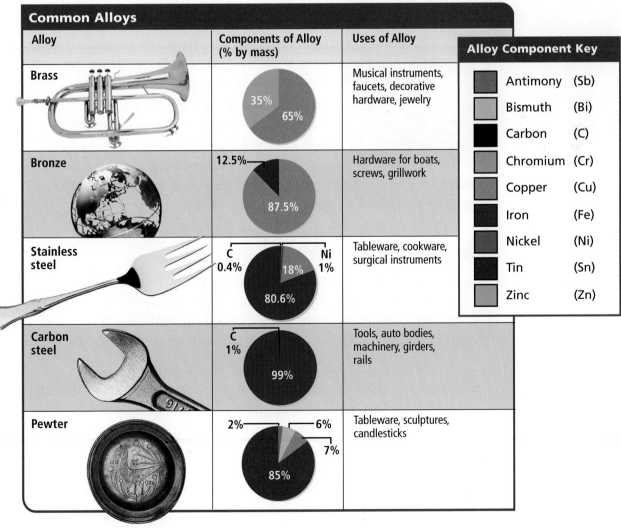

Common Alloys

Alloy	Components of Alloy (% by mass)	Uses of Alloy
Brass	35% / 65%	Musical instruments, faucets, decorative hardware, jewelry
Bronze	12.5% / 87.5%	Hardware for boats, screws, grillwork
Stainless steel	C 0.4% / Ni 1% / 18% / 80.6%	Tableware, cookware, surgical instruments
Carbon steel	C 1% / 99%	Tools, auto bodies, machinery, girders, rails
Pewter	2% / 6% / 7% / 85%	Tableware, sculptures, candlesticks

Alloy Component Key

- Antimony (Sb)
- Bismuth (Bi)
- Carbon (C)
- Chromium (Cr)
- Copper (Cu)
- Iron (Fe)
- Nickel (Ni)
- Tin (Sn)
- Zinc (Zn)

READING VISUALS How are brass and bronze different from each other? How are stainless steel and carbon steel different from each other?

Alloys have many uses in modern life.

The advances in materials science that began with bronze almost 6000 years ago continue today. Modern industry uses many different alloys. Some alloys, based on lightweight metals such as aluminum and titanium, are relatively recent developments. However, the most important alloy used today—steel—has been around for many years.

A major advance in technology occurred in the 1850s with the development of the Bessemer process. This process made it possible to manufacture large amounts of steel in a short time. Until then, steel could be made only in batches of less than 100 pounds. The Bessemer process made it possible to produce up to 30 tons of steel in about 20 minutes. Since it began to be mass-produced, steel has been used in everything from bridges to cars to spoons.

Steel is the main material used in the structure of this sphere at Epcot Center in Florida.

Most steel used in construction is an alloy of iron and carbon. Iron is too soft to be a good building material by itself, but adding only a small amount of carbon—about 1 percent by mass—makes a very hard and strong material. Some types of steel contain small amounts of other metals as well, which give the alloys different properties. As you can see on the chart on page 635, one type of stainless steel contains only 1 percent nickel. However, different types of stainless steel can be made, and they have different uses. For instance, stainless steel used in appliances has 8 to 10 percent nickel and 18 percent chromium in it.

Alloys in Transportation

Different forms of transportation rely on steel. Wooden sailing ships were replaced by steel ships in the late 1800s. Today, steel cargo ships carry steel containers. Railroads depended on steel from their very beginning. Today's high-speed trains still run on steel wheels and tracks.

Modern vehicles use more recently developed alloys as well. For example, aluminum and titanium are lightweight metals that are relatively soft, like iron. However, their alloys are strong, like steel, and light. Airplane engines are made from aluminum alloys, and both aluminum and titanium alloys are used in aircraft bodies. Aluminum alloys are also commonly used in high-speed passenger ferries and in the bodies of cars. Because the alloys are light, they help to improve the fuel efficiency of these vehicles.

CHECK YOUR READING How are alloys used in transportation?

Alloys in Medicine

You may have noticed that most medical equipment is shiny and silver-colored. This equipment is made of stainless steel, which contains nickel and chromium in addition to iron and carbon. Surgical instruments are often made of stainless steel because it can be honed to a very sharp edge and is also rust resistant.

Cobalt and titanium alloys are also widely used in medicine because they do not easily react with substances in the body, such as blood and digestive juices. These alloys can be surgically placed inside the body with a minimum of harm to either the body or the metal. The photographs on the right show one use of alloys—making artificial joints.

Memory alloys similar to the nitinol alloy described earlier also have a wide range of medical uses. These alloys are used in braces for teeth, and as implants that hold open blocked arteries or correct a curve in the spine. Medical devices made of memory alloys can be made in a particular shape and then reshaped for implantation. After the device is in place, the person's body heat causes it to return to its original shape.

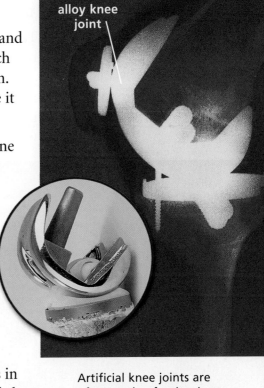

alloy knee joint

Artificial knee joints are often made of a titanium alloy. The x-ray image shows the device in place.

 CHECK YOUR READING What properties make alloys useful in medicine?

INVESTIGATE Alloys

How is a pure metal different from its alloy?

PROCEDURE

1. Examine the iron nails and the alloy (steel or stainless steel) nails. Record your observations.

2. Find and record the mass of the three iron nails. Repeat with the three alloy nails.

3. Find the volume of the nails by displacement, as follows: Into the empty graduated cylinder, pour water to a height that is higher than the nails are long. Note the water level. Add the iron nails and record the change in water level. Repeat this step with the alloy nails.

4. Calculate the density of each type of nail. **Density = $\frac{mass}{Volume}$**

WHAT DO YOU THINK?

- Compare your observations of the metals contained in the nails.
- Which metal has the greater density? How might a metal's density be important in how it is used?

CHALLENGE How can you identify different alloys of a metal?

SKILL FOCUS
Observing

MATERIALS
- 3 iron nails
- 3 steel nails or 3 stainless steel nails
- balance
- graduated cylinder
- water

TIME
30 minutes

Alloys in Space Flight

The aerospace industry develops and uses some of the newest and most advanced alloys. The same qualities that make titanium and aluminum alloys useful in airplanes—lightness, strength, and heat resistance—also make them useful in spacecraft. Titanium alloys were used in the Gemini space program of the 1960s. Large portions of the wings of today's space shuttle are made of aluminum alloys.

Research on the International Space Station may lead to the development of new alloys.

For more than 20 years, the heat shield on the shuttle's belly has been made from ceramic tiles. However, engineers have experimented with a titanium heat shield as well.

Construction of the International Space Station, which is shown in the photograph on the left, began in 1998. Alloys are a major part of the space station's structure. More important, research on the space station may lead to the development of new alloys.

One of the goals of research on the space station is to make alloys in a microgravity environment, which cannot be done on Earth. For example, astronauts have experimented with thick liquids, made with iron, that harden or change shape when a magnet is placed nearby, and then return to their previous shapes when the magnet is removed. These liquid alloys may be useful in robots or in artificial organs for humans.

CHECK YOUR READING Why is research into new alloys on the International Space Station important?

19.4 Review

KEY CONCEPTS

1. How can one metal be made to dissolve in another metal?

2. Name three metal alloys and a use for each one.

3. Why are alloys of cobalt or titanium, instead of pure iron, used for medical devices that are implanted inside people?

CRITICAL THINKING

4. **Infer** In industry, all titanium alloys are simply called titanium. What might this tell you about the use of pure titanium?

5. **Compare and Contrast** How are modern alloys similar to alloys made hundreds or thousands of years ago? How are they different?

CHALLENGE

6. **Synthesize** The melting point of copper is 1083°C. Tin is dissolved in copper to make bronze. Will bronze have a melting point of 1083°C? Why or why not?

MATH in SCIENCE

MATH TUTORIAL
CLASSZONE.COM
Click on Math
Tutorial for more help
understanding percents.

The Mixtures in Alloys

An alloy is a mixture of a metal with other substances. Because even a small change in the percentages of materials in an alloy can change its properties, alloys are made according to strict specifications. For example, steel is an alloy of iron and carbon. Steel that contains 0.6 percent carbon by mass is used in steel beams, whereas steel that contains 1.0 percent carbon by mass, which makes the steel harder, is used to make tools and springs. How can the percentages of materials in an alloy be calculated?

Example

Calculate the percentage of nickel in an alloy if a small portion of the alloy has 10 atoms, 3 of which are nickel.

(1) Convert the number of atoms into a fraction.

3 of 10 atoms in the alloy are nickel $= \dfrac{3}{10}$

(2) To calculate a percentage, first find an equivalent fraction that has a denominator of 100. Use x as the numerator.

$$\dfrac{3}{10} = \dfrac{x}{100}$$

(3) Convert the fraction into a percentage by using cross products

$$3 \cdot 100 = 10 \cdot x$$
$$300 = 10x$$
$$30 = x$$

ANSWER The percentage of nickel atoms in the alloy is 30%.

Answer the following questions.

1. A sample of an alloy contains 4 iron atoms, 3 zinc atoms, 2 aluminum atoms, and 1 copper atom.

   a. What percentage of the alloy is aluminum by number of atoms?

   b. What percentage is zinc by number of atoms?

2. A sample of an alloy contains 12 titanium atoms, 4 niobium atoms, and 4 aluminum atoms.

   a. What percentage of the alloy is titanium by number of atoms?

   b. What percentage is niobium by number of atoms?

CHALLENGE Suppose there is an alloy in which 2 of every 3 atoms are silver atoms, 1 of every 4 atoms is a copper atom, and 1 of every 12 atoms is a tin atom. What are the percentages of each metal in the alloy by number of atoms?

The steel in girders like these contains iron and 0.6 percent carbon by mass.

Chapter Review

the BIG idea

When substances dissolve to form a solution, the properties of the mixture change.

CONTENT REVIEW
CLASSZONE.COM

KEY CONCEPTS SUMMARY

1 **A solution is a type of mixture.**

- A solution is a mixture in which one or more solutes are dissolved in a solvent.
- A solution is a homogeneous mixture.

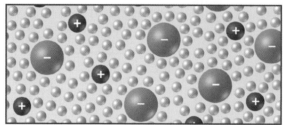

Ionic compound dissolved in solvent

VOCABULARY
solution p. 611
solute p. 612
solvent p. 612
suspension p. 613

2 **The amount of solute that dissolves can vary.**

- The amount of dissolved solute determines a solution's concentration.
- The more soluble a substance is, the more of it will dissolve in a solution.

Dilute

Concentrated

VOCABULARY
concentration p. 617
dilute p. 618
saturated p. 618
solubility p. 619

3 **Solutions can be acidic, basic, or neutral.**

- Acids donate protons (H+) in solutions, and bases accept protons in solutions.
- Acidity is measured by the H+ concentration on the pH scale.

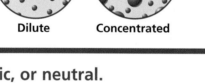

Acid   HCl $\xrightarrow{H_2O}$ H^+ + Cl^-

Base   NaOH $\xrightarrow{H_2O}$ Na^+ + OH^-

VOCABULARY
acid p. 626
base p. 626
pH p. 629
neutral p. 629

4 **Metal alloys are solid mixtures.**

- Many of the metals used in modern transportation and medicine are alloys.
- The properties of a metal can be changed by adding one or more substances to produce a more useful material.

VOCABULARY
alloy p. 634

Reviewing Vocabulary

Draw a diagram similar to the example shown below to connect and organize the concepts of related vocabulary terms. After you have completed your diagram, explain in two or three sentences why you organized the terms in that way. Underline each of the terms in your explanation.

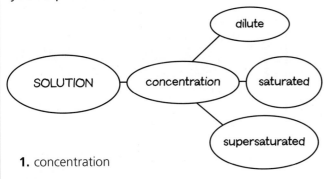

1. concentration

2. acid

3. base

4. neutral

5. pH

Latin Roots *Several of the vocabulary terms in this chapter come from the Latin word* solvere, *which means "to loosen." Describe how each of the following terms is related to the Latin word.*

6. solution

7. solute

8. solvent

9. solubility

Reviewing Key Concepts

Multiple Choice *Choose the letter of the best answer.*

10. What makes a solution different from other types of mixtures?
    - **a.** Its parts can be separated.
    - **b.** It is the same throughout.
    - **c.** Its parts can be seen.
    - **d.** It is a liquid.

11. When a solute is dissolved in a solvent, the solvent's
    - **a.** boiling point decreases
    - **b.** boiling point decreases and its freezing point increases
    - **c.** freezing point increases
    - **d.** freezing point decreases and its boiling point increases

12. When a compound held together by ionic bonds dissolves, the compound
    - **a.** releases molecules into the solution
    - **b.** forms a suspension
    - **c.** releases ions into the solution
    - **d.** becomes nonpolar

13. Water is called the universal solvent because it
    - **a.** dissolves many substances
    - **b.** dissolves very dense substances
    - **c.** has no charged regions
    - **d.** is nonpolar

14. How does an increase in temperature affect the solubility of solids and gases?
    - **a.** It increases solubility of most solids and decreases the solubility of gases.
    - **b.** It decreases solubility of most solids and gases.
    - **c.** It increases solubility of gases and decreases the solubility of most solids.
    - **d.** It increases solubility of both solids and gases.

15. A solution with a very high H^+ concentration has a
    - **a.** very high pH
    - **b.** very low pH
    - **c.** pH close to 5
    - **d.** pH close to 7

16. Why are oils insoluble in water?
    - **a.** They are acids.
    - **b.** They are polar.
    - **c.** They are bases.
    - **d.** They are nonpolar.

Short Answer *Write a short answer to each question.*

17. Describe the reaction that occurs when a strong acid reacts with a strong base.

18. How might an alloy be changed for different uses? Explain.

Thinking Critically

The illustration below shows the results of pH tests of four different solutions. Assume the solutions are made with strong acids or strong bases. Use the diagram to answer the next four questions.

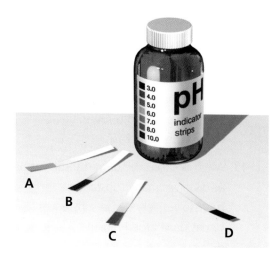

19. OBSERVE Which of the indicator strips show an acidic solution? Which show a basic solution?

20. INFER Which strip of indicator paper detected the highest concentration of H^+ ions? How do you know?

21. PREDICT What would happen if you mixed together equal amounts of the solutions that produced the results of strip B and strip D?

22. INFER Suppose you mix together equal amounts of the solutions that produced the results of strip C and strip D, then test the pH of this new solution. What color will the indicator paper be? Explain.

23. CAUSE AND EFFECT Suppose that you place a beaker containing a solution in a refrigerator. An hour later there is a white solid on the bottom of the beaker. What happened? Why?

24. INFER Do you think iron by itself would be a good material to use in the frame of a bridge? Why or why not?

25. SYNTHESIZE How might the concentration of a solute in an alloy be related to the properties of the alloy? Explain.

Using Math Skills in Science

Use the graph below to answer the next three questions.

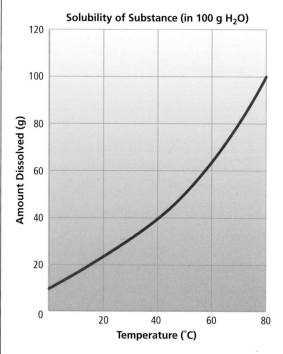

26. What happens to the solubility of the substance as the temperature increases? decreases?

27. Approximately how many grams of the substance dissolve at 20°C? 60°C?

28. Is the substance a solid or a gas? Explain.

the BIG idea

29. APPLY Look back at pages 608–609. Think about the answer you gave to the question about the photograph. How has your understanding of solutions and their properties changed?

30. COMPARE Describe the similarities and differences between solutions of table salt (NaCl) in water and sugar in water. Do both solutes have similar effects on the properties of the solvent? Explain.

UNIT PROJECTS

Evaluate all data, results, and information from your project. Prepare to present your project.

Interpreting Graphs

Use the information in the paragraph and the graph to answer the questions.

Acid rain is an environmental concern in the United States and in other countries. Acid rain is produced when the burning of fuels releases certain chemicals into the air. These chemicals can react with water vapor in Earth's atmosphere to form acids. The acids then fall back to the ground in either rain or snow. The acids can damage plants, animals, and buildings. Normally, rain has a pH of about 5.6, which is slightly acidic. But rain in some areas of the United States has a pH that is lower than 4.0. The graph shows the pH of water in several lakes.

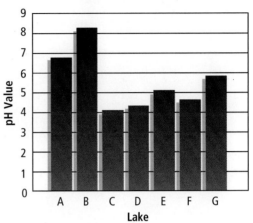

Lake Water pH Values

1. Which lake is the most acidic?
   a. Lake A   **c.** Lake C
   b. Lake B   **d.** Lake D

2. Which lake is the least acidic?
   a. Lake A   **c.** Lake C
   b. Lake B   **d.** Lake D

3. Which lake has water the closest to neutral?
   a. Lake A   **c.** Lake E
   b. Lake B   **d.** Lake G

4. Lakes that form on a bed of limestone are less likely to suffer from high acidity. The limestone reacts with acids to neutralize them. Which of the following lakes is most likely to have a limestone bed?
   a. Lake C   **c.** Lake F
   b. Lake D   **d.** Lake G

5. Lake trout are fish that live in many freshwater lakes. When the pH of the water in a lake drops below 5.5, this species of fish can no longer reproduce, because its eggs cannot hatch. Which of the following statements is most likely true?
   a. Lake trout have probably stopped reproducing in all the lakes.
   b. In terms of reproducing, lake trout are not in danger in any of the lakes.
   c. Lake trout will probably be able to reproduce in lakes A, B, and G but not in the others.
   d. Lake trout have probably stopped reproducing only in lakes C, D, and F.

Extended Response

Answer the following two questions in detail. Include some of the terms from the list in the box. Underline each term you use in your answers.

concentration	solute	solubility
polar	solution	solvent

6. Suppose you are trying to make two solutions. One contains water and salt. The other contains water and oil. What do you think will happen in both cases? How might charges on particles affect your results?

7. Explain why some substances dissolve more easily than others. How can this characteristic of a solute be changed by changing the temperature or pressure of a solution?

South Carolina Essentials

7–2.3 Compare the body shapes of bacteria (spiral, coccus, and bacillus) and the body structures that protists (euglena, paramecium, amoeba) use for food gathering and locomotion.

Bacteria and Protists

In Chapter 1, you read that organisms can be classified by their cell type. Organisms that belong to the domain Bacteria are prokaryotes. Prokaryotes are unicellular organisms made of prokaryotic cells. Their cytoplasm contains ribosomes but no organelles, so the structure of a prokaryote is simple. In addition, a prokaryote has a tough cell wall that protects the organism. Organisms in the domain Eukarya have cells with a nucleus. This domain includes all multicellular organisms on Earth, such as plants, animals, and fungi. The domain Eukarya also includes many unicellular organisms called protists. In this section, you will learn more about the body shapes of bacteria and the body structures that protists use for food gathering and locomotion.

BACTERIA CHARACTERISTICS

Bacteria are the simplest kind of life known on Earth. All bacteria are composed of just one cell without a nucleus. Their genetic material is contained in a single loop within the cell. A bacterium reproduces using binary fission.

Bacterial cells are different from the cells of other organisms. A bacteria cell is about 1/10 to 1/20 the size of a typical cell from organisms such as animals, plants, fungi, or protists. These four groups include organisms made up of cells with true nuclei. The nucleus is a structure that is enclosed by a membrane and that holds the genetic material.

CLASSIFICATION OF BACTERIA

Scientists often classify bacteria by their external shapes.

- Spiral-shaped bacteria, called spirilla, occur in single strands.
- Rod-shaped bacteria, called bacilli, may occur singly or in chains.
- Round-shaped bacteria, called cocci, may occur singly or in pairs, chains, or clusters.

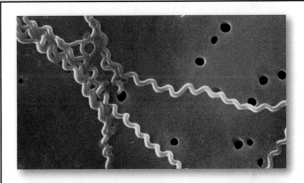

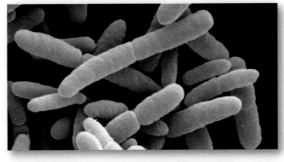

Bacteria are classified by their external shapes. Bacteria may be spiral-shaped (top), rod-shaped (middle), or round-shaped (bottom).

PROTIST CHARACTERISTICS

Protists are organisms that make up one of the six kingdoms of living things. Most protists are microscopic. Protists differ from bacteria in that protist cells contain nuclei with nuclear membranes. Most protists are single-celled, but some, such as seaweeds, are multicellular. The protists are the most diverse of all kingdoms. A person has more in common with an animal such as an ant than some protists have in common with each other. Protists live in all moist environments, including fresh water, salt water, and forest floors.

ALGAE

Plantlike protists, called algae, obtain energy from sunlight. Like plants, algae carry out the process of photosynthesis. Photosynthetic organisms play important roles in ecosystems. They serve as food for other organisms and supply oxygen to the atmosphere. Some algae, such as *Euglenas* and *Pfiesteria,* can obtain energy from sunlight, or, when food is available, from feeding on other organisms.

PROTOZOA

Protists that eat other organisms or decaying parts of other organisms are protozoa. The name *protozoa* means "primitive animals." Like animals, these protists gather food from their environment. They come in many shapes and sizes, but all are single-celled. Protozoa cannot use sunlight as a source of energy; instead they must move to obtain the food they need to survive. Examples of protozoa are *Paramecia* and *Amoebas*. Although the vast majority of protozoa are harmless, a number of them live as parasites. One of the world's most destructive human diseases, malaria, is caused by a protozoan called *Plasmodium.*

OTHER PROTISTS

Protists that absorb food from their environment are funguslike protists. These protists take in materials from the soil or from other organisms to obtain energy. The term *mold* usually refers to fungi, but some molds are protists. Slime molds are single-celled protists that live on decaying plants on forest floors. When their food is scarce, individual cells group together to produce a multicellular colony that functions like a larger organism.

Life Functions of Protists

	Euglena	*Amoeba*	*Paramecia*
Source of energy	makes food from sunlight or absorbs nutrients from environment	has flexible shape and engulfs food by wrapping around it	sweeps food into groove that functions like mouth
Method of movement	swims using flagellum, or whiplike appendage	moves by stretching and bending projections called pseudopods	swims by beating fine hairs called cilia

South Carolina Essentials

7–3.4 Explain the effects of disease on the major organs and body systems (including infectious diseases such as colds and flu, AIDS, and athlete's foot and noninfectious diseases such as diabetes, Parkinson's and skin cancer).

Infectious and Noninfectious Diseases

In Chapter 10, you read about how diseases affect the human body. In this section, you will learn more about several infectious and noninfectious diseases.

INFECTIOUS DISEASES

Infectious diseases are diseases that can be spread. Viruses, bacteria, and other pathogens cause infectious diseases.

NONINFECTIOUS DISEASES

Noninfectious diseases are diseases that cannot be spread by pathogens. They are not contagious. Some noninfectious diseases are inherited; others develop later in life.

Infectious Diseases	
DISEASE	DESCRIPTION
Colds	The common cold is caused by a virus infection centered in the respiratory system. Symptoms include sneezing, coughing, and a runny nose.
Influenza (flu)	The flu is a highly contagious viral infection of the respiratory system. Symptoms include fever, muscle aches, and severe cough.
Strep throat	Strep throat is a disease caused by a bacterial infection. Symptoms include fever, pain, and swelling of the throat and tonsils.
Athlete's foot	Athlete's foot is a fungal infection of the skin of the feet. Symptoms include itchy, scaly skin between the toes.
AIDS	Acquired immunodeficiency syndrome (AIDS) is caused by the human immuno-deficiency virus (HIV). The virus attacks immune system cells, making the body unable to fight off other pathogens.

Noninfectious Diseases	
DISEASE	DESCRIPTION
Diabetes	Diabetes is a disease that results in higher than normal glucose (sugar) levels in the blood. This disease results from a person's inability to either produce or properly use insulin. Complications from diabetes include poor blood circulation, kidney disease, and heart disease.
Asthma	Asthma is a respiratory disease that affects the lungs and airways that bring air to the lungs.
Parkinson's disease	Parkinson's disease occurs when certain nerve cells in the brain become damaged or die. Symptoms vary among those afflicted. Tremor (the uncontrollable shaking of limbs) is a major symptom.
Skin cancer	Skin cancer is a disease in which cancer cells are found in the outer layers of the skin. Sunburn and UV light, along with heredity and environmental factors, may lead to skin cancer.

South Carolina Essentials

7–4.4 Explain the effects of soil quality on the characteristics of an ecosystem.

Characteristics of Soil

In Chapter 11, you read that soil is an important abiotic factor in an ecosystem. In this section, you will learn about the properties and characteristics of soil.

Soil is a mixture of rock particles, air, water, and organic matter. Organic matter is matter that has come from the waste and remains of living organisms. Soils vary greatly in the types and amounts of materials they contain and in their ability to support plant growth. Soil scientists study the physical and chemical properties of soil. These properties include soil profile, color, structure, consistency, texture, particle size, infiltration, fertility, acidity, temperature, and moisture.

HORIZON PROFILE

The layers that soil forms in the ground are called soil horizons. A cross-section view of the horizons in a specific location is a soil profile. Dark-colored soil typically makes up the uppermost layer of soil, or topsoil. This layer has the most organic matter, and its rock particles are most weathered. Topsoil is nutrient-rich. The layer beneath the topsoil is often reddish in color, due to the clay and minerals it contains. The lowest layer of soil is often yellowish brown in color and contains the largest and least-weathered rock particles.

STRUCTURE

Soil structure refers to the shape of masses of soil in the ground. The structure of soil can be granular, blocky, prismatic, columnar, or platy, as described in the table below. Granular, blocky, and prismatic structures are the best for plant growth because these soils contain spaces that can hold air and water, similar to a sponge. Because these structures are not too firm, plant roots can spread easily through them. Soil can also be structured as a single large mass (massive) or as individual particles (single-grained). In general, massive and single-grained soils are the least helpful for plant growth.

Soil Structures	
STRUCTURE	**DESCRIPTION**
Granular	like cookie crumbs, with most pieces less than 0.5 cm across
Blocky	blocks of different shapes, each 1.5–5.0 cm across
Prismatic	thin columns, each several centimeters long
Columnar	vertical columns that have salt at the top
Platy	thin, flat plates
Single-grained	small individual particles that do not stick together
Massive	single large block that is difficult to break apart

Distinct layers of soil can be seen in a soil horizon.

CONSISTENCY

Single-grained soil, such as sand, always has a loose consistency—that is, the grains of soil do not stick together. On the other hand, massive soil has an extremely firm consistency—that is, it is very difficult to break the soil apart. Soil structure and consistency determine a soil's ability to hold air and nutrient-containing water, both of which plants need to grow. Water and air cannot easily move through soils that are too firm. In contrast, water drains out of soils that are too loose. Water and nutrients must therefore be added frequently to loose soils.

TEXTURE

The texture of soil is related to, but different from, its structure. Soil texture depends on the sizes of the small rock particles in a soil. It is determined by the relative amounts of sand, silt, and clay in the soil. Sand particles are the largest and can be seen without a microscope. Silt particles are smaller and can be seen only with a microscope. The pieces of silt that are visible in the photograph below contain many, many particles. Clay particles are the smallest and, like silt, can be seen only with a microscope. Clay particles stick together, forming large chunks, as shown in the picture.

Like structure and consistency, soil texture affects how well water and nutrients move through a soil. Very sandy soils have a high infiltration rate—that is, water drains into the soil easily. However, water also drains out of sandy soil easily and can take certain nutrients with it, such as nitrogen (N), phosphorus (P), and potassium (K). The best soil texture for retaining water—and therefore the best soil for growing plants—contains equal amounts of sand, silt, clay, and organic matter.

Soil Texture

SAND	SILT	CLAY
gritty in texture	silky, smooth, or lumpy	sticky, or hard and lumpy

Measurable Properties

PERMEABILITY

Permeability refers to how easily water flows through soil. Smaller particles of soil are able to pack closer together, making the soil less permeable. Larger particles of soil cannot pack as tightly together, making the soil more permeable, as water can more easily flow through the open spaces between particles.

When conducting a soil test, a soil scientist measures the fertility, acidity, and organic content of a soil sample.

SOIL TESTING

A soil test is an analysis of soil fertility in which the mineral nutrients in a soil are chemically removed and measured. Acidity and organic matter are also measured. The information provided by a soil test indicates what, if anything, should be added to the soil to promote plant growth. For example, lime can be added to the soil to make it less acidic (increase its pH). If the test shows a low level of nitrogen, phosphorus, or potassium, a fertilizer can be added that is highest in that nutrient. Results from a soil test can help growers add to the soil what is needed only. This practice improves the soil conditions for plants while saving money and reducing pollution. Excess fertilizer can pollute rivers, streams, and lakes.

IMPORTANT ABIOTIC FACTOR

Soil is an important abiotic factor in an ecosystem, because all organisms depend on soil, either directly or indirectly. A soil's quality, such as its nutrient content, determines which types of organisms can survive in an ecosystem. When the quality of an ecosystem's soil changes, the characteristics and organisms found in the ecosystem change as well. For example, the global loss of topsoil, at a rate of 7 percent each decade, is increasing the amount and size of deserts on Earth. This process is called desertification.

Soil is a key abiotic factor in an ecosystem. The loss of topsoil results in desertification.

South Carolina Essentials

7–4.5 Summarize how the location and movement of water on Earth's surface through groundwater zones and surface-water drainage basins, called watersheds, are important to ecosystems and to human activities.

Location and Movement of Water on Earth

In Chapter 11, you read that water cycles through ecosystems. You also read about freshwater and saltwater biomes. In this section, you will learn about groundwater zones and watersheds, and their importance to ecosystems and to human activities.

WATERSHED SYSTEMS

No matter where you live, your home is in a watershed. A **watershed** is an area of land that drains into a body of water, such as a river or lake. A watershed is also called a drainage basin.

WATER BELOW THE GROUND

Water that soaks into the ground is called **groundwater** when it reaches the water table. The **water table** is the surface of the region in the ground in which all spaces are filled with water. The **zone of saturation** is a term used to describe the area in which water has filled in all the spaces in the

soil. The water table is found at the top of this zone. In many parts of the United States, as well as throughout the world, people depend on groundwater as their main source of water.

Just as surface water flows in a river, groundwater flows in an aquifer. An aquifer is an underground layer of sediment or rock that stores and transmits water. The sediment or rock is permeable—that is, it has interconnected spaces through which water can flow. The **zone of aeration** is a term used to describe this permeable area that is not saturated with water. If people dig wells from an aquifer faster than precipitation can soak into the ground and replace it, the aquifer can dry up.

Groundwater flows from one watershed to another. It can also flow back to the surface. Where the land dips below the water table, water fills the low

Groundwater

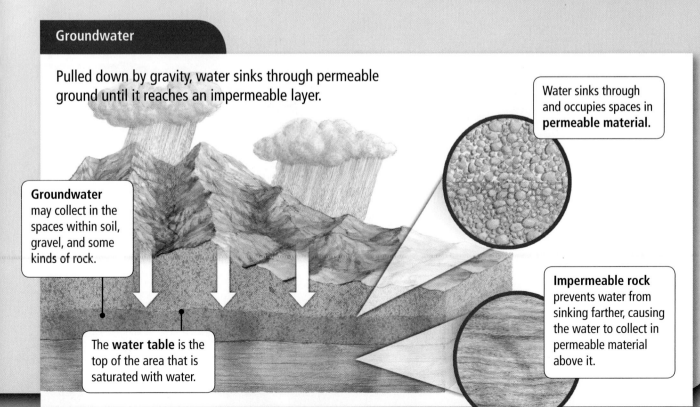

Pulled down by gravity, water sinks through permeable ground until it reaches an impermeable layer.

Water sinks through and occupies spaces in **permeable material**.

Groundwater may collect in the spaces within soil, gravel, and some kinds of rock.

Impermeable rock prevents water from sinking farther, causing the water to collect in permeable material above it.

The **water table** is the top of the area that is saturated with water.

area. The result might be a spring or a river. The surface of a lake is part of the water table. The flow of groundwater through underground rock such as limestone may result in the formation of caverns, caves, and tunnels.

WATER ABOVE THE GROUND

In a watershed, water moves aboveground in streams, rivers, and lakes. Streams and rivers gain water from runoff—water from precipitation or irrigation that flows over the land. Streams and rivers also get bigger when tributaries join them.

Water can fall from the same cloud as rain or snow onto either side of a ridge. This water can end up in different rivers—or even in different oceans. The ridge forms a **divide**, or boundary of high ground between two watersheds. In the illustration, you can see a river and its **tributaries**, or branches. There are divides on either side of the river. Rain that falls on a divide flows toward lower ground on

either side of the divide. Water from melting snow also flows downhill. Everywhere on Earth, the force of gravity pulls water downhill.

LAND

Land in a watershed consists of all the rocks and soil over which, and through which, water flows. The shape and makeup of the land in a watershed affects the water that moves through it in several ways. For example, water flows faster down steep slopes, and fast-moving water is less likely to soak into the ground.

Solid rock does not soak up water. Unless the rock has cracks or other openings, there are no spaces for water to sink into it. The depth of the soil is also important. If a layer of soil is thick and contains a lot of sand, water from a heavy rainstorm can quickly sink into it. If a soil is rich in clay, more water will remain at the surface. Particles of clay are tiny, and the spaces between them are so small that water moves very slowly through soil with a lot of clay.

Divides and Drainage Basins

Divides exist in mountain ranges as well as in flatter regions.

Water falling on a divide flows into the **drainage basins** on wither side of the divide.

Water in a drainage basin flows downhill in streams and rivers, usually to the ocean.

ORGANISMS

All the living things within a watershed—including people—are part of the watershed system. When you drink water from an underground well or aquifer, you are interacting with the watershed.

Watersheds support many types of ecosystems. A wetland is an ecosystem in which the water table is at the surface for at least part of the year. Plants that require wet soil grow there. Wetlands help provide protection from floods. They absorb runoff and slow the flow of water. As water moves through a wetland, much of the sediment and other material is filtered out. The water becomes cleaner.

STREAMS AND RIVER PROCESSES

Some of the water that falls on land becomes runoff. As runoff moves downhill, it can erode, or pick up and carry, sediment. It can also dissolve some of the material with which it comes in contact. As runoff enters a stream channel or other body of water, it can carry both solid and dissolved materials with it. As smaller streams flow into larger streams, materials are carried far from their starting points.

The faster that water moves, the more likely it is to cause erosion. Also, fast-moving water can move larger particles than slow-moving water. You can see these factors at work in a steep mountain area. Streams and rivers cut narrow, V-shaped valleys into the land. In the streams and rivers you might see rounded rocks that look too large for the water to move. But when floodwater races down the valleys, the water picks up rocks or tumbles them along. As the rocks move, they hit against other rocks, knocking off sharp edges. In this way, the rocks in the river become rounder.

When water slows down, it deposits, or drops, sediment. You can explore this process by examining a floodplain—the area that is covered by water when a stream or river overflows. A floodplain becomes flat over time as sediment from many floods fills in low areas. As floodwater leaves the channel of a stream or river, it spreads out and slows down quickly. Larger particles are deposited first, close to the channel. As a result, banks, or higher areas, may build up along the channel's edges. Smaller particles are carried farther away, causing a well-developed floodplain to slope very gently away from the banks. The soil in a floodplain is nutrient-rich and both natural vegetation and crops grow well in it.

A stream or river usually slows down as it flows into another body of water. It may deposit enough sediment to build up a delta above the water surface. A delta is not a stable area of land. These unique ecosystems can grow, erode, and change shape quickly. Examples of deltas include the Santee delta in South Carolina and the Mississippi delta in Louisiana.

Meandering waterways and saltwater marshland are evident in this aerial photo of Capers Island, a barrier island off the coast of South Carolina.

Human Impact on Water Quality

Although 71 percent of Earth's surface is covered by water, only 3 percent of that amount is usable freshwater. Clean water is necessary for drinking, food production, transportation, recreation, and habitats for plants and animals.

People need water—not just for drinking but for farming, manufacturing, the production of hydro-electric power, transportation, and many other uses, such as recreation. Water bodies such as lakes and rivers provide a valuable source of nutrients to a number of organisms, including humans. The water that people use comes from a watershed. When people build dams, they affect the flow of water above and below the ground. Water shortages can result when people take water from a river, lake, or aquifer faster than the water is replaced through precipitation and runoff.

LAND USE AND WATER QUALITY

How people use land is important to water quality. When people cover parts of a watershed with buildings and paved roads, less land is available to absorb precipitation. Runoff increases, which increases erosion and flooding. The plowing of fields can cause greater erosion. Planting trees and shrubs can decrease erosion because the plants' roots help hold the soil in place.

The pumping of groundwater from an aquifer can affect water quality. Consider groundwater near a coast. Fresh water in the aquifer prevents salt water from intruding. If people pump too much fresh water from the ground, salt water can move in from the ocean and replace it—making the water too salty to drink.

What can people do to solve water-quality problems? Government agencies and concerned citizens can monitor water quality within a watershed by measuring and recording water properties over time. They measure such properties as the types and amounts of materials in water, the level of water in a lake, and the depth of the water table. These data help identify areas where water quality is decreasing or a water resource is being overused. Then people can work to find solutions to these problems.

People can help maintain water quality by making good choices. For example, they can conserve water by repairing dripping faucets and leaky water pipes. When people add plants to yards and parks, they can use ones that are native to the area. Native plants do not need extra fertilizer or water. People can also avoid polluting water sources by disposing items such as batteries and used motor oil properly.

The construction of a dam changes a river's ecosystems.

South Carolina Essentials

7–5.3 Compare the physical properties of metals and nonmetals.

Physical Properties of Metals and Nonmetals

In Chapter 17, you read that substances' properties depend on their bonds. In this section, you will learn about the physical properties of metals and nonmetals.

PROPERTIES OF METALS

Metal atoms bond together by sharing their electrons with one another. Atoms in all directions share electrons equally. This equal sharing lets the electrons move easily among the atoms of the metal. This type of bond is called a metallic bond. The physical properties of metals are determined by their metallic bonds. The table below summarizes the unique physical properties of metals.

PROPERTIES OF NONMETALS

The properties of nonmetals tend to be the opposite of those of metals. The properties of nonmetals also tend to vary more from element to element than the properties of metals do. Many of them are gases at room temperature, and one—bromine—is a liquid. The solid nonmetals often have dull surfaces and cannot be shaped by hammering or drawing into wires. Nonmetals are generally poor conductors of heat and electric current.

The table below summarizes the physical properties of nonmetals.

Physical Properties of Metals	
PROPERTY	DESCRIPTION
Conductor	Heat and electricity flow easily through metals.
High melting point	All metals, except mercury, are solid at room temperature.
Malleable	Metals are easily shaped by pounding.
Ductile	Metals can be drawn into a wire.
Luster	Metals have a shiny surface or brightly reflect light.
High density	Metals are heavy for their size.

Physical Properties of Nonmetals	
PROPERTY	DESCRIPTION
Brittle	Nonmetals shatter or break easily.
Nonconductor	Heat and electricity do not flow easily through nonmetals.
Dull	Nonmetals do not have a shiny surface.

Nonmetallic elements (shown clockwise from the top left) include sulfur, bromine, phosphorus, iodine, and carbon.

Student Resource Handbooks

Scientific Thinking Handbook — R2

Making Observations	R2
Predicting and Hypothesizing	R3
Inferring	R4
Identifying Cause and Effect	R5
Recognizing Bias	R6
Identifying Faulty Reasoning	R7
Analyzing Statements	R8

Lab Handbook — R10

Safety Rules	R10
Using Lab Equipment	R12
The Metric System and SI Units	R20
Precision and Accuracy	R22
Making Data Tables and Graphs	R23
Designing an Experiment	R28

Math Handbook — R36

Describing a Set of Data	R36
Using Ratios, Rates, and Proportions	R38
Using Decimals, Fractions, and Percents	R39
Using Formulas	R42
Finding Areas	R43
Finding Volumes	R43
Using Significant Figures	R44
Using Scientific Notation	R44

Note-Taking Handbook — R45

Note-Taking Strategies	R45
Vocabulary Strategies	R50

Scientific Thinking Handbook

Making Observations

An **observation** is an act of noting and recording an event, characteristic, behavior, or anything else detected with an instrument or with the senses.

Observations allow you to make informed hypotheses and to gather data for experiments. Careful observations often lead to ideas for new experiments. There are two categories of observations:

- **Quantitative observations** can be expressed in numbers and include records of time, temperature, mass, distance, and volume.

- **Qualitative observations** include descriptions of sights, sounds, smells, and textures.

EXAMPLE

A student dissolved 30 grams of Epsom salts in water, poured the solution into a dish, and let the dish sit out uncovered overnight. The next day, she made the following observations of the Epsom salt crystals that grew in the dish.

Table 1. Observations of Epsom Salt Crystals

> To determine the mass, the student found the mass of the dish before and after growing the crystals and then used subtraction to find the difference.

> The student measured several crystals and calculated the mean length. (To learn how to calculate the mean of a data set, see page R36.)

Quantitative Observations	Qualitative Observations
• mass = 30 g	• Crystals are clear.
• mean crystal length = 0.5 cm	• Crystals are long, thin, and rectangular.
• longest crystal length = 2 cm	• White crust has formed around edge of dish.

> Photographs or sketches are useful for recording qualitative observations.

Epsom salt crystals

MORE ABOUT OBSERVING

- Make quantitative observations whenever possible. That way, others will know exactly what you observed and be able to compare their results with yours.

- It is always a good idea to make qualitative observations too. You never know when you might observe something unexpected.

Predicting and Hypothesizing

A **prediction** is an expectation of what will be observed or what will happen. A **hypothesis** is a tentative explanation for an observation or scientific problem that can be tested by further investigation.

EXAMPLE

Suppose you have made two paper airplanes and you wonder why one of them tends to glide farther than the other one.

1. Start by asking a question.

2. Make an educated guess. After examination, you notice that the wings of the airplane that flies farther are slightly larger than the wings of the other airplane.

3. Write a prediction based upon your educated guess, in the form of an "If . . . , then . . ." statement. Write the independent variable after the word *if*, and the dependent variable after the word *then*.

4. To make a hypothesis, explain why you think what you predicted will occur. Write the explanation after the word *because*.

1. Why does one of the paper airplanes glide farther than the other?

2. The size of an airplane's wings may affect how far the airplane will glide.

3. Prediction: If I make a paper airplane with larger wings, then the airplane will glide farther.

To read about independent and dependent variables, see page R30.

4. Hypothesis: If I make a paper airplane with larger wings, then the airplane will glide farther, because the additional surface area of the wing will produce more lift.

Notice that the part of the hypothesis after *because* adds an explanation of why the airplane will glide farther.

MORE ABOUT HYPOTHESES

- The results of an experiment cannot prove that a hypothesis is correct. Rather, the results either support or do not support the hypothesis.

- Valuable information is gained even when your hypothesis is not supported by your results. For example, it would be an important discovery to find that wing size is not related to how far an airplane glides.

- In science, a hypothesis is supported only after many scientists have conducted many experiments and produced consistent results.

Inferring

An **inference** is a logical conclusion drawn from the available evidence and prior knowledge. Inferences are often made from observations.

EXAMPLE

A student observing a set of acorns noticed something unexpected about one of them. He noticed a white, soft-bodied insect eating its way out of the acorn.

The student recorded these observations.

Observations

- There is a hole in the acorn, about 0.5 cm in diameter, where the insect crawled out.
- There is a second hole, which is about the size of a pinhole, on the other side of the acorn.
- The inside of the acorn is hollow.

Here are some inferences that can be made on the basis of the observations.

Inferences

- The insect formed from the material inside the acorn, grew to its present size, and ate its way out of the acorn.
- The insect crawled through the smaller hole, ate the inside of the acorn, grew to its present size, and ate its way out of the acorn.
- An egg was laid in the acorn through the smaller hole. The egg hatched into a larva that ate the inside of the acorn, grew to its present size, and ate its way out of the acorn.

When you make inferences, be sure to look at all of the evidence available and combine it with what you already know.

MORE ABOUT INFERENCES

Inferences depend both on observations and on the knowledge of the people making the inferences. Ancient people who did not know that organisms are produced only by similar organisms might have made an inference like the first one. A student today might look at the same observations and make the second inference. A third student might have knowledge about this particular insect and know that it is never small enough to fit through the smaller hole, leading her to the third inference.

Identifying Cause and Effect

In a **cause-and-effect relationship,** one event or characteristic is the result of another. Usually an effect follows its cause in time.

SCIENTIFIC THINKING HANDBOOK

There are many examples of cause-and-effect relationships in everyday life.

Cause	Effect
Turn off a light.	Room gets dark.
Drop a glass.	Glass breaks.
Blow a whistle.	Sound is heard.

Scientists must be careful not to infer a cause-and-effect relationship just because one event happens after another event. When one event occurs after another, you cannot infer a cause-and-effect relationship on the basis of that information alone. You also cannot conclude that one event caused another if there are alternative ways to explain the second event. A scientist must demonstrate through experimentation or continued observation that an event was truly caused by another event.

EXAMPLE

Make an Observation

Suppose you have a few plants growing outside. When the weather starts getting colder, you bring one of the plants indoors. You notice that the plant you brought indoors is growing faster than the others are growing. You cannot conclude from your observation that the change in temperature was the cause of the increased plant growth, because there are alternative explanations for the observation. Some possible explanations are given below.

- The humidity indoors caused the plant to grow faster.

- The level of sunlight indoors caused the plant to grow faster.

- The indoor plant's being noticed more often and watered more often than the outdoor plants caused it to grow faster.

- The plant that was brought indoors was healthier than the other plants to begin with.

To determine which of these factors, if any, caused the indoor plant to grow faster than the outdoor plants, you would need to design and conduct an experiment.

See pages R28–R35 for information about designing experiments.

Recognizing Bias

Television, newspapers, and the Internet are full of experts claiming to have scientific evidence to back up their claims. How do you know whether the claims are really backed up by good science?

Bias is a slanted point of view, or personal prejudice. The goal of scientists is to be as objective as possible and to base their findings on facts instead of opinions. However, bias often affects the conclusions of researchers, and it is important to learn to recognize bias.

When scientific results are reported, you should consider the source of the information as well as the information itself. It is important to critically analyze the information that you see and read.

SOURCES OF BIAS

There are several ways in which a report of scientific information may be biased. Here are some questions that you can ask yourself:

1. **Who is sponsoring the research?**

   Sometimes, the results of an investigation are biased because an organization paying for the research is looking for a specific answer. This type of bias can affect how data are gathered and interpreted.

2. **Is the research sample large enough?**

   Sometimes research does not include enough data. The larger the sample size, the more likely that the results are accurate, assuming a truly random sample.

3. **In a survey, who is answering the questions?**

   The results of a survey or poll can be biased. The people taking part in the survey may have been specifically chosen because of how they would answer. They may have the same ideas or lifestyles. A survey or poll should make use of a random sample of people.

4. **Are the people who take part in a survey biased?**

   People who take part in surveys sometimes try to answer the questions the way they think the researcher wants them to answer. Also, in surveys or polls that ask for personal information, people may be unwilling to answer questions truthfully.

SCIENTIFIC BIAS

It is also important to realize that scientists have their own biases because of the types of research they do and because of their scientific viewpoints. Two scientists may look at the same set of data and come to completely different conclusions because of these biases. However, such disagreements are not necessarily bad. In fact, a critical analysis of disagreements is often responsible for moving science forward.

Identifying Faulty Reasoning

Faulty reasoning is wrong or incorrect thinking. It leads to mistakes and to wrong conclusions. Scientists are careful not to draw unreasonable conclusions from experimental data. Without such caution, the results of scientific investigations may be misleading.

EXAMPLE

Scientists try to make generalizations based on their data to explain as much about nature as possible. If only a small sample of data is looked at, however, a conclusion may be faulty. Suppose a scientist has studied the effects of the El Niño and La Niña weather patterns on flood damage in California from 1989 to 1995. The scientist organized the data in the bar graph below.

The scientist drew the following conclusions:

1. The La Niña weather pattern has no effect on flooding in California.
2. When neither weather pattern occurs, there is almost no flood damage.
3. A weak or moderate El Niño produces a small or moderate amount of flooding.
4. A strong El Niño produces a lot of flooding.

Flood and Storm Damage in California

Estimated damage (millions of dollars)

- Weak–moderate El Niño
- Strong El Niño

Starting year of season (July 1–June 30)

SOURCE: *Governor's Office of Emergency Services, California*

For the six-year period of the scientist's investigation, these conclusions may seem to be reasonable. However, a six-year study of weather patterns may be too small of a sample for the conclusions to be supported. Consider the following graph, which shows information that was gathered from 1949 to 1997.

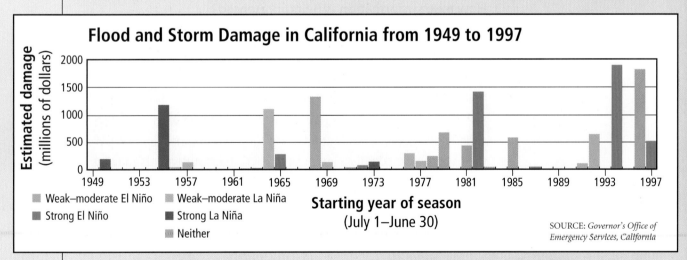

Flood and Storm Damage in California from 1949 to 1997

Estimated damage (millions of dollars)

- Weak–moderate El Niño
- Strong El Niño
- Weak–moderate La Niña
- Strong La Niña
- Neither

Starting year of season (July 1–June 30)

SOURCE: *Governor's Office of Emergency Services, California*

The only one of the conclusions that all of this information supports is number 3: a weak or moderate El Niño produces a small or moderate amount of flooding. By collecting more data, scientists can be more certain of their conclusions and can avoid faulty reasoning.

Analyzing Statements

To **analyze** a statement is to examine its parts carefully. Scientific findings are often reported through media such as television or the Internet. A report that is made public often focuses on only a small part of research. As a result, it is important to question the sources of information.

Evaluate Media Claims

To **evaluate** a statement is to judge it on the basis of criteria you've established. Sometimes evaluating means deciding whether a statement is true.

Reports of scientific research and findings in the media may be misleading or incomplete. When you are exposed to this information, you should ask yourself some questions so that you can make informed judgments about the information.

1. **Does the information come from a credible source?**

   Suppose you learn about a new product and it is stated that scientific evidence proves that the product works. A report from a respected news source may be more believable than an advertisement paid for by the product's manufacturer.

2. **How much evidence supports the claim?**

   Often, it may seem that there is new evidence every day of something in the world that either causes or cures an illness. However, information that is the result of several years of work by several different scientists is more credible than an advertisement that does not even cite the subjects of the experiment.

3. **How much information is being presented?**

   Science cannot solve all questions, and scientific experiments often have flaws. A report that discusses problems in a scientific study may be more believable than a report that addresses only positive experimental findings.

4. **Is scientific evidence being presented by a specific source?**

   Sometimes scientific findings are reported by people who are called experts or leaders in a scientific field. But if their names are not given or their scientific credentials are not reported, their statements may be less credible than those of recognized experts.

Differentiate Between Fact and Opinion

Sometimes information is presented as a fact when it may be an opinion. When scientific conclusions are reported, it is important to recognize whether they are based on solid evidence. Again, you may find it helpful to ask yourself some questions.

1. **What is the difference between a fact and an opinion?**

   A **fact** is a piece of information that can be strictly defined and proved true. An **opinion** is a statement that expresses a belief, value, or feeling. An opinion cannot be proved true or false. For example, a person's age is a fact, but if someone is asked how old they feel, it is impossible to prove the person's answer to be true or false.

2. **Can opinions be measured?**

   Yes, opinions can be measured. In fact, surveys often ask for people's opinions on a topic. But there is no way to know whether or not an opinion is the truth.

HOW TO DIFFERENTIATE FACT FROM OPINION

Human Activities and the Environment

Opinions

Notice words or phrases that express beliefs or feelings. The words *unfortunately* and *careless* show that opinions are being expressed.

Unfortunately, human use of fossil fuels is one of the most significant developments of the past few centuries. Humans rely on fossil fuels, a non-renewable energy resource, for more than 90 percent of their energy needs.

This careless misuse of our planet's resources has resulted in pollution, global warming, and the destruction of fragile ecosystems. For example, oil pipelines carry more than one million barrels of oil each day across tundra regions. Transporting oil across such areas can only result in oil spills that poison the land for decades.

Facts

Statements that contain statistics tend to be facts. Writers often use facts to support their opinions.

Opinion

Look for statements that speculate about events. These statements are opinions, because they cannot be proved.

Lab Handbook

Safety Rules

Before you work in the laboratory, read these safety rules twice. Ask your teacher to explain any rules that you do not completely understand. Refer to these rules later on if you have questions about safety in the science classroom.

Directions

- Read all directions and make sure that you understand them before starting an investigation or lab activity. If you do not understand how to do a procedure or how to use a piece of equipment, ask your teacher.
- Do not begin any investigation or touch any equipment until your teacher has told you to start.
- Never experiment on your own. If you want to try a procedure that the directions do not call for, ask your teacher for permission first.
- If you are hurt or injured in any way, tell your teacher immediately.

Dress Code

goggles

apron

gloves

- Wear goggles when
  — using glassware, sharp objects, or chemicals
  — heating an object
  — working with anything that can easily fly up into the air and hurt someone's eye
- Tie back long hair or hair that hangs in front of your eyes.
- Remove any article of clothing—such as a loose sweater or a scarf—that hangs down and may touch a flame, chemical, or piece of equipment.
- Observe all safety icons calling for the wearing of eye protection, gloves, and aprons.

Heating and Fire Safety

fire safety

heating safety

- Keep your work area neat, clean, and free of extra materials.
- Never reach over a flame or heat source.
- Point objects being heated away from you and others.
- Never heat a substance or an object in a closed container.
- Never touch an object that has been heated. If you are unsure whether something is hot, treat it as though it is. Use oven mitts, clamps, tongs, or a test-tube holder.
- Know where the fire extinguisher and fire blanket are kept in your classroom.
- Do not throw hot substances into the trash. Wait for them to cool or use the container your teacher puts out for disposal.

Electrical Safety

electrical safety

- Never use lamps or other electrical equipment with frayed cords.
- Make sure no cord is lying on the floor where someone can trip over it.
- Do not let a cord hang over the side of a counter or table so that the equipment can easily be pulled or knocked to the floor.
- Never let cords hang into sinks or other places where water can be found.
- Never try to fix electrical problems. Inform your teacher of any problems immediately.
- Unplug an electrical cord by pulling on the plug, not the cord.

Chemical Safety

chemical safety

poison

fumes

- If you spill a chemical or get one on your skin or in your eyes, tell your teacher right away.
- Never touch, taste, or sniff any chemicals in the lab. If you need to determine odor, waft. Wafting consists of holding the chemical in its container 15 centimeters (6 in.) away from your nose, and using your fingers to bring fumes from the container to your nose.
- Keep lids on all chemicals you are not using.
- Never put unused chemicals back into the original containers. Throw away extra chemicals where your teacher tells you to.
- Pour chemicals over a sink or your work area, not over the floor.
- If you get a chemical in your eye, use the eyewash right away.
- Always wash your hands after handling chemicals, plants, or soil.

Wafting

Glassware and Sharp-Object Safety

sharp objects

- If you break glassware, tell your teacher right away.
- Do not use broken or chipped glassware. Give these to your teacher.
- Use knives and other cutting instruments carefully. Always wear eye protection and cut away from you.

Animal Safety

- Never hurt an animal.
- Touch animals only when necessary. Follow your teacher's instructions for handling animals.
- Always wash your hands after working with animals.

Cleanup

disposal

- Follow your teacher's instructions for throwing away or putting away supplies.
- Clean your work area and pick up anything that has dropped to the floor.
- Wash your hands.

Using Lab Equipment

Different experiments require different types of equipment. But even though experiments differ, the ways in which the equipment is used are the same.

Beakers

- Use beakers for holding and pouring liquids.
- Do not use a beaker to measure the volume of a liquid. Use a graduated cylinder instead. (See page R16.)
- Use a beaker that holds about twice as much liquid as you need. For example, if you need 100 milliliters of water, you should use a 200- or 250-milliliter beaker.

Test Tubes

- Use test tubes to hold small amounts of substances.
- Do not use a test tube to measure the volume of a liquid.
- Use a test tube when heating a substance over a flame. Aim the mouth of the tube away from yourself and other people.
- Liquids easily spill or splash from test tubes, so it is important to use only small amounts of liquids.

Test-Tube Holder

- Use a test-tube holder when heating a substance in a test tube.
- Use a test-tube holder if the substance in a test tube is dangerous to touch.
- Make sure the test-tube holder tightly grips the test tube so that the test tube will not slide out of the holder.
- Make sure that the test-tube holder is above the surface of the substance in the test tube so that you can observe the substance.

Test-Tube Rack

- Use a test-tube rack to organize test tubes before, during, and after an experiment.

- Use a test-tube rack to keep test tubes upright so that they do not fall over and spill their contents.

- Use a test-tube rack that is the correct size for the test tubes that you are using. If the rack is too small, a test tube may become stuck. If the rack is too large, a test tube may lean over, and some of its contents may spill or splash.

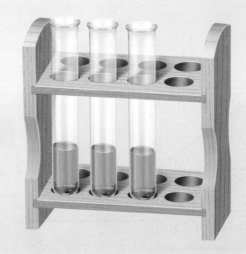

Forceps

- Use forceps when you need to pick up or hold a very small object that should not be touched with your hands.

- Do not use forceps to hold anything over a flame, because forceps are not long enough to keep your hand safely away from the flame. Plastic forceps will melt, and metal forceps will conduct heat and burn your hand.

Hot Plate

- Use a hot plate when a substance needs to be kept warmer than room temperature for a long period of time.

- Use a hot plate instead of a Bunsen burner or a candle when you need to carefully control temperature.

- Do not use a hot plate when a substance needs to be burned in an experiment.

- Always use "hot hands" safety mitts or oven mitts when handling anything that has been heated on a hot plate.

Microscope

Scientists use microscopes to see very small objects that cannot easily be seen with the eye alone. A microscope magnifies the image of an object so that small details may be observed. A microscope that you may use can magnify an object 400 times—the object will appear 400 times larger than its actual size.

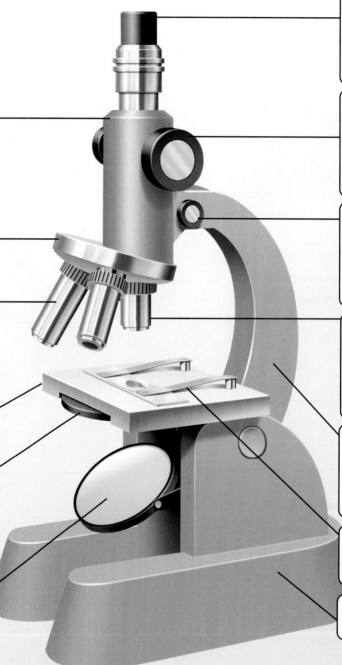

Body The body separates the lens in the eyepiece from the objective lenses below.

Nosepiece The nosepiece holds the objective lenses above the stage and rotates so that all lenses may be used.

High-Power Objective Lens This is the largest lens on the nosepiece. It magnifies an image approximately 40 times.

Stage The stage supports the object being viewed.

Diaphragm The diaphragm is used to adjust the amount of light passing through the slide and into an objective lens.

Mirror or Light Source Some microscopes use light that is reflected through the stage by a mirror. Other microscopes have their own light sources.

Eyepiece Objects are viewed through the eyepiece. The eyepiece contains a lens that commonly magnifies an image 10 times.

Coarse Adjustment This knob is used to focus the image of an object when it is viewed through the low-power lens.

Fine Adjustment This knob is used to focus the image of an object when it is viewed through the high-power lens.

Low-Power Objective Lens This is the smallest lens on the nosepiece. It magnifies an image approximately 10 times.

Arm The arm supports the body above the stage. Always carry a microscope by the arm and base.

Stage Clip The stage clip holds a slide in place on the stage.

Base The base supports the microscope.

VIEWING AN OBJECT

1. Use the coarse adjustment knob to raise the body tube.

2. Adjust the diaphragm so that you can see a bright circle of light through the eyepiece.

3. Place the object or slide on the stage. Be sure that it is centered over the hole in the stage.

4. Turn the nosepiece to click the low-power lens into place.

5. Using the coarse adjustment knob, slowly lower the lens and focus on the specimen being viewed. Be sure not to touch the slide or object with the lens.

6. When switching from the low-power lens to the high-power lens, first raise the body tube with the coarse adjustment knob so that the high-power lens will not hit the slide.

7. Turn the nosepiece to click the high-power lens into place.

8. Use the fine adjustment knob to focus on the specimen being viewed. Again, be sure not to touch the slide or object with the lens.

MAKING A SLIDE, OR WET MOUNT

1 Place the specimen in the center of a clean slide.

2 Place a drop of water on the specimen.

3 Place a cover slip on the slide. Put one edge of the cover slip into the drop of water and slowly lower it over the specimen.

4 Remove any air bubbles from under the cover slip by gently tapping the cover slip.

5 Dry any excess water before placing the slide on the microscope stage for viewing.

Spring Scale (Force Meter)

- Use a spring scale to measure a force pulling on the scale.

- Use a spring scale to measure the force of gravity exerted on an object by Earth.

- To measure a force accurately, a spring scale must be zeroed before it is used. The scale is zeroed when no weight is attached and the indicator is positioned at zero.

- Do not attach a weight that is either too heavy or too light to a spring scale. A weight that is too heavy could break the scale or exert too great a force for the scale to measure. A weight that is too light may not exert enough force to be measured accurately.

Graduated Cylinder

- Use a graduated cylinder to measure the volume of a liquid.

- Be sure that the graduated cylinder is on a flat surface so that your measurement will be accurate.

- When reading the scale on a graduated cylinder, be sure to have your eyes at the level of the surface of the liquid.

- The surface of the liquid will be curved in the graduated cylinder. Read the volume of the liquid at the bottom of the curve, or meniscus (muh-NIHS-kuhs).

- You can use a graduated cylinder to find the volume of a solid object by measuring the increase in a liquid's level after you add the object to the cylinder.

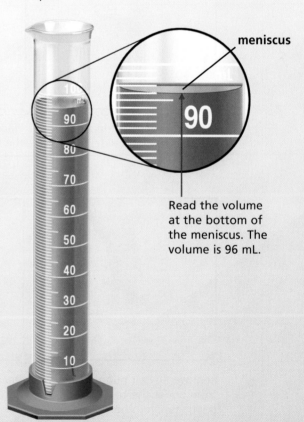

meniscus

Read the volume at the bottom of the meniscus. The volume is 96 mL.

Metric Rulers

- Use metric rulers or meter sticks to measure objects' lengths.

- Do not measure an object from the end of a metric ruler or meter stick, because the end is often imperfect. Instead, measure from the 1-centimeter mark, but remember to subtract a centimeter from the apparent measurement.

- Estimate any lengths that extend between marked units. For example, if a meter stick shows centimeters but not millimeters, you can estimate the length that an object extends between centimeter marks to measure it to the nearest millimeter.

- **Controlling Variables** If you are taking repeated measurements, always measure from the same point each time. For example, if you're measuring how high two different balls bounce when dropped from the same height, measure both bounces at the same point on the balls—either the top or the bottom. Do not measure at the top of one ball and the bottom of the other.

EXAMPLE

How to Measure a Leaf

1. Lay a ruler flat on top of the leaf so that the 1-centimeter mark lines up with one end. Make sure the ruler and the leaf do not move between the time you line them up and the time you take the measurement.

2. Look straight down on the ruler so that you can see exactly how the marks line up with the other end of the leaf.

3. Estimate the length by which the leaf extends beyond a marking. For example, the leaf below extends about halfway between the 4.2-centimeter and 4.3-centimeter marks, so the apparent measurement is about 4.25 centimeters.

4. Remember to subtract 1 centimeter from your apparent measurement, since you started at the 1-centimeter mark on the ruler and not at the end. The leaf is about 3.25 centimeters long (4.25 cm – 1 cm = 3.25 cm).

Triple-Beam Balance

This balance has a pan and three beams with sliding masses, called riders. At one end of the beams is a pointer that indicates whether the mass on the pan is equal to the masses shown on the beams.

1. Make sure the balance is zeroed before measuring the mass of an object. The balance is zeroed if the pointer is at zero when nothing is on the pan and the riders are at their zero points. Use the adjustment knob at the base of the balance to zero it.

2. Place the object to be measured on the pan.

3. Move the riders one notch at a time away from the pan. Begin with the largest rider. If moving the largest rider one notch brings the pointer below zero, begin measuring the mass of the object with the next smaller rider.

4. Change the positions of the riders until they balance the mass on the pan and the pointer is at zero. Then add the readings from the three beams to determine the mass of the object.

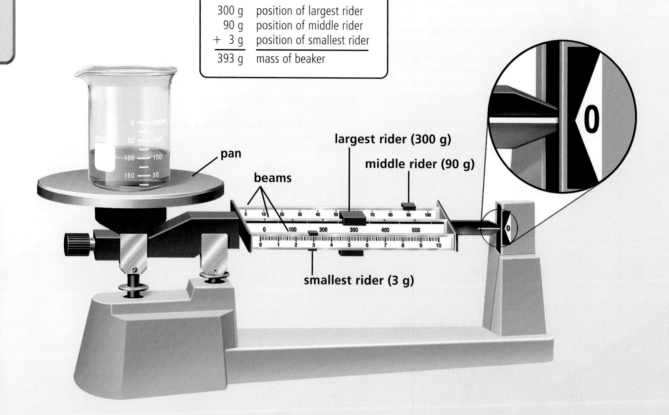

300 g	position of largest rider
90 g	position of middle rider
+ 3 g	position of smallest rider
393 g	mass of beaker

pan

beams

largest rider (300 g)

middle rider (90 g)

smallest rider (3 g)

Double-Pan Balance

This type of balance has two pans. Between the pans is a pointer that indicates whether the masses on the pans are equal.

1. Make sure the balance is zeroed before measuring the mass of an object. The balance is zeroed if the pointer is at zero when there is nothing on either of the pans. Many double-pan balances have sliding knobs that can be used to zero them.

2. Place the object to be measured on one of the pans.

3. Begin adding standard masses to the other pan. Begin with the largest standard mass. If this adds too much mass to the balance, begin measuring the mass of the object with the next smaller standard mass.

4. Add standard masses until the masses on both pans are balanced and the pointer is at zero. Then add the standard masses together to determine the mass of the object being measured.

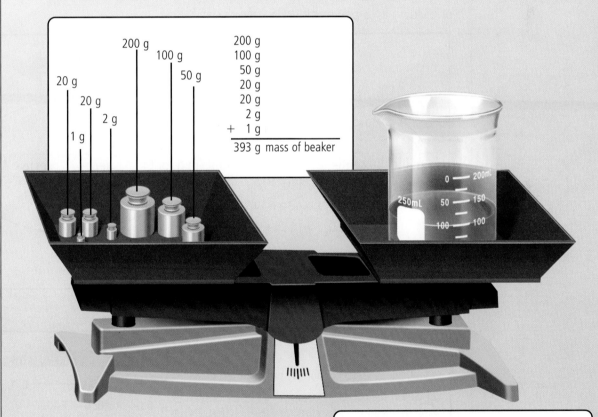

	200 g
	100 g
	50 g
	20 g
	20 g
	2 g
+	1 g
393 g	mass of beaker

Never place chemicals or liquids directly on a pan. Instead, use the following procedure:

❶ Determine the mass of an empty container, such as a beaker.

❷ Pour the substance into the container, and measure the total mass of the substance and the container.

❸ Subtract the mass of the empty container from the total mass to find the mass of the substance.

The Metric System and SI Units

Scientists use International System (SI) units for measurements of distance, volume, mass, and temperature. The International System is based on multiples of ten and the metric system of measurement.

Basic SI Units		
Property	**Name**	**Symbol**
length	meter	m
volume	liter	L
mass	kilogram	kg
temperature	kelvin	K

SI Prefixes		
Prefix	**Symbol**	**Multiple of 10**
kilo-	k	1000
hecto-	h	100
deca-	da	10
deci-	d	$0.1 \left(\frac{1}{10}\right)$
centi-	c	$0.01 \left(\frac{1}{100}\right)$
milli-	m	$0.001 \left(\frac{1}{1000}\right)$

Changing Metric Units

You can change from one unit to another in the metric system by multiplying or dividing by a power of 10.

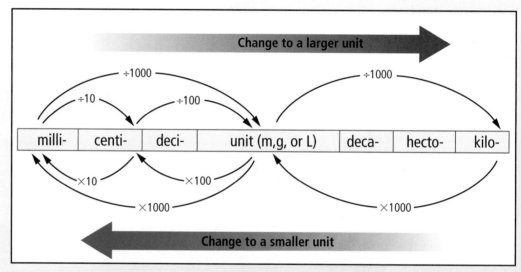

Example

Change 0.64 liters to milliliters.

(1) Decide whether to multiply or divide.

(2) Select the power of 10.

ANSWER 0.64 L = 640 mL

Change to a smaller unit by multiplying.

mL ◄——— × 1000 ——— L

0.64 × 1000 = 640.

Example

Change 23.6 grams to kilograms.

(1) Decide whether to multiply or divide.

(2) Select the power of 10.

ANSWER 23.6 g = 0.0236 kg

Change to a larger unit by dividing.

g ——— ÷ 1000 ——► kg

23.6 ÷ 1000 = 0.0236

Temperature Conversions

Even though the kelvin is the SI base unit of temperature, the degree Celsius will be the unit you use most often in your science studies. The formulas below show the relationships between temperatures in degrees Fahrenheit (°F), degrees Celsius (°C), and kelvins (K).

$$°C = \frac{5}{9} (°F - 32)$$

$$°F = \frac{9}{5} °C + 32$$

$$K = °C + 273$$

See page R42 for help with using formulas.

Examples of Temperature Conversions		
Condition	**Degrees Celsius**	**Degrees Fahrenheit**
Freezing point of water	0	32
Cool day	10	50
Mild day	20	68
Warm day	30	86
Normal body temperature	37	98.6
Very hot day	40	104
Boiling point of water	100	212

Converting Between SI and U.S. Customary Units

Use the chart below when you need to convert between SI units and U.S. customary units.

SI Unit	From SI to U.S. Customary			From U.S. Customary to SI		
Length	**When you know**	**multiply by**	**to find**	**When you know**	**multiply by**	**to find**
kilometer (km) = 1000 m	kilometers	0.62	miles	miles	1.61	kilometers
meter (m) = 100 cm	meters	3.28	feet	feet	0.3048	meters
centimeter (cm) = 10 mm	centimeters	0.39	inches	inches	2.54	centimeters
millimeter (mm) = 0.1 cm	millimeters	0.04	inches	inches	25.4	millimeters
Area	**When you know**	**multiply by**	**to find**	**When you know**	**multiply by**	**to find**
square kilometer (km²)	square kilometers	0.39	square miles	square miles	2.59	square kilometers
square meter (m²)	square meters	1.2	square yards	square yards	0.84	square meters
square centimeter (cm²)	square centimeters	0.155	square inches	square inches	6.45	square centimeters
Volume	**When you know**	**multiply by**	**to find**	**When you know**	**multiply by**	**to find**
liter (L) = 1000 mL	liters	1.06	quarts	quarts	0.95	liters
	liters	0.26	gallons	gallons	3.79	liters
	liters	4.23	cups	cups	0.24	liters
	liters	2.12	pints	pints	0.47	liters
milliliter (mL) = 0.001 L	milliliters	0.20	teaspoons	teaspoons	4.93	milliliters
	milliliters	0.07	tablespoons	tablespoons	14.79	milliliters
	milliliters	0.03	fluid ounces	fluid ounces	29.57	milliliters
Mass	**When you know**	**multiply by**	**to find**	**When you know**	**multiply by**	**to find**
kilogram (kg) = 1000 g	kilograms	2.2	pounds	pounds	0.45	kilograms
gram (g) = 1000 mg	grams	0.035	ounces	ounces	28.35	grams

Precision and Accuracy

When you do an experiment, it is important that your methods, observations, and data be both precise and accurate.

low precision

precision, but not accuracy

precision and accuracy

Precision

In science, **precision** is the exactness and consistency of measurements. For example, measurements made with a ruler that has both centimeter and millimeter markings would be more precise than measurements made with a ruler that has only centimeter markings. Another indicator of precision is the care taken to make sure that methods and observations are as exact and consistent as possible. Every time a particular experiment is done, the same procedure should be used. Precision is necessary because experiments are repeated several times and if the procedure changes, the results will change.

EXAMPLE

Suppose you are measuring temperatures over a two-week period. Your precision will be greater if you measure each temperature at the same place, at the same time of day, and with the same thermometer than if you change any of these factors from one day to the next.

Accuracy

In science, it is possible to be precise but not accurate. **Accuracy** depends on the difference between a measurement and an actual value. The smaller the difference, the more accurate the measurement.

EXAMPLE

Suppose you look at a stream and estimate that it is about 1 meter wide at a particular place. You decide to check your estimate by measuring the stream with a meter stick, and you determine that the stream is 1.32 meters wide. However, because it is hard to measure the width of a stream with a meter stick, it turns out that you didn't do a very good job. The stream is actually 1.14 meters wide. Therefore, even though your estimate was less precise than your measurement, your estimate was actually more accurate.

Making Data Tables and Graphs

Data tables and graphs are useful tools for both recording and communicating scientific data.

Making Data Tables

You can use a **data table** to organize and record the measurements that you make. Some examples of information that might be recorded in data tables are frequencies, times, and amounts.

EXAMPLE

Suppose you are investigating photosynthesis in two elodea plants. One sits in direct sunlight, and the other sits in a dimly lit room. You measure the rate of photosynthesis by counting the number of bubbles in the jar every ten minutes.

1. Title and number your data table.

2. Decide how you will organize the table into columns and rows.

3. Any units, such as seconds or degrees, should be included in column headings, not in the individual cells.

Table 1. Number of Bubbles from Elodea

Time (min)	Sunlight	Dim Light
0	0	0
10	15	5
20	25	8
30	32	7
40	41	10
50	47	9
60	42	9

Always number and title data tables.

The data in the table above could also be organized in a different way.

Table 1. Number of Bubbles from Elodea

Light Condition	Time (min)						
	0	10	20	30	40	50	60
Sunlight	0	15	25	32	41	47	42
Dim light	0	5	8	7	10	9	9

Put units in column heading.

Making Line Graphs

You can use a **line graph** to show a relationship between variables. Line graphs are particularly useful for showing changes in variables over time.

EXAMPLE

Suppose you are interested in graphing temperature data that you collected over the course of a day.

Table 1. Outside Temperature During the Day on March 7

	Time of Day						
	7:00 A.M.	9:00 A.M.	11:00 A.M.	1:00 P.M.	3:00 P.M.	5:00 P.M.	7:00 P.M.
Temp (°C)	8	9	11	14	12	10	6

1. Use the vertical axis of your line graph for the variable that you are measuring—temperature.

2. Choose scales for both the horizontal axis and the vertical axis of the graph. You should have two points more than you need on the vertical axis, and the horizontal axis should be long enough for all of the data points to fit.

3. Draw and label each axis.

4. Graph each value. First find the appropriate point on the scale of the horizontal axis. Imagine a line that rises vertically from that place on the scale. Then find the corresponding value on the vertical axis, and imagine a line that moves horizontally from that value. The point where these two imaginary lines intersect is where the value should be plotted.

5. Connect the points with straight lines.

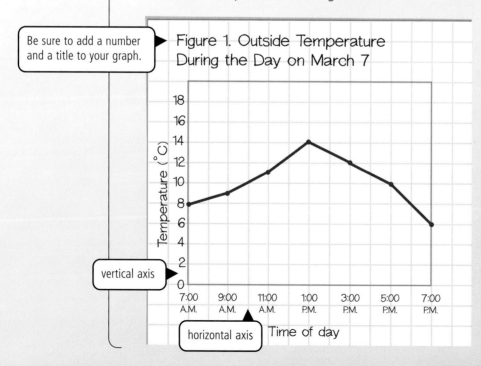

Be sure to add a number and a title to your graph. ▶

Figure 1. Outside Temperature During the Day on March 7

vertical axis ▶

horizontal axis

Making Circle Graphs

You can use a **circle graph,** sometimes called a pie chart, to represent data as parts of a circle. Circle graphs are used only when the data can be expressed as percentages of a whole. The entire circle shown in a circle graph is equal to 100 percent of the data.

EXAMPLE

Suppose you identified the species of each mature tree growing in a small wooded area. You organized your data in a table, but you also want to show the data in a circle graph.

1. To begin, find the total number of mature trees.

    56 + 34 + 22 + 10 + 28 = 150

2. To find the degree measure for each sector of the circle, write a fraction comparing the number of each tree species with the total number of trees. Then multiply the fraction by 360°.

    Oak: $\frac{56}{150} \times 360° = 134.4°$

3. Draw a circle. Use a protractor to draw the angle for each sector of the graph.

4. Color and label each sector of the graph.

5. Give the graph a number and title.

Table 1. Tree Species in Wooded Area

Species	Number of Specimens
Oak	56
Maple	34
Birch	22
Willow	10
Pine	28

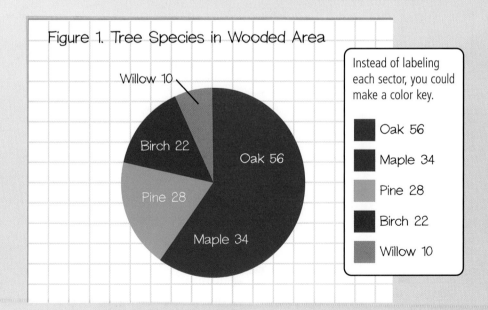

Figure 1. Tree Species in Wooded Area

Instead of labeling each sector, you could make a color key.

- Oak 56
- Maple 34
- Pine 28
- Birch 22
- Willow 10

Bar Graph

A **bar graph** is a type of graph in which the lengths of the bars are used to represent and compare data. A numerical scale is used to determine the lengths of the bars.

EXAMPLE

To determine the effect of water on seed sprouting, three cups were filled with sand, and ten seeds were planted in each. Different amounts of water were added to each cup over a three-day period.

Table 1. Effect of Water on Seed Sprouting

Daily Amount of Water (mL)	Number of Seeds That Sprouted After 3 Days in Sand
0	1
10	4
20	8

1. Choose a numerical scale. The greatest value is 8, so the end of the scale should have a value greater than 8, such as 10. Use equal increments along the scale, such as increments of 2.

2. Draw and label the axes. Mark intervals on the vertical axis according to the scale you chose.

3. Draw a bar for each data value. Use the scale to decide how long to make each bar.

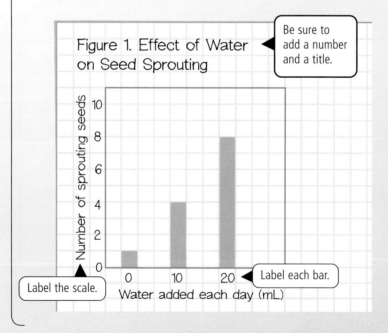

Figure 1. Effect of Water on Seed Sprouting

Be sure to add a number and a title.

Number of sprouting seeds

Water added each day (mL)

Label the scale.

Label each bar.

LAB HANDBOOK

Double Bar Graph

A **double bar graph** is a bar graph that shows two sets of data. The two bars for each measurement are drawn next to each other.

EXAMPLE

The seed-sprouting experiment was done using both sand and potting soil. The data for sand and potting soil can be plotted on one graph.

1. Draw one set of bars, using the data for sand, as shown below.
2. Draw bars for the potting-soil data next to the bars for the sand data. Shade them a different color. Add a key.

Table 2. Effect of Water and Soil on Seed Sprouting

Daily Amount of Water (mL)	Number of Seeds That Sprouted After 3 Days in Sand	Number of Seeds That Sprouted After 3 Days in Potting Soil
0	1	2
10	4	5
20	8	9

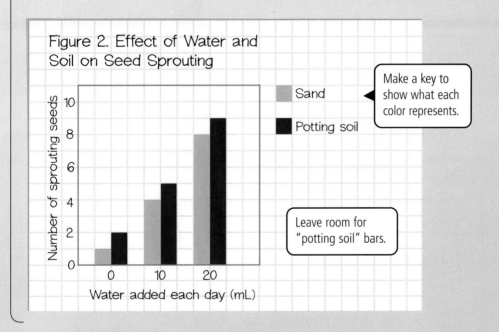

Figure 2. Effect of Water and Soil on Seed Sprouting

Make a key to show what each color represents.

Leave room for "potting soil" bars.

Designing an Experiment

Use this section when designing or conducting an experiment.

Determining a Purpose

You can find a purpose for an experiment by doing research, by examining the results of a previous experiment, or by observing the world around you. An **experiment** is an organized procedure to study something under controlled conditions.

1. Write the purpose of your experiment as a question or problem that you want to investigate.

2. Write down research questions and begin searching for information that will help you design an experiment. Consult the library, the Internet, and other people as you conduct your research.

> Don't forget to learn as much as possible about your topic before you begin.

LAB HANDBOOK

EXAMPLE

Middle school students observed an odor near the lake by their school. They also noticed that the water on the side of the lake near the school was greener than the water on the other side of the lake. The students did some research to learn more about their observations. They discovered that the odor and green color in the lake came from algae. They also discovered that a new fertilizer was being used on a field nearby. The students inferred that the use of the fertilizer might be related to the presence of the algae and designed a controlled experiment to find out whether they were right.

Problem

How does fertilizer affect the presence of algae in a lake?

Research Questions

• Have other experiments been done on this problem? If so, what did those experiments show?

• What kind of fertilizer is used on the field? How much?

• How do algae grow?

• How do people measure algae?

• Can fertilizer and algae be used safely in a lab? How?

> **Research**
> As you research, you may find a topic that is more interesting to you than your original topic, or learn that a procedure you wanted to use is not practical or safe. It is OK to change your purpose as you research.

Writing a Hypothesis

A **hypothesis** is a tentative explanation for an observation or scientific problem that can be tested by further investigation. You can write your hypothesis in the form of an "If . . . , then . . . , because . . ." statement.

Hypothesis

If the amount of fertilizer in lake water is increased, then the amount of algae will also increase, because fertilizers provide nutrients that algae need to grow.

Hypotheses
For help with hypotheses, refer to page R3.

Determining Materials

Make a list of all the materials you will need to do your experiment. Be specific, especially if someone else is helping you obtain the materials. Try to think of everything you will need.

Materials

- 1 large jar or container
- 4 identical smaller containers
- rubber gloves that also cover the arms
- sample of fertilizer-and-water solution
- eyedropper
- clear plastic wrap
- scissors
- masking tape
- marker
- ruler

Determining Variables and Constants

EXPERIMENTAL GROUP AND CONTROL GROUP

An experiment to determine how two factors are related always has two groups—a control group and an experimental group.

1. Design an experimental group. Include as many trials as possible in the experimental group in order to obtain reliable results.

2. Design a control group that is the same as the experimental group in every way possible, except for the factor you wish to test.

Experimental Group: two containers of lake water with one drop of fertilizer solution added to each

Control Group: two containers of lake water with no fertilizer solution added

> Go back to your materials list and make sure you have enough items listed to cover both your experimental group and your control group.

VARIABLES AND CONSTANTS

Identify the variables and constants in your experiment. In a controlled experiment, a **variable** is any factor that can change. **Constants** are all of the factors that are the same in both the experimental group and the control group.

> **Hypothesis**
> If the amount of fertilizer in lake water is increased, then the amount of algae will also increase, because fertilizers provide nutrients that algae need to grow.

1. Read your hypothesis. The **independent variable** is the factor that you wish to test and that is manipulated or changed so that it can be tested. The independent variable is expressed in your hypothesis after the word *if*. Identify the independent variable in your laboratory report.

2. The **dependent variable** is the factor that you measure to gather results. It is expressed in your hypothesis after the word *then*. Identify the dependent variable in your laboratory report.

Table 1. Variables and Constants in Algae Experiment

Independent Variable	Dependent Variable	Constants
Amount of fertilizer in lake water	Amount of algae that grow	• Where the lake water is obtained • Type of container used • Light and temperature conditions where water will be stored

> Set up your experiment so that you will test only one variable.

MEASURING THE DEPENDENT VARIABLE

Before starting your experiment, you need to define how you will measure the dependent variable. An **operational definition** is a description of the one particular way in which you will measure the dependent variable.

Your operational definition is important for several reasons. First, in any experiment there are several ways in which a dependent variable can be measured. Second, the procedure of the experiment depends on how you decide to measure the dependent variable. Third, your operational definition makes it possible for other people to evaluate and build on your experiment.

EXAMPLE 1

An operational definition of a dependent variable can be qualitative. That is, your measurement of the dependent variable can simply be an observation of whether a change occurs as a result of a change in the independent variable. This type of operational definition can be thought of as a "yes or no" measurement.

Table 2. Qualitative Operational Definition of Algae Growth

Independent Variable	Dependent Variable	Operational Definition
Amount of fertilizer in lake water	Amount of algae that grow	Algae grow in lake water

A qualitative measurement of a dependent variable is often easy to make and record. However, this type of information does not provide a great deal of detail in your experimental results.

EXAMPLE 2

An operational definition of a dependent variable can be quantitative. That is, your measurement of the dependent variable can be a number that shows how much change occurs as a result of a change in the independent variable.

Table 3. Quantitative Operational Definition of Algae Growth

Independent Variable	Dependent Variable	Operational Definition
Amount of fertilizer in lake water	Amount of algae that grow	Diameter of largest algal growth (in mm)

A quantitative measurement of a dependent variable can be more difficult to make and analyze than a qualitative measurement. However, this type of data provides much more information about your experiment and is often more useful.

Writing a Procedure

Write each step of your procedure. Start each step with a verb, or action word, and keep the steps short. Your procedure should be clear enough for someone else to use as instructions for repeating your experiment.

> If necessary, go back to your materials list and add any materials that you left out.

Procedure

1. Put on your gloves. Use the large container to obtain a sample of lake water.

2. Divide the sample of lake water equally among the four smaller containers.

> **Controlling Variables**
> The same amount of fertilizer solution must be added to two of the four containers.

3. Use the eyedropper to add one drop of fertilizer solution to two of the containers.

4. Use the masking tape and the marker to label the containers with your initials, the date, and the identifiers "Jar 1 with Fertilizer," "Jar 2 with Fertilizer," "Jar 1 without Fertilizer," and "Jar 2 without Fertilizer."

5. Cover the containers with clear plastic wrap. Use the scissors to punch ten holes in each of the covers.

> **Controlling Variables**
> All four containers must receive the same amount of light.

6. Place all four containers on a window ledge. Make sure that they all receive the same amount of light.

7. Observe the containers every day for one week.

8. Use the ruler to measure the diameter of the largest clump of algae in each container, and record your measurements daily.

Recording Observations

Once you have obtained all of your materials and your procedure has been approved, you can begin making experimental observations. Gather both quantitative and qualitative data. If something goes wrong during your procedure, make sure you record that too.

Observations
For help with making qualitative and quantitative observations, refer to page R2.

For more examples of data tables, see page R23.

Table 4. Fertilizer and Algae Growth

Date and Time	Experimental Group		Control Group		
	Jar 1 with Fertilizer (diameter of algae in mm)	Jar 2 with Fertilizer (diameter of algae in mm)	Jar 1 without Fertilizer (diameter of algae in mm)	Jar 2 without Fertilizer (diameter of algae in mm)	Observations
5/3 4:00 P.M.	0	0	0	0	condensation in all containers
5/4 4:00 P.M.	0	3	0	0	tiny green blobs in jar 2 with fertilizer
5/5 4:15 P.M.	4	5	0	3	green blobs in jars 1 and 2 with fertilizer and jar 2 without fertilizer
5/6 4:00 P.M.	5	6	0	4	water light green in jar 2 with fertilizer
5/7 4:00 P.M.	8	10	0	6	water light green in jars 1 and 2 with fertilizer and in jar 2 without fertilizer
5/8 3:30 P.M.	10	18	0	6	cover off jar 2 with fertilizer
5/9 3:30 P.M.	14	23	0	8	drew sketches of each container

Notice that on the sixth day, the observer found that the cover was off one of the containers. It is important to record observations of unintended factors because they might affect the results of the experiment.

Use technology, such as a microscope, to help you make observations when possible.

Drawings of Samples Viewed Under Microscope on 5/9 at 100x

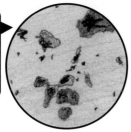

Jar 1 with Fertilizer

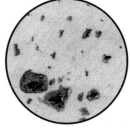

Jar 2 with Fertilizer

Jar 1 without Fertilizer

Jar 2 without Fertilizer

Summarizing Results

To summarize your data, look at all of your observations together. Look for meaningful ways to present your observations. For example, you might average your data or make a graph to look for patterns. When possible, use spreadsheet software to help you analyze and present your data. The two graphs below show the same data.

EXAMPLE 1

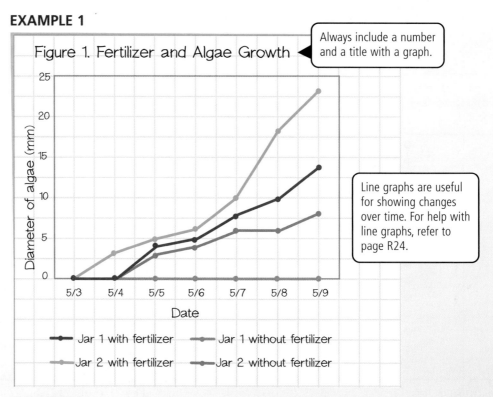

Always include a number and a title with a graph.

Line graphs are useful for showing changes over time. For help with line graphs, refer to page R24.

EXAMPLE 2

Bar graphs are useful for comparing different data sets. This bar graph has four bars for each day. Another way to present the data would be to calculate averages for the tests and the controls, and to show one test bar and one control bar for each day.

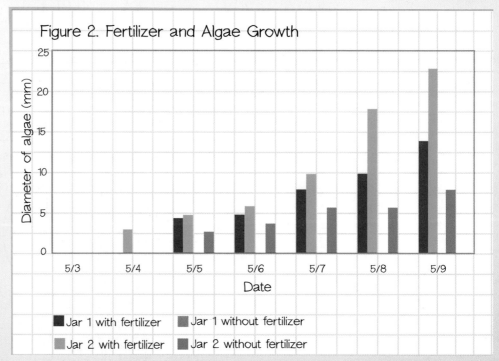

Drawing Conclusions

RESULTS AND INFERENCES

To draw conclusions from your experiment, first write your results. Then compare your results with your hypothesis. Do your results support your hypothesis? Be careful not to make inferences about factors that you did not test.

> For help with making inferences, see page R4.

Results and Inferences

The results of my experiment show that more algae grew in lake water to which fertilizer had been added than in lake water to which no fertilizer had been added. My hypothesis was supported. I infer that it is possible that the growth of algae in the lake was caused by the fertilizer used on the field.

> Notice that you cannot conclude from this experiment that the presence of algae in the lake was due only to the fertilizer.

QUESTIONS FOR FURTHER RESEARCH

Write a list of questions for further research and investigation. Your ideas may lead you to new experiments and discoveries.

Questions for Further Research

- What is the connection between the amount of fertilizer and algae growth?
- How do different brands of fertilizer affect algae growth?
- How would algae growth in the lake be affected if no fertilizer were used on the field?
- How do algae affect the lake and the other life in and around it?
- How does fertilizer affect the lake and the life in and around it?
- If fertilizer is getting into the lake, how is it getting there?

Math Handbook

Describing a Set of Data

Means, medians, modes, and ranges are important math tools for describing data sets such as the following widths of fossilized clamshells.

13 mm   25 mm   14 mm   21 mm   16 mm   23 mm   14 mm

Mean

The **mean** of a data set is the sum of the values divided by the number of values.

> **Example**
>
> To find the mean of the clamshell data, add the values and then divide the sum by the number of values.
>
> $$\frac{13\text{ mm} + 25\text{ mm} + 14\text{ mm} + 21\text{ mm} + 16\text{ mm} + 23\text{ mm} + 14\text{ mm}}{7} = \frac{126\text{ mm}}{7} = 18\text{ mm}$$
>
> **ANSWER** The mean is 18 mm.

Median

The **median** of a data set is the middle value when the values are written in numerical order. If a data set has an even number of values, the median is the mean of the two middle values.

> **Example**
>
> To find the median of the clamshell data, arrange the values in order from least to greatest. The median is the middle value.
>
> 13 mm   14 mm   14 mm   16 mm   21 mm   23 mm   25 mm
>
> **ANSWER** The median is 16 mm.

Mode

The **mode** of a data set is the value that occurs most often.

Example

To find the mode of the clamshell data, arrange the values in order from least to greatest and determine the value that occurs most often.

13 mm   14 mm   14 mm   16 mm   21 mm   23 mm   25 mm

ANSWER The mode is 14 mm.

A data set can have more than one mode or no mode. For example, the following data set has modes of 2 mm and 4 mm:

2 mm   2 mm   3 mm   4 mm   4 mm

The data set below has no mode, because no value occurs more often than any other.

2 mm   3 mm   4 mm   5 mm

Range

The **range** of a data set is the difference between the greatest value and the least value.

Example

To find the range of the clamshell data, arrange the values in order from least to greatest.

13 mm   14 mm   14 mm   16 mm   21 mm   23 mm   25 mm

Subtract the least value from the greatest value.

13 mm is the least value.
25 mm is the greatest value.

25 mm − 13 mm = 12 mm

ANSWER The range is 12 mm.

Using Ratios, Rates, and Proportions

You can use ratios and rates to compare values in data sets. You can use proportions to find unknown values.

Ratios

A **ratio** uses division to compare two values. The ratio of a value a to a nonzero value b can be written as $\frac{a}{b}$.

Example

The height of one plant is 8 centimeters. The height of another plant is 6 centimeters. To find the ratio of the height of the first plant to the height of the second plant, write a fraction and simplify it.

$$\frac{8 \text{ cm}}{6 \text{ cm}} = \frac{4 \times \overset{1}{\cancel{2}}}{3 \times \underset{1}{\cancel{2}}} = \frac{4}{3}$$

ANSWER The ratio of the plant heights is $\frac{4}{3}$.

You can also write the ratio $\frac{a}{b}$ as "a to b" or as $a:b$. For example, you can write the ratio of the plant heights as "4 to 3" or as $4:3$.

Rates

A **rate** is a ratio of two values expressed in different units. A unit rate is a rate with a denominator of 1 unit.

Example

A plant grew 6 centimeters in 2 days. The plant's rate of growth was $\frac{6 \text{ cm}}{2 \text{ days}}$. To describe the plant's growth in centimeters per day, write a unit rate.

Divide numerator and denominator by 2: $\quad \frac{6 \text{ cm}}{2 \text{ days}} = \frac{6 \text{ cm} \div 2}{2 \text{ days} \div 2}$

Simplify: $\quad = \frac{3 \text{ cm}}{1 \text{ day}}$

> You divide 2 days by 2 to get 1 day, so divide 6 cm by 2 also.

ANSWER The plant's rate of growth is 3 centimeters per day.

Proportions

A **proportion** is an equation stating that two ratios are equivalent. To solve for an unknown value in a proportion, you can use cross products.

Example

If a plant grew 6 centimeters in 2 days, how many centimeters would it grow in 3 days (if its rate of growth is constant)?

Write a proportion:	$\dfrac{6 \text{ cm}}{2 \text{ days}} = \dfrac{x}{3 \text{ days}}$
Set cross products:	$6 \text{ cm} \cdot 3 = 2x$
Multiply 6 and 3:	$18 \text{ cm} = 2x$
Divide each side by 2:	$\dfrac{18 \text{ cm}}{2} = \dfrac{2x}{2}$
Simplify:	$9 \text{ cm} = x$

ANSWER The plant would grow 9 centimeters in 3 days.

Using Decimals, Fractions, and Percents

Decimals, fractions, and percentages are all ways of recording and representing data.

Decimals

A **decimal** is a number that is written in the base-ten place value system, in which a decimal point separates the ones and tenths digits. The values of each place is ten times that of the place to its right.

Example

A caterpillar traveled from point *A* to point *C* along the path shown.

A   **36.9 cm**   **B**   **52.4 cm**   **C**

ADDING DECIMALS To find the total distance traveled by the caterpillar, add the distance from *A* to *B* and the distance from *B* to *C*. Begin by lining up the decimal points. Then add the figures as you would whole numbers and bring down the decimal point.

```
  36.9 cm
+ 52.4 cm
─────────
  89.3 cm
```

ANSWER The caterpillar traveled a total distance of 89.3 centimeters.

Example continued

SUBTRACTING DECIMALS To find how much farther the caterpillar traveled on the second leg of the journey, subtract the distance from *A* to *B* from the distance from *B* to *C*.

$$
\begin{array}{r}
52.4 \text{ cm} \\
- \ 36.9 \text{ cm} \\
\hline
15.5 \text{ cm}
\end{array}
$$

ANSWER The caterpillar traveled 15.5 centimeters farther on the second leg of the journey.

Example

A caterpillar is traveling from point *D* to point *F* along the path shown. The caterpillar travels at a speed of 9.6 centimeters per minute.

D   E   **33.6 cm**   F

MULTIPLYING DECIMALS You can multiply decimals as you would whole numbers. The number of decimal places in the product is equal to the sum of the number of decimal places in the factors.

For instance, suppose it takes the caterpillar 1.5 minutes to go from *D* to *E*. To find the distance from *D* to *E*, multiply the caterpillar's speed by the time it took.

9.6	1	decimal place
× 1.5	+ 1	decimal place
480		
96		
14.40	2	decimal places

[Align as shown.]

ANSWER The distance from *D* to *E* is 14.4 centimeters.

DIVIDING DECIMALS When you divide by a decimal, move the decimal points the same number of places in the divisor and the dividend to make the divisor a whole number.

For instance, to find the time it will take the caterpillar to travel from *E* to *F*, divide the distance from *E* to *F* by the caterpillar's speed.

9.6)33.6   ◄ Move each decimal point one place to the right.

$$
\begin{array}{r}
3.5 \\
96 \overline{)336.} \\
\underline{288} \\
480 \\
\underline{480} \\
0
\end{array}
$$

◄ Line up decimal points.

ANSWER The caterpillar will travel from *E* to *F* in 3.5 minutes.

Fractions

A **fraction** is a number in the form $\frac{a}{b}$, where b is not equal to 0. A fraction is in **simplest form** if its numerator and denominator have a greatest common factor (GCF) of 1. To simplify a fraction, divide its numerator and denominator by their GCF.

Example

A caterpillar is 40 millimeters long. The head of the caterpillar is 6 millimeters long. To compare the length of the caterpillar's head with the caterpillar's total length, you can write and simplify a fraction that expresses the ratio of the two lengths.

Write the ratio of the two lengths:	$\dfrac{\text{Length of head}}{\text{Total length}}$	$= \dfrac{6 \text{ mm}}{40 \text{ mm}}$
Write numerator and denominator as products of numbers and the GCF:		$= \dfrac{3 \times 2}{20 \times 2}$
Divide numerator and denominator by the GCF:		$= \dfrac{3 \times \overset{1}{\cancel{2}}}{20 \times \underset{1}{\cancel{2}}}$
Simplify:		$= \dfrac{3}{20}$

ANSWER In simplest form, the ratio of the lengths is $\frac{3}{20}$.

Percents

A **percent** is a ratio that compares a number to 100. The word *percent* means "per hundred" or "out of 100." The symbol for *percent* is %.

For instance, suppose 43 out of 100 caterpillars are female. You can represent this ratio as a percent, a decimal, or a fraction.

Percent	Decimal	Fraction
43%	0.43	$\dfrac{43}{100}$

Example

In the preceding example, the ratio of the length of the caterpillar's head to the caterpillar's total length is $\frac{3}{20}$. To write this ratio as a percent, write an equivalent fraction that has a denominator of 100.

Multiply numerator and denominator by 5:	$\dfrac{3}{20} =$	$\dfrac{3 \times 5}{20 \times 5}$
		$= \dfrac{15}{100}$
Write as a percent:		$= 15\%$

ANSWER The caterpillar's head represents 15 percent of its total length.

Using Formulas

A **formula** is an equation that shows the general relationship between two or more quantities.

The term *variable* is also used in science to refer to a factor that can change during an experiment.

In science, a formula often has a word form and a symbolic form. The formula below expresses Ohm's law.

Word Form

$$\text{Current} = \frac{\text{voltage}}{\text{resistance}}$$

Symbolic Form

$$I = \frac{V}{R}$$

In this formula, I, V, and R are variables. A mathematical **variable** is a symbol or letter that is used to represent one or more numbers.

Example

Suppose that you measure a voltage of 1.5 volts and a resistance of 15 ohms. You can use the formula for Ohm's law to find the current in amperes.

Write the formula for Ohm's law: $\quad I = \frac{V}{R}$

Substitute 1.5 volts for V and 15 ohms for R: $\quad I = \frac{1.5 \text{ volts}}{15 \text{ ohms}}$

Simplify: $\quad I = 0.1$ amp

ANSWER The current is 0.1 ampere.

If you know the values of all variables but one in a formula, you can solve for the value of the unknown variable. For instance, Ohm's law can be used to find a voltage if you know the current and the resistance.

Example

Suppose that you know that a current is 0.2 amperes and the resistance is 18 ohms. Use the formula for Ohm's law to find the voltage in volts.

Write the formula for Ohm's law: $\quad I = \frac{V}{R}$

Substitute 0.2 amp for I and 18 ohms for R: $\quad 0.2 \text{ amp} = \frac{V}{18 \text{ ohms}}$

Multiply both sides by 18 ohms: $\quad 0.2 \text{ amp} \cdot 18 \text{ ohms} = V$

Simplify: $\quad 3.6 \text{ volts} = V$

ANSWER The voltage is 3.6 volts.

MATH HANDBOOK

Finding Areas

The area of a figure is the amount of surface the figure covers.

Area is measured in square units, such as square meters (m^2) or square centimeters (cm^2). Formulas for the areas of three common geometric figures are shown below.

Area = (side length)²
$A = s^2$

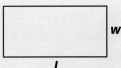

Area = length × width
$A = lw$

Area = $\frac{1}{2}$ × base × height
$A = \frac{1}{2} bh$

Example

Each face of a halite crystal is a square like the one shown. You can find the area of the square by using the steps below.

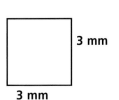

Write the formula for the area of a square:	$A = s^2$
Substitute 3 mm for s:	$= (3 \text{ mm})^2$
Simplify:	$= 9 \text{ mm}^2$

ANSWER The area of the square is 9 square millimeters.

Finding Volumes

The volume of a solid is the amount of space contained by the solid.

Volume is measured in cubic units, such as cubic meters (m^3) or cubic centimeters (cm^3). The volume of a rectangular prism is given by the formula shown below.

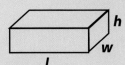

Volume = length × width × height
$V = lwh$

Example

A topaz crystal is a rectangular prism like the one shown. You can find the volume of the prism by using the steps below.

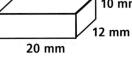

Write the formula for the volume of a rectangular prism:	$V = lwh$
Substitute dimensions:	$= 20 \text{ mm} \times 12 \text{ mm} \times 10 \text{ mm}$
Simplify:	$= 2400 \text{ mm}^3$

ANSWER The volume of the rectangular prism is 2400 cubic millimeters.

Using Significant Figures

The **significant figures** in a decimal are the digits that are warranted by the accuracy of a measuring device.

When you perform a calculation with measurements, the number of significant figures to include in the result depends in part on the number of significant figures in the measurements. When you multiply or divide measurements, your answer should have only as many significant figures as the measurement with the fewest significant figures.

Example

Using a balance and a graduated cylinder filled with water, you determined that a marble has a mass of 8.0 grams and a volume of 3.5 cubic centimeters. To calculate the density of the marble, divide the mass by the volume.

Write the formula for density: $\text{Density} = \dfrac{\text{mass}}{\text{Volume}}$

Substitute measurements: $= \dfrac{8.0 \text{ g}}{3.5 \text{ cm}^3}$

Use a calculator to divide: $\approx 2.285714286 \text{ g/cm}^3$

ANSWER Because the mass and the volume have two significant figures each, give the density to two significant figures. The marble has a density of 2.3 grams per cubic centimeter.

Using Scientific Notation

Scientific notation is a shorthand way to write very large or very small numbers. For example, 73,500,000,000,000,000,000,000 kg is the mass of the Moon. In scientific notation, it is 7.35×10^{22} kg.

Example

You can convert from standard form to scientific notation.

Standard Form	Scientific Notation
720,000 5 decimal places left	7.2×10^5 Exponent is 5.
0.000291 4 decimal places right	2.91×10^{-4} Exponent is −4.

You can convert from scientific notation to standard form.

Scientific Notation	Standard Form
4.63×10^7 Exponent is 7.	46,300,000 7 decimal places right
1.08×10^{-6} Exponent is −6.	0.00000108 6 decimal places left

Note-Taking Handbook

Note-Taking Strategies

Taking notes as you read helps you understand the information. The notes you take can also be used as a study guide for later review. This handbook presents several ways to organize your notes.

Content Frame

1. Make a chart in which each column represents a category.
2. Give each column a heading.
3. Write details under the headings.

NAME	GROUP	CHARACTERISTICS	DRAWING
snail	mollusks	mantle, shell	
ant	arthropods	six legs, exoskeleton	
earthworm	segmented worms	segmented body, circulatory and digestive systems	
heartworm	roundworms	digestive system	
sea star	echinoderms	spiny skin, tube feet	
jellyfish	cnidarians	stinging cells	

categories

details

Combination Notes

1. For each new idea or concept, write an informal outline of the information.
2. Make a sketch to illustrate the concept, and label it.

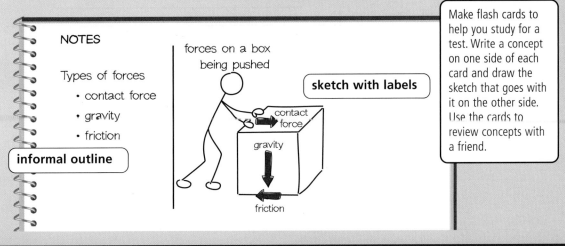

NOTES

Types of forces
- contact force
- gravity
- friction

informal outline

forces on a box being pushed

sketch with labels

contact force

gravity

friction

Make flash cards to help you study for a test. Write a concept on one side of each card and draw the sketch that goes with it on the other side. Use the cards to review concepts with a friend.

Main Idea and Detail Notes

1. In the left-hand column of a two-column chart, list main ideas. The blue headings express main ideas throughout this textbook.

2. In the right-hand column, write details that expand on each main idea.

You can shorten the headings in your chart. Be sure to use the most important words.

When studying for tests, cover up the detail notes column with a sheet of paper. Then use each main idea to form a question—such as "How does latitude affect climate?" Answer the question, and then uncover the detail notes column to check your answer.

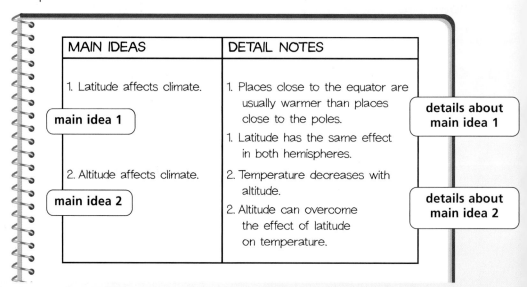

MAIN IDEAS	DETAIL NOTES
1. Latitude affects climate.	1. Places close to the equator are usually warmer than places close to the poles.
main idea 1	1. Latitude has the same effect in both hemispheres.
2. Altitude affects climate.	2. Temperature decreases with altitude.
main idea 2	2. Altitude can overcome the effect of latitude on temperature.

details about main idea 1

details about main idea 2

Main Idea Web

1. Write a main idea in a box.

2. Add boxes around it with related vocabulary terms and important details.

You can find definitions near highlighted terms.

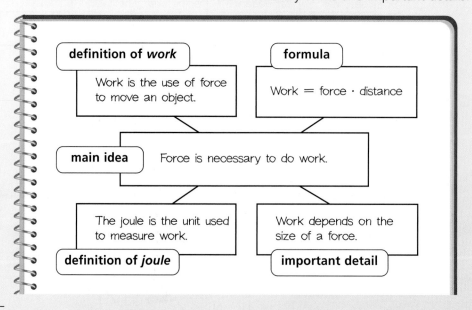

definition of *work*
Work is the use of force to move an object.

formula
Work = force · distance

main idea
Force is necessary to do work.

The joule is the unit used to measure work.
definition of *joule*

Work depends on the size of a force.
important detail

Mind Map

1. Write a main idea in the center.

2. Add details that relate to one another and to the main idea.

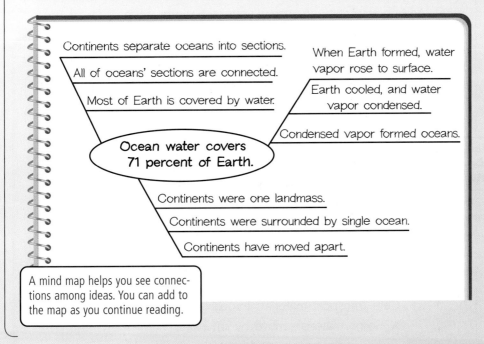

Continents separate oceans into sections.

All of oceans' sections are connected.

Most of Earth is covered by water.

When Earth formed, water vapor rose to surface.

Earth cooled, and water vapor condensed.

Condensed vapor formed oceans.

Ocean water covers 71 percent of Earth.

Continents were one landmass.

Continents were surrounded by single ocean.

Continents have moved apart.

A mind map helps you see connections among ideas. You can add to the map as you continue reading.

Supporting Main Ideas

1. Write a main idea in a box.

2. Add boxes underneath with information—such as reasons, explanations, and examples—that supports the main idea.

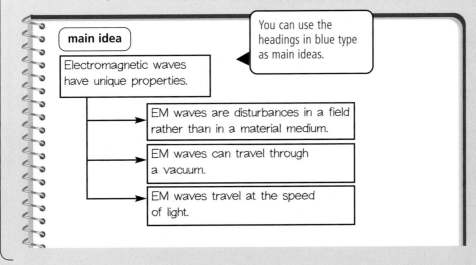

main idea

Electromagnetic waves have unique properties.

You can use the headings in blue type as main ideas.

EM waves are disturbances in a field rather than in a material medium.

EM waves can travel through a vacuum.

EM waves travel at the speed of light.

Outline

1. Copy the chapter title and headings from the book in the form of an outline.

2. Add notes that summarize in your own words what you read.

Cell Processes

I. Cells capture and release energy.
    A. All cells need energy.
    B. Some cells capture light energy.
       1. Process of photosynthesis
       2. Chloroplasts (site of photosynthesis)
       3. Carbon dioxide and water as raw materials
       4. Glucose and oxygen as products
    C. All cells release energy.
       1. Process of cellular respiration
       2. Fermentation of sugar to carbon dioxide
       3. Bacteria that carry out fermentation

II. Cells transport materials through membranes.
    A. Some materials move by diffusion.
       1. Particle movement from higher to lower concentrations
       2. Movement of water through membrane (osmosis)
    B. Some transport requires energy.
       1. Active transport
       2. Examples of active transport

1st key idea

1st subpoint of I

2nd subpoint of I

1st detail about B

2nd detail about B

Correct Outline Form
Include a title.

Arrange key ideas, subpoints, and details as shown.

Indent the divisions of the outline as shown.

Use the same grammatical form for items of the same rank. For example, if A is a sentence, B must also be a sentence.

You must have at least two main ideas or subpoints. That is, every A must be followed by a B, and every 1 must be followed by a 2.

Concept Map

1. Write an important concept in a large oval.
2. Add details related to the concept in smaller ovals.
3. Write linking words on arrows that connect the ovals.

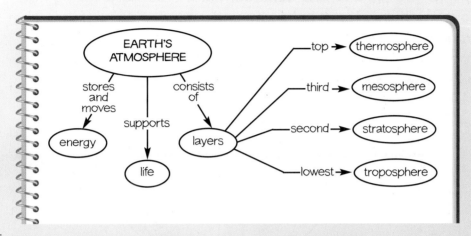

The main ideas or concepts can often be found in the blue headings. An example is "The atmosphere stores and moves energy." Use nouns from these concepts in the ovals, and use the verb or verbs on the lines.

Venn Diagram

1. Draw two overlapping circles, one for each item that you are comparing.
2. In the overlapping section, list the characteristics that are shared by both items.
3. In the outer sections, list the characteristics that are peculiar to each item.
4. Write a summary that describes the information in the Venn diagram.

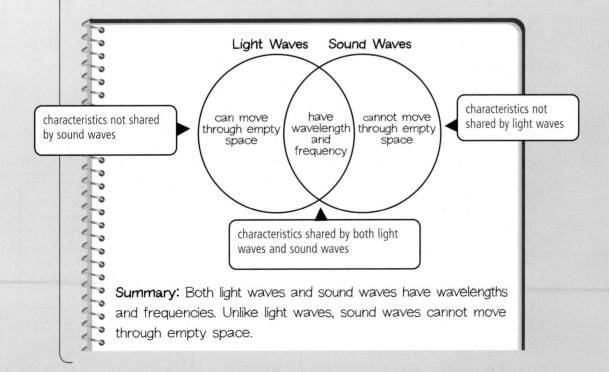

Summary: Both light waves and sound waves have wavelengths and frequencies. Unlike light waves, sound waves cannot move through empty space.

Vocabulary Strategies

Important terms are highlighted in this book. A definition of each term can be found in the sentence or paragraph where the term appears. You can also find definitions in the Glossary. Taking notes about vocabulary terms helps you understand and remember what you read.

Description Wheel

1. Write a term inside a circle.
2. Write words that describe the term on "spokes" attached to the circle.

When studying for a test with a friend, read the phrases on the spokes one at a time until your friend identifies the correct term.

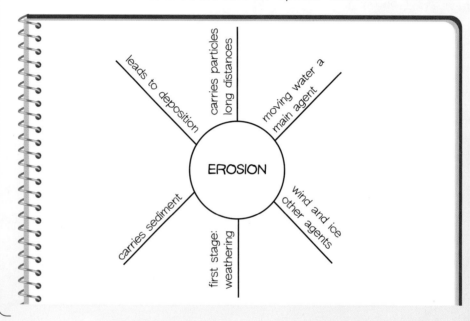

Four Square

1. Write a term in the center.
2. Write details in the four areas around the term.

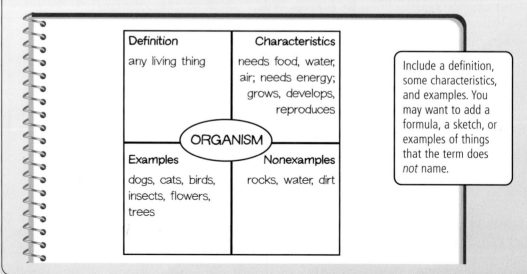

Include a definition, some characteristics, and examples. You may want to add a formula, a sketch, or examples of things that the term does *not* name.

Frame Game

1. Write a term in the center.

2. Frame the term with details.

Include examples, descriptions, sketches, or sentences that use the term in context. Change the frame to fit each new term.

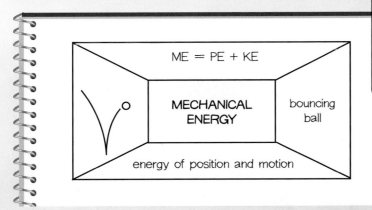

Magnet Word

1. Write a term on the magnet.

2. On the lines, add details related to the term.

You can also use phrases or sentences on the lines.

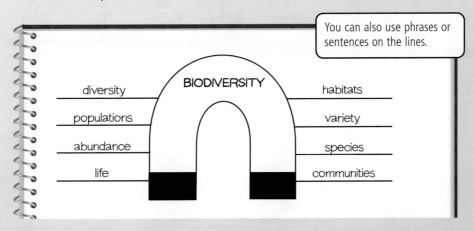

Word Triangle

1. Write a term and its definition in the bottom section.

2. In the middle section, write a sentence in which the term is used correctly.

3. In the top section, draw a small picture to illustrate the term.

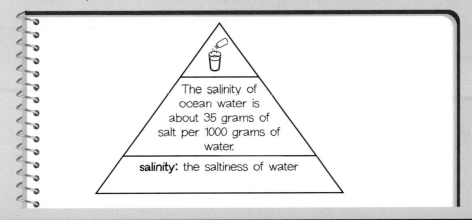

The Periodic Table of the Elements

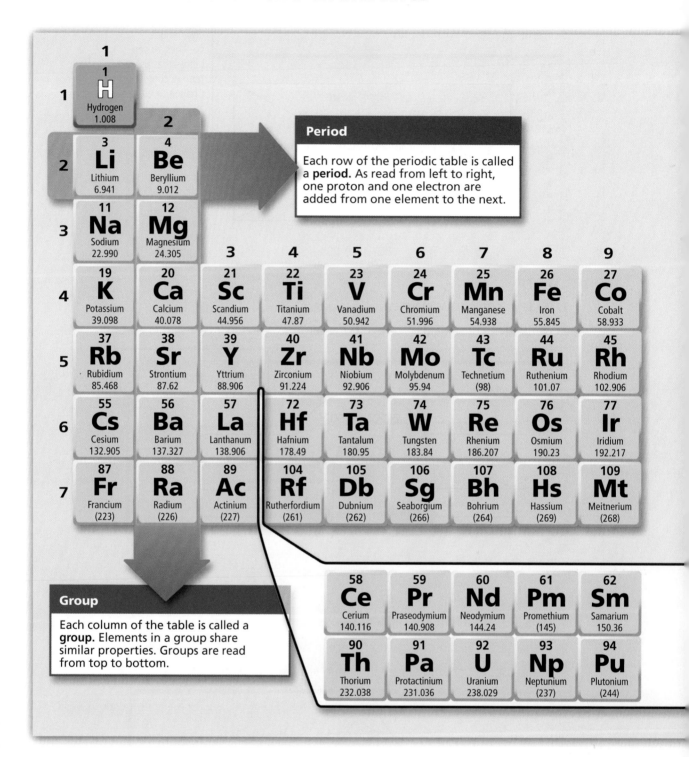

Period

Each row of the periodic table is called a **period.** As read from left to right, one proton and one electron are added from one element to the next.

Group

Each column of the table is called a **group.** Elements in a group share similar properties. Groups are read from top to bottom.

Metal	Metalloid	Nonmetal

 Solid   Liquid   Gas

APPENDIX

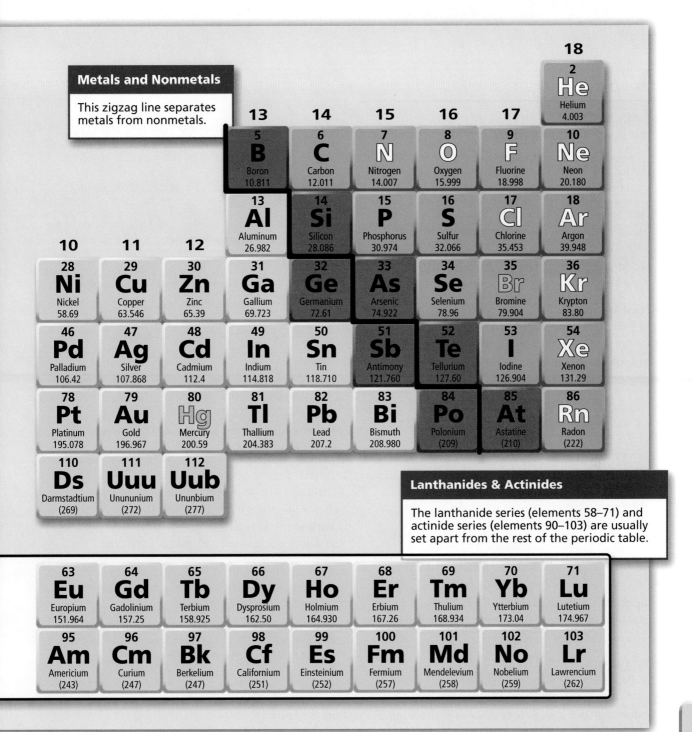

Metals and Nonmetals

This zigzag line separates metals from nonmetals.

18
2 **He** Helium 4.003

13	14	15	16	17	
5 **B** Boron 10.811	**6** **C** Carbon 12.011	**7** **N** Nitrogen 14.007	**8** **O** Oxygen 15.999	**9** **F** Fluorine 18.998	**10** **Ne** Neon 20.180
13 **Al** Aluminum 26.982	**14** **Si** Silicon 28.086	**15** **P** Phosphorus 30.974	**16** **S** Sulfur 32.066	**17** **Cl** Chlorine 35.453	**18** **Ar** Argon 39.948

10	11	12						
28 **Ni** Nickel 58.69	**29** **Cu** Copper 63.546	**30** **Zn** Zinc 65.39	**31** **Ga** Gallium 69.723	**32** **Ge** Germanium 72.61	**33** **As** Arsenic 74.922	**34** **Se** Selenium 78.96	**35** **Br** Bromine 79.904	**36** **Kr** Krypton 83.80
46 **Pd** Palladium 106.42	**47** **Ag** Silver 107.868	**48** **Cd** Cadmium 112.4	**49** **In** Indium 114.818	**50** **Sn** Tin 118.710	**51** **Sb** Antimony 121.760	**52** **Te** Tellurium 127.60	**53** **I** Iodine 126.904	**54** **Xe** Xenon 131.29
78 **Pt** Platinum 195.078	**79** **Au** Gold 196.967	**80** **Hg** Mercury 200.59	**81** **Tl** Thallium 204.383	**82** **Pb** Lead 207.2	**83** **Bi** Bismuth 208.980	**84** **Po** Polonium (209)	**85** **At** Astatine (210)	**86** **Rn** Radon (222)
110 **Ds** Darmstadtium (269)	**111** **Uuu** Unununium (272)	**112** **Uub** Ununbium (277)						

Lanthanides & Actinides

The lanthanide series (elements 58–71) and actinide series (elements 90–103) are usually set apart from the rest of the periodic table.

63 **Eu** Europium 151.964	**64** **Gd** Gadolinium 157.25	**65** **Tb** Terbium 158.925	**66** **Dy** Dysprosium 162.50	**67** **Ho** Holmium 164.930	**68** **Er** Erbium 167.26	**69** **Tm** Thulium 168.934	**70** **Yb** Ytterbium 173.04	**71** **Lu** Lutetium 174.967
95 **Am** Americium (243)	**96** **Cm** Curium (247)	**97** **Bk** Berkelium (247)	**98** **Cf** Californium (251)	**99** **Es** Einsteinium (252)	**100** **Fm** Fermium (257)	**101** **Md** Mendelevium (258)	**102** **No** Nobelium (259)	**103** **Lr** Lawrencium (262)

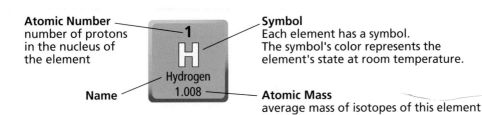

Atomic Number number of protons in the nucleus of the element

1 **H** Hydrogen 1.008

Symbol Each element has a symbol. The symbol's color represents the element's state at room temperature.

Name

Atomic Mass average mass of isotopes of this element

Glossary

GLOSSARY

A

abiotic factor (AY-by-AHT-ihk)
A nonliving physical or chemical part of an ecosystem. (p. 330)

factor abiótico Una parte física o química sin vida de un ecosistema.

acid
A substance that can donate a proton to another substance and has a pH below 7. (p. 626)

ácido Una sustancia que puede donar un protón a otra sustancia y que tiene un pH menor a 7.

active transport
The process of using energy to move materials through a membrane. (p. 60)

transporte activo El proceso de usar energía para mover sustancias a través de una membrana.

adaptation
A characteristic, a behavior, or any inherited trait that makes a species able to survive and reproduce in a particular environment. (p. xxxi)

adaptación Una característica, un comportamiento o cualquier rasgo heredado que permite a una especie sobrevivir o reproducirse en un medio ambiente determinado.

addiction
A physical or psychological need for a habit-forming substance, such as alcohol or drugs. (p. 306)

adicción Una necesidad física o psicológica de una sustancia que forma hábito, como el alcohol o las drogas.

adolescence (ad-uhl-EHS-uhns)
The stage of life from the time a human body begins to mature sexually to adulthood. (p. 295)

adolescencia La etapa de la vida que va desde que el cuerpo humano empieza a madurar sexualmente hasta la edad adulta.

adulthood
The stage of life that begins once a human body completes its growth and reaches sexual maturity. (p. 296)

edad adulta La etapa de la vida que empieza una vez que el cuerpo humano completa su crecimiento y alcanza la madurez sexual.

allele (uh-LEEL)
An alternate form of a gene for a specific trait or gene product. (p. 103)

alelo Una forma alterna de un gen para un rasgo específico o un producto del gen.

alloy
A solid mixture composed of a metal and one or more other substances. (p. 634)

aleación Una mezcla sólida compuesta de un metal y una o más sustancias adicionales.

antibiotic
A medicine that can block the growth and reproduction of bacteria. (p. 241)

antibiótico Una medicina que puede impedir el crecimiento y la reproducción de las bacterias.

antibody
A protein produced by some white blood cells to attack specific foreign materials. (p. 235)

anticuerpo Una proteína producida por algunos glóbulos blancos para atacar materiales extraños específicos.

antigen
A particular substance that the body recognizes as foreign and that stimulates a response. (p. 238)

antígeno Una sustancia que el cuerpo reconoce come extraña y que causa una respuesta.

appendicular skeleton (AP-uhn-DIHK-yuh-luhr)
The bones of the skeleton that function to allow movement, such as arm and leg bones. (p. 176)

esqueleto apendicular Los huesos del esqueleto cuya función es permitir el movimiento, como los huesos del brazo y los huesos de la pierna.

artery
A blood vessel with strong walls that carries blood away from the heart. (p. 229)

arteria Un vaso sanguíneo con paredes fuertes que lleva la sangre del corazón hacia otras partes del cuerpo.

asexual reproduction
The process by which a single organism produces offspring that have the same genetic material. (p. 88)

reproducción asexual El proceso mediante el cual un solo organismo produce crías que tienen el mismo material genético.

atmosphere (AT-muh-SFEER)
The outer layer of gases of a large body in space, such as a planet or star; the mixture of gases that surrounds the solid Earth; one of the four parts of the Earth system. (p. xxxiii)

atmósfera La capa externa de gases de un gran cuerpo que se encuentra en el espacio, como un planeta o una estrella; la mezcla de gases que rodea la Tierra sólida; una de las cuatro partes del sistema terrestre.

atom
The smallest particle of an element that has the chemical properties of that element. (p. 448)

átomo La partícula más pequeña de un elemento que tiene las propiedades químicas de ese elemento.

atomic mass
The average mass of the atoms of an element. (p. 517)

masa atómica La masa promedio de los átomos de un elemento.

atomic number
The number of protons in the nucleus of an atom. (p. 512)

número atómico El número de protones en el núcleo de un átomo.

autonomic nervous system
The part of the nervous system that controls involuntary action and responses. (p. 267)

sistema nervioso autónomo La parte del sistema nervioso que controla la acción involuntaria y las respuestas.

axial skeleton
The central part of the skeleton, which includes the cranium, the spinal column, and the ribs. (p. 176)

esqueleto axial La parte central del esqueleto que incluye al cráneo, a la columna vertebral y a las costillas.

B

bacteria (bak-TEER-ee-uh)
A large group of one-celled organisms that sometimes cause disease. *Bacteria* is a plural word; the singular is *bacterium*. (pp. 14, 309)

bacterias Un grupo grande de organismos unicelulares que algunas veces causan enfermedades.

base
A substance that can accept a proton from another substance and has a pH above 7. (p. 626)

base Una sustancia que puede aceptar un protón de otra sustancia y que tiene un pH superior a 7.

binary fission
A form of asexual reproduction by which some single-celled organisms reproduce. The genetic material is copied, and one cell divides into two independent cells that are each a copy of the original cell. Prokaryotes such as bacteria reproduce by binary fission. (p. 89)

fisión binaria Una forma asexual de reproducción mediante la cual algunos organismos unicelulares se reproducen. El material genético se copia y una célula se divide en dos células independientes las cuales son copias de la célula original. Los organismos procariotas, tales como las bacterias, se reproducen mediante fisión binaria.

biodiversity
The number and variety of living things found on Earth or within an ecosystem. (p. 411)

biodiversidad La cantidad y variedad de organismos vivos que se encuentran en la Tierra o dentro de un ecosistema.

biology
The scientific study of life and all living things; ecology, zoology, and botany are examples of biological sciences.

biología El estudio científico de la vida y de todos los organismos vivos; la ecología, la zoología y la botánica son ejemplos de ciencias biológicas.

biome (BY-ohm)
A region of Earth that has a particular climate and certain types of plants. Examples are tundra, taiga, desert, grassland, temperate and tropical forests. (p. 350)

bioma Una región de la Tierra que tiene un clima particular y ciertos tipos de plantas. La tundra, la taiga, el desierto, la estepa, la selva tropical y el bosque templado son ejemplos de biomas.

biosphere (BY-uh-SFEER)
All living organisms on Earth in the air, on the land, and in the waters; one of the four parts of the Earth system. (p. xxxiii)

biosfera Todos los organismos vivos de la Tierra, en el aire, en la tierra y en las aguas; una de las cuatro partes del sistema de la Tierra.

biotic factor (by-AHT-ihk)
A living thing in an ecosystem. (p. 330)

factor biótico Un organismo vivo en un ecosistema.

blood
A fluid in the body that delivers oxygen and other materials to cells and removes carbon dioxide and other wastes. (p. 225)

sangre Un fluido en el cuerpo que reparte oxígeno y otras sustancias a las células y elimina dióxido de carbono y otros desechos.

boiling
A process by which a substance changes from its liquid state to its gas state. The liquid is heated to a specific temperature at which bubbles of vapor form within the liquid. (p. 486)

> **ebullición** Un proceso mediante el cual una sustancia cambia de su estado líquido a su estado gaseoso se calienta el líquido a una determinada temperatura a la cual se forman burbujas de vapor dentro del líquido.

boiling point
The temperature at which a substance changes from its liquid state to its gas state through boiling. (p. 486)

> **punto de ebullición** La temperatura a la cual una sustancia cambia de su estado líquido a su estado gaseoso mediante ebullición.

budding
A process of asexual reproduction in which an organism develops as an outgrowth of the parent. Each bud can grow into a new organism, breaking free and becoming separate and independent. (p. 89)

> **gemación** Un proceso de reproducción asexual en el cual un organismo se desarrolla a partir de una porción del progenitor. Cada yema puede convertirse en un nuevo organismo, separándose del progenitor y volviéndose independiente.

C

capillary
A narrow blood vessel that connects arteries with veins. (p. 229)

> **capilar** Un vaso sanguíneo angosto que conecta a las arterias con las venas.

carbohydrate (KAHR-boh-HY-drayt)
A type of molecule made up of subunits of sugars and used for energy and structure. (p. 42)

> **carbohidrato** Un tipo de molécula compuesta de unidades de azúcares y usada como fuente de energía y como material estructural.

carbon cycle
The continuous movement of carbon through Earth, its atmosphere, and the living things on Earth. (p. 338)

> **ciclo del carbono** El movimiento continuo del carbono en la Tierra, su atmósfera y todos los seres vivos en ella.

cardiac muscle
The muscle that makes up the heart. (p. 184)

> **músculo cardiaco** El músculo del cual está compuesto el corazón.

carrying capacity
The maximum size that a population can reach in an ecosystem. (p. 385)

> **capacidad de carga** El tamaño máximo que una población puede alcanzar en un ecosistema.

catalyst
A substance that increases the rate of a chemical reaction but is not consumed in the reaction. (p. 576)

> **catalizador** Una sustancia que aumenta lel a ritmo velocidad de una reacción química pero que no es consumida en la reacción.

cell
The smallest unit that is able to perform the basic functions of life. (p. xxxi)

> **célula** La unidad más pequeña capaz de realizar las funciones básicas de la vida.

cell cycle
The normal sequence of growth, maintenance, and division in a cell. (p. 80)

> **ciclo celular** La secuencia normal de crecimiento, mantenimiento y división en una célula.

cell membrane
The outer boundary of the cytoplasm, a layer that controls what enters or leaves the cell; a protective covering enclosing an entire cell. (p. 20)

> **membrana celular** El límite exterior del citoplasma, una capa que controla lo que entra y sale de la célula, una cubierta protectora que encierra una célula entera.

cellular respiration
A process in which cells use oxygen to release energy stored in sugars. (pp. 50, 199)

> **respiración celular** Un proceso en el cual las células usan oxígeno para liberar energía almacenada en las azúcares.

cell wall
A protective outer covering that lies just outside the cell membrane of plant cells. (p. 21)

> **pared celular** Una cubierta exterior protectora que se encuentra justo fuera de la membrana celular de las células vegetales.

central nervous system
The brain and spinal cord. The central nervous system communicates with the rest of the nervous system through electrical signals sent to and from neurons. (p. 264)

> **sistema nervioso central** El cerebro y la médula espinal. El sistema nervioso central se comunica con el resto del sistema nervioso mediante señales eléctricas enviadas hacia y desde las neuronas.

chemical change
A change of one substance into another substance. (p. 478)

cambio químico La transformación de una sustancia a otra sustancia.

chemical energy
Energy that is stored in the chemical composition of matter. The amount of chemical energy in a substance depends on the types and arrangement of its atoms. When wood or gasoline burns, chemical energy produces heat. The energy used by the cells in your body comes from chemical energy in the foods you eat. (p. 47)

energía química Energía almacenada en la composición química de la materia. La cantidad de energía química en una sustancia depende de los tipos y la disposición de sus átomos. Cuando se quema madera o gasolina, la energía química produce calor. La energía usada por las células en tu cuerpo proviene de la energía química en los alimentos que comes.

chemical formula
An expression that shows the number and types of atoms joined in a compound. (p. 543)

fórmula química Una expresión que muestra el número y los tipos de átomos unidos en un compuesto.

chemical property
A characteristic of a substance that describes how it can form a new substance. (p. 478)

propiedad química Una característica de una sustancia que describe como puede formar una nueva sustancia.

chemical reaction
The process by which chemical changes occur. In a chemical reaction, atoms are rearranged, and chemical bonds are broken and formed. (pp. 42, 569)

reacción química El proceso mediante el cual ocurren cambios químicos. En una reacción química, se reacomodan átomos y se rompen y se forman enlaces químicos.

childhood
The stage of life after infancy and before the beginning of sexual maturity. (p. 294)

niñez La etapa de la vida después de la infancia y antes del comienzo de la madurez sexual.

chlorophyll (KLAWR-uh-fihl)
A light-absorbing chemical, a pigment, that traps the energy in sunlight and converts it to chemical energy. Found in chloroplasts of plant cells and the cells of other photosynthetic organisms. (p. 48)

clorofila Una sustancia química que absorbe luz, un pigmento, que atrapa la energía de la luz solar y la convierte a energía química. Se encuentra en los cloroplastos de células vegetales y en las células de otros organismos fotosintéticos.

chloroplast (KLAWR-uh-PLAST)
An organelle in a plant cell that contains chlorophyll, a chemical that uses the energy from sunlight to make sugar. (p. 23)

cloroplasto Un organelo en una célula vegetal que contiene clorofila, una sustancia química que usa la energía de la luz solar para producir azúcar.

chromosome
The physical structure in a cell that contains the cell's genetic material. (p. 75)

cromosoma Una estructura corporal en la célula que contiene el material genético de la célula.

circulatory system
The group of organs, consisting of the heart and blood vessels, that circulates blood through the body. (p. 225)

sistema circulatorio El grupo de órganos, que consiste del corazón y los vasos sanguíneos, que hace circular la sangre por el cuerpo.

classification
The systematic grouping of different types of organisms by their shared characteristics.

clasificación La agrupación sistemática de diferentes tipos de organismos en base a las características que comparten.

cloning
The process of using DNA technology to produce an offspring that is genetically identical to its one parent. (p. 154)

clonación El proceso de usar tecnología de ADN para producir una cría que es genéticamente idéntica a su único progenitor.

commensalism (kuh-MEHN-suh-LIHZ-uhm)
An interaction between two species in which one species benefits without harming the other; a type of symbiosis. (p. 379)

comensalismo Una interacción entre dos especies en la cual una especie se beneficia sin causar daño a la otra; un tipo de simbiosis.

community

All the populations that live and interact with each other in a particular place. The community can live in a place as small as a pond or a park, or it can live in a place as large as a rain forest or the ocean. (p. 368)

comunidad Todas las poblaciones que viven e interactúan entre sí en un lugar. La comunidad puede vivir en un lugar tan pequeño como una laguna o un parque o en un lugar tan grande como un bosque tropical o el océano.

compact bone

The tough, hard outer layer of a bone. (p. 175)

hueso compacto La capa exterior, resistente y dura de un hueso.

competition

The struggle between two or more living things that depend on the same limited resource. (p. 375)

competencia La lucha entre dos o más organismos vivos que dependen del mismo recurso limitado.

compound

A substance made up of two or more different types of atoms bonded together. (p. 455)

compuesto Una sustancia formada por dos o más diferentes tipos de átomos enlazados.

condensation

The process by which a gas becomes a liquid. (p. 487)

condensación El proceso mediante el cual un gas se convierte en un líquido.

coniferous (koh-NIHF-uhr-uhs)

A term used to describe cone-bearing trees and shrubs that usually keep their leaves or needles during all the seasons of the year; examples are pine, fir, and spruce trees. (p. 352)

conífero Un término usado para describir a los árboles y los arbustos que producen conos o piñas y que generalmente conservan sus hojas o agujas durante todas las estaciones del año; el pino, el abeto y la picea son ejemplos de coníferas.

conservation

The process of saving or protecting a natural resource. (p. 419)

conservación El proceso de salvar o proteger un recurso natural.

consumer

A living thing that gets its energy by eating other living things in a food chain; consumers are also called heterotrophs. (p. 344)

consumidor Un organismo vivo que obtiene su energía alimentándose de oros organismos vivos en una cadena alimentaria; los consumidores también son llamados heterótrofos.

cooperation

A term used to describe an interaction between two or more living things in which they are said to work together. (p. 377)

cooperación Un término que describe la interacción entre dos o más organismos vivos en la cual se dice que trabajan juntos.

covalent bond

A pair of electrons shared by two atoms. (p. 550)

enlace covalente Un par de electrones compartidos por dos átomos.

cycle

n. A series of events or actions that repeat themselves regularly; a physical and/or chemical process in which one material continually changes locations and/or forms. Examples include the water cycle, the carbon cycle, and the rock cycle.

v. To move through a repeating series of events or actions. (p. 336)

ciclo Una serie de eventos o acciones que se repiten regularmente; un proceso físico y/o químico en el cual un material cambia continuamente de lugar y/o forma. Ejemplos: el ciclo del agua, el ciclo del carbono y el ciclo de las rocas.

cytokinesis (SY-toh-kuh-NEE-sihs)

The division of a parent cell's cytoplasm following mitosis. (p. 81)

citocinesis La división del citoplasma de la célula madre después de la mitosis.

cytoplasm (SY-tuh-PLAZ-uhm)

A thick, gelatin-like material contained within the cell membrane. Most of the work of the cell is carried out in the cytoplasm. (p. 20)

citoplasma Un material espeso, parecido a la gelatina, contenido dentro de la membrana celular. La mayor parte del trabajo de la célula se realiza en el citoplasma.

D

data
Information gathered by observation or experimentation that can be used in calculating or reasoning. *Data* is a plural word; the singular is *datum*.

> **datos** Información reunida mediante observación o experimentación y que se puede usar para calcular o para razonar.

deciduous (dih-SIHJ-oo-uhs)
A term used to describe trees and shrubs that drop their leaves when winter comes; examples are maple, oak, and birch trees. (p. 353)

> **caducifolio** Un término usado para describir árboles y arbustos que dejan caer sus hojas cuando llega el invierno; el arce, el roble y el abedul son ejemplos de árboles caducifolios.

decomposer
An organism that feeds on and breaks down dead plant or animal matter. (p. 345)

> **organismo descomponedor** Un organismo que se alimenta de y degrada materia vegetal o animal.

density
A property of matter representing the mass per unit volume. (p. 475)

> **densidad** Una propiedad de la materia que representa la masa por unidad de volumen.

dermis
The inner layer of the skin. (p. 244)

> **dermis** La capa interior de la piel.

diffusion (dih-FYOO-zhuhn)
The tendency of a substance to move from an area of higher concentration to an area of lower concentration. (p. 56)

> **difusión** La tendencia de una sustancia a moverse de un área de mayor concentración a un área de menor concentración.

digestion
The process of breaking down food into usable materials. (p. 206)

> **digestión** El proceso de descomponer el alimento en sustancias utilizables.

digestive system
The structures in the body that work together to transform the energy and materials in food into forms the body can use. (p. 206)

> **sistema digestivo** Las estructuras en el cuerpo que trabajan juntas para transformar la energía y las sustancias en el alimento a formas que el cuerpo puede usar.

dilute
adj. Having a low concentration of solute.

v. To add solvent in order to decrease the concentration of a solution. (p. 618)

> **diluido** *adj.* Que tiene una baja concentración de soluto.
>
> **diluir** *v.* Agregar solvente para disminuir la concentración de una solución."

diversity
A term used to describe the quality of having many differences; *biodiversity* describes the great variety and many differences found among living things.

> **diversidad** Un término usado para describir la cualidad de tener muchas diferencias; la biodiversidad describe la gran variedad y las muchas diferencias encontradas entre organismos vivos.

DNA
The genetic material found in all living cells that contains the information needed for an organism to grow, maintain itself, and reproduce. Deoxyribonucleic acid (dee-AHK-see-RY-boh-noo-KLEE-ihk). (p. 74)

> **ADN** El material genético que se encuentra en todas las céulas vivas y que contiene la información necesaria para que un organismo crezca, se mantenga a sí mismo y se reproduzca. Ácido desoxiribunucleico.

dominant
A term that describes the allele that determines the phenotype of an individual organism when two different copies are present in the genotype. (p. 107)

> **dominante** Un término que describe al alelo que determina el fenotipo de un organismo cuando están presentes dos copias diferentes en el genotipo.

E

ecology
The scientific study of how living things interact with each other and their environment. (p. 329)

> **ecología** El estudio científico de cómo interactúan los organismos vivos entre sí y con su medio ambiente.

ecosystem
All the living and nonliving things that interact in a particular environment. An ecosystem can be as small as a meadow or a swamp or as large as a forest or a desert. (p. 329)

> **ecosistema** Todos los organismos vivos y las cosas que interactúan en un medio ambiente específico. Un ecosistema puede ser tan pequeño como un prado o un pantano, o tan grande como un bosque o un desierto.

egg
A female reproductive cell (gamete) that forms in the reproductive organs of a female and has just a single copy of the genetic material of the parent. (p. 118)

> **óvulo** Una célula reproductiva femenina (gameto) que se forma en los órganos reproductivos de una hembra y tiene una sola copia del material genético de la madre.

electron
A negatively charged particle located outside an atom's nucleus. An electron is about 2000 times smaller than either a proton or neutron. (p. 511)

> **electrón** Una partícula con carga negativa localizada fuera del núcleo de un átomo. Un electrón es como aproximadamente 2000 veces más pequeño que un protón o un neutrón.

element
A substance that cannot be broken down into a simpler substance by ordinary chemical changes. An element consists of atoms of only one type. (p. 454)

> **elemento** Una sustancia que no puede descomponerse en otra sustancia más simple por medio de cambios químicos normales. Un elemento consta de átomos de un solo tipo.

embryo (EHM-bree-OH)
A multicellular organism, plant or animal, in its earliest stages of development. (p. 281)

> **embrión** Una planta o un animal en su estadio mas temprano de desarrollo.

endocrine system
A group of organs called glands and the hormones they produce that help regulate conditions inside the body. (p. 270)

> **sistema endocrino** Un grupo de órganos llamados glándulas y las hormonas que producen que ayudan a regular las condiciones dentro del cuerpo.

endothermic reaction
A chemical reaction that absorbs energy. (p. 587)

> **reacción endotérmica** Una reacción química que absorbe energía.

energy
The ability to do work or to cause a change. For example, the energy of a moving bowling ball knocks over pins; energy from food allows animals to move and to grow; and energy from the Sun heats Earth's surface and atmosphere, which causes air to move. (p. xxxiii)

> **energía** La capacidad para trabajar o causar un cambio. Por ejemplo, la energía de una bola de boliche en movimiento tumba los pinos; la energía proveniente de su alimento permite a los animales moverse y crecer; la energía del Sol calienta la superficie y la atmósfera de la Tierra, lo que ocasiona que el aire se mueva.

energy pyramid
A model used to show the amount of energy available to living things in an ecosystem. (p. 348)

> **pirámide de energía** Un modelo usado para mostrar la cantidad de energía disponible para organismos vivos en un ecosistema.

environment
Everything that surrounds a living thing. An environment is made up of both living and nonliving factors. (p. xxxi)

> **medio ambiente** Todo lo que rodea a un organismo vivo. Un medio ambiente está compuesto de factores vivos y factores sin vida.

epidermis
The outer layer of the skin. (p. 244)

> **epidermis** La capa exterior de la piel.

estuary
The lower end of a river where it meets the ocean and fresh and salt waters mix. (p. 356)

> **estuario** La parte baja de un río donde desemboca en el océano y donde el agua dulce del río se mezcla con el agua salada del mar.

eukaryotic cell (yoo-KAR-ee-AHT-ihk)

> A cell in which the genetic material is enclosed within a nucleus, surrounded by its own membrane. (p. 20)

> **célula eucariota** Una célula en la cual el material genético esta dentro de un núcleo, rodeado por su propia membrana.

evaporation
A process by which a substance changes from its liquid state to its gas state by random particle movement. Evaporation usually occurs at the surface of a liquid over a wide range of temperatures. (p. 485)

> **evaporación** Un proceso mediante el cual una sustancia cambia de su estado líquido a su estado gaseoso por medio del movimiento aleatorio de las partículas. La evaporación normalmente ocurre en la superficie de un líquido en una amplia gama de temperaturas.

exothermic reaction

A chemical reaction that releases energy. (p. 587)

   reacción exotérmica Una reacción química que libera energía.

experiment

An organized procedure to study something under controlled conditions. (p. xxiv)

   experimento Un procedimiento organizado para estudiar algo bajo condiciones controladas.

extinction

The permanent disappearance of a species. (p. xxxi)

   extinción La desaparición permanente de una especie.

F

fermentation

A chemical process by which cells release energy from sugar when no oxygen is present. (p. 52)

   fermentación Un proceso químico mediante el cual las células liberan energía del azúcar cuando no hay oxígeno presente.

fertilization

Part of the process of sexual reproduction in which a male reproductive cell and a female reproductive cell combine to make a new cell that can develop into a new organism. (pp. 118, 281)

   fertilización El proceso mediante el cual una célula reproductiva masculina y una célula reproductiva femenina se combinan para formar una nueva célula que puede convertirse en un organismo nuevo.

fetus

The developing human embryo from eight weeks to birth. (p. 282)

   feto El embrión humano en desarrollo de las ocho semanas al nacimiento.

food chain

A model used to show the feeding relationship between a single producer and a chain of consumers in an ecosystem. In a typical food chain, a plant is the producer that is eaten by a consumer, such as an insect; then the insect is eaten by a second consumer, such as a bird. (p. 346)

   cadena alimentaria Un modelo usado para mostrar la relación de ingestión entre un solo productor y una cadena de consumidores en un ecosistema. En una cadena alimentaria típica, una planta es la productora que es ingerida por un consumidor como un insecto, y luego el insecto es ingerido por un segundo consumidor como un pájaro.

food web

A model used to show a feeding relationship in which many food chains overlap in an ecosystem. (p. 346)

   red trófica Un modelo usado para mostrar una relación de consumo en la cual muchas cadenas alimentarias se empalman en un ecosistema.

force

A push or a pull; something that changes the motion of an object. (p. xxxiii)

   fuerza Un empuje o un jalón; algo que cambia el movimiento de un objeto.

freezing

The process by which a substance changes from its liquid state into its solid state. (p. 484)

   congelación El proceso mediante el cual una sustancia cambia de su estado líquido a su estado sólido.

freezing point

The temperature at which a substance changes from its liquid state to its solid state through freezing. (p. 484)

   punto de congelación La temperatura a la cual una sustancia cambia de su estado líquido a su estado sólido mediante congelación.

friction

A force that resists the motion between two surfaces in contact. (p. xxxv)

   fricción Una fuerza que resiste el movimiento entre dos superficies en contacto.

G

gamete

A sperm or egg cell, containing half the usual number of chromosomes of an organism (one chromosome from each pair), which is found only in the reproductive organs of a plant or animal. (p. 118)

   gameto Un óvulo o un espermatozoide, que contiene la mitad del número usual de cromosomas de un organismo (un cromosoma de cada par), que se encuentra sólo en los órganos reproductivos de una planta o de un animal.

gas

Matter with no definite volume and no definite shape. The molecules in a gas are very far apart, and the amount of space between them can change easily. (p. 460)

   gas Materia sin volumen definido ni forma definida. Las moléculas en un gas están muy separadas unas de otras, y la cantidad de espacio entre ellas puede cambiar fácilmente.

gene
The basic unit of heredity that consists of a segment of DNA on a chromosome. (p. 102)

gen La unidad básica de herencia que consiste en un segmento de ADN en un cromosoma.

genetic engineering
The scientific process in which DNA is separated from an organism, changed, and then reinserted into the same or a different organism. (p. 151)

ingeniería genética El proceso científico en el cual se extrae el ADN de un organismo, se modifica y luego se reinserta en el mismo organismo o en uno diferente.

genetic material
The nucleic acid DNA that is present in all living cells and contains the information needed for a cell's growth, maintenance, and reproduction.

material genético El ácido nucleico ADN, ue esta presente en todas las células vivas y que contiene la información necesaria para el crecimiento, el mantenimiento y la reproducción celular.

genome (JEE-nohm)
All the DNA of an organism, including its genes; the genetic material of an organism. (p. 154)

genoma Todo el ADN de un organismo, incluyendo sus genes; el material genético de un organismo.

genotype (JEHN-uh-typ)
The genetic makeup of an organism; all the genes that an organism has. (p. 106)

genotipo La estructura genética de un organismo; todos los genes que tiene un organismo.

geosphere (JEE-uh-SFEER)
All the features on Earth's surface—continents, islands, and seafloor—and everything below the surface—the inner and outer core and the mantle; one of the four parts of the Earth system. (p. xxxiii)

geosfera Todas las características de la superficie de la Tierra, es decir, continentes, islas y el fondo marino, y de todo bajo la superficie, es decir, el núcleo externo e interno y el manto; una de las cuatro partes del sistema de la Tierra.

gland
An organ in the body that produces a specific substance, such as a hormone. (p. 271)

glándula Un órgano en el cuerpo que produce una sustancia específica, como una hormona.

glucose
A sugar molecule that is a major energy source for most cells, produced by the process of photosynthesis. (p. 47)

glucosa Una molécula de azúcar que es la principal fuente de energía para la mayoría de las células, producida mediante el proceso de fotosíntesis.

gravity
The force that objects exert on each other because of their masses. (p. xxxv)

gravedad La fuerza que los objetos ejercen entre sí debido a sus masas.

group
A vertical column in the periodic table of the elements. Elements in a group have similar properties. (p. 522)

grupo Una columna vertical en la tabla periódica de los elementos. Los elementos en un grupo tienen propiedades similares.

H

habitat
The natural environment in which a living thing gets all that it needs to live; examples include a desert, a coral reef, and a freshwater lake. (p. 366)

hábitat El medio ambiente natural en el cual un organismo vivo consigue todo lo que requiere para vivir; ejemplos incluyen un desierto, un arrecife coralino y un lago de agua dulce.

half-life
The amount of time it takes for half of the nuclei of a radioactive isotope to decay into atoms of another element. (p. 532)

vida media La cantidad de tiempo que se necesita para que le toma a la mitad del núcleo de un isótopo radioactivo se en descomponganerse en átomos de otro elemento.

heredity
The passing of genes from parents to offspring; the genes are expressed in the traits of the offspring. (p. 102)

herencia La transferencia de genes de los progenitores a las crías; los genes se expresan en los rasgos de las crías.

homeostasis (HOH-mee-oh-STAY-sihs)
A condition needed for health and functioning in which an organism or cell maintains a relatively stable internal environment. (p. 172)

homeostasis Una condición necesaria para la salud y el funcionamiento en la cual un organismo o una célula mantiene un medio ambiente estable e interna.

hormone
A chemical that is made in one organ and travels through the blood to another organ. (p. 271)

hormona Una sustancia química que se produce en un órgano y viaja por la sangre a otro órgano.

hydrosphere (HY-druh-SFEER)
All water on Earth—in the atmosphere and in the oceans, lakes, glaciers, rivers, streams, and underground reservoirs; one of the four parts of the Earth system. (p. xxxiii)

hidrosfera Toda el agua de la Tierra: en la atmósfera y en los océanos, lagos, glaciares, ríos, arroyos y depósitos subterráneos; una de las cuatro partes del sistema de la Tierra.

hypothesis
A tentative explanation for an observation or phenomenon. A hypothesis is used to make tentative predictions. (p. xxiv)

hipótesis Una explicación provisional de una observación o de un fenómeno. Una hipótesis se usa para hacer predicciones que se pueden probar.

I, J, K

immune system
A group of organs that provides protection against disease-causing agents. (p. 235)

sistema inmune o inmunológico Un grupo de órganos que provee protección contra agentes que causan enfermedades.

immunity
Resistance to a disease. Immunity can result from antibodies formed in the body during a previous attack of the same illness. (p. 240)

inmunidad La resistencia a una enfermedad. La inmunidad puede resultar de anticuerpos formados en el cuerpo durante un ataque previo de la misma enfermedad.

infancy
The stage of life that begins at birth and ends when a baby begins to walk. (p. 294)

infancia La etapa de la vida que inicia al nacer y termina cuando el bebe empieza a caminar.

integumentary system (ihn-TEHG-yu-MEHN-tuh-ree)
The body system that includes the skin and its associated structures. (p. 243)

sistema tegumentario El sistema corporal que incluye a la piel y a sus estructuras asociadas.

interaction
The condition of acting or having an influence upon something. Living things in an ecosystem interact with both the living and nonliving parts of their environment. (p. xxxi)

interacción La condición de actuar o influir sobre algo. Los organismos vivos en un ecosistema interactúan con las partes vivas y las partes sin vida de su medio ambiente.

interphase
The period in the cell cycle in which a cell grows, maintains itself, and prepares for division. (p. 81)

interfase El período en el ciclo celular en el cual una célula crece, se mantiene y se prepara para la división.

involuntary muscle
A muscle that moves without conscious control. (p. 184)

músculo involuntario Un músculo que se mueve sin control consciente.

ion
An atom or group of atoms that has a positive or negative electric charge. (p. 514)

ión Un átomo o un grupo de átomos que tiene una carga eléctrica positiva o negativa.

ionic bond
The electrical attraction between a negative ion and a positive ion. (p. 548)

enlace iónico La atracción eléctrica entre un ión negativo y un ión positivo.

isotope
An atom of one element that has a different number of neutrons than another atom of the same element. (p. 512)

isótopo Un átomo de un elemento que tiene un número diferente de neutrones que otro átomo del mismo elemento.

L

law
In science, a rule or principle describing a physical relationship that always works in the same way under the same conditions. The law of conservation of energy is an example.

ley En las ciencias, una regla o un principio que describe una relación física que siempre funciona de la misma manera bajo las mismas condiciones. La ley de la conservación de la energía es un ejemplo.

law of conservation of energy
A law stating that no matter how energy is transferred or transformed, it continues to exist in one form or another. (p. xxxv)

ley de la conservación de la energía Una ley que establece que no importa cómo se transfiere o transforma la energía, toda la energía sigue presente en alguna forma u otra.

law of conservation of mass
A law stating that atoms are not created or destroyed in a chemical reaction. (p. 579)

ley de la conservación de la masa Una ley que establece que los átomos ni se crean ni se destruyen en una reacción química.

limiting factor
A factor or condition that prevents the continuing growth of a population in an ecosystem. (p. 384)

factor limitante Un factor o una condición que impide el crecimiento continuo de una población en un ecosistema.

lipid
A type of molecule made up of subunits of fatty acids. Lipids are found in the fats, oils, and waxes used for structure and to store energy. (p. 43)

lípido Un tipo de molécula compuesta de unidades de ácidos grasos. Los lípidos se encuentran en las grasas, los aceites y las ceras usadas como materiales estructurales y para almacenar energía.

liquid
Matter that has a definite volume but does not have a definite shape. The molecules in a liquid are close together but not bound to one another. (p. 460)

líquido Materia que tiene un volumen definido pero no tiene una forma definida. Las moléculas en un líquido están cerca unas de otras pero no están ligadas.

M

mass
A measure of how much matter an object is made of. (p. 442)

masa Una medida de la cantidad de materia de la que está compuesto un objeto.

matter
Anything that has mass and volume. Matter exists ordinarily as a solid, a liquid, or a gas. (p. 441)

materia Todo lo que tiene masa y volumen. Generalmente la materia existe como sólido, líquido o gas.

meiosis (my-OH-sihs)
A part of sexual reproduction in which cells divide to form sperm cells in a male and egg cells in a female. Meiosis occurs only in reproductive cells. (p. 119)

meiosis Una parte de la reproducción sexual en la cual las células se dividen para formar espermatozoides en los machos y óvulos en las hembras. La meiosis sólo ocurre en las células reproductivas.

melting
The process by which a substance changes from its solid state to its liquid state. (p. 483)

fusión El proceso mediante el cual una sustancia cambia de su estado sólido a su estado líquido.

melting point
The temperature at which a substance changes from its solid state to its liquid state through melting. (p. 483)

punto de fusión La temperatura a la cual una sustancia cambia de su estado sólido a su estado líquido mediante fusión.

menstruation
A period of about five days during which blood and tissue exit the body through the vagina. (p. 279)

menstruación Un período de aproximadamente cinco días durante el cual salen del cuerpo sangre y tejido por la vagina.

metal
An element that tends to be shiny, easily shaped, and a good conductor of electricity and heat. (p. 527)

metal Un elemento que tiende a ser brilloso, fácilmente deformable moldeado y buen conductor de electricidad y calor.

metallic bond
A certain type of bond in which nuclei float in a sea of electrons. (p. 556)

enlace metálico Cierto tipo de enlace en el cual los núcleos flotan en un mar de electrones.

metalloid
An element that has properties of both metals and nonmetals. (p. 530)

metaloide Un elemento que tiene propiedades de los metales así como de los no metales.

microorganism
A very small organism that can be seen only with a microscope. Bacteria are examples of microorganisms. (p. 308)

microorganismo Un organismo muy pequeño que solamente puede verse con un microscopio. Las bacterias son ejemplos de microorganismos.

microscope
An instrument that uses glass lenses to magnify an object. (p. 12)

microscopio Un instrumento que usa lentes de vidrio para magnificar un objeto.

mitochondria (MY-tuh-KAWN-dree-uh)
Organelles that release energy by using oxygen to break down sugars. (p. 23)

mitocondrias Organelos que liberan energía usando oxígeno para romper los azúcares.

mitosis
The phase in the cell cycle during which the nucleus divides. (p. 81)

mitosis La fase en el ciclo celular durante la cual se divide el núcleo.

mixture
A combination of two or more substances that do not combine chemically but remain the same individual substances. Mixtures can be separated by physical means. (p. 455)

mezcla Una combinación de dos o más sustancias que no se combinan químicamente sino que permanecen como sustancias individuales. Las mezclas se pueden separar por medios físicos.

molecule
A group of atoms that are held together by covalent bonds so that they move as a single unit. (pp. 450, 551)

molécula Un grupo de átomos que están unidos mediante enlaces covalentes de tal manera que se mueven como una sola unidad.

multicellular
A term used to describe an organism that is made up of many cells. (p. 11)

multicelular Un término usado para describir a un organismo que esta formado por muchas células.

muscular system
The muscles of the body that, together with the skeletal system, function to produce movement. (p. 183)

sistema muscular Los músculos del cuerpo que, junto con el sistema óseo, sirven para producir movimiento.

mutation
Any change made to DNA. (p. 145)

mutación Cualquier cambio hecho al ADN.

mutualism (MYOO-choo-uh-LIHZ-uhm)
An interaction between two species in which both benefit; a type of symbiosis. (p. 378)

mutualismo Una interacción entre dos especies en la cual ambas se benefician; un tipo de simbiosis.

N

natural resource
Any type of matter or energy from Earth's environment that humans use to meet their needs. (p. 404)

recurso natural Cualquier tipo de materia o energía del medio ambiente de la Tierra que usan los humanos para satisfacer sus necesidades.

neuron
A nerve cell. (p. 265)

neurona Una célula nerviosa.

neutral
Describing a solution that is neither an acid nor a base. A neutral solution has a pH of 7. (p. 629)

neutro Que describe una solución que no es un ácido ni una base. Una solución neutra tiene un pH de 7.

neutron
A particle that has no electric charge and is located in an atom's nucleus. (p. 511)

neutrón Una partícula que no tiene carga eléctrica y que se encuentra en el núcleo de un átomo.

niche (nihch)
The role a living thing plays in its habitat. A plant is a food producer, whereas an insect both consumes food as well as provides food for other consumers. (p. 367)

nicho El papel que juega un organismo vivo en su hábitat. Una planta es un productor de alimento mientras que un insecto consume alimento y a la vez sirve de alimento a otros consumidores.

nitrogen cycle
The continuous movement of nitrogen through Earth, its atmosphere, and the living things on Earth. (p. 339)

ciclo del nitrógeno El movimiento ntinuo de nitrógeno por la Tierra, su atmósfera y los organismos vivos de la Tierra.

nonmetal
An element that is not a metal and has properties generally opposite to those of a metal. (p. 529)

no metal Un elemento que no es un metal y que tiene propiedades generalmente opuestas a las de los metales.

nucleic acid (noo-KLEE-ihk)
A type of molecule, made up of subunits of nucleotides, that is part of the genetic material of a cell and is needed to make proteins. DNA and RNA are nucleic acids. (p. 43)

ácido nucleico Un tipo de molécula, compuesto de unidades de nucleótidos, que es parte del material genético de una célula y se necesita para producir proteínas. El ADN y el ARN son ácidos nucleicos.

nucleus (NOO-klee-uhs)
1. The central region of an atom where most of the atom's mass is found in protons and neutrons. 2. The structure in a eukaryotic cell that contains the genetic material a cell needs to reproduce and function. (pp. 20, 511)

> **núcleo** 1. La región central de un átomo donde se encuentra la mayor parte de la masa del átomo en la forma de protones y neutrones. 2. La estructura en una célula eucariota que contiene el material genético que la célula necesita para reproducirse y funcionar.

nutrient (NOO-tree-uhnt)
A substance that an organism needs to live. Examples include water, minerals, and materials that come from the breakdown of food particles. (p. 205)

> **nutriente** Una sustancia que un organismo necesita para vivir. Ejemplos incluyen agua, minerales y sustancias que provienen de la descomposición de partículas de alimento.

nutrition
The study of the materials that nourish the body. (p. 300)

> **nutrición** El estudio de las sustancias que dan sustento al cuerpo.

offspring
The new organisms produced by one or two parent organisms.

> **crías** Los nuevos organismos producidos por uno o dos organismos progenitores.

organ
A structure in a plant or animal that is made up of different tissues working together to perform a particular function. (pp. 30, 171)

> **órgano** Una estructura en una planta o en un animal compuesta de diferentes tejidos que trabajan juntos para realizar una función determinada.

organelle (AWR-guh-NEHL)
A structure in a cell that is enclosed by a membrane and that performs a particular function. (p. 20)

> **organelo** Una estructura en una célula, envuelta en una membrana, que realiza una función determinada.

organism
An individual living thing, made up of one or many cells, that is capable of growing and reproducing. (p. 9)

> **organismo** Un individuo vivo, compuesto de una o muchas células, que es capaz de crecer y reproducirse.

organ system
A group of organs that together perform a function that helps the body meet its needs for energy and materials. (p. 172)

> **sistema de órganos** Un grupo de órganos que juntos realizan una función que ayuda al cuerpo a satisfacer sus necesidades energéticas y de materiales.

osmosis (ahz-MOH-sihs)
The movement of water through a membrane from an area of higher concentration to an area of lower concentration. (p. 59)

> **osmosis** El movimiento de agua a través de una membrana desde un área de mayor concentración hacia un área de menor concentración.

P, Q

parasitism (PAR-uh-suh-TIHZ-uhm)
A relationship between two species in which one species is harmed while the other benefits; a type of symbiosis. (p. 379)

> **parasitismo** Una relación entre dos especies en la cual una especie es perjudicada mientras que la otra se beneficia; un tipo de simbiosis.

parent
An organism that produces a new organism or organisms similar to or related to itself. (p. 93)

> **progenitor** Un organismo que produce un nuevo organismo u organismos parecidos a o relacionados a él.

passive transport
The movement of materials through a membrane without any input of energy. (p. 58)

> **transporte pasivo** El movimiento de sustanciasa través de una membrana sin aporte de energía.

pathogen
An agent that causes disease. (p. 234)

> **patógeno** Un agente que causa una enfermedad.

pedigree
A chart that shows family relationships, including two or more generations. (p. 147)

> **pedigrí** Un diagrama de las relaciones de dos o más generaciones de una familia.

percentage
A ratio that states the number of times an outcome is likely to occur out of a possible 100 times. (p. 112)

> **porcentaje** Una razón que establece el número de veces que es probable que ocurra un resultado en 100 veces.

period
A horizontal row in the periodic table of the elements. Elements in a period have varying properties. (p. 522)

período Un renglón horizontal en la tabla periódica de los elementos. Los elementos en un período tienen distintas propiedades.

periodic table
A table of the elements, arranged by atomic number, that shows the patterns in their properties. (p. 518)

tabla periódica Una tabla de los elementos, organizada en base a número atómico, que muestra los patrones en sus propiedades.

peripheral nervous system
The part of the nervous system that lies outside the brain and spinal cord. (p. 266)

sistema nervioso periférico La parte del sistema nervioso que se encuentra fuera del cerebro y la médula espinal.

peristalsis (PEHR-ih-STAWL-sihs)
Wavelike contractions of smooth muscles in the organs of the digestive tract. The contractions move food through the digestive system. (p. 206)

peristalsis Contracciones ondulares de músculos lisos en los órganos del tracto digestivo. Las contracciones mueven el alimento por el sistema digestivo.

pH
The concentration of hydrogen ions in a solution; a measurement of acidity. (p. 629)

pH La concentración de iones de hidrógeno en una solución; una medida de acidez.

phenotype
The observable characteristics or traits of an organism. (p. 106)

fenotipo Las características o rasgos visibles de un organismo.

photosynthesis (FOH-toh-SIHN-thih-sihs)
The process by which green plants and other producers use simple compounds and energy from light to make sugar, an energy-rich compound. (pp. 48, 590)

fotosíntesis El proceso mediante el cual las plantas verdes y otros productores usan compuestos simples y energía de la luz para producir azúcares, compuestos ricos en energía.

physical change
A change in a substance that does not change the substance into a different one. (p. 476)

cambio físico Un cambio en una sustancia que no transforma la sustancia a otra sustancia.

physical property
A characteristic of a substance that can be observed without changing the identity of the substance. (p. 473)

propiedad física Una característica de una sustancia que se puede observar sin cambiar la identidad de la sustancia.

pioneer species
The first species to move into a lifeless environment. Plants like mosses are typical pioneer species on land. (p. 386)

especie pionera La primera especie que ocupa un medio ambiente sin vida. Las plantas como los musgos son típicas especies pioneras terrestres.

polar covalent bond
The unequal sharing of electrons between two atoms that gives rise to negative and positive regions of electric charge. (p. 551)

enlace polar covalente El compartir electrones desigualmente entre dos átomos y que lleva a la formación de regiones de carga eléctrica positiva y regiones de carga eléctrica negativa.

pollution
The release of harmful substances into the air, water, or land. (p. 411)

contaminación La descarga de sustancias nocivas al aire, al agua o a la tierra.

population
A group of organisms of the same species that live in the same area. For example, a desert will have populations of different species of lizards and cactus plants. (p. 366)

población Un grupo de organismos de la misma especie que viven en la misma área. Por ejemplo, un desierto tendrá poblaciones de distintas especies de lagartijas y de cactus.

population density
A measure of the number of organisms that live in a given area. The population density of a city may be given as the number of people living in a square kilometer. (p. 406)

densidad de población Una medida de la cantidad de organismos que viven un área dada. La densidad de población de una ciudad puede expresarse como el número de personas que viven en un kilómetro cuadrado.

precipitate

n. A solid substance that forms as a result of a reaction between chemicals in two liquids.

v. To come out of solution. (p. 572)

precipitado *s.* Una sustancia sólida que se forma como resultado de la reacción entre sustancias químicas en dos líquidos.

precipitar *v.* Salir de solución.

predator

An animal that hunts other animals and eats them. An owl is a predator that feeds on small animals such as mice. (p. 375)

predador Un animal que caza otros animales y se los come. Un búho es un predador que se alimenta de animales pequeños como los ratones.

prey

An animal that other animals hunt and eat. A mouse is prey that is eaten by other animals, such as owls and snakes. (p. 375)

presa Un animal que otros animales cazan y se comen. Un ratón es una presa que es comido por otros animales como los búhos y las serpientes.

probability

The likelihood or chance that a specific outcome will occur out of a total number of outcomes. (p. 112)

probabilidad La posibilidad de que ocurra un resultado específico en un número total de resultados.

producer

An organism that captures energy from sunlight and transforms it into chemical energy that is stored in energy-rich carbon compounds. Producers are a source of food for other organisms. (p. 343)

productor Un organismo que capta energía de la luz solar y la transforma a energía química que se almacena en compuestos de carbono ricos en energía. Los productores son una fuente de alimento para otros organismos.

product

A substance formed by a chemical reaction. A product is made by the rearrangement of atoms and bonds in reactants. (p. 571)

producto Una sustancia formada por una reacción química. Un producto se hace mediante la reorganización de los átomos y los enlaces en los reactivos.

prokaryotic cell (proh-KAR-ee-AWT-ihk)

A cell that lacks a nucleus and other organelles, with DNA that is not organized into chromosomes. (p. 20)

célula procariota Una célula que carece de núcleo y otros organelos, con ADN que no esta organizado en cromosomas.

protein

One of many types of molecules made up of chains of amino acid subunits. Proteins control the chemical activity of a cell and support growth and repair. (p. 43)

proteína Uno de muchos tipos de moléculas formadas por cadenas de aminoácidos. Las proteínas controlan la actividad química de una célula y sustentan el crecimiento y la reparación.

proton

A positively charged particle located in an atom's nucleus. (p. 511)

protón Una partícula con cargada positivamente localizada en el núcleo de un átomo.

Punnett square

A chart used to show all the ways genes from two parents can combine and be passed to offspring; used to predict all genotypes that are possible. (p. 110)

cuadro de Punnett Una tabla que se usa para mostrar todas las formas en que los genes de dos progenitores pueden combinarse y pasarse a la crías; se usa para predecir todos los genotipos que son posibles.

R

radiation (RAY-dee-AY-shuhn)

Energy that travels across distances in the form of electromagnetic waves. (p. xxxiii)

radiación Energía que viaja a través de la distancia en forma de ondas electromagnéticas.

radioactivity

The process by which the nucleus of an atom of an element releases energy and particles. (p. 530)

radioactividad El proceso mediante el cual el núcleo de un átomo de un elemento libera energía y partículas.

ratio

A comparison between two quantities, often written with a colon, as 3 : 4. (p. 112)

razón Una comparación entre dos cantidades, a menudo se escribe con dos puntos, como 3 : 4.

reactant

A substance that is present at the beginning of a chemical reaction and is changed into a new substance. (p. 571)

reactante Una sustancia que está presente en el comienzo de una reacción química y que se convierte en una nueva sustancia.

reactive

Likely to undergo a chemical change. (p. 526)

reactivo Que es probable que sufra un cambio químico.

recessive

A term that describes an allele that is not expressed when combined with a dominant form of the gene. (p. 107)

recesivo Un término que describe un alelo que no se expresa cuando se combina con una forma dominante del gen.

red blood cell

A type of blood cell that picks up oxygen in the lungs and delivers it to cells throughout the body. (p. 227)

glóbulos rojos Un tipo de célula sanguínea que toma oxígeno en los pulmones y lo transporta a células en todo el cuerpo.

regeneration

In some organisms, the process by which certain cells produce new tissue growth at the site of a wound or lost limb; also a form of asexual reproduction. (p. 90)

regeneración En algunos organismos, el proceso mediante el cual ciertas células producen crecimiento de tejido nuevo en el sitio de una herida o de una extremidad perdida; también un tipo de reproducción asexual.

replication

The process by which DNA is copied before it condenses into chromosomes. Replication takes place before a cell divides. (p. 137)

replicación El proceso mediante el cual el ADN se copia antes de condensarse en los cromosomas. La replicación se realiza antes de que una célula se divida.

resistance

The ability of an organism to protect itself from a disease or the effects of a substance. (p. 313)

resistencia La habilidad de un organismo para protegerse de una enfermedad o de los efectos de una sustancia.

respiration

The physical and chemical processes by which a living thing exchanges gases with the environment. In cellular respiration, cells take in oxygen and release the energy stored in carbon compounds. (p. 594)

respiración Los procesos físicos y químicos mediante los cuales un organismo vivo toma oxígeno y libera energía. En la respiración celular, las células absorben oxígeno y liberan la energía almacenada en compuestos de carbono.

respiratory system

A system that interacts with the environment and with other body systems to bring oxygen to the body and remove carbon dioxide. (p. 197)

sistema respiratorio Un sistema que interactúa con el medio ambiente y con otros sistemas corporales para traer oxígeno al cuerpo y eliminar dióxido de carbono.

RNA

A molecule that carries genetic information from DNA to a ribosome, where the genetic information is used to bring together amino acids to form a protein. Ribonucleic acid (RY-boh-noo-KLEE-ihk). (p. 138)

ARN Una molécula que lleva información genética del ADN al ribosoma, donde la información genética se usa para unir aminoácidos para formar una proteína. Ácido ribonucleico.

S

saturated

Containing the maximum amount of a solute that can be dissolved in a particular solvent at a given temperature and pressure. (p. 618)

saturado Que contiene la máxima cantidad de soluto que se puede disolver en un solvente en particular a determinada temperatura y presión.

selective breeding

The process of breeding plants and animals with specific traits to produce offspring that have these traits. (p. 151)

reproducción selectiva El proceso de reproducir plantas y animales con rasgos específicos para producir crías que tengan estos rasgos.

sexual reproduction

A type of reproduction in which male and female reproductive cells combine to form offspring with genetic material from both cells. (p. 102)

reproducción sexual Un tipo de reproducción en el cual se combinan las células reproductivas femeninas y masculinas para formar una cría con material genético de ambas células.

skeletal muscle

A muscle that attaches to the skeleton. (p. 184)

músculo esquelético Un músculo que está sujeto al esqueleto.

skeletal system

The framework of bones that supports the body, protects internal organs, and anchors all the body's movement. (p. 174)

> **sistema óseo** El armazón de huesos que sostiene al cuerpo, protege a los órganos internos y sirve de ancla para todo el movimiento del cuerpo.

smooth muscle

Muscle that performs involuntary movement and is found inside certain organs, such as the stomach. (p. 184)

> **músculo liso** Músculos que realizan movimiento involuntario y se encuentran dentro de ciertos órganos, como el estómago.

solid

Matter that has a definite shape and a definite volume. The molecules in a solid are in fixed positions and are close together. (p. 460)

> **sólido** La materia que tiene una forma definida y un volumen definido. Las moléculas en un sólido están en posiciones fijas y cercanas unas a otras.

solubility

The amount of solute that dissolves in a certain amount of a solvent at a given temperature and pressure to produce a saturated solution. (p. 619)

> **solubilidad** La cantidad de soluto que se disuelve en cierta cantidad de solvente a determinada temperatura y presión para producir una solución saturada.

solute

In a solution, a substance that is dissolved in a solvent. (p. 612)

> **soluto** En una solución, una sustancia que se disuelve en un solvente.

solution

A mixture of two or more substances that is identical throughout; a homogeneous mixture. (p. 611)

> **solución** Una mezcla de dos o más sustancias que es idéntica en su totalidad;, una mezcla homogénea.

solvent

In a solution, the substance that dissolves a solute and makes up the largest percentage of a solution. (p. 612)

> **solvente** En una solución, la sustancia que disuelve un soluto y que compone el porcentaje mayor de la una solución.

specialization

The specific organization of a cell and its structure that allows it to perform a specific function. (p. 28)

> **especialización** La organización específica de una célula y de su estructura que le permite realizar una función específica.

species

A group of living things that are so closely related that they can breed with one another and produce offspring that can breed as well. (p. 365)

> **especie** Un grupo de organismos que están tan estrechamente relacionados que pueden aparearse entre sí y producir crías que también pueden aparearse.

sperm

A male reproductive cell (gamete) that forms in the reproductive organs of a male and has just a single copy of the genetic material of the parent. (p. 118)

> **espermatozoide** Una célula reproductiva masculina (gameto) que se forma en los órganos reproductivos de un macho y tiene una sola copia del material genético del progenitor.

spongy bone

Strong, lightweight tissue inside a bone. (p. 175)

> **hueso esponjoso** Tejido fuerte y de peso ligero dentro de un hueso.

states of matter

The different forms in which matter can exist. Three familiar states are solid, liquid, and gas. (p. 459)

> **estados de la materia** Las diferentes formas en las cuales puede existir la materia. Los tres estados conocidos son sólido, líquido y gas.

stimulus

Something that causes a response in an organism or a part of the body. (p. 262)

> **estímulo** Algo que causa una respuesta en un organismo o en una parte del cuerpo.

sublimation

The process by which a substance changes directly from its solid state to its gas state without becoming a liquid first. (p. 485)

> **sublimación** El proceso mediante el cual una sustancia cambia directamente de su estado sólido a su estado gaseoso sin convertirse primero en líquido.

subscript

A number written slightly below and to the right of a chemical symbol that shows how many atoms of an element are in a compound. (p. 543)

subíndice Un número que se escribe en la parte inferior a la derecha de un símbolo químico y que muestra cuantos átomos de un elemento están en un compuesto.

succession (suhk-SEHSH-uhn)

A natural process that involves a gradual change in the plant and animal communities that live in an area. (p. 386)

sucesión Un proceso natural que involucra un cambio gradual en las comunidades de plantas y animales que viven en un área.

suspension

A mixture in which the different parts are identifiable as separate substances; a heterogeneous mixture. (p. 613)

suspensión Una mezcla en la cual las diferentes partes son identificables como sustancias distintas; una mezcla heterogénea.

sustainable

A term that describes the managing of certain natural resources so that they are not harmed or used up. Examples include maintaining clean groundwater and protecting top soil from erosion. (p. 422)

sostenible Un término que describe el manejo de ciertos recursos naturales para que no se deterioren o se terminen. Ejemplos incluyen mantener limpia el agua subterránea y proteger de la erosión a la capa superficial del suelo.

symbiosis (SIHM-bee-OH-sihs)

The interaction between individuals from two different species that live closely together. (p. 378)

simbiosis La interacción entre individuos de dos especies distintas que viven en proximidad.

system

A group of objects or phenomena that interact. A system can be as simple as a rope, a pulley, and a mass. It also can be as complex as the interaction of energy and matter in the four parts of the Earth system.

sistema Un grupo de objetos o fenómenos que interactúan. Un sistema puede ser algo tan sencillo como una cuerda, una polea y una masa. También puede ser algo tan complejo como la interacción de la energía y la materia en las cuatro partes del sistema de la Tierra.

T

technology

The use of scientific knowledge to solve problems or engineer new products, tools, or processes.

tecnología El uso de conocimientos científicos para resolver problemas o para diseñar nuevos productos, herramientas o procesos.

theory

In science, a set of widely accepted explanations of observations and phenomena. A theory is a well-tested explanation that is consistent with all available evidence.

teoría En las ciencias, un conjunto de explicaciones de observaciones y fenómenos que es ampliamente aceptado. Una teoría es una explicación bien probada que es consecuente con la evidencia disponible.

tissue

A group of similar cells that are organized to do a specific job. (pp. 29, 170)

tejido Un grupo de células parecidas que juntas realizan una función específica en un organismo.

U

unicellular

A term used to describe an organism that is made up of a single cell. (p. 11)

unicelular Un término usado para describir a un organismo que está compuesto de una sola célula.

urban

A term that describes a city environment.

urbano Un término que describe el medio ambiente de una ciudad.

urinary system

A group of organs that filter waste from an organism's blood and excrete it in a liquid called urine. (p. 213)

sistema urinario Un grupo de órganos que filtran desechos de la sangre de un organismo y los excretan en un líquido llamado orina.

urine

Liquid waste that is secreted by the kidneys. (p. 213)

orina El desecho líquido que secretan los riñones.

V

vaccine
A small amount of a weakened pathogen that is introduced into the body to stimulate the production of antibodies. (p. 240)

vacuna Una pequeña cantidad de un patógeno debilitado que se introduce al cuerpo para estimular la producción de anticuerpos.

variable
Any factor that can change in a controlled experiment, observation, or model. (p. R30)

variable Cualquier factor que puede cambiar en un experimento controlado, en una observación o en un modelo.

vein
A blood vessel that carries blood back to the heart. (p. 229)

vena Un vaso sanguíneo que lleva la sangre de regreso al corazón.

virus
A nonliving, disease-causing particle that uses the materials inside cells to reproduce. A virus consists of genetic material enclosed in a protein coat. (p. 309)

virus Una particular sin vida, que causa enfermedad y que usa los materiales dentro de las células para reproducirse. Un virus consiste de material genético encerrado en una cubierta proteica.

volume
An amount of three-dimensional space, often used to describe the space that an object takes up. (p. 443)

volumen Una cantidad de espacio tridimensional; a menudo se usa este término para describir el espacio que ocupa un objeto.

voluntary muscle
A muscle that can be moved at will. (p. 184)

músculo voluntario Un músculo que puede moverse a voluntad.

voluntary nervous system
The nerves that govern consciously controlled function and movement. (p. 267)

sistema nervioso voluntario Los nervios que gobiernan las funciones y el movimiento cuyo control es consciente.

W, X, Y, Z

water cycle
The continuous movement of water through Earth, its atmosphere, and the living things on Earth. (p. 337)

ciclo del agua El movimiento continuo de agua por la Tierra, su atmósfera y los organismos vivos de la Tierra.

weight
The force of gravity on an object. (p. 443)

peso La fuerza de la gravedad sobre un objeto.

Index

Page numbers for definitions are printed in **boldface** type.
Page numbers for illustrations, maps, and charts are printed in *italics.*

A

AB blood, 231
abdominal breathing, 204, *204*
abiotic factors, **330**, 350, 385
  effect on ecosystems, *331*, 331–333
  light as, 332
  soil as, 648, 650, *650*
  temperature as, 331, *331*
  water as, 333
A blood, 231
accuracy, **R22**
acetic acid, 612, 628
acid(s), 208, **626**
  chapter investigation into, 632–633
  characteristics of, 627, *627*
  common, *630*
  measuring strengths of, 628–629
  neutralization of bases by, 631
  properties of, 625–627
acid-base indicators, 627, 629
acidic solutions, 629
acidity, measuring, 629
acid rain, 412, *412*, 631
acquired immunodeficiency syndrome (AIDS), 313, *647*
acquired traits, 101, 102
active immunity, 240
active transport, **60**, 60–61, *61*
adaptations, 375
addiction, 305, **306**
adenine (A), 136, 138, 139
Adirondack Mountains, acid rain in, 412, *412*
adolescents, **295**, 298
  skeleton in, 178
adrenal glands, **271**, *271, 272*
adrenaline, *271, 272*
adulthood, **296**
  later, 296
  skeleton in, 178
aeration, zone of, 651
aerogel, *491*
aging, 4
  stress of, 298
air, xxxi. *See also* atmosphere.
  investigation into particles of, 411
  quality of, 412, *412*
  in spread of disease, 310
air pollution, 413, *413*
albinism, 146
alcohol, 305
  fermentation of, 52–53
algae, 384, 646
alkali metals, 527
alkaline earth metals, 527

alleles, *102,* **103,** 105
  dominant, 107, *107,* 110, 114
  in producing traits, 106–107
  recessive, 107, *107,* 110, 114
  sickle cell, 147
alloys, 528, **634**
  common, *635*
  Internet activity on, 609
  investigation of, 637
  in medicine, 637, *637*
  memory, 637
  mixtures in, 639
  in space flight, 638, *638*
  in transportation, 636
  uses of, 636–638
alternative energy sources, development of, 423
aluminum, 492, 519, 636
alveoli, 200
Alvin (three-person submarine), 436
Alzheimer's disease, 146
amino acids, 43, *43,* 136
ammonia, 542, 619
Amoeba, 646, *646*
amphetamines, 305
analysis, critical, R8
anaphase, 82, *83*
anaphase I, **120,** *121*
anaphase II, **120,** *121*
angular movement, 179, *180*
animal(s)
  as biotic factors, 330
  contact with, 310
  distribution of, in habitat, 370
  fibers of, 46
  protecting species, 395
  wetland, 416
animal cells, *22,* 23
  cytokinesis in, *85*
  investigation into, 21
anorexia nervosa, 306
antibiotics, **241,** 309, 313
antibodies, **235,** 236, 239, 240
  investigation into, 239
antidiuretic hormone, *271*
antifreeze, 616, *616*
antigen, **238**
anvil, *263,* **263**
Apgar score, *294*
appearance in separating minerals, 495
appendicular skeleton, **175,** *177*
aquatic ecosystems, water pollution and, 413, *413*
aquifers, 624, 651
  pumping of groundwater from, 654
Archaea, 27, *27*
Arctic National Wildlife Refuge (ANWR), 397
area, **R43**

arginine, 137
argon gas, 529
arteries, **228,** *228, 229,* **229**
 pulmonary, 229, *229*
artificial polymer, 249
artificial skin, 249, *249*
asexual reproduction, **88,** 88–91
 comparison of sexual reproduction and, *92*
 health and, 90–91
 investigation into, 91
astatine, 522
asthma, *647*
athlete's foot, *647*
atmosphere, **xxx**
atomic masses, **517,** 518
 chapter investigation into modeling, 524–525
atomic mass number, **512,** 512–513
atomic model, 511, *511*
atomic numbers, **512,** 519
atomic particles, investigation into masses of, 513
atomic structure, timeline of, 604–607, *604–607*
atoms, **xxxv,** 42, 441, **448,** 448–449, 452, *452*
 chemical changes in, 530–531
 combination of, in predictable numbers, 542
 in matter, 509–510, *510*
 motion of, 451, *451,* 452
 sharing of electrons, 550–551
 size of, 448, 449, 512, 523
 structure of, *511,* 511–512
 transfer of electrons and, 548–549
auditory canal, 263
autonomic nervous system, *266,* 266–267, *267,* **267**
averages, calculating, **R36**
axial skeleton, **175,** *177*

B

bacilli, 645, *645*
bacteria, **14,** 27, 170, 308, *309,* **309,** 310, 645
 characteristics of, 645
 classification of, 645, *645*
 nitrogen-fixing, 340, *380,* 388
 spontaneous generation and, 14–15
bacteria cell, 645
balanced hormone action, 276
ball-and-socket joint, 180
Ballard, Robert, 436
banded sea snake, 435, *435*
bar graphs, R26, R31
 double, R27
bases, **626**
 chapter investigation into, 632–633
 characteristics of, 627, *627*
 common, *630*
 measuring strengths of, 628–629
 neutralization of acids by, 631
 properties of, 625–627
B blood, 231
B cells, **239,** 240
beam balances, 442
behavior
 of gases, 465, *465*
 learned, 101
bends, 622

Bessemer process, 636
bias, **R6**
 scientific, R6
 sources of, R6
bile, *210*
binary fission, *89,* **89,** 90
biodiversity, **411**
 habitat loss impact on, 414–416, *415, 416*
 impact of pollution on, 411
biology, importance of cell theory in, 14
biomagnification, 349, *349*
biomes, **350, 368,** *369*
 freshwater, 355–356, 651
 land, *351,* 351–354, *352, 353, 354*
 marine, 356–357, *357*
biosphere, **xxxiii**
biosphere 2, carbon dioxide levels in, 55, *55*
biotic factors, **330,** 385
 animals as, 330
 interaction with ecosystem, 330
 plants as, 330
birth rates, 384
 populations and, 389
bismuth, 530
Black, Joseph, 604
bladder, 213
blood, **225,** *227,* 227–228, 516
 clotting of, 227
 removal of waste from, 213
 types of, 231, *231*
blood cells, 28, 175
blood pressure, *215,* 229–230, *230,* 296
 high, 230
blood vessels, *175,* 229, *229,* 296
bluebirds, 370
body systems, interaction of, in maintaining human
  body, 296–297
body temperature, 277, 296
 maintaining, 183, *183*
Bohr, Niels, 606
boiling, *486,* **486**
boiling point, **486**
 raising the, 616, *616*
bond energy, **586**
bonding as Internet Activity, 539
bonds
 chemical, 42, 541, 553–554
 covalent, **550,** 550–551, *551, 552,* 558
 ionic, *552*
 metallic, **556,** 556–557, 655
 polar covalent, *551,* **551,** *552,* 622
bone density, test of, 178, *178*
bone marrow, 235
bones, 516
 compact, 175
 flat, 174
 irregular, 174
 as lever, 174
 as living tissue, 174–175
 long, 174
 movement of, 186, *186*
 short, 174
 spongy, 175
Borrelia burgdorferi, 311
Boyle, Robert, 604

Brady, Mathew, 394
Braille, 164
brain, 265, *265*
   senses in, 163
brain stem, 267
brass, 528, *635*
breathing
   abdominal, 204, *204*
   lung, 204, *204*
   nostril, 204, *204*
broadleaf trees, 354, *354*
bromine, 522, 529, 655
bronchial tubes, 200, *201*
bronze, 612, 634, 635, *635*
Brown, Robert, 129
bubbles, formation of, as sign of chemical change, 480
buckminsterfullerene, 559, *559*
budding, 89, *89*
burns, 247, *324*
Busch, Gil, 164
Bush, George W., 397

C

cactus, 332, 352, 367, *367*, 368
calcitonin, 272
calcium, 527, 542
calcium carbonate, 627, 631
calcium chloride, 542, 553
cancer, 313
   effect of, on cell cycle, 148
   skin, *647*
cancer cells, *148*
Capers Island, *653*
capillaries, *229*, **229**
carbohydrates, *42*, **42**, 205, 206, **301**
   complex, 42
   simple, 42
carbon, 529, 636
   investigation into, 339
carbonate, 627
carbon cycles, *338*, **338**, 338–339, 424
carbon dioxide, 543, 580, *580*
   in carbon cycle, 338
   exchanging oxygen and, 198, *198*
   levels of, in biosphere 2, 55, *55*
carbon monoxide, 305
   air quality and, 412
carbon steel, *635*
carcinogens, 148
cardiac cells, 184
cardiac muscle, **184**, *185*
Carolina parakeet, *395*
carpooling, 424
carrying capacity, **385**, 402
   as Internet Activity, 363
Carson, Rachel, 396
case study of Colorado River, 405, *405*
castes, 377
catalysts, *576*, **576**, 595
catalytic converters, 596
   chemical reactions in, *597*
caterpillar, 346
cattail, 346

cause-and-effect relationship, **R5**
Cavendish, Henry, 604
Celera, 131
cell(s), 7, 128, 170
   animal, *22*
   bacteria, 645
   blood, 175
   cardiac, 184
   diffusion in, 57–58
   discovery of, 12
   diversity of, 20
   DNA of, 128
   effect of size on transport, 62–63
   elements in, 41–42
   epidermal, 246
   eukaryotic, *20*, **20**, 21, *22*, 23–24, 27
   features of, *33*
   as Internet Activity, 7
   investigation into, 62
   mast, *236*
   in multicellular organisms, 28, *29*, 29–31, *30*
   muscle, 63
   need for energy, 47
   nerve, 63
   origin of, 13, *13*
   parts of, *129*
   plant, *22*
   prokaryotic, *20*, **20**, 27
   red blood, 170, *222*, 231, 273
   release of energy by, 50
   size of, 18, *18*
   structure of, *129*
   use of active transport, 60–61
   use of diffusion, 56
   white blood, 131, 227, 235, 236, 237, 272
cell cycle, **80**, *81*, 81–82, *83*, 84
   chapter investigation of stages in, 86–87
   effect of cancer on, 148
cell division, 281
   in both sexual and asexual reproduction, 92
   cancer and, 148
   functions of, 73
   in growth, development and repair, 76–78, *78*
   as Internet Activity, 71
   investigation into, 84
   in meiosis, 119–120, *121*
   in multicellular organisms, 76
   phase of, *81*, 81–82
   in unicellular organisms, *89*, 89–90
cell function, 42–44
cell membrane, **20**, 45, *45*, 85
cell models, investigation into, 31
cell plate, 84
cells, prokaryotic, *20*, **20**, 27, 645
cell theory, *13*
   development of, 18
   importance of, in biology, 14
cellular respiration, **50**, *51*, 54, 58, **199**, 275, 303
   comparison of photosynthesis and, 52, *52*
cell wall, 21, *21*, 84
central nervous system, 264–265, *266*
central vacuoles, 24, *24*
cerebellum, 267
cerebral cortex, 163

chapter investigations. *See also* investigations.
    acids and bases, 632–633
    chemical bonds, 560–561
    cleaning oil spills, 426–427
    cleaning your hands, 314–315
    diffusion, 64–65
    estimating populations, 372–373
    exothermic or endothermic, 592–593
    extract and observe DNA, 142–143
    freezing point, 488–489
    heart rate and exercise, 232–233
    mass and volume, 446–447
    modeling a kidney, 216–217
    modeling atomic masses, 524–525
    muscles, 188–189
    offspring models, 108–109
    soil samples, 334–335
    stages of cell cycle, 86–87
    taste, 268–269
    using microscope, 16–17, *16–17*
chemical bonds, 42, 541, 547–554, 557–558
    chapter investigation into, 560–561
chemical changes, 471, **478**, 478–480, 571
    in atoms, 530–531
    as Internet Activity, 471
    investigation into, 479
    signs of, 480, *480*
chemical digestion, 207, 208
    investigation into, 207
chemical dyes in showing nerve growth, 79
chemical energy, **47,** 343
chemical equations, 580
    balancing, 581–582, *583*
chemical formulas, **543,** 543–544, *544,* 546
chemical pollution, *413,* 414, *414*
chemical properties, *478,* **478,** 478–480, *480,* 522
chemical reactions, 42, 44, **569,** 569–576
    atom intervention in, 569
    in catalytic converters, *597*
    classification of, 573, *573*
    description of, by chemical equations, 580
    energy changes in, 586–591
    evidence of, 572, *572*
    industrial uses of, 598–599, *599*
    investigation into, 574
    need for, in living things, 594–595
    rates of, 574–576
    use of, in technology, 596, *597*
chemical symbols, 519
chemistry in firefighting, 585, *585*
chemosynthesis, 343
childhood, **294**
    skeleton in, 178
children, 298
chlorine, 522, 542, 548
chlorophyll, **48**
chloroplasts, 23, **23,** 48, *48,* 50
chromium, 528
chromosome(s), **75,** *102, 129*
    of fruit flies, 129
    investigation into, 76
chromosome pairs, genes on, *102,* 102–103
cicadas, 371, *371,* 375
cilia, 28, *28,* 200, 235, *235*
circle graph, making, 458

circle graphs, 458, R25
circulatory system, **225,** 225–231, *228,* 235, 296, 297, 303
    structures in, *226,* 226–227, 229
    working with other body systems, 225
citric acid, *630*
clay, 649, *649,* 652
    physical properties of, 474, *474*
Clean Air Act, 420
Clean Water Act, 420
climate
    exploring, 436
    investigation into, 355
    in land biomes, 350
cloning, *154,* **154**
coal, 411
    as renewable resource, *410*
coat coloring, 116
cobalt alloy, 637
cocaine, 305
cocci, 645, *645*
cochlea, *263,* **263**
coefficients, **582**
    balancing equations with, 582, *583*
colds, *647*
collared lizard, 352, *352*
collecting duct, *214,* **214**
Colorado River, case study of, 405, *405*
color change, 572, *572*
    as sign of chemical change, 480
color fixers, 46, *46*
combustibility, 478
combustion, 339, 573, *573,* 578
commensalism, *379,* **379,** *380*
communication, chemistry of, 606
community, **368,** *369*
compact bone, *175,* **175**
competition, **375,** 375–376
complex carbohydrates, 42
compounds, 42, **455,** 541–545
    comparing mixtures and, 456
    covalent, 554, *554,* 558, 614, *614*
    ionic, 549, 553, 557–558, 614, *614*
    modeling, 543
    properties of, 541–542, 557–558
    synthetic, 504
computerized tomography (CT) systems scan, 256
concentration, 57, *57, 58, 575,* **617**
    chemical reactions and, 574
    degrees of, 618
condensation, *487,* **487**
conduction, 277
cones, 262
coniferous trees, *352,* **352,** 354, *386*
Connecting Sciences
    Life Science and Physical Science, 79, 277, 349
    Physical Science and Earth Science, 495, 516, 624
connective tissue, 170, 171
conservation, *419,* **419**
    in protecting ecosystems, 422–423
    wilderness, 394–397, *394–397*
conservation of mass
    investigation into, 579
    observations leading to discovery of, 578–579
    using, 584, *584*
conservation tillage, 422

constants, **R30**
consumers, *344,* **344,** 375, 388
   primary, 344, *344, 348*
   secondary, 344, *344,* 346, *348*
   tertiary, 344, *344, 348*
controlled burns, *324*
   in ecosystems, 322–325
convection, 277
Coolidge, William, 254
cooling, 277
cooperation, *377,* **377**
copper, 510, 522, 527, 528, 612, 634, 635
   chemical properties of, 478
corn, shapes and sizes of, *128*
cornea, *262,* **262**
corpuscles, 604
covalent bonds, **550,** 550–551, *551, 552,* 558
   polar, *551,* **551,** *552,* 622
covalent compounds, 554, *554,* 558, 614, *614*
cowbird chick, 381, *381*
crabs, 367, *367,* 368
cranium, 176
creosote bushes, 370, 375
Crick, Francis, 32, 74, 130
critical analysis, R8
   of statements, R8–R9
crying, 203
crystals, investigation into, 553
Curie, Marie, 255, 530, 606, *606*
Curie, Pierre, 606
cycles, **336**
   carbon, *338,* 338–339, 424
   cell, 80, *81,* 81–82, *83,* 84, 86–87, 148
   defined, 80
   nitrogen, 339–340, *340,* 424
   water, 337, *337,* 341, 410, 424
cystic fibrosis, 146, 312
cytokinesis, 80, **81,** *83,* 84, *85,* 89, **120,** *121*
cytoplasm, **20,** 27, 645
   division of, 84
cytosine (C), 136, 138, 139

D

Dalton, John, 511, 605, *605*
Damadian, Raymond, 256
dams, construction of, *654*
data
   analyzing, xxxix
   choosing display, 307
   describing set of, R36–R37
   graphing, 355
data tables, making, R23
Davy, Humphrey, 605
DDT, food chain and, 349, *349*
decay, radioactive, 532, *532*
deciduous trees, **353,** 353–354
decimals, **R39,** R40
   adding, R39
   dividing, R40
   multiplying, R40
   subtracting, R40
decomposers, 340, *345,* **345,** 388
   investigation into, 345

decomposition, 573, *573*
deep-sea, 435, *435*
   exploring vents, 436
De Forest, Lee, 606
deforestation, *415*
delivery, 282
delta, 653
density, **475**
   calculating, 475
   of elements, 523
   in identifying substances, 491
   of materials, 481
   in separating minerals, 495
deoxyribonucleic acid (DNA), 3, 32, 43, *74,* **74,** 75
   of cells, 128
   changes in sequences, 144–145
   chapter investigation into extracting and
      observing, 142–143
   characteristics of, 130
   effect of changes in, on organisms, 150–152
   of extinct animals, 155
   genetic code and, *136,* 136–137
   model of, 32, *32*
   recombined, 130
   storage of information, 135–138
deoxyribonucleic acid (DNA) double helix molecule, 130
deoxyribonucleic acid (DNA) fingerprints, 130, 153
deoxyribonucleic acid (DNA) identification, 153
deoxyribonucleic acid (DNA) technology, applications
      of, 153–154
dermis, *244,* **244**
desert, 352–353, *353*
desert ecosystems, 332, 333
desertification, 650
design
   of experiments, 493
   technological, xl–xli
DeSilva, Ashanti, *131*
development, role of cell division in, 77, *77*
dew, 482, *482*
diabetes mellitus, 276, *647*
diamonds, 529, 558
diaphragm, 200, *201,* 203
diet, effect of, on health, 300–302
diffusion, **56,** *57*
   in cells, 57–58
   chapter investigation into, 64–65
digestion, **206**
   chemical, 207, 208
   mechanical, 207
digestive system, 205, *209,* 212, 225, 297
   as defense from harmful materials, 235
   in moving and breaking down food, **206**
   organs in, 208, *209,* 210
digestive tract, movement of material through, 208
digital imaging, *257*
dilute solution, *618,* **618**
diploid cell, 118, 119
diseases
   germ theory on, *309*
   infectious, 647, *647*
   in later life, 312
   noninfectious, 647, *647*
   prevention and treatment, 240–241
   science in fighting, 308

displacement, measuring volume by, 445, *445*
divide, *652*, **652**
divides, **652**, *652*
dodo bird, 155
Dolly, 154, *154*
dominant alleles, *107,* **107,** 110, 114
Donald, Ian, 256
double bar graphs, R27
drainage basins, *652*
drawing conclusions, 91
drug abuse, 304, 305
dry ice, *454,* 485
Duwamish River (Washington), 413, *413*
dyes, 46
dystrophin, 136

E

ear. *See also* hearing.
   infections of, 309
eardrum, 263, *263,* **263**
Earth
   atoms in crust of, 510, *510*
   change over time, xxxiii
   gravity, xxxv
   heat, xxxiii
   location and movement of water on, 651–653
   processes, xxxiii
   surface, xxxiii
   system, xxxiii
Earth Science, xxxii, 495, 516
   connecting Physical Science to, 624
eating disorders, 306
ecologists, 389
ecology, **329**
   in urban planning, 408
ecosystem-management approach, 423
ecosystems, **329, 368,** *369,* 407
   biotic factors interaction with, 330
   changes in, over time, 386–388
   competition in, 375
   conservation in protecting, 422–423
   constant changes in, 383–388
   consumers in, 344, *344*
   controlled burns in, 322–325
   decomposers in, 345, *345*
   effect of abiotic factors on, *331,* 331–333
   efforts to protect, 418–425
   energy flows through, 342–345
   on fire, 322–325
   interactions in, 365–371, 381, *381*
   matter cycles through, 336–340
   movement of energy through, 348
   needs of, 336
   pressure of human populations on, 402–407
   producers in, 343, *343*
   recovery of, *421*
   support for life, 329–333
ecosystem services, 325, 397
eddies, 437, *437*
egg, **118**
egg cells, 278, 279
Einstein, Albert, 510
einsteinium, 510

electric properties, **492**
electron microscope, *130*
electrons, 19, **511**
   atoms sharing of, 550–551
   size of, 512
   transfer of, by atoms, 548–549
elements, 41–42, *454,* **454**
   atoms in, 511–513
   chemical properties of, 522
   densities of, 523
   in human body, *42*
   investigation into ratios, 543
   of life, 516
   location on periodic table, 548
   names and symbols of, 510
   organization of, by similarities, 517–519
   predicting new, 519
   rare Earth, 528, *528*
elephant, *370*
embryo, **281**
emphysema, 146
endangered species, helping, 420, *420*
Endangered Species Act, 420
endocrine glands, 271
endocrine system, **270,** 270–273, *273,* 295, 296
   control of, 274–276
endocytosis, 61, *61*
endoplasmic reticulum, *22,* 23–24
endothermic reactions, **587**
   absorption of energy in, *589,* 589–590
   chapter investigation into, 592–593
   exothermic reaction in combination with, 590–591
energy, **xxxiii, xxxv**
   bond, 586
   chemical, **47,** 343
   Earth system, xxxiii
   exercise and, 54, *54*
   flows through ecosystems, 342–345
   heat, xxxiii
   transport need for, 59
energy pyramid, *348,* **348**
environment
   growth of awareness of, 418–420, *421,* 422
   as Internet Activity, 399
   living things dependence on, 329–330
   organization of, into levels, 368, *369*
environmental pollution, 152
Environmental Protection Agency (EPA), 420
enzymes, 43, 576, *576,* 595
epidermal cells, 246
epidermis, *244,* **244**
epiglottis, 200, *201*
epithelial tissue, 170, 171
erosion, 653
Escherichia coli, 311
esophagus, **208**
   digestion in, 208
estrogen (females), *271*
estuary, **356,** *356*
ethylene glycol, 616
Euglena, 646, *646*
Eukarya, 28
   organisms in the domain, 645

eukaryotic cells, *20,* **20,** 21, *22,* 23–24, 27, 138
    genetic material of, 74
europium, 528
evaluating, **R8**
    media claims, R8
evaporation, 245, 277, 337, *485,* **485**
evidence, coillection of, xxxviii
exercise, 303
    chapter investigation into heart rate and, 232–233
    energy and, 54, *54*
    investigating response into, 274
    muscles and, 187, *187*
exocytosis, 61, *61*
exothermic reactions, **587**
    chapter investigation into, 592–593
    in combination with endothermic reaction, 590–591
    release of energy in, 587–589, *588*
experimental group, R30
experiments, **xxxviii.** *See also* labs.
    conclusions, drawing, R35
    constants, determining, R30
    controlled, **R28,** R30
    designing, 493, R28–R35
    hypothesis, writing, R29
    materials, determining, R29
    observations, recording, R33
    procedure, writing, R32
    purpose, determining, R28
    results, summarizing, R34
    variables, R30–R31, R32
exponential growth, 93
exponent, using, 93
extinct animals, DNA of, 155
Extreme Science
    DNA of extinct animals, 155
    growing new skin, 249, *249*
    looking at atoms, 452, *452*
eye, 30, *30*

F

face, aging, 299, *299*
fact, **R9**
    difference from opinion, R9
family groups, 377
farmland, loss of productive, 407
fast-twitch muscles, 184
fats, 205, **301**
fatty acids, 43, 627, *630*
faulty reasoning, **R7**
feedback
    mechanisms, 274–276
    negative, 275, *275*
    positive, *275,* 275–276
feeding relationships, models in explaining, 346
female reproductive system, 279, *279*
femur, *177*
fermentation, **52,** 52–53, 54
    investigation into, 53
Fermi, Enrico, 510
fermium, 510
ferns, 332
fertilization, *118,* **118,** 118–119, *281,* **281**
    investigation into, 119

fetus, **282**
    growth of, *283*
fibers, 46, *46,* 301
    animal, 46
    plant, 46
fibrin, 276
fibula, *177*
fight or flight response, 267
firefighter, 585, *585*
firefighting, chemistry in, 585, *585*
first generation, 104, *105*
flat bones, 174
Fleming, Alexander, 309
Flemming, Walther, 129
floodplain, 653
flu, *647*
fluorine, 522
food
    breaking down of, in digestive system, 206
    in spread of disease, 310
food chains, **346,** *347,* 355, 357, 375
    DDT and, 349, *349*
food labels, 302
    investigation into, 303
food web, **346**
force, **xxxv**
    friction, **xxxv**
    gravitational, **xxxv**
    physical, xxxv
forest fires, 323
forest habitat, *415*
forestry practices, changes in, 423
Forest Service, U.S., 423
formulas, **R42**
    chemical, 543–544, *544,* 546
    determining volume by, 444
fossil fuels, 411
    air quality and, 412
fossils, **xvii**
fractions, **R41**
    multiplying, by whole number, 389
Franklin, Rosalind, 32, 130
fraternal twins, 284
freezing, **484**
freezing point
    chapter investigation into, 488–489
    lowering, 615, *615*
Fresh Kills Landfill, 403, *403*
freshwater biomes, 355–356, *356,* 651
friction, **xxxv**
Frontiers in Science
    ecosystems on fire, 322–325
    exploring the water planet, 434–437, *434–437*
    genes that map the body, 2–3
    medicines from nature, 502–505, *502–505*
    surprising senses, 162–165
frostbite, 248
fruit flies
    chromosomes of, 129
    genes of, 129
fullerene, 559
functional magnetic resonance imaging (FMRI), 163–165
fungi, 241, *345*

G

Galápagos Islands, 366, *366, 367,* 368
gallbladder, 208, **210**
    in digestion, 210
gallium, 519, 530
Galveston Island State Park, *421*
gambling, 306
gametes, **118**
gases, **460,** *461*
    behavior of, 465, *465*
    collecting and studying, 604
    composition of, 464
    formation of, 572, *572*
    volume and, *464*
gas exchange, *198*
gas solution, 612, *612*
Geiger counter, 530
generation, spontaneous, 14–15
genes, 3, *102,* **102,** 105, 137, 312
    on chromosome pairs, *102,* 102–103
    of fruit flies, 129
    Hox, 3, *3*
    identification of, 131
    mutation of, 149
genetically modified fish, 130
genetically modified plants, 151–152, *152*
genetic code, DNA and, *136,* 136–137
genetic disorders, 312
    mutations as cause of, *146,* 146–147
genetic engineering, **151,** 151–152, *152*
    risks and benefits associated with, 152–153
genetic fingerprints, *131*
genetic material
    of eukaryotic cells, 74
    organization of, *75*
genetic profiles, 131
genomes, **154**
    studying, 154
genotypes, *106,* **106,** 113
geosphere, **xxxiii**
geothermal power plants, 423
germanium, 530
germs, 14, 309
germ theory, 309
Geronimo, Michelle, 164
Giardia lamblia, 311
glaciers, 337
glands, **271,** 271–272
    adrenal, *271,* 272
    endocrine, 271
    oil, 245
    pineal, 271, 272
    pituitary, 271, *271,* 272, 274, 275, 279
    salivary, 208, 209
    sweat, 245
    thymus, 235
    thyroid, 271, *271,* 272, 275
glaucoma, 146
Glen Canyon, 396
gliding movement, 180
global information systems (GIS), 396
glomerulus, 214, **214**
glow stick, 594, *594*

glucagon, 272, 276
glucose, 47, **47,** 48, 50, 58, 271
glycerol, 43
gold, *454,* 510, 527, 634
Goldsmith, Michael, 256
Golgi apparatus, 24
grams (g), 442
Grand Canyon, 396
Grant, Ulysses S., 394
graphing, 297
graphite, 529, 559, *559*
graphs
    bar, R26, R31
    circle, 458, R25
    double bar, R27
    interpreting, 55
    line, 242, 577, R24, R34
grasses, 351, 353
grassland, 352–353, *353*
grassroots efforts, 419, *419*
gravity, **xxxv,** 443
Great Salt Lake, 27
Green, Kevin, *130*
ground squirrel, 352
groundwater, *651,* **651,** 651–652
    pumping of, from aquifers, 654
group, **522**
growth, role of cell division in, 77, *77*
growth hormone, *271*
guanine (G), 136, 138, 139

H

habitats, **366,** 366–367, *367*
    changing, 415–416, *416*
    distribution of animals in, 370
    human impact on, 414–415
    impact on biodiversity of loss, 414–416, *415, 416*
    natural, 407
    populations in, 376
    removing, 414–415, *415*
hair, 246, *246*
Hales, Stephen, 604
half-life, **532**
hallucinations, 306
halogens, 522, 529, *529*
hammer, *263,* **263**
hands, chapter investigation into cleaning, 314–315
Hanson, David, 249, *249*
haploid cells, 118, 119
hard water, 624
healing, 247, *247*
health, 300
    asexual reproduction and, 90–91
    effect of diet on, 300–302
hearing, 263, **263,** *263. See also* ear.
heart, *226,* 226–227, **228,** *228,* 303
    pumping of, as Internet Activity, 223
heart rates, 307
    chapter investigation into exercise and, 232–233
heat. *See also* energy.
    Earth's, xxxiii
heath hen, *395*

heating, 277
    properties of, *492*, **492**
helium, 622
hemoglobin, 146
hemophilia, 149
heredity, *102*, **102**
    Gregor Mendel's discoveries about, 104–105, *105*
herring, 370, 375
heterogeneous mixture, 457
hiccup, 203
high blood pressure, 230
hinge joint, 179
histamine, 237
homeostasis, **172**, 183, 215, 245, 261, 274, 275
homogeneous mixture, 457, 611
homologs, 102–103, 119
Hooke, Robert, 12, 13, 128
    microscope of, *12*
hormone balance, 276
hormones, 270–271, *271*, **271**, 279, 295, 296
Hox genes, 3, *3*
    limb development and, 4, *4*
    as switches, 4
human body
    changes in, over time, 293–298
    elements in, *42*
    as Internet Activity, 167
    need for energy and materials, 205–206
    need for oxygen, 197
human chromosomes, *103*
human development, 293–298
    as Internet Activity, 291
human genome as Internet Activity, 133
Human Genome Project, 131
human populations
    growth of, 401–402, *402*
    pressure of, on ecosystems, 402–407
    projection of, 402, *402*
humans
    impact on water quality, 654
    resource use by, 409
humerus, *177*
Huntington's disease, 312
hydras, *89*
hydrazoic acid, 542
hydrochloric acid, 626, 628, *630*
hydrogen, 44, 542
    in water cycle, 337
hydrogen chloride, 628
hydrogen peroxide, 545, *545*
hydropower plants, 423
hydrosphere, **xxxiii**
hypothalamus, **271**, *272*, 274, 275
hypothesis, **xxxviii**, **R3**, R29

identical twins, 284
iguanas, 60, 61, 368
immune system, 234–241
    response structures in, *235*, 235–236
    response to attack, 236–240, *237*

immunity, **240**
    active, 240
    development of, 240, *240*
    passive, 240
impermeable rock, *651*
implantation, 282
impurities, filtering, 624
incineration, 404
Individuals with Disabilities Education Act (IDEA), 224, *224*
infancy, *294*, **294**
    skeleton in, 178
infants, 298
infectious diseases, 309, 647, *647*
    causes of, *311*
    spread of, 310
    treating, 309
inference, **R4**, R35
inferring, 173, 382, 456, 574, 595
influenza, *647*
influenza virus, *311*
infrared (IR) spectroscopy, 504
inherited traits, 101
injuries, 247, *247*
insulin, *271*, 272, 276
integers, adding, 341
integumentary system, **243**, 243–245
    as defense from harmful materials, 235
internal measurement, 211
International Space Station, 638, *638*
International System of Units, R20–R21
Internet Activities
    alloys, 609
    bonding, 539
    carrying capacity, 363
    cell division, 71
    cells, 7
    environment, 399
    heart pumping, 223
    human body, 167
    human development, 291
    human genome, 133
    lung movement, 195
    Mendel's experiment, 99
    periodic table, 507
    photosynthesis, 39
    physical and chemical changes, 471
    prairie ecosystem, 327
    reactions, 567
    scale, 439
    senses, 259
interphase, 80, **81**, *81*
invasive species, 415, *416*
investigations. *See also* chapter investigations.
    alloys, 637
    antibodies, 239
    asexual reproduction, 91
    carbon, 339
    cell division, 84
    cell models, 31
    cells, 62
    chemical changes, 479
    chemical digestion, 207
    chemical reactions, 574
    chromosomes, 76

climate, 355
conservation of mass, 579
crystals, 553
decomposers, 345
element ratios, 543
fermentation, 53
fertilization, 119
food labels, 303
life expectancy, 297
limiting factors, 385
liquids, 463
lungs, 199
mass, 449
masses of atomic particles, 513
mixtures, 456
movable joints, 179
multiple probabilities, 114
neutral mutations, 146
oil and water, 44
particles in the air, 411
plant and animal cells, 21
radioactivity, 531
resources, 404
response to exercise, 274
separating mixtures, 493
skin protection, 245
solubility, 620
solutions, 612
species interactions, 377
sugar combustion, 595
systems, 170
involuntary muscles, **184**
iodine, 522, *550*
iodine clock, 577
ionic bonds, **548,** 548–549, *549, 552*
ionic compounds, 553, 557–558, 614, *614*
names of, 549
ions, **514,** 626
formation of, 514, *514,* 515, *515*
negative, 548
positive, 548
iron, 492, 510, 527, 528, 636
irregular bones, 174
Isle Royale, 385
Isle Royale National Park, 384, *384*
isotopes, **512,** 513, *513,* 517, 530
radioactive, 530, 531

J

Jackson, William Henry, 394
joints
ball-and-socket, 180
hinge, 179
investigation into movable, 179

K

kalanchoe, 89
kangaroo, 352
Kenyon, Cynthia, 4, *4*

kidneys, 61, 213, 273
chapter investigation into modeling, 216–217
as filters, 214, *214*
killer whales, 377
kilogram (kg), 442
Koch, Robert, 309
krypton, 529

L

labor, 282
laboratory equipment
beakers, R12, *R12*
double-pan balances, R19, *R19*
force meter, R16, *R16*
forceps, R13, *R13*
graduated cylinder, R16, *R16*
hot plate, R13, *R13*
meniscus, R16, *R16*
microscope, *R14,* R14–R15
ruler, metric, R17, *R17*
spring scale, R16, *R16*
test-tube holder, R12, *R12*
test-tube racks, R13, *R13*
test tubes, R12, *R12*
triple-beam balances, R18, *R18*
labs, R10–R35. *See also* experiments.
lactic acid, 54
fermentation of, 52–53
Lake Erie, 413
land, in a watershed, 652
land biomes, *351,* 351–354, *352, 353, 354*
desert, 352–353, *353*
grassland, 352–353, *353*
taiga, 351–352, *352*
temperate forest, *353,* 353–354
tropical forest, *353,* 353–354
tundra, 351–352, *352*
land ecosystems, plants as producers in, 343, *343*
landfills, 403, *403*
land use
pressures of expanding, 407
water quality and, 654
Langmuir, Irving, 606
lanthanides, 528
lanthanum, 528
large intestine, **208,** *209*
digestion in, 208
larynx, 202
Las Vegas, *406,* 406–407
later adulthood, 296
laughing, 203
Lavoisier, Antoine, 578–579, *579*
law of conservation of mass, **579**
laws, physical, xxxv
lead, 510
leaf, 30, *30*
learned behaviors, 101
Leeuwenhoek, Anton van, 12, 13, 128
length, choosing units of, 211
lens, 262, *262,* **262**
lever, bones as, 174
Lewis, G. N., 606
lichens, 351, *380, 386*

life expectancy, investigation into, 297
Life Science, connecting Physical Science to, 79, 277, 349
lifestyle, 304
ligaments, 179
light, 262, 441
    as abiotic factor, 332
light microscope, 41
    invention of, 18
lightning, 339
light waves, 263
limiting factors, **384**
    investigation into, 385
line graphs, 577, R24, R34
    analyzing, 577
    making, 242
lionfish, 435
lipids, 43, *43*, 45, *45*
liquids, **460,** *461*
    boiling of, 486, *486*
    comparison of solids and, 459
    condensation of, 487, *487*
    definite volume of, 463
    evaporation of, 485, *485*
    investigation into, 463
liquid solution, 612, *612*
Lister, Robert, 309
liters (L), 417, 445
lithium, 510, 522
litmus, 627
liver, 208, **210**
    in digestion, 210
living space, patterns in, 370, *370*
living things
    cells in, 11
    characteristics of, 10
    differences between nonliving things, 9
    need for chemical reactions, 594–595
    needs of, 10, *10*
long bones, 174
loosestrife, 415, *416*
lung cancer, 146
lungs, 200, 226, **228,** *228*
    in breathing, 204, *204*
    investigation into, 199
    movement of, as Internet Activity, 195
Lyme disease, 310
lymph, 229, 236
lymphatic system, 229, 236
lymph nodes, 235
lysosomes, 24
lysozyme, 136

M

magnesium, 510, 527
magnesium fluoride, 549
magnesium hydroxide, 631
magnetic properties, *492,* **492**
magnetic resonance imaging (MRI), 254, *256,* 257, *257*
magnetism in separating minerals, 495
malaria, 147, 646
male reproductive system, 280, *280*
manganese, 528
marine biomes, 356–357, *357*

marrow, 175, *175*
masses, **442**
    of atomic particles, 513
    chapter investigation into, 446–447
    investigation into, 449
    measuring, 442, *442,* **442**
    as physical properties, 474
mast cell, *236*
materials, density of, 481
Mather, Stephen, 395
Math in Science
    adding integers, 341
    analyzing line graphs, 577
    calculating percentages, 639
    calculating ratios, 546
    choosing data display, 307
    choosing units of length, 211
    comparing rates, 181
    finding percent of whole, 149
    finding volumes, 417
    interpreting graphs, 55
    making circle graph, 458
    making line graph, 242
    multiplying fraction by whole number, 389
    solving proportions, 481
    solving Propranolol, 285
    using exponents, 93
    using Punnett squares, 116
    using scientific notation, 25, 533
math skills
    area, **R43**
    averages, **R36, R37**
    decimal, **R39,** R40
    describing set of data, R36–R37
    formulas, **R42**
    fractions, **R41**
    mean, **R36**
    median, **R36**
    mode, **R37**
    percents, **R41**
    proportions, **R39**
    range, **R37**
    rates, **R38**
    scientific notation, **R44**
    significant figures, **R44**
    volume, **R43**
matter, **xxxiii, xxxv, 441**
    atoms in, 448–451, 509–510, *510*
    mass as measure of, 442–44
    observable properties of, 473–480
    particle arrangement and motion determining
        state of, 459
    physical changes from one state to another, 482
    physical states of, 459–465
    in substances, 453–457
meadow ecosystem, 344, *344*
meadowlark, 375
mean, **R36**
measurement, 463, 479, 579
    internal, 211
    International System of Units (SI), R20–R21
    of strengths of acids and bases, 628–629
    temperature, R21
mechanical digestion, 207
median, **R36**

medicines
  alloys in, 637, *637*
  from nature, 502–505, *502–505*
  radioactivity in, 531, *531*
  testing, 504–505
meiosis
  cell division in, 119–120, *121*
  defined, **119**
  differences between mitosis and, 122, *122*
  in sexual reproduction, 117–119
meiosis I, 120, *121*
meiosis II, 120, *121*
melanin, 248
melting, *483,* 483–484
melting point, **483,** 484, 556
  in separating minerals, 495
memory alloys, 637
Mendel, Gregor
  discoveries about heredity, 104–105, *105*
  experiments of, as Internet Activity, 99
Mendeleev, Dmitri, 518, *518,* 519, 523
menstruation, 279, *279*
messenger RNA (mRNA), 138, 141
metal alloys, 634–638
metallic bonds, **556,** 556–557, 655
metallic properties, 557, *557*
metalloids, *530,* **530**
metals, **527,** 550
  acid reactions with, 627
  properties of, 655, *655*
  reactive, 527, *527*
  transition, *527,* 527–528
  unique bonds of, 556–557
metaphase, 82, *83*
metaphase I, **120,** *121*
metaphase II, **120,** *121*
methane, 544, *550*
metric system, R20–R21
  changing metric units, R20, *R20*
  converting between U.S. customary units, R21, *R21*
  temperature conversion, R21, *R21*
mice, *380*
microchips, 598
microorganisms, **308**
microscope, **12,** 128, *R14,* R14–R15
  chapter investigation into using, 16–17, *16–17*
  importance of, 18–19
  invention of, 308
  light, 18, 41
  making a slide or wet mount, R15, *R15*
  role of, in discovery of cells, 12, *12*
  scanning electron, 19, *19*
  scanning tunneling, 607
  transmission electron, 19, *19*
  viewing an object, R15
mid-ocean ridge, 436
milliliters (mL), 445
mineral hot springs, 558, *558*
minerals, 302, *302*
  separating, 495
Minkoff, Larry, 256
Mississippi delta, 653
mistletoe, *380*
mitochondria, **23,** 50
mitosis, 80, **81,** 89

differences between meiosis and, 122, *122*
  modeling, 84
  steps of, 82, *83*
mixed substances, 453–454
mixtures, *455,* **455,** 611
  in alloys, 639
  comparing compounds and, 456
  heterogeneous, 457
  homogeneous, 457, 611
  investigation into, 456, 493
  separation of, 493–494, *494*
model(s)
  atomic, 511, *511*
  cell, 31
  of deoxyribonucleic acid (DNA), 32, *32*
  in explaining feeding relationships, 346
  making, 31, 84
  scientific, 32, *32*
  in studying cells, 32, *32*
modeling, 62, 76, 449, 513
  atomic masses, 524–525
  compounds, 543
  of kidney, 216–217
  of mitosis, 84
  molecules, 503–504
modes, **R37**
Mojave desert, 370
molds, slime, 646
molecules, 42, *450,* **450,** 462, *462,* **551**
  DNA double helix, 130
  modeling, 503–504
  motion of, 451, *451*
moon jellyfish, 379, *379*
mordant, 46, *46*
Morgan, Thomas Hunt, 123, 129
mosses, 332, 351, 379, *386*
Mount St. Helens, 414
mouth, **208,** *209*
  digestion in, 208
movement, 183
  angular, 179
  of bones and skeletal muscles, 186, *186*
  of energy through ecosystems, 348
  gliding, 180
  lung, 195
  rotational, 180, *180*
  of water on Earth, 651–653
mucus, 200, 235
Muir, John, 395
multicellular organisms, *11,* **11,** 20
  asexual reproduction in, 88
  cell division in, 76, 88
  cells in, 28, *29,* 29–31, *30*
multiple births, 284, *284*
multi-slice CT, *257*
muscle cells, 47, 63
muscles
  cardiac, 184, *185*
  chapter investigation into, 188–189
  developing, 187
  exercise and, 187, *187*
  fast-twitch, 184
  functions performed by, 182–183, *183*
  involuntary, 184
  skeletal, 184, *185*

slow-twitch, 184
smooth, 184, *185*
voluntary, 184, 213
muscle tissue, 170, 171, *171, 185*
muscular coordination, 187
muscular system, 182–187, **183**
mushrooms, *345*
musk ox, *331*
mutations, **145,** 146–147
as cause of genetic disorders, *146,* 146–147
gene, 149
investigation into neutral, 146
mutualism, *378,* **378,** 378–379, *380*

N

nail, 246, *246*
narcotics, 305
National Environmental Policy Act, 420
national park, 394
National Park Service, 395
native species, 415–416, *416*
natural gas, 411
natural habitats, 407
natural remedies, finding, 503
natural resource, **404**
natural sugars, 301
Nature Conservancy, 324, 396
negative feedback, 275, *275*
negative ions, 548
formation of, 515, *515*
neon, 529
nephron, 214, **214**
neptunium, 510
nerve cells, 63, *258*
nerve growth, chemical dyes in showing, 79
nerve tissue, 170, 171
nervous system, 261–267, 296
autonomic, *266,* 266–267, *267,* **267**
central, 264–265, *266*
peripheral, *266,* **266**
voluntary, 267
neurons, **265**
neutralization reaction, 631
neutral solution, 629
neutrons, *511,* **511,** 530
size of, 512
newton (N), 443
niche, **367**
nickel, 527, 528, 635
nicotine, 148
nitinol, 635
nitrogen, 529, 544, *552,* 649
in nitrogen system, 339–340
nitrogen cycle, **339,** 339–340, *340,* 424
nitrogen dioxide, air quality and, 412
nitrogen-fixing bacteria, 340, *380,* 388
noble gases, 529, *529*
noninfectious diseases, 312, *312,* 647, *647*
nonliving things, differences between living thing and, 9
nonmetals, *529,* **529,** 548, 550
properties of, 655, *655*
nonrenewable resources, *410,* 410–411, 424

nonspecific response, 237
nose, 200
nostril breathing, 204, *204*
notation, scientific, 25, 533, **R44**
note taking, **R45–R49**
combination notes, 72, *72,* 100, *100,* 328, *328,* 568, *568,* R45, *R45*
concept map, R49, *R49*
content frame, 292, *292,* R45, *R45*
description wheel diagram, 540, *540*
detail notes, 224, *224,* 260, *260,* 440, *440,* 540, *540*
main idea, 440, *440,* 540, *540*
main idea and detail notes, R46, *R46*
main idea web, 8, *8,* 100, *100,* 168, *168,* 260, *260,* 472, *472,* 508, *508,* R46, *R46*
mind maps, 100, *100,* 610, R47, *R48*
outlines, 40, *40,* 196, *196,* 260, *260,* 364, *364,* R48, *R48*
supporting main ideas, 134, *134,* 400, *400,* R47, *R47*
Venn diagram, R49, *R49*
nuclear magnetic resonance (NMR) spectroscopy, 504
nuclear radiation, 148
nucleic acids, *43,* 43–44
nucleotides, *43,* 43–44, 137
nucleus, *20,* **20,** 23, 129, *511,* **511,** 645
nutrients, **205,** 300
getting, *301,* 301–302
ocean, 437, *437*
nutrition, **300**
understanding, 302

O

O blood, 231
observations, xxxviii, 21, 44, 53, 411, **R2,** R5, R33
qualitative, R2
quantitative, R2
ocean
exploring, xxxiii, 436
nutrients in, 437, *437*
ocean ecosystems
commensal relationships in, 379
light in, 332
octopus, 435, *435*
odor, production of, 480
offspring
chapter investigation into models, 108–109
similarity of parents and, 101–102
oil
investigation into combining water and, 44
as renewable resource, *410*
oil glands, 245
oil spills
chapter investigation into, 426–427
cleaning, 426–427
operational definition, **R31**
opinion, **R9**
different from fact, R9
orchids, 379
organ, *30,* **30,** *171,* **171**
organelles, *20,* **20,** 27
organic chemists, 504
organic farmers, 422
organic matter, 648

organisms, **368,** *369*
   classification by cell type, 26
   interaction of, 374–379, *380,* 381
   multicellular, 11, *11,* 20
   cells in, 28, *29*
   occupation of specific living areas by, 365
   types of, 131
   unicellular, 11, *11,* 20, 26, 28
   in watershed, 653
organ system, 31, *171,* **172**
osmium, 523
osmosis, *59,* **59**
Outcome Assessment System Information Set (OASIS), *333*
outcomes, probability of, 112
ovaries, **271,** *271, 272,* 279
overeating, 306
oxygen, 50, 542, 544, *552,* 579
   body's need for, 197
   exchanging carbon dioxide and, 198, *198*
   in water cycle, 337
ozone, 450

P

pan balance, 442, *442*
pancreas, 208, **210, 271,** *271, 272*
   in digestion, 210
panoramic x-ray, *255*
Paramecia, 646, *646*
paramecium, 28, *28*
parasites, 241, 646
parasitism, 379, **379,** *380,* 381
parents, similarity of offspring and, 101–102
Parkinson's disease, *647*
particle accelerators, 607, *607*
Pascual-Leone, Alvaro, 164
passive immunity, 240
passive transport, *58,* **58**
Pasteur, Louis, 14, 309
   experiments of, 15, *15*
pasteurization, 14
patella, *177*
pathogens, **234,** 235, 240, 308, 310, 647
   types of, *241*
patterns
   in living space, 370, *370*
   in populations, 368, 370–371
   in time, 371, *371*
pedigree, **147**
   for sickle cell disease, *147*
penicillin, discovery of, 309
percent, **R41**
   of whole, finding, 149
percentage, **112**
percentages, 112
   calculating, 639
period, **522**
periodic table, 507, *518,* **518**
   distinct regions on, 526
   elements' location on, 548
   groups in, 522
   halogens, 529, *529*
   as Internet Activity, 507

   metalloids on, 530, *530*
   metals on, *527,* 527–528
   noble gases, 529, *529*
   nonmetals on, 529, *529*
   organization of, 519, *520–521,* 522–523
   periods in, 522
   trends in, 522–523, *523*
peripheral nervous system, *266,* **266**
peristalsis, *206,* **206,** 207, 208
permafrost, 351
permeable material, *651*
person-to-person contact, 310
petroleum, 411
pewter, *635*
Pfiesteria, 646
phagocytes, *238,* **238,** 238–239
phenotypes, *106,* **106,** 113
phosphorus, 649
photoresist, 598
   reaction of, with ultraviolet light, 599
photosynthesis, 39, **48,** *49,* 57, 332, 338, 343, **590,** 646
   comparison of cellular respiration and, 52, *52*
   as Internet Activity, 39
pH scale, 629
physical changes, 471, **476,** *477,* 570, *570*
   changes of state as, 482–487
   as Internet Activity, 471
physical dependency, 306
physical properties, **473,** 473–476, *477*
Physical Science, 495, 516
   connecting Earth Science to, 624
   connecting Life Science to, 79, 277, 349
phytoplankton, 355, 357
Pinchot, Gifford, 395
pineal gland, **271,** *272*
pioneer species, *386,* **386,** 388
pituitary gland, **271,** *271, 272,* 274, 275, 279
placenta, 282, *282*
plant(s)
   as biotic factors, 330
   effect of osmosis on, 59, *59*
   genetically modified, 151–152, *152*
   as producers in land ecosystems, 343, *343*
   true-breeding, 104
plant cells, *22, 23,* **23**
   cytokinesis in, *85*
   investigation into, 21
plant fibers, 46
plasma, 227
platelets, 227
platinum, 528
pneumonia, 309
pods, 377
polar covalent bonds, *551,* **551,** *552,* 622
polar ice sheets, 337
polar substances, 58
pollen counts, 242
pollution, **411**
   across systems, 414, *414*
   air, 413, *413*
   chemical, *413,* 414, *414*
   environmental, 152
   impact on biodiversity, 411
   reducing, 424–425
   water, 413, *413*

polymer, artificial, 249
population density, **406,** 406–407
populations, *366,* **366, 368,** *369. See also* human
    populations.
  birth rates and, 389
  changes in, over time, 383–385
  chapter investigation into estimating, 372–373
  growth and decline, 384, *384*
  growth of human, 401–402, *402*
  patterns in, 368, 370–371
pores, 245
positive feedback, *275,* 275–276
positive ions, 548
  formation of, 514, *514*
positron emission tomography (PET) scanners, *164,* 256
posture, maintaining, 183
potassium, 522, 527, 649
potassium bromide, 549
pound (lb), 443
prairie ecosystem as Internet Activity, 327
prairie falcon, 375
praseodymium, 528
precipitate, 618, *619*
precipitation, 337, **572**
  formation of, 572, *572*
precision, **R22**
predator-prey interactions, 384, *384*
predators, 351, **375**
prediction, **xxxviii, R3**
pregnancy, 282
pressure, solubility and, 622, *622*
prey, **375**
Priestley, Joseph, 604
primary consumers, 344, *344, 348*
primary producer, 346
primary succession, *386,* 386–387
probabilities, **112**
  investigation into multiple, 114
  Punnett square in calculating, *113, 115*
producers, *343,* **343,** *348,* 375
  primary, 346
  of tundra ecosystems, 351
production, rates of, 181
products, **571**
projection of human populations, 402, *402*
prokaryotes, 28, 645
prokaryotic cells, *20,* **20,** 27, 645
propane, 544
properties
  characteristics, of substances, 490–492
  chemical, *478,* 478–480, *480*
  electric, 492
  magnetic, 492, *492*
  metallic, 557, *557*
  physical, **473,** 473–476, *477*
prophase, 82, *83*
prophase I, **120,** *121*
prophase II, **120,** *121*
proportions, **R39**
  solving, 285, 481
proteins, 43, *43,* 136, 205, 206, **301**
  RNA in making, 138–139, *139, 140*
protists, 28, 645, 646
  characteristics of, 646

protons, *511,* **511,** 626
  size of, 512
protozoa, 646
puberty, 272, 295
pulmonary arteries, 229, *229*
pulmonary veins, 229, *229*
Punnett squares, **110,** 110–111, 114
  in calculating probability, *113, 115*
  using, 116
pupil, *262,* **262**
pure substance, 453–454

Q

quarks, 607
quartz, 598, *598*

R

rabies, 310
radiation, 277
  nuclear, 148
  ultraviolet, 148
radioactive decay, 532, *532*
radioactive isotopes, 530, 531
radioactivity, 255, **530**
  investigation into, 531
  uses of, in medicine, 531, *531*
radius, *177*
range, **R37**
rare Earth elements, 528, *528*
rates, **R38**
  comparing, 181
  of production, 181
ratios, **112,** 542, **R38**
  calculating, 546
reactants, **571**
reactions, 567
  as Internet Activity, 567
reactive metals, **526,** 527, *527*
reasoning, faulty, **R7**
recessive alleles, *107,* **107,** 110, 114
recycling, *424,* 424–425
red blood cells, 170, **222, 227,** 231, 273
regeneration, *90,* **90**
relevance, determining, 123
renewable resources, 410, *410*
  coal as, *410*
  oil as, *410*
  trees as, *410*
  water as, 410, *410*
repair, role of cell division in, 78, *78*
replication, *137,* **137,** 137–138
reproduction
  asexual, 88–91
  sexual, 92, 102
reproductive system, 278–284
  production of specialized cells, 278–279
resistance, **313**
resources
  human pressures on, 404–405, *405*
  human use of, 409
  improving use of, 422–423, *423*

investigation into, 404
nonrenewable, *410*, 410–411, 424
renewable, 410, *410*
respiration, 338, **594**
cellular, 199
respiratory system, **197**, 197–203, *201*, 212, 225, 296, 297
cellular, 199
as defense from harmful materials, 235
speech, *202*, 202–203
structures in, 200
retina, 262, *262*, **262**
rib bones, 176
ribonucleic acid (RNA), 43, 44, **138**
in making proteins, 138–139, *139, 140*
ribosomal RNA (rRNA), 138
ribosomes, 23, 27, 645
ribs, *177*
ringworms, 310, 379
risk-taking, 306
rods, 262
Roentgen, William Conrad, *254*
rotational movement, 180, *180*
ruddy ducks, 346
runoff, 652, 653, 654
rust, 478
Rutherford, Ernest, 606

S

safety, R10–R11
animal, R11
chemical, R11
clean up, R11
directions, R10
dress code, R10
electrical, R11
fire, R10
glassware, R11
heating, R10
icons, R10–R11
lab, R10–R11
sharp object, R11
salamanders, *29*, 382, *382*
saliva, 235
salivary glands, 208, *209*
salt, 631
table, 614
saltwater biome, 651
sand, 649, *649*
Santee delta, 653
saturated solution, 618, *618,* 619
saturation, zone of, 651
scale as Internet Activity, 439
scale worms, *436*
scanning electron microscopes (SEMs), 19, *19*
scanning tunneling microscopes (STMs), 452, *452,* 607
scapula, *177*
scavengers, 344
science
in fighting disease, 308
nature of, xxxvi–xxxix
Science on the Job
firefighter, 585, *585*
stage makeup artist, 299

textile designer, 46
urban planner, 408
yoga instructor, 204, *204*
scientific models, 32, *32*
scientific notation, 25, 533, **R44**
using, 25, 533
scientific theory, 14
scientists, efforts to prevent and treat illness, 313, *313*
seaweeds, 646
secondary consumers, 344, *344,* 346, *348*
secondary sexual characteristics, 295
secondary succession, 387, *387*
second generation, 104, *105*
selective breeding, *151,* **151**
self-pollination, 104
semen, 280
semiconductor devices, 533, *533*
semiconductors, 530
senses, 261–264
in brain, 163
as Internet Activity, 259
sensory receptors, 246
separation
of minerals, 495
of mixtures, 493–494, *494*
sex chromosomes, 103, *103*
sexual reproduction, 92, **102**
comparison of asexual reproduction and, *92*
meiosis in, 117–119
Shackleton, Ernest, 173
short bones, 174
sickle cell, *147*
sickle cell allele, 147
sickle cell disease, 146, 312
pedigree for, *147*
Sierra Club, 395
sigh, 203
sight, *262*, **262**
significant figures, **R44**
Silent Spring (Carson), 396, 419
silicon, 530, 598
silt, 649, *649*
silver, 527
simple carbohydrates, 42
single-cell organisms, cell division in, 88
sizes, comparing, 25
skeletal muscles, **184,** *185*
movement of bones and, 186, *186*
skeletal system, **174,** 174–180, *177*
bones in, 174–175, *175*
joints in, *179,* 179–180, *180*
skeleton
appendicular, 175, 176
axial, 175, 176
changes in, as body develops and ages, 178
skill focus
analyzing data, 114, 303, 377
designing experiments, 119, 385, 493, 620
drawing conclusions, 91
graphing data, 297, 355
inferring, 456, 574, 595
interpreting, 404
measuring, 463, 479, 579

modeling, 31, 62, 76, 84, 146, 199, 207, 239, 449, 513, 531, 543
observing, 21, 44, 53, 179, 245, 274, 339, 345, 411, 553, 612, 637
predicting, 170
skin, 212
artificial, 249, *249*
functions of, 243, *247*, 247–248
growing new, 249, *249*
investigation into protection of, 245
structure of, *244*, 244–245
skin cancer, *647*
skull, 176, *177*
slides, making, R15, *R15*
slime molds, 646
slow-twitch muscles, 184
small intestine, **208**, *209*
digestion in, 208
smell, 264
smooth muscle, **184**, *185*
social insects, 377
sodium, 522, 527, 548
sodium azide, decomposition of, 584, *584*
sodium bicarbonate, 631
sodium chloride, 549, *552*, 553
sodium hydroxide, 626, 627, 628, 629, *630*
soil
as abiotic factor, *332*, 332–333, 648, 650, *650*
chapter investigation into samples of, 334–335
characteristics of, 648
consistency of, 649
permeability of, 650
structure of, 648, *648*
testing, 650, *650*
texture of, 649, *649*
soil horizons, 648, *648*
soil profile, 648
soil scientists, 648
solar energy, *423*
solids, **460**, *461*
comparison of liquids and, 459
definite volume and shape of, 462, *462*
formation of, as sign of chemical change, 480
freezing of, 484, *484*
melting of, *483*, 483–484
solid solution, 612, *612*
solitaire bird, 155, *155*
solubility, **492,** 619
investigation of, 620
molecular structure and, 622–623
pressure and, 622, *622*
of a solute, 620–622
temperature and, 620–621, *621*
solute, **612**
solubility of a, 620–622
solution(s), **611,** *613*
acidic, 629
changes of properties of solvents in, *615*, 615–616, *616*
concentration of, 617
dilute, 618, *618*
effect of temperature on, 617
investigation of, 612
neutral, 629
saturated, 618, *618,* 619
supersaturated, 618–619, *619,* 621

types of, 612, *612*
wastewater, 624
water-based, 626
solvents, **612**
changes of properties of, in solutions, *615,* 615–616, *616*
universal, 623
sound, 441
sound waves, 263
space flight, alloys in, 638, *638*
spacesuits, features of, *33*
specialization, **28,** *29*
species, **365**
competition between, and within, 376, *376*
investigation into interactions of, 377
pioneer, 388
survival of, 378–379, *380,* 381
specific response, 238–239
spectroscopy, types of, 504
speech, *202,* 202–203
sperm, **118,** *280,* **280**
sperm cells, 278
sphygmomanometer, 230
spices, mixture of, 458
spinal column, 176
spinal cord, 265
spirilla, 645, *645*
spleen, 235
sponge, 29, 31
spongy bone, *175,* **175**
spontaneous generation, bacteria and, 14–15
spring scale, 443
stage makeup artist, 299
stainless steel, *635,* 636, 637
starch, 48, *48*
starfish, *90,* **90**
states of matter, **459**
gases, **460,** *461,* 464–465, *465*
liquids, **460,** *461,* 463
solids, **460,** *461,* 462, *462*
steel, 528, 636
stimulus, *262,* **262**
stirrup, 263, *263,* **263**
stomach, **208,** *209*
digestion in, 208
strangler fig, 375, *375*
streams and river processes, 653
strep throat, 309, *647*
Streptococcus, 130
stress, 298
Sturtevant, Alfred, 123
sublimation, **485**
subscripts, **543,** 580
substances
characteristic properties of, 490–492
chemical properties of, *478,* 478–480, *480*
identifying unknown, 491
mixed, 453–454
physical properties of, 473–476, *477*
properties used for identifying, *491,* 491–492, *492*
pure, 453–454
succession, **386,** 388
primary, *386,* 386–387
secondary, 387, *387*

sugar, 48, 50, 542
   investigation into combustion of, 595
   natural, 301
   table, 614
sulfur, 529
sulfur dioxide, air quality and, 412
sunburns, 248
Superfund Program, 422, *422*
supersaturated solutions, 618–619, *619,* 621
supertasting, chapter investigation into, 268–269
surface area, *575*
   chemical reactions and, 574–575
surprising senses, 162–165
suspensions, *613,* **613**
sustainable, **422,** 422–423
sweat glands, 245
sweating, **172**
symbiosis, **378,** 378–379, *380,* 381
synesthesia, 164–165
synthesis, 573, *573*
synthetic compound, 504
systems
   investigation into, 170
   pollution across, 414, *414*

T

tables, R23
table salt, 614
table sugar, 614
taiga, 351–352, *352*
talipes, 312
Tall Grass Prairie Restoration Preserve, 324
tapeworms, 379
tarnish, 478
taste, 264, *264*
Taxol, 503, 504
Taylor-Clarke, Marisa, 164
Tay-Sachs disease, 146
T cells, *238,* **238,** 238–239, 272
technology, nature of, xl–xli
teeth, 516
telophase, 82, *83*
telophase I, **120,** *121*
telophase II, **120,** *121*
temperate forest, *353,* 353–354
temperate rain forests, 354
temperature, *575*
   as abiotic factor, 331, *331*
   body, 183, *183,* 277, 296
   changes in, 572, *572*
   chemical reactions and, 575
   effect of, on a solution, 617
   solubility and, 620–621, *621*
   unit conversion, R21, *R21*
   water cycle and, 341
templates, 135, 138, 139
termites, 379
tertiary consumers, 344, *344, 348*
testes, **271,** *271, 272, 280,* **280**
testosterone (males), *271*
textile designer, 46
theory, cell, 18

Think Science
   determining relevance, 123
   inferring, 173, 382
   isolating variables, 555
   making comparisons, 33
Thomson, Joseph John, 605
thoracic cavity, 200
3-D ultrasound, *257*
throat, 200
thymine (T), 136
thymus, 235, **271,** *272*
thyroid gland, **271,** *271, 272,* 275
thyroxine, *271,* 275
tibia, *177*
ticks, *380*
tidal pools, 356
time
   changes in populations over, 383–385
   patterns in, 371, *371*
Timelines in Science
   seeing inside the body, 254–257, *254–257*
   story of atomic structure, 604–607, *604–607*
   story of genetics, 128–131
   wilderness conservation, 394–397, *394–397*
tin, 634, 635
tissues, **29,** 29–30, *30,* **170,** 170–171
   bones, 174–175
   connective, 170, 171
   epithelial, 170, 171
   muscle, 170, 171, *171, 185*
   nerve, 170, 171
titanium, 635, 636
titanium alloy, 637, *637*
tobacco, 305
tongue, 208
touch, 263
trachea, 200, *201*
traits
   acquired, 101, 102
   alleles in producing, 106–107
   inherited, 101
   linking, 123
transcription, 138–139, *139*
transfer RNA (tRNA), 138, 141
transfusions, 231
transition metals, *527,* 527–528
translation, 139, *140,* 141
transmission electron microscope (TEM), 19, *19*
transpiration, 337
transport
   active, **60,** 60–61, *61*
   effect of cell size on, 62–63
   need for energy, 59
   passive, *58,* **58**
transportation, alloys in, 636
trees as renewable resource, *410*
tremor, 647
tributaries, **652**
triplet code, 137
triplets, 285
tropical forest, *353,* 353–354, 354, *354*
tropical rain forests, 331, 333, 354, 375
true-breeding plant, 104

INDEX

tundra, 351–352, *352*
    producers on, 351
tungsten, 528, 529
twins, 285
    fraternal, 284
    identical, 284

U

ulna, *177*
ultrasound, *256*
ultraviolet radiation, 148
umbilical cord, 282
unicellular organisms, *11,* **11,** 20, 26, 28
    asexual reproduction in, 88
    cell division in, *89,* 89–90
United Nations Environment Programme, 422
U.S. Division of Forestry, 395
U.S. Geological Survey, 394
unit projects
    brain: then and now, 165
    building an ecosystem, 325
    conservation campaign, 325
    design an experiment, 5, 165
    design a park, 325
    DNA detective work, 5
    life in the water, 437
    living cell, 5
    medicines around you, 505
    model medicine, 505
    ocean news report, 437
    remedies, 505
    track drop of water, 437
    your body system, 165
universal pH indicator, 629
universal solvent, 623
uracil (U), 138, 139
urban growth, pressures of, *406,* 406–407
urban planner, 408
urban planning, ecology in, 408
ureters, 213, 214
urethra, 213
urinary system, 212–215, *213,* **213,** 297
    kidneys in, *214,* 214–215
    removal of waste from blood, 213
urine, **213,** 214, 215
uterus, 279, *282*

V

vaccination, 240–241
vaccines, **240,** 313
vacuoles, 24
vagina, 279
variables, 555, **R30,** R31, R32
    controlling, R17
    dependent, **R30,** R31
    independent, **R30**
    isolating, 555
veins, **228,** *228, 229,* **229**
    pulmonary, 229, *229*
vertebrae, 176, *177,* 265
vesicles, 24

veterinarian, 310
vibrations, 263
villi, 208, *208*
vinegar, 612
viruses, 241, 308, **309,** 310
vitamins, 302, *302*
vocabulary strategies, R50–R51
    description wheel, 260, *260,* 292, *292,* 540, *540,*
        610, R50, *R50*
    four square, 8, *8,* 134, *134,* 168, *168,* 292, *292,* 364,
        364, 440, *440,* 568, *568,* 610, R50, *R50*
    frame game, 72, *72,* 134, *134,* 224, *224,* 292, *292,*
        328, *328,* 508, *508,* 610, R51, *R51*
    magnet word, 100, *100,* 134, *134,* 196, *196,* 292,
        292, 400, *400,* 472, *472,* R51, *R51*
    word triangle, 40, *40,* 134, *134,* R51, *R51*
vocal cords, 202, 203
voice box, 202
Volta, Alessandro, 605, *605*
volumes, **443, R43**
    chapter investigation into, 446–447
    determining, by formula, 444
    finding, 417
    gas and, *464*
    measuring, by displacement, 445, *445*
    as physical properties, 474
voluntary muscles, **184,** 213
voluntary nervous system, **267**

W

warbler, 381, *381*
waste
    human pressures on disposal of, 403–404
    production of, in life processes, 212
    reducing, 424–425
wastewater solutions, 624
water, xxxi, xxxiii, 44, *44,* 205, 302, *552*
    as abiotic factor, 333
    filtering out impurities, 624
    hydrosphere, xxxiii
    investigation into combining oil and, 44
    location and movement of, on Earth, 651–653
    molecules of, 450
    nonpolar substances in, *623*
    polar substances in, *623*
    as renewable resource, 410, *410*
    in spread of disease, 310
water buffalo, 331, *331*
water cycle, *337,* **337,** 410, 424
    temperature and, 341
water ecosystems, 338
water planet, exploring, 434–437
water pollution, 413, *413*
water quality, 413, *413*
    human impact on, 654
    land use and, 654
water removal, 203, *203*
watersheds, 405, **651**
    land in, 652
    organisms in, 653
    protecting natural, 397
watershed systems, 651
water table, *651,* **651,** 653

water-treatment plants, 494, *494*
water vapor, 337
Watson, James, 32, 74, 130
waves
   light, 263
   sound, 263
weight, **443**
   measuring, 443, *443*
West Nile virus, 313
wetland animals, 416
wetlands, 653
wet mount, making a, R15, *R15*
white blood cells, 131, 227, 235, 236, 237, 272
whole number, multiplying fraction by, 389
wildebeests, 370, *370*
wilderness conservation, 394–397, *394–397*
Wilkins, Maurice, 130
wind, 423
windpipe, 200
withdrawal, 306
woody shrubs, 351

X

X-chromosome, 103, *103,* 114
xenon, 529
x-ray, *254*
   panoramic, *255*
x-ray crystallography, 130
x-ray studies, 504

Y

yawn, 203
Y-chromosome, 103, *103,* 114
yeast, growth of, 383
Yellowstone National Park, 27, 394, 418, 558, *558*
yoga instructor, 204, *204*
yogurt, 53

Z

zebrafish, 4, *4,* 5, *5*
   Hox genes of, 5
Zhu, Zuoyan, 130
zinc, 527, 528
zone of aeration, **651**
zone of saturation, **651**

Acknowledgments

Photography

Cover © David Nardini/Getty Images; **i** © David Nardini/Getty Images; **iii** Photograph of James Trefil by Evan Cantwell; Photograph of Rita Ann Calvo by Joseph Calvo; Photograph of Kenneth Cutler by Kenneth A. Cutler; Photograph of Douglas Carnine by McDougal Littell; Photograph of Linda Carnine by Amilcar Cifuentes; Photograph of Donald Steely by Marni Stamm; Photograph of Sam Miller by Samuel Miller; Photograph of Vicky Vachon by Redfern Photographics; **vi** *bottom* © Kent Foster Photographs/Bruce Coleman, Inc.; **viii** © Larry Dale Gordon/Getty Images; **ix** © Professors P.M. Motta & S. Correr/Photo Researchers, Inc.; **x** © Jeff Schultz/Alaska Stock.com; **xi** © Wolcott Henry/National Geographic Image Collection; **xii** © Steve Allen/Brand X Pictures; **xiii** © David Leahy/Getty Images; **xiv** © Digital Vision/PictureQuest; **xv** © Stephen Frink/Index Stock; **xx–xxi** Photographs by Sharon Hoogstraten; **xxx–xxxi** © Ron Sanford/Corbis; **xxxii–xxxiii** © Tim Fitzharris/Masterfile; **xxxiv–xxxv** © Jack Affleck/SuperStock; **xxxvi** *left* © Michael Gadomski/Animals Animals; *right* © Shin Yoshino/Minden Pictures; **xxxvii** © Laif Elleringmann/Aurora Photos; **xxxviii** © Pascal Goetgheluck/Science Photo Library/Photo Researchers, Inc.; **xxxix** *top left* © David Parker/Science Photo Library/Photo Researchers, Inc.; *top right* © James King-Holmes/Science Photo Library/Photo Researchers, Inc.; *bottom* Sinsheimer Labs/University of California, Santa Cruz; **xl–xli** *background* © Maximillian Stock/Photo Researchers, Inc.; **xl** Courtesy, John Lair, Jewish Hospital, University of Louisville; **xli** *top* © Brand X Pictures/Alamy; *center* Courtesy, AbioMed; **xlvi** © Chedd-Angier Production Company.

Cells and Heredity

1 © Dr. Gopal Murti/Photo Researchers, Inc.; **2, 3** © Mark Smith/Photo Researchers, Inc.; **4** *top left to right* © Dr. Richard Kessel and Dr. Gene Shih/Visuals Unlimited; *bottom* © Chedd-Angier Production Company; **5** *left* © Carolina Biological/Visuals Unlimited; *right* © Inga Spence/Visuals Unlimited; **6, 7** © Biophoto Associates/Photo Researchers, Inc.; **7** *top right* Photograph by Ken O'Donoghue; *center right* Photograph by Frank Siteman; **9** Photograph by Ken O'Donoghue; **10** © Heintges/Premium Stock/PictureQuest; **11** *bottom* © David Stone/Rainbow/ PictureQuest; *inset* © Science VU/Visuals Unlimited; **12** *left* © American Registry of Photography; *right* Library of Congress, Prints and Photographs Division, #LC-USZ62-95187; **13** *bottom* © Tom Walker/Visuals Unlimited; *inset* © Greg Theiman; **14** © Will & Demi McIntyre/Corbis; **16** *top* © Science VU/Visuals Unlimited; *center* Photograph by Frank Siteman; *bottom left, bottom right* Photographs by Ken O'Donoghue; **18** *left* Photograph by Ken O'Donoghue; *right* © Dr. Gary Gaugler/Visuals Unlimited **19** © Eye of Science/Photo Researchers, Inc.; **20** *left* © Eric Grave/Photo Researchers, Inc.; *right* © CNRI/Photo Researchers, Inc.; **21** *bottom left* © Biophoto Associates/Science Source/Photo Researchers, Inc.; *bottom right* © Dennis Kunkel/Phototake; **22** *background* © John Edwards/Getty Images; *inset* © Gary Braasch/Getty Images; **23** © Dr. Martha Powell/Visuals Unlimited; **24** *top* © Dr. Henry Aldrich/Visuals Unlimited; *bottom* © Biophoto Associates/Photo Researchers, Inc.; **25** *top* © Dr. Gary Gaugler/Visuals Unlimited; *bottom* © Dr. Tony Brain and David Parker/Photo Researchers, Inc.; **26** Photograph by Ken O'Donoghue; **27** *center* © Ralph White/Corbis; *inset* © Alfred Pasieka/Photo Researchers, Inc.; **28** © Stan Flegler/Visuals Unlimited; **29** *left to right* © Ted Whittenkraus/Visuals Unlimited; © Gustav Verderber/Visuals Unlimited; © Dwight R. Kuhn; **30** *left* © Eric and David Hosking/Corbis; *right* © Frans Lanting/Minden Pictures; **31** Photograph by Ken O'Donoghue; **32** *top* © Ken Eward/BioGrafx/Photo Researchers, Inc.; *inset* © A. Barrington Brown/Photo Researchers, Inc.; **33** *left* © Photo Researchers, Inc.; *inset* © Dr. Linda Stannard, UCT/Photo Researchers, Inc.; **34** *top left* David Stone/Rainbow/PictureQuest; *top right* © Science VU/Visuals Unlimited; *center left* © CNRI/Photo Researchers, Inc.; © *bottom* Frans Lanting/Minden Pictures; **35** © Dr. Martha Powell/Visuals Unlimited; **36** *top* © Tom Walker/Visuals Unlimited; *inset* © Greg Theiman; **38, 39** © Kent Foster Photographs/Bruce Coleman, Inc.; **39** *top, center* Photographs by Ken O'Donoghue; **41** Photograph by Ken O'Donoghue; **42** © Corbis-Royalty Free; **44** *top* © Alfred Pasieka/Photo Researhers, Inc.; *bottom* Photograph by Ken O'Donoghue; **46** *background* © Andrew Syred/Photo Researchers, Inc.; *bottom left* © Anna Clopet/Corbis; *center right* Photograph by Tim Nihoff; *montage top to bottom* © Dr. Jeremy Burgess/Photo Researchers, Inc.; © Andrew Syred/Photo Researchers, Inc.; **47** *top right* © David Young-Wolff/PhotoEdit; *top inset* John Durham/Photo Researchers, Inc.; *bottom inset* © Innerspace Imaging/Photo Researchers, Inc.; **48** © Dr. Jeremy Burgess/Photo Researchers, Inc.; **49** *top center* © Biophoto Associates/Science Source/Photo Researchers, Inc.; **51** *top left* © Dr. Gopal Murti/Photo Researchers, Inc.; *top right* © Biophoto Associates/Science Source/Photo Researchers, Inc.; **53** Photograph by Ken O'Donoghue;

54 © Bob Daemmrich Photo, Inc.; 55 © Roger Ressmeyer/Corbis; 56 Photograph by Ken O'Donoghue; 59 © Marilyn Schaller/Photo Researchers, Inc.; 60 © Fred Bavendam/Peter Arnold, Inc.; 62 Photograph by Frank Siteman; 64 *top* Corbis/Royalty Free; *all others* Photograph by Frank Siteman; 66 *bottom left* Photograph by Frank Siteman; *bottom right* © Fred Bavendam/Peter Arnold, Inc.; 70, 71 © CNRI/Photo Researchers, Inc.; 71 *top right* Photograph by Ken O'Donoghue; *center right* Photograph by Frank Siteman; 73 Photograph by Ken O'Donoghue; 74 © Will & Deni McIntyre/Photo Researchers, Inc.; 76 Photograph by Frank Siteman; 77 *background* © Rudiger Lehnen/Photo Researchers, Inc.; *left inset* © Alexis Rosenfeld/Photo Researchers, Inc.; *right inset* © David Hughes/Bruce Coleman, Inc.; 79 *left* © Nancy Kedersha/UCLA/Photo Researchers, Inc.; *top right* Photograph of Elizabeth Gould by Denise Applewhite; 80 © IFA/eStock Photo/PictureQuest; 83 © Ed Reschke; 84 Photograph by Ken O'Donoghue; 85 *left* © Dr. Gopal Murti/Photo Researchers, Inc.; *right* © Carolina Biological/Visuals Unlimited; 86 *top* © Michael Newman/PhotoEdit, Inc.; *top right, bottom left, bottom right* Photographs by Ken O'Donoghue; *center right* © Science VU/Visuals Unlimited; *center* © Custom Medical Stock Photo; 88 © M.I. Walker/Photo Researchers, Inc.; 89 *top* © CNRI/Photo Researchers, Inc.; *bottom* © Biophoto Associates/Photo Researchers, Inc.; 90 © David B. Fleetham/Visuals Unlimited; 91 *top* © Cytographics/Visuals Unlimited; *bottom* Photograph by Ken O'Donoghue; 93 © CNRI/Phototake; 94 © Will & Deni McIntyre/Photo Researchers, Inc.; 98, 99 © Norbert Rosing/National Geographic Image Collection; 99 *top right* © Photodisc/Getty Images; *center right* Photograph by Ken O'Donoghue; 101 © Florence Delva/Getty Images; 103 *left* © CNRI/Photo Researchers, Inc.; *right* © Biophoto Associates/Photo Researchers, Inc.; 106 © Mary Kate Denny/PhotoEdit; 107 © Ken Weingart/Corbis; 108 *top* © Johnny Johnson/Animals Animals; *bottom* Photograph by Ken O'Donoghue; 109, 110 Photographs by Ken O'Donoghue; 113 *background* © Ludovic Maisant/Corbis; *bottom right* © Jane Burton/Bruce Coleman, Inc.; 114 Photograph by Frank Siteman; 116 © Robert Dowling/Corbis; 117 Photograph by Ken O'Donoghue; 118 © Pascal Goetgheluck/Photo Researchers, Inc.; 119 Photograph by Ken O'Donoghue; 123 © David M. Phillips/Photo Researchers, Inc.; 128 *center* Library of Congress, Prints and Photographs Division, #LC-USZ62-95187; *center right* Courtesy of The Royal Society of London; *bottom* Courtesy of Professor John Doebley, Genetics Department, University of Wisconsin; 129 *top left* Library and Archives of the Royal Botanical Gardens, Kew; *center* Drawing by Edward Strasburger; *center left* © Margaret Stones; *center right* © Oliver Meckes/Photo Researchers, Inc.; *bottom* © Vic Small; 130 *top left* Reproduced from *The Journal of Experimental Medicine*, 1944, vol. 79, 158-159, by copyright permission of the Rockefeller University Press; *top right* © Dr. Gopal Murti/Photo Researchers, Inc.; *center* © Omikron/Photo Researchers, Inc.; *bottom left* © Lennart Nilsson/Albert Bonniers Forlag AB; 131 *top* © David Parker/Photo Researchers, Inc.; *center* Courtesy of The Whitehead Institute/MIT Center for Genome Research and reprinted by permission of Nature, 409:745-964 (2001), Macmillan Publishers Ltd.; *bottom* Courtesy of the USC-Keck School of Medicine and Ashanti DeSilva; 132, 133 © Ted Horowitz/Corbis; 133 *top right* Photograph by Ken O'Donoghue; *bottom right* © Corbis-Royalty Free; 135 Photography by Ken O'Donoghue; 139 Photograph by Ken O'Donoghue; 142 *top* © Ken Eward/Photo Researchers, Inc.; *center* Photograph by Frank Siteman; *bottom* Photography by Ken O'Donoghue; 143 Photograph by Frank Siteman; 144 Photograph by Ken O'Donoghue; 145 © David Pollack/Corbis; 146 Photograph by Frank Siteman; 147 © Meckes/Ottawa/Photo Researchers, Inc.; 148 © Gladden Willis/Visuals Unlimited, Inc; 149 © Dennis Kunkel Microscopy, Inc.; 150 © Geoff Tompkinson/Photo Researchers, Inc.; 151 © Doug Loneman/AP Wide World Photos; 152 © Richard T. Nowitz/Corbis; 153 © Mark C. Burnett/Stock Boston, Inc./PictureQuest ; 154 © Getty Images; 155 *left* © ImageState-Pictor/PictureQuest; *right* © PJ Green/Ardea London Limited; 156 © Getty Images.

Human Biology

161 RNHRD NHS Trust; 162–163 © Peter Byron/PhotoEdit; 163 *top right* © ISM/Phototake; 164 *top* © Wellcome Department of Cognitive Neurology/Photo Researchers, Inc., *bottom* Chedd-Angier Production Company; 165 © Myrleen Ferguson Cate/PhotoEdit; 166–167 © Chris Hamilton/Corbis; 167 *top* Frank Siteman, *bottom* Ken O'Donoghue; 169 © SuperStock; 170 Frank Siteman; 171 *left* © Martin Rotker/Phototake; 172 © SW Production/Index Stock Imagery/PictureQuest; 173 *background* © Hulton-Deutsch Collection/Corbis, *center* © Underwood & Underwood/Corbis; 174 Frank Siteman; 175 © Prof. P. Motta/Dept. of Anatomy/University "La Sapienza," Rome/Photo Researchers, Inc.; 176 © Photodisc/Getty Images; 178 *bottom* © Science Photo Library/Photo Researchers, Inc., *bottom left* © Zephyr/Photo Researchers, Inc.; 179 *top* © Zephyr/Photo Researchers, Inc., *bottom* Frank Siteman; 180 *top left* © Stock Image/SuperStock, *top right* © Science Photo Library/Photo Researchers, Inc.; 181 © Dennis Kunkel/Phototake; 182 Frank Siteman; 183 © Kevin R. Morris/Corbis; 185 *background* © Mary Kate Denny/PhotoEdit, *top* © Martin Rotker/Phototake, *left* © Triarch/Visuals Unlimited, *bottom* © Eric Grave/Phototake; 186 © Ron Frehm/AP Wide World Photos; 187 © Jeff Greenberg/PhotoEdit; 188 *top* © Gunter Marx Photography/Corbis, *bottom, all* Frank Siteman; 190 © Martin Rotker/Phototake; 191 *top* © Stock Image/SuperStock; 194–195 © Larry Dale Gordon/Getty Images; 195 *top* Frank

Siteman, *bottom* Ken O'Donoghue; **197** Frank Siteman; **198** © Amos Nachoum/Corbis; **199** Ken O'Donoghue; **201** *bottom left* © Michael Newman/PhotoEdit, *bottom right* © Science Photo Library/Photo Researchers, Inc.; **203** © Kennan Harvey/Getty Images; **204** *background* © Jim Cummins/Getty Images, *center* © Steve Casimiro/Getty Images; **205** Ken O'Donoghue; **207** Ken O'Donoghue; **208** © Professors P. Motta & A. Familiari/University "La Sapienza," Rome/Photo Researchers, Inc.; **209** © David Young-Wolff/PhotoEdit; **210** © Dr. Gladden Willis/Visuals Unlimited; **211** © David Gifford/SPL/Custom Medical Stock Photo; **212** Frank Siteman; **215** © LWA-Dann Tardif/Corbis; **216** *top* © Myrleen Ferguson Cate/PhotoEdit, *bottom left* Ken O'Donoghue, *bottom right* Frank Siteman; **217** Frank Siteman; **222–223** © Professors P.M. Motta & S. Correr/Photo Researchers, Inc.; **223** *both* Frank Siteman; **225** Frank Siteman; **227** © Science Photo Library/Photo Researchers, Inc.; **228** © Myrleen Ferguson Cate/PhotoEdit; **229** © Susumu Nishinaga/Photo Researchers, Inc.; **231** © Journal-Courier/The Image Works; **232** *top left* © Michael Newman/PhotoEdit, *bottom left* Ken O'Donoghue, *center right, bottom right* Frank Siteman; **234** Frank Siteman; **235** *top* © Eddy Gray/Photo Researchers, Inc., *bottom* © Mary Kate Denny/PhotoEdit; **236** © Science Photo Library/Photo Researchers, Inc.; **237** *top* © Dr. P. Marazzi/Photo Researchers, Inc., *top right* © Dr. Jeremy Burgess/Photo Researchers, Inc.; **238** © Science Photo Library/Photo Researchers, Inc.; **239** Frank Siteman; **240** © Bob Daemmrich/The Image Works; **241** © Richard Lord/The Image Works; **242** *background* © SCIMAT/Photo Researchers, Inc., *inset* © Vision/Photo Researchers; **243** Ken O'Donoghue; **244** RMIP/Richard Haynes; **245** Frank Siteman; **246** *top inset* © Dennis Kunkel/Phototake, *bottom inset* © Andrew Syred/Photo Researchers, Inc., *center* © Photodisc/Getty Images; **247** *all* © Eric Schrempp/Photo Researchers, Inc.; **248** © The Image Bank/Getty Images; **249** *background* © James King-Holmes/Photo Researchers, Inc., *top right* © Sygma/Corbis, *bottom right* © David Hanson; **254** *top* © Hulton Archive/Getty Images, *bottom* © Simon Fraser/Photo Researchers, Inc.; **255** *top* © Bettmann/Corbis, *center* © Underwood & Underwood/Corbis, *bottom* © George Bernard/Photo Researchers, Inc.; **256** *top left* © Collection CNRI/Phototake, *top right* © Geoff Tompkinson/Photo Researchers, Inc., *bottom* © Josh Sher/Photo Researchers, Inc.; **257** *top* © Simon Fraser/Photo Researchers, Inc., *bottom* © GJLP/Photo Researchers, Inc.; **258–259** © Photo Researchers, Inc.; **259** *top* Ken O'Donoghue, *center* © Photospin; **261** Ken O'Donoghue; **263** RMIP/Richard Haynes; **264** © David Young-Wolff/PhotoEdit; **267** © Royalty-Free/Corbis; **268** *top* © Ed Young/Corbis, *bottom* Ken O'Donoghue; **269** *top* Frank Siteman, *bottom* Ken O'Donoghue; **270** © David Young-Wolff/PhotoEdit; **271** © Kwame Zikomo/SuperStock; **272** © ISM/Phototake; **274** Frank Siteman; **275** © CNRI/Photo Researchers, Inc.; **277** *left* © David Young-Wolff/PhotoEdit, *bottom right* © Glenn Oakley/ImageState/PictureQuest; **278** Ken O'Donoghue; **283** *background* © Yoav Levy/Phototake, *top left* © Dr. Yorgos Nikas/Photo Researchers, Inc.; **284** © David Degnan/Corbis; **285** *left* © Christopher Brown/Stock Boston, Inc./PictureQuest, *right* © Nissim Men/Photonica; **290–291** © Brooklyn Productions/Corbis; **291** *top* Ken O'Donoghue; **293** Frank Siteman; **294** © Tom Galliher/Corbis; **295** © Tom Stewart/Corbis; **296** © Novastock/Index Stock Imagery, Inc.; **298** *left* © Spencer Grant/PhotoEdit, *right* © Michael Newman/PhotoEdit; **299** *all* from STAGE MAKEUP, STEP BY STEP. Courtesy of Quarto Publishing, Inc.; **300** © Ed Young/Corbis; **301** © Ronnie Kaufman/Corbis; **302** © Photodisc/Getty Images; **304** © Don Smetzer/PhotoEdit; **306** © Brett Coomer/HO/AP Wide World Photos; **307** *left* © Eric Kamp/Index Stock Photography, Inc., *top right* © Ariel Skelley/Corbis; **308** Frank Siteman; **309** © Mediscan/Visuals Unlimited; **311** *top left* © Dr. Kari Lounatmaa/Science Photo Library/Photo Researchers, Inc., *top right* © Dr. Gopal Murti/Photo Researchers, Inc., *bottom left* © Professors P.M. Motta & F.M. Magliocca/Photo Researchers, Inc., *bottom right* © Microworks/Phototake, *bottom right inset* © Andrew Spielman/Phototake; **312** © Mary Steinbacher/PhotoEdit; **313** © Srulik Haramary/Phototake; **314** *top left* © Kwame Zikomo/Superstock, *bottom left* Ken O'Donoghue, *bottom right* Frank Siteman; **315** Ken O'Donoghue; **316** © Mediscan/Visuals Unlimited.

Ecology
321 © Richard du Toit/Nature Picture Library; **322, 323** *background* © Mark Thiessen/National Geographic Image Collection; **323** *top* © Frank Oberle/Getty Images; *bottom* © Hal Horwitz/Corbis; **324** *top (both)* © Lawrence J. Godson; *bottom* Chedd-Angier Production Company; **326, 327** © Jeff Schultz/Alaska Stock.com; **327** *top* Photograph by Ken O'Donoghue; *center* Photograph by Frank Siteman; **329** Photograph by Frank Siteman; **330** © Mark Allen Stack/Tom Stack & Associates; **331** *left* © Jim Brandenburg/Minden Pictures; *right* © Ted Kerasote/Photo Researchers, Inc.; **332** *bottom left* © Grant Heilman Photography; **333** © Frans Lemmens/Getty Images; **334** *top* © Michael J. Doolittle/The Image Works, Inc.; *bottom* Photograph by Ken O'Donoghue; **336** Photograph by Ken O'Donoghue; **339** Photograph by Frank Siteman; **341** © Randy Wells/Corbis; **342** Photograph by Frank Siteman; **343** *left* © Eric Crichton/Corbis; *top right* © E.R. Degginger/Color-Pic, Inc.; *bottom right* © T.E. Adams/Visuals Unlimited, Inc.; **344** © Anthony Mercieca Photo/Photo Researchers, Inc.; **345** *top* © Fred Bruemmer/DRK Photo; *bottom* Photograph by Ken O'Donoghue; **347** *background* © Raymond Gehman/Corbis; **349** *left* © Arthur Gurmankin & Mary Morina/Visuals Unlimited, Inc.; *top right* © Carmela Leszczynski/Animals Animals; **350** © Charles Melton/Visuals Unlimited, Inc.; **351** © Michio Hoshino/Minden Pictures; **352** *top left* © Tom Bean;

top right © E.R. Degginger/Color-Pic, Inc.; *bottom* © Joe McDonald/Visuals Unlimited, Inc.; **353** *left* © David Wrobel/Visuals Unlimited, Inc.; *right* © Tom Bean; **354** *left* © Owaki-Kulla/Corbis; *right* © Frans Lanting/Minden Pictures; **355** *top* Photograph by Ken O'Donoghue; *bottom* © Stephen Dalton/Photo Researchers, Inc.; **356** *left* © Aaron Horowitz/Corbis; *center* © Hans Pfletschinger/Peter Arnold, Inc.; *right* © Arthur Gurmankin & Mary Morina/Visuals Unlimited, Inc.; **357** *left* © Paul Rezendes; *center* © Richard Herrmann/Visuals Unlimited, Inc.; *right* © Norbert Wu; **362, 363** © Wolcott Henry/National Geographic Image Collection; **363** *top* Photograph by Frank Siteman; *center* Photograph by Ken O'Donoghue; **365** Photograph by Frank Siteman; **366** *left and center* © Frans Lanting/Minden Pictures; *right* © Robin Karpan/Visuals Unlimited, Inc.; **370** © Walt Anderson/Visuals Unlimited, Inc.; **371** © Alan & Linda Detrick/Photo Researchers, Inc.; **372** *top* © Patrick J. Endres/Visuals Unlimited, Inc.; *bottom left* Photograph by Frank Siteman; *bottom right* Photograph by Ken O'Donoghue; **373** Photograph by Ken O'Donoghue; **374** © Spencer Grant/PhotoEdit, Inc.; **375** © Gary Braasch; **376** *top* © Joe McDonald/Visuals Unlimited, Inc.; *bottom* © Stephen J. Krasemann/Photo Researchers, Inc.; **377** *top* Photograph by Ken O'Donoghue; *bottom* © Michael Fogden/Bruce Coleman Inc.; **378** © Michael & Patricia Fogden/Minden Pictures; **379** © Bradley Sheard; **380** *clockwise from top* © S.J. Krasemann/Peter Arnold, Inc.; © Ray Coleman/Visuals Unlimited, Inc.; © Astrid & Hanns-Frieder Michler/Science Photo Library; © E.R. Degginger/Color-Pic, Inc.; © Dwight R. Kuhn; © Phil Degginger/Color-Pic, Inc.; **381** © Arthur Morris/Visuals Unlimited, Inc.; **382** *left* © Kevin Fleming/Corbis; *inset* © David M. Dennis/Animals Animals; **383** Photograph by Ken O'Donoghue; **384** *top* © Shin Yoshino/Minden Pictures; *bottom* © Tim Fitzharris/Minden Pictures; **385** Photograph by Frank Siteman; **386** *bottom (background)* © Leo Collier/Getty Images; **387** *bottom (background)* © David R. Frazier/Getty Images; **389** © A. & J. Visage/Peter Arnold, Inc.; **390** *top left* © Frans Lanting/Minden Pictures; **394** *bottom left* Denver Public Library, Western History Collection, call#F-4659; *top center* © James Randklev/Getty Images; *bottom right* Library of Congress, Prints and Photographs Division (LC-USZ62-16709 DLC) cph 3a18915; **395** *top left* © H.H. French/Corbis; *top right* © Bill Ross/Corbis; *center left* The Bancroft Library, University of California, Berkeley; *center right* © Corbis; *bottom* © Michael Sewell/Peter Arnold, Inc.; **396** *top left* © Alfred Eisenstaedt/Getty Images; *top right* © Tom Bean/DRK Photo; *center right* © David Muench/Corbis; *bottom left* © Kevin Schafer/Corbis; *bottom right* Habitat Quality for San Joaquin Kit Fox on Managed and Private Lands reprinted from ESRI Map Book, Vol. 16 and used herein with permission. Copyright © 2001 ESRI. All rights reserved.; **397** *top* © Tom Soucek/Alaska Stock Images; *bottom* © Richard Galosy/Bruce Coleman, Inc.; **398, 399** © Alex Maclean/Photonica; **399** *top and center* Photographs by Ken O'Donoghue; **401** Photograph by Frank Siteman; **403** © Ray Pfortner/Peter Arnold, Inc.; **404** Photograph by Ken O'Donoghue; **405** *top* © John Elk III; *bottom* © Ted Spiegel/Corbis; **406** *background* © ChromoSohm/Sohm/Photo Researchers, Inc.; *insets* Courtesy, USGS: EROS Data Center; **407** © Mark E. Gibson/Visuals Unlimited, Inc.; **408** © David Zimmerman/Corbis; **409** © David Young-Wolff/PhotoEdit, Inc.; **410** *left* © Richard Stockton/Iguazu Falls/Index Stock Imagery, Inc.; *right* © Bill Ross/Corbis; **411** Photograph by Ken O'Donoghue; **412** *bottom* © Tom Bean/DRK Photo; *inset* © Jenny Hager/The Image Works, Inc.; **413** *bottom* © Natalie Fobes/Corbis; *inset* © Natalie Fobes/Getty Images; **415** © Kent Foster Photgraphs/Visuals Unlimited, Inc.; **416** *top* © Andrew J. Martinez/Photo Researchers, Inc.; *inset* © D. Cavagnaro/Visuals Unlimited, Inc.; **417** © Tom Edwards/Visuals Unlimited, Inc.; **418** Photographs by Ken O'Donoghue and Frank Siteman; **419** © Frank Pedrick/The Image Works, Inc.; **420** © Joe McDonald/Visuals Unlimited, Inc.; **421** *top (background)* © Jim Wark/Airphoto; *top (inset)* Photograph by Scott Williams/U.S. Fish and Wildlife Service; *bottom (background)* © Tom Bean/Corbis; *bottom (insets)* Courtesy, San Diego State University, Soil Ecology and Restoration Group; **422** © Melissa Farlow/National Geographic Image Collection; **423** © Klein/Hubert/Peter Arnold, Inc.; **424** *top* © Janis Miglavs; *bottom* © David Young-Wolff/PhotoEdit, Inc.; **425** © Kevin Schafer/Corbis; **426** *top* Tom Myers/Photo Researchers, Inc.; *bottom* Photograph by Frank Siteman; **428** *center left* © Natalie Fobes/Corbis; *center right* © Kent Foster Photographs/Visuals Unlimited, Inc.; *bottom left* © Joe McDonald/Visuals Unlimited, Inc.; *bottom right* © Klein/Hubert/Peter Arnold, Inc.

Matter
433 © Robert F. Sisson/Getty Images; **434–435** © Ralph White/Corbis; **435** *center* © Roger Steene/imagequestmarine.com; *bottom* Wolcott Henry/National Geographic Image Collection; **436** *top* NOAA/Pacific Marine Environmental Laboratory; *bottom* © The Chedd-Angier Production Company; **437** © Orbital Imaging Corporation and processing by NASA Goddard Space Flight Center. Image provided by ORBIMAGE; **438–439** © Steve Allen/Brand X Pictures; **439, 441** Photographs by Sharon Hoogstraten; **442** *left* © Antonio Mo/Getty Images; *right* © ImageState/Alamy; **443** © Tom Stewart/Corbis; **444, 445** Photographs by Sharon Hoogstraten; **446** *top* © Stewart Cohen/Getty Images; *bottom* Photograph by Sharon Hoogstraten; **446–447, 447** Photographs by Sharon Hoogstraten; **448** © Royalty-Free/Corbis; **449** Photograph by Sharon Hoogstraten; **450** © NatPhotos/Tony Sweet/Digital Vision; **451** © Jake Rajs/Getty Images; **452** Courtesy IBM Archives; **453** Photograph by Sharon Hoogstraten; **454** *left* © James L. Amos/Corbis; *right* © Omni Photo Communications, Inc./Index Stock; **455** ©

ACKNOWLEDGMENTS

Richard Laird/Getty Images; **456** Photograph by Sharon Hoogstraten; **457** © Royalty-Free/Corbis; **458** © Nik Wheeler/Corbis; **459** Photograph by Sharon Hoogstraten; **462** © Robert F. Sisson/Getty Images; **463** Photograph by Sharon Hoogstraten; **466** *top* Photograph by Sharon Hoogstraten; *bottom left* © James L. Amos/Corbis; *bottom right* © Royalty-Free/Corbis; **468** Photographs by Sharon Hoogstraten; **470–471** © David Leahy/Getty Images; **471, 473** Photographs by Sharon Hoogstraten; **474** *left* Photograph by Sharon Hoogstraten; *right* © Dan Lim/Masterfile; **477** *top left* © Maryellen McGrath/Bruce Coleman Inc.; *top center* © Jean-Bernard Vernier/Corbis Sygma; *top right* © Angelo Cavalli/Getty Images; *bottom* © Garry Black/Masterfile; *inset* Photograph by Sharon Hoogstraten; **478** © Mark C. Burnett/Stock, Boston Inc./PictureQuest; **479** Photograph by Sharon Hoogstraten; **480** © J. Westrich/Masterfile; **481** *left* © Owen Franken/Corbis; *right* © Erich Lessing/Art Resource, New York; **482** © ImageState/Alamy; **483** *left* © Brand X Pictures; *right* © Peter Bowater/Alamy; **484** © Royalty-Free/Corbis; **485** © Winifred Wisniewski/Frank Lane Picture Agency/Corbis; **486** © A. Pasieka/Photo Researchers; **487** © Sean Ellis/Getty Images; **488** *top* © Royalty-Free/Corbis; *bottom* Photograph by Sharon Hoogstraten; **489, 490** Photographs by Sharon Hoogstraten; **491** © Lawrence Livermore National Laboratory/Photo Researchers; **492** *top left* © SPL/Photo Researchers; *top right* © Felix St. Clair Renard/Getty Images; *bottom* © David Young-Wolff/PhotoEdit; **493** Photograph by Sharon Hoogstraten; **494** © Alan Towse/Ecoscene/Corbis; **495** © Robert Essel NYC/Corbis; *inset* © The Cover Story/Corbis; **496** *top left* © Dan Lim/Masterfile; *top right* © Mark C. Burnett/Stock, Boston Inc./PictureQuest; *bottom* © David Young-Wolff/PhotoEdit; **498** © Winifred Wisniewski/Frank Lane Picture Agency/Corbis.

Chemical Interactions

501 © Photodisc/Getty Images; **502–503** © David Cavagnaro/Peter Arnold, Inc.; **503** Joel Sartore/National Geographic Image Collection; **504** © The Chedd-Angier Production Company; **505** © Colin Cuthbert/Photo Researchers; **506–507** IBM Research, Almaden Research Center; **507, 509** Photographs by Sharon Hoogstraten; **510** NASA; **512** © Pascal Goetgheluck/Photo Researchers; **513** Photograph by Sharon Hoogstraten; **516** © Cnri/Photo Researchers; **517** Photograph by Sharon Hoogstraten; **518** *left, right* The Granger Collection, New York; **524** *top* © A. Hart-Davis/Photo Researchers; *bottom* Photograph by Sharon Hoogstraten; **526** Photograph by Sharon Hoogstraten; **527** *left* © Charles D. Winters/Photo Researchers; *center* © Rich Treptow/Visuals Unlimited; *right* © Corbis Images/PictureQuest; **528** © Peter Christopher/Masterfile; **529** © M. Gibbon/Robertstock.com; **530** © Superstock; **531** *top* © Simon Fraser/Photo Researchers; *bottom* Photograph by Sharon Hoogstraten; **533** © Alfred Pasieka/Photo Researchers; *inset* © John Walsh/Photo Researchers; **538–539** © Digital Vision/PictureQuest; **539, 541** Photographs by Sharon Hoogstraten; **542** *left* © Rich Treptow/Visuals Unlimited; *center, right* © E. R. Degginger/Color-Pic, Inc.; **543, 545** Photograph by Sharon Hoogstraten; **546** © Lawrence M. Sawyer/Photodisc/PictureQuest; **547** © IFA/eStock Photography (PQ price control)/PictureQuest; **549** © Runk and Schoenberger/Grant Heilman Photography, Inc.; **552** © The Image Bank/Getty Images; **553** Photograph by Sharon Hoogstraten; **555** © Astrid & Hanns-Frieder Michler/Photo Researchers; *inset* © Volker Steger/Photo Researchers; **556** Photograph by Sharon Hoogstraten; **557** © David Wrobel/Visuals Unlimited; **558** © Rob Blakers/photolibrary/PictureQuest; **559** *left* © E. R. Degginger/Robertstock.com; *right* © C. Swartzell/Visuals Unlimited; **560** *top* © David Young-Wolff/Getty Images; *bottom* Photograph by Sharon Hoogstraten; **561** Photograph by Sharon Hoogstraten; **562** *left* © Rich Treptow/Visuals Unlimited; *center, right* © E. R. Degginger/Color-Pic, Inc.; **566–567** From *General Chemistry* by P. W. Atkins, © 1989 by Peter Atkins. Used with permission of W.H. Freeman and Company; **567, 569** Photographs by Sharon Hoogstraten; **570** © Daryl Benson/Masterfile; **572** *top left* © Science VU/Visuals Unlimited; *top right* © 1992 Richard Megna/Fundamental Photographs, NYC; *bottom left* © E. R. Degginger/Color-Pic, Inc.; *bottom right* © Larry Stepanowicz/Visuals Unlimited; **574** Photograph by Sharon Hoogstraten; **577** © Corbis Images/PictureQuest; *inset* © Andrew Lambert Photography/Photo Researchers; **578** © Wally Eberhart/Visuals Unlimited; **579** *top* The Granger Collection, New York; *bottom* Photograph by Sharon Hoogstraten; **580** © William Ervin/Photo Researchers; **582** © Maximilian Stock Ltd./Photo Researchers; **584** © Index Stock; **585** *left, inset* Courtesy of Chicago Fire Department; *center* Uline; *bottom right* Photograph by Sharon Hoogstraten; **586** Photograph by Sharon Hoogstraten; **587** *top* NASA; *bottom* © 1992 Richard Megna/Fundamental Photographs, NYC; **588** © Jeffrey L. Rotman/Corbis; **589** Thomas Eisner and Daniel Aneshansley, Cornell University; **591** © Harald Sund/Brand X Pictures/PictureQuest; **592** *top* AP/Wide World Photos; *bottom* Photographs by Sharon Hoogstraten; **593** Photograph by Sharon Hoogstraten; **594** © Runk and Schoenberger/Grant Heilman Photography, Inc.; **595** Photograph by Sharon Hoogstraten; **596** © Tom Yhlman/Visuals Unlimited; **597** *background* © Conor Caffrey/Photo Researchers; **598** © Arnold Fisher/Photo Researchers; **599** *left to right* © Bruce Forster/Getty Images; © Colin Cuthbert/Photo Researchers; © Fontarnau-Gutiérrez/age fotostock america, inc.; © D. Roberts/Photo Researchers; **600** © 1992 Richard Megna/Fundamental Photographs, NYC; **604** From Hales, *Vegetable Statiks* [1727]; **605** *top* The Granger Collection, New York; *bottom* Mary Evans Picture Library; **606** *top* AP/Wide World Photos; *bottom* © Dorling Kindersley; **607** *top, bottom* © David Parker/Photo Researchers; **608–609** © Stephen Frink/Index Stock; **609, 611** Photographs by Sharon Hoogstraten; **612**

© Richard Cummins/Corbis; **613, 615** Photographs by Sharon Hoogstraten; **616** © Peter & Georgina Bowater/Stock Connection/PictureQuest; *inset* © 2001 Kim Fennema/Visuals Unlimited; **617, 618** Photographs by Sharon Hoogstraten; **619** *left, right* © 1990 Richard Megna/Fundamental Photographs, NYC; **620–621** Photographs by Sharon Hoogstraten; **622** © Stephen Frink/StephenFrink.com; **623** Photograph by Sharon Hoogstraten; **624** © Thom Lang/Corbis; **625, 627, 629** Photographs by Sharon Hoogstraten; **630** *top left* © Martyn F. Chillmaid/Photo Researchers; *top right* © Chuck Swartzell/Visuals Unlimited; *center left* © E. R. Degginger/Color-Pic, Inc.; *center right* © Phil Degginger/Color-Pic, Inc.; *bottom left* © Stockbyte; *bottom right* © E. R. Degginger/Color-Pic, Inc.; **632** © Runk and Schoenberger/Grant Heilman Photography, Inc.; **632–633, 633, 634** Photographs by Sharon Hoogstraten; **635** *top to bottom* © Photodisc/Getty Images; © Greg Pease/Stock Connection/PictureQuest; © Stockbyte; © S. Feld/Robertstock.com; Jellinek & Sampson, London/Bridgeman Art Library; **636** © Joachim Messerschmidt/Bruce Coleman, Inc.; **637** *top* © Princess Margaret Rose Hospital/Photo Researchers; *inset* © Klaus Rose/Okapia/Photo Researchers; *bottom* Photograph by Sharon Hoogstraten; **638** NASA; **639** © IFA/eStock Photography (PQ price control)/PictureQuest; **640** © Joachim Messerschmidt/Bruce Coleman, Inc.

South Carolina Essentials

645 *top* © Tina Carvalho/Visuals Unlimited; *center* © Scimat/Photo Researchers, Inc.; *bottom* © CNRI/Photo Researchers, Inc.; **646** *left* © M. I. Walker/Photo Researchers, Inc.; *center* © Visuals Unlimited; *right* © Gary Retherford/Photo Researchers, Inc.; **648** © Kenneth W. Fink/Photo Researchers, Inc.; **649** © Wally Eberhart/Visuals Unlimited; **650** *left* © Comstock Images/Alamy; *right* © Reuters/Corbis; **653** © Jupiter Images; **654** © Mira/Alamy Images; **655** © Andrew Lambert Photography/Photo Researchers, Inc.

Illustrations and Maps

Ampersand Design Group **461, 585, 597;** Richard Bonson/Wildlife Art Ltd. **348, 367, 369, 380** *(background),* **390** *(top right),* **651;** Peter Bull/Wildlife Art Ltd. **32;** Sandra Doyle/Wildlife Art Ltd. **347** *(all),* **358** *(bottom);* Stephen Durke **442, 443, 450, 452, 454, 462, 464, 465, 466, 511, 512, 513, 514, 515, 534, 548, 549, 550, 551, 552, 554, 559, 562, 564, 570, 571, 573, 588, 589, 597, 602, 614, 642;** Chris Forsey **652;** Luigi Galante **386–387** *(all insets),* **390** *(bottom);* Patrick Gnan/Deborah Wolfe Ltd. **61;** Dan Gonzalez **408, 414;** Gary Hincks **332** *(bottom right),* **337, 338, 340, 356–357** *(background),* **358** *(center),* **403, 624;** Keith Kasnot **49, 51, 52, 66;** George Kelvin **15, 17;** George Kelvin and Richard McMahon **19** *(montage);* Myriam Kirkman-Oh/KO Studios **43** *(center),* **140;** Debbie Maizels **3** *(right),* **22, 30, 34, 42, 43** *(top, bottom),* **45, 58, 60, 61, 75** *(center right),* **136** *(bottom),* **175, 186, 244, 250, 262, 264, 288;** MapQuest.com, Inc. **351, 367** *(top right),* **369** *(top),* **405;** Linda Nye **171, 190, 206, 226, 230, 250, 252, 279, 280, 281, 282, 283, 286;** Steve Oh/KO Studios **75** *(left),* **83, 96** *(right),* **121, 122, 124, 136, 137, 139, 238, 265;** Laurie O'Keefe, **349;** Mick Posen/Wildlife Art Ltd. **78, 105, 111, 113, 116;** Dan Stuckenschneider **R11–R19, R22, R32;** Bart Vallecoccia and Richard McMahon **3** *(montage),* **171, 177, 190, 192, 201, 202, 204, 206, 209, 213, 214, 218, 220, 228, 263, 265, 266, 273, 279, 280, 286.**

ACKNOWLEDGMENTS